£5.00

* 1,000,000 *

Free E-Books

@

www.ForgottenBooks.org

* Alchemy *

The Secret is Revealed

@

www.TheBookofAquarius.com

Forgotten Books

A Short History of Freethought, Ancient and Modern

By

J. M. Robertson

Published by Forgotten Books 2012
Originally Published 1906

PIBN 1000245568

Copyright © 2012 Forgotten Books
www.forgottenbooks.org

A SHORT HISTORY OF FREETHOUGHT

BY THE SAME AUTHOR.

ESSAYS TOWARDS A CRITICAL METHOD.
NEW ESSAYS TOWARDS A CRITICAL METHOD.
MONTAIGNE AND SHAKSPERE.
BUCKLE AND HIS CRITICS: a Sociological Study.
THE SAXON AND THE CELT: a Sociological Study.
MODERN HUMANISTS: Studies of Carlyle, Mill, Emerson, Arnold, Ruskin, and Spencer.
THE FALLACY OF SAVING: a Study in Economics.
THE EIGHT HOURS QUESTION: a Study in Economics.
THE DYNAMICS OF RELIGION: an Essay in English Culture-History. (By "M. W. Wiseman.")
PATRIOTISM AND EMPIRE.
STUDIES IN RELIGIOUS FALLACY.
AN INTRODUCTION TO ENGLISH POLITICS.
WRECKING THE EMPIRE.
CHRISTIANITY AND MYTHOLOGY.
A SHORT HISTORY OF CHRISTIANITY.
PAGAN CHRISTS.
CRITICISMS. 2 vols.
TENNYSON AND BROWNING AS TEACHERS.
ESSAYS IN ETHICS.
ESSAYS IN SOCIOLOGY. 2 vols.
LETTERS ON REASONING.
COURSES OF STUDY.
CHAMBERLAIN: a Study.
DID SHAKESPEARE WRITE "TITUS ANDRONICUS"?

A SHORT HISTORY

OF

FREETHOUGHT

ANCIENT AND MODERN

BY
JOHN M. ROBERTSON

SECOND EDITION, REWRITTEN AND GREATLY ENLARGED

IN TWO VOLUMES
VOL. II.

[ISSUED FOR THE RATIONALIST PRESS ASSOCIATION, LTD.]

WATTS & CO.,
17, JOHNSON'S COURT, FLEET STREET, LONDON, E.C.
1906

CONTENTS

VOLUME II.

CHAP. XIII.—THE RISE OF MODERN FREETHOUGHT.

§ 1. *The Italian Influence.* The Sozzini. Unitarianism in Europe. Effects in England. Aconzio. The Catholic Reaction in Italy - - - - 1
§ 2. *France.* Desperiers. Rabelais. Dolet. Montaigne. Charron - - - - - - 5
§ 3. *England.* Charges of Atheism. Executions under Elizabeth. Hammond. Kett. Marlowe. Raleigh. Shakespeare. Executions under James. Bacon 23
§ 4. *Popular Thought in Europe.* Callidius. Flade. Wier. Coornhert. Grotius. Gorlæus. Koerbagh. Beverland. Socinianism. The case of Spain. Cervantes - - - - - - 49
§ 5. *Scientific Thought.* Copernicus. Giordano Bruno. Vanini. Sanchez. Galileo. The Aristotelian strife. Vives. Ramus. Descartes. Gassendi 60

CHAP. XIV.—BRITISH FREETHOUGHT IN THE SEVENTEENTH CENTURY.

§ 1. Lord Herbert of Cherbury. Hobbes. Selden - 85
§ 2. The popular ferment: attempted suppression of heresy by Parliament. Lawrence Clarkson. The Levellers and Toleration. Forms of unbelief. The term "rationalist." Propaganda against atheism. Culverwel. Freethought at the Restoration. The protests of Howe, Stillingfleet, and Baxter. Freethought in Scotland. The argument of Mackenzie. English Apologetics of Casaubon, Ingelo, Temple, Wilkins, Tillotson, Cudworth, Boyle, and others. Martin Clifford. Emergence of Deism. Avowals of Archdeacon Parker. Charles Blount. Leslie's polemic. Growth of apologetic literature. Toland. The Licensing Act - - - - - 92
§ 3. Literary and academic developments. Sir Thomas Browne. Jeremy Taylor. John Spencer. Joseph Glanvill. Cartesianism. Glisson. Influence of

Gassendi. Unitarianism. Lord Falkland. Colonel Fry. Locke. The Marquis of Halifax. Newton. Penn. Tillotson. Firmin. Latitudinarianism. Dr. T. Burnet. Dr. B. Connor. John Craig. The "rationalists" - - - - - 110

CHAP. XV.—BRITISH FREETHOUGHT IN THE EIGHTEENTH CENTURY.

§ 1. Toland. Strifes among believers. Cudworth. Bishops Browne and Berkeley. Heresy in the Church. The Schools of Newton, Leibnitz, and Clarke. Hutchinson. Halley. Provincial deism. Whiston. Saunderson. Literary orthodoxy. Addison. Steele. Berkeley. Swift. New deism. **Shaftesbury. Trenchard. Unitarianism. Asgill.** Coward. Dodwell - - - - - 126

§ 2. Anthony Collins. Bentley's attack. Mandeville. Woolston. Middleton. Deism at Oxford. Tindal. Elwall. Berkeley's polemic. Lady Mary Montagu. Pope. Deism and Atheism. Strutt. Parvish. Influence of Spinoza. William Pitt. Chubb. Morgan. Peter Annet. Dodwell the Younger. The work achieved by deism. The social situation. The intellectual success. Recent disparagements and German testimony. The arrest of English science. Effects of imperialism. Contrast with France - 134

§ 3. Supposed "decay" of deism. Butler. William Law. Hume - - - - - 155

§ 4. Freethought in Scotland. Execution of Thomas Aikenhead. Confiscation of innovating books. Legislation against deism. Halyburton's polemic. Strife over creeds. John Johnston. William Dudgeon. Hutcheson. Leechman. Forbes. Millar. Smith. Ferguson. Kames. Church riots. Freethought in Ireland. Lord Molesworth. Archbishop Synge. Bishop Clayton - - 158

§ 5. Situation in England in 1750. Richardson's lament. Middleton. Deism among the clergy. Sykes. The deistic evolution. Materialism. La Mettrie. Shifting of the social centre: the industrial and political forces. Gray's avowal. Hume's estimate. Goldsmith's. The later deism. Bolingbroke. Diderot's diagnosis. Influence of Voltaire. Low state of popular culture. Prosecutions of poor freethinkers. Jacob Ilive. Peter Annet. Later deistic literature. The Wesleyan revival. The contribution of Gibbon. Burke's miscalculation.

		PAGE
The religion of the younger Pitt. Geology. Hutton. Cowper's anger. Paley's complaints. Commonness of unbelief. Erasmus Darwin. Panic and reaction after the French Revolution. New aristocratic orthodoxy. Thomas Paine. New democratic freethought		165

CHAP. XVI.—EUROPEAN FREETHOUGHT FROM DESCARTES TO THE FRENCH REVOLUTION.

§ I. *France and Holland.*

1. Influence of Montaigne and Charron. La Mothe le Vayer. Gui Patin. Naudé. Richelieu — 181
2. Descartes's influence. Boileau. Malherbe. Jean Fontanier. Theophile de Viau. Claude Petit. Corneille. Moliere. Cyrano de Bergerac — 182
3. Pascal. Jansenism. Bossuet - 185
4. Huet. Le Vassor's complaint. Jesuit polemic 188
5. Gassendi - 190
6. St. Evremond. Regnard. La Bruyere. Fontenelle - 193
7. The Cartesian school. Régis. Desgabets. Malebranche - 194
8. Richard Simon. La Peyrere - 196
9. Influence of Descartes in Holland. Louis Meyer. Spinoza - 197
10. Dutch rationalism. Le Clerc. Spinozistic movements. Deurhoff. Bekker. Discussion on witchcraft. "Juan di Posos." Leenhoff. Booms - 201
11. Bayle - 203
12. Bayle's influence. Passerano. Dutch literary conditions - 206
13. Spinozism in France. Abbadie's complaints. Decline in French intellectual prestige. Influence of Louis XIV. Boulainvilliers. Fenelon. Chevalier Ramsay. Huard. Marie Huber. Persecution of the *philosophes* - 207
14. The *Testament* of Jean Meslier - 212
15. Voltaire. Buckle's chronological error. Frederick the Great. Marchioness du Chatelet. Voltaire's influence - 215
16. The *Encyclopédie*. The French intellectual evolution. Bibliographical outline. Burigny. Freret. Dumarsais. Premontval - 222
17. The orthodox defence. Bergier. English estimates and misconceptions - 228

CONTENTS

			PAGE
	18.	The main body of deists. Raynal an exception. Rousseau	232
	19.	The literary development. Montesquieu. Official toleration	234
	20.	La Mettrie. The scientific movement. Buffon. Maupertuis. Robinet. Helvetius. Beccaria	236
	21.	Diderot	239
	22.	D'Alembert. D'Holbach	243
	23.	Situation at the Revolution. Volney. Dupuis. Condorcet	244
	24.	The anti-deistic legend	245
		(*a*) The leading revolutionists deistic, not atheistic. The orthodox types: Gregore. Action of the clergy	246
		(*b*) Deistic measures. No new State cult. The alleged Cult of Reason. Free-thought among the priests. Reason and Deity. Hebert. Chaumette. Clootz	248
		(*c*) Robespierre. The Terror: its deistic associations. Salaville the atheist	250
	25.	Origination of the legend. Rivarol. Influence of the " philosophic " schools. Frederick's estimate. The Revolution and Rousseau	250
II.	*Germany.*		
	1.	The Lutheran decadence. Orthodox apologetics. Alsted. The Thirty Years' War. The Peace of Westphalia. Traces of unbelief during the war. Resulting skepticism. New apologetics. Knutzen and his movement	254
	2.	Influence of Spinoza. Favour shown to him. Opposition. F. W. Stosch. Bibliographical sketch	257
	3.	Leibnitz	259
	4.	Influence of Leibnitz. Pietism. Rationalist reaction. The name *Freigeist*	261
	5.	Christian Thomasius. His influence	263
	6.	Dippel	264
	7.	T. L. Lau	265
	8.	Wolff	266
	9.	New rationalism. J. L. Schmidt. Edelmann. J. F. W. Jerusalem	266
	10.	English and French influences. Optimism and pessimism. Haller. Euler. The argument from ignorance. Decay of orthodoxy. Influence of the king	269
	11.	Frederick	272

			PAGE
	12.	Nicolai and his publications. Riem. Schade. Basedow. Eberhard. Spalding. Teller	274
	13.	Clerical rationalism. Semler	277
	14.	Bahrdt	278
	15.	Mendelssohn. Reimarus. Lessing	281
	16.	Vogue of deism. Wieland. Isenbiehl. Further clerical rationalism. Schulz. Orthodox and official reaction. The *Moroccan Letters*. Mauvillon. The edict of repression. Herder	285
	17.	Goethe	290
	18.	Schiller	292
	19.	Kant	293
	20.	Influence of Kant. The sequel. Fichte. Erhard. Hamann	300
	21.	Other philosophic movements. Crusius. Tetens. Platner. Pyrrhonism of Beausobre. Fichte's development. Strifes of the post-Kantians. Nugatoriness of the theistic constructions. Thought in Austria. Rule of the Jesuits. Jahn. Beethoven	302

§ III. *The remaining European States.*

	1.	The reformation in Denmark and Sweden. Gustavus Vasa. Christina. Puffendorf. Count Struensee	306
	2.	Poland. Liszinski. Russia. Peter the Great and the monks. Catherine	308
	3.	Italy. Spanish misrule. Tuscany. The two Ferdinands. Naples under Carpi. Vico. His influence	309
	4.	Beccaria and the economists	312
	5.	Algarotti. Filangieri. Galiani. Genovesi. Alfieri. Bettinelli. Dandolo. Leopold of Tuscany. Fall of the Jesuits	313
	6.	Spain. Aranda. The rule of Charles III. The Catholic reaction	314
	7.	Portugal. Pombal	315
	8.	Switzerland	315

CHAP. XVII.—EARLY FREETHOUGHT IN THE UNITED STATES.

	1.	Deism of the revolutionary statesmen	317
	2.	First traces of unbelief. Franklin	317
	3.	Jefferson. John Adams. Washington	318
	4.	Thomas Paine	320
	5.	Paine's treatment in America	321
	6.	Palmer. Houston. Deism and Unitarianism	322

CHAP. XVIII.—FREETHOUGHT IN THE NINETEENTH CENTURY.

General outline - - - - - 325

§ I. *Popular Propaganda.*

1. The influence of Paine. Watson's Reply. Translations from the French. Houston. Wedderburn. Richard Carlile and his co-adjutors. Taylor. Southwell and his co-adjutors. Hetherington - - - 327
2. Robert Owen and his movement. G. and A. Combe. G. J. Holyoake. Bradlaugh and the Secularist movement. The Bradlaugh struggle. Trial of G. W. Foote. Results to freethought. Case of Mrs. Besant - 332
3. The United States. France. Movements of Fourier, Saint-Simon, and Comte. Other Catholic countries. Spain. Holland. Freethought journalism - - - - 336
4. Germany. Freethought after the war of Liberation. Religious reaction. The "Friends of Light." Freethought in 1848. "Free-religious" societies. Organised freethought. German police laws. Marx, Bebel, and Liebknecht. German freethought in the United States - - 338
5. "Free-religious" societies in America and England. Fox, Conway, and South Place Chapel. The Ethical Societies. The Labour Churches - - - - 342
6. Unitarianism - - - - - 343
7. Academic freethinking in France. Opinion in 1830. Academic freethought in Switzerland. The religious revolt. Decline of Swiss clericalism and orthodoxy. Critical thought in Holland. The Transvaal. Results of the South African War - - 345
8. Popular freethought in the Catholic countries. Belgium. Spain. Portugal. France. Italy. The South American Republics - - 348
9. Popular freethought in Sweden - - 349

Scholarly and other Biblical Criticism.

1. German rationalism. Schleiermacher. The evolution to Strauss. Persecution. Leeway in research. Unsuccessful new departures. Ghillany. Daumer - - - - 351
2. The German academic evolution. Decay of interest in theology - - - - 354
3. Progress in England and the United States. Unitarianism. Hennell. Parker. F. W. Newman. R. W. Mackay. Greg. Thomas Scott. W. R. Cassels' *Supernatural Religion* 356

			PAGE
	4.	Rationalism in France. Larroque. D'Eichthal. Peyrat. Renan. Havet	358
	5.	The higher criticism. Eichhorn's successors. Geddes. Colenso. Kuenen. Wellhausen. Smith. Kalisch. New Testament criticism to Schmiedel. Unitarian propaganda	358
	6.	Assyriology	360
§ III.	*The Natural Sciences.*		
	1.	*Astronomy.* Effects of the Copernican and Newtonian systems. Laplace's theory. Readjustment of theism. Miracles	361
	2.	*Biology.* Lawrence	362
	3.	*Geology.* Werner and Hutton. Hugh Miller	363
	4.	*Zoology.* Erasmus Darwin. Saint-Hilaire. Goethe. The Orthodox resistance	365
	5.	*Evolutionary Biology.* Robert Chambers. Orthodox vilification	366
	6.	*Darwinism.* C. Darwin and Wallace. The orthodox attack. Wilberforce and Huxley. Luthardt. Carlyle on Darwin	366
	7.	Collapse of deism. Developments of Darwinism. Haeckel	368
§ IV.	*Abstract Philosophy and Ethics.*		
	1.	The German successors of Kant. Hegel and his school. Bruno Bauer. Schopenhauer. Hartmann. Nietzsche	369
	2.	Feuerbach. Buchner	371
	3.	Philosophy in France after the Revolution. Maine de Biran. De Maistre. Cousin. Jouffroy. Lamennais. Damiron	372
	4.	Auguste Comte. Taine	374
	5.	Philosophy in Britain. Bentham. James Mill. George Grote. Influence of Utilitarianism	375
	6.	Hamilton. Mansel. Spencer. The Hegelians	376
	7.	Rationalism within the Church. Influence of Coleridge. Maurice. Parr	377
	8.	Unitarianism. Emerson. Parker	378
V.	*The Sociological Sciences.*		
	1.	Deism and sociology. Salverte. Charles Comte. Auguste Comte. Draper. Buckle. Spencer. Recent sociology	379
	2.	Anthropology and mythology	380
	3.	Psychology. Phrenology	381
§ VI.	*Poetry and Fine Letters.*		
	1.	France after the Revolution. Chateaubriand and his school	382

		PAGE
2.	Later French literature. Michelet. The novelists	384
3.	French poetry. Beranger. De Musset. Hugo. Leconte de Lisle. Neurotic religion	385
4.	English poetry. Shelley. Coleridge. Scott. Byron. Southey. Keats	386
5.	Tennyson. Browning. Clough. Arnold. Swinburne. James Thomson	388
6.	The case of Charles Lamb	389
7.	Carlyle. Emerson. Ruskin. Arnold	391
8.	The novelists. George Eliot. Recent fiction	392
9.	The case of Richard Jefferies	393
10.	*Belles Lettres* in the United States. Hawthorne. Poe. Emerson. Thoreau. Whitman. Howells. H. James. Holmes. Higginson. Conway	394
11.	Italy. Leopardi. Germany. Kleist. Heine. Auerbach. Heyse. Wagner	395
12.	Russia. Bielinsky. Granovsky. Tourguenief. Tolstoy. Gorky. The Scandinavian States	398

CHAP. XIX.—THE STATE OF THOUGHT IN THE NATIONS.

§ 1. *Britain and the United States.* Conventional dissimulation. Romilly. Brougham. Carlyle. Mill. Froude. Macaulay. Bain on Carlyle, Macaulay, and Lyell. The economic pressure. Mr. Morley. Sir L. Stephen. Difficulties as to endowing rationalism. Position of freethought lecturers. Optimistic miscalculations. Cases of reversion. Vogue of paralogism. Drummond. Rarity of best propagandist type. Clifford. Huxley. Pressures in the United States. Lincoln. Douglass. Grant. Ingersoll. Journalism. Clerical obscurantism. Conflicting forces in the churches. Politics and freethought. Neutral propaganda. The Free Church quarrel in Scotland. Stress of life in the United States. Australia and New Zealand. Unitarianism. Romanism and Ritualism. Welcome given to new works of apologetics. Intellect in the Church of England. Freethought among women. Harriet Martineau. George Eliot. Mrs. Besant. Frances Wright -   400

§ 2. *The Catholic Countries.* Sharp division between faith and rationalism. Revival of Italy. Leopardi. Mazzini. Garibaldi. Gubernatis. France. Gambetta. Paris Municipal Council. Position of women. Socialism   414

§ 3. *Germany.* Bureaucratism and reaction. Virchow.

		PAGE
	Catholicism. The theological chairs. Tendencies to reversion. Harnack. The Social Democrats. Influence of Marx, Engels, and Bebel - - - - - - -	417
§ 4.	*Russia and the Scandinavian States.* The Scandinavian conditions. Russia. Popular ignorance. The *intelliguentia*. Present prospects - -	419
§ 5.	*Modern Jewry.* Part played by Jews in freethought history. Jewish deism in eighteenth century. Rabbi Elijah. Krochmal. Present tendencies -	421
§ 6.	*The Oriental Civilisations.* Asiatic ignorance. The new birth of Japan. Popular religion there. Attitude of Fukuzawa. The social problem. Vogue of religion. Estimates of Japanese thought: Chamberlain, Griffis, Tracy, Dixon, Hearn, Gulick, Parker. Dependence of rationalism on culture. Iyevasu. Transition from old to new. Thought in China. Freethought in Islam. Prospects in India. Buddhism in Burmah. Modern Brahmanism. Chaitanya. Nanak and the Sikhs. The Jainas. The Brahmo-Somaj movement. Turkey. Christian Greece. Conclusion: preoccupations of social and intellectual problems - - - -	422

Chapter XIII.

THE RISE OF MODERN FREETHOUGHT

§ 1. *The Italian Influence.*

THE negative bearing of the Reformation on freethought is made clear by the historic fact that the new currents of thought which broadly mark the beginning of the "modern spirit" arose in its despite, and derive originally from outside its sphere. It is to Italy, where the political and social conditions always tended to frustrate the Inquisition, that we trace the rise alike of modern deism, modern Unitarianism, modern pantheism, modern physics, and the tendency to rational atheism. The deistic way of thinking, of course, prevailed long before it got that name; and besides the vogue of Averroism we have noted the virtual deism of More's *Utopia* (1515). The first explicit mention of deism noted by Bayle, however, is in the epistle dedicatory to the second and expanded edition of the *Instruction Chretienne* of the Swiss Protestant Viret (1563), where professed deists are spoken of as a new species bearing a new name. On the admission of Viret, who was the friend and bitter disciple of Calvin, they rejected all revealed religion, but called themselves deists by way of repudiating atheism; some keeping a belief in immortality, some rejecting it. In the theological manner he goes on to call them all execrable atheists, and to say that he has added to his treatise on their account an exposition of natural religion grounded on the "Book of Nature"; stultifying himself by going on to say that he has also dealt with the professed atheists.[1] Of the deists

---

[1] Bayle, *Dictionnaire*, art. VIRET, note D.

he admits that among them were men of the highest repute for science and learning. Thus within ten years of the burning of Servetus we find privately avowed deism and atheism in the area of French-speaking Protestantism.

Doubtless the spectacle of Protestant feuds and methods would go far to foster such unbelief; but though, as we have seen, there were aggressive Unitarians in Germany before 1530, who, being scholars, may or may not have drawn on Italian thought, thereafter there is reason to look to Italy as the source of the propaganda. Thence came the two Sozzini, the founders of Socinianism, of whom Lelio, the uncle of Fausto, travelled much in northern Europe (including England) between 1546 and 1552.[1] Before Socinianism had taken form it was led up to, as we have seen, in the later writings of the ex-monk Bernardino Ochino (1487–1564), who, in the closing years of a much chequered career, combined mystical and Unitarian tendencies with a leaning to polygamy and freedom of divorce.[2] His influence was considerable among the Swiss Protestants, though they finally expelled him for his heresies. From Geneva or from France, in turn, apparently came some of the English freethought of the middle period of the sixteenth century;[3] for in 1562 Speaker Williams in the House of Commons, in a list of misbelievers, speaks of "Pelagians, *Libertines*, Papists, and such others, leaving God's commandments to follow their own traditions, affections, and minds"[4]—using theologically the foreign term, which never became naturalised in English

---

[1] Calvin, scenting his heresy, warned him in 1552 (Bayle, art. MARIANUS SOCIN, the first, note B); but they remained on surprisingly good terms till Lelio's death in 1562. Cp. Stahelin, *Johannes Calvin*, ii, 321-8.
[2] Cp. Bayle, art. OCHIN; Miss M. E. Lowndes, *Michel de Montaigne*, p. 266; Owen, *Skeptics of the French Renaissance*, p. 588; Benrath, *Bernardino Ochino of Siena*, Eng. trans. 1876, pp. 268-272. McCrie mentions (*Reformation in Italy*, ed. 1856, p. 228, *note*) that Ochino's dialogue on polygamy has been translated and published in England "by the friends of that practice."
[3] Above, vol. i, pp. 473-4.
[4] D'Ewes, *Journals of Parliament in the Reign of Elizabeth*, 1682, p. 65.

in its foreign sense. It was about the year 1563, again, that Roger Ascham wrote his *Scholemaster*, wherein are angrily described, as a species new in England, men who, "where they dare," scorn both Protestant and Papist, rejecting scripture, and counting the Christian mysteries as fables."[1] He describes them as "$\alpha\theta\epsilon o\iota$ in doctrine"; adding, "this last word is no more unknowne now to plane Englishe men than the Person was unknown somtyme in England, untill some Englishe man took peines to fetch that develish opinion out of Italie."[2] The whole tendency he connects in a general way with the issue of many new translations from the Italian, mentioning in particular Petrarch and Boccaccio. Among good Protestants his view was general; and so Lord Burghley in his *Advice to his Son* writes: "Suffer not thy sons to pass the Alps, for they shall learn nothing there but pride, blasphemy, and atheism." As it happened, his grandson the second Earl of Exeter, and his great-grandson Lord Roos, went to Rome and became not atheists but Roman Catholics.

Like the old Averroïsm, the new pietistic Unitarianism persisted in Italy and radiated thence afresh when it had flagged in other lands. The exploded Unitarian tradition[3] runs that the doctrine arose in the year 1546 among a group of more than forty learned men who were wont to assemble in secret at Vicenza, near Venice. In point of fact, Melanchthon comments on Unitarianism at Venice in 1538,[4] and Servetus, the alleged source of the earlier Venetian movement, after intercourse with Lutherans in Germany, had put forth his anti-trinitarian doctrines as early as 1531 and 1532. Claudius of Savoy, too, emphatically gave out his at Berne in 1534, after having been imprisoned at Strasburg and banished thence;[5] and Ochino and Lelio

[1] See above, vol. i, p. 474.
[2] *The Scholemaster*, Arber's rep. p. 82.
[3] See McCrie, *Reformation in Italy*, ed. 1856, pp. 96-99.
[4] *Id.* p. 96.
[5] Trechsel, *Die Protestantischen Antitrinitarier vor Faustus Socinus*, i (1839), 56; Mosheim, 16 Cent. 3rd sec. Pt. ii, ch. iv, § 3.

Sozzini left Italy in 1543. But there seems to have been a continuous evolution of Unitarian heresy in the south after the German movement had ceased. Giorgio Biandrata, whom we have seen flying to Poland from Geneva, had been seized by the Inquisition at Pavia for such opinion. Still it persisted. In 1562, Giulio Guirlando of Treviso, and in 1566 Francesco Saga of Rovigo, were burned at Venice for anti-Trinitarianism. Giacomo Aconzio, too, who dedicated his *Stratagems of Satan* (Basel, 1565) to Queen Elizabeth, and who pleaded notably for the toleration of heresy,[1] was a decided latitudinarian.[2]

It is remarkable that the whole ferment occurs in the period of the Catholic Reaction, the Council of Trent, and the subjection of Italy, when the Papacy was making its great effort to recover its ground. It would seem that in the compulsory peace which had now fallen on Italian life men's thoughts turned more than ever to mental problems, as had happened in Greece after the rise of Alexander's empire. The authority of the church was outwardly supreme; the Jesuits had already begun to do great things for education;[3] the revived Inquisition was everywhere in Italy; its prisons, as we have seen, were crowded with victims of all grades during a whole generation; Pius V and the hierarchy everywhere sought to enforce decorum in life; the "pagan" academies formed on the Florentine model were dissolved; and classic culture rapidly decayed with the arts, while clerical learning flourished,[4] and a new religious music began with Palestrina; yet on the death of Paul IV the Roman populace burned the Office of the Inquisition to the ground and cast the Pope's statue into

---

[1] Hallam, *Lit. of Europe*, ii, 82.
[2] Art. ACONTIUS, in *Dict. of National Biog.* Cp. J. J. Tayler, *Retrospect of the Religious Life of England*, 2nd ed. pp. 205-6. As to the attack on latitudinarianism in the Thirty-nine Articles, see above, vol. i, p. 475.
[3] Bacon, *Advancement of Learning*, B. i; *Filum Labyrinthi*, § 7 (Routledge's ed. pp. 50, 63, 209).
[4] Cp. Zeller, *Hist. de l'Italie*, pp. 400-412; Greene, *Short Hist.* ch.

the Tiber;[1] and in that age (1548) was born Giordano Bruno, one of the types of modern freethought.

§ 2. *France*.

In the other countries influenced by Italian culture in the sixteenth century the rationalist spirit had various fortune. The true renascence of letters in France had begun before and gone on during the Reformation period; and all along it showed a tincture of freethought. From the midst of the group who laid the foundations of French Protestantism by translations of the Bible there comes forth the most articulate freethinker of that age, BONAVENTURE DESPERIERS, author of the *Cymbalum Mundi* (1537). Early associated with Calvin and Olivetan in revising the translation of the Bible by Lefevre d'Etaples (rev. 1535), Desperiers turned away from the Protestant movement, as did Rabelais and Dolet, caring as little for the new presbyter as for the old priest; and all three were duly accused by the Protestants of atheism and *libertinage*.[2] In the same year Desperiers aided Dolet to produce his much-praised *Commentarii linguae latinae;* and within two years he had printed his own satire, *Cymbalum Mundi*,[3] wherein, by way of pagan dialogues, are allegorically ridiculed the Christian scheme, its miracles, Bible contradictions, and the spirit of persecution, then in full fire in France against the Protestants. The allegory is not always clear to modern eyes; but there was no question then about its general bearing; and Desperiers, though groom of the chamber (after Clement Marot) to Marguerite of France (later of Navarre), had to fly for his

---

[1] McCrie, p. 164. It was said by Senliger that "in the time of Pius IV [between Paul IV and Pius V] people talked very freely in Rome." *Id. ib.* note.

[2] *Notice* of Bonaventure Desperiers, by Bibliophile Jacob, in 1841 ed. of *Cymbalum Mundi*, etc.

[3] For a solution of the enigma of the title see the *Clef* of Eloi Johanneau in ed. cited, p. 83. The book is dedicated by *Thomas Du Clevier a son ami Pierre Tyrocan*, which is found to be, with one letter altered (perhaps by a printer's error), an anagram for *Thomas Incrédule a son ami Pierre Croyant*, "Unbelieving Thomas to his friend Believing Peter." *Clef* cited, pp. 80–85.

life as Marot did before him. The first edition of his book, secretly printed at Paris, was seized and destroyed; and the second (1538), printed for him at Lyons, whither he had taken his flight, seems to have had a similar fate. From that time he disappears, probably dying, whether or not by suicide is doubtful,[1] before 1544, when his miscellaneous works were published. They include his *Œuvres Diverses*—many of them graceful poems addressed to his royal mistress, Marguerite—which, with his verse translation of the *Andria* of Terence and his *Discours non plus Melancoliques que Divers*, make up his small body of work. In the *Discours* may be seen applied to matters of history and scholarship the same critical spirit that utters itself in the *Cymbalum*, and the same literary gift; but for orthodoxy his name became a hissing and a byword, and it is only in modern times that French scholarship has recognised in Desperiers the true literary comrade and potential equal of Rabelais and Marot.[2] The age of Francis was too inclement for such literature as his *Cymbalum;* and it was much that it spared Gringoire (d. 1544), who, without touching doctrine, satirised in his verse both priests and Protestants.

It is something of a marvel, further, that it spared RABELAIS (? 1493–1553), whose enormous raillery so nearly fills up the literary vista of the age for modern retrospect. It has been said by a careful student that "the free and universal inquiry, the philosophic doubt, which were later to work the glory of Descartes, proceed from Rabelais";[3] and it is indeed an impression of boundless intellectual curiosity and wholly unfettered thinking that is set up by his entire career. Educated at a convent school, he had the luck to have for schoolfellows the four famous brothers Du Bellay, so well able

---

[1] The readiness of piety in all ages to invent frightful deaths for unbelievers must be remembered in connection with this and other records. Cp. *Notice* cited, p. xx, and note.

[2] So Charles Nodier, cited in the *Notice* by Bibliophile Jacob, pp. xxiii–xxiv.

[3] Perrens, *Les Libertins en France au XVIIe siecle*, 1896, p. 41.

to protect him in later life ; and, forced to spend fifteen years of his young life (1509-24) as a Franciscan monk, he turned the time to account by acquiring an immense erudition, including a knowledge of Greek, then rare.[1] Naturally the book-lover was not popular among his fellow-monks; and his Greek books were actually confiscated by the chapter, who found in his cell certain writings of Erasmus. Thereafter, by the help of the friendly bishop of the diocese, Rabelais received papal permission to join the order of the Benedictines (1524); but soon after, though he was a fully-ordained priest, we find him broken loose, and living for some six years a life of wandering freedom, winning friends in high places by his learning and his gaiety, everywhere studying and observing. In 1530 he is found at Montpellier, extending his studies in medicine, in which he speedily won distinction, becoming a lecturer in the following year. He was esteemed one of the chief anatomists of his day, being one of the first to dissect the human body and to insist on the need of such training for physicians ;[2] and in 1532 he published at Lyons an edition of the Latin letters of the Ferrarese physician Mandard; and his own commentaries on Galen and Hippocrates.[3] At Lyons he made the acquaintance of Dolet, Marot, and Desperiers; and his letter (of the same year) to Erasmus, addressed as Bernard de Salignac, showed afresh how his intellectual sympathies went.

In 1533 began his series of almanacks, continued till 1550, presumably as printer's hack-work. Only one of them seems to have been comic; and this, which alone has been preserved entire, passes hardy ridicule on astrology,[4] one of the most popular superstitions of the

---

[1] *Notice historique* in Bibliophile Jacob's ed. of Rabelais, 1841 ; Stapfer, *Rabelais*, pp. 6, 10.
[2] Le Double, *Rabelais anatomiste et physiologiste*, 1889, pp. 12, 425; and pref. by Professor Duval, p. xiii; Stapfer, p. 42.
[3] In the same year he was induced to publish what turned out to be two spurious documents purporting to be ancient Roman remains. See Heulhard, *Rabelais légiste*.   [4] Stapfer, pp. 24-25.

day, among high and low alike. Just before, he had begun to handle the famous names and figures of Pantagruel and Gargantua; and almost immediately the Sorbonne was on his track, condemning his *Pantagruel* in 1533. A journey soon afterwards to Rome, in the company of his friend Bishop Jean du Bellay, the French ambassador, may have saved him some personal experience of persecution. Two years later, when the Bishop went to Rome to be made cardinal, Rabelais again accompanied him; and this time he obtained from Pope Clement VII an absolution for his breach of his monastic vows, with permission to practise medicine in a Benedictine monastery. Shortly before, his little son Theodule had died;[1] and it may have been grief that inspired such a desire: in any case, the papal permission was never used,[2] though the pardon was doubtless serviceable. Taking his degree as doctor at Montpelier in 1537, he recommenced a wandering life.

In this period Rabelais had seen cause to modify a number of the hardier utterances in the original issues of the first two books of his *Pantagruel*, notably his many epithets aimed at the Sorbonne.[3] In the reprints there are substituted for Biblical names some drawn from heathen mythology; expressions too strongly savouring of Calvinism are withdrawn; and disrespectful allusions to the kings of France are elided. Calvin, who had once been his friend, had in his book *De Scandalis* angrily accused him of *libertinage*, profanity, and atheism; and henceforth, like Desperiers, he was as little in sympathy with Protestantism as with the zealots of Rome. In his concern to keep himself safe with the Sorbonne he even made a rather unworthy attack (1542) on his former friend ETIENNE DOLET for the mere

---

[1] Rathery, *Notice biog.* in edit. Firmin Didot, i, 71; Stapfer, pp. 42–43.
[2] Stapfer, p. 53.
[3] See the list in the avertissement of M. Burgaud des Marets to éd. Firmin Didot. Cp. Stapfer, pp. 63, 64. For example, the "theologian" who makes the ludicrous speech in Liv. i, ch. 19, becomes (cc. 18 and 20) a "sophist"; and the *sorbonistes, sorbonicoles,* and *sorbonagres* of cc. 20 and 21 become mere *maistres, magistres,* and *sophistes* likewise.

oversight of reprinting one of his books without deleting passages which Rabelais had expunged;[1] but no expurgation could make his *evangile*, as he called it, a Christian treatise, or keep for him an orthodox reputation; and it was with much elation that he obtained in 1545 from King Francis—whose private reader was his friend Duchatel, Bishop of Tulle—a privilege to print the third book of *Pantagruel*, which he issued in 1546, signed for the first time with his name, and prefaced by a cry of jovial defiance to the "petticoated devils" of the Sorbonne. They at once sought to convict him of fresh blasphemies; but even the thrice-repeated substitution of an *n* for an *m* in *âme*, making "ass" out of "soul," was carried off, by help of Bishop Duchatel, as a printer's error; and the king, having laughed like other readers, maintained the imprimatur.

It was on the death of Francis in 1547 that Rabelais ran his greatest danger, having to fly to Metz, where for a time he acted as salaried physician of the city. In 1549, however, on the birth of a son to Henri II, his friend Cardinal Bellay returned to power, and Rabelais to court favour with him. The derider of astrology did not scruple to cast a prosperous horoscope for the infant prince—justifying by strictly false predictions his own estimate of the art, since the child died in the cradle. There was now effected the dramatic scandal of the appointment of Rabelais in 1550 to two parish cures, one of which, Meudon, has given him his most familiar *sobriquet*. He seems to have left both to be served by vicars;[2] but the wrath of the church was so great that early in 1552 he resigned them;[3] proceeding immediately

---

[1] R. Christie, *Étienne Dolet*, pp. 369-372. Mr. Christie, in his vacillating way, severely blames Dolet, and then admits that the book may have been printed while Dolet was in prison, and that in any case there was no malice in the matter. This point, and the persistent Catholic calumnies against Dolet, are examined by the author in art. "The Truth about Etienne Dolet," in *National Reformer*, June 2nd and 9th, 1889.

[2] Jacob, *Notice*, p. lxiii; Stapfer, p. 76.

[3] So Rathery, p. 60, and Stapfer, p. 78. Jacob, p. lxii, says he resigned only one. Rathery makes the point clear by giving a copy of the act of resignation as to Meudon.

afterwards to publish the fourth book of *Pantagruel*, for which he had duly obtained official privilege. As usual, the Sorbonne rushed to the pursuit ; and the Parlement of Paris forbade the sale of the book despite the royal permission. That permission, however, was reaffirmed ; and this, the most audacious of all the writings of Rabelais, went forth freely throughout France. In the following year, his work done, he died.

It is difficult to estimate the intellectual effect of his performance, which was probably much greater at the end of the century than during his life. His vast innuendoes by way of jests about the people of *Ruach* (the Spirit) who lived solely on wind ;[1] his quips about the "reverend fathers in devil," of the "diabological faculty";[2] his narratives about the *Papefigues* and *Papimanes*;[3] and his gibes at the Decretals,[4] were doubtless enjoyed by many good Catholics, otherwise placated by his attacks on the "demoniacal Calvins, impostors of Geneva";[5] and so careful was he on matters of dogma that it remains impossible to say with confidence whether or not he finally believed in a future state.[6] That he was a deist or Unitarian seems the reasonable inference as to his general creed ;[7] but there also he throws out no negations—even indicates a genial contempt for the *philosophe ephectique et pyrrhonien*[8] who opposes a halting doubt to two contrary doctrines. In any case, he was anathema to the heresy-hunters of the Sorbonne, and only powerful protection could have saved him. Dolet was at least no more of an unbeliever than he ; but where Rabelais could with ultimate impunity ridicule the whole machinery of the church,[9] Dolet, after several iniquitous prosecutions, in which

---

[1] Liv. iv, ch. 43.   [2] Liv. iii, ch. 23.
[3] Liv. iv, ch. 45-48.   [4] Liv. iv, ch. 49 sq.   [5] Liv. iv, ch. 32.
[6] Professor Stapfer, *Rabelais, sa personne, son génie, son œuvre*, 1889, pp. 365-8. Cp. the *Notice* of Bibliophile Jacob, ed. 1841 of Rabelais, pp. lvii-lviii ; and Perrens, *Les Libertins*, p. 39. In his youth he affirmed the doctrine. Stapfer, p. 23.
[7] Cp. Rene Millet, *Rabelais*, 1892, pp. 172-180. Ramus, whom Rabelais had derided, accused him of atheism. Jacob, p. lxx.
[8] Liv. iii, ch. 36.   [9] Cp. Voltaire, *Lettres sur Rabelais*, etc., i.

his jealous rivals in the printing business took part, was finally done to death in priestly revenge[1] for his youthful attack on the religion of inquisitorial Toulouse, where gross pagan superstition and gross orthodoxy went hand in hand.[2] The second last attack on him was for publishing Protestant books and French translations of the Bible: the last was a hypocritical charge of mistranslating the dying speech of Socrates. Of the freethought of such an age there could be no adequate record. Its tempestuous energy, however, implies not a little of private unbelief; and at a time when in England, two generations behind France in point of literary evolution, there was, as we have seen, a measure of rationalism among religionists, there must have been at least as much in the land of Rabelais and Desperiers. The work of Guillaume Postell, *De causis seu principiis et originibus Naturæ contra Atheos*, published in 1552, testifies to kinds of unbelief that outwent the doubt of Rabelais; though Postell's general extravagance discounts all of his utterances. It is said of Guillaume Pellicier (1527–1568), Bishop of Montpellier, who first turned Protestant and afterwards atheist, that he would have been burned but for the fact of his consecration.[3]

Among the eminent ones then surmised to lean somewhat to unbelief was the sister of King Francis, Marguerite of Navarre, whom we have noted as a protectress of the pantheistic *Libertini*, denounced by Calvin. She is held to have been substantially skeptical until her forty-fifth year;[4] though her final religiousness seems also beyond doubt.[5] In her youth she bravely protected the Protestants from the first persecution of 1523 onwards; and the strongly Protestant drift of her *Miroir de l'ame pecheresse* exasperated the Catholic theologians; but after the Protestant violences of 1546

[1] Cp. author's art. above cited.
[2] Christie, *Etienne Dolet*, pp. 105-6.
[3] Perrens, *Les Libertins*, p. 43, citing Patin, *Lettres*, i, 210.
[4] Ch. Nodier, quoted by Bibliophile Jacob in ed. of *Cymbalum Mundi*, as cited, p. xviii.
[5] Cp. Brantome, *Des dames illustres*. Œuvres, ed. 1838, ii, 186.

she seems to have sided with her brother against the Reform.[1] The strange taste of the *Heptameron*, of which again her part-authorship seems certain,[2] constitutes a moral paradox not to be solved save by recognising in her a woman of genius, whose alternate mysticism and bohemianism expressed a very ancient duality in human nature.

A similar mixture will explain the intellectual life of the poet Ronsard. A persecutor of the Huguenots,[3] he was denounced as an atheist by two of their ministers;[4] and the pagan fashion in which he handled Christian things scandalised his own side, albeit he was hostile to Rabelais. But though the spirit of the French Renaissance, so eagerly expressed in the *Défense et Illustration de la langue françoise* of Joachim du Bellay (1549), is at its outset as emancipated as that of the Italian, we find Ronsard in his latter years edifying the pious.[5] Any ripe and consistent rationalism, indeed, was then impossible. One of the most powerful minds of the age was BODIN (1530–96), whose *République* is one of the most scientific treatises on government between Aristotle and our own age, and whose *Colloquium Heptaplomeres*[6] is no less original an outline of a naturalist[7] philosophy. It consists of six dialogues, in which seven men take part, setting forth the different religious standpoints of Jew, Christian, pagan, Lutheran, Calvinist, and Catholic, the whole leading up to a doctrine of tolerance and universalism. Bodin was repeatedly and emphatically accused of unbelief by

---

[1] Bayle, *Dictionnaire*, art. MARGUERITE DE NAVARRE (the First), notes F and G.

[2] Bayle, note N. Cp. Nodier, as cited, p. xix, as to the collaboration of Desperiers and others.

[3] Bayle, art. RONSARD, note D.

[4] Garasse, *La Doctrine Curieuse des Beaux Esprits de ce Temps*, 1623, pp. 126-7. Ronsard replied to the charge in his poem, *Des miseres du temps*.

[5] Bayle, art. RONSARD, note O. Cp. Perrens, *Les Libertins*, p. 43.

[6] MS. 1588. First printed in 1841 by Guhrauer, again in 1857 by L. Noack.

[7] As before noted, he seems to have coined the word. Cp. Lechler, *Geschichte des englischen Deismus*, pp. 31, 455, *notes*.

friends and foes;[1] and his rationalism on some heads is beyond doubt; yet he not only held by the belief in witchcraft, but wrote a furious treatise in support of it;[2] and he dismissed the system of Copernicus as too absurd for discussion.[3] He also formally vetoes all discussion on faith, declaring it to be dangerous to religion;[4] and by these conformities he probably saved himself from ecclesiastical attack.[5] Nonetheless, he essentially stood for religious toleration: the new principle that was to change the face of intellectual life. A few liberal Catholics shared it with him to some extent[6] long before St. Bartholomew's Day; eminent among them being L'Hopital,[7] whose humanity, tolerance, and concern for practical morality and the reform of the church brought upon him the charge of atheism. He was, however, a believing Catholic.[8] Deprived of power, his edict of tolerance repealed, he saw the long and ferocious struggle of Catholics and Huguenots renewed, and crowned by the massacre of St. Bartholomew's Day (1572). Broken-hearted, and haunted by that monstrous memory, he died within six months.

Two years later there was put to death at Paris, by

---

[1] Bayle, art. BODIN, note O. Cp. Renan, *Averroes*, 3e edit. p. 424; and the *Lettres de Gui Patin*, iii, 679 (letter of 27 juillet, 1668), cited by Perrens, *Les Libertins*, p. 43. Leibnitz, in an early letter to Jac. Thomasius, speaks of the MS. of the *Colloquium*, then in circulation, as proving its writer to be "the professed enemy of the Christian religion," adding: "Vanini's dialogues are a trifle in comparison." (*Philosophische Schriften*, ed. Gerhardt, i, 26; Martineau, *Study of Spinoza*, 1882, p. 77.) Carriere, however, notes (*Weltanschauung*, p. 317) that in later years Leibnitz learned to prize Bodin's treatise highly.

[2] Cp. Lecky, *Rationalism in Europe*, ed. 1887, i, 66, 87-91. In the *République*, too, he has a chapter on astrology, to which he leans somewhat. [3] *République*, Liv. iv, ch. 2.

[4] *Id.* Liv. iv, ch. 7. "Bodin in this sophistry was undoubtedly insincere" (Hallam, *Lit. of Europe*, ii, 159). [5] Cp. Perrens, *Les Libertins*, p. 43.

[6] Cp. Villemain, *Vie de L'Hopital*, in *Etudes de l'histoire moderne*, 1846, pp. 363-8, 428.

[7] Buckle (3-vol. ed. ii, 10; 1 vol. ed. p. 291) errs in representing L'Hopital as the only statesman of the time who dreamt of toleration. It is to be noted, on the other hand, that the Huguenots themselves protested against any toleration of atheists or Anabaptists; and even the reputed freethinker Gabriel Naudé, writing in 1639, defended the massacre on political grounds (Owen, *Skeptics of the French Renaissance*, p. 470, *note*). Bodin implicitly execrated it. Cp. Hallam, *Lit. of Europe*, ii, 162. [8] Villemain, p. 429.

hanging and burning, on the charge of atheism, Geoffroi Vallee, a man of good family in Orleans. Long before, at the age of sixteen, he had written a freethinking treatise entitled *La Beatitude des Chretiens, ou le fleau de la foy*. He had been the associate of Ronsard, who renounced him, and helped, it is said, to bring him to execution.[1] It is not unlikely that a similar fate would have overtaken the famous Protestant scholar and lexicographer, Henri Estienne (1532-1598), had he not died unexpectedly. His repute of being "the prince of atheists"[2] and the " Pantagruel of Geneva" was probably due in large part to his sufficiently audacious *Apologie pour Herodote* (1566) and to his having translated into Latin (1562) the *Hypotyposes* of Sextus Empiricus, a work which clearly made for freethinking. In that book he had spoken, either ignorantly or ironically, of the "detestable work of Bonaventure Desperiers,"[3] but his own performance was nearly as well fitted to cause scandal.

One literary movement towards better things had begun before the crowning infamy of the Massacre appalled men into questioning the creed of intolerance. Castalio, whom we have seen driven from Geneva by Calvin in 1544 for repugning to the doctrine of predestination, published pseudonymously, in 1554, in reply to Calvin's vindication of the slaying of Servetus, a tract, *De Haereticis quomodo cum iis agendum sit variorum Sententiæ*, in which he contrived to collect some passage from the Fathers and from modern writers in favour of toleration. To these he prefaced, by way of a letter to the Duke of Wirtemberg, an argument of his own, the starting-point of much subsequent propaganda.[4] Aconzio, mentioned above, followed in his

---

[1] Garasse, *Doctrine Curieuse*, pp. 125-6; *Mémoires de Garasse*, ed. Ch. Nisard, 1860, pp. 77-78; Perrens, p. 43.
[2] Bibliophile Jacob, Introd. to Beroalde de Verville.
[3] *Cymbalum Mundi*, ed. Bibliophile Jacob, pp. xx, 13.
[4] Bayle, *Dictionnaire*, art. CASTALION; Hallam, *Lit. of Europe*, ii, 81; Lecky, *Rationalism in Europe*, ii, 46-49. Hallam finds Castalio's letter to the Duke of Wirtemberg "cautious"; but Mr. Lecky quotes some strong expressions from what he describes as the preface of Martin

steps; and later came Mino Celso of Siena, with his "long and elaborate argument against persecution," *De Haereticis capitali supplicio non afficiendis* (1584).[1] Withal, Castalio died in beggary, ostracised alike by Protestants and Catholics, and befriended only by the Sozzini, whose sect was the first to earn collectively the praise of condemning persecution.[2] But in the next generation there came to reinforce the cause of humanity a more puissant pen than any of these; while at the same time the recoil from religious cruelty was setting many men secretly at utter variance with faith.

In France in particular a generation of insane civil war for religion's sake must have gone far to build up unbelief. Already in 1552 we have seen Guillaume Postell publishing his book, *Contra Atheos*. Unbelief increasing, there is published in 1564 an *Atheomachie* by one De Bourgeville; but the Massacre must have gone far to frustrate him. In 1581 appears another *Atheomachie, ou réfutation des erreurs et impietes des Atheistes, Libertins, etc.*, issued at Geneva, but bearing much on French life; and in the same year is issued the long-time popular work of Philippe de Mornay, *De la verite de la religion Chrestienne, Contre les Athees, Epicuriens, Payens, Juifs, Mahumedistes, et autres Infidèles*.

> Published at Antwerp. It was reprinted in 1582, 1583, and 1590; translated into Latin in 1583, and frequently reprinted in that form; translated into English in 1587, and in that form at least thrice reprinted. In both the Epistle Dedicatory (to Henry of Navarre) and the Preface the author speaks of the great multiplication of unbelief, the refutation of which he declares to be more needful among Christians than it ever had been among the heathen. But, like most of the writers against atheism in that age, he declares (Eng. trans. ed. 1604, p. 10) that there are no atheists save a few young fools and utterly bad men.

Bellius (Castalio's pseudonym) to Cluten's *De Haereticis persequendis*, ed. 1610. Castalio died in 1563. As to his translations from the Bible, see Bayle's note.

[1] Hallam, ii, 83; McCrie, *Ref. in Italy*, ed. 1856, p. 231.
[2] Even Stahelin (*Johannes Calvin*, ii, 303) condemns Calvin's action and tone towards Castalio, though he makes the significant remark that the latter "treated the Bible pretty much as any other book."

Yet again, in 1586, Christophe Cheffontaines published his *Epitome novæ illustrationis Christianae Fidei adversus Impios, Libertinos et Atheos;* and still skepticism gained ground, having found a new and potent mouthpiece.

In the greatest French writer of that age, a professed Catholic, but in mature life averse alike to Catholic and to Protestant bigotry, the shock of the Massacre can be seen disintegrating once for all the spirit of faith. MONTAIGNE typifies the pure skepticism produced in an unscientific age by the practical demonstration that religion can avail immeasurably more for evil than for good.[1] A few years before the Massacre he had translated for his dying father[2] the old *Theologia Naturalis* of Raymond of Sebonde; and we know from the later *Apology* in the Essays that freethinking contemporaries declared the argument of Raymond to be wholly insufficient.[3] It is clear from the same essay that Montaigne felt as much; though the gist of his polemic is a vehement attack upon all forms of confident opinion, religious and anti-religious alike. "In replying to arguments of so opposite a tenour, Montaigne leaves Christianity, as well as Raimond Sebonde, without a leg to stand upon. He demolishes the arguments of Sebonde with the rest of human presumption, and allows Christianity, neither held by faith nor provable by reason, to fall between the two stools."[4] The truth is that Montaigne's essays are the product of a mental evolution spread over at least twenty years. In his youth his vivid temperament kept him both credulous and fanatical, so much so that in 1562 he took the reckless oath prescribed by the Catholic Parlement of Paris.

---

[1] "Our religion," he writes, "is made to extirpate vices; it protects, nourishes, and incites them" (*Essais*, B. ii, ch. 12; ed. Firmin-Didot, ii, 464). "There is no enmity so extreme as the Christian."
[2] Mr. Owen was mistaken (*Skeptics of the French Renaissance*, 1893, p. 414) in supposing that Montaigne spent several years over this translation. It was done rapidly. Cp. Miss M. E. Lowndes' excellent monograph, *Michel de Montaigne*, 1898, pp. 103, 106.
[3] Ed. Firmin-Didot, ii, 469.
[4] Miss Lowndes, as cited, p. 145. Cp. E. Champion, *Introduction aux Essais de Montaigne*, 1900.

Beginning to recoil from the ferocities and iniquities of the League, he remained for a time hotly anti-Protestant; and it seems to have been his dislike of Protestant criticism that led him to run amuck against reason, at the cost of overthrowing the treatise he had set out to defend. The common end of such petulant skepticism is a plunge into uneasy yet unreasoning faith; but, though Montaigne professed Catholicism to the end, the utter wickedness of the Catholic policy made it impossible for him to hold sincerely to the creed any more than to the cause.[1] It was the Massacre that above all made Montaigne renounce public life;[2] it must have affected likewise his working philosophy.

That philosophy was not, indeed, an original construction: he found it to his hand partly in the deism of his favourite Seneca; partly in the *Hypotyposes* of Sextus Empiricus, of which the Latin translation is known to have been among his books; from which he took several of the mottoes inscribed on his library ceiling,[3] and from which he frequently quotes towards the end of his *Apology*. The body of ideas compacted on these bases cannot be called a system: it was not in Montaigne's nature to frame a logical scheme of thought; and he was far from being the philosophic skeptic he set out to be[4] by way of confounding at once the bigots and the atheists. As he put it in a passage added to the later editions of the *Essais*,[5] he was a kind of *metis*, belonging neither to the camp of ignorant faith nor to that of philosophic conviction, whether believing or

---

[1] For a view of Montaigne's development see M. Champion's excellent *Introduction*—a work indispensable to a full understanding of the *Essais*.

[2] Cp. the *Essais*, B. iii, ch. i (ed. Firmin-Didot, ii, 208). Mr. Owen gives a somewhat misleading idea of the passage (*French Skeptics*, p. 486).

[3] Miss Lowndes, *Michel de Montaigne*, p. 131. Cp. Mr. Owen, p. 111.

[4] He was consistent enough to doubt the new cosmology of Copernicus (*Essais*, as cited, i, 615); and he even made a childish attack on the reform of the Calendar (liv. iii, cc. x, xi); but he was a keen and convinced critic of the prevailing abuses in law and education. Mr. Owen's discussion of his opinions is illuminating; but that of Champion makes a still more searching analysis as regards the conflicting tendencies in Montaigne.

[5] Liv. i, ch. 54.

unbelieving. But on the other hand his whole habit of mind is perfectly fatal to orthodox religion; and it is clear that, despite his professions of conformity, he did not hold the ordinary Christian beliefs.[1] Whatever he might say in the *Apology*, in the other essays he repeatedly reveals a radical unbelief. The essay on Custom strikes at the root of all orthodoxy, with its thrusts at "the gross imposture of religions, wherewith so many worthy and sufficient men have been besotted and drunken," and its terse avowal that "miracles are according to the ignorance wherein we are by nature, and not according to nature's essence."[2] Above all, he rejected the great superstition of the age, the belief in witchcraft. His function in literature was thus to set up a certain mental atmosphere,[3] and this the extraordinary vitality of his utterance enabled him to do to an incalculable extent. He had the gift to disarm or at least to baffle hostility, to charm kings,[4] to stand free between warring factions. No book ever written conveys more fully the sensation of a living voice; and after three hundred years he has as friendly an audience as ever.

   Mr. Owen notes (*French Skeptics*, p. 446; cp. Champion, pp. 168-9) that, though the Papal curia requested him to alter certain passages in the Essays, "it cannot be shown that he erased or modified a single one of the points." Sainte-Beuve, indeed, has noted many safeguarding clauses added to the later versions of the essay on Prayers (i, 56); but they really carry further the process of doubt. M. Champion has well shown how the profession of personal indecision and mere self-portraiture served as a passport for utterances which would have brought instant punishment on an author who showed any clear purpose. As it was, nearly a century passed before the *Essais* were placed upon the Roman *Index Librorum Prohibitorum* (1676).

The momentum of such an influence is seen in the

---

[1] Cp. the clerical protests of Sterling (*Lond. and Westm. Review*, July, 1838, p. 346) and Dean Church (*Oxford Essays*, p. 279) with the judgment of M. Champion, pp. 159-173.
[2] Liv. i, ch. 22.
[3] Cp. citations in Buckle, 3-vol. ed. ii, 18, note 42 (1-vol. ed. p. 296); Lecky, *Rationalism*, i, 92-5; and Perrens, *Les Libertins*, p. 44.
[4] As to Henri IV see Perrens, p. 53.

work of CHARRON (1541-1603), Montaigne's friend and disciple. The *Essais* had first appeared in 1580; the expanded and revised issue in 1588; and in 1601 there appeared Charron's *De la Sagesse,* which gives methodic form and as far as was permissible a direct application to Montaigne's naturalistic principles. Charron's is a curious case of mental evolution. First a lawyer, then a priest, he became a highly successful popular preacher and champion of the Catholic League; and as such was favoured by the notorious Marguerite (the Second[1]) of Navarre. Becoming the friend of Montaigne in 1586, he shows already in 1593, in his *Three Truths*, the influence of the essayist's skepticism,[2] though Charron's book was expressly framed to refute, first, the atheists; second, the pagans, Jews, Mohammedans; and third, the Christian heretics and schismatics. The *Wisdom,* published only eight years later, is a work of a very different cast, proving a mental change. Even in the first work " the growing teeth of the skeptic are discernible beneath the well-worn stumps of the believer";[3] but the second almost testifies to a new birth. Professedly orthodox, it was yet recognised at once by the devout as a "seminary of impiety,"[4] and brought on its author a persecution that lasted till his sudden death from apoplexy, which his critics pronounced to be a divine dispensation. In the second and rearranged edition, published a year after his death, there are some modifications; but they are so far from essential[5] that Buckle found the book as it stands a kind of pioneer manual of rationalism.[6] Its

---

[1] Not, as Mr. Owen states (*French Skeptics*, p. 569), the sister of Francis I, who died when Charron was eight years old, but the daughter of Henri II, and first wife of Henri of Navarre, afterwards Henri IV.

[2] Cp. Sainte Beuve, as cited by Owen, p. 571, note, and Owen's own words, p. 572. [3] Owen, p. 571. Cp. pp. 573, 574.

[4] Bayle, art. CHARRON. "A brutal atheism" is the account of Charron's doctrine given by the Jesuit Garasse. Cp. Perrens, p. 57.

[5] Mr. Owen (p. 570) comes to this conclusion after carefully collating the editions. Cp. p. 587, *note*. The whole of the alterations, including those proposed by President Jeannin, will be found set forth in the edition of 1607, and the reprints of that.

[6] "The first......attempt made in a modern language to construct a system of morals without the aid of theology" (*Introd. to Hist. of Civ. in England*, 3-vol. ed. ii, 19; 1-vol. ed. p. 296).

way of putting all religions on one level, as being alike grounded on bad evidence and held on prejudice, is only the formal statement of an old idea, found, like so many others of Charron's, in Montaigne ; but the didactic purpose and method turn the skeptic's shrug into a resolute propaganda. So with the formal and earnest insistence that true morality cannot be built on religious hopes and fears—a principle which Charron was the first to bring directly home to the modern intelligence,[1] as he did the principle of development in religious systems.[2] Attempting as it does to construct a systematic practical philosophy of life, it puts aside so positively the claims of the theologians,[3] and so emphatically subordinates religion to the rule of natural reason,[4] that it constitutes a virtual revolution in public doctrine for Christendom. As Montaigne is the effective beginner of modern literature, so is Charron the beginner of modern secular teaching. He is a Naturalist, professing theism.

It was only powerful protection that could save such a book from proscription ; but Charron and his book had the support at once of Henri IV and the President Jeannin—the former a proved indifferentist to religious forms ; the latter the author of the remark that a peace with two religions was better than a war which had none. Such a temper had become predominant even among professed Catholics, as may be gathered from the immense popularity of the *Satyre Menippee* (1594). Ridiculing as it did the insensate fanaticism of the Catholic League, it was naturally described as the work of atheists ; but there seems to have been no such element in the case, the authors being all Catholics of good standing, and some of them even having a record for zeal.[5] On the other hand, it is expressly testified by

---

[1] Cp. Owen, pp. 580–5.   [2] Buckle, ii, 21 ; 1-vol. ed. p. 297.
[3] *E.g.*, the preface to the first edition, *ad init.*
[4] *E.g.*, Liv. ii, ch. 28 of revised ed. (ed. 1609, p. 399).
[5] See the biog. pref. of M. Labitte to the Charpentier edition, p. xxv. The *Satyre* in its own turn freely charges atheism and incest on Leaguers ; *e.g.*, the *Harangue de M. de Lyon,* ed. cited, pp. 78, 86. This was by Rapin, whom Garasse particularly accuses of *libertinage*. See the *Doctrine Curieuse*, as cited, p. 124.

the Catholic historian De Thou that all the rich and the aristocracy held the League in abomination.[1] In such an atmosphere rationalism must needs germinate, especially when the king's acceptance of Catholicism dramatised the unreality of the grounds of strife.

After the assassination of the king in 1610, the last of the bloody deeds which had kept France on the rack of uncertainty in religion's name for three generations, the spirit of rationalism naturally did not wane. In the Paris of the early seventeenth century, doubtless, the new emancipation came to be associated, as "libertinism," with license as well as with freethinking. In the nature of the case there could be no serious and free literary discussion of the new problems either of life or belief, save in so far as they had been handled by Montaigne and Charron ; and, inasmuch as the accounts preserved of the freethought of the age are almost invariably those of its worst enemies, it is chiefly their side of the case that has been presented. Thus in 1623 the Jesuit Father François Garasse published a thick quarto of over a thousand pages, entitled *La Doctrine Curieuse des Beaux Esprits de ce temps, ou pretendu tels*, in which he assails the "libertins" of the day with an infuriated industry. The eight books into which he divides his treatise proceed upon eight alleged maxims of the freethinkers, which run as follows :—

I. There are very few good wits [*bons Esprits*] in the world ; and the fools, that is to say, the common run of men, are not capable of our doctrine ; therefore it will not do to speak freely, but in secret, and among trusting and cabalistic souls.

II. Good wits [*beaux Esprits*] believe in God only by way of form, and as a matter of public policy (*par Maxime d'Etat*).

III. A *bel Esprit* is free in his belief, and is not readily to be taken in by the quantity of nonsense that is propounded to the simple populace.

IV. All things are conducted and governed by Destiny, which is irrevocable, infallible, immovable, necessary, eternal, and inevitable to all men whomsoever.

V. It is true that the book called the Bible, or the Holy

---

[1] Cited by Buckle.

Scripture, is a good book (*un gentil livre*), and contains a lot of good things; but that a *bon esprit* should be obliged to believe under pain of damnation all that is therein, down to the tail of Tobit's dog, does not follow.

VI. There is no other divinity or sovereign power in the world but NATURE, which must be satisfied in all things, without refusing anything to our body or senses that they desire of us in the exercise of their natural powers and faculties.

VII. Supposing there be a God, as it is decorous to admit, so as not to be always at odds with the superstitious, it does not follow that there are creatures which are purely intellectual and separated from matter. All that is in Nature is composite, and therefore there are neither angels nor devils in the world, and it is not certain that the soul of man is immortal.

VIII. It is true that to live happily it is necessary to extinguish and drown all scruples; but all the same it does not do to appear impious and abandoned, for fear of offending the simple or losing the support of the superstitious.

This is obviously neither candid[1] nor competent writing; and as it happens there remains proof, in the case of the life of La Mothe le Vayer, that "earnest freethought in the beginning of the seventeenth century afforded a *point d'appui* for serious-minded men, which neither the corrupt Romanism nor the narrow Protestantism of the period could furnish."[2] Garasse's own doctrine was that "the true liberty of the mind consists in a simple and docile (*sage*) belief in all that the church propounds, indifferently and without distinction."[3] The later social history of Catholic France is the sufficient comment on the efficacy of such teaching to regulate life. In any case the new ideas steadily gained ground; and on the heels of the treatise of Garasse appeared that of Marin Mersenne, *L'impieté des Déistes, Athées et Libertins de ce temps combattue, avec la refutation des opinions de*

---

[1] M. Labitte, himself a Catholic, speaks of Garasse's "forfanterie habituelle" and "ton d'insolence sincere qui deguise tant de mensonges" (Pref. cited, p. xxxi).

[2] Owen, *French Skeptics*, p. 659. Cp. Lecky, *Rationalism*, i, 97, citing Maury, as to the resistance of *libertins* to the superstition about witchcraft.

[3] *Doctrine Curieuse des Beaux Esprits*, as cited, p. 208. This is one of the passages which fully explain the opinion of the orthodox of that age that Garasse "helped rather than hindered atheism" (Reimmann, *Hist. Atheismi*, 1725, p. 408).

Charron, de Cardan, de Jordan Brun, et des quatraines du Deiste (1624). In a previous treatise, *Quæstiones celeberrimæ in Genesim in quo volumine Athei et Deisti impugnantur* (1623), Mersenne set agoing the often-quoted assertion that, while atheists abounded throughout Europe, they were so specially abundant in France that in Paris alone there were some fifty thousand. Even taking the term "atheist" in the loosest sense in which such writers used it, the statement was never credited by any contemporary; but neither did anyone doubt that there was an unprecedented amount of unbelief. Such were the signs of the times when Pascal was in his cradle.

> Mersenne's statistical assertion was made in two sheets of the *Quæstiones Celeberrimæ*, "qui ont été supprime dans la plupart des exemplaires, a cause, sans doute, de leur exaggération" (Bouillier, *Hist. de la philos. cartesienne*, 1854, i, 28, where the passage is cited). The suppressed sheets included a list of the "atheists" of the time, occupying five folio columns. Julian Hibbert, *Plutarchus and Theophrastus on Superstition*, etc., 1828; App. Catal. of Works written against Atheism, p. 3; Prosper Marchand, *Lettre sur le Cymbalum Mundi*, in ed. Bibliophile Jacob, 1841, p. 17, *note*.

§ 3. *England.*

While France was thus passing from general fanaticism to a large measure of freethought, England was passing by a less tempestuous path to a hardly less advanced stage of opinion. The comparative bloodlessness of the strife between Protestant and Catholic under Mary and Elizabeth, the treatment of the Jesuit propaganda under the latter queen as a political rather than a doctrinal question, prevented any such vehemence of recoil from religious ideals as took place in France.

Unbelief, as we have seen, however, there certainly was; and it is recorded that Walter, Earl of Essex, on his deathbed at Dublin in 1576, murmured that among his countrymen neither Popery nor Protestantism prevailed: "there was nothing but infidelity, infidelity,

infidelity ; atheism, atheism ; no religion, no religion."[1] And when we turn aside from the beaten paths of Elizabethan literature we see clearly what is partly visible from those paths—a number of freethinking variations from the norm of faith. Ascham, as we saw, found some semblance of atheism shockingly common among the travelled upper class of his day; and the testimonies continue. Lyly, in his *Euphues* (1579), referring to England in general or Oxford in particular as Athens, asks: " Be there not many in Athens which think there is no God, no redemption, no resurrection ?" Further, he complains that " it was openly reported of an old man in Naples that there was more lightness in Athens than in all Italy   more Papists, more *Atheists*, more sects, more schisms, than in all the monarchies in the world ";[2] and he proceeds to frame an absurd dialogue of " Euphues and Atheos," in which the latter, "monstrous, yet tractable to be persuaded,"[3] is converted with a burlesque facility. Lyly, a commonplace pietist, is a poor witness as to the atheistic arguments current, but those he cites are so much better than his own, up to the point of terrified collapse on the atheist's part, that he had doubtless heard them. The atheist speaks as a pantheist, identifying deity with the universe ; and readily meets a simple appeal to Scripture with the reply that "whosoever denieth a godhead denieth also the Scriptures which testifie of him."[4] Evidently, then, such opinions were in some vogue, else they had not been handled in a book so essentially planned for the general reader. But however firmly held, they could not be published ; and fourteen years later, over thirty years after the outburst of Ascham, we still find only a sporadic and unwritten freethought, however abundant, going at times in fear of its life.

---

[1] Froude, *History of England*, ed. 1875, xi, 199, citing *MSS. Ireland*.
[2] *Euphues: The Anatomy of Wit*, Arber's reprint, pp. 140, 153. That the reference was mainly to Oxford is to be inferred from the address " To my verie good friends the Gentlemen Schollers of Oxford," prefixed to the ed. of 1581. *Id.* p. 207.
[3] *Id.* p. 158.   [4] *Id.* pp. 161, 166.

Private discussion, indeed, there must have been, if there be any truth in Bacon's phrase that "atheists will ever be talking of that opinion, as if they would be glad to be strengthened by the consent of others"[1]—an argument which would make short work of the vast literature of apologetic theism—but even private talk had need be cautious, and there could be no publication of atheistic opinions. Printed rationalism could go no further than such a protest against superstition as Reginald Scot's *Discoverie of Witchcraft* (1584), which, however, is a sufficiently remarkable expression of reason in an age in which a Bodin held angrily by the delusion.[2] Elizabeth was herself substantially irreligious,[3] and preferred to keep the clergy few in number and subordinate in influence;[4] but her Ministers regarded the church as part of the State system, and punished all open or at least aggressive heresy in the manner of the Inquisition. A sect called the "Family of Love," deriving from Holland (already "a country fruitfull of heretics"),[5] went so far as to hold that "Christ doth not signify any one person, but a quality whereof many are partakers"—a doctrine which we have seen ascribed by Calvin to the *libertins* of Geneva a generation before;[6] but it does not appear

---

[1] Essay *Of Atheism*.
[2] Lecky, *Rationalism*, i, 103-4. Scot's book (now made accessible by a reprint, 1886) had practically no influence in his own day; and King James, who wrote against it, caused it to be burned by the hangman in the next. Scot inserts the "infidelitie of atheists" in the list of intellectual evils on his title-page; but save for an allusion to "the abhomination of idolatrie" all the others indicted are aspects of the black art.
[3] "No woman ever lived who was so totally destitute of the sentiment of religion" (Green, *Short History*, ch. vii, § 3, p. 369).
[4] Cp. Soames, *Elizabethan Religious History*, 1839, p. 225. Yet when Morris, the attorney of the Duchy of Lancaster, introduced in Parliament a Bill to restrain the power of the ecclesiastical courts, she had him dismissed and imprisoned for life, being determined that the control should remain in her own hands. Heylyn, *Hist. of the Ref.* ed. 1849, pref. vol. i, pp. xiv-xv.
[5] Camden, *Annals of Elizabeth*, sub. ann. 1580; 3rd ed. 1635, p. 218.
[6] Hooker, Pref. to *Ecclesiastical Polity*, ch. iii, § 9, ed. 1850. Camden (p. 219) states that the Dutch teacher Henry Nichalai, whose works were translated for the sect, "gave out that he did partake of God, and God of his humanity."

that they were persecuted.[1] Some isolated propagandists, however, paid the last penalty. One Matthew Hamont or Hamond, a ploughwright, of Hetherset, was in 1579 tried by the Bishop and Consistory of Norwich "for that he denyed Christe," and, being found guilty, was burned, after having had his ears cut off "because he spake wordes of blasphemie against the Queen's Maiistie and others of her Counsell."[2] The victim would thus seem to have been given to violence of speech; but the record of his negations, which suggest developments from the Anabaptist movement, is none the less notable. In Stow's wording,[3] they run:—

> "That the newe Testament and Gospell of Christe are but mere foolishnesse, a storie of menne, or rather a mere fable.
> "Item, that man is restored to grace by the meere mercy of God, wythout the meane of Christ's bloud, death, and passion.
> "Item, that Christe is not God, nor the Saviour of the world, but a meere man, a sinfull man, and an abhominable Idoll.
> "Item, that al they that worshippe him are abhominable Idolaters; And that Christe did not rise agayne from death to life by the power of his Godhead, neither, that hee did ascende into Heaven.
> "Item, that the holy Ghoste is not God, neither, that there is any suche holy Ghoste.
> "Item, that Baptisme is not necessarie in the Churche of God, neither the use of the sacrament of the body and bloude of Christ."

There is trace of a freethinker named Lewis, who appears to have been burned at the same place in the same year.[4] Further one Peter Cole, an Ipswich tanner, was burned in 1587 (also at Norwich) for similar doctrine; and Francis Kett, a young clergyman, ex-fellow of Corpus Christi College, Cambridge, was burned at the same

---

[1] See above, i, 474, as to a much more pronounced heresy in 1549, which also seems to have escaped punishment. Camden tells that the books of the "Family of Love" were burnt in 1580, but mentions no other penalties.
[2] May 13th, 1579. The burning was on the 20th.
[3] Stow's *Chronicle*, 1580, pp. 1194-5.
[4] *David's Evidence*, by William Burton, Preacher of Reading, 1592 (?), p. 125.

place in 1589 for heresy of the Unitarian order.[1] Hamond and Cole seem, however, to have been in their own way religious men,[2] and Kett a devout mystic, with ideas of a Second Advent.[3] All founded on the Bible.

> Most surprising of all perhaps is the record of the trial of one John Hilton, clerk in holy orders, before the Upper House of Convocation on December 22nd, 1584, on the charge of having "said in a sermon at St. Martin's-in-the-Fields that the Old and New Testaments are but fables." (Lansdowne MSS. British Museum, No. 982, fol. 46, cited by Professor Storojenko, *Life of Robert Greene*, Eng. trans. in Grosart's "Huth Library" ed. of Greene's Works, i, 39, *note*.) As Hilton confessed to the charge and made abjuration, it may be surmised that he had spoken under the influence of liquor. Even on that view, however, such an episode tells of a considerable currency of unbelieving criticism.

Apart from constructive heresy, the perpetual religious dissensions of the time were sure to stimulate doubt; and there appeared quite a number of treatises directed wholly or partly against explicit unbelief, as: "The Faith of the Church Militant," translated from the Latin of the Danish divine Hemming (1581), and addressed "to the confutation of the Jewes, Turks, Atheists, Papists, Hereticks, and all other adversaries of the truth whatsoever"; "The Touchstone of True Religion......against the impietie of Atheists, Epicures, Libertines, Hippocrites, and Temporisours of these times" (1590); "An Enemie to Atheisme," translated by T. Rogers from the Latin of Avenar (1591); Henry Smith's "God's Arrow against Atheists" (1593); an English translation of the second volume of La Primaudaye's *L'Academie Française*, containing a refutation of atheistic doctrine; and no fewer than three "Treatises of the Nature of God"—two anonymous, the third by Bishop Thomas Morton—all appearing in the year 1599.

All this smoke implies some fire; and the translator

---

[1] Burton, as cited.
[2] Art. MATTHEW HAMOND, in *Dict. of Nat. Biog.*
[3] Art. FRANCIS KETT, in *Dict. of Nat. Biog.*

of La Primaudaye, one "T. B.," declares in his dedication that there has been a general growth of atheism in England and on the continent, which he traces to "that Monster Machiavell." Among English atheists of that school he ranks the dramatist Robert Greene, who had died in 1592 ; and it has been argued, not quite convincingly, that it was to Machiavelli that Greene had pointed, in his death-bed recantation *A Groatsworth of Wit* (1592), as the atheistic instructor of his friend Marlowe,[1] who introduces "Machiavel" as cynical prologist to his *Jew of Malta*. Greene's own "atheism" had been for the most part a matter of bluster and disorderly living ; and we find his friend Thomas Nash, in his *Strange News* (1592), calling the Puritan zealot who used the pseudonym of Martin Marprelate "a mighty platformer of atheism"; even as his own and Greene's enemy, Gabriel Harvey, called Nash an atheist.[2] But Nash in his *Christ's Tears over Jerusalem* (1592), though he speaks of the "atheistical Julian," discusses contemporary atheism in a fashion descriptive of an actual growth of the opinion, concerning which he alleges that there is no "sect now in England so scattered [*i.e.*, so widely spread] as atheisme." The "outward atheist," he declares, "establishes reason as his God"; and he offers some sufficiently primitive arguments by way of confutation.[3] There had arisen, in short, a ferment of rationalism which was henceforth never to disappear from English life.

In 1593, indeed, we find atheism formally charged against two famous men, CHRISTOPHER MARLOWE and Sir WALTER RALEIGH, of whom the first is

[1] Professor Storojenko, *Life of Greene*, Eng. trans. in Grosart's "Huth Library" ed. of Greene's Works, i, 42-50. It is quite clear that Malone and the critics who have followed him were wrong in supposing the unnamed instructor to be Francis Kett, who was a devout Unitarian. Professor Storojenko speaks of Kett as having been made an Arian at Norwich, after his return there in 1585, by the influence of Lewes and Haworth. Query Hamond?
[2] In *Pierce's Supererogation*, Collier's ed. p. 85, cited by Storojenko.
[3] Rep. of Nash's Works in Grosart's "Huth Library" ed. vol. iv, pp. 172, 173, 178, 182, 183.

documentarily connected with Kett, and the second in turn with Marlowe. An official document,[1] preserved by some chance, reveals that Marlowe was given—whether or not over the wine-cup—to singularly audacious derision of the received beliefs; and so explicit is the evidence that it is nearly certain he would have been executed for blasphemy had he not been privately killed (1593) while the proceedings were pending. The "atheism" imputed to him is not made out in any detail; but many of the other utterances are notably in keeping with Marlowe's daring temper; and they amount to unbelief of a stringent kind. In *Doctor Faustus*[2] he makes Mephistopheles affirm that "Hell hath no limits......but where we are is hell"—a doctrine which we have seen to be current before his time; and in his private talk he had gone much further. Not only did he question, with Raleigh, the Biblical chronology: he affirmed "that Moyses was but a juggler, and that one Heriots" [*i.e.*, Thomas Harriot, the astronomer, one of Raleigh's circle] "can do more than he"; and concerning Jesus he used language incomparably more offensive to orthodox feeling than that of Hamond and Kett. There is more in all this than a mere assimilation of Machiavelli; though the further saying "that the first beginning of religion was only to keep men in awe" —put also by Greene, with much force of versification, in the mouth of a villain-hero in the play of *Selimus*[3]— tells of that influence. Marlowe was indeed not the man to swear by any master without adding something of his own. Atheism, however, is not inferrible from any of his works: on the contrary, in the second part of his famous first play he makes his hero, described by the repentant Greene as the "atheist Tamburlaine," declaim

---

[1] MS. Harl. 6853, fol 320 It is given in full in the appendix to the first issue of the selected plays of Marlowe in the Mermaid Series, edited by Mr. Havelock Ellis; and, with omissions, in the editions of Cunningham, Dyce, and Bullen.   [2] Act II, sc. i.

[3] Grosart's ed. in "Temple Dramatists" series, ll. 246-371. There is plenty of "irreligion" in the passage, but not atheism, though there is a denial of a future state (365-70).

of deity with signal eloquence, though with a pantheistic cast of phrase. In another passage, a Moslem personage claims to be on the side of a Christ who would punish perjury; and in yet another the hero is made to trample under foot the pretensions of Mohammed.[1] It was probably his imputation of perjury to Christian rulers in particular that earned for Marlowe the malignant resentment which inspired the various edifying comments published after his unedifying death. Had he not perished as he did in a tavern brawl, he might have had the nobler fate of a martyr.

Concerning Raleigh, again, there is no shadow of proof of atheism, though his circle, which included the Earls of Northumberland and Oxford, was called a "school of atheism" in a Latin pamphlet by the Jesuit Parsons,[2] published at Rome in 1593; and at his trial he was called an atheist by the Chief Justice, and his friend Harriot a "devil."[3] It is matter of literary history, however, that he, like Montaigne, had been influenced by the *Hypotyposes* of Sextus Empiricus;[4] his short essay *The Sceptick* being a naïf exposition of the thesis that "the sceptick doth neither affirm neither deny any position; but doubteth of it, and applyeth his Reason against that which is affirmed, or denied, to justifie his non-consenting."[5] The essay itself, nevertheless, proceeds upon a set of wildly false propositions in natural history, concerning which the adventurous reasoner has no doubts whatever; and altogether we may be sure that his artificial skepticism did not carry him far in philosophy. In *Discovery of Guiana* (1600) he declares that he is "resolved" of the truth of the stories of men whose heads grow beneath their shoulders. In other directions, however, he was less credulous. In his *History of the World* (1603-16) he pointed out, as

---

[1] *Tamburlaine*, Part II, Acts II, sc. ii, iii; V, sc. i.
[2] Writing as Andrew Philopater. See *Dict. of Nat. Biog.*, art. ROBERT PARSONS, and Storojenko, as cited, i, 36, and *note*.
[3] Edwards, *Life of Sir Walter Raleigh*, 1868, i, 432, 436.
[4] Translated into Latin by Henri Estienne in 1562.
[5] *Remains of Sir Walter Raleigh*, ed. 1657, p. 123.

Marlowe had done in talk, how incompatible was such a phenomenon as the mature civilisation of ancient Egypt in the days of Abraham with the orthodox chronology.[1] This, indeed, was heresy enough, then and later, seeing that not only did Bishop Pearson, in 1659, in a work on *The Creed* which has been circulated down to the nineteenth century, indignantly denounce all who departed from the figures in the margin of the Bible; but Coleridge, a century and a half later, took the very instance of Egyptian history as triumphantly establishing the accuracy of the Bible record against the French atheists.[2] As regards Raleigh's philosophy, the evidence goes to show only that he was ready to read a Unitarian essay, presumably that already mentioned, supposed to be Kett's; and that he had intercourse with Marlowe and others (in particular his secretary, HARRIOTT) known to be freethinkers. A prosecution begun against him on this score, at the time of the inquiry concerning Marlowe (when Raleigh was in disgrace with the Queen), came to nothing. It had been led up to by a translation of Parsons' pamphlet, which affirmed that his private group was known as "Sir Walter Rawley's school of Atheisme," and that therein "both Moyses and our Savior, the Old and the New Testaments, are jested at, and the scholars taught among other things to spell God backwards."[3] This seems to have been idle gossip, though it tells of unbelief somewhere; and Raleigh's own writings always indicate[4] belief in the Bible; though his dying speech and epitaph are noticeably deistic. That he was a deist, given to free discussion, seems the probable truth.[5]

---

[1] B. II, ch. i, sec. 7.   [2] Essay on the *Prometheus*
[3] Art. RALEIGH, in *Dict. of Nat. Biog.* xlvii, 192.
[4] *Id.* pp. 200–1.
[5] It is asserted by Francis Osborn, who had known Raleigh, that he got his title of *Atheist* from Queen Elizabeth. See the preface (*Author to Reader*) to Osborn's *Miscellany of Sundry Essays*, etc., in 7th ed. of his *Works*, 1673. As to atheism at Elizabeth's court, see Taylor, *Retrospect of Relig. Life of England*, 2nd ed. p. 198, and ref. Lyly makes one of his characters write of the ladies at court that "they never jar about matters of religion, because they never mean to reason of them" (*Euphues*, Arber's ed. p. 194).

The latest documentary evidence as to the case of Marlowe is produced by Mr. F. S. Boas in his article, "New Light on Marlowe and Kyd," in the *Fortnightly Review*, February, 1899, reproduced in his edition of the works of Thomas Kyd (Clarendon Press, 1901). In addition to the formerly known data as to Marlowe's "atheism," it is now established that Thomas Kyd, his fellow-dramatist, was arrested on the same charge, and that there was found among his papers one containing "vile hereticall conceiptes denyinge the divinity of Jhesus Christe our Saviour." This Kyd declared he had had from Marlowe, denying all sympathy with its views. Nevertheless, he was put to the torture. The paper, however, proves to be a vehement Unitarian argument on Scriptural grounds, and is much more likely to have been written by Francis Kett than by Marlowe. In the MSS. now brought to light, one Cholmeley, who "confessed that he was persuaded by Marlowe's reasons to become an Atheiste," is represented by a spy as speaking "all evil of the Counsell, saying that they are all Atheistes and Machiavillians, especially my Lord Admirall." The same "atheist," who imputes atheism to others as a vice, is described as regretting he had not killed the Lord Treasurer, "sayenge that he could never have done God better service."

For the rest, the same spy tells that Cholmeley believed Marlowe was "able to shewe more sound reasons for Atheisme than any devine in Englande is able to geve to prove devinitie, and that Marloe told him that he hath read the Atheist lecture to Sir Walter Raleigh and others." On the last point there is no further evidence, save that Sir Walter, his dependant Thomas Harriott, and Mr. Carewe Rawley, were on March 21st, 1593-4, charged upon sworn testimonies with holding "impious opinions concerning God and Providence." Harriott had published in 1588 a work on his travels in Virginia, at the close of which is a passage in the devoutest vein telling of his missionary labours (quoted by Mr. Boas, art. cited, p. 225). Yet by 1592 he had, with his master, a reputation for atheism; and that it was not wholly on the strength of his great scientific knowledge is suggested by the statement of Anthony a Wood that he "made a philosophical theology, wherein he cast off the Old Testament."

Of this no trace remains; but it is established that he was a highly accomplished mathematician, much admired by Kepler; and that he "applied the telescope to celestial purposes almost simultaneously with Galileo" (art. HARRIOTT in *Dict. of Nat. Biog.*). "Harriott......was the first who dared to say $A = B$ in the form $A - B = O$, one of the greatest sources of progress ever opened in algebra" (Professor A. De Morgan,

Newton, his Friend and his Niece, 1885, p. 91). Further, he improved algebraic notation by the use of small italic letters in place of Roman capitals, and struck out the hypothesis of secondary planets as well as of stars invisible from their size and distance. "He was the first to verify the results of Galileo." Rev. Baden Powell, *Hist. of Nat. Philos.* 1834, pp. 126, 168. Cp. Rigaud, as cited by Powell; Ellis's notes on Bacon, in Routledge's 1-vol. ed. 1905, pp. 674-6; and Storojenko, as above cited, p. 38, *note*.

The frequency of such traces of rationalism at this period is to be understood in the light of the financial and other scandals of the Reformation; the bitter strifes of church and dissent; and the horrors of the wars of religion in France, concerning which Bacon remarks in his essay *Of Unity in Religion* that the spectacle would have made Lucretius "seven times more Epicure and atheist than he was." The proceedings against Raleigh and Kyd, accordingly, did not check the spread or the private avowal of unbelief. A few years later we find Hooker, in the Fifth Book of his *Ecclesiastical Polity* (1597), bitterly avowing that the unbelievers in the higher tenets of religion are much strengthened by the strifes of believers;[1] and a dozen years earlier Bishop Pilkington tells of "young whelps" who "in corners make themselves merry with railing and scoffing at the holy scriptures."[2]

From Hooker's account it is clear that, at least with comparatively patient clerics like himself, the freethinkers would at times deliberately press the question of theism, and avow the conviction that belief in God was "a kind of harmless error, bred and confirmed by the sleights of wiser men." He further notes with even greater bitterness that some—an "execrable crew"—who were themselves unbelievers, would in the old pagan manner argue for the fostering of religion as a matter of State policy, herein conning the lesson of Machiavelli. For his own part Hooker was confessedly ill-prepared to

---

[1] B. v, ch. ii, §§ 1-4. *Works*, ed. 1850, i, 432-6.
[2] *Exposition upon Nehemiah* (1585) in Parker Society's ed. of *Works*, 1842, p. 401.

debate with the atheists, and his attitude was not fitted to shake their opinions. His one resource is the inevitable plea that atheists are such for the sake of throwing off all moral restraint[1]—a theorem which could hardly be taken seriously by those who knew the history of the English and French aristocracies, Protestant and Catholic, for the past hundred years. Hooker's own measure of rationalism, though remarkable as compared with previous orthodoxy, went no further than the application of the argument of Pecock that reason must guide and control all resort to Scripture and authority ;[2] and he came to it under stress of dispute, as a principle of accommodation for warring believers, not as an expression of any independent skepticism. The unbelievers of his day were for him a frightful portent, menacing all his plans of orthodox toleration ; and he would have had them put down by force—a course which in some cases, as we have seen, had been actually taken, and was always apt to be resorted to in that age. But orthodoxy all the while had a sure support in the social and political conditions which made impossible the publication of rationalistic opinions. While the whole machinery of public doctrine remained in religious hands or under ecclesiastical control, the mass of men of all grades inevitably held by the traditional faith. What is remarkable is the amount of unbelief, either privately explicit or implicit in the higher literature, of which we have trace.

Above all there remains the great illustration of the rationalistic spirit of the English literary renascence of the sixteenth century—the drama of SHAKESPEARE. Of that it may confidently be said that every attempt to find for it a religious foundation has failed.[3] A clerical historian sums up concerning Shakespeare that "the

---

[1] *Works*, i, 432 ; ii, 762–3.
[2] *Eccles. Pol.* B. i, ch. 7 ; B. ii, ch. 1, 7 ; B. iii, ch. 8 ; B. v, ch. 8 ; B. vii, ch. 11 ; B. viii, § 6 (*Works*, i, 165, 231, 300, 446 ; ii, 388, 537). See the citations in Buckle, 3-vol. ed. iii, 341–2 ; 1-vol. ed. pp. 193–4.
[3] Some typical attempts of the kind are discussed in the author's two lectures on *The Religion of Shakespeare*, 1887 (South Place Institute).

religious phrases which are thinly scattered over his work are little more than expressions of a distant and imaginative reverence. And on the deeper grounds of religious faith his silence is significant.......The riddle of life and death he leaves......a riddle to the last, without heeding the common theological solutions around him."[1] The practical wisdom in which he rose above his rivals, no less than in dramatic and poetic genius, kept him prudently reticent on his opinions, as it set him upon building his worldly fortunes while the others with hardly an exception lived in shallows and miseries. As so often happens, it was among the ill-balanced types that there was found the heedless courage to cry aloud what others thought ; but Shakespeare's significant silence reminds us that the largest spirits of all could live in disregard of contemporary creeds. For, while there is no record of his having privately avowed unbelief, much less any explicit utterance of it in his plays, in no genuine work of his is there any conformity to current habits of religious speech. In *Measure for Measure* the Duke, counselling as a friar the condemned Claudio, discusses the ultimate issues of life and death without a hint of Christian credence.

So silent is the dramatist on the ecclesiastical issues of his day that Protestants and Catholics are enabled to go on indefinitely claiming him as theirs; the latter dwelling on his generally kindly treatment of friars ; the former citing the fact that some Protestant preacher—evidently a protege of his daughter Susannah—was allowed lodging at his house. But the preacher was not hospitably treated;[2] and other clues fail. There is good reason to think that Shakespeare was much influenced by Montaigne's Essays, read by him in Florio's translation, which was issued when he was recasting the old *Hamlet;* and his whole treatment of life in the great tragedies and serious comedies produced by him from

[1] Green, *Short History,* ch. vii, § vii, *end.* Compare Ruskin's *Sesame and Lilies,* Lect. III, § 115.
[2] The record is that the town paid for his bread and wine.

that time forward is even more definitely untheological than Montaigne's own doctrine.[1] Nor can he be supposed to have disregarded the current disputes as to fundamental beliefs, implicating as they did his fellow-dramatists Marlowe, Kyd, and Greene. The treatise of De Mornay, of which Sir Philip Sidney began and Golding finished the translation,[2] was in his time widely circulated in England; and its very inadequate argumentation might well strengthen in him the anti-theological leaning.

A serious misconception has been set up as to Shakespeare's cast of mind by the persistence of editors in including among his works without discrimination plays which are certainly not his, as the *Henry VI* group, to which he contributed little, and in particular the First Part, of which he wrote probably nothing. It is on the assumption that that play is Shakespeare's work that Mr. Lecky (*Rationalism in Europe*, ed. 1887, i, 105 6) speaks of "that melancholy picture of Joan of Arc which is perhaps the darkest blot upon his genius." Now, whatever passages Shakespeare may have contributed to the Second and Third Parts, it is certain that he has barely a scene in the First, and that there is not a line from his hand in the La Pucelle scenes. Many students think that Dr. Furnivall has even gone too far in saying that "the only part of it to be put down to Shakespeare is the Temple Garden scene of the red and white roses" (Introd. to *Leopold* Shakespeare, p. xxxviii); so little is there to suggest even the juvenile Shakespeare there. But that any critical and qualified reader can still hold him to have written the worst of the play is unintelligible. The whole work would be a "blot on his genius" in respect of its literary weakness. The doubt was raised long before Mr. Lecky wrote, and was made good a generation ago. When Mr. Lecky further proceeds, with reference to the witches in *Macbeth*, to say (*id. note*) that it is "probable that Shakespeare......believed with an unfaltering faith in the reality of witchcraft," he strangely misreads that play. Nothing is clearer than that it grounds Macbeth's action from the first in Macbeth's own character and his wife's, employing the witch machinery (already used by Middleton) to meet the popular taste, but never once making the witches really causal forces. An "unfaltering" believer in witchcraft

---

[1] Cp. the author's *Montaigne and Shakespeare*, pp. 136-155.
[2] *A Woorke concerning the trewnesse of the Christian Religion*, 1587. Reprinted in 1592, 1604, and 1617.

who wrote for the stage would surely have turned it to serious account in other tragedies. This Shakespeare never does. On Mr. Lecky's view, he is to be held as having believed in the fairy magic of the *Midsummer Night's Dream* and the *Tempest*, and in the actuality of such episodes as that of the ghost in *Macbeth*. But who for a moment supposes him to have held any such belief? It is probable that the entire undertaking of *Macbeth* (1605?) and later of the *Tempest* (1610?) was due to a wish on the part of the theatre management to please King James (acc. 1603), whose belief in witchcraft and magic was notorious. Even the use of the Ghost in *Hamlet* is an old stage expedient, common to the pre-Shakespearean play and to others of Kyd's and Peele's. Shakespeare significantly altered the dying words of Hamlet from the " heaven receive my soul " of the old version to " the rest is silence." The bequest of his soul to the Deity in his will is merely the regulation testamentary formula of the time. In his sonnets, which hint his personal cast if anything does, there is no trace of religious creed.

Nor is Shakespeare in this aspect abnormal among his colleagues. To say nothing of Marlowe and the weak though gifted Greene, the bulk of his dramatic rivals are similarly unconcerned with religion : indeed, the quarrelsome Nash, with his *Christ's Tears over Jerusalem*, is almost the only pietistic type among them. Hence, in fact, the bitter hostility of the Puritans to the stage. Some of the Elizabethans do indeed take up matters of creed in their plays; for instance, Peele, whose *David and Bethsabe* is the first regular English drama on a Biblical subject, frequently writes as a Protestant zealot,[1] though his career was very much on the lines of those of Marlowe and Greene ; and perhaps Fletcher had a similar leaning, since it is clearly his hand that penned the part of *Henry VIII* in which occurs the Protestant tag, " In her [Elizabeth's] days......God shall be truly known."[2] To the queen's reign, too, probably belongs *The Atheist's Tragedy* of

---

[1] The allusion to " popish ceremonies " in *Titus Andronicus* is probably from his hand. See the author's work, *Did Shakespeare Write " Titus Andronicus "?* where it is argued that the play in question is substantially Peele's and Greene's.

[2] As to the expert analysis of this play, which shows it to be in large part Fletcher's, see Furnivall, as cited, pp. xciii–xcvi.

Cyril Tourneur, first published in 1611, but evidently written in its author's early youth—a coarse and worthless performance, full of extremely bad imitations of Shakspere.[1] To the age of Elizabeth also belongs, perhaps, the sententious tragedy of *Mustapha* by Fulke Greville, Lord Brooke, first surreptitiously published in 1609. A century and a half later the deists were fond of quoting[2] the concluding *Chorus Sacerdotum*, beginning:

> O wearisome condition of humanity,
>   Born under one law, to another bound ;
> Vainly begot, and yet forbidden vanity ;
>   Created sick, commanded to be sound :
> If nature did not take delight in blood
> She would have made more easy ways to good.

It is natural to suspect that the author of such lines was less orthodox than his own day had reputed him ; and yet the whole of his work shows him much pre-occupied with religion, though perhaps in a deistic spirit. But Brooke's introspective and undramatic poetry is an exception : the prevailing colour of the whole drama of the Shakesperean period is pre-Puritan and semi-pagan ; and the theological spirit of the next generation, intensified by King James, was recognised by cultured foreigners as a change for the worse.[3]

Not that rationalism became extinct. The "Italianate" incredulity as to a future state, which Sir John Davies had sought to repel by his poem, *Nosce Teipsum* (1599), can hardly have been overthrown even by that remarkable production ; and there were other forms of doubt. In 1602 appeared *The Unmasking of the Politique Atheist, by J. H.* [John Hull], *Batchelor of Divinitie*, which, however, is in the main a mere attempt to retort upon Catholics the charge of atheism laid by them against Protestants. Soon after, in 1605, we find

---

[1] Cp. Seccombe and Allen, *The Age of Shakspere*, 1903, ii, 189.
[2] See Alberti, *Briefe betreffende den Zustand der Religion in Gross-Britannien*, Hanover, 1752, ii, 429. Alberti reads "God" at the end of the passage ; but Dr. Grosart's edition is here followed.
[3] Hallam, *Lit. Hist. of Europe*, ed. 1872, ii, 371, 376, and *notes ;* Pattison, *Isaac Casaubon*, 2nd ed. 1892, p. 286 sq.

Dr. John Dove producing a *Confutation of Atheisme* in the manner of previous continental treatises, making the word "atheism" cover many shades of theism; and an essayist writing in 1608 asserts that, on account of the self-seeking and corruption so common among churchmen, "prophane Atheisme hath taken footing in the hearts of ignorant and simple men."[1] Such assertions prove merely a frequent coolness towards religion, not a vogue of reasoned unbelief. But the existence of rationalising heresy is attested by the burning of two men, Bartholomew Legate and Edward Wightman, for avowing Unitarian views, in 1612. These, the last executions for heresy in England, were results of the theological zeal of King James, stimulated by the Calvinistic fanaticism of Archbishop Abbot, the predecessor of Laud. A Dutch Arminian theologian of Socinian leanings, named Conrad Vorstius, professor at Steinfurth, had produced in 1606 a heretical treatise, *De Deo*, but had nevertheless been appointed in 1610 professor of theology at Leyden, in succession to Arminius. His opinions were "such as in our own day would certainly disqualify him from holding such an office in any Christian University";[2] and James, worked upon by Abbot, went so far as to make the appointment of Vorstius a diplomatic question. The stadhouder Maurice and the bulk of the Dutch clergy being of his view, the more tolerant statesmen of Holland, and the mercantile aristocracy, yielded from motives of prudence, and Vorstius was dismissed in order to save the English alliance. As regarded his own dominions, James drew up with his own hands a catalogue of the heresies found by him in Vorstius' book, and caused it to be burned in London and at the two universities.[3]

On the heels of this amazing episode came the cases of Wightman and Legate. Finding, in a personal

---

[1] *Essaies Politicke and Morall*, by D. T. Gent, 1608, fol. 9.

[2] Gardiner, *History of England, 1603-1642*, 4th ed. ii, 128. Cp. Bayle, art. VORSTIUS, Note *N*. By his theological opponents and by James, Vorstius was of course called an atheist.

[3] Bayle, art. cited, Note *F*.

conversation, that Legate had "ceased to pray to Christ," the king had him brought before the Bishop of London's Consistory Court, which sentenced the heretic to Newgate. Being shortly released, he had the imprudence to threaten an action for false imprisonment, whereupon he was re-arrested. Chief Justice Coke held that, technically, the Consistory Court could not sentence to burning; but Hobart and Bacon, the law officers of the Crown, and other judges, were of opinion that it could. Legate, accordingly, was duly tried, sentenced, and burned at Smithfield; and Wightman a few days later was similarly disposed of at Lichfield.[1]

Bacon's share in this matter is obscure, and has not been discussed by either his assailants or his vindicators. As for the general public, the historian records that "not a word was uttered against this horrible cruelty. As we read over the brief contemporary notices which have reached us, we look in vain for the slightest intimation that the death of these two men was regarded with any other feelings than those with which the writers were accustomed to hear of the execution of an ordinary murderer. If any remark was made it was in praise of James for the devotion which he showed to the cause of God."[2] That might have been reckoned on. It was not twenty years since Hamond and Kett had been burned on similar grounds; and there had been no outcry then. Little had gone on in the average intellectual life in the interim save religious discussion and Bibliolatry, and not from such culture could there come any growth of human kindness or any clearer conception of the law of reciprocity. But whether by force of recoil from a revival of the fires of Smithfield or from a perception that mere cruelty did not avail to destroy heresy, the *ultima ratio* was never again resorted to on English ground. That rationalism persisted is clear from the *Atheomastix* of Bishop Fotherby (1622), which

---

[1] Gardiner, pp. 129–130.
[2] Gardiner, as cited. Fuller is quite acquiescent.

notes among other things that as a result of constant disputing "the Scriptures (with many) have lost their authority, and are thought onely fit for the ignorant and idiote."[1] And while the growing stress of the strife between the ecclesiasticism of the Crown and the forces of nonconformity more and more thrust to the front religio-political issues, there began alongside of those strifes the new and powerful propaganda of deism, which, beginning with the Latin treatise, *De Veritate*, of Lord Herbert of Cherbury (1624), was gradually to leaven English thought for over a century.

Above all, there now came into play the manifold influence of FRANCIS BACON, whose case illustrates perhaps more fully than any other the difficulties, alike external and internal, in the way of right thinking. Taken as a whole, his work is on account of those difficulties divided against itself, insisting as it does alternately on a strict critical method and on the subjection of reason to the authority of revelation. He sounds a trumpet call to a new and universal effort of free and circumspect intelligence; and on the instant he stipulates for the prerogative of Scripture. Though only one of many who assailed alike the methodic tyranny of Aristotelianism[2] and the methodless empiricism of the ordinary "scientific" thought of the past, he made his attack with a sustained and manifold force of insight and utterance which still entitles him to pre-eminence as the great critic of wrong methods and the herald of better. Yet he not only transgresses often his own principal precepts in his scientific reasoning: he falls below several of his contemporaries and predecessors in point of his formal insistence on the final supremacy of theology over reason, alike in physics and in ethics. Where Hooker is ostensibly seeking to widen the field of rational judgment on the side of creed, Bacon, the

[1] *Atheomastix*, pref.
[2] In the *Advancement of Learning*, B. i. (Routledge's 1-vol. ed. p. 54), he himself notes how, long before his time, the new learning had in part discredited the schoolmen.

very champion of mental emancipation in the abstract, declares the boundary to be fixed.

Of those lapses from critical good faith, part of the explanation is to be found in the innate difficulty of vital innovation for all intelligences; part in the special pressures of the religious environment. On the latter head Bacon makes such frequent and emphatic protest that we are bound to infer on his part a personal experience in his own day of the religious hostility which long followed his memory. In the works which he wrote at the height of his powers, especially in his masterpiece, the *Novum Organum* (1620), where he comes closest to the problems of exact inquiry, he specifies again and again both popular superstition and orthodox theology as hindrances to scientific research, commenting on "those who out of faith and veneration mix their philosophy with theology and traditions,"[1] and declaring that of the drawbacks science had to contend with "the corruption of philosophy by superstition and an admixture of theology is far the more widely spread, and does the greatest harm, whether to entire systems or to their parts. For the human understanding is obnoxious to the influence of the imagination no less than to the influence of common notions."[2] In the same passage he exclaims at the "extreme levity" of those of the moderns who have attempted to "found a system of natural philosophy on the first chapter of Genesis, on the book of Job, and other parts of the sacred writings";[3] and yet again, coupling as obstinate adversaries of Natural Philosophy "superstition, and the blind and immoderate zeal of religion," he roundly affirms that "by the simpleness of certain divines access to any philosophy, however pure, is well nigh closed."[4] These

---

[1] *Novum Organum*, B. i, Aph. 62 (*Works*, Routledge's 1 vol. ed. p. 271). [2] *Id*. Aph. 65. (Ed. cited, p. 272.)
[3] *Id. ib.* Cp. the *Advancement of Learning*, B. ii, and the *De Augmentis*, B. ix, near end. (Ed. cited, pp. 173, 634.)
[4] *Id*. Aph. 89. (Ed. cited, p. 285.) Compare Aph. 46, 49, 96; the *Valerius Terminus*, cap. 25; the English *Filum Labyrinthi*, § 7; and the *De Principiis atque Originibus*. (Ed. cited, pp. 204, 208, 265, 267, 288, 650.)

charges are repeatedly salved by such claims as that "true religion" puts no obstacles in the way of science;[1] that the book of Job runs much to natural philosophy;[2] and, in particular, in the last book of the *De Augmentis Scientiarum*, redacted after his disgrace, by the declaration—more emphatic than those of the earlier *Advancement of Learning*—that "Sacred Theology ought to be derived from the word and oracles of God, and not from the light of nature or the dictates of reason."[3] In this mood he goes so far as to declare, with the thoroughgoing obscurantists, that "the more discordant and incredible the divine mystery is, the more honour is shown to God in believing it, and the nobler is the victory of faith."

Yet even in the calculated extravagance of this last pronouncement there is a ground for question whether the fallen Chancellor, hoping to retrieve himself, and trying every device of his ripe sagacity to minimise opposition, was not straining his formal orthodoxy beyond his real intellectual habit. As against such wholesale affirmation we have his declarations that "certain it is that God worketh nothing in nature but by second causes," and that any pretence to the contrary "is mere imposture as it were in favour towards God, and nothing else but to offer to the author of truth the unclean sacrifice of a lie";[4] his repeated objection to the discussion of Final Causes;[5] his attack on Plato and Aristotle for rejecting the atheistic scientific method of Democritus;[6] his peremptory assertion that motion

---

[1] *Valerius Terminus*, cap. i. (Ed. cited, p. 188.)

[2] *Id.* p. 187; *Filum Labyrinthi*, p. 209.

[3] B. iv, ch. 1 (Ed. cited, p. 691.) Compare *Valerius Terminus* cap. i (p. 186), and *De Aug*. B. iii, ch. 2 (p. 456), as to the impossibility of knowing the will and character of God from Nature, though (*De Aug.* last cit.) it reveals his power and glory.

[4] *Advancement of Learning*, B. i. (Ed. cited, p. 45.) Cp. *Valerius Terminus*, cap. 1 (p. 187).

[5] *Advancement*, B. ii; *De Augmentis*, B. iii, cc. 4 and 5; *Valerius Terminus*, cap. 25; *Novum Organum*, B. i, Aph. 48. B. ii, Aph. 2. (Ed. cited, pp. 96, 205, 266, 302, 471, 473.)

[6] *De Principiis atque Originibus*. (Ed. cited, pp. 649-50.) Elsewhere (*De Aug.* B. iii, ch. 4, p. 471) he expressly puts it that the system of

is a property of matter;[1] and his almost Democritean handling of the final problem, in which he insists that primal matter is, "next to God, the cause of causes, itself only without a cause."[2] Further, though he speaks of Scriptural miracles in a conventional way,[3] he drily pronounces in one passage that, "as for narrations touching the prodigies and miracles of religions, they are either not true or not natural, and, therefore, impertinent for the story of nature."[4] Finally, as against the formal capitulation to theology at the close of the *De Augmentis*, he has left standing in the first book of the Latin version the ringing doctrine of the original *Advancement of Learning* (1605), that "there is no power on earth which setteth up a throne or chair in the spirits and souls of men, and in their cogitations, imaginations, opinions, and beliefs, but knowledge and learning";[5] and in his *Wisdom of the Ancients*[6] he has contrived to turn a crude myth into a subtle allegory in behalf of toleration.

Thus, despite his many resorts to and prostrations before the Scriptures, the general effect of his writings in this regard is to set up in the minds of his readers the old semi-rationalistic equivoque of a "two-fold truth"; reminding us as he does that he "did in the beginning separate the divine testimony from the human." When, therefore, he announces that "we know by faith" that "matter was created from nothing,"[7] he has the air of juggling with his problem; and his further suggestion as to the possibility of matter being endowed with a force of evolution, however cautiously put, is far removed from orthodoxy. Accordingly, the charge of atheism—which he notes as commonly brought against all who dwell

---

Democritus, which "removed God and mind from the structure of things," was more favourable to true science than the teleology and theology of Plato and Aristotle.

[1] *Id.* pp. 651, 657.   [2] *Id.* p. 648.
[3] *De Augmentis*, B. iii, ch. 2; B. iv, ch. 2. (Ed. cited, pp. 456, 482.)
[4] *De Augmentis*, B. ii, ch. 1. (Ed. cited, p. 428.)
[5] Ed. cited, p. 73.
[6] No. xviii, *Diomedes*. Ed. cited, p. 841.
[7] *De Principiis atque Originibus*, p. 664.

solely on second causes'—was actually cast at his memory in the next generation.² It was of course false: on the issue of theism he is continually descanting with quite conventional unction; as in the familiar essay on atheism.³ His dismissal of final causes as "barren" meant merely that the notion was barren of scientific result;⁴ and he refers the question to metaphysic.⁵ But if his theism was of a kind disturbing to believers in a controlling Providence, as little was it satisfactory to Christian fervour; and it can hardly be doubted that the main stream of his argument made for a non-Biblical deism, if not for atheism; his dogmatic orthodoxies being undermined by his own scientific teaching.⁶

As regards his intellectual inconsistencies, we can but say that they are such as meet us in men's thinking at every new turn. Though we can see that Bacon's orthodoxy "doth protest too much," with an eye on king and commons and public opinion, we are not led to suppose that he had ever in his heart cast off his inherited creed. He shows frequent Christian prejudice in his references to pagans; and can write that " To seek to extinguish anger utterly is but the bravery of the Stoics,"⁷ pretending that the Christian books are more accommodating, and ignoring the Sermon on the Mount. In arguing that the "religion of the heathen" set men

---

¹ *Nov. Org.* i, 89; *Filum Labyrinthi*, § 7; Essay 16.

² See Francis Osborn's pref. (*Author to Reader*) to his "Miscellany," in *Works*, 7th ed. 1673.

³ Cp. *Valerius Terminus*, cap. 1.

⁴ This is pointed out by Glassford in his translation of the *Novum Organum* (1844, p. 26); and by Ellis in his and Spedding's edition of the *Works*. (Routledge's rep. pp. 32, 473, *note.*)

⁵ *De Augmentis*, B. iii, ch. 4, *end.*

⁶ Lechler (*Gesch. des englischen Deismus*, pp. 23-25) notes that Bacon involuntarily made for deism. Cp. Amand Saintes *Hist. de la philos. de Kant*, 1844, p. 69; and Kuno Fischer, *Francis Bacon*, Eng. trans. 1857, ch. xi, pp. 341-3. Dean Church (*Bacon*, in "Men of Letters" series, pp. 174, 205) insists that Bacon held by revelation and immortality; and can, of course, cite his profession of such belief, which is not to be disputed. (Cp. the careful judgment of Professor Fowler in his *Bacon*, pp. 180-191, and his ed. of the *Novum Organum*, 1878, pp. 43-53.) But the tendency of the specific Baconian teaching is none the less to put these beliefs aside, and to overlay them with a naturalistic habit of mind. At the first remove from Bacon we have Hobbes.

⁷ Essay 57, *Of Anger.*

upon ending "all inquisition of nature in metaphysical or theological discourse," and in charging the Turks with a special tendency to "ascribe ordinary effects to the immediate workings of God,"[1] he is playing not very scrupulously on the vanity of his co-religionists. As he was only too well aware, both tendencies ruled the Christian thought of his own day, and derive direct from the sacred books—not from "abuse," as he pretends. And on the metaphysical as on the common-sense side of his thought he is self-contradictory, even as most men have been before and since, because judgment cannot easily fulfil the precepts it frames for itself in illuminated hours. Latter-day students have been impressed, as was Leibnitz, by the original insight with which Bacon negated the possibility of our forming any concrete conception of a primary form of matter, and insisted on its necessary transcendence of our powers of knowledge.[2] On the same principle he should have negated every modal conception of the still more recondite Something which he put as antecedent to matter, and called God.[3] Yet in his normal thinking he seems to have been content with the commonplace formula given in his essay on Atheism—that we cannot suppose the totality of things to be "without a mind." He has here endorsed in its essentials what he elsewhere calls "the heresy of the Anthropomorphites,"[4] failing to apply his own law in his philosophy, as elsewhere in his physics. When, however, we realise that similar inconsistency is fallen into after him by Spinoza, and wholly escaped perhaps by no thinker, we are in a way to understand that with all his deflections from his own higher law Bacon may have profoundly and fruitfully influenced the thought of the next generation, if not his own.

The fact of this influence has been somewhat obscured

---

[1] *Valerius Terminus*, ch. 25.
[2] *De Principiis*, ed. cited, pp. 648-9. Cp. pp. 642-3.
[3] *Id.* p. 648.
[4] *Valerius Terminus*, cap. ii ; *De Augmentis*, B. v, ch. 4. Ed. cited, pp. 199, 517.

by the modern dispute as to whether he had any important influence on scientific progress.[1] At first sight the old claim for him in that regard seems to be heavily discounted by the simple fact that he definitely rejected the Copernican system of astronomy.[2] Though, however, this gravely emphasises his fallibility, it does not cancel his services as a stimulator of scientific thought. At that time, only a few were yet intelligently convinced Copernicans; and we have the record of how, in Bacon's day, Harvey lost heavily in credit and in his medical practice by propounding his discovery of the circulation of the blood,[3] which, it is said, no physician over forty years old at that time believed in. For men of that century it was thus no fatal shortcoming in Bacon to have failed to grasp the true scheme of sidereal motion,[4] any more than it was one on Galileo's side to be wrong about the tides. They could realise that it was precisely in astronomy, for lack of special study and expert knowledge, that Bacon was least qualified to judge. Intellectual influence on science is not necessarily dependent on actual scientific achievement, though that of course furthers and establishes it; and the fact of Bacon's impact on the mind of the next age is abundantly proved by testimonies.

For a time the explicit tributes came chiefly from

[1] Cp. Brewster, *Life of Newton*, 1855, ii, 400-4; Draper, *Intel. Devel. of Europe*, ed. 1875, ii, 258-60; Dean Church, *Bacon*, pp. 180-201; Fowler, *Bacon*, ch. vi; Professor Lodge, *Pioneers of Science*, pp. 145, 151; Lange, *Gesch. d. Mater.* i, 197 sq. (Eng. trans. i, 236-7), and cit. from Liebig—as to whom, however, see Fowler, pp. 133, 157.

[2] *Novum Organum*, ii, 46 and 48, § 17; *De Aug.* iii, 4; *Thema Coeli*. Ed. cited, pp. 364, 375, 461, 705, 709. Whewell (*Hist. of Induct. Sciences*, 3rd ed. i, 296, 298) ignores the second and third of these passages in denying Hume's assertion that Bacon rejected the Copernican theory with "disdain." It is true, however, that Bacon had vacillated. The facts are fairly faced by Professor Fowler in his *Bacon*, 1881, pp. 151-2, and his ed. of *Novum Organum*, Introd. pp. 30-36. See also the summing up of Ellis in notes to passages above cited, and at p. 675.

[3] Aubrey, *Lives of Eminent Persons*, ed. 1813, vol. ii, Pt. ii, p. 383.

[4] As Professor Masson points out (*Poet. Works of Milton*, 1874, Introd. i, 92 sq.), not only does Milton seem uncertain to the last concerning the truth of the Copernican system, but his friends and literary associates, the "Smectymnuans," in their answer to Bishop Hall's *Humble Remonstrance* (1641), had pointed to the Copernican doctrine as an unquestioned instance of a supreme absurdity.

abroad ; though at all times, even in the first shock of his disgrace, there were Englishmen perfectly convinced of his greatness. To the winning of foreign favour he had specially addressed himself in his adversity. Grown wary in act as well as wise in theory, he deleted from the Latin *De Augmentis* a whole series of passages of the *Advancement of Learning* which disparaged Catholics and Catholicism;[1] and he had his reward in being appreciated by many Jesuit and other Catholic scholars.[2] But Protestants such as Comenius and Leibnitz were ere long more emphatic than any Catholics;[3] and at the time of the Restoration we find Bacon enthusiastically praised among the more open-minded and scientifically biassed thinkers of England, who included some zealous Christians.[4] It was not that his special "method" enabled them to reach important results with any new facility: its impracticability is now insisted on by friends as well as foes.[5] It was that he arraigned with extraordinary psychological insight and brilliance of phrase the mental vices which had made discoveries so rare; the alternate self-complacency and despair of the average indolent mind; the "opinion of store" which was "cause of want"; the timid or superstitious evasion of research. In all this he was using his own highest powers, his comprehension of human character and his genius for speech. And though his own scientific results were not to be compared with those of Galileo and Descartes, the

[1] See notes in ed. cited, pp. 50, 53, 61, 63, 68, 75, 76, 84, 110.
[2] Fowler, ed. of *Nov. Org.* § 14, pp. 101-4.
[3] Fowler, ed. of *Nov. Org.* § 14, p. 108 ; Ellis in ed. cited, p. 643.
[4] Rawley's *Life*, in ed. cited, p. 9 ; Osborn, as above cited ; Fowler, ed. of *Nov. Org.* Introd. § 14 ; T. Martin, *Character of Bacon*, 1835, pp. 216, 227, 222-3.
[5] Cp. Fowler, *Bacon*, pp. 139-141 ; Mill, *System of Logic*, B. vi, ch. v, § 5 ; Jevons, *Principles of Science*, 1-vol. ed. p. 576 ; Tyndall, *Scientific Use of the Imagination*, 3rd ed. pp. 4, 8-9, 42 3 ; T. Martin, as cited, pp. 210-238 ; Bagehot, *Postulates of English Political Economy*, ed. 1885, pp. 18-19, Ellis and Spedding, in ed. cited, pp. x, xii, 22, 389. The notion of a dialectic method which should mechanically enable any man to make discoveries is an irredeemable fallacy, and must be abandoned. Bacon's own remarkable anticipation of modern scientific thought in the formula that heat is a mode of motion (*Nov. Org.* ii, 20) is not mechanically yielded by his own process, noteworthy and suggestive though that is.

wonderful range of his observation and his curiosity, the unwearying zest of his scrutiny of well-nigh all the known fields of Nature, must have been an inspiration to multitudes of students besides those who have recorded their debt to him. It is probable that but for his literary genius, which though little discussed is of a very rare order, his influence would have been both narrower and less durable; but, being one of the great writers of the modern world, he has swayed men down till our own day.

§ 4. *Popular Thought in Europe.*

Of popular freethought in the rest of Europe there is little to chronicle for a hundred and fifty years after the Reformation. The epoch-making work of COPERNICUS, published in 1543, had little or no immediate effect in Germany, where, as we have seen, physical and verbal strifes had begun with the ecclesiastical revolution, and were to continue to waste the nation's energy for a century. In 1546, all attempts at ecclesiastical reconciliation having failed, the emperor Charles V, in whom Melanchthon had seen a model monarch,[1] decided to put down the Protestant heresy by war. Luther had just died, apprehensive for his cause. Civil war now raged till the peace of Augsburg in 1555; whereafter Charles abdicated in favour of his son Philip. Here were in part the conditions which in France and elsewhere were later followed by a growth of rational unbelief; and there are some traces even at this time of skepticism in high places in the German world, notably in the case of the Emperor Maximilian II, who, "grown up in the spirit of doubt,"[2] would never identify himself with either Protestants or Catholics.[3] But in Germany there was still too little intellectual light, too little brooding over experience, to permit of the spread of such a temper; and the balance of forces amounted only to a

[1] Kohlrausch, *Hist. of Germany*, Eng. trans. p. 385.
[2] Moritz Ritter, *Geschichte der deutschen Union*, 1867-73, II, 55.
[3] Menzel, *Geschichte der Deutschen*, 3te Aufl. Cap. 416.

deadlock between the ecclesiastical parties. Protestantism on the intellectual side, as already noted, had sunk into a bitter and barren polemic[1] among the reformers themselves; and many who had joined the movement reverted to Catholicism.[2] Meanwhile the teaching and preaching Jesuits were zealously at work, turning the dissensions of the enemy to account, and contrasting its schism upon schism with the unity of the church. But Protestantism was well welded to the financial interest of the many princes and others who had acquired the church lands confiscated at the Reformation; since a return to Catholicism would mean the surrender of these.[3] Thus there wrought on the one side the organised spirit of anti-heresy[4] and on the other the organised spirit of Bibliolatry, neither gaining ground; and between the two intellectual life was paralysed. Protestantism saw no way of advance; and the prevailing temper began to be that of the Dark Ages, expectant of the end of the world.[5] Superstition abounded, especially the belief in witchcraft, now acted on with frightful cruelty throughout the whole Christian world;[6] and in the nature of the case Catholicism counted for nothing on the opposite side.

The only element of rationalism that one historian of culture can detect is the tendency of the German moralists of the time to turn the devil into an abstraction by identifying him with the different aspects of human folly and vice.[7] There was, as a matter of fact, a somewhat higher manifestation of the spirit of reason

[1] Cp. Gardiner, *The Thirty Years' War*, 8th ed. pp. 12-13; Kohlrausch, p. 438; Pusey, *Histor. Enq. into German Rationalism*, pp. 9-25; Henderson, *Short History of Germany*, i, ch. 16.
[2] Kohlrausch, p. 439. A specially strong reaction set in about 1573. Ritter, *Geschichte der deutschen Union*, i, 19. Cp. Menzel, Cap. 433.
[3] Cp. Gardiner, *The Thirty Years War*, pp. 16, 18, 21; Kohlrausch, p. 370.
[4] As to this see Moritz Ritter, as cited, i, 9, 27; ii, 122 sq.; Dunham, *History of the Germanic Empire*, iii, 186; Henderson, i, 411 sq.
[5] Freytag, *Bilder aus der deutschen Vergangenheit*, Bd. ii, Abth. ii, 1883, p. 381; Bd. iii, *ad init.*
[6] Cp. Lecky, *Rationalism in Europe*, small ed. i, 53-83.
[7] Freytag, *Bilder*, Bd. ii, Abth. ii, p. 378.

in the shape of some new protests against the superstition of sorcery. About 1560 a Catholic priest named Cornelius Loos Callidius was imprisoned by a papal nuncio for declaring that witches' confessions were merely the results of torture. Forced to retract, he was released; but again offended, and was again imprisoned, dying in time to escape the fate of a councillor of Treves, named Flade, who was burned alive for arguing, on the basis of an old canon (mistakenly named from the Council of Ancyra), that sorcery is an imaginary crime.[1] Then appeared the famous John Wier's treatise on witchcraft,[2] a work which, though fully adhering to the belief in the devil and things demoniac, argued against the notion that witches were conscious workers of evil. Wier[3] was a physician, and saw the problem partly as one in pathology. Other laymen, and even priests, as we have seen, had reacted still more strongly against the prevailing insanity; but it had the authority of Luther on its side, and with the common people the protests counted for little.

Reactions against Protestant bigotry in Holland on other lines were not much more successful, and indeed were not numerous. One of the most interesting is that of DIRK COORNHERT (1522-1590), who by his manifold literary activities[4] became one of the founders of Dutch prose. In his youth Coornhert had visited Spain and Portugal, and had there, it is said, seen an execution of victims of the Inquisition,[5] deriving thence the aversion to intolerance which stamped his whole life's work. It does

---

[1] *The Pope and the Council*, Eng. trans. p. 260; French trans. p. 285.
[2] *De Praestigiis Daemonum*, 1563. See it described by Lecky, *Rationalism*, i, 85-7; Hallam, *Lit. Hist.* ii, 76.
[3] By Dutch historians Wier is claimed as a Dutchman. He was born at Grave, in North Brabant, but studied medicine at Paris and Orleans, and after practising physic at Arnheim in the Netherlands was called to Düsseldorf as physician to the Duke of Jülich, to whom he dedicated his treatise. His ideas are probably traceable to his studies in France.
[4] His collected works (1632) amount to nearly 7,000 folio pages. J. Ten Brink, *Kleine Geschiedenis der Nederlandsche Letteren*, 1882, p. 91.
[5] Ten Brink, p. 86. Jonckbloet (*Beknopte Geschiedenis der Nederl. Letterkunde*, ed. 1880, p. 148) is less specific.

not appear, however, that any such peninsular experience was required, seeing that the Dutch Inquisition became abundantly active about the same period. Learning Latin at thirty, in order to read Augustine, he became a translator of Cicero and singularly enough—of Boccaccio. An engraver to trade, he became first notary and later secretary to the burgomaster of Haarlem; and, failing to steer clear of the strifes of the time, was arrested and imprisoned at the Hague in 1567. On his release he sought safety at Kleef in Santen, whence he returned after the capture of Brill to become secretary of the new national Government at Haarlem; but he had again to take to flight, and lived at Kleef from 1572 to 1577. In 1578 he debated at Leyden with two preachers of Delft on predestination, which he declared to be unscriptural; and was officially ordered to keep silence. Thereupon he published a protest, and got into fresh trouble by drawing up, as notary, an appeal to the Prince of Orange on behalf of his Catholic fellow-countrymen for freedom of worship, and by holding another debate at the Hague.[1] Always his master-ideal was that of toleration, in support of which he wrote strongly against Beza and Calvin (this in a Latin treatise published only after his death), declaring the persecution of heretics to be a crime in the kingdom of God; and it was as a moralist that he gave the lead to Arminius on the question of predestination.[2] "Against Protestant and Catholic sacerdotalism and scholastic he set forth humanist world-wisdom and Biblical ethic,"[3] to that end publishing a translation of Boethius (1585), and composing his chief work on *Zedekunst* (Ethics). Christianity, he insisted, lay not in profession or creed, but in practice. By way of restraining the ever-increasing malignity of theological strifes, he made the quaint proposal that the clergy should not be allowed to utter anything but the actual

---

[1] Ten Brink, pp. 89-90.   [2] Hallam, *Lit. of Europe*, ii, 83.
[3] Ten Brink, p. 87.

words of the Scriptures, and that all works of theology should be sequestrated. For these and other heteroclite suggestions he was expelled from Delft (where he sought finally to settle, 1587) by the magistrates, at the instance of the preachers, but was allowed to die in peace at Gouda, where he wrote to the last.[1]

All the while, though he drew for doctrine on Plutarch, Cicero, Seneca, and Marcus Aurelius equally with the Bible, Coornhert habitually founded on the latter as the final authority.[2] On no other footing could anyone in his age and country stand as a teacher. It was not till after generations of furious intolerance that a larger outlook was possible in the Netherlands; and the first steps towards it were naturally taken independently of theology. Although Grotius figured for a century as one of the chief exponents of Christian evidences, it is certain that his great work on the Law of War and Peace (1625) made for a rationalistic conception of society. "Modern historians of jurisprudence, like Lerminier and Bluntschli, represent it as the distinctive merit of Grotius that he freed the science from bondage to theology."[3] The breach, indeed, is not direct, as theistic sanctions are paraded in the Prolegomena; but along with these goes the avowal that natural ethic would be valid even were there no God, and—as against the formula of Horace, *Utilitas justi mater*—that "the mother of natural right is human nature itself."[4]

Where Grotius, defender of the faith, figured as a heretic, unbelief could not speak out, though there are traces of its underground life. The charge of atheism was brought against the *Exercitationes Philosophicae* of Gorlæus, published in 1620; but the book

---

[1] Jonckbloet, *Beknopte Geschiedenis*, p. 149; Ten Brink, p. 91; Bayle, *Dictionnaire*, art. KOORNHERT; Punjer, *Hist. of the Chr. Philos. of Religion*, Eng. trans. p. 269; Dr. E. Gosse, art. on Dutch Literature in *Encyc. Brit.* 9th ed. xii, 93.

[2] Ten Brink, p. 91. [3] Professor Flint, *Vico*, p. 142.

[4] *De Jure Belli et Pacis*, proleg. §§ 11, 16.

being posthumous, conclusions could not be tried. Views far short of atheism, however, were dangerous to their holders; for the merely Socinian work of Voelkel, published at Amsterdam in 1642, was burned by order of the authorities, and a second impression shared the same fate.[1] In 1653 the States of Holland forbade the publication of all Unitarian books and all Socinian worship; and though the veto as to books was soon evaded, that on worship was enforced.[2] Descartes, as we shall see, during his stay in Holland was menaced by clerical fanaticism. Some fared worse. In the generation after Grotius, one Koerbagh, a doctor, for publishing (1668) a dictionary of definitions containing advanced ideas, had to fly from Amsterdam. At Culenberg he translated a Unitarian work and began another; but was betrayed, tried for blasphemy, and sentenced to ten years' imprisonment, to be followed by ten years' banishment. He compromised by dying in prison within the year. Even as late as 1678 Hadrian Beverland (afterwards appointed, through Isaac Vossius, to a lay office under the Church of England) was imprisoned and struck off the rolls of Leyden University for his *Peccatum Originale*, in which he speculated erotically as to the nature of the sin of Adam and Eve. The book was furiously answered, and publicly burned.[3] It was only after an age of such intolerance that Holland, at the end of the seventeenth century, began to become for England a model of freedom in opinion as formerly in trade.

Unitarianism, which we have seen thus invading Holland somewhat persistently during half a century, was then as now impotent beyond a certain point by reason of its divided allegiance, though it has always had the support of some good minds. Its denial of the deity of Jesus could not be made out without a certain superposing of reason on Scripture; and yet to Scripture it always finally appealed. The majority of men

[1] Bayle, art. VOELKEL.
[2] Schlegel's note on Mosheim, Reid's ed. p. 862.
[3] Niceron, *Mémoires pour servir*, etc. xiv (1731), 340 sq.

accepting such authority have always tended to believe more uncritically ; and the majority of men who are habitually critical will always repudiate the Scriptural jurisdiction. In Poland, accordingly, the movement, so flourishing in its earlier years, was soon arrested, as we have seen, by the perception that it drove many Protestants back to Catholicism ; among these being presumably a number whose critical insight showed them that there was no firm standing-ground between Catholicism and Naturalism. Every new advance within the Unitarian pale terrified the main body, many of whom were mere Arians, holding by the term Trinity, and merely making the Son subordinate to the Father. Thus when one of their most learned ministers, Simon Budny, followed in the steps of Ferencz Davides (whom we have seen dying in prison in Transylvania in 1579) and represented Jesus as a "mere" man, he was condemned by a synod (1582) and deposed from his office (1584). He recanted, and was reinstated,[1] but his adherents seem to have been excommunicated. The sect thus formed were termed Semi-Judaizers by another heretic, Martin Czechowicz, who himself denied the pre-existence of Jesus, and made him only a species of demigod ;[2] yet Fausto Sozzini, better known as Faustus Socinus, who also wrote against them, and who had worked with Biandrata to have Davides imprisoned, conceded that prayer to Christ was optional.[3]

Faustus, who arrived in Poland in 1579, seems to have been moved to his strenuously "moderate" policy, which for a time unified the bulk of the party, mainly by a desire to keep on tolerable terms with Protestantism. That, however, did not serve him with the Catholics ; and when the reaction set in he suffered severely at their hands. His treatise, *De Jesu Christu Servatore*, created bitter resentment ; and in 1598 the Catholic rabble of Cracow, led "as usual by the students of the

---

[1] Krasinski, *Ref. in Poland*, 1840, ii, 363 ; Mosheim, 16 Cent. sec. iii, Pt. ii, ch. iv, § 22. Budny translated the Bible, with rationalistic notes.
[2] Krasinski, p. 361. [3] Mosheim, last cit. § 23, note 4.

university," dragged him from his house. His life was saved only by the strenuous efforts of the rector and two professors of the university; and his library was destroyed, with his manuscripts, whereof " he particularly regretted a treatise which he had composed against the atheists ";[1] though it is not recorded that the atheists had ever menaced either his life or his property. He seems to have been zealous against all heresy save his own, preaching passive obedience in politics as emphatically as any churchman, and condemning alike the rising of the Dutch against Spanish rule and the resistance of the French Protestants to their king.[2]

This attitude may have had something to do with the better side of the ethical doctrines of the sect, which leant considerably to non-resistance. Czechowicz (who was deposed by his fellow-Socinians for schism) seems not only to have preached a patient endurance of injuries, but to have meant it;[3] and to the Socinian sect belongs the main credit of setting up a humane compromise on the doctrine of eternal punishment.[4] The time, of course, had not come for any favourable reception of such a compromise in Christendom; and it is noted of the German Socinian, Ernst Schoner (Sonerus), who wrote against the orthodox dogma, that his works are "exceedingly scarce."[5] Unitarianism as a whole, indeed, made little headway outside of Poland and Transylvania.

In Spain, meantime, there was no recovery from the paralysis wrought by the combined tyranny of church and crown, incarnate in the Inquisition. The monstrous multiplication of her clergy might alone have sufficed to set up stagnation in her mental life; but,

[1] Krasinski, p. 367; Wallace, *Antitrin. Biog.* 1850, ii, 320.
[2] Bayle, art. FAUSTE SOCIN. Krasinski, p. 374.
[3] Krasinski, pp. 361-2. Fausto Sozzini also could apparently forgive everybody save those who believed less than he did.
[4] Cp. the inquiry as to Locke's Socinianism in J. Milner's *Account of Mr. Lock's Religion out of his own Writings*, 1706, and Lessing's *Zur Geschichte und Literatur*, i, as to Leibnitz's criticism of Sonerus.
[5] Enfield's *History of Philosophy* (an abstract of Brucker), ed. 1840 p. 537.

not content with the turning of a vast multitude[1] of men and women away from the ordinary work of life, her rulers set themselves to expatriate as many more on the score of heresy. A century after the expulsion of the Jews came the turn of the Moors, whose last hold in Spain, Granada, had been overthrown in 1492. Within a generation they had been deprived of all exterior practice of their religion;[2] but that did not suffice, and the Inquisition never left them alone. Harried, persecuted, compulsorily baptised, deprived of their Arabic books, they repeatedly revolted, only to be beaten down. At length, in the opening years of the seventeenth century (1610-1613), under Philip III, on the score that the great Armada had failed because heretics were tolerated at home, it was decided to expel the whole race; and now a million Moriscoes, among the most industrious inhabitants of Spain, were driven the way of the Jews. It is needless here to recall the ruinous effect upon the material life of Spain:[3] the aspect of the matter which specially concerns us is the consummation of the policy of killing out all intellectual variation. The Moriscoes may have counted for little in positive culture; but they were one of the last and most important factors of variation in the country; and when Spain was thus successively denuded of precisely the most original and energetic types among the Jewish, the Spanish, and the Moorish stocks, her mental ruin was complete.

To modern freethought, accordingly, she has till our own age contributed practically nothing. The brilliant dramatic literature of the reigns of the three Philips, which influenced the rising drama alike of France and

[1] In the dominions of Philip II there are said to have been 58 archbishops, 684 bishops, 11,400 abbeys, 23,000 religious fraternities, 46,000 monasteries, 13,500 nunneries, 312,000 secular priests, 400,000 monks, 200,000 friars and other ecclesiastics. H. E. Watts, *Miguel de Cervantes*, 1895, pp. 67-68. Spain alone had 9,088 monasteries.

[2] Buckle, 3-vol. ed. ii, 484; 1-vol. ed. p. 564, and refs.

[3] Cp. Buckle, 3-vol. ed. ii, 497-9; 1-vol. ed. pp. 572-3; La Rigaudiere, *Hist. des Perséc. Relig. en Espagne*, 1860, pp. 220-6.

England, is notably unintellectual,[1] dealing endlessly in plot and adventure, but yielding no great study of character, and certainly doing nothing to further ethics. Calderon was a thorough fanatic, and became a priest;[2] Lope de Vega found solace under bereavement in zealously performing the duties of an Inquisitor; and was so utterly swayed by the atrocious creed of persecution which was blighting Spain that he joined in the general exultation over the expulsion of the Moriscoes. Even the mind of Cervantes had not on this side deepened beyond the average of his race and time;[3] his old wrongs at Moorish hands perhaps warping his better judgment. His humorous and otherwise kindly spirit, so incongruously neighboured, must indeed have counted for much in keeping life sweet in Spain in the succeeding centuries of bigotry and ignorance. But from the seventeenth century till the other day the brains were out, in the sense that genius was lacking. That species of variation had been too effectually extirpated during two centuries to assert itself until after a similar duration of normal conditions. The "immense advantage of religious unity," which even a modern Spanish historian[4] has described as a gain balancing the economic loss from the expulsion of the Moriscoes, was precisely the condition of minimum intellectual activity—the unity of stagnation.

It has been held by one historian that at the death of Philip II there arose some such sense of relief throughout Spain as was felt later in France at the death of Louis XIV; that "the Spaniards now ventured to sport with the chains which they had not the power to break"; and that Cervantes profited by the change in conceiving

---

[1] Cp. Lewes, *Spanish Drama*, passim.
[2] "He inspires me only with horror for the faith which he professes. No one ever so far disfigured Christianity, no one ever assigned to it passions so ferocious, or morals so corrupt" (Sismondi, *Lit. of South of Europe*, Bohn trans. ii, 379).
[3] Ticknor, *Hist. of Spanish Lit.*, 6th ed. ii, 501; *Don Quixote*, Pt. II, ch. liv.
[4] Lafuente, *Historia de España*, 1856, xvii, 340. It is not quite certain that Lafuente expressed his sincere opinion.

and writing his Don Quixote.¹ But the same historian had before seen that "poetic freedom was circumscribed by the same shackles which fettered moral liberty. Thoughts which could not be expressed without fear of the dungeon and the stake were no longer materials for the poet to work on. His imagination, instead of improving them into poetic ideas......had to be taught to reject them. But the eloquence of prose was more completely bowed down under the inquisitorial yoke than poetry, because it was more closely allied to truth, which of all things was the most dreaded."² Cervantes, Lope de Vega, and Calderon proved that within the iron wall of Catholic orthodoxy, in an age when conclusions were but slowly being tried between dogma and reason, there could be a vigorous play of imaginative genius on the field of human nature; even as in Velasquez, sheltered by royal favour, the genius of portraiture could become incarnate. But after these have passed away, the laws of social progress are revealed in the defect of all further Spanish genius. Even of Cervantes it is recorded—on very doubtful authority, however—that he said "I could have made Don Quixote much more amusing if it were not for the Inquisition"; and it is matter of history that a passage in his book[3] disparaging perfunctory works of charity was in 1619 ordered by the Holy Office to be expunged as impious and contrary to the faith.⁴ When the total intellectual life of a nation falls ever further in the rear of the world's movement, even the imaginative arts are stunted. Turkey excepted, the civilised nations of Europe which for two centuries have contributed the fewest great names to the world's bead-roll have been

---

[1] Bouterwek, *Hist. of Spanish and Portuguese Literature*, Eng. trans. 1823, I, 331.
[2] *Id.* p. 151.   [3] Part II, ch. xxxvi.
[4] H. E. Watts, *Miguel de Cervantes*, p. 167. *Don Quixote* was "always under suspicion of the orthodox" *Id.* p. 166. Mr. Watts, saying nothing of Cervantes' approval of the expulsion of the Moriscoes, claims that his "head was clear of the follies and extravagances of the reigning superstition" (*Id.* p. 231).

Spain, Austria, Portugal, Belgium, and Greece, all noted for their "religious unity." And of all of these Spain is the supreme instance of positive decadence, she having exhibited in the sixteenth century a greater complex of energy than any of the others.[1] The lesson is monumental.

§ 5. *Scientific Thought.*

It remains to trace briefly the movement of scientific and speculative thought which constituted the transition between the Scholastic and the modern philosophy. It may be compendiously noted under the names of Copernicus, Bruno, Vanini, Sanchez, Galileo, Ramus, Gassendi, Bacon, and Descartes.

The great performance of COPERNICUS, given to the world with an editor's treacherous preface as he lay on his deathbed in 1543, did not become a general possession for over a hundred years. It was, in fact, the most momentous challenge that had been offered in the modern world to established beliefs, alike theological and lay, for it seemed to flout "common sense" as completely as it did the cosmogony of the sacred books. Its gradual victory, therefore, is the first great instance of a triumph of reason over spontaneous and instilled prejudice; and Galileo's account of his reception of it should be a classic document in the history of rationalism. It was when he was a student in his teens that there came to Pisa one Christianus Urstitius of Rostock, a follower of Copernicus, to lecture on the new doctrine. The young Galileo, being satisfied that "that opinion could be no other than a solemn madness," did not attend; and those of his acquaintance who did made a jest of the matter, all save one, "very intelligent and wary," who told him that "the business

[1] Bouterwek, whose sociology, though meritorious, is ill-clarified, argues that the Inquisition was in a manner congenial to Spain because before its establishment the suspicion of heresy was already "more degrading in Spain than the most odious crimes in other countries." But the same might have been said of the other countries also. As to earlier Spanish heresy see above, vol. i, p. 382 sq.

was not altogether to be laughed at." Thenceforth he began to inquire of Copernicans, with the result inevitable to such a mind as his. "Of as many as I examined I found not so much as one who told me not that he had been a long time of the contrary opinion, but to have changed it for this, as convinced by the strength of the reasons proving the same ; and afterwards questioning them one by one, to see whether they were well possessed of the reasons of the other side, I found them all to be very ready and perfect in them, so that I could not truly say that they took this opinion out of ignorance, vanity, or to show the acuteness of their wits." On the other hand, the opposing Aristotelians and Ptolomeans had seldom even superficially studied the Copernican system, and had in no case been converted from it. "Whereupon, considering that there was no man who followed the opinion of Copernicus that had not been first on the contrary side, and that was not very well acquainted with the reasons of Aristotle and Ptolemy, while, on the contrary, there was not one of the followers of Ptolemy that had ever been of the judgment of Copernicus, and had left that to embrace this of Aristotle," he began to realise how strong must be the reasons that thus drew men away from beliefs "imbibed with their milk."[1] We can divine how slow would be the progress of a doctrine which could only thus begin to find its way into one of the most gifted scientific minds of the modern world. It was only the *elite* of the intellectual life who could at first receive it.

> The doctrine of the earth's two-fold motion, as we have seen, had actually been taught in the fifteenth century by Nicolaus of Cusa (1401-64), who, instead of being prosecuted, was made a cardinal, so little was the question then considered (Ueberweg, ii, 23-24). See above, vol. i, p. 358, as to Pulci. Only very slowly did the work even of Copernicus make its impression. Mr. Green (*Short History*, ed. 1881, p. 297) makes first the blunder of stating that it influenced thought in the *fifteenth* century, and then the further mistake of saying that it was brought home to the general intelligence by Galileo

[1] Galileo, *Dialogi sui Sistemi del Mondo*, ii (*Opere*, ed. 1811, xi, 303-4).

and Kepler in the later years of the *sixteenth* century (*Id.* p. 412). Galileo's European notoriety dates from 1616; his *Dialogues of the Two Systems of the World* appeared only in 1632; and his *Dialogues of the New Sciences* in 1638. Kepler's indecisive *Mysterium Cosmographicum* appeared only in 1597; his treatise on the motions of the planet Mars not till 1609.

One of the first to bring the new cosmological conception to bear on philosophic thought was GIORDANO BRUNO (1548-1600), whose life and death of lonely chivalry have won him his place as the typical martyr of modern freethought.[1] He may be conceived as a blending of the pantheistic and naturalistic lore of ancient Greece,[2] assimilated through the Florentine Platonists, with the spirit of modern science (itself a revival of the Greek) as it first takes firm form in Copernicus, whose doctrine Bruno early and ardently embraced. Baptised Filippo, he took Giordano as his cloister-name when he entered the great convent of S. Domenico Maggiore at Naples in 1563, in his fifteenth year. No human being was ever more unfitly placed among the Dominicans, punningly named the "hounds of the Lord" (*domini canes*) for their work as the corps of the Inquisition; and very early in his cloister life he came near being formally proceeded against for showing disregard of sacred images, and making light of the

[1] A good study of Bruno is supplied by Mr. Owen in his *Skeptics of the Italian Renaissance*. He has, however, omitted to embody the later discoveries of Dufour and Berti, and has some wrong dates. Mrs. Frith's *Life of Giordano Bruno* (1887) gives all the data, but is uncritical on the philosophic side. A competent estimate is given in the late Professor Adamson's lectures on *The Development of Modern Philosophy*, etc., 1903, vol. ii, p. 23 sq.; also in his art. in *Encyc. Brit.* For a hostile view see Hallam, *Lit. of Europe*, as cited, ii, 105-111. The biography of M. Bartholmess, *Jordano Bruno*, 1846, is extremely full and sympathetic, but unavoidably loose as to dates. Much new matter has since been collected, for which see the *Vita di Giordano Bruno* of Domenico Berti, rev. and enlarged ed. 1889, and the doctoral treatise of C. Sigwart, *Die Lebensgeschichte Giordano Brunos*, Tubingen, 1880. For other authorities see Mr. Owen's and Mrs. Frith's lists, and the final *Literaturnachweis* in Gustav Louis's *Giordano Bruno, seine Weltanschauung und Lebensverfassung*, Berlin, 1900. The study of Bruno has been carried further in Germany than in England; but Mr. Whittaker (*Essays and Notices*, 1895) makes up much leeway.

[2] Cp. Bartholmèss, i, 49-53; Lange, *Gesch. des Mater.* i, 191-4 (Eng. trans. i, 232); Gustav Louis, as cited, pp. 11, 88.

sanctity of the Virgin.[1] He passed his novitiate, however, without further trouble, and was fully ordained a priest in 1572, in his twenty-fourth year. Passing then though several Neapolitan monasteries during a period of three years, he seems to have become not a little of a freethinker on his return to his first cloister, as he had already reached Arian opinions in regard to Christ, and soon proceeded to substitute a mystical and Pythagorean for the orthodox view of the Trinity.[2]

For the second time a "process" was begun against him, and he took flight to Rome (1576), presenting himself at a convent of his Order. News speedily came from Naples of the process against him, and of the discovery that he had possessed a volume of the works of Chrysostom and Jerome with the scholia of Erasmus—a prohibited thing. Only a few months before Bartolomeo Carranza, Bishop of Toledo, who had won the praise of the Council of Trent for his index of prohibited books, had been condemned to abjure for the doctrine that "the worship of the relics of the saints is of human institution," and had died in the same year at the convent to which Bruno had now gone. Thus doubly warned, he threw off his priestly habit, and fled to the Genoese territory,[3] where, in the commune of Noli, he taught grammar and astronomy. In 1578 he visited successively Turin, Venice, Padua, Bergamo, and Milan, resuming at the last-named town his monk's habit. Thereafter he again returned to Turin, passing thence to Chambery at the end of 1578, and thence to Geneva early in 1579.[4] His wish, he said, was "to live in liberty and security," but for that he must first renounce his Dominican habit, other Italian refugees, of whom there were many at Geneva, helping him to a layman's suit. Becoming a corrector of the press, he seems to have conformed externally to

[1] Berti, *Vita di Giordano Bruno*, 1889, pp. 40-41, 420. Bruno gives the facts in his own narrative before the Inquisitors at Venice.
[2] *Id.* pp. 42-43, 47; Owen, p. 265.
[3] Not to Genoa, as Berti stated in his first ed. See ed. 1889, pp. 54, 392.
[4] Berti, p. 65. Mr. Owen has the uncorrected date, 1576.

Calvinism ; but after a stay of two and a half months he published a short diatribe against one Antonio de La Faye, who professed philosophy at the Academy ; and for this he was arrested and sentenced to excommunication, while his bookseller was subjected to one day's imprisonment and a fine.[1] After three weeks the excommunication was raised ; but he nevertheless left Geneva, and afterwards spoke of Calvinism as the "*de*formed religion." After a few weeks' sojourn at Lyons he went to Toulouse, the very centre of inquisitional orthodoxy, and there, strangely enough, he was able to stay for more than a year,[2] taking his degree as Master of Arts, and becoming professor of astronomy. But the civil wars made Toulouse unsafe ; and at length, probably in 1581 or 1582, he reached Paris, where for a time he lectured as professor extraordinary.[3] In 1583 he reached England, where he remained till 1585, lecturing, debating at Oxford on the Copernican theory, and publishing a number of his works, four of them dedicated to his patron Castelnau, the French ambassador. He had met Sir Philip Sidney at Milan in 1578; and his dialogue, *Cena de le Ceneri*, gives a vivid account of a discussion in which he took a leading part at a banquet given by Sir Fulke Greville. His picture of "Oxford ignorance and English ill-manners"[4] is not lenient ; and there is no reason to suppose that his doctrine was then assimilated by many ;[5] but his stay in the household of Castlenau was one of the happiest periods of his chequered life. While in England he wrote no fewer than seven works, four of them dedicated

[1] Dufour, *Giordano Bruno a Géneve: Documents Inedits,* 1884; Berti, pp. 95-97; Gustav Louis, *Giordano Bruno*, pp. 73-75. Mr. Owen (p. 269) has overlooked these facts, set forth by Dufour in 1884. The documents are given in full in Mrs. Frith's *Life*, 1887, p. 60 sq.
[2] The dates are in doubt. Cp. Berti, p. 115, and Mrs. Frith, p. 65.
[3] See his own narrative before the Inquisitors in 1592. Berti, p. 394.
[4] Mrs. Frith's *Life*, p. 121, and refs.; Owen, p. 275; Bartholmess, *Jordano Bruno*, i, 136-8.
[5] Cp. Hallam, *Lit. of Europe*, ii, 111, *note*. As to Bruno's supposed influence on Bacon and Shakspere, cp. Bartholmess, i, 134-5; Mrs. Frith's *Life*, pp. 104-8 ; and the author's *Montaigne and Shakspere*, pp. 82-7.

to Castlenau, and two—the *Heroic Fervours* and the *Expulsion of the Triumphant Beast*—to Sir Philip Sidney.

Returning to Paris on the recall of Castlenau in 1585, he made an attempt to reconcile himself to the church, but it was fruitless; and thereafter he went his own way. After a public disputation at the university in 1586, he set out on a new peregrination, visiting first Mayence, Marburg, and Wittemberg. At Marburg he was refused leave to debate; and at Wittemberg he seems to have been carefully conciliatory, as he not only matriculated, but taught for over a year (1586-88), till the Calvinist party carried the day over the Lutheran.[1] Thereafter he reached Prague, Helmstadt, Frankfort, and Zurich. At length, on the fatal invitation of the Venetian youth Mocenigo, he re-entered Italian territory, where, in Venice, he was betrayed to the Inquisition by his treacherous and worthless pupil.

What had been done for freethought by Bruno in his fourteen years of wandering, debating, and teaching through Europe it is impossible to estimate; but it is safe to say that he was one of the most powerful antagonists to orthodox unreason that had yet appeared. Of all men of his time he had perhaps the least affinity with the Christian creed, which was repellent to him alike in the Catholic and the Protestant versions. The attempt to prove him a believer on the strength of a non-autograph manuscript[2] is idle. In the *Spaccio della bestia trionfante* he derides the notion of a union of divine and human natures, and substantially proclaims a natural (theistic) religion, negating all "revealed" religions alike. Where Boccaccio had accredited all the three leading religions, Bruno disallows all with paganism, though he puts that above Christianity.[3] And his

---

[1] His praise of Luther, and his compliments to the Lutherans, are in notable contrast to his verdict on Calvinism. What happened was that at Wittemberg he was on his best behaviour, and was well treated accordingly.

[2] Noroff, as cited by Mrs. Frith, p. 345.

[3] Cp. Berti, pp. 187-8; Whittaker, *Essays and Notices*, 1895, p. 89; and Louis's section, *Stellung zu Christenthum und Kirche*.

disbelief grew more stringent with his years. Among the heretical propositions charged against him by the Inquisition were these: that there is transmigration of souls; that magic is right and proper; that the Holy Spirit is the same thing as the soul of the world; that the world is eternal; that Moses, like the Egyptians, wrought miracles by magic; that the sacred writings are but a romance (*sogno*); that the devil will be saved; that only the Hebrews are descended from Adam, other men having descended from progenitors created by God before Adam; that Christ was not God, but was a notorious sorcerer (*insigne mago*), who, having deceived men, was deservedly hanged, not crucified; that the prophets and the apostles were bad men and sorcerers, and that many of them were hanged as such. A number of these propositions are professedly drawn, always, of course, by forcing his language, but not without some colourable pretext, from his two "poems," *De triplice, minimo, et mensura*, and *De monade, numero et figura*, published at Frankfort in 1591, in the last year of his freedom.[1]

Alike in the details of his propaganda and the temper of his utterance, he expresses from first to last the spirit of freethought and free speech. *Libertas philosophica*[2] is the breath of his nostrils; and by his life and his death alike he upholds the ideal for men as no other before him did. The wariness of Rabelais and the noncommittal skepticism of Montaigne are alike alien to him; he is too lacking in reticence, too explosive, to give due heed even to the common-sense amenities of life, much more to hedge his meaning with safeguarding qualifications. And it was doubtless as much by the contagion of his mood as by his lore that he impressed men.

[1] Berti, pp. 297-8. It takes much searching in the two poems to find the ideas in question, and Berti has attempted no collation; but, allowing for distortions, the Inquisition has sufficient ground for outcry.
[2] In the treatise *De Lampade combinatoria Lulliana* (1587). According to Berti (p. 220) he is the first to employ this phrase, which becomes the watchword of Spinoza (*libertas philosophandi*) a century later.

His personal and literary influence was probably most powerful in respect of his eager propaganda of the Copernican doctrine, which he of his own force vitally expanded and made part of a pantheistic conception of the universe.[1] Where Copernicus adhered by implication to the idea of an external and limitary sphere—the last of the eight of the Ptolemaic theory—Bruno reverted boldly to the doctrine of Anaxarchos, and declared firmly for the infinity of space and of the series of the worlds. In regard to biology he makes an equivalent advance, starting from the thought of Empedocles and Lucretius, and substituting an idea of natural selection for that of creative providence.[2] The conception is definitely thought out, and marks him as one of the renovators of scientific no less than of philosophic thought for the modern world; though the special paralysis of science under Christian theology kept his ideas on this side pretty much a dead letter for his own day. And indeed it was to the universal and not the particular that his thought chiefly and most enthusiastically turned. A philosophic poet rather than a philosopher or man of science, he yet set abroad for the modern world that conception of the physical infinity of the universe which, once psychologically assimilated, makes an end of the medieval theory of things. On this head he was eagerly affirmative; and the merely Pyrrhonic skeptics he assailed as he did the "asinine" orthodox, though he insisted on doubt as the beginning of wisdom.

Of his extensive literary output not much is stamped with lasting scientific fitness or literary charm; and some of his treatises, as those on mnemonics, have no more value than the product of his didactic model, Raymond Lully. As a writer he is at his best in the

---

[1] Berti. cap. iv; Owen, p. 249; Ueberweg, ii, 27; Pünjer, p. 93 sq.; Whittaker, *Essays and Notices*, 1895, p. 66. As to Bruno's debt to Nicolaus of Cusa cp. Gustav Louis, as cited, p. 11; Pünjer, as cited; Carriere, *Die philosophische Weltanschauung der Reformationszeit*, p. 25; and Whittaker, p. 68. The argument of Carriere's second edition is analysed and rebutted by Mr. Whittaker, p. 253 sq.

[2] *De Immenso*, vii, c. 18, cited by Whittaker, *Essays and Notices*, p. 70.

sweeping expatiation of his more general philosophic treatises, where he attains a lifting ardour of inspiration, a fervour of soaring outlook, that puts him in the front rank of the thinkers of his age. And if his literary character is at times open to severe criticism in respect of his lack of balance, sobriety, and self-command, his final courage atones for such shortcomings.

His case, indeed, serves to remind us that at certain junctures it is only the unbalanced types that aid humanity's advance. The perfectly prudent and self-sufficing man does not achieve revolutions, does not revolt against tyrannies: he wisely adapts himself and subsists, letting the evil prevail as it may. It is the more impatient and unreticent, the eager and hot-brained—in a word, the faulty—who clash with oppression and break a way for quieter spirits through the hedges of enthroned authority. The serenely contemplative spirit is rather a possession than a possessor for his fellows: he may inform and enlighten, but is not in himself a countering or inspiriting force: a Shelley avails more than a Goethe against tyrannous power. And it may be that the battling enthusiast in his own way wins liberation for himself from "fear of fortune and death," as he wins for others liberty of action.[1] Even such a liberator, bearing other men's griefs and taking stripes that they might be kept whole, was Bruno.

And when the end came he vindicated human nature as worthily as could any quietist. Charged on the traitor's testimony with many "blasphemies," he denied them all,[2] but stood to his published writings[3] and vividly expounded his theories,[4] professing in the usual manner to believe in conformity with the church's teachings, whatever he might write on philosophy. It is impossible to trust the Inquisition records as to his

---

[1] As to Bruno's own claim in the *Eroici Furori*, cp. Whittaker, *Essays and Notices*, p. 90.
[2] Documents in Berti, pp. 407-418.
[3] See the document in Berti, p. 398 sq.; Mrs. Frith's *Life*, pp. 270-281.
[4] Berti, p. 400 sq.

words of self-humiliation;[1] though on the other hand no blame can rationally attach to anyone who, in his place, should try to deceive such enemies, morally on a level with hostile savages seeking one's life. It is certain that the Inquisitors frequently wrung recantations by torture.[2]

What is historically certain is that Bruno was not released, but sent on to Rome, and was kept there in prison for seven years. He was not the sort of heretic likely to be released; though the fact of his being a Dominican, and the desire to maintain the church's intellectual credit, delayed so long his execution. Certainly not an atheist (he called himself in several of his book-titles *Philotheus;* and his quasi-pantheism or monism often lapses into theistic modes),[3] he yet was from first to last essentially though not professedly anti-Christian in his view of the universe. If the Church had cause to fear any philosophic teaching, it was his, preached with the ardour of a prophet and the eloquence of a poet. His doctrine that the worlds in space are innumerable was as offensive to orthodox ears as his specific negations of Christian dogma, outgoing as it did the later idea of Kepler and Galileo. He had, moreover, finally refused to make any fresh recantation; and the only detailed document extant concerning his final trial describes him as saying to his judges: "With more fear, perchance, do you pass sentence on me than I receive it." According to all accessible records, he was burned alive at Rome in February, 1600, in the Field of Flowers, near where his statue now stands.

An attempt has been made by Professor Desdouits in a pamphlet (*La légende tragique de Jordano Bruno:* Paris, 1885)

---

[1] See Berti, p. 396; Owen, pp. 285-6; Mrs. Frith, pp. 282-3.

[2] The controversy as to whether Galileo was tortured leaves it clear that torture was common. See Dr. Parchappe, *Galilée, sa vie,* etc., 1866, Ptie. ii, ch. 7.

[3] Professor Carriere has contended that a transition from pantheism to theism marks the growth of his thought; but, as is shown by Mr. Whittaker, he is markedly pantheistic in his latest work of all, though his pantheism is not merely naturalistic. *Essays and Notices,* pp. 72, 253-8.

to show that there is no evidence that Bruno was burned; and an anonymous writer in the *Scottish Review* (October, 1888, Art. 11), rabidly hostile to Bruno, has maintained the same proposition. Doubt on the subject dates from Bayle. Its main ground is the fewness of the documentary records, of which, further, the genuineness is now called in question. But no good reason is shown for doubting them. They are three in number.

1. The Latin letter of Gaspar Schopp (Scioppius), dated February 17, 1600, is an eye-witness's account of the sentencing and burning of Bruno at that date. (See it in full, in the original Latin, in Berti, p. 461 sq. and in App. V to Mrs. Frith's *Life of Bruno*, and partly translated in Professor Adamson's lectures, as cited.) It was not printed till 1621, but the grounds urged for its rejection are totally inadequate, and involve assumptions, which are themselves entirely unproved, as to what Scioppius was likely to do. Finally, no intelligible reason is suggested for the forging of such a document. The remarks of Professor Desdouits on this head have no force whatever. The writer in the *Scottish Review* (p. 263, and *note*) suggests as "at least as possible an hypothesis as any other that he [Bruno] was the author of the forged accounts of his own death." Such are the conceptions offered as substitutes for the existing view.

2. There are preserved two extracts from a Roman news-letter (*Avvisa*) of the time; one, dated February 12th, 1600, commenting on the case; the other, dated February 19th, relating the execution on the 17th. (See both in *S. R.* pp. 264-5. They were first printed by Signor Berti in *Documenti intorno a Giordano Bruno*, Rome, 1880, and are reprinted in his *Vita*, ed. 1889, cap. xix.) Against these testimonies the sole plea is that they mis-state Bruno's opinions and the duration of his imprisonment—a test which would reduce to mythology the contents of most newspapers in our own day. The writer in the *Scottish Review* makes the suicidal suggestion that, inasmuch as the errors as to dates occur in Schopp's letter, "the so-called Schopp was fabricated from these notices, or they from Schopp"—thus admitting that one ranked as a historical document.

3. There has been found, by a Catholic investigator, a double entry in the books of the Lay Brotherhood of *San Giovanni Decollato*, whose function was to minister to prisoners under capital sentence, giving a circumstantial account of Bruno's execution. (See it in *S. R.* pp. 266, 269, 270.) In this case, the main entry being dated "1600. Thursday. February 16th," the anonymous writer argues that "the whole

thing resolves itself into a make-up," because February 16th was the Wednesday. The entry refers to the procedure of the Wednesday night and the Thursday morning; and such an error could easily occur in any case. Whatever may be one day proved, the cavils thus far count for nothing. All the while, the records as to Bruno remain in the hands of the Catholic authorities; but, despite the discredit constantly cast on the church on the score of Bruno's execution, they offer no official denial of the common statement; while they do officially admit (*S. R.* p. 252) that on February 8th Bruno was sentenced as an "obstinate heretic," and "given over to the Secular Court." On the other hand, the episode is well vouched; and the argument from the silence of ambassadors' letters is so far void. No pretence is made of tracing Bruno anywhere after February, 1600.

Since the foregoing note appeared in the first edition I have met with the essay of Mr. R. Copley Christie, "Was Giordano Bruno Really Burned?" (*Macmillan's Magazine*, October, 1885; rep. in Mr. Christie's *Selected Essays and Papers*, 1902). This is a crushing answer to the thesis of M. Desdouits, showing as it does clear grounds not only for affirming the genuineness of the letter of Scioppius, but for doubting the diligence of M. Desdouits. Mr. Christie points out (1) that in his book *Ecclesiasticus*, printed in 1612, Scioppius refers to the burning of Bruno almost in the words of his letter of 1600; (2) that in 1607 Kepler wrote to a correspondent of the burning of Bruno, giving as his authority J. M. Wacker, who in 1600 was living at Rome as the imperial ambassador; and (3) that the tract *Machiavellatio*, 1621, in which the letter of Scioppius was first printed, was well known in its day, being placed on the *Index*, and answered by two writers without eliciting any repudiation from Scioppius, who lived till 1649. As M. Desdouits staked his case on the absence of allusions to the subject before 1661 (overlooking even the allusion by Mersenne, in 1624, cited by Bayle), his theory may be regarded as utterly exploded.

Bruno has been zealously blackened by Catholic writers for the obscenity of some of his writing[1] and the alleged freedom of his life—piquant charges, when we remember the life of the Papal Italy in which he was born. LUCILIO VANINI (otherwise Julius Cæsar Vanini), the next martyr of freethought, also an Italian (b. at Taurisano, 1585), is open to the more relevant charges of an inordinate vanity and some duplicity. Figuring

[1] Notably his comedy *Il Candelaio*.

as a Carmelite friar, which he was not, he came to England (1612) and deceitfully professed to abjure Catholicism,[1] gaining, however, nothing by the step, and contriving to be reconciled to the church. Previously he had figured, like Bruno, as a wandering scholar at Amsterdam, Brussels, Cologne, Geneva, and Lyons; and afterwards he taught natural philosophy for a year at Genoa. His treatise, *Amphitheatrum Æternæ Providentiæ* (Lyons, 1615), is professedly directed against "Atheists, Epicureans, Peripatetics, and Stoics," and is ostensibly quite orthodox.[2] As usual, it leaves us in doubt as to the amount of real atheism current at the time. The preface asserts that "'Αθεοτητο *autem secta pestilentissima quotidie, latius et latius vires acquirit eundo*" and there are various allusions to atheists in the text;[3] but their arguments are such as might be brought by deists against miracles and the Christian doctrine of sin; and there is an allusion of the customary kind to "*Nicolaus Machiavellus Atheorum facile princeps*,"[4] which puts all in doubt. The later *Dialogues*, while discussing many questions of creed and science in a free fashion, no less profess orthodoxy; and, while one passage is pantheistic,[5] they also denounce atheism, and profess faith in immortality.[6] Other passages imply doubt;[7] but it is to be remembered that the Dialogues were penned not by Vanini, but by his disciples at Paris, he only tardily giving his consent to their publication.[8] And whereas one passage does avow that the author in his *Amphitheatrum* had said

---

[1] Owen, *Skeptics of the Italian Renaissance*, p. 357. A full narrative, from the documents, is given in R. C. Christie's essay, "Vanini in England," in the *English Historical Review* of April, 1895, reprinted in his *Selected Essays and Papers*, 1902.
[2] See it analysed by Owen, pp. 361-8, and by Carriere, *Weltanschauung*, pp. 496-504.
[3] *Amphitheatrum*, ed. 1615, pp. 72, 73, 113, etc.
[4] P. 35.
[5] See Rousselot's French trans. 1842, p. 227.
[6] *Id.* pp. 219-221.   [7] *E.g.*, pp. 347-8.
[8] Owen, pp. 369, 370. It is thus possible that the passages on the score of which Vanini is charged with wild conceit were not written by him at all.

many things he did not believe, the context clearly suggests that the reference was not to the main argument, but to some of its dubious facts.¹ In any case, Vanini cannot be shown to be an atheist;² and the attacks upon him as an immoral writer are not any better supported.³ The publication of the work was in fact formally authorised by the Sorbonne, and it does not even appear that when he was charged with atheism and blasphemy at Toulouse that work was at all founded on.⁴ The charges rested on the testimony of a treacherous associate as to his private conversation; and if true, it only amounted to proving his pantheism, expressed in his use of the word "Nature." At his trial he expressly avowed and argued for theism. Yet he was convicted,⁵ and burned alive (February 9th, 1619) on the day of his sentence. Drawn on a hurdle, in his shirt, with a placard on his shoulders inscribed "Atheist and Blasphemer of the name of God," he went to his death with a high heart, rejoicing, as he cried in Italian, to die like a philosopher.⁶ A Catholic historian,⁷ who was present, says he hardily declared that "Jesus facing death sweated with fear: I die undaunted." But before burning him they tore out his tongue by the roots; and the Christian historian is humorous over the victim's long cry of agony.⁸ No martyr ever faced death with a more dauntless courage than this

¹ Cp. the passages cited by Hallam, *Lit. Hist.* ii, 461, with Mr. Owen's defence, p. 368, *note*.
² Cp. Carriere's analysis of the Dialogues, pp. 505-9.
³ See Mr. Owen's vindication, pp. 371-4. Renan's criticism (*Averroes*, pp. 420-3) is not quite judicial. See many others cited by Carriere, p. 516.
⁴ Owen, p. 395.
⁵ Personal enmity on the part of the prosecuting official was commonly held to explain the trial. Owen, p. 393; Carriere, p. 521.
⁶ *Mercure Français*, 1619, tom. v. p. 64.
⁷ Gramond (Barthélemi de Grammont), *Historia Galliæ ab excessu Henri IV*, 1643, p. 209. Carriere translates the passage in full, pp. 500-12, 515.
⁸ Gramond, p. 210. Of Vanini, as of Bruno, it is recorded that at the stake he repelled the proffered crucifix. Mr. Owen and other writers, who justly remark that he well might, overlook the once received belief that it was the official practice, with obstinate heretics, to proffer a *red-hot* crucifix, so that the victim should be sure to spurn it with open anger.

> Lonely antagonist of Destiny
> That went down scornful before many spears;[1]

and if the man had all the faults falsely imputed to him[2] his death might shame his accusers.

Contemporary with Bruno and Vanini was SANCHEZ, a physician of Portuguese-Jewish descent, settled as a Professor at Toulouse, who contrived to publish a treatise (written 1576, printed 1581) affirming "That Nothing is Known" (*Quod Nihil Scitur*) without suffering any molestation. It is a formal putting of the Pyrrhonist skepticism of Montaigne, which is thus seen to have been to some extent current before he wrote; but there is no sign that Sanchez' formal statement had any philosophic influence, save perhaps on Descartes in the next generation.[3] His most important aspect is as a thinker on natural science; and here he is really corrective and constructive rather than Pyrrhonist; his poem on the comet of 1577 being one of the earliest rational utterances on the subject in the Christian period.[4]

But it was with Galileo that there began the practical application of the Copernican theory to astronomy, and, indeed, the decisive demonstration of its truth. With him, accordingly, began the positive rejection of the Copernican theory by the church; for thus far it had never been officially vetoed. Almost immediately after the publication of Galileo's *Sidereus Nuncius* (1610) his name is found in the papers of the Inquisition, with that

---

[1] Stephen Phillips, *Marpessa*.

[2] Cp. Owen, pp. 389, 391, and Carriere, pp. 512-13, as to the worst calumnies. It is significant that Vanini was tried *solely* for blasphemy and atheism. What is proved against him is that he and an associate practised a rather gross fraud on the English ecclesiastical authorities, having apparently no higher motive than gain and a free life. Mr. Christie notes, however, that Vanini in his writings always speaks very kindly of England and the English, and so did not add ingratitude to his act of imposture.

[3] Cp. Bartholmess, *Hist. crit. des doctr. relig. de la philos. moderne*, 1855, i, 21-22.

[4] See Owen, *Skeptics of the French Renaissance*, pp. 631-6—a fairer and more careful estimate than that of Hallam, *Lit. Hist. of Europe*, ii, 111-113.

of Cremonini of Padua, as a subject of investigation.[1] The juxtaposition is noteworthy. Cremonini was an Aristotelian, with Averroïst leanings, and reputed an atheist;[2] and it was presumably on this score that the Inquisition was looking into his case. At the same time, as an Aristotelian he was strongly opposed to Galileo, and is said to have been one of those who refused to look through Galileo's telescope.[3] Galileo, on the other hand, was ostensibly a good Catholic; but his discovery of the moons of Jupiter was a signal confirmation of the Copernican theory, and the new status at once given to that made a corresponding commotion in the church. Thus he had against him both the unbelieving pedants of the schools and the priests.

The fashion in which Galileo's sidereal discoveries were met is indeed typical of the whole history of freethought: the clergy pointed to the story of Joshua stopping the sun and moon; some schoolmen insisted that "the heavens are unchangeable," and that there was no authority in Aristotle for the new assertions; with such minds the man of science had to argue, and in deference to such he had at length to affect to doubt his own demonstrations.[4] The Catholic Reaction had finally created as bitter a spirit of hostility to free science in the church as existed among the Protestants; and in Italy even those who saw the moons of Jupiter through his telescope dared not avow what they had seen.[5] It was therefore an unfortunate step on his part to go from Padua, which was under the rule of Venice, then antipapal,[6] to Tuscany, on the invitation of the Grand Duke.

[1] Karl von Gebler, *Galileo Galilei and the Roman Curia*, Eng. trans. 1879, pp. 36 37.
[2] This appears from the letters of Sagredo to Galileo. Gebler, p 37. Cp. Bayle, art. CREMONIN, notes C and D; and Renan, *Averroes*, 3e edit. pp. 408–413.
[3] Lange, *Geschichte des Materialismus*, i, 183 (Eng. trans. i, 220); Gebler, p. 25.
[4] Gebler, pp. 54, 129, and *passim*; *The Private Life of Galileo*, Boston, 1870, pp. 67–72.
[5] Galileo's letter to Kepler, cited by Gebler, p. 26.
[6] The Jesuits had been expelled from Venice in 1616, in retaliation for a papal interdict.

When in 1613 he published his treatise on the solar spots, definitely upholding Copernicus against Jesuits and Aristotelians, trouble became inevitable; and his letter to his pupil, Father Castelli, professor of mathematics at Pisa, discussing the Biblical argument with which they had both been met, at once evoked a general explosion. An outcry of ignorant Dominican monks[1] sufficed to set at work the machinery of the Index, the first result of which (1616) was to put on the list of condemned books the great treatise of Copernicus, published seventy-three years before. Galileo personally escaped for the present through the friendly intervention of the Pope, Paul V, on the appeal of his patron, the Grand Duke of Tuscany, apparently on the ground that he had not publicly taught the Copernican theory. It would seem as if some of the heads of the church were at heart Copernicans,[2] but were obliged to disown a doctrine felt by so many others to be subversive of the church's authority.

> See the details of the procedure in Domenico Berti, *Il Processo Originale de Galileo Galilei*, ed. 1878, cap. iv, and in Gebler, ch. vi. The latter writer claims to show that, of two records of the "admonition" to Galileo, one, the more stringent in its terms, was false, *though made at the date it bears*, to permit of subsequent proceedings against Galileo. But the whole thesis is otiose. It is admitted (Gebler, p. 89) that Galileo was admonished "not to defend or hold the Copernican doctrine." Gebler contends, however, that this was not a command to keep "entire silence," and that therefore Galileo is not justly to be charged with having disobeyed the injunction of the Inquisition when, in his *Dialogues on the Two Principal Systems of the World, the Ptolemaic and Copernican* (1632), he dealt dialectically with the subject, neither affirming nor denying, but treating both theories as hypotheses. But the real issue is not Galileo's cautious disobedience (see

---

[1] The measure of reverence with which the orthodox handled the matter may be inferred from the fact that the Dominican Caccini, who preached against Galileo in Florence, took as one of his texts the verse in Acts i: "*Viri Galilaei, quid statis aspicientes in cælum,*" making a pun on the Scripture.

[2] See *The Private Life of Galileo*, Boston, 1870, pp. 86-7, 91, 99; Gebler, p. 44; Berti, *Il Processo Originale de Galileo Galilei*, 1878, p. 53.

Gebler's own admissions, p. 149) to an irrational decree, but the crime of the church in silencing him. It is not likely that the "enemies" of Galileo, as Gebler supposes (pp. 90, 338), anticipated his later dialectical handling of the subject, and so falsified the decision of the Inquisition against him in 1616. Gebler had at first adopted the German theory that the absolute command to silence was forged in 1632; and, finding the document certainly belonged to 1616, framed the new theory, quite unnecessarily, to save Galileo's credit. The two records are quite in the spirit and manner of Inquisitorial diplomacy. As Berti remarks, "the Holy Office proceeded with much heedlessness (*legerezza*) and much confusion" in 1616. Its first judgment, in either form, merely emphasises the guilt of the second.

Thus officially "admonished" for his heresy, but not punished, in 1616, Galileo kept silence for some years, till in 1618 he published his (erroneous) theory of the tides, which he sent with an ironical epistle to the friendly Archduke Leopold of Austria, professing to be propounding a mere dream, disallowed by the official veto on Copernicus.[1] This, however, did him less harm than his essay *Il Saggiatore* ("The Scales"), in which he confuted the Jesuit Grassi on the question of comets. Receiving the *imprimatur* in 1623, it was dedicated to the new pope, Urban VIII, who, as the Cardinal Maffeo Barberini, had been Galileo's friend. The latter could now hope for freedom of speech, as he had all along had a number of friends at the papal court, besides many priests, among his admirers and disciples. But the enmity of the Jesuits countervailed all. They did not succeed in procuring a censure of the *Saggiatore,* though that subtly vindicates the Copernican system while professing to hold it disproved by the fiat of the church;[2] but when, venturing further, he after another lapse of years produced his *Dialogues on the Two Systems,* for which he obtained the papal *imprimatur* in 1632, they caught him in their net. Having constant access to the Pope, they contrived to make him believe that Galileo had

[1] Gebler (p. 101) solemnly comments on this letter as a lapse into "servility" on Copernicus' part.
[2] Gebler, pp. 112-113.

ridiculed him in one of the personages of his Dialogues. It was quite false; but one of the Pope's anti-Copernican arguments was there unconsciously made light of; and his wounded vanity was probably a main factor in the impeachment which followed.[1] His Holiness professed to have been deceived into granting the *imprimatur*;[2] a Special Commission was set on foot; the proceedings of 1616 were raked up; and Galileo was again summoned to Rome. He was old and frail, and sent medical certificates of his unfitness for such travel; but it was insisted on, and as under the papal tyranny there was no help, he accordingly made the journey. After many delays he was tried, and, on his formal abjuration, sentenced to formal imprisonment (1633) for teaching the "absurd" and "false doctrine" of the motion of the earth and the non-motion of the sun from east to west. In this case the Pope, whatever were his motives, acted as a hot anti-Copernican, expressing his personal opinion on the question again and again, and always in an anti-Copernican sense. In both cases, however, the Popes, while agreeing to the verdict, abstained from officially ratifying it,[3] so that, in proceeding to force Galileo to abjure his doctrine, the Inquisition technically exceeded its powers—a circumstance in which some Catholics appear to find comfort. Seeing that three of the ten cardinals named in the preamble to the sentence did not sign, it has been inferred that they dissented; but there is no good reason to suppose that either the Pope or they wilfully abstained from signing. They had gained their point—the humiliation of the great discoverer.

> Compare Gebler, p. 241; *Private Life*, p. 257, quoting Tiraboschi. For an exposure of the many perversions of the facts as to Galileo by Catholic writers see Parchappe, *Galilee, sa vie*, etc., 2e Partie. To such straits has the Catholic Church been reduced in this matter that part of its defence of the treatment of Galileo is the plea that he unwarrantably

---

[1] *Private Life*, pp. 216-218; Gebler, pp. 157-162.
[2] Berti, pp. 61-64; *Private Life*, pp. 212-213; Gebler, p. 162.
[3] Gebler, p. 239; *Private Life*, p. 256.

asserted that the fixity of the sun and the motion of the earth were *taught in the Scriptures*. (See *Galileo e l' Inquisizione*, by Monsignor Marini, Roma, 1850, pp. 1, 53-4, etc.) Had he really done so he would only have been assenting to what his priestly opponents constantly dinned in his ears. But in point of fact he had not so assented; for in his letter to Castelli (see Gebler, pp. 46-50) he had earnestly deprecated the argument from the Bible, urging that though Scripture could not err its interpreters might misunderstand it; and even going so far as to argue, with much ingenuity, that the story of Joshua, literally interpreted, could be made to harmonise with the Copernican theory, but not at all with the Ptolemaic.

The thesis of Monsignor Marini deserves to rank as the highest flight of absurdity and effrontery in the entire discussion. Every step in both procedures of the Inquisition insists on the falsity and the anti-scriptural character of the doctrine that the earth moves round the sun (see Berti, *Il Processo*, p. 115 sq.; Gebler, pp. 76-7, 230-4); and never once is it hinted that Galileo's error lay in ascribing to the Bible the doctrine of the earth's fixity.

The stories of his being tortured and blinded, and saying "Still it moves," are indeed myths.[1] The broken-spirited old man was in no mood so to speak; he was, moreover, in all respects save his science, an orthodox Catholic,[2] and as such not likely to defy the Church to its face. In reality he was formally in the custody of the Inquisition—and this not in a cell, but in the house of an official—for only twenty-two days. After the sentence he was again formally detained for some seventeen days in the Villa Medici, but was then allowed to return to his own rural home at Acatri,[3] on condition that he lived in solitude, receiving no visitors. He was thus much more truly a prisoner than the so-called "prisoner of the Vatican" in our own day. The worst part of the sentence, however, was the placing of all his

[1] Gebler, pp. 249-263; *Private Life*, pp. 255-6; Marini, pp. 55-57. The "e pur si muove" story is first heard of in 1774. As to the torture, it is to be remembered that Galileo recanted under *threat* of it. See Berti, pp 93-101; Marini, p 59; Professor Lodge, *Pioneers of Science*, 1893, pp. 128-131. Berti argues that only the special humanity of the Commissary-General, Macolano, saved him from the torture. Cp. Gebler, p. 259, *note*.
[2] Gebler, p. 281.
[3] *Private Life*, pp. 255-260, 268; Gebler, p. 252.

works, published and unpublished, on the *Index Expurgatorius*, and the gag thus laid on all utterance of rational scientific thought in Italy—an evil of incalculable influence. "The lack of liberty and speculation," writes a careful Italian student, "was the cause of the death first of the Accademia dei Lincei, an institution unique in its time ; then of the Accademia del Cimento. Thus Italy, after the marvellous period of vigorous native civilisation in the thirteenth century, after a second period of civilisation less native but still its own, as being Latin, saw itself arrested on the threshold of a third and not less splendid period. Vexations and prohibitions expelled courage, spontaneity, and universality from the national mind ; literary style became uncertain, indeterminate ; and, forbidden to treat of government, science, or religion, turned to things frivolous and fruitless. For the great academies, instituted to renovate and further the study of natural philosophy, were substituted small ones without any such aim. Intellectual energy, the love of research and of objective truth, greatness of feeling and nobility of character, all suffered. Nothing so injures a people as the compulsion to express or conceal its thought solely from motives of fear. The nation in which those conditions were set up became intellectually inferior to those in which it was possible to pass freely in the vast regions of knowledge. Her culture grew restricted, devoid of originality, vaporous, umbratile ; there arose habits of servility and dissimulation ; great books, great men, great purposes were denaturalised."[1]

It was thus in the other countries of Europe that Galileo's teaching bore its fruit, for he speedily got his condemned Dialogues published in Latin by the Elzevirs ; and in 1638, also at the hands of the Elzevirs, appeared his *Dialogues of the New Sciences* [*i.e.*, of mechanics and motion], the "foundation of mechanical physics." By this time he was totally blind, and then

[1] Berti, *Il Processo di Galileo,* ed. 1878, pp. 111-112.

only, when physicians could not help him save by prolonging his life, was he allowed to live under strict surveillance in Florence, needing a special indulgence from the Inquisition to permit him even to go to church at Easter. The desire of his last blind days, to have with him his best-beloved pupil, Father Castelli, was granted only under rigid limitation and supervision, though even the Papacy could not keep from him the plaudits of the thinkers of Europe. Finally he passed away in his rural "prison"—after five years of blindness—in 1642, the year of Newton's birth. Not till 1757 did the Papacy permit other books teaching his system; not until 1820 was permission given to treat it as true; and not until 1835 was it withdrawn from the *Index Expurgatorius*.[1]

While modern science was thus being placed on its special basis, a continuous resistance was being made in the schools to the dogmatism which held the mutilated lore of Aristotle as the sum of human wisdom. Like the ecclesiastical revolution, this had been protracted through centuries. Aristotelianism, whether theistic or pantheistic, whether orthodox or heterodox,[2] had become a dogmatism like another, a code that vetoed revision, a fetter laid on the mind. Even as a negation of Christian superstition it had become impotent, for the Peripatetics were not only ready to make common cause with the Jesuits against Galileo, as we have seen; some of them were content even to join in the appeal to the Bible.[3] The result of such uncritical partisanship was that the immense service of Aristotle to mental life—

---

[1] Gebler, pp. 312-315.

[2] See Ueberweg, ii, 12, as to the conflicting types. In addition to Cremonini, several leading Aristotelians in the sixteenth and seventeenth centuries were accused of atheism (Hallam, *Lit. Hist.* ii, 101-2), the old charge against the Peripatetic school. Hallam (p. 102) complains that CESALPINI of Pisa "substitutes the barren unity of pantheism for religion." Cp. Ueberweg, ii, 14; Renan, *Averroès*, 3e édit. p. 417. An Averroïst on some points, he believed in separate immortality.

[3] Gebler, pp. 37, 45. Gebler appears to surmise that Cremonini may have escaped the attack upon himself by turning suspicion upon Galileo, but as to this there is no evidence.

the comprehensive grasp which gave him his long supremacy as against rival system-makers, and makes him still so much more important than any of the thinkers who in the sixteenth century revolted against him—was by opponents disregarded and denied, though the range and depth of his influence is apparent in all the polemic against him, notably in that of Bacon, who is constantly citing him, and relates his reasoning to him, however antagonistically, at every turn.

Naturally, the less sacrosanct dogmatism was the more freely assailed; and in the sixteenth century the attacks became numerous and vehement. Luther was a furious anti-Aristotelian,[1] as were also some Calvinists; but in 1570 we find Beza declaring to Ramus[2] that "the Genevese have decreed, once and for ever, that they will never, neither in logic nor in any other branch of learning, turn away from the teaching of Aristotle." In Italy, Telesio, who notably anticipates the tone of Bacon as to natural science, and is largely followed by him, influenced Bruno in the anti-Aristotelian direction,[3] though it was in a long line from Aristotle that he got his principle of the eternity of the universe. The Spaniard Ludovicus Vives, too (1492-1540), pronounced by Lange one of the clearest heads of his age, had insisted on progress beyond Aristotle in the spirit of naturalist science.[4] But the typical anti-Aristotelian of the century was RAMUS (Pierre de la Ramee, 1515-72), whose long and strenuous battle against the ruling school at Paris brought him to his death in the Massacre of St. Bartholomew,[5] and who hardily laid it down that "there is no authority over reason, but reason ought to

---

[1] Ueberweg, ii, 17. [2] *Epist.* 36.
[3] Bartholmess, *Jordano Bruno*, i, 49.
[4] Lange, *Gesch. des Materialismus*, i, 189-190 (Eng. trans. i, 228). Born in Valencia and trained at Paris, Vives became a humanist teacher at Louvain, and was called to England (1523) to be tutor to the Princess Mary, and taught at Oxford. Being opposed to the divorce of Henry VIII, he was imprisoned for a time, afterwards living at Bruges.
[5] See the copious monograph, *Ramus, sa vie, ses écrits, et ses opinions*, par Ch. Waddington, 1855. Mr. Owen has a good account of Ramus in his *French Skeptics of the Renaissance*.

be queen and ruler over authority."[1] Such a message was of more value than his imperfect attempt to supersede the Aristotelian logic. Bacon, who carried on in England the warfare against the Aristotelian tradition, never ventured so to express himself as against the theological tyranny, though, as we have seen, the general energy and vividness of his argumentation gave him an influence which undermined the orthodoxies to which he professed to conform. On the other hand, he did no such service to exact science as was rendered in his day by Kepler and Galileo and their English emulators; and his full didactic influence came much later into play.

Like fallacies to Bacon's may be found in DESCARTES; but he in turn, next to Copernicus, Kepler, and Galileo,[2] unquestionably laid a good part of the foundation of modern philosophy and science,[3] GASSENDI largely aiding. Though he never does justice to Galileo, from his fear of provoking the church, it can hardly be doubted that he owes to him in large part the early determination of his mind to scientific methods; for it is difficult to believe that the account he gives of his mental development in the *Discours de la Methode* (1637) is biographically true. It is rather the schemed statement, by a ripened mind, of how it might best have been developed. Nor did Descartes, any more than Bacon, live up to the intellectual idea he had framed. All through his life he anxiously sought to propitiate the church;[4] Gassendi was a priest; and both were unmenaced in France under Richelieu and

---

[1] *Scholæ math.* l. iii, p. 78, cited by Waddington, p. 343.
[2] "In many respects Galileo deserves to be ranked with Descartes as inaugurating modern philosophy." Professor Adamson, *The Development of Modern Philosophy*, 1903, i, 5. "We may compare his [Hobbes's] thought with Descartes's, but the impulse came to him from the physical reasonings of Galileo." Professor Croom Robertson, *Hobbes*, 1886, p. 42.
[3] Buckle, 1-vol. ed. pp. 327-336; 3-vol. ed. ii, 77-85. Cp. Lange (Eng. trans. i, 248, *note*); Adamson, *The Philosophy of Kant*, 1879, p. 194.
[4] Cp. Lange, i, 425 (Eng. trans. i, 248-9, *note*); Bouillier, *Hist. de la philos. cartésienne*, 1854, i, 40-47, 185-6; Bartholmess, *Jordano Bruno*, i, 354-5; Memoir in Garnier ed. of *Œuvres Choisies*, p. v, also pp. 6, 17, 19, 21. Bossuet pronounced his precautions excessive. But cp. Dr. Land's notes in *Spinoza: Four Essays*, 1882, p. 55.

Mazarin; but the unusual rationalism of Descartes's method, avowedly aiming at the uprooting of all his own prejudices[1] as a first step to truth, displeased the Jesuits, and could not escape the hostile attention of the Protestant theologians of Holland, where Descartes passed so many years of his life. Despite his constant theism, accordingly, he had at length to withdraw.[2] A Jesuit, Pere Bourdin, sought to have the *Discours de la Methode* condemned by the French clergy, but the attempt failed. France was for the time, in fact, the most freethinking part of Europe;[3] and Descartes, though not so unsparing with his prejudices as he set out to be, was the greatest innovator in philosophy that had arisen in the Christian era. He made real scientific discoveries where Bacon only inspired an approach and schemed a wandering road to them; and, though his timorous conformities deprive him of any heroic status, it is perhaps not too much to pronounce him "the great reformer and liberator of the European intellect."[4] One not given to warm sympathy with freethought has avowed that "the common root of modern philosophy is the doubt which is alike Baconian and Cartesian."[5] From Descartes, then, as regards philosophy, more than from any professed thinker of his day, but also from the other thinkers we have noted, from the reactions of scientific discovery, from the terrible experience of the potency of religion as a breeder of strife and its impotence as a curber of evil, and from the practical freethinking of the more open-minded of that age in general, derives the great rationalistic movement which, taking clear literary form first in the seventeenth century, has with some fluctuations broadened and deepened down to our own day.

[1] *Discours de la Méthode*, pties. i, ii, iii, iv (*Œuvres Choisies*, pp. 8, 10, 11, 22, 24); *Meditation I* (*id.* pp. 73-74).
[2] Full details in Kuno Fischer's *Descartes and his School*, Eng. trans. 1890, B. i, ch. 6; Bouillier, i, cc. xii, xiii.
[3] Buckle, 1-vol. ed. pp. 337-9; 3-vol. ed. ii, 94, 97.
[4] Buckle, p. 330; ii, 82.
[5] Kuno Fischer, *Francis Bacon*, Eng. trans. 1857, p, 74.

Chapter XIV.

BRITISH FREETHOUGHT IN THE SEVENTEENTH CENTURY

§ 1.

THE propagandist literature of deism begins with an English diplomatist, Lord HERBERT of Cherbury, the friend of Bacon, who stood in the full stream of the current freethought of England and France[1] in the first quarter of the seventeenth century. English deism, as literature, is thus at its very outset affiliated with French; all of its elements, critical and ethical, are germinal in Bodin, Montaigne, and Charron, each and all of whom had a direct influence on English thought; and we shall find later French thought, as in the cases of Gassendi, Bayle, Simon, St. Evremond, and Voltaire, alternately influenced by and reacting on English. But, apart from the undeveloped rationalism of the Elizabethan period, which never found literary expression, the French ferment seems to have given the first effective impulse.

We have seen the state of upper-class and middle-class opinion in France about 1624. It was in Paris in that year that Herbert published his *De Veritate*, after acting for many years as the English ambassador at the French court. Hitherto deism had been represented by unpublished arguments disingenuously dealt with in published answers; henceforth there slowly grows up a deistic literature. Herbert was a powerful and audacious nobleman, with a weak king; and he could venture on a publication which would have cost an ordinary man dear. Yet even he saw fit to publish in Latin; and he

---

[1] Jenkin Thomasius in his *Historia Atheismi* (1709) joins Herbert with Bodin as having five points in common with him (ch. ix, § 2, pp. 76-77).

avowed hesitations.[1] His work has two aspects, a philosophical and a political, and in both it is remarkable.[2] Rejecting tacitly the theological basis of current philosophy, he divides the human mind into four faculties—Natural Instinct, Internal Sense, External Sense, and the Discursive faculty—through one or other of which all our knowledge emerges. Of course, he makes the first the verification of his idea of God, pronouncing that to be primary, independent, and universally entertained, and therefore not lawfully to be disputed (already a contradiction in terms); but, inasmuch as scriptural revelation has no place in the process, the position is conspicuously more advanced than that of Bacon in the *De Augmentis*, published the year before, and even than that of Locke, sixty years later. On the question of concrete religion Herbert is still more aggressive. His argument[3] is, in brief, that no professed revelation can have a decisive claim to rational acceptance; that none escapes sectarian dispute in its own field; that as each one misses most of the human race none seems to be divine; and that human reason can do for morals all that any one of them does. The negative generalities of Montaigne here pass into a positive anti-Christian argument; for Herbert goes on to pronounce the doctrine of forgiveness for faith immoral. Like all pioneers, Herbert falls into some inconsistencies on his own part; the most flagrant being his claim to have had a sign from heaven—that is, a private and special revelation—encouraging him to publish his book.[4] But his criticism is none the less telling and persuasive so far as it goes, and remains

[1] The book was reprinted at Paris in Latin in 1633, and again at London in 1645. It was translated and published in French in 1639, but never in English.
[2] Compare the verdict of Hamilton in his ed. of Reid, Note A, § 6, 35 (p. 781).
[3] For a good analysis see Pünjer, *Hist. of the Christ. Philos. of Religion*, Eng. trans. 1887, pp. 292–9; also Noack, *Die Freidenker in der Religion*, Bern, 1853, i, 17–40; and Lechler, *Geschichte des englischen Deismus*, pp. 36–54.
[4] See his Autobiography, Murray's reprint, p. 93.

valid to this day. Nor do his later and posthumous works[1] add to it in essentials, though they do much to construct the deistic case on historical lines. The *De religione gentilium* in particular is a noteworthy study of pre-Christian religions, apparently motived by doubt or challenge as to his theorem of the universality of the God-idea. It proves only racial universality without agreement; but it is so far a scholarly beginning of rational hierology.

The next great freethinking figure in England is THOMAS HOBBES (1588-1679), the most important thinker of his age, after Descartes, and hardly less influential. But the purpose of Hobbes being always substantially political and regulative, his unfaith in the current religion is only incidentally revealed in the writings in which he seeks to show the need for keeping it under monarchic control.[2] Hobbes is in fact the anti-Presbyterian or anti-Puritan philosopher; and to discredit anarchic religion in the eyes of the majority he is obliged to speak as a judicial churchman. Yet nothing is more certain than that he was no orthodox Christian; and even his professed theism resolves itself somewhat easily into virtual agnosticism on logical pressure. No thought of prudence could withhold him from showing, in a discussion on words, that he held the doctrine of the *Logos* to be meaningless.[3] Of atheism he was repeatedly accused[4] by both royalists and rebels; and his answer was forensic rather than fervent, alike as to his scripturalism, his Christianity, and his impersonal conception of Deity.[5] In affirming "one God eternal"

---

[1] *De causis errorum, una cum tractate de religione laici et appendice ad sacerdotes* (1645); *De religione gentilium* (1663). The latter was translated into English in 1705. The former are short appendices to the *De Veritate*.

[2] It is to be remembered that the doctrine of the supremacy of the civil power in religious matters (Erastianism) was maintained by some of the ablest men on the Parliamentary side, in particular Selden.

[3] *Leviathan*, ch. iv. Morley's ed. p. 26.

[4] Reviving as he did the ancient rationalistic doctrine of the eternity of the world (*De Corpore*, Pt. ii, ch. viii, § 20), he gave a clear footing for atheism as against the Judæo-Christian view.

[5] Cp. his letter to an opponent, *Considerations upon the Reputation*,

of whom men "cannot have any idea in their mind, answerable to his nature," he was negating all creeds. He expressly contends, it is true, for the principle of a Providence ; but it is hard to believe that he laid any store by prayer, public or private ; and it would appear that whatever thoughtful atheism there was in England in the latter part of the century looked to him as its philosopher, in so far as it did not derive from Spinoza.[1] Nor could the Naturalist school of that day desire a better, terser, or more drastic scientific definition of religion than Hobbes gave them : " Fear of power invisible, *feigned by the mind or imagined from tales publicly allowed*, RELIGION; *not allowed*, SUPERSTITION."[2] As the churchmen readily saw, his insistence on identifying the religion of a country with its law plainly implied that no religion is any more "revealed" than another. With him too begins (1651) the public criticism of the Bible on literary or documentary grounds ;[3] though, as we have seen, this had already gone far in private ;[4] and he gave a new lead, partly as against Descartes, to a materialistic philosophy.[5] He was, in fact, in a special and peculiar degree for his age, a freethinker ; and so deep was his intellectual hostility to the clergy of all species that he could not forego enraging those of his own political side by his sarcasms.[6] Here he is in marked contrast with Descartes, who dissembled his opinion about Copernicus and Galileo for peace' sake ;[7] and was always the

---

etc., *of Thomas Hobbes*, 1680, with cc. xi and xii of *Leviathan*, and *De Corpore Politico*, Pt. ii, ch. 6. One of his most explicit declarations for theism is in the *De Homine*, ch. i, where he employs the design argument, declaring that he who will not see that the bodily organs are *a mente aliqua conditas ordinatasque ad sua quasque officia* must be himself without mind. This ascription of "mind," however, he tacitly negates in *Leviathan*, ch. xi, and *De Corpore Politico*, Pt. ii, ch. 6.

[1] Cp. Bentley's letter to Bernard, 1692, cited in the author's *Dynamics of Religion*, pp. 82-3.
[2] *Leviathan*, Pt. i, ch. 6. Morley's ed. p. 34.
[3] *Leviathan*, Pt. iii, ch. 33.
[4] Above, p. 41.
[5] On this see Lange, *Hist. of Materialism*, sec. iii, ch. ii.
[6] *E.g.*, *Leviathan*, Pt. iv, ch. 47.
[7] Kuno Fischer, *Descartes and his School*, pp. 232-5.

close friend of the orthodox champion Mersenne down to his death.[1]

With the partial exception of the more refined and graceful Pecock, Hobbes has of all English thinkers down to his period the clearest and hardest head for all purposes of reasoning, save in the single field of mathematics, where he meddled without mastery; and against the theologians of his time his argumentation is as a two-edged sword. That such a man should have been resolutely on the side of the king in the Civil War is one of the proofs of the essential fanaticism and arbitrariness of the orthodox Puritans, who plotted more harm to the heresies they disliked than was ever wreaked on themselves. Hobbes came near enough being clerically ostracised among the Royalists; but among the earlier Puritans, or under an Independent Puritan Parliament at any time, he would have stood a fair chance of execution. It was doubtless largely due to the anti-persecuting influence of Cromwell, as well as to his having ostensibly deserted the royalists, that Hobbes was allowed to settle quietly in England after making his submission to the Rump Parliament in 1651. In 1666 his *Leviathan* and *De Cive* were together condemned by the Restoration Parliament in its grotesque panic of piety after the Great Fire of London; but Charles II protected and pensioned him, though he was forbidden to publish anything further on burning questions, and *Leviathan* was not permitted in his lifetime to be republished in English.[2] He was thus for his generation the typical "infidel," the royalist clergy being perhaps his bitterest enemies. His spontaneous hostility to fanaticism shaped his literary career, which

[1] Hobbes also was of Mersenne's acquaintance, but only as a man of science. When, in 1647, Hobbes was believed to be dying, Mersenne for the first time sought to discuss theology with him; but the sick man instantly changed the subject. In 1648 Mersenne died. He thus did not live to meet the strain of Hobbes's *Leviathan* (1651), which enraged the French no less than the English clergy. See Professor Croom Robertson's *Hobbes*, pp. 63-65.

[2] Croom Robertson, *Hobbes*, p. 196; Pepys's Diary, Sept. 3rd, 1668.

began in 1628 with a translation of Thucydides, undertaken by way of showing the dangers of democracy. Next came the *De Cive* (Paris, 1642), written when he was already an elderly man; and thenceforth the Civil War tinges his whole temper.

It is in fact by way of a revolt against all theological ethic, as demonstrably a source of civil anarchy, that Hobbes formulates a strictly civic or legalist ethic, denying the supremacy of an abstract or *a priori* natural moral law (though he founded on natural law), as well as rejecting all supernatural illumination of the conscience.[1] In the Church of Rome itself there had inevitably arisen the practice of Casuistry, in which to a certain extent ethics had to be rationally studied; and early Protestant Casuistry, repudiating the authority of the priest, had to rely still more on reason.

> Compare Whewell, *Lectures on the History of Moral Philosophy*, ed. 1862, pp. 25–38, where it is affirmed that, after the Reformation, "Since the assertions of the teacher had no inherent authority, he was obliged to give his proofs as well as his results," and "the determination of *cases* was replaced by the discipline of *conscience*" (p. 29). There is an interesting progression in English Protestant casuistry from W. Perkins (1558–1602) and W. Ames (pub. 1630), through Bishops Hall and Sanderson, to Jeremy Taylor. Mosheim (17 Cent. sec. ii, Pt. ii, § 9) pronounces Ames "the first among the Reformed who attempted to elucidate and arrange the science of morals as distinct from that of dogmatics." See biog. notes on Perkins and Ames in Whewell, pp. 27–29, and Reid's Mosheim, p. 681.

But Hobbes passed in two strides to the position that natural morality is a set of demonstrable inferences as to what adjustments promote general well-being; and further that there is no practical code of right and wrong apart from positive social law.[2] He thus practically introduced once for all into modern Christendom the fundamental dilemma of rationalistic ethics, not only

---

[1] *Leviathan*, ch. ii: Morley's ed. p. 19; cc. xiv, xv, pp. 66, 71, 72, 78; ch. xxix, pp. 148, 149.

[2] *Leviathan*, cc. xv, xvii, xviii. Morley's ed. pp. 72, 82, 83, 85.

positing the problem for his own generation,[1] but anticipating it as handled in later times.[2]

How far his rationalism was ahead of that of his age may be realised by comparing his positions with those of John Selden, the most learned and, outside of philosophy, one of the shrewdest of the men of that generation. Selden was sometimes spoken of by the Hobbists as a freethinker; and his *Table Talk* contains some sallies which would startle the orthodox if publicly delivered;[3] but not only is there explicit testimony by his associates as to his orthodoxy:[4] his own treatise, *De Jure Naturali et Gentium juxta disciplinam Ebræorum*, maintains the ground that the "Law of Nature" which underlies the variants of the Laws of Nations is limited to the precepts and traditions set forth in the Talmud as delivered by Noah to his posterity.[5] Le Clerc said of the work, justly enough, that in it "Selden only copies the Rabbins, and scarcely ever reasons." He illustrates, in fact, the extent to which a scholar could in that day be anti-clerical without being rationalistic. Like the bulk of the Parliamentarians, though without their fanaticism, he was thoroughly opposed to the political pretensions of the church,[6] desiring, however, to leave episcopacy alone, as a matter outside of legislation, when the House of Commons abolished it. Yet he spoke of the name of Puritan as one which he "trusted he was not either mad enough or foolish enough to deserve."[7] There were thus in the Parliamentary party men of very different shades of opinion. The largest party, perhaps, was that of the fanatics who, as Mrs.

---

[1] "For two generations the effort to construct morality on a philosophical basis takes more or less the form of answers to Hobbes" (Sidgwick, *Outlines of the History of Ethics*, 3rd ed. p. 169).
[2] As when he presents the law of Nature as "dictating peace, for a means of the conservation of men in multitudes" (*Leviathan*, ch. xv. Morley's ed. p. 77).
[3] See the headings, COUNCIL, RELIGION, etc.
[4] G. W. Johnson, *Memoirs of John Selden*, 1835, pp. 348, 362.
[5] *Id.* p. 264.
[6] *Id.* pp. 258, 302.
[7] *Id.* p. 302. Cp. in the *Table Talk*, art. TRINITY, his view of the Roundheads.

Hutchinson—herself fanatical enough—tells concerning her husband, "would not allow him to be religious because his hair was not in their cut."[1] Next in strength were the more or less devout and anti-clerical but less pious Scripturalists, of whom Selden was the most illustrious. By far the smallest group of all were the freethinkers, men of their type being as often repelled by the zealotry of the Puritans as by the sacerdotalism of the State clergy. The Rebellion, in short, though it evoked rationalism, was not evoked by it.

§ 2.

When, however, we turn from the higher literary propaganda to the verbal and other transitory debates of the period of the Rebellion, we realise how much partial rationalism had hitherto subsisted without notice. In that immense ferment some very advanced opinions, such as quasi-Anarchism in politics[2] and anti-Scripturalism in religion, were more or less directly professed. In 1645-6 the authorities of the City of London, alarmed at the unheard-of amount of discussion, petitioned Parliament to put down all private meetings;[3] and on February 6th, 1646 (N.S.), a solemn fast, or "day of publique humiliation," was proclaimed on the score of the increase of "errors, heresies, and blasphemies." On the same grounds, the Presbyterian party in Parliament pressed an "Ordinance for the *suppression* of Blasphemies and Heresies," which, long held back by Vane and Cromwell, was carried in their despite in 1648, by large majorities, when the royalists renewed hostilities. It enacted the death penalty against all who should deny the doctrine of the Trinity, the divinity of

---

[1] *Memoirs of Colonel Hutchinson*, ed. 1810, i, 181. Cp. i, 292; ii. 44.
[2] Cp. Overton's pamphlet, *An Arrow against all Tyrants and Tyranny* (1646), cited in the *History of Passive Obedience since the Reformation*, 1689, i, 59; Pt. ii of Thomas Edwards' *Gangræna*, 1646, p. 179; and Pt. iii, pp. 14-17.
[3] *Lords Journals*, January 16th, 1645-6; cp. Gardiner, *Hist. of the Civil War*, ed. 1893, iii, 11.

Christ, the inspiration of the Bible, a day of judgment, or a future state; and prescribed imprisonment for Arminianism, rejection of infant baptism, anti-Sabbatarianism, anti-Presbyterianism, or defence of the doctrine of Purgatory or the use of images.[1] And of aggressive heresy there are some noteworthy traces. In a pamphlet entitled "*Hell Broke Loose:* a Catalogue of the many spreading Errors, Heresies, and Blasphemies of these Times, for which we are to be humbled" (March 9th, 1646, N.S.), the first entry is a citation of the notable thesis, "That the Scripture, whether a true manuscript or no, whether Hebrew, Greek, or English, is but humane, and not able to discover a divine God." This is cited from "Pilgrim of Saints, by Clarkson," presumably the Lawrence Clarkson who for his book *The Single Eye* was sentenced by resolution of Parliament on September 27th, 1650, to be imprisoned, the book being burned by the common hangman. He is further cited as teaching that even unbaptised persons may preach and baptise. Of the other heresies cited the principal is the old denial of a future life.

Against the furious intolerance of the Puritan legislature some pleaded with new zeal for tolerance all round. Notable among the new parties were the Levellers, who insisted that the State should leave religion entirely alone, tolerating all creeds, including even atheism; and who put forward a new and striking ethic, grounding on "universal reason" the right of all men to the soil.[2] In the strictly theological field, the most striking innovation, apart from simple Unitarianism, is the denial of the eternity or even the existence of future torments—a position first taken up, as we have seen, either by the continental Socinians or by the unnamed English heretics of the Tudor period, who passed on their heresy

[1] Green, *Short History*, ch. viii, § 8, pp. 551-2; Gardiner, *Hist. of the Civil War*, ed. 1893, iv, 22.
[2] See G. P. Gooch's *History of Democratic Ideas in England in the Seventeenth Century*, 1898, ch. vi.

to the time of Marlowe.[1] In this connection the learned booklet[2] entitled *Of the Torments of Hell: the foundations and pillars thereof discover'd, search'd, shaken, and removed* (1658) was rightly thought worth translating into French by d'Holbach over a century later.[3]

Humane feeling of this kind counted for much in the ferment. The Presbyterian Thomas Edwards, writing about the same time, speaks of " monsters " unheard-of theretofore, "now common among us—as denying the Scriptures, pleading for a toleration of all religions and worships, yea, for blasphemy, and denying there is a God."[4] Among the 180 sects named by him[5] there were " Libertines," " Antiscripturists," " Skeptics and Questionists,"[6] who held nothing save the doctrine of free speech and liberty of conscience ;[7] as well as Socinians, Arians, and Anti-trinitarians ; and he speaks of serious men who had not only abandoned their religious beliefs, but sought to persuade others to do the same.[8] Under the rule of Cromwell, tolerant as he was of Christian sectarianism, and even of Unitarianism as represented by Biddle, the more advanced heresies would get small liberty. It was only privately that such men as Henry Marten and Thomas Chaloner, the regicides, could avow themselves to be of "the natural religion." The statement of Bishop Burnet, following Clarendon, that "many of the republicans began to profess deism," cannot be taken literally, though it is broadly intelligible that "almost all of them were for destroying all clergymen and for leaving religion free, as they called it, without either encouragement or restraint."

---

[1] Above, pp. 26–29.
[2] In the British Museum copy the name Richardson is penned, not in a contemporary hand, at the end of the preface.
[3] The fourth English edition appeared in 1754.
[4] *Gangræna*, 1645 (or 1646), ep. ded. (p. 5). Cp. *Second Part of Gangræna*, 1646, pp. 178–9, and Bailie's *Letters*, ed. 1841, ii, 234-7 , iii, 393.
[5] *Gangræna*, pp. 18–36.
[6] *Id*. p. 15. As to other sects mentioned by him, cp. Tayler, p. 194.
[7] On the intense aversion of most of the Presbyterians to toleration, see Tayler, *Retrospect of Relig. Life of Eng.* p. 136. They insisted, rightly enough, that the principle was never recognised in the Bible.
[8] See the citations in Buckle, 3-vol. ed. i, 347 ; 1-vol. ed. p. 196.

See Burnet's *History of His Own Time*, B. I, ed. 1838, p. 43. The phrase, "They were for pulling down the churches," again, cannot be taken literally. Of those who "pretended to little or no religion and acted only upon the principles of civil liberty," Burnet goes on to name Sidney, Henry Nevill, Marten, Wildman, and Harrington. The last was certainly of Hobbes's way of thinking in philosophy (Croom Robertson, *Hobbes*, p. 223, *note*); but Wildman was one of the signers of the Anabaptist petition to Charles II in 1658 (Clarendon, *Hist. of the Rebellion*, B. xv, ed. 1843, p. 855). As to Marten and Challoner, see Carlyle's *Cromwell*, iii, 194; and articles in *Nat. Dict. of Biog.* Vaughan (*Hist. of England*, 1840, ii, 477, *note*) speaks of Walwyn and Overton as "among the freethinkers of the times of the Commonwealth." They were, however, Biblicists, not unbelievers. Professor Gardiner (*History of the Commonwealth and Protectorate*, ii, 253, citing a News-letter in the Clarendon MSS.) finds record in 1653 of "a man [who] preached flat atheism in Westminster Hall, uninterrupted by the soldiers of the guard"; but this obviously counts for little.

But between the advance in speculation forced on by the disputes themselves, and the usual revolt against the theological spirit after a long and ferocious display of it, there spread even under the Commonwealth a new temper of secularity. On the one hand, the temperamental distaste for theology, antinomian or other, took form in the private associations for scientific research which were the antecedents of the Royal Society. On the other hand, the spirit of religious doubt spread widely in the middle and upper classes; and it is noteworthy that the term "rationalist" emerges as the label of a sect of Independents or Presbyterians who declare that "What their reason dictates to them in church or State stands for good, until they be convinced with better."[1] The "rationalism," so-called, of that generation remained ostensibly scriptural; but on other lines thought went further. Of atheism there are at this stage only dubious biographical and controversial traces, such as Mrs. Hutchinson's characterisation of a Nottingham physician, possibly a deist, as a "horrible atheist,"[2] and the Rev. John Dove's *Confutation of*

[1] See above, vol. i, p. 5.
[2] *Memoirs of Colonel Hutchinson*, 3rd ed. i, 200.

Atheism (1640), which does not bear out its title. Ephraim Pagitt, in his *Heresiography* (1644), speaks loosely of an "atheistical sect who affirm that men's soules sleep with them *until the day of judgment*"; and tells of some alleged atheist merely that he "mocked and jeared at Christ's Incarnation."[1] Similarly a work, entitled *Dispute betwixt an Atheist and a Christian* (1646), shows the existence not of atheists, but of deists, and the deist in the dialogue is a Fleming.

More trustworthy is the allusion in Nathaniel Culverwel's *Discourse of the Light of Nature* (written in 1646, published posthumously in 1652) to "those lumps and dunghills of all sects......that young and upstart generation of gross anti-scripturalists, that have a powder-plot against the Gospel, that would very compendiously behead all Christian religion at one blow, a device which old and ordinary heretics were never acquainted withal."[2] The reference is presumably to the followers of Lawrence Clarkson. Yet even here we have no mention of atheism, which is treated as something almost impossible. Indeed, the very course of arguing in favour of a "Light of Nature" seems to have brought suspicion on Culverwel himself, who shows a noticeable liking for Herbert of Cherbury.[3] He is, however, as may be inferred from his angry tone towards anti-scripturalists, substantially orthodox, and not very important.

> It is contended for Culverwel by modern admirers (ed. cited, p. xxi) that he deserves the praise given by Hallam to the later Bishop Cumberland as "the first Christian writer who sought to establish systematically the principle of moral right independent of revelation." [See above, p. 90, the similar tribute of Mosheim to Ames.] But Culverwel does not really make this attempt. His proposition is that reason, "the candle of the Lord," discovers "that all the moral law is founded in natural and common light, in the light of reason, and that there is

---

[1] *Heresiography: The Heretics and Sectaries of these Times*, 1644, Epistle Dedicatory.
[2] *Discourse*, ed. 1857, p. 226.
[3] Dr. J. Brown's pref. to ed. of 1857, p. xxii.

nothing in the mysteries of the Gospel *contrary* to the light of reason" (Introd. *end*); yet he contends not only that faith transcends reason, but that Abraham's attempt to slay his son was a dutiful obeying of "the God of nature" (pp. 225-6). He does not achieve the simple step of noting that the recognition of revelation as such must be performed by reason, and thus makes no advance on the position of Bacon, much less on those of Pecock and Hooker. His object, indeed, was not to justify orthodoxy by reason against rationalistic unbelief, but to make a case for reason in theology against the Lutherans and others who, "because Socinus has burnt his wings at this candle of the Lord," scouted all use of it (Introd.). Culverwel, however, was one of the learned group in Emanuel College, Cambridge, whose tradition developed in the next generation into Latitudinarianism ; and he may be taken as a learned type of a number of the clergy who were led by the abundant discussion all around them into professing and encouraging a ratiocinative habit of mind. Thus we find Dean Stuart, Clerk of the Closet to Charles I, devoting one of his short homilies to Jerome's text, *Tentemus animas quae deficiunt a fide naturalibus rationibus adjurare*. "It is not enough," he writes, "for you to rest in an imaginary faith, and easiness in beleeving, except yee know also what and why and how you come to that beleef. Implicite beleevers, ignorant beleevers, the adversary may swallow, but the understanding beleever hee must chaw, and pick bones before hee come to assimilate him, and make him like himself. The implicite beleever stands in an open field, and the enemy will ride over him easily: the understanding beleever is in a fenced town." (*Catholique Divinity*, 1657, pp. 133-4—a work written many years earlier.)

The discourse on Atheism, again, in the posthumous works of John Smith of Cambridge (d. 1652) is entirely retrospective ; but soon another note is sounded. As early as 1652, the year after the issue of Hobbes's *Leviathan*, the prolific Walter Charleton, who had been physician to the king, published a book entitled *The Darkness of Atheism expelled by the Light of Nature*, wherein he asserted that England "hath of late produced and doth foster more swarms of atheistical monsters......than any age, than any Nation hath been infested withal." In the following year Henry More, the Cambridge Platonist, published his *Antidote against Atheism*, which assumes that the atheistic way of thinking had lately become rather fashionable. In 1654, again, there is noted[1] a treatise called *Atheismus Vapulans*, by William Towers, whose message can in part be inferred from his title;[2] and in 1657 Charleton issued his *Immortality of the Human Soul demonstrated by the Light of Nature,* wherein the argument, which says nothing of revelation, is so singularly unconfident, and so much broken in upon by excursus, as to leave it doubtful whether the author was more lacking in dialectic skill or in conviction. And traces of unbelief multiply. Baxter and Howe were agreed, in 1658, that there were both "infidels and papists" at work around them; and in 1659 Howe writes: "I know some leading men are not Christians."[3] "Seekers, Vanists, and Behmenists" are specified as groups to which both infidels and papists attach themselves. And Howe, recognising how religious strifes promote unbelief, calls his hearers to witness "What a cloudy, wavering, uncertain, lank, spiritless thing is the faith of Christians in this age become! Most content themselves to profess it only as the religion of their country."[4]

From the *Origines Sacræ* (1662) of Stillingfleet, further, it would appear that both deism and atheism were becoming more and more common.[5] He states

---

[1] Fabricius, *Delectus Argumentorum et Syllabus Scriptorum*, 1725, p. 341.

[2] No copy in British Museum.

[3] Urwick, *Life of John Howe*, with 1846 ed. of Howe's Select Works, pp. xiii, xix. Urwick, a learned evangelical, fully admits the presence of "infidels" on both sides in the politics of the time.

[4] *Discourse Concerning Union Among Protestants*, ed. cited, pp. 146, 156, 158. In the preface to his treatise, *The Redeemer's Tears Wept over Lost Souls*, Howe complains of "the atheism of some, the avowed mere theism of others," and of a fashionable habit of ridiculing religion. This sermon, however, appears to have been first published in 1584; and the date of its application is uncertain.

[5] The preface begins: "It is neither to satisfie the importunity of friends, nor to prevent false copies (which and such like excuses I know are expected in usual prefaces), that I have adventured abroad this following treatise: but it is out of a just resentment of the affronts and indignities which have been cast on religion, by such who account it a matter of judgment to disbelieve the Scriptures, and a piece of wit to dispute themselves out of the possibility of being happy in another world."

that "the most popular pretences of the atheists of our age have been the irreconcilableness of the account of times in Scripture with that of the learned and ancient heathen nations, the inconsistency of the belief of the Scriptures with the principles of reason; and the account which may be given of the origin of things from the principles of philosophy without the Scriptures." These positions are at least as natural to deists as to atheists; and Stillingfleet is later found protesting against the policy of some professed Christians who give up the argument from miracles as valueless.[1] His whole treatise, in short, assumes the need for meeting a very widespread unbelief in the Bible, though it rarely deals with the atheism of which it so constantly speaks. After the Restoration, naturally, all the new tendencies were greatly reinforced,[2] alike by the attitude of the king and his companions, all influenced by French culture, and by the general reaction against Puritanism. Whatever ways of thought had been characteristic of the Puritans were now in more or less complete disfavour; the belief in witchcraft was scouted as much on this ground as on any other;[3] and the deistic doctrines found a ready audience among royalists,[4] whose enemies had been above all things Bibliolaters.

We gather this, however, still from the apologetic treatises and the histôrians, not from new deistic literature; for in virtue of the Press Licensing Act, passed on behalf of the church in 1662, no heretical book could be printed; so that Herbert was thus far the only professed deistic writer in the field, and Hobbes the only other of similar influence. Baxter, writing in 1655 on *The Unreasonableness of Infidelity*, handles chiefly Anabaptists; and in his *Reformed Pastor* (1656),

[1] See B. ii, ch. 10. P. 338, 3rd ed. 1666.
[2] Cp. Glanvill, pref. *Address* to his *Scepsis Scientifica*, Owen's ed. 1885, pp. lv-lvii; and Henry More's *Divine Dialogues*, Dial. i, ch. 32.
[3] Cp. Lecky, *Rationalism in Europe*, i, 109.
[4] There is evidence that Charles II, at least up to the time of his becoming a Catholic, was himself at heart a deist. See Burnet's *History of his Own Time*, ed. 1838, pp. 61, 175, and notes; and cp. refs. in Buckle, 3-vol. ed. i, 362, *note;* 1-vol. ed. p. 205.

though he avows that "the common ignorant people," seeing the endless strifes of the clergy, "are hardened by us against all religion," the only specific unbelief he mentions is that of "the devil's own agents, the unhappy Socinians," who had written "so many treatises for......unity and peace."[1] But in his *Reasons of the Christian Religion*, issued in 1667, he thinks fit to prove the existence of God and a future state, and the truth and the supernatural character of the Christian religion. Any deist or atheist who took the trouble to read through it would have been rewarded by the discovery that the learned author has annihilated his own case. In his first part he affirms: "If there were no life of Retribution after this, Obedience to God would be finally men's loss and ruine: But Obedience to God shall not be finally men's loss and ruine: Ergo, there is another life."[2] In the second part he writes that "Man's personal interest is an unfit rule and measure of God's goodness";[3] and, going on to meet the new argument against Christianity based on the inference that an infinity of stars are inhabited, he writes:—

> Ask any man who knoweth these things whether all this earth be any more in comparison of the whole creation than one Prison is to a Kingdom or Empire, or the paring of one nail in comparison of the whole body. And if God should cast off *all this earth*, and use *all the sinners* in it as they deserve, it is no more sign of a want of benignity or mercy in him than it is for a King to cast *one subject* of a *million* into a jail or than it is to *pare a man's nails*, or cut off a wart, or a hair, or to pull out a rotten aking tooth.[4]

Thus the second part absolutely destroys one of the fundamental positions of the first. No semblance of levity on the part of the freethinkers could compare with the profound intellectual insincerity of such a propaganda as this; and that deism and atheism continued to gain ground is proved by the multitude of apologetic

---

[1] *The Reformed Pastor*, abr. ed. 1826, pp. 236, 239.
[2] Work cited, ed. 1667, p. 136. The proposition is reiterated.
[3] *Id.* p. 388. [4] *Id.* pp. 388-9.

treatises. Even in church-ridden Scotland they were found necessary; at least the young advocate George Mackenzie, afterwards to be famous as the "bloody Mackenzie" of the time of persecution, thought it expedient to make his first appearance in literature with a *Religio Stoici* (1663), wherein he sets out with a refutation of atheism. It is difficult to believe that his counsel to Christians to watch the "horror-creating beds of dying atheists"[1]—a false pretence as it stands—represented any knowledge whatever of professed atheism in his own country; and his discussion of the subject is wholly on the conventional lines—notably so when he uses the customary plea that the theist runs no risk even if there is no future life, whereas the atheist runs a tremendous risk if there is one;[2] but when he writes of "that mystery why the greatest wits are most frequently the greatest atheists,"[3] he must be presumed to refer at least to deists. And other passages show that he had listened to freethinking arguments. Thus he speaks[4] of those who "detract from Scripture by attributing the production of miracles to natural causes"; and again[5] of those who "contend that the Scriptures are written in a mean and low style; are in some places too mysterious, in others too obscure; contain many things incredible, many repetitions, and many contradictions." His own answers are conspicuously weak. In the latter passage he continues: "But those miscreants should consider that much of the Scripture's native splendour is impaired by its translators"; and as to miracles he makes the inept answer that if secondary causes were in operation they acted by God's will; going on later to suggest on his own part that prophecy may be not a miraculous gift, but "a natural (though the highest) perfection of our human nature."[6] Apart from his weak dialectic, he writes in general with cleverness and literary finish, but

---

[1] *Religio Stoici*, Edinburgh, 1663, p. 19. The essay was reprinted in London in 1693 under the title of *The Religious Stoic*.
[2] *Id.* p. 18.   [3] *Id.* p. 124.   [4] *Id.* p. 76.   [5] *Id.* p. 69.   [6] *Id.* p. 116.

without any note of sincerity; and his profession of concern that reason should be respected in theology[1] is as little acted on in his later life as his protest against persecution.[2] The inference from the whole essay is that in Scotland, as in England, the civil war had brought up a considerable crop of reasoned unbelief; and that Mackenzie, professed defender of the faith as he was at twenty-five, and official persecutor of nonconformists as he afterwards became, met with a good deal of it in his cultured circle.

When such thought could subsist in the ecclesiastical climate of Puritan Scotland, it must needs flourish in England. In 1667 appeared *A Philosophicall Essay towards an eviction of the Being and Attributes of God*, etc., of which the preface proclaims "the bold and horrid pride of Atheists and Epicures" who "have laboured to introduce into the world a general Atheism, or at least a doubtful Skepticisme in matters of Religion." In 1668 was published Meric Casaubon's treatise, *Of Credulity and Incredulity in things Natural, Civil, and Divine*, assailing not only "the Sadducism of these times in denying spirits, witches," etc., but " Epicurus......and the juggling and false dealing lately used to bring Atheism into Credit"—a thrust at Gassendi. A similar polemic is entombed in a ponderous folio "romance" entitled *Bentivolio and Urania*, by Nathaniel Ingelo, D.D., a fellow first of Emanuel College, and afterwards of Queen's College, Cambridge (1660; 4th ed. amended, 1682). The second part, edifyingly dedicated to the Earl of Lauderdale, one of the worst men of his day, undertakes to handle the "Atheists, Epicureans, and Skepticks"; and in the preface the atheists are duly vituperated; while Epicurus

---

[1] *Religio Stoici*, p. 122.

[2] This last is interesting as a probable echo of opinions he had heard from some of his older contemporaries: "Opinion kept within its proper bounds is an [=the Scottish "ane"] pure act of the mind; and so it would appear that to punish the body for that which is a guilt of the soul is as unjust as to punish one relation for another" (pref. pp. 10-11). He adds that "the Almighty hath left no warrand upon holy record for persecuting such as dissent from us."

is decried as a gross sensualist, in terms of the legend, and the skeptics as "resigned to the slavery of vice." In the sixth book the atheists are allowed a momentary hearing in defence of their "horrid absurdities," from which it appears that there were current arguments alike anthropological and metaphysical against theism. The most competent part of the author's own argument, which is unlimited as to space, is that which controverts the thesis of the invention of religious beliefs by "politicians"[1]—a notion first put in currency, as we have seen, by those who insisted on the expediency and value of such inventions; as, Polybius among the ancients, and Machiavelli among the moderns.

Dr. Ingelo's folio seems to have had readers; but he avowedly did not look for converts; and defences of the faith on a less formidable scale were multiplied. A "Person of Honour"[2] produced in 1669 an essay on *The Unreasonableness of Atheism made Manifest*, which, without supplying any valid arguments, gives some explanation of the growth of unbelief in terms of the political and other antecedents;[3] and in 1670 appeared Richard Barthogge's *Divine Goodness Explicated and Vindicated from the Exceptions of the Atheists*. Baxter in 1671[4] complains that "infidels are grown so numerous and so audacious, and look so big and talk so loud"; and still the process continues. In 1672 Sir William Temple writes indignantly of "those who would pass for wits in our age by saying things which, David tells us, the fool said in his heart."[5] In the same year appeared *The Atheist Silenced*, by one J. M.; in 1674, Dr. Thomas Good's *Firmianus et Dubitantius, or Dialogues concerning Atheism, Infidelity, and Popery;*

---

[1] Work cited, 2nd ed. Pt. ii, pp. 106-115.
[2] Said to be Sir Charles Wolseley.
[3] Cp. *Dynamics of Religion*, pp. 86-7, 89-90. This explanation is also given by Bishop Wilkins in his treatise on *Natural Religion*, 7th ed. p. 354.
[4] Replying to Herbert's *De Veritate*, which he seems not to have read before.
[5] Pref. to *Observations upon the United Provinces of the Netherlands*, in Works, ed. 1814, i. 36.

in 1675, the posthumous treatise of Bishop Wilkins (d. 1672), *Of the Principles and Duties of Natural Religion*, with a preface by Tillotson; and a *Brevis Demonstratio*, with the modest sub-title, "The Truth of Christian Religion Demonstrated by Reasons the best that have yet been out in English"; in 1677, Bishop Stillingfleet's *Letter to a Deist;* and in 1678 the massive work of Cudworth on *The True Intellectual System of the Universe*, attacking atheism (not deism) on philosophic lines which sadly compromised the learned author.[1] English dialectic being found insufficient, there was even produced in 1679 a translation by the Rev. Joshua Bonhome of the French *L'Atheisme Convaincu* of David Dersdon, published twenty years before.

All of these works explicitly avow the abundance of unbelief; Tillotson, himself accused of it, pronounces the age "miserably overrun with Skepticism and Infidelity"; and Wilkins, avowing that these tendencies are common "not only among sensual men of the vulgar sort, but even among those who pretend to a more than ordinary measure of wit and learning," attempts to meet them by a purely deistic argument, with a claim for Christianity appended, as if he were concerned chiefly to rebut atheism, and held his own Christianity on a very rationalistic tenure. The fact was that the orthodox clergy were as hard put to it to repel religious antinomianism on the one hand as to repel atheism on the other; and no small part of the deistic movement seems to have been set up by the reaction against pious lawlessness.[2] Thus we have Tillotson, writing as Dean of Canterbury, driven to plead in his preface to the work of Wilkins that "it is a great mistake" to think the obligation of moral duties "doth solely depend upon the revelation of God's will made to us in the Holy Scriptures." It was such reasoning that brought upon him the charge of freethinking.

---

[1] Cp. *Dynamics of Religion*, pp. 87, 94–98, 111, 112.
[2] As to the religious immorality, see Mosheim, 17 Cent. sec. ii, Pt. ii, ch. ii, § 23, and Murdock's notes.

All the while, the censorship of the press, which was one of the means by which the clerical party under Charles combated heresy, prevented any new and outspoken writing on the deistic side. The *Treatise of Humane Reason* (1674) of Martin Clifford, a scholarly man-about-town, who was made Master of the Charterhouse, went indeed to the bottom of the question of authority by showing, as Spinoza had done shortly before,[1] that the acceptance of authority is itself in the last resort grounded in reason, and pointed out that many modern wars had been on subjects of religion. Still, it was sufficiently guarded concerning creed to allow of his putting his name to the second edition. But the tendency of such claims was obvious enough to inspire Boyle's *Discourse of Things above Reason* (1681), an attempt which anticipates Berkeley's argument against freethinking mathematicians.[2] The stress of new discussion is further to be gathered from the work of Howe, *On the Reconcilableness of God's Prescience of the Sins of Men with the Wisdom and Sincerity of his Counsels and Exhortations*, produced in 1677 at Boyle's request. As a modern admirer admits that the thesis was a hopeless one,[3] it is not to be supposed that it did anything to lessen doubt in its own day. The preface to Stillingfleet's *Letter to a Deist* (1677), which for the first time brings that appellation into prominence in English controversy, tacitly abandoning the usual ascription of atheism to all unbelievers, avows that "a mean esteem of the Scriptures and the Christian Religion" has become very common "among the Skepticks of this Age," and complains very much, as Butler did sixty years later, of the spirit of "Raillery and Buffoonery" in which the matter was too commonly approached. The "Letter" shows that a multitude of the inconsistencies and other blemishes of the Old Testament were being eagerly discussed on all hands; and it

---

[1] *Tract. Theol. Polit.* c. 15.
[2] Work cited, pp. 10, 14, 30, 55.
[3] Dr. Urwick, *Life of Howe*, as cited, p. xxxii.

cannot be said that the Bishop's vindication was well calculated to check the tendency. Indeed, we have the angry and reiterated declaration of Archdeacon Parker, writing in 1681, that "the ignorant and the unlearned among ourselves are become the greatest pretenders to skepticism ; and it is the common people that nowadays set up for Skepticism and Infidelity"; that "Atheism and Irreligion are at length become as common as Vice and Debauchery"; and that "Plebeans and Mechanicks have philosophised themselves into Principles of Impiety, and read their Lectures of Atheism in the Streets and Highways. And they are able to demonstrate out of the *Leviathan* that there is no God nor Providence," and so on.[1] As the Archdeacon's method of refutation consists mainly in abuse, he doubtless had the usual measure of success.

Meanwhile, during an accidental lapse of the press laws, the deist CHARLES BLOUNT[2] produced his *Anima Mundi* (1679), in which there is set forth a measure of cautious unbelief : following it up (1680) by his much more pronounced essay, *Great is Diana of the Ephesians*, a keen attack on the principle of revelation and clericalism in general, and his translation of Philostratus' *Life of Apollonius of Tyana*, so annotated as to be an ingenious counterblast to the Christian claims. The book was condemned to be burnt ; and only the influence of Blount's family,[3] probably, prevented his

---

[1] *A Demonstration of the Divine Authority of the Law of Nature and of the Christian Religion*, by Samuel Parker, D.D., 1681, pref. The first part of this treatise is avowedly a popularisation of the argument of Cumberland's *Disquisitio de Legibus Naturæ*, 1672. Parker had previously published in Latin a *Disputatio de Deo et Providentia Divina*, in which he raised the question *An Philosophorum ulli, et quinam Athei fuerunt* (1678).

[2] Concerning whom see Macaulay's *History*, ch. xix, ed. 1877, ii, 411-412—a grossly prejudiced account. Blount is there spoken of as "one of the most unscrupulous plagiaries that ever lived," and as having "stolen" from Milton, because he issued a pamphlet "By Philopatris," largely made up from the *Areopagitica*. Compare Macaulay's treatment of Locke, who adopted Dudley North's currency scheme (ch. xxi, vol. ii, p. 547).

[3] As to these, see the *Dict. of Nat. Biog.* The statements of Anthony Wood as to the writings of Blount's father, relied on in the author's *Dynamics of Religion*, appear to be erroneous.

being prosecuted. The propaganda, however, was resumed by Blount and his friends in small tracts, and after his suicide[1] in 1693 these were collected as the *Oracles of Reason* (1693), his collected works (without the *Apollonius*) appearing in 1695. By this time the political tension of the Revolution of 1688 was over; Le Clerc's work on the inspiration of the Old Testament, raising many doubts as to the authorship of the Pentateuch, had been translated in 1690; Spinoza's *Tractatus Theologico-Politicus* (1670) had been translated into English in 1689, and had impressed in a similar sense a number of scholars; his *Ethica* had given a new direction to the theistic controversy; the Boyle Lecture had been established for the confutation of unbelievers; and after the political convulsion of 1688 has subsided it rains refutations.

Much account was made of one of the most compendious, the *Short and Easy Method with the Deists* (1697), by the nonjuror Charles Leslie; but this handy argument (which is really adopted without acknowledgment from an apologetic treatise by a French Protestant refugee, published in 1688[2]) was not only much bantered by deists, but was sharply censured as incompetent by the French Protestant Le Clerc;[3] and many other disputants had to come to the rescue. A partial list will suffice to show the rate of increase of the ferment :—

1683. Dr. Rust, *Discourse on the Use of Reason in......Religion, against Enthusiasts and Deists.*
1685. Duke of Buckingham, *A Short Discourse upon the Reasonableness of men's having a religion or worship of God.*
,, *The Atheist Unmask'd.* By a Person of Honour.
1688. Peter Allix, D.D. *Reflexions*, etc., as above cited.
1691. Archbishop Tenison, *The Folly of Atheism.*
,, *Discourse of Natural and Revealed Religion.*

[1] All that is known of this tragedy is that Blount loved his deceased wife's sister and wished to marry her; but she held it unlawful, and he was in despair. An overstrung nervous system may be diagnosed from much of his writing.
[2] *Reflexions upon the Books of the Holy Scriptures to establish the Truth of the Christian Religion*, by Peter Allix, D.D., 1688, i, 6–7.
[3] As cited by Leslie, *Truth of Christianity Demonstrated*, 1711, pp. 17–21.

1691. John Ray, *Wisdom of God manifested in the Works of the Creation.* (Many reprints.)
1692. C. Ellis, *The Folly of Atheism Demonstrated.*
,, Bentley's *Sermons on Atheism.* (First Boyle Lectures.)
1693. Archbishop Davies, *An Anatomy of Atheism.* A poem.
,, *A Conference between an Atheist and his Friend.*
1694. J. Goodman, *A Winter Evening Conference between Neighbours.*
,, Bishop Kidder, *A Demonstration of the Messias.* (Boyle Lect.)
1695. John Locke, *The Reasonableness of Christianity.*
,, John Edwards, B.D., *Some Thoughts concerning the Several Causes and occasions of Atheism.* (Directed against Locke.)
1696. *An Account of the Growth of Deism in England.*
,, *Reflections on a Pamphlet, etc.* (the last named).
,, Sir Charles Wolseley, *The Unreasonableness of Atheism Demonstrated.* (Reprint.)
,, Dr. Nichols' *Conference with a Theist.* Pt. I. (Answer to Blount.)
,, J. Edwards, D.D., *A Demonstration of the Evidence and Providence of God.*
,, E. Pelling, *Discourse......on the Existence of God* (Pt. II in 1705).
1697. Stephen Eye, *A Discourse concerning Natural and Revealed Religion.*
,, Bishop Gastrell, *The Certainty and Necessity of Religion.* (Boyle Lect.)
,, H. Prideaux, *Discourse vindicating Christianity*, etc.
,, C. Leslie, *A Short and Easy Method with the Deists.*
1698. Dr. J. Harris, *A Refutation of Atheistical Objections.* (Boyle Lect.)
,, Thos. Emes, *The Atheist turned Deist, and the Deist turned Christian.*
1699. C. Lidgould, *Proclamation against Atheism*, etc.
,, J. Bradley, *An Impartial View of the Truth of Christianity.* (Answer to Blount.)
1700. Bishop Bradford, *The Credibility of the Christian Revelation.* (Boyle Lect.)
,, Rev. P. Berault, *Discourses on the Trinity, Atheism*, etc.
1701. T. Knaggs, *Against Atheism.*
,, W. Scot, *Discourses concerning the wisdom and goodness of God.*
1702. *A Confutation of Atheism.*
,, Dr. Stanhope, *The Truth and Excellency of the Christian Religion.* (Boyle Lect.)

1704. *An Antidote of Atheism* (? Reprint of More).
1705. Translation of Herbert's *Ancient Religion of the Gentiles.*
,, Charles Gildon, *The Deist's Manual* (a recantation).
,, Ed. Pelling, *Discourse concerning the existence of God.* Part II.
,, Dr. Samuel Clarke, *A Demonstration of the Being and Attributes of God*, etc. (Boyle Lect. of 1704.)
1706. *A Preservative against Atheism and Infidelity.*
,, Th. Wise, B.D., *A Confutation of the Reason and Philosophy of Atheism* (recast and abridgment of Cudworth).
,, T. Oldfield, *Mille Testes; against the Atheists, Deists, and Skepticks.*
,, *The Case of Deism fully and fairly stated, with Dialogue*, etc.
1707. Dr. John Hancock, *Arguments to prove the Being of a God.* (Boyle Lect.)

Still there was no new deistic literature apart from Toland's *Christianity not Mysterious* (1696) and his unauthorised issue (of course without his name) of Shaftesbury's *Inquiry Concerning Virtue* in 1699; and in that there is little direct conflict with orthodoxy, though it plainly enough implied that scripturalism would injuriously affect morals. It seems at that date, perhaps through the author's objection to its circulation, to have attracted little attention; but he tells that it incurred hostility.[1] Blount's famous stratagem of 1693[2] had led to the dropping of the official censorship of the press, the Licensing Act having been renewed for only two years in 1693 and dropped in 1695; but after the prompt issue of Blount's collected works in that year, and the appearance of Toland's *Christianity not Mysterious* in the next, the new Blasphemy Law of 1698 served sufficiently to terrorise writers and printers in

[1] *Characteristics*, ii, 263 (*Moralists*, Pt. ii, § 3). One of its most dangerous positions from the orthodox point of view would be the thesis that while religion could do either great good or great harm to morals, atheism could do neither. (B. I, Pt. iii, § 1.) Cp. Bacon's Essay, *Of Atheism*.

[2] Blount, after assailing in anonymous pamphlets Bohun the licenser, induced him to license a work entitled *King William and Queen Mary Conquerors*, which infuriated the nation. Macaulay calls the device "a base and wicked scheme." It was almost innocent in comparison with Blount's promotion of the "Popish plot" mania. See *Who Killed Sir Edmund Godfrey Berry?* by Alfred Marks, 1905, pp. 133-5, 150.

that regard for the time being.¹ Bare denial of the Trinity, of the truth of the Christian religion, or of the divine authority of the Scriptures, was made punishable by disability for any civil office ; and on a second offence by three years' imprisonment, with withdrawal of all legal rights. The first clear gain from the freedom of the press was thus simply a cheapening of books in general. By the Licensing Act of Charles II, and by a separate patent, the Stationers' Company had a monopoly of printing and selling all classical authors ; and while their editions were disgracefully bad, the importers of the excellent editions printed in Holland had to pay them a penalty of 6s. 8d. on each copy. By the same Act, passed under clerical influence, the number even of master printers and letter-founders had been reduced, and the number of presses and apprentices strictly limited ; and the total effect of the monopolies was that when Dutch-printed books were imported in exchange for English, the latter sold more cheaply at Amsterdam than they did in London, the English consumer, of course, bearing the burden.² The immediate effect, therefore, of the lapse of the Licensing Act must have been to cheapen greatly all foreign books by removal of duties, and at the same time to cheapen English books by leaving printing free. It will be seen above that the output of treatises *against* freethought at once increases in 1696. But the revolution of 1688, like the Great Rebellion, had doubtless given a new stimulus to freethinking ; and the total effect of freer trade in books, even with a veto on "blasphemy," could only be to further it. This was ere long to be made plain.

§ 3.

Alongside of the more popular and native influences, there were at work others, foreign and more academic ;

¹ The Act of 1698 had been preceded by a proclamation of the king, dated February 24th, 1697.
² See Locke's notes on the Licensing Act in Lord King's *Life of Locke*, 1829, pp. 203-6; Fox Bourne's *Life of Locke*, ii, 313-4 ; Macaulay's *History*, Student's ed. ii, 504.

and even in professedly orthodox writers there are signs of the influence of deistic thought. Thus Sir Thomas Browne's *Religio Medici* (written about 1634, published 1642) has been repeatedly characterised[1] as tending to promote deism by its tone and method ; and there can be no question that it assumes a great prevalence of critical unbelief, to which its attitude is an odd combination of humorous cynicism and tranquil dogmatism, often recalling Montaigne,[2] and at times anticipating Emerson. There is little savour of confident belief in the smiling maxim that " to confirm and establish our belief 'tis best to argue with judgments below our own "; or in the avowal, " in divinity I love to keep the road ; and though not in an implicit yet an humble faith, follow the great wheel of the church, by which I move."[3] The pose of the typical believer : " I can answer all the objections of Satan and my rebellious reason with that odd resolution I learned of Tertullian, *Certum est quia impossibile est,*"[4] tells in his case of no anxious hours ; and such smiling incuriousness is not promotive of conviction in others, especially when followed by a recital of some of the many insoluble dilemmas of Scripture. When he reasons he is merely self-subversive, as in the saying, " 'Tis not a ridiculous devotion to say a prayer before a game at tables ; *for* even in sortileges and matters of greatest uncertainty there is a settled and *preordered* course of effects ";[5] and after remarking that the notions of Fortune and astral influence " have perverted the devotion of many into atheism," he proceeds to avow that his many doubts never inclined him " to any point of

---

[1] Trinius, *Freydenker-Lexicon*, 1759, p. 120 ; Pünjer, i, 291, 300-1. Mr. A. H. Bullen, in his introduction to his ed. of Marlowe (1885, vol. i, p. lviii), remarks that Browne, who "kept the road in divinity, "exposed the vulnerable points in the Scriptural narratives with more acumen and gusto than the whole army of freethinkers, from Anthony Collins downwards." This is of course an extravagance, but, as Mr. Bullen remarks in the *Dict. of Nat. Biog.* vii, 66, Browne discusses "with evident relish" the "seeming absurdities in the Scriptural narrative."
[2] Browne's Annotator points to the derivation of his skepticism from "that excellent French writer Monsieur Mountaign, in whom I often trace him" (Sayle's ed. 1904, i, p. xviii.).
[3] *Religio Medici*, i, 6.   [4] *Id.* i, 9.   [5] *Id.* i, 18.

infidelity or desperate positions of atheism ; for I have been these many years of opinion there never was any."[1] The broad fact remains that he avows " reason is a rebel unto faith "; and in his later treatise on *Vulgar Errors* (1645) he shows much of the practical play of the new skepticism.[2] Yet it is on record that in 1664, on the trial of two women for witchcraft, Browne declared that the fits suffered from by the children said to have been bewitched " were natural, but heightened by the devil's cooperating with the malice of the witches, at whose instance he did the villainies."[3] This amazing deliverance is believed to have " turned the scale " in the minds of the jury against the poor women, and they were sentenced by the sitting judge, Sir Matthew Hale, to be hanged. It would seem that in Browne's latter years the irrational element in him overpowered the rational. In other men, happily, the progression was different.

The opening even of Jeremy Taylor's *Ductor Dubitantium*, so far as it goes, falls little short of the deistic position.[4] A new vein of rationalism, too, is opened in the theological field by the great Cambridge scholar John Spencer, whose *Discourse concerning Prodigies* (1663 ; 2nd ed. 1665), though quite orthodox in its main positions, has in part the effect of a plea for naturalism as against supernaturalism ; and whose great work, *De legibus Hebræorum* (1685), is, apart from Spinoza, the most scientific view of Hebrew institutions produced before the rise of German theological rationalism in the latter part of the eighteenth century. Holding most of the Jewish rites to have been planned by the deity as substitutes for or safeguards against

---

[1] *Religio Medici*, i, 20.
[2] By an odd error of the press, Browne is made in Mr. Sayle's excellent reprint (p. 108) to begin a sentence : " I do confess I am an Atheist. I cannot persuade myself to honour that the world adores." The passage should obviously read : "to that subterraneous Idol [avarice] and God of the Earth I do confess I am an Atheist," etc.
[3] Hutchinson, *Historical Essay Concerning Witchcraft*, 1718, p. 118 ; 2nd ed. 1720, p. 151.
[4] Cp. Whewell, *Lectures on the History of Moral Philosophy*, ed. 1862, p. 33.

those of the Gentiles which they resembled, he unconsciously laid, with Herbert, the foundations of comparative hierology, bringing to the work a learning which is still serviceable to scholars.[1] And there were yet other new departures by clerical writers, who of course exhibit the difficulty of attaining a consistent rationalism. One clergyman, Joseph Glanvill, is found publishing a treatise on *The Vanity of Dogmatising* (1661; amended in 1665 under the title *Scepsis Scientifica*), wherein, with careful reservation of religion, the spirit of critical science is applied to the ordinary processes of opinion with much energy, and the "mechanical philosophy" of Descartes is embraced with zeal. Following Hobbes,[2] Glanvill also states clearly the positive view of causation[3] afterwards fully developed by Hume.[4] Yet he not only vetoed all innovation in "divinity," but held stoutly by the belief in witchcraft, and was its chief English champion in his day against rational disbelief.[5]

Apart from the influence of Hobbes, who, like Descartes, shaped his thinking from the starting-point of Galileo, the Cartesian philosophy played in England a great transitional part. At the university of Cambridge it was already naturalised;[6] and the influence of Glanvill, who was an active member of the Royal Society, must have carried it further. The remarkable treatise of the anatomist Glisson,[7] *De natura substantiæ*

---

[1] See Professor Robertson Smith, *The Religion of the Semites*, 1889, pref. p. vi.
[2] See the *Humane Nature* (1640), ch. iv, §§ 7–9.
[3] *Scepsis Scientifica*, ch. xxiii, § 1.
[4] See the passages compared by Lewes, *History of Philosophy*, 4th ed. ii, 338.
[5] In his *Blow at Modern Sadducism* (4th ed. 1668), *Sadducismus Triumphatus* (1681, 3rd ed. 1689), and *A Whip to the Droll, Fidler to the Atheist* (1668—a letter to Henry More, who was zealous on the same lines). These works seem to have been much more widely circulated than the *Scepsis Scientifica*.
[6] Owen, pref. to ed. of *Scepsis Scientifica*, p. ix.
[7] Of whom, however, a high medical authority declares that "as a physiologist he was sunk in realism" (that is, metaphysical apriorism). Professor T. Clifford Allbutt, Harveian Oration on *Science and Medieval Thought*, 1901, p. 44.

energetica (1672), suggests the influence of either Descartes or Gassendi; and it is remarkable that the clerical moralist Cumberland, writing his *Disquisitio de legibus Naturæ* (1672) in reply to Hobbes, not only takes up a utilitarian position akin to Hobbes's own, and expressly avoids any appeal to the theological doctrine of future punishments, but introduces physiology into his ethic to the extent of partially figuring as an ethical materialist.[1] In regard to Gassendi's direct influence it has to be noted that in 1659 there appeared *The Vanity of Judiciary Astrology*, translated by "A Person of Quality," from P. Gassendus; and further that, as is remarked by Reid, Locke borrowed more from Gassendi than from any other writer.[2]

> It is stated by Sir Leslie Stephen (*English Thought in the Eighteenth Century*, 2nd ed. i, 32) that in England the philosophy of Descartes made no distinguished disciples; and that John Norris "seems to be the only exception to the general indifference." This overlooks (1) Glanvill, who constantly cites and applauds Descartes (*Scepsis Scientifica*, Owen's ed. pp. 20, 28, 30, 38, 43, 46, 64, 70, etc.). (2) In Henry More's *Divine Dialogues*, again (1668), one of the disputants is made to speak (*Dial.* i, ch. 24) of "that admired wit Descartes." More had been one of the admirers in his youth, but changed his view; and his *Enchiridion Metaphysicum* (1671) is an attack on the Cartesian system as tending to atheism. (3) The continual objections to Descartes on the same score throughout Cudworth's *True Intellectual System*, further, imply anything but "general indifference"; and (4) Barrow's tone in venturing to oppose him (cit. in Whewell's *Philosophy of Discovery*, 1860, p. 179) pays tribute to his great influence. (5) Maxwell, in a note to his translation (1727) of Bishop Cumberland's *Disquisitio de legibus Naturæ*, remarks that the doctrine of a universal *plenum* was accepted from the Cartesian philosophy by Cumberland, "in whose time that philosophy prevailed much" (p. 120). See again (6) Clarke's Answer to Butler's Fifth Letter (1718) as to the "universal prevalence" of Descartes's notions in natural philosophy. (7) The Scottish Lord President Forbes (d. 1747) summed up that "Descartes's

---

[1] Cp. Whewell, as last cited, pp. 75-83; Hallam, *Literature of Europe*, iv, 159-171.
[2] Reid, *Intellectual Powers*, Essay I, ch. i; Hamilton's ed. of Works, p. 226.

romance kept entire possession of men's belief for full fifty years" (*Works*, ii, 132). (8) And his fellow-judge, Sir William Anstruther, in his "Discourse against Atheism" (*Essays, Moral and Divine*, 1701, pp. 6, 8, 9), cites with much approval the theistic argument of "the celebrated Descartes" as "the last evidences which appeared upon the stage of learning" in that connection.

Cp. Berkeley, *Siris*, § 331. Of Berkeley himself, Professor Adamson writes (*Encyc. Brit.* iii, 589) that "Descartes and Locke......are his real masters in speculation." The Cartesian view of the eternity and infinity of matter had further become an accepted ground for "philosophical atheists" in England before the end of the century (Molyneux, in *Familiar Letters of Locke and his Friends*, 1708, p. 46). As to the many writers who charged Descartes with promoting atheism, see Mosheim's notes in Harrison's ed. of Cudworth's *Intellectual System*, i, 276-6; and Leibnitz's letter to Philipp, cited by Latta, *Leibniz*, 1898, p. 8, *note*.

Sir Leslie Stephen seems to have followed, under a misapprehension, Whewell, who contends merely that the Cartesian doctrine of vortices was never widely accepted in England (*Philosophy of Discovery*, pp. 177-8; cp. *Hist. of the Inductive Sciences*, ed. 1857, ii, 107, 147-8). Buckle was perhaps similarly misled when he wrote in his note-book: "Descartes was never popular in England" (*Misc. Works*, abridged ed. i, 269). Whewell himself mentions that Clarke, soon after taking his degree at Cambridge, "was actively engaged in introducing into the academic course of study, first, the philosophy of Descartes in its best form, and, next, the philosophy of Newton" (*Lectures on Moral Philosophy*, ed. 1862, pp. 97-98). And Professor Fowler, in correcting his first remarks on the point, decides that "many of the mathematical teachers at Cambridge continued to teach the Cartesian system for some time after the publication of Newton's Principia" (ed. of *Novum Organum*, 1878, p. xi).

At the same time there was growing up not a little Socinian and other Unitarianism, for some variety of which we have seen two men burned in 1612. Church measures had been taken against the importation of Socinian books as early as 1640. The famous Lord Falkland, slain in the Civil War, is supposed to have leant to that opinion;[1] and Chillingworth, whose *Religion*

---

[1] J. J. Tayler, *Retrospect of the Religious Life of England*, Martineau's ed. p. 204; Wallace, *Antitrinitarian Biography*, iii, 152-3.

of Protestants (1637) was already a remarkable application of rational tests to ecclesiastical questions in defiance of patristic authority,[1] seems in his old age to have turned Socinian.[2] Violent attacks on the Trinity are noted among the heresies of 1646.[3] Colonel John Fry, one of the regicides, who in Parliament was accused of rejecting the Trinity, cleared himself by explaining that he simply objected to the terms "persons" and "subsistence," but was one of those who sought to help the persecuted Unitarian Biddle. In 1652 the Parliament ordered the destruction of a certain Socinian Catechism; and by 1655 the heresy seems to have become common.[4] It is now certain that Milton was substantially a Unitarian,[5] and that Locke and Newton were at heart no less so.[6]

Indeed, the theism of Locke's *Essay on the Human Understanding* undermined even his Unitarian Scripturalism, inasmuch as it denies, albeit confusedly, that revelation can ever override reason. This compromise appears to be borrowed from Spinoza, who had put it with similar vagueness in his great *Tractatus*,[7] of which pre-eminent work Locke cannot have been ignorant, though he protested himself little read in the works of Hobbes and Spinoza, "those justly decried names."[8] The *Tractatus* being translated into English in the same year with the publication of the *Essay*, its influence would concur with Locke's in a widened circle of readers; and the substantially naturalistic doctrine of both books inevitably promoted the deistic movement. We have Locke's own avowal that he had many doubts as to the Biblical narratives;[9] and he never attempts to remove

---

[1] Cp. Buckle, 3-vol. ed. ii, 347–351; 1-vol. ed. pp. 196–9.
[2] Tayler, *Retrospect*, pp. 204–5; Wallace, iii, 154–6.
[3] *Gangræna*, Pt. i, p. 38.
[4] Tayler, p. 221. As to Biddle, the chief propagandist of the sect, see pp. 221–4, and Wallace, Art. 285.
[5] Macaulay, *Essay on Milton*. Cp. Browne's ed. (Clarendon Press) of the poems of Milton, ii, 30.   [6] Cp. *Dynamics of Religion*, ch. 5.
[7] *Tractatus Theologico-Politicus*, c. 15.
[8] *Third Letter to the Bishop of Worcester*.
[9] *Some Familiar Letters between Mr. Locke and Several of his Friends*, 1708, pp. 302–4.

the doubts of others. Since, however, his doctrine provided a sphere for revelation on the territory of ignorance, giving it prerogative where its assertions were outside knowledge, it counted substantially for Unitarianism in so far as it did not lead to deism.

> See the *Essay*, B. iv, c. 18. Locke's treatment of revelation may be said to be the last and most attenuated form of the doctrine of "two-fold truth." On his principle, any proposition in a professed revelation that was not provable or disprovable by reason and knowledge must pass as true. His final position, that "whatever *is* divine revelation ought to overrule *all* our opinions" (B. iv, c. 18, § 10), is tolerably elastic, inasmuch as he really reserves the question of the actuality of revelation. Thus he evades the central issue. Naturally he was by critical foreigners classed as a deist. Cp. Gostwick, *German Culture and Christianity*, 1882, p. 36. The German historian Tennemann sums up that Clarke wrote his apologetic works because "the consequences of the empiricism of Locke had become so decidedly favourable to the cause of atheism, skepticism, materialism, and irreligion" (*Manual of the Hist. of Philos.* Eng. trans. Bohn ed. § 349).

In his "practical" treatise *On the Reasonableness of Christianity* (1695) Locke played a similar part. It was inspired by the genuine concern for social peace which had moved him to write an essay on Toleration as early as 1667,[1] and to produce from 1685 onwards his famous *Letters on Toleration*, by far the most persuasive appeal of the kind that had yet been produced;[2] all the more successful so far as it went, doubtless, because the first Letter ended with a memorable capitulation to bigotry: "Lastly, those are not at all to be tolerated who deny the being of God. Promises, covenants, and oaths, which are the bonds of human society, can have no hold upon an atheist. The taking away of God, though but even in thought, dissolves all. *Besides, also, those that by their atheism undermine and destroy all religion can have no pretence of religion whereupon to challenge the privilege of a toleration*" This handsome endorsement

---
[1] Fox Bourne, *Life of Locke*, 1876, ii, 34.
[2] The first Letter, written while he was hiding in Holland in 1685, was in Latin, but was translated into French, Dutch, and English.

of the religion which had repeatedly "dissolved all" in a pandemonium of internecine hate, as compared with the one heresy which had never broken treaties or shed blood, is presumably more of a prudent surrender to normal fanaticism than an expression of the philosopher's own state of mind;[1] and his treatise on *The Reasonableness of Christianity* is an attempt to limit religion to a humane ethic, with sacraments and mysteries reduced to ceremonies, while claiming that the gospel ethic was "now with divine authority established into a legible law, far surpassing all that philosophy and human reason had attained to."[2] Its effect was, however, to promote rationalism without doing much to mitigate the fanaticism of belief.

> Locke's practical position has been fairly summed up by Professor Bain: "Locke proposed, in his *Reasonableness of Christianity*, to ascertain the exact meaning of Christianity, by casting aside all the glosses of commentators and divines, and applying his own unassisted judgment to spell out its teachings.
>
> The fallacy of his position obviously was that he could not strip himself of his education and acquired notions.......He seemed unconscious of the necessity of trying to make allowance for his unavoidable prepossessions. In consequence, he simply fell into an old grove of received doctrines; and these he handled under the set purpose of simplifying the fundamentals of Christianity to the utmost. Such purpose was not the result of his Bible study, but of his wish to overcome the political difficulties of the time. He found, by keeping close to the Gospels and making proper selections from the Epistles, that the belief in Christ as the Messiah could be shown to be the central fact of the Christian faith; that the other main doctrines followed out of this by a process of reasoning; and that, as all minds might not perform the process alike, these doctrines could not be essential to the practice of Christianity. He got out of the difficulty of framing a creed, as many others have done, by simply using Scripture language, without subjecting

---

[1] Mr. Fox Bourne, in his biography (ii, 41), apologises for the lapse, so alien to his own ideals, by the remark that "the atheism then in vogue was of a very violent and rampant sort." It is to be feared that this palliation will not hold good—at least, the present writer has been unable to trace the atheism in question. For "atheism" we had better read "religion."

[2] *Second Vindication of "The Reasonableness of Christianity"* 1697, pref.

it to any very strict definition; certainly without the operation of stripping the meaning of its words, to see what it amounted to. That his short and easy method was not very successful the history of the deistical controversy sufficiently proves" (*Practical Essays*, 1884, pp. 226-7).

That Locke was felt to have injured orthodoxy is further proved by the many attacks made on him from the orthodox side. Even the first Letter on Toleration elicited retorts, one of which claims to demonstrate "the Absurdity and Impiety of an Absolute Toleration."[1] On his positive teachings he was assailed by Bishop Stillingfleet; by the Rev. John Milner, B.D.; by the Rev. John Morris; by William Carrol; and by the Rev. John Edwards, B.D.; his only assailant with a rationalistic repute being Dr. Thomas Burnet. Some attacked him on his *Essays;* some on his *Reasonableness of Christianity;* orthodoxy finding in both the same tendency to "subvert the nature and use of divine revelation and faith."[2] In the opinion of the Rev. Mr. Bolde, who defended him in *Some Considerations* published in 1699, the hostile clericals had treated him "with a rudeness peculiar to some who make a profession of the Christian religion, and seem to pride themselves in being the clergy of the Church of England."[3] This is especially true of Edwards, a notably ignoble type; but hardly of Milner, whose later *Account of Mr. Lock's Religion out of his Own Writings, and in his Own Words* (1700), pressed him shrewdly on the score of his "Socinianism." In the eyes of a pietist like William Law, again, Locke's conception of the infant mind as a *tabula rasa* was "dangerous to religion," besides being philosophically false.[4] Yet Locke agreed with Law[5] that moral obligation is dependent solely on the will of

[1] Fox Bourne, *Life of Locke*, ii, 181.
[2] Said by Carrol, *Dissertation on Mr. Lock's Essay*, 1706, cited by Anthony Collins, *Essay Concerning the Use of Reason*, 1709, p. 30.
[3] Cited by Fox Bourne, *Life of Locke*, ii, 438.
[4] *Confutation of Warburton* (1757) in *Extracts from Law's Works*, 1768, i, 208-9.
[5] Cp. the *Essay*, B. I, ch. iii, § 6, with Law's *Case of Reason*, in *Extracts*, as cited, p. 36.

God—a doctrine denounced by Shaftesbury from a deistic standpoint as the negation of morality.

> See the *Inquiry Concerning Virtue or Merit*, Pt. iii, § 2; and the *Letters to a Student*, under date June 3rd, 1709 (p. 403 in Rand's *Life, Letters, etc., of Shaftesbury*, 1900). The extraordinary letter of Newton to Locke, written just after or during a spell of insanity, first apologises for having believed that Locke "endeavoured to embroil me with women and by other means," and goes on to beg pardon "for representing that you struck at the root of morality, in a principle you laid down in your book of ideas." In his subsequent letter, replying to that of Locke granting forgiveness and gently asking for details, he writes: "What I said of your book I remember not." (Letters of September 16th and October 5th, 1693, given in Fox Bourne's *Life of Locke*, ii, 226-7, and Sir D. Brewster's *Memoirs of Sir Isaac Newton*, 1855, ii, 148-151.) Newton, who had been on very friendly terms with Locke, must have been repeating, when his mind was disordered, criticisms otherwise current. After printing in full the letters above cited, Brewster insists, on his principle of sacrificing all other considerations to Newton's glory (cp. De Morgan, *Newton: his Friend: and his Niece*, 1885, pp. 99-111), that all the while Newton was "in the full possession of his mental powers." The whole diction of the first letter tells the contrary. If we are not to suppose that Newton had been temporarily insane, we must think of his judgment as even less rational, apart from physics, than it is seen to be in his dissertations on prophecy. Certainly Newton was at all times apt to be suspicious of his friends to the point of moral disease (see his attack on Montague, in his letter to Locke of January 26th, 1691-92: in Fox Bourne, ii, 218; and cp. De Morgan, as cited, p. 146); but the letter to Locke indicates a point at which the normal malady had upset the mental balance. It remains, nevertheless, evidence as to bitter orthodox criticism of Locke.

On the whole, it is clear, the effect of his work, especially of his naturalistic psychology, was to make for rationalism; and his compromises furthered instead of checking the movement of unbelief. His ideal of practical and undogmatic Christianity, indeed, was hardly distinguishable from that of Hobbes,[1] and, as previously set forth by the Rev. Arthur Bury in his *Naked Gospel* (1690), was so repugnant to the church

---
[1] Cp. *Dynamics of Religion*, p. 122.

that that book was burned at Oxford as heretical.[1] Locke's position as a believing Christian was indeed extremely weak, and could easily have been demolished by a competent deist, such as Collins,[2] or a skeptical dogmatist who could control his temper and avoid the gross misrepresentation so often resorted to by Locke's orthodox enemies. But by the deists he was valued as an auxiliary, and by many latitudinarian Christians as a helper towards a rationalistic if not a logical compromise.

Rationalism of one or the other tint, in fact, seems to have spread in all directions. The accomplished and influential George Savile, Marquis of Halifax, often spoken of as a deist, and even as an atheist, by his contemporaries,[3] appears clearly from his own writings to have been either that or a Unitarian.[4] That Sir Isaac Newton was "some kind of Unitarian"[5] is proved by documents long withheld from publication, and disclosed only in the second edition of Sir David Brewster's *Memoirs*. There is indeed no question that he remained a mere scripturalist, handling the texts as such,[6] and wasting much time in vain interpretations of Daniel and the Apocalypse.[7] Temperamentally, also, he was averse to anything like bold discussion, declaring that " those at Cambridge ought not to judge and censure their superiors, but to obey and honour them, according to the law and the doctrine of passive obedience "[8] —this after he had sat on the Convention which deposed James II. In no aspect, indeed, apart from his supreme

---

[1] Fox Bourne, ii, 404-5.
[2] An ostensibly orthodox Professor of our own day has written that Locke's doctrine as to religion and ethics " shows at once the sincerity of his religious convictions and the inadequate conception he had formed to himself of the grounds and nature of moral philosophy " (Fowler, *Locke*, 1880, p. 76).
[3] Cp. Macaulay, *History*, ch. ii. Student's ed. i, 120.
[4] Compare his *Advice to a Daughter*, § 1 (in *Miscellanies*, 1700), and his *Political Thoughts and Reflections : Religion*.
[5] De Morgan, as cited, p. 107.
[6] See Brewster, ii, 318, 321-2, 323, 331 sq., 342 sq.
[7] *Id.* p. 327 sq.
[8] *Id.* p. 115.

scientific genius, does he appear as morally[1] or intellectually pre-eminent. There is therefore more than usual absurdity in the proclamation of his pious biographer that "the apostle of infidelity cowers beneath the implied rebuke"[2] of his orthodoxy. The very anxiety shown by Newton and his friends[3] to checkmate " the infidels " is a proof that his religious work was not scientific even in inception, but the expression of his neurotic side ; and the attempt of some of his scientific admirers to show that his religious researches belong solely to the years of his decline is a corresponding oversight. Newton was always pathologically prepossessed on the side of his religion, and subordinated his science to his theology even in the *Principia*. It is therefore all the more significant of the set of opinion in his day that, tied as he was to Scriptural interpretations, he drew away from orthodox dogma as to the Trinity. Not only does he show himself a destructive critic of Trinitarian texts and an opponent of Athanasius[4]: he expressly formulates the propositions (1) that "there is one God the Father......and one mediator between God and man, the man Christ Jesus"; (2) that "the Father is the invisible God whom no eye hath seen or can see. All other beings are sometimes visible"; and (3) that "the Father *hath* life in himself, and hath *given* the Son to have life in himself."[5] Such opinions, of course, could not be published : under the Act of 1697 they would have made Newton liable to loss of office and all civil rights. In his own day, therefore, his opinions were rather gossipped-of than known ;[6] but in so far as his heresy was realised, it must have wrought much more for unbelief than could be achieved for orthodoxy by his surprisingly commonplace strictures on atheism, which show the ordinary inability to see what atheism means.

[1] Cp. De Morgan, pp. 133-145.
[2] Brewster, ii, 314.
[3] *Id.* pp. 315-316.
[4] *Id.* pp. 342-6.
[5] *Id.* p. 349. See the remaining articles, and App. XXX, p. 532.'
[6] *Id.* p. 388.

The argument of his *Short Scheme of True Religion* brackets atheism with idolatry, and goes on: "Atheism is so senseless and odious to mankind that it never had many professors. *Can it be by accident* that all birds, beasts, and men have their right side and left side alike shaped (except in their bowels), and just two eyes, and no more, on either side of the face?" etc. (Brewster, ii, 347). The logical implication is that a monstrous organism, with the sides unlike, represents "accident," and that in that case there has either been no causation or no "purpose" by Omnipotence. It is only fair to remember that no avowedly "atheistic" argument could in Newton's day find publication; but his remarks are those of a man who had never contemplated philosophically the negation of his own religious sentiment at the point in question. Brewster, whose judgment and good faith are alike precarious, writes that "When Voltaire asserted that Sir Isaac explained the prophecies in the same manner as those who went before him, he only exhibited his ignorance of what Newton wrote, and what others had written" (ii, 331, *note;* 355). The writer did not understand what he censured. Voltaire meant that Newton's treatment of prophecy is on the same plane of unscientific credulity as that of his orthodox predecessors.

Other distinguished men of the period were more overt in their dissent from orthodoxy. William Penn, the Quaker, held a Unitarian attitude;[1] and in the Church itself sad confusion arose on the attempt being made to define the orthodox view[2] in opposition to a widely-circulated anti-Trinitarian treatise.[3] Archbishop Tillotson (d. 1694) was often accused of Socinianism; and in the next generation was smilingly spoken of by Anthony Collins as a leading Freethinker. Positive Unitarianism all the while was being pushed by a number of tracts which escaped prosecution, being prudently handled by Locke's friend, Thomas Firmin;[4] and the heresy must have been encouraged even within the Church by the scandal which broke out when Dean Sherlock's *Vindication* of the Trinity (1693) was attacked

---

[1] Tayler, *Retrospect*, p. 226; Wallace, *Antitrin. Biog.* i, 160-9.
[2] Tayler, p. 227; *Dynamics*, pp. 113-115.
[3] This was by William Freeke, who was prosecuted and fined £500. The book was burnt by the hangman (1693). Wallace, Art. 354.
[4] Fox Bourne, ii, 405; Wallace, Art. 353.

by Dean South[1] as the work of a Tritheist. The plea of Dr. Wallis, Locke's old teacher, that a doctrine of "three somewhats"—he objected to the term "persons"—in one God was as reasonable as the concept of three dimensions,[2] was of course only a heresy the more. The fray waxed so furious, and the discredit cast on orthodoxy was so serious,[3] that in the year 1700 an Act of Parliament was passed forbidding the publication of any more works on the subject.

Meanwhile the so-called Latitudinarians,[4] all the while aiming as they did at a non-dogmatic Christianity, served as a connecting medium for the different forms of liberal thought; and a new element of critical disintegration was introduced by a speculative treatment of Genesis in the *Archæologia* (1692) of Dr. T. Burnet, a professedly orthodox scholar, who nevertheless treated the Creation story as an allegory, and threw doubt on the Mosaic authorship of the Pentateuch. His ideas were partly popularised through Blount's *Oracles of Reason*. Much more remarkable, but outside of popular discussion, were the *Evangelium medici* (1697) of Dr. B. CONNOR, wherein the Gospel miracles were explained away, on lines later associated with German rationalism, as natural phenomena; and the curious treatise of Newton's friend, John Craig,[5] *Theologiæ christianæ principia mathematica* (1699), wherein it is argued that all evidence grows progressively less valid in course of time;[6] and that accordingly the Christian religion will

---

[1] "Locke's ribald schoolfellow of nearly fifty years ago" (Fox Bourne, last cit.).
[2] *Id. ib.*
[3] Cp. *Dynamics of Religion*, pp. 113-115.
[4] As to whom see Tayler, *Retrospect*, ch. v, § 4. They are spoken of as "the new sect of Latitude-Men" in 1662; and in 1708 are said to be "at this day Low Churchmen." See *A Brief Account of the New Sect of Latitude-Men* by "S. P." of Cambridge, 1662, reprinted in *The Phœnix*, vol. ii, 1708, and pref. to that vol. From S. P.'s account it is clear that they connected with the new scientific movment, and leant to Cartesianism. As above noted, they included such prelates as Wilkins and Tillotson.
[5] See Brewster's *Memoirs of Newton*, 1855, ii, 315-316, for a letter indicating his religious attitude.
[6] See the note of Pope and Warburton on the *Dunciad*, iv, 462.

cease to be believed about the year 3144, when probably will occur the Second Coming. Connor, when attacked, protested his orthodoxy; Craig held successively two prebends of the Church of England;[1] and both lived and died unmolested, probably because they had the prudence to write in Latin. About this time, further, the title of "Rationalist" made some fresh headway as a designation, not of unbelievers, but of believers who sought to ground themselves on reason. Such books as those of Clifford and Boyle tell of much discussion as to the efficacy of "reason" in religious things, and in 1686 there appears *A Rational Catechism*[2] a substantially deistic or Unitarian production, notable for its aloofness from evangelical feeling, despite its many references to Biblical texts in support of its propositions. In the *Essays Moral and Divine* of the Scotch judge, Sir William Anstruther, published in 1701, there is a reference to "those who arrogantly term themselves Rationalists"[3] in the sense of claiming to find Christianity not only, as Locke put it, a reasonable religion, but one making no strain upon faith. Already the term had become potentially one of vituperation, and it is applied by the learned judge to "the wicked reprehended by the Psalmist."[4] Forty years later, however, it was still applied rather to the Christian who claimed to believe upon rational grounds than to the deist or unbeliever.[5]

---

[1] See arts. in *Dict. of Nat. Biog.*
[2] Reprinted at Amsterdam, 1712.
[3] *Essays* as cited, p. 84.
[4] *Id.* p. 30.
[5] See *Christianity not Founded on Argument* (by Henry Dodwell, jr.), 1741, pp. 11, 34. Waterland, as cited by Bishop Hurst, treats the terms *Reasonist* and *Rationalist* as labels or nicknames of those who untruly profess to reason more scrupulously than other people. The former term may, however, have been set up as a result of Le Clerc's rendering of "the *Logos*" in John i, 1, by "Reason"—an argument to which Waterland repeatedly refers.

Chapter XV.

BRITISH FREETHOUGHT IN THE EIGHTEENTH CENTURY

§ 1.

IT appears from the last chapter that the "deistic movement," commonly assigned to the eighteenth century, had been abundantly prepared for in the seventeenth, which, in turn, was but developing ideas current in the sixteenth. When, in 1696, JOHN TOLAND published his *Christianity Not Mysterious*, the sensation it made was due not so much to any unheard-of boldness in its thought as to the simple fact that deistic ideas had thus found their way into print.[1] So far the deistic position was represented in English literature only by the works of Herbert, Hobbes, and Blount; and of these only the first (who wrote in Latin) and the third had put the case at any length. Against the deists or atheists of the school of Hobbes, and the Scriptural Unitarians who thought with Newton and Locke, there stood arrayed the great mass of orthodox intolerance which clamoured for the violent suppression of every sort of "infidelity." It was this feeling, of which the army of ignorant rural clergy were the spokesmen, that found vent in the Blasphemy Act of 1697. The new literary growth dating from the time of Toland is the evidence of the richness of the rationalistic soil already created. Thinking men craved a new atmosphere. Locke's *Reasonableness of Christianity* is an unsuccessful compromise: Toland's book begins a new propagandist era.

---

[1] As Voltaire noted, Toland was persecuted in Ireland for his circumspect and cautious first book, and left unmolested in England when he grew much more aggressive.

Toland's treatise,[1] heretical as it was, professedly founded on Locke's anonymous *Reasonableness of Christianity*, its young author being on terms of acquaintance with the philosopher.[2] Toland, however, lacked alike the timidity and the prudence which so safely guided Locke in his latter years; and though his argument was only a logical and outspoken extension of Locke's position, to the end of showing that there was nothing supernatural in Christianity of Locke's type, it separated him from "respectable" society in England and Ireland for the rest of his life. The book was "presented" by the Grand Juries of Middlesex and Dublin;[3] the dissenters in Dublin being chiefly active in denouncing it—with or without knowledge of its contents;[4] half-a-dozen answers appeared immediately; and when in 1698 he produced another, entitled *Amyntor*, showing the infirm foundation of the Christian canon, there was again a speedy crop of replies. Despite the oversights inevitable to such pioneer work, it opens, from the side of freethought, the era of documentary criticism of the New Testament; and in some of his later freethinking books, as the *Nazarenus* (1718) and the *Pantheisticon* (1720), he continues to show himself in advance of his time in "opening new windows" for his mind.[5] The latter work represents in particular the influence of Spinoza, whom he had formerly criticised somewhat forcibly[6] for his failure to recognise that motion is inherent in matter. On that head he lays down[7] the doctrine that "motion is but matter under a certain consideration"—an essentially "materialist"

---

[1] First ed. anonymous. Second ed., of same year, gives author's name. Another ed. in 1702.

[2] Cp. *Dynamics of Religion*, p. 129.

[3] As late as 1701 a vote for its prosecution was passed in the Lower House of Convocation. Farrar, *Crit. Hist. of Freethought*, p. 180.

[4] Molyneux, in *Familiar Letters of Locke*, etc., p. 228.

[5] No credit for this is given in Sir Leslie Stephen's notice of Toland in *English Thought in the Eighteenth Century*, i, 101-112. Compare the estimate of Lange, *Gesch. des Materialismus*, i, 272-6 (Eng. trans. i, 324-330). Lange perhaps idealises his subject somewhat.

[6] In two letters published along with the *Letters to Serena*, 1704.

[7] *Letters to Serena*, etc., 1704, pref.

position, deriving from the pre-Socratic Greeks, and incidentally affirmed by Bacon.[1] He was not exactly an industrious student or writer; but he had scholarly knowledge and instinct, and several of his works show close study of Bayle.

As regards his more original views on Christian origins, he is not impressive to the modern reader; but theses which to-day stand for little were in their own day important. Thus in his *Hodegus* (Part I of the *Tetradymus*, 1720) it is elaborately argued that the "pillar of fire by night and of cloud by day" was no miracle, but the regular procedure of guides in deserts, where night marches are the rule; the "cloud" being simply the smoke of the vanguard's fire. Later criticism decides that the whole narrative of the Exodus is myth. Toland's method, however, was relatively so advanced that it had not been abandoned by theological "rationalists" a century later. Of that movement he must be ranked an energetic pioneer; though he lacked somewhat the strength of character that in his day was peculiarly needed to sustain a freethinker. Much of his later life was spent abroad; and his *Letters to Serena* (1704) show him permitted to discourse to the Queen of Prussia on such topics as the origin and force of prejudice, the history of the doctrine of immortality, and the origin of idolatry. He pays his correspondent the compliment of treating his topics with much learning; and his manner of assuming her own orthodoxy in regard to revelation could have served as a model to Gibbon.[2] But, despite such distinguished patronage, his life was largely passed in poverty, cheerfully endured,[3] with only chronic help from well-to-do sympathisers, such as Shaftesbury, who was not over-sympathetic. When it

---

[1] *De Principiis atque Originibus* (Routledge's 1-vol. ed. pp. 651, 667).
[2] Work cited, pp. 19, 67.
[3] Sir Henry Craik (cited by Temple Scott, Bohn ed. of Swift's Works, iii, 9) speaks of Toland as "a man of utterly worthless character." This is mere malignant abuse. Toland is described by Pope in a note to the *Dunciad* (ii, 399) as a spy to Lord Oxford. There could hardly be a worse authority for such a charge.

is noted that down to 1761 there had appeared no fewer than fifty-four answers to his first book,[1] his importance as an intellectual influence may be realised.

A certain amount of evasion was forced upon Toland by the Blasphemy Law of 1697; inferentially, however, he was a thorough deist until he became pantheist; and the discussion over his books showed that views essentially deistic were held even among his antagonists. One, an Irish bishop, got into trouble by setting forth a notion of deity which squared with that of Hobbes.[2] The whole of our present subject, indeed, is much complicated by the distribution of heretical views among the nominally orthodox, and of orthodox views among heretics.[3] Thus the school of Cudworth, zealous against atheism, was less truly theistic than that of Blount,[4] who, following Hobbes, pointed out that to deny to God a continual personal and providential control of human affairs was to hold to atheism under the name of theism;[5] whereas Cudworth, the champion of theism against the atheists, entangled himself hopelessly[6] in a theory which made deity endow Nature with "plastic" powers and leave it to its own evolution. The position was serenely demolished by Bayle,[7] as against Le Clerc, who sought to defend it; and in England the clerical outcry was so general that Cudworth gave up authorship.[8] Over the same crux, in Ireland, Bishop Browne and Bishop Berkeley accused each other of promoting atheism; and Archbishop King was embroiled in the dispute.[9] On the other hand, the theistic Descartes had laid down a

---

[1] Gostwick, *German Culture and Christianity*, 1882, p. 26.
[2] Cp. Stephen, as cited, p. 115.
[3] "The Christianity of many writers consisted simply in expressing deist opinions in the old-fashioned phraseology" (Stephen, i, 91).
[4] Cp. Pünjer, *Christ. Philos. of Religion*, pp. 289-290; and *Dynamics of Religion*, pp. 94-98. Mr. Morley's reference to "the godless deism of the English school" (*Voltaire*, 4th ed. p. 69) is puzzling.
[5] Macaulay's description of Blount as an atheist is therefore doubly unwarranted.
[6] Cp. *Dynamics of Religion*, pp. 94-98.
[7] *Continuation des Pensées Diverses......a l'occasion de la Comete......de 1680*, Amsterdam, 1705, i, 91.
[8] Warburton, *Divine Legation*, vol. ii, preface.
[9] Stephen, *English Thought*, i, 114-118.

"mechanical" theory of the universe which perfectly comported with atheism, and partly promoted that way of thinking;[1] and a selection from Gassendi's ethical writings, translated into English[2] (1699), wrought in the same direction. The Church itself contained Cartesians and Cudworthians, Socinians and deists.[3] Each group, further, had inner differences as to free-will[4] and Providence; and the theistic schools of Newton, Clarke, and Leibnitz rejected each other's philosophies as well as that of Descartes. Leibnitz complained grimly that Newton and his followers had "a very odd opinion concerning the Work of God," making the universe an imperfect machine, which the deity had frequently to mend; and treating space as an organ by which God perceives things, which are thus regarded as not produced or maintained by him.[5] Newton's principles of explanation, he insisted, were those of the materialists.[6] John Hutchinson, a professor at Cambridge, in his *Treatise of Power, Essential and Mechanical*, also bitterly assailed Newton as a deistical and anti-scriptural sophist.[7] Clarke, on the other hand, declared that the philosophy of Leibnitz was "tending to banish God from the world."[8] Alongside of such internecine strife, it was not surprising that the great astronomer Halley, who accepted Newton's principles in physics, was commonly reputed an atheist;

---

[1] This, according to John Craig, was Newton's opinion. "The reason of his [Newton's] showing the errors of Cartes's philosophy was because he thought it made on purpose to be the foundation of infidelity." Letter to Conduitt, April 7th, 1727, in Brewster's *Memoirs of Newton*, ii, 315. Clarke, in his Answer to Butler's Fifth Letter, expresses a similar view.

[2] "*Three Discourses of Happiness, Virtue, and Liberty*, Collected from the Works of the Learn'd Gassendi by Monsieur Bernier. Translated out of the French, 1699."

[3] Cp. W. Sichel, *Bolingbroke and His Times*, 1901, i, 175.

[4] Sir Leslie Stephen (i, 33) makes the surprising statement that a "dogmatic assertion of free-will became a mark of the whole deist and semi-deist school." On the contrary, Hobbes and Anthony Collins, not to speak of Locke, wrote with uncommon power against the conception of free-will, and had many disciples on that head.

[5] Letter to the Princess of Wales, November 1715, in Brewster, ii, 284-5.

[6] Second Letter to Clarke, par. 1.

[7] *Abstract from the Works of John Hutchinson*, 1755, pp. 149-163.

[8] Clarke's Answer to Leibnitz's First Letter, *end*.

and that the freethinkers pitted his name in that connection against Newton's.[1] It can hardly be doubted that if intellectual England could have been polled in 1710, under no restraints from economic, social, and legal pressure, some form of rationalism inconsistent with Christianity would have been found to be fully as common as orthodoxy. In outlying provinces, in Devon and Cornwall, in Ulster, in Edinburgh and Glasgow, as well as in the metropolis, the pressure of deism on the popular creed evoked expressions of Arian and Socinian thought among the clergy.[2] It was, in fact, the various pressures under notice that determined the outward fortunes of belief and unbelief, and have substantially determined them since. When the devout Whiston was deposed from his professorship for his Arianism, and the unbelieving Saunderson was put in his place,[3] and when Simson was suspended from his ministerial functions in Glasgow,[4] the lesson was learned that outward conformity was the sufficient way to income.[5]

Hard as it was, however, to kick against the pricks of law and prejudice, it is clear that many in the upper and middle classes privately did so. The clerical and the new popular literature of the time prove this abundantly. In the *Tatler* and its successors,[6] the decorous Addison

[1] Berkeley, *Defence of Freethinking in Mathematics*, par. vii; and Stock's Memoir of Berkeley. Cp. Brewster, *Memoirs of Newton*, ii, 408.
[2] Lecky, *Hist. of Engl. in the Eighteenth Cent.* ed. 1892, iii, 22–24.
[3] The tradition of Saunderson's unbelief is constant. In the memoir prefixed to his *Elements of Algebra* (1740) no word is said of his creed, though at death he received the sacrament.
[4] See *The State of the Process depending Against Mr. John Simson*, Edinburgh, 1728. Simson always expressed himself piously, but had thrown out such expressions as *Ratio est principium et fundamentum theologiæ*, which "contravened the Act of Assembly, 1717" (vol. cited, p. 316). The "process" against him began in 1714, and dragged on for nearly twenty years, with the result of his resigning his professorship of theology at Glasgow in 1729, and seceding from the Associate Presbytery in 1733. Burton, *History of Scotland*, viii, 399–400.
[5] Cp. the pamphlet by "A Presbyter of the Church of England," attributed to Bishop Hare, cited in *Dynamics of Religion*, pp. 177–8, and by Lecky, iii, 25.
[6] *Tatler*, Nos. 12, 111, 135; *Spectator*, Nos. 234, 381, 389, 599; *Guardian*, Nos. 3, 9, 27, 35, 39, 55, 62, 70, 77, 83, 88, 126, 130, 169. Most of the *Guardian* papers cited are by Berkeley. They are extremely virulent; but Steele's run them hard.

and the indecorous Steele, neither of them a competent thinker, frigidly or furiously asperse the new tribe of freethinkers; the evangelically pious Berkeley and the extremely unevangelical Swift rival each other in the malice of their attacks on those who rejected their creed. Berkeley, a man of philosophic genius but intense prepossessions, maintained Christianity on grounds which are the negation of philosophy.[1] Swift, the genius of neurotic misanthropy, who, in the words of Macaulay, "though he had no religion, had a great deal of professional spirit,"[2] fought venomously for the creed of salvation. And still the deists multiplied. In the Earl of SHAFTESBURY[3] they had a satirist with a finer and keener weapon than was wielded by either Steele or Addison, and a much better temper than was owned by Swift or Berkeley. He did not venture to parade his unbelief: to do so was positively dangerous; but his thrusts at faith left little doubt as to his theory. He was at once dealt with by the orthodox as an enemy, and as promptly adopted by the deists as a champion, important no less for his ability than for his rank. Nor, indeed, is he lacking in boldness in comparison with contemporary writers. The anonymous pamphlet entitled *The Natural History of Superstition*, by the deist, John Trenchard, M.P. (1709), does not venture on overt heresy. But Shaftesbury's *Letter Concerning Enthusiasm* (1708), his *Essay on the Freedom of Wit and Humour* (1709), and his treatise, *The Moralists* (1709), had need be anonymous because of their essential hostility to the reigning religious ethic.

Such writing marks a new stage in rationalistic propaganda. Swift, writing in 1709, angrily proposes to "prevent the publishing of such pernicious works as

---

[1] *Analyst*, Queries 60 and 62: *Defence of Freethinking in Mathematics*, §§ 5, 6, 50. Cp. *Dynamics of Religion*, pp. 141-2.
[2] Letter in De Morgan's *Newton: his Friend: and his Niece*, 1885, p. 69.
[3] The essays in the *Characteristics* (excepting the *Inquiry Concerning Virtue and Merit*, which was published by Toland, without permission, in 1699) appeared between 1708 and 1711, being collected in the latter year. Shaftesbury died in 1713, in which year appeared his paper on *The Judgment of Hercules*.

under pretence of freethinking endeavour to overthrow those tenets in religion which have been held inviolable in almost all ages."[1] But his further protest that "the doctrine of the Trinity, the divinity of Christ, the immortality of the soul, and even the truth of all revelation, are daily exploded and denied in books openly printed," points mainly to the Unitarian propaganda. Among freethinkers he names, in his *Argument Against Abolishing Christianity* (1708), Asgill, Coward, Toland, and Tindal. But the first was an ultra-Christian; the second was a Christian upholder of the thesis that spirit is not immaterial; and the last, at that date, had published only his *Four Discourses* (collected in 1709) and his *Rights of the Christian Church*, which are anti-clerical, but not anti-Christian. Professor Henry Dodwell, who in 1706 published an *Epistolary Discourse Concerning the Soul's Natural Mortality*, maintaining the doctrine of conditional immortality,[2] which he made dependent on baptism in the apostolical succession, was a devout Christian; and no writer of that date went further. It would appear that Swift spoke mainly from hearsay, and on the strength of the conversational freethinking so common in society.[3] But the anonymous essays of Shaftesbury which were issued in 1709 might be the immediate provocation of his outbreak.[4]

---

[1] *A Project for the Advancement of Religion.* Bohn ed. of *Works*, iii, 44. In this paper Swift reveals his moral standards by the avowal (p. 40) that "hypocrisy is much more eligible than open infidelity and vice: it wears the livery of religion......and is cautious of giving scandal."

[2] Sir Leslie Stephen (*English Thought*, i, 283) speaks of Dodwell's thesis as deserving only "pity or contempt." Cp. Macaulay, Student's ed. ii, 107-8. But a doctrine of conditional immortality had been explicitly put by Locke in his *Reasonableness of Christianity*, 1695, p. 13. Cp. Professor Fraser's *Locke*, 1890, pp. 259-260, and Fox Bourne's *Life of Locke*, ii, 287. The difference was that Dodwell elaborately gave his reasons, which, as Dr. Clarke put it, made "all good men sorry, and all profane men rejoice."

[3] Compare his ironical *Argument Against Abolishing Christianity*, 1708.

[4] He had, however, hailed the anonymous *Letter Concerning Enthusiasm* as "very well writ," believing it to be by a friend of his own. "Enthusiasm," as meaning "popular fanaticism," was of course as repellent to a churchman as to the deists.

§ 2.

Deism had been thus made in a manner fashionable[1] when, in 1713, ANTHONY COLLINS began a new development by his *Discourse of Freethinking*. He had previously published a notably freethinking *Essay Concerning the Use of Reason* (1707); carried on a discussion with Clarke on the question of the immateriality of the soul; and issued treatises entitled *Priestcraft in Perfection* (1709, dealing with the history of the Thirty-nine Articles)[2] and *A Vindication of the Divine Attributes* (1710), exposing the Hobbesian theism of Archbishop King on lines followed twenty years later by Berkeley in his *Minute Philosopher*. But none of these works aroused such a tumult as the *Discourse of Freethinking*, which may be said to sum up and unify the drift not only of previous English freethinking, but of the great contribution of Bayle, whose learning and temper influence all English deism from Shaftesbury onwards.[3] Collins's book, however, was unique in its outspokenness. To the reader of to-day, indeed, it is no very aggressive performance: the writer was a man of imperturbable amenity and genuine kindliness of nature; and his style is the completest possible contrast to that of the furious replies it elicited. It was to Collins that Locke wrote, in 1703: "Believe it, my good friend, to love truth for truth's sake is the principal part of human perfection in this world, and the secd-plot of all other virtues; and, if I mistake not, you have as much of it as I ever met with in anybody." The *Discourse* does no

---

[1] Dr. E. Synge, of Dublin (afterwards Archbishop of Tuam), in his *Religion Tryed by the Test of Sober and Impartial Reason*, published in 1713, seems to be writing before the issue of Collins's book when he says (*Dedication*, p. 11) that the spread of the "disease not only of Heterodoxy but of Infidelity" is "too plain to be either denied or dissembled."

[2] Leslie affirms in his *Truth of Christianity Demonstrated* (1711, p. 14) that the satirical *Detection* of his *Short Method with the Deists*, to which the *Truth* is a reply, was by the author of *Priestcraft in Perfection*; but, while the *Detection* has some of Collins's humour, it lacks his amenity, and is evidently not by him.

[3] An English translation of the Dictionary, in 5 vols. folio, with "many passages restored," appeared in 1734.

discredit to this uncommon encomium, being a luminous and learned plea for the conditions under which alone truth can be prosperously studied, and the habits of mind which alone can attain it. Of the many replies, the most notorious is that of Bentley writing as *Phileleutherus Lipsiensis*, a performance which, on the strength of its author's reputation for scholarship, has been uncritically applauded by not a few critics of whom some of the most eminent do not appear to have read Collins's treatise.[1] Bentley's is in reality pre-eminent only for insolence and bad faith, the latter quality being sometimes complicated by lapses of scholarship hardly credible on its author's part.[2] One mistranslation which was either a joke or a printer's error, and one misspelling of a Greek name, are the only heads on which Bentley confutes his author. He had, in fact, neither the kind of knowledge nor the candour that could fit him to handle the problems raised. It was Bentley's cue to represent Collins as an atheist, though he was a very pronounced deist;[3] and in the first uproar Collins had to fly to Holland to avoid arrest.[4] But deism was too general to permit of such a representative being exiled; and he returned to study quietly, leaving Bentley's vituperation and prevarication unanswered, with the other attacks made upon him. In 1715 he published his brief but masterly *Inquiry Concerning Human Liberty*—anonymous, like all his works—which remains unsurpassed in its essentials as a statement of the case for Determinism.[5]

[1] The worst case is that of Mark Pattison, who calls Collins's book of 178 pages a "small tract."
[2] See the details in *Dynamics of Religion*, ch. vii.
[3] "Ignorance," Collins writes, "is the foundation of Atheism, and Freethinking the cure of it" (*Discourse of Freethinking*, p. 105). Like Newton, he contemplated only an impossible atheism, never formulated by any writer.
[4] Mr. Temple Scott, in his Bohn ed. of Swift's Works (iii, 166), asserts that Swift's satire "frightened Collins into Holland." For this statement there is no evidence whatever, and as it stands it is unintelligible.
[5] Second ed. 1717. Another writer, William Lyons, was on the same track, publishing *The Infallibility of Human Judgment, its Dignity and Excellence* (2nd ed. 1720), and *A Discourse of the Necessity of Human Actions* (1730).

Not till 1723 did he publish his next work, *A Discourse of the Grounds and Reasons of the Christian Religion*, a weighty attack on the argument from prophecy, to which the replies numbered thirty-five; on which followed in 1727 his *Scheme of Literal Prophecy Considered*, a reply to criticisms. The former work was pronounced by Warburton one of the most plausible ever written against Christianity, and the replies might have been left to confute each other. The movement was now in full flood, the acute MANDEVILLE[1] having issued in 1720 his *Free Thoughts on Religion*, and in 1723 a freshly expanded edition of his very anti-theological *Fable of the Bees*; while the half-deranged ex-clergyman, THOMAS WOOLSTON, contributed in 1726-28 his rather ribald *Discourses on Miracles*, of which Voltaire, who was in England in 1728, tells that thirty thousand copies were sold;[2] while sixty pamphlets were written in opposition. It was in the middle of the debate that CONYERS MIDDLETON, Fellow of Trinity College, Cambridge, produced his *Letter from Rome* (1729), wherein the part of paganism in Christianity is so set forth as to carry inference further than the argument ostensibly goes. In that year the heads of Oxford University publicly lamented the spread of open deism among the students; and the proclamation did nothing to check the contagion. In *Fogg's Weekly Journal* of July 4th, 1730, it is announced that "one of the principal colleges in Oxford has of late been infested with deists; and that three deistical students have been expelled; and a fourth has had his degree

---

[1] As to whose positions see a paper in the writer's *Essays Towards a Critical Method*, 1889.

[2] There were six separate *Discourses*. Voltaire speaks of "three editions *coup sur coup* of ten thousand each" (*Lettre sur les auteurs Anglais*—in *Œuvres*, ed. 1792, lxviii, 359). This seems extremely unlikely as to any one *Discourse*; and even 5,000 copies of each *Discourse* is a hardly credible sale. In any case, Woolston's *Discourses* are now much seldomer met with than Collins's *Discourse of Freethinking*. Alberti (*Briefe betreffend den Zustand der Religion in Gross-Brittannien*) writes in 1752 that the *Discourses* are in that day somewhat rare, and seldom found together. Many copies were probably destroyed by the orthodox, and many would doubtless be thrown away, as tracts so often

deferred two years, during which he is to be closely confined in college ; and, among other things, is to translate Leslie's *Short and Easy Method with the Deists* "[1] It is not hard to divine the effect of such apologetic methods. In 1731, the author of an apologetic pamphlet in reply to Woolston laments that even at the universities young men "too often" become tainted with "infidelity"; and, on the other hand, directing his battery against those who "causelessly profess to build their skeptical notions" on the writings of Locke, he complains of Dr. Holdsworth and other academic polemists who had sought to rob orthodoxy of the credit of such a champion as Locke by "consigning him over to that class of freethinkers and skeptics to which he was an adversary."[2]

With MATTHEW TINDAL'S *Christianity as Old as Creation* (1730) the excitement seems to have reached high-water mark, that work eliciting from first to last over a hundred and fifty replies, at home and abroad. Its directness and simplicity of appeal to what passed for theistic common-sense were indeed fitted to give it the widest audience yet won by any deist; and its anti-clericalism would carry it far among his fellow Whigs to begin with.[3] One tract of the period, dedicated to the Queen Regent, complains that "the present raging infidelity threatens an universal infection," and that it is not confined to the capital, but "is disseminated even to the confines of your kingdom."[4] Tindal, like Collins, wrote anonymously, and so escaped prosecution, dying in 1733, when the second part of his book, left ready for publication, was deliberately destroyed by Bishop Gibson, into whose hands it came. In 1736 he and Shaftesbury are described by an orthodox apologist as the "two oracles of deism."[5] Woolston, who put his name to his books,

[1] Tyerman's *Life of Wesley*, ed. 1871, i, 65-66.
[2] *The Infidel Convicted*, 1731, pp. 33, 62.
[3] Tindal (Voltaire tells) regarded Pope as devoid of genius and imagination, and so trebly earned his place in the *Dunciad*.
[4] *A Layman's Faith* "By a Freethinker and a Christian," 1732.
[5] Title-page of Rev. Elisha Smith's *Cure of Deism*, 1st ed. 1736; 3rd ed. 1740.

is commonly said to have paid the penalty of imprisonment for the rest of his life (d. 1733), being unable to pay a fine of £100 ; but Voltaire positively asserts that "nothing is more false" than the statement that he died in prison ; adding: "Several of my friends have seen him in his house: he died there, at liberty."[1] In any case, he was sentenced ; and the punishment was the measure of the anger felt at the continuous advance of deistic opinions, or at least against hostile criticism of the Scriptures. Unitarianism, formerly a hated heresy, was now in comparison leniently treated, because of its deference to Scriptural authority. Thus the Unitarian Edward Elwall, who had published a book called *A True Testimony for God and his Sacred Law* (1724), for which he was prosecuted at Stafford in 1726, was allowed by the judge to argue his cause fully, and was unconditionally acquitted, to the displeasure of the clergy. Anti-scriptural writers could not hope for such toleration, being doubly odious to the church. Berkeley, in 1721, had complained bitterly[2] of the general indifference to religion, which his writings had done nothing to alter ; and in 1736 he angrily demanded that blasphemy should be punished like high treason.[3] His *Minute Philosopher* (1732) betrays throughout his angry consciousness of the vogue of freethinking after twenty years of resistance from his profession ; and that performance is singularly ill fitted to alter the opinions of unbelievers. In his earlier papers attacking them he had put a stress of malice that, in a mind of his calibre, is startling even to the student of religious history.[4] It reveals him as no less possessed by the passion of creed than the most ignorant priest of his church. For him all freethinkers were detested disturbers of his emotional life ; and of the best of them, as Collins, Shaftesbury, and Spinoza, he

---

[1] *Lettre sur les auteurs Anglais*, as cited. Voltaire tells that, when a she-bigot one day spat in Woolston's face, he calmly remarked: "It was so that the Jews treated your God."
[2] *Essay Towards Preventing the Ruin of Great Britain.*
[3] *Discourse to Magistrates.*
[4] *Guardian*, Nos. 3, 55, 88.

speaks with positive fury. In the *Minute Philosopher*, half-conscious of the wrongness of his temper, he sets himself to make the unbelievers figure in dialogue as ignorant, pretentious, and coarse-natured, while his own mouthpieces are meant to be benign, urbane, wise, and persuasive. Yet in the very pages so planned he unwittingly reveals that the freethinkers whom he goes about to caricature were commonly good-natured in tone, while he becomes as virulent as ever in his eagerness to discredit them. Not a paragraph in the book attains to the spirit of judgment or fairness: all is special pleading, overstrained and embittered sarcasm, rankling animus. No man was less qualified to write a well-balanced dialogue as between his own side and its opponents; unless it be in the sense that his passion recoils on his own case. Even while setting up ninepins of ill-put "infidel" argument to knock down, he elaborates futilities of rebuttal, indicating to every attentive reader the slightness of his rational basis.

On the strength of this performance he might fitly be termed the most ill-conditioned sophist of his age, were it not for the perception that religious feeling in him has become a pathological phase, and that he suffers incomparably more from his own passions than he can cause his enemies to suffer by his eager thrusts at them. More than almost any gifted pietist of modern times he sets us wondering at the power of creed in certain cases to overgrow judgment and turn to naught the rarest faculties. No man in Berkeley's day had a finer natural lucidity and suppleness of intelligence; yet perhaps no polemist on his side did less either to make converts or to establish a sound intellectual practice. Plain men on the freethinking side he must either have bewildered by his metaphysic or revolted by his spite: while to the more efficient minds he stood revealed as a kind of inspired child, rapt in the construction and manipulation of a set of brilliant sophisms which availed as much for any other creed as for his own. To the armoury of Christian apologetic now growing up he contributed a special form of the sceptical argument: freethinkers, he declared, made certain arbitrary or irrational assumptions in accepting Newton's doctrine of fluxions, and it was only their prejudice that prevented them from being similarly accommodating to Christian mysteries.[1] It is a kind of argument dear to minds pre-convinced and incapable of a logical revision, but worse than inept as against opponents. To theosophy, indeed, Berkeley rendered a more successful service in presenting it with the no better formula of "existence dependent upon consciousness"—a verbalism which has served the purposes of theology in the philosophic schools down till our own day. For his, however, the popular polemic value of such a theorem must have been sufficiently countervailed by his vehement championship of the doctrine of passive obedience in its most extreme form—"that loyalty is a virtue or moral duty; and disloyalty or rebellion, in the most strict and proper sense, a vice or crime against the law of nature."[2]

It belonged to the overstrung temperament of Berkeley that, like a nervous artist, he should figure to himself all his freethinking antagonists as personally odious, himself growing odious under the obsession; and he solemnly asserts, in his *Discourse to Magistrates*, that there had been "lately set up within this city of Dublin" an "execrable fraternity of blasphemers," calling themselves "blasters," and forming "a distinct society, whereof the proper and avowed business shall be to shock all serious Christians by the most impious and horrid blasphemies, uttered in the most public manner."[3] There appears to be not a grain of truth in this astonishing assertion, to which no subsequent historian has paid the slightest attention. In a period in which freethinking books had been again and again burned in Dublin by the public hangman, such a society could be projected only in a nightmare; and Berkeley's

---

[1] *The Analyst*, Queries 55 67.
[2] *Discourse of Passive Obedience*, § 26.
[3] *Works*, ed. 1837, p. 352.

hallucination may serve as a sign of the extent to which his judgment had been deranged by his passions.[1]

When educated Christians could be so habitually envenomed as was Berkeley, there was doubtless a measure of contrary heat among English unbelievers; but, apart altogether from what could be described as blasphemy, unbelief abounded in the most cultured society of the day. Bolingbroke's rationalism had been privately well known; and so distinguished a personage as the brilliant and scholarly Lady Mary Wortley Montagu, hated by Pope, is one of the reputed freethinkers of her time.[2] In the very year of the publication of Berkeley's *Minute Philosopher*, the first two epistles of the *Essay on Man* of his own friend and admirer, Pope, gave a new currency to the form of optimistic deism created by Shaftesbury, and later elaborated by Bolingbroke. Pope was always anxiously hostile in his allusions to the professed freethinkers[3]—among whom Bolingbroke only posthumously enrolled himself—and in private he specially aspersed Shaftesbury, from whom he had taken so much;[4] but his prudential tactic gave all the more currency to the virtual deism he enunciated. Given out without any critical allusion to Christianity, and put forward as a vindication of the ways of God to men, it gave to heresy the status of a well-bred piety. A good authority pronounces that "the *Essay on Man*

---

[1] See the whole context, which palpitates with excitement.

[2] Mr. Walter Sichel (*Bolingbroke and his Times*, 1901, i, 175) thinks fit to dispose of her attitude as " her aversion to the church and to everything that transcended her own faculties." So far as the evidence goes, her faculties were much superior to those of most of her orthodox contemporaries. For her tone see her letters.

[3] E.g., *Dunciad*, ii, 399; iii, 212; iv, 492.

[4] Voltaire commented pointedly on Pope's omission to make any reference to Shaftesbury, while vending his doctrine. (*Lettres Anglaises*, xxii.) As a matter of fact Pope does in the *Dunciad* (iv, 488) refer maliciously to the Theocles of Shaftesbury's *Moralists* as maintaining a Lucretian theism or virtual atheism. The explanation is that Shaftesbury had sharply criticised the political course of Bolingbroke, who in turn ignored him as a thinker. See the present writer's introd. to Shaftesbury's *Characteristics*, ed. 1900; and cp. W. R. Scott, *Francis Hutcheson*, 1900, p. 101.

did more to spread English deism in France than all the works of Shaftesbury."[1]

> The line of the *Essay* which now reads
> > The soul, uneasy and confined *from* home,
>
> originally ran "*at* home"; but, says Warton, "this expression seeming to exclude a future existence, *as, to speak the plain truth, it was intended to do*, it was altered"—presumably by Warburton. (Warton's *Essay on Pope*, 4th ed. ii, 67.) The Spinozistic or pantheistic character of much of the *Essay on Man* was noted by various critics, in particular by the French Academician De Crousaz (*Examen de l'Essay de M. Pope sur l'Homme*, 1748). When the younger Racine, writing to the Chevalier Ramsay in 1742, charged the *Essay* with irreligion, Pope wrote him repudiating alike Spinoza and Leibnitz. (Warton, ii, 121.) In 1755, however, the Abbé Gauchat renewed the attack, declaring that the *Essay* was "neither Christian nor philosophic" (*Lettres Critiques*, i, 346). Warburton at first charged the poem with rank atheism, and afterwards vindicated it in his manner. (Warton, i, 125.) But in Germany, in the youth of Goethe, we find the *Essay* regarded by Christians as an unequivocally deistic poem. (Goethe's *Wahrheit und Dichtung*, Th. II, B. vii : *Werke*, ed. 1866, xi, 263.) And by a modern Christian polemist the *Essay* is described as "the best positive result of English deism in the eighteenth century" (Gostwick, *German Culture and Christianity*, 1882, p. 31).

In point of fact, though Voltaire testifies from personal knowledge that there were in England in his day many principled atheists,[2] there was little overt atheism,[3] whether by reason of the special odium attaching to that way of thinking, or of a real production of theistic belief by the concurrence of the deistic propaganda on this head with that of the clergy, themselves in so many cases deists.[4] Collins observed that nobody

---

[1] Texte, *Rousseau and the Cosmopolitan Spirit in Literature*, Eng. trans. pp. 117 118.
[2] *Dict. Philos.* art. ATHÉE, § 2.
[3] Wise, in his adaptation of Cudworth, *A Confutation of the Reason and Philosophy of Atheism* (1706), writes that "the philosophical atheists are but few in number," and their objections so weak "as that they deserve not a hearing but rather neglect"; but goes on to admit that "one or two broachers of 'em may be thought able to infect a whole nation, as......sad experience tells us" (work cited, i, 5).
[4] Complaint to this effect was made by orthodox writers. The Scotch Professor Halyburton, for instance, complains that in many sermons in

had doubted the existence of God until the Boyle lecturers began to prove it ; and Clarke had more than justified the jest by arguing, in his Boyle Lectures for 1705, that all deism logically leads to atheism. But though the apologists roused much discussion on the theistic issue, the stress of the apologetic literature passed from the theme of atheism to that of deism. Shaftesbury's early *Inquiry Concerning Virtue* had assumed the existence of a good deal of atheism ; but his later writings, and those of his school, do not indicate any great atheistic opposition.[1] Even the discussion on the immateriality and immortality of the soul—which began with the *Grand Essay* of Dr. William Coward,[2] in 1704, and was taken up, as we have seen, by the non-juror Dodwell[3]—was conducted on either orthodox or deistic lines. Coward wrote as a professed Christian,[4] to maintain, "against impostures of philosophy," that "matter and motion must be the foundation of thought in men and brutes." Collins maintained against Clarke the proposition that matter is capable of thought ; and SAMUEL STRUTT ("of the Temple"), whose *Philosophical Inquiry into the Physical Spring of Human Actions, and the Immediate Cause of Thinking* (1732), is a most tersely cogent sequence of materialistic argument, never raises any question of deity. The result was that the problem of "materialism" was virtually dropped, Strutt's essay in particular passing into general oblivion.

his day "*Heathen Morality* has been substituted in the room of *Gospel Holiness*. And Ethicks by some have been preached instead of the *Gospels* of Christ." *Natural Religion Insufficient* (Edinburgh), 1714, p. 25. Cp. pp. 23, 26-27, 59, etc.

[1] *The Moralists* deals rather with strict skepticism than with substantive atheism

[2] *The Grand Essay ; or, a Vindication of Reason and Religion Against Impostures of Philosophy*. The book was condemned to be burned by the House of Commons.

[3] Above, p. 133.

[4] Mr. Herbert Paul, in his essay on Swift (*Men and Letters*, 1901, p. 267), lumps as deists the four writers named by Swift in his *Argument*. Not having read them, he thinks fit to asperse all four as bad writers. Asgill, as was noted by Coleridge, was one of the best writers of his time. He was, in fact, a master of the staccato style, practised by Mr. Paul with less success.

It was replied to, however, with the *Inquiry* of Collins, as late as 1760, by a Christian controversialist who admits Strutt to have been "a gentleman of an excellent genius for philosophical inquiries, and a close reasoner from those principles he laid down" (*An Essay towards demonstrating the Immateriality and Free Agency of the Soul*, 1760, p. 94). The Rev. Mr. Monk, in his *Life of Bentley* (2nd ed. 1833, ii, 391), absurdly speaks of Strutt as having "dressed up the arguments of Lord Herbert of Cherbury and other enemies of religion in a new shape." The reverend gentleman cannot have paid any attention to the arguments either of Herbert or of Strutt, which have no more in common than those of Toland and Hume. Strutt's book was much too closely reasoned to be popular. His name was for the time, however, associated with a famous scandal at Cambridge University. When in 1739 proceedings were taken against what was described as an "atheistical society" there, Strutt was spoken of as its "oracle." One of the members was Paul Whitehead, satirised by Pope. Another, Tinkler Ducket, a Fellow of Caius College, in holy orders, was prosecuted in the Vice-Chancellor's Court on the twofold charge of proselytising for atheism and of attempting to seduce a "female." In his defence he explained that he had been for some time "once more a believer in God and Christianity"; but was nevertheless expelled. See Monk's *Life of Bentley*, as cited, ii, 391 sq.

No less marked is the failure to develop the "higher criticism" from the notable start made in 1739 in the very remarkable *Inquiry into the Jewish and Christian Revelations* by Samuel Parvish, who made the vital discovery that Deuteronomy is a product of the seventh century B.C.[1] His book, which is in the form of a dialogue between a Christian and a Japanese, went into a second edition (1746), but his idea struck too deep for the critical faculty of that age; and not till the nineteenth century was the clue found again by De Wette, in Germany.[2] Parvish came at the end of the main deistic movement,[3] and by that time the more open-

---

[1] Work cited, p. 324.
[2] Cp. Cheyne, *Founders of Old Testament Criticism*, 1893, p. 2.
[3] Dr. Cheyne expresses surprise that a "theological writer" who got so far should not have been "prompted by his good genius to follow up his advantage." It is, however, rather remarkable that Parvish, who was a bookseller at Guildford (Alberti, *Briefe*, p. 426), should have achieved what he did. It was through not being a theological writer that he went so far, no theologian of his day following him.

minded men had come to a point of view from which it did not greatly matter when Deuteronomy was written, or precisely how a cultus was built up; while orthodoxy could not dream of abandoning its view of inspiration. There was thus an arrest alike of historical criticism and of the higher philosophic thought under the stress of the concrete disputes over ethics, miracles, prophecy, and politics; and a habit of taking deity for granted became normal, with the result that when the weak point was pressed upon by Law and Butler there was a sense of blankness on both sides. But among men theistically inclined, the argument of Tindal against revelationism was extremely telling, and it had more literary impressiveness than any writing on the orthodox side before Butler. By this time the philosophic influence of Spinoza—seen as early as 1699 in Shaftesbury's *Inquiry Concerning Virtue*,[1] and avowed by Clarke when he addressed his *Demonstration* (1705) "more particularly in answer to Mr. Hobbs, Spinoza, and their followers"— had spread among the studious class, greatly reinforcing the deistic movement; so that in 1732 Berkeley, who ranked him among "weak and wicked writers," described him as "the great leader of our modern infidels."

See the *Minute Philosopher*, Dial. vii, § 29. Similarly Leland, in the *Supplement* (1756) to his *View of the Deistical Writers* (afterwards incorporated as Letter VI), speaks of Spinoza as "the most applauded doctor of modern atheism." Sir Leslie Stephen's opinion (*English Thought*, i, 33), that "few of the deists, probably," read Spinoza, seems to be thus outweighed. If they did not in great numbers read the *Ethica*, they certainly read the *Tractatus* and the letters. As early as 1677 we find Stillingfleet, in the preface to his *Letter to a Deist*, speaking of Spinoza as "a late author [who] I hear is mightily in vogue among many who cry up anything on the atheistical side, though never so weak and trifling"; and further of a mooted proposal to translate the *Tractatus Theologico-Politicus* into English. A translation was published in 1689. In Gildon's work of recantation, *The Deist's Manual* (1705, p. 192), the indifferent Pleonexus, who "took more delight in bags

[1] See the author's introduction to ed. of the *Characteristics*, 1900.

than in books," and demurs to accumulating the latter, avows that he has a few, among them being Hobbes and Spinoza. Evelyn, writing about 1680-90, speaks of "that infamous book, the *Tractatus Theologico-Politicus* " as "a wretched obstacle to the searchers of holy truth" (*The History of Religion*, 1850, p. xxvii). Cp. Halyburton, *Natural Religion Insufficient*, Edinburgh, 1714, p. 31, as to the "great vogue among our young Gentry and Students" of Hobbes, Spinoza, and others.

Among the deists of the upper classes was the young William Pitt, afterwards Lord Chatham, if, as has been alleged, it was he who in 1733, two years before he entered Parliament, contributed to the *London Journal* a "Letter on Superstition," the work of a pronounced freethinker.[1] On the other hand, such deistic writing as that of THOMAS CHUBB, an energetic tallow-chandler of Salisbury (d. 1747), in a multitude of tracts brought an ethical "Christian rationalism" within the range of the unscholarly many; while THOMAS MORGAN (d. 1741), a physician, began in the *Moral Philosopher*, 1739-1740,[2] to sketch a rationalistic theory of Christian origins, besides putting the critical case with new completeness. At the same time PETER ANNET (1693-1769), a schoolmaster and inventor of a system of shorthand, widened the propaganda in other directions. He seems to have been the first freethought lecturer, for his first pamphlet, *Judging for Ourselves: or, Freethinking the Great Duty of Religion*, "By P. A., Minister of the Gospel" (1739), consists of "Two Lectures delivered at Plaisterer's Hall." Through all his propaganda, of which the more notable portions are his *Supernaturals Examined* and a series of controversies on the Resurrection, there runs a train of shrewd critical sense, put forth in crisp and vivacious English, which made him a popular force. At length, when in 1761 he issued nine numbers of *The Free Inquirer*, in which he attacked the Pentateuch with much insight and cogency, but with a

---

[1] The question remains obscure. Cp. the Letter cited, reprinted at end of Carver's 1830 ed. of Paine's Works (New York); F. Thackeray's *Life of Chatham*, ii, 405; and Chatham's "scalping-knife" speech.
[2] *A Vindication of the Moral Philosopher* appeared in 1741.

certain want of rational balance (shown also in his treatise, *Social Bliss Considered,* 1749), he was made a victim of the then strengthened spirit of persecution, being sentenced to stand thrice in the pillory with the label "For Blasphemy," and to suffer a year's hard labour. Nevertheless, he was popular enough to start a school on his release.

Such popularity, of course, was alien to the literary and social traditions of the century, and from the literary point of view the main line of deistic propaganda, as apart from the essays and treatises of Hume and the posthumous works of Bolingbroke, ends with the younger HENRY DODWELL'S (anonymous) ironical essay, *Christianity not Founded on Argument* (1741). So rigorously congruous is the reasoning of that brilliant treatise that some have not quite unjustifiably taken it for the work of a dogmatic believer, standing at some such position as that taken up before him by Huet, and in recent times by Cardinal Newman.[1] He argues, for instance, not merely that reason can yield none of the confidence which belongs to true faith, but that it cannot duly strengthen the moral will against temptations.[2] But it at once elicited a number of replies, all treating it unhesitatingly as an anti-Christian work; and Leland handles it as bitterly as he does any openly freethinking treatise.[3] Its thesis might have been seriously supported by reference to the intellectual history of the preceding thirty years, wherein much argument had certainly failed to establish the reigning creed or to discredit the unbelievers.

Of the work done by English deism thus far, it may suffice to say that within two generations it had more profoundly altered the intellectual temper of educated men than any religious movement had ever done in the same time. This appears above all from the literature produced by orthodoxy in reply, where the mere

---

[1] Cp. Cairns, *Unbelief in the Eighteenth Century,* 1881, p. 101.
[2] Ed. 1741, p. 30 sq.
[3] *View of the Deistical Writers,* Letter XI (X in 1st ed.).

defensive resort to reasoning, apart from the accounts of current rationalism, outgoes anything in the previous history of literature. Could the discussion have been continuous—could England have remained what she was in the main deistic period, a workshop of investigation and a battleground of ideas—all European development might have been indefinitely hastened. But the deists, for the most part educated men appealing to educated men or to the shrewdest readers among the artisans, had not learned to reckon with the greater social forces ; and beyond a certain point they could not affect England's intellectual destinies. The clergy, who could not argue them down in the court of culture, had in their own jurisdiction the great mass of the uneducated lower classes, and the great mass of the women of all classes, whom the ideals of the age kept uneducated with a difference. With the multitude remaining a ready hotbed for new "enthusiasm," and the women of the middle and upper orders no less ready nurturers of new generations of young believers, the work of emancipation was but begun when deism was made "fashionable." And with England on the way to a new era at once of industrial and imperial expansion, in which the energies that for a generation had made her a leader of European thought were diverted to arms and to commerce, the critical and rationalising work of the deistical generation could not go on as it had begun. That generation left its specific mark on the statute-book in a complete repeal of the old laws relating to witchcraft ;[1] on literature in a whole library of propaganda and apology ; on moral and historic science in a new movement of humanism, which was to culminate in the French Revolution. But for reasons lying in the environment as well as in its own standpoint, deism was not destined to rise on continuous stepping-stones to social dominion.

Currency has been given to a misconception of intellectual

[1] Act 9th Geo. II (1736), ch. 5.

history by the authoritative statement that in the deistic controversy "all that was intellectually venerable in England" appeared "on the side of Christianity" (Sir Leslie Stephen, *English Thought in the Eighteenth Century*, i, 86). The proposition seems to be an echo of orthodox historiography, as Buckle had before written in his note-book: "In England skepticism made no head. Such men as Toland and Tindal, Collins, Shaftesbury, Woolston, were no match for Clarke, Warburton, and Lardner. They could make no head till the time of Middleton" (*Misc. Works*, abridged ed. i, 321)—a strain of assertion which clearly proceeds on no study of the period. In the first place, all the writing on the freethinking side was done under peril of Blasphemy Laws, and under menace of all the calumny and ostracism that in Christian society follow on advanced heresy; while the orthodox side could draw on the entire clerical profession, over ten thousand strong, and trained for and pledged to defence of the faith. Yet, when all is said, the ordinary list of deists amply suffices to disprove Sir L. Stephen's phrase. His "intellectually venerable" list runs: Bentley, Locke, Berkeley, Clarke, Butler, Waterland, Warburton, Sherlock, Gibson, Conybeare, Smalbroke, Leslie, Law, Leland, Lardner, Foster, Doddridge, Lyttelton, Barrington, Addison, Pope, Swift. He might have added Newton and Boyle. Sykes,[1] Balguy, Stebbing, and a "host of others," he declares to be "now for the most part as much forgotten as their victims"; Young and Blackmore he admits to be in similar case. All told, the list includes only three or four men of any permanent interest as thinkers, apart from Newton; and only three or four more important as writers. To speak of Waterland,[2] Warburton,[3] Smalbroke,[4] Sherlock, Leslie, and half-a-dozen more as "intellectually venerable" seems grotesque; even Bentley is a strange subject for veneration.

On the other hand, the list of "the despised deists," who

---

[1] Really an abler man than half the others in the list, but himself a good deal of a heretic.

[2] Whose doctrine Sir Leslie Stephen elsewhere (p. 258) pronounces a "brutal theology which gloried in trampling on the best instincts of its opponents," and a "most unlovely product of eighteenth-century speculation."

[3] Of Warburton Sir Leslie writes elsewhere (p. 353) that "this colossus was built up of rubbish." See p. 352 for samples. Again he speaks (p. 368) of the bishop's pretensions as "colossal impudence." It should be noted, further, that Warburton's teaching in the *Divine Legation* was a gross heresy in the eyes of William Law, who in his *Short but Sufficient Confutation* pronounced its main thesis a "most horrible doctrine." Ed. 1768, as cited, i, 217.

[4] As to whose "senile incompetence" see same vol. p. 234.

"make but a poor show when compared with this imposing list," runs thus: Herbert, Hobbes, Blount, Halley (well known to be an unbeliever, though he did not write on the subject), Toland, Shaftesbury, Collins, Mandeville, Tindal, Chubb, Morgan, Dodwell, Middleton, Hume, Bolingbroke, Gibbon. It would be interesting to know on what principles this group is excluded from the intellectual veneration so liberally allotted to the other. It is nothing to the purpose that Shaftesbury and Mandeville wrote "covertly" and "indirectly." The law and the conditions compelled them to do so. It is still more beside the case to say that "Hume can scarcely be reckoned among the deists. He is already [when?] emerging into a higher atmosphere." Hume wrote explicitly as a deist; and only in his posthumous Dialogues did he pass on to the atheistic position. At no time, moreover, was he "on the side of Christianity." On the other hand, Locke and Clarke and Pope were clearly "emerging into a higher atmosphere" than Christianity, since Locke is commonly reckoned by the culture-historians, and even by Sir Leslie Stephen, as making for deism; Pope was the pupil of Bolingbroke, and wrote as such; and Clarke was shunned as an Arian. Newton, again, was a Unitarian, and Leibnitz accused his system of making for irreligion. It would be hard to show, further, who are the "forgotten victims" of Balguy and the rest. Balguy criticised Shaftesbury, whose name is still a good deal better known than Balguy's. The main line of deists is pretty well remembered. And if we pair off Hume against Berkeley, Hobbes against Locke, Middleton (as historical critic) against Bentley, Shaftesbury against Addison, Mandeville against Swift, Bolingbroke against Butler, Collins against Clarke, Herbert against Lyttelton, Tindal against Waterland, and Gibbon against shall we say?—Warburton, it hardly appears that the overplus of merit goes so overwhelmingly as Sir Leslie Stephen alleges, even if we leave Newton, with brain unhinged, standing against Halley. The statement that the deists "are but a ragged regiment," and that "in speculative ability most of them were children by the side of their ablest antagonists," is simply unintelligible unless the names of all the ablest deists are left out. Locke, be it remembered, did not live to meet the main deistic attack on Christianity; and Sir Leslie admits the weakness of his pro-Christian performance.

The bases of Sir Leslie Stephen's verdict may be tested by his remarks that "Collins, a *respectable country gentleman*, showed considerable acuteness; Toland, *a poor denizen of Grub Street*, and Tindal, a Fellow of All Souls, made a *certain* display of learning, and succeeded in planting some effective arguments."

Elsewhere (pp. 217-227) Sir Leslie admits that Collins had the best of the argument against his "venerable" opponents on Prophecy; and Professor Huxley credits him with equal success in the argument with Clarke. The work of Collins on *Human Liberty*, praised by a whole series of students and experts, and entirely above the capacity of Bentley, is philosophically as durable as any portion of Locke, who made Collins his chosen friend and trustee, and who did not live to meet his anti-Biblical arguments. Tindal, who had also won Locke's high praise by his political essays, profoundly influenced such a student as Laukhard (Lechler, p. 451). And Toland, whom even Mr. Farrar (Bampton Lectures, p. 179) admitted to possess "much originality and learning," has struck Lange as a notable thinker, though he *was* a poor man. Leibnitz, who answered him, praises his acuteness, as does Pusey, who further admits the uncommon ability of Morgan and Collins (*Historical Enquiry into German Rationalism*, 1828, p. 126). It is time that the conventional English standards in these matters should be rectified.

The unfortunate effect of Sir Leslie Stephen's dictum is seen in the assertion of Professor Höffding (*Hist. of Modern Philos.* Eng. trans. 1900, i, 403), that Sir Leslie "rightly remarks of the English deists that they were altogether inferior to their adversaries"; and further (p. 405), that by the later deists, "Collins, Tindal, Morgan, etc., the dispute as to miracles was carried on with great violence." It is here evident that Professor Höffding has not read the writers he depreciates, for those he names were far from being violent. Had he known the literature, he would have named Woolston, not Collins and Tindal and Morgan. He is merely echoing, without inquiring for himself, a judgment which he regards as authoritative. In the same passage he declares that "only one of all the men formerly known as the 'English deists' [Toland] has rendered contributions of any value to the history of thought." If this is said with a knowledge of the works of Collins, Shaftesbury, and Middleton, it argues a sad lack of critical judgment. But there is reason to infer here also that Professor Höffding writes in ignorance of the literature he discusses.

While some professed rationalists thus belittle a series of pioneers who did so much to make later rationalism possible, some eminent theologians do them justice. Thus does Professor Cheyne begin his series of lectures on *Founders of Old Testament Criticism* (1893): "A well-known and honoured representative of progressive German orthodoxy (J. A. Dorner) has set a fine example of historical candour by admitting the obligations of his country to a much-disliked form of English heterodoxy. He says that English deism, which found so many apt disciples in Germany, 'by clearing away dead matter, prepared the way for a reconstruction of theology from the very depths of the heart's beliefs, and also subjected man's nature to stricter observation.'¹ This, however, as it appears to me, is a very inadequate description of the facts. It was not merely a new constructive stage of German theoretic theology, and a keener psychological investigation, for which deism helped to prepare the way, but also a great movement, which has in our own day become in a strict sense international, concerned with the literary and historical criticism of the Scriptures. Beyond all doubt, the Biblical discussions which abound in the works of the deists and their opponents contributed in no slight degree to the development of that semi-apologetic criticism of the Old Testament of which J. D. Michaelis, and in some degree even Eichhorn, were leading representatives.......It is indeed singular that deism should have passed away in England without having produced a great critical movement among ourselves." Not quite so singular, perhaps, when we note that in our own day Sir Leslie Stephen and Professor Höffding could sum up the work of the deists without a glance at what it did for Biblical criticism.

If we were to set up a theory of intellectual possibilities from what has actually taken place in the history of thought, and without regard to the economic and political conditions above mentioned, we might reason that deism failed permanently to overthrow the current creed because it was not properly preceded by discipline in natural science. There might well be stagnation in the higher criticism of the Hebrew Scriptures when all natural science was still coloured by them. In nothing, perhaps, is the danger of Sacred Books more fully exemplified than in their influence for the suppression of true scientific thought. A thousandfold more potently than the faiths of ancient Greece has that of Christendom blocked the way to all intellectually vital discovery. If even the fame and the pietism of Newton could not save him from the charge of promoting atheism, much less could obscure men hope to set up any view of natural

¹ *History of Protestant Theology*, Eng. trans. ii, 77. For the influence of deism on Germany, see Tholuck (*Vermischte Schriften*, Bd. ii) and Lechler (*Gesch. des englischen Deismus*).—*Note by Dr. Cheyne.*

things which clashed with pulpit prejudice. But the harm lay deeper, inasmuch as the ground was preoccupied by pseudo-scientific theories which were at best fanciful modifications of the myths of Genesis. Types of these performances are the treatise of Sir Matthew Hale on *The Primitive Origination of Mankind* (1685); Dr. Thomas Burnet's *Sacred Theory of the Earth* (1680-89); and Whiston's *New Theory of the Earth* (1696)—all devoid of scientific value; Hale's work being pre-Newtonian; Burnet's anti-Newtonian, though partly critical as regards the sources of the Pentateuch; and Whiston's a combination of Newton and myth with his own quaint speculations. Even the *Natural History of the Earth* of Professor John Woodward (1695), after recognising that fossils were really prehistoric remains, decided that they were deposited by the Deluge.[1] Beyond this, science made little advance for many years. Moral and historical criticism, then, as regards some main issues, had gone further than scientific; and men's thinking on certain problems of cosmic philosophy was thus arrested for lack of a basis in experiential science. But the true reason of the arrest of exact Biblical criticism in the eighteenth century is that which explains also the arrest of the sciences. English energy, broadly speaking, was diverted into other channels. In the age of Chatham it became more and more military and industrial, imperialist and commercial; and the scientific work of Newton was considerably less developed by English hands than was the critical work of the first deists. Long before the French Revolution, mathematical and astronomical science were being advanced by French hands, the English doing nothing. Lagrange and Euler, Clairaut and D'Alembert, carried on the work, till Laplace consummated it in his great theory, which is to Newton's what Newton's was to that of Copernicus. It was Frenchmen, freethinkers to a man, who built up the new astronomy, while England

[1] White, *Warfare of Science with Theology*, i, 227.

was producing only eulogies of Newton's greatness. "No British name is ever mentioned in the list of mathematicians who followed Newton in his brilliant career and completed the magnificent edifice of which he laid the foundation."[1] "Scotland contributed her Maclaurin, but England no European name."[2] Throughout the latter half of the eighteenth century "there was hardly an individual in this country who possessed an intimate acquaintance with the methods of investigation which had conducted the foreign mathematicians to so many sublime results."[3] "The English mathematicians seem to have been so dazzled with the splendour of Newton's discoveries that they never conceived them capable of being extended or improved upon";[4] and Newton's name was all the while vaunted, unwarrantably enough, as being on the side of Christian orthodoxy. There was nothing specially incidental to deism, then, in the non-development of the higher criticism in England after Collins and Parvish, or in the lull of critical speculation in the latter half of the century. It was part of a general social readjustment in which English attention was turned from the mental life to the physical, from intension of thought to extension of empire.

> Playfair (as cited, p. 39 ; Brewster, p. 348, *note*) puts forward the theory that the progress of the higher science in France was due to the "small pensions and great honours" bestowed on scientific men by the Academy of Sciences. The lack of such an institution in England he traces to "mercantile prejudices," without explaining these in their turn. They are to be understood as the consequences of the special expansion of commercial and industrial life in England in the eighteenth century, when France, on the contrary, losing India and North America, had her energies in a proportional degree thrown back on the life of the mind. French freethought, it will be observed, expanded *with* science, while in England there

---
[1] Playfair, in the *Edinburgh Review*, January, 1808, cited by Brewster, *Memoirs of Newton*, 1855, i, 347.
[2] Brewster, as cited.
[3] Grant, *History of Physical Astronomy*, 1852, p. 108.
[4] Baden Powell, *Hist. of Nat. Philos.* 1834, p. 363.

occurred, not a spontaneous reversion to orthodoxy any more than a surrender of the doctrine of Newton, but a general turning of attention in other directions. It is significant that the most important names in the literature of deism after 1740 are those of Hume and Smith, late products of the intellectual atmosphere of pre-industrial Scotland ; of Bolingbroke, an aristocrat of the deistic generation, long an exile in France, who left his works to be published after his death ; and of Gibbon, who also breathed the intellectual air of France.

§ 3.

It is commonly assumed that after Chubb and Morgan the deistic movement in England "decayed," or "passed into skepticism" with Hume ; and that the decay was mainly owing to the persuasive effect of Bishop Butler's *Analogy* (1736).[1] This appears to be a complete misconception, arising out of the habit of looking to the succession of books without considering the accompanying social conditions. Butler's book had very little influence till long after his death,[2] being indeed very ill-fitted to turn contemporary deists to Christianity. It does but develop one form of the skeptical argument for faith, as Berkeley had developed another ; and that form of reasoning never does attain to anything better than a success of despair. The main argument being that natural religion is open to the same objections as revealed, on the score (1) of the inconsistency of Nature with divine benevolence, and (2) that we must be guided in opinion as in conduct by probability, a Mohammedan could as well use the theorem for the Koran as could a Christian for the Bible ; and the argument against the justice of Nature tended logically to atheism. But the deists had left to them the resource of our modern theists —that of surmising a beneficence above human comprehension ; and it is clear that if Butler made any converts they must have been of a very unenthusiastic kind. It is therefore safe to say with Pattison that " To whatever

---

[1] Sir James Stephen, *Horæ Sabbaticæ*, ii, 281 ; Lechler, p. 451.
[2] See details in *Dynamics of Religion*, ch. viii.

causes is to be attributed the decline of deism from 1750 onwards, the books polemically written against it cannot be reckoned among them."[1]

On the other hand, even deists who were affected by the plea that the Bible need not be more consistent and satisfactory than Nature, could find refuge in Unitarianism, a creed which, as industriously propounded by Priestley[2] towards the end of the century, made a numerical progress out of all proportion to that of orthodoxy. The argument of William Law,[3] again, which insisted on the irreconcilability of the course of things with human reason, and called for an abject submission to revelation, could appeal only to minds already thus prostrate. Both his and Butler's methods, in fact, prepared the way for HUME. And in the year 1741, five years after the issue of the *Analogy,* and seven before the issue of Hume's *Essay on Miracles,* we find the thesis of that essay tersely affirmed in a note to Book II of an anonymous translation (ascribed to T. FRANCKLIN) of Cicero's *De Natura Deorum.*

> The passage is worth comparing with Hume : " Hence we see what little credit ought to be paid to facts said to be done out of the ordinary course of nature. These miracles [cutting the whetstone, etc., told by Cicero, *De Div.* i, c. xvii] are well attested. They were recorded in the annals of a great people, believed by many learned and otherwise sagacious persons, and received as religious truths by the populace; but the testimonies of ancient records, the credulity of some learned men, and the implicit faith of the vulgar, can never prove that

---

[1] Essay on "Tendencies of Religious Thought in England: 1688-1750," in *Essays and Reviews,* 9th ed. p. 304.

[2] In criticising whom Sir Leslie Stephen barely notices his scientific work, but dwells much on his religious fallacies, a course which would make short work of the fame of Newton.

[3] In his *Case of Reason : or, Natural Religion Fully and Fairly Stated,* in answer to Tindal (1732). See the argument set forth by Sir Leslie Stephen, i, 158-163. It is noteworthy, however, that in his *Spirit of Prayer* (1750) Part II, Dial. i, Law expressly argues that " No other religion can be right but that which has its foundation in Nature. For the God of Nature can require nothing of his creatures but what the state of their nature calls them to." Like Baxter, Berkeley, Butler, and so many other orthodox polemists, Law uses the argument from ignorance when it suits him, and ignores or rejects it when used by others.

to have been, which is impossible in the nature of things ever to be." *M. Tullius Cicero Of the Nature of the Gods*......with Notes, London, 1741, p. 85.

What Hume did was to elaborate the skeptical argument with a power and fulness which forced attention once for all, alike in England and on the Continent. It is not to be supposed, however, that Hume's philosophy, in so far as it was strictly skeptical—that is, suspensory —drew away deists from their former attitude of confidence to one of absolute doubt. Nor did Hume ever aim at such a result. What he did was to countermine the minds of Berkeley and others, who, finding their supra-rational dogmas set aside by rationalism, deistic or atheistic, sought to discredit at once deistic and atheistic philosophies based on study of the external world, and to establish their creed anew on the basis of their subjective consciousness. As against that method, Hume showed the futility of all apriorism alike, destroying the sham skepticism of the Christian theists by forcing their method to its conclusions; but, knowing that strict skepticism is practically null in life, he counted on leaving the ground cleared for experiential rationalism. And he did, in so far as he was read. His essay, *Of Miracles* (with the rest of the *Inquiries* of 1748-51, which recast his early *Treatise of Human Nature,* 1739), posits a principle valid against all supernaturalism whatever; while his *Natural History of Religion* (1757), though affirming deism, rejected the theory of a primordial monotheism, and laid the basis of the science of Comparative Hierology.[1] Finally, his posthumous *Dialogues Concerning Natural Religion* (1779) admit, though indirectly, the untenableness of deism, and fall back decisively upon the atheistic or agnostic position. Like Descartes, he lacked the heroic fibre; but like him

[1] The general reader should take note that in A. Murray's issue of Hume's Essays (now or lately published by Ward, Lock, & Co.), which omits altogether the essays on Miracles and a Future State, the *Natural History of Religion* is much mutilated, though the book professes to be a verbatim reprint.

he recast philosophy for modern Europe; and its subsequent course is but a development of or a reaction against his work.

§ 4.

It is remarkable that this development of opinion took place in that part of the British Islands where religious fanaticism had gone furthest, and speech and thought were socially least free. Freethought in Scotland before the middle of the seventeenth century can have existed only as a thing furtive and accursed; and though, as we have seen from the *Religio Stoici* of Sir George Mackenzie, unbelief had emerged in some abundance at or before the Restoration, only wealthy men could dare openly to avow their deism.[1] In 1697 the clergy had actually succeeded in getting a lad of eighteen, Thomas Aikenhead, hanged for professing deism in general, and in particular for calling the Old Testament "Ezra's Fables," and denying the divinity of Jesus, though he broke down and pleaded penitence.[2] At this date the clergy were hounding on the Privy Council to new activity in trying witches; and all works of supposed heretical tendency imported from England were confiscated in the Edinburgh shops, among them being Thomas Burnet's *Sacred Theory of the Earth*.[3] Scottish intellectual development had in fact been arrested by the Reformation, so that, save for Napier's *Logarithms* (1614) and such a political treatise as Rutherford's *Lex Rex* (1644), the nation of Dunbar and Lyndsay produced for two centuries no secular literature of the least value, and not even a theology of any enduring interest. Deism, accordingly, seems in the latter half of the seventeenth and the early part of the eighteenth century

---

[1] See Burton, *Hist. of Scotland*, viii, 549-50, as to the case of Pitcairne.
[2] Macaulay, *History*, ch. xxii; student's ed. ii. 620-1; Burton, *History of Scotland*, viii, 76-77. Aikenhead seems to have been a boy of unusual capacity, even by the bullying account of Macaulay. See his arguments on the bases of ethics, set forth in his "dying speech," as cited by Halyburton, *Natural Religion Insufficient*, 1714, pp. 119-123, 131.
[3] Macaulay, as cited.

to have made fully as much progress in Scotland as in England; and the bigoted clergy could offer little intellectual resistance.

> As early as 1696 the Scottish Parliament passed an Act "against the Atheistical opinions of the Deists." (Macaulay, ch. xxii; Cunningham, *Hist. of the Ch. of Scotland*, ii, 313.) Sir W. Anstruther (a judge in the Court of Session), in the preface to his *Essays Moral and Divine*, Edinburgh, 1710, speaks of "the spreading contagion of *atheism*, which threatens the ruin of our excellent and holy religion." To atheism he devotes two essays; and neither in these nor in one on the Incarnation does he discuss deism, the arguments he handles being really atheistic. Scottish freethought seems thus to have gone further than English at the period in question. As to the prevalence of deism, however, see the posthumous work of Professor Halyburton, of St. Andrews, *Natural Religion Insufficient* (Edinburgh, 1714), Epist. of Recom.; pref. pp. 25, 27, and pp. 8, 15, 19, 23, 31, etc. Halyburton's treatise is interesting as showing the psychological state of argumentative Scotch orthodoxy in his day. He professes to repel the deistical argument throughout by reason; he follows Huet and concurs with Berkeley in contending that mathematics involves anti-rational assumptions; and he takes entire satisfaction in the execution of the lad Aikenhead for deism. Yet in a second treatise, *An Essay Concerning the Nature of Faith*, he contends, as against Locke and the "Rationalists," that the power to believe in the word of God is "expressly deny'd to man in his natural estate," and is a supernatural gift. Thus the Calvinists, like Baxter, were at bottom absolutely insincere in their profession to act upon reason, while insolently charging insincerity on others.

Even apart from deism there had arisen a widespread aversion to dogmatic theology and formal creeds, so that an apologist of 1715 speaks of his day as "a time when creeds and Confessions of Faith are so generally decried, and not only exposed to contempt, as useless inventions but are loaded by many writers of distinguished wit and learning with the most fatal and dangerous consequences."[1] This writer admits the intense bitterness

---

[1] *A Full Account of the Several Ends and Uses of Confessions of Faith*, first published in 1719 as a preface to a Collection of Confessions of Faith, by Professor W. Dunbar, of Edinburgh University, 3rd ed. 1775, p. 1.

of the theological disputes of the time;[1] and he speaks, on the other hand, of seeing "the most sacred mysteries of godliness impudently denied and impugned" by some, while the "distinguishing doctrines of Christianity are by others treacherously undermined, subtilised into an airy phantom, or at least doubted, if not disclaimed."[2] His references are probably to works published in England, notably those of Locke, Toland, Shaftesbury, and Collins, since in Scotland no such literature could be published; but he doubtless has an eye to Scottish opinion.

While, however, the rationalism of the time could not take book form, there are clear traces of its existence among educated men, even apart from the general complaints of the apologists. Thus the Professor of Medicine at Glasgow University in the opening years of the eighteenth century, John Johnston, was a known freethinker.[3] In the way of moderate or Christian rationalism, the teaching of the prosecuted Simson seems to have counted for something, seeing that Francis Hutcheson at least imbibed from him "liberal" views about future punishment and the salvation of the heathen, which gave much offence in the Presbyterian pulpit in Ulster.[4] And Hutcheson's later vindication of the ethical system of Shaftesbury in his *Inquiry Concerning the Ideas of Beauty and Virtue* (1725) must have tended to attract attention in Scotland to the *Characteristics* after his instalment as a Professor at Glasgow. In an English pamphlet, in 1732, he was satirised as introducing Shaftesbury's system into a University,[5] and it is from the Shaftesbury camp that the first literary expression of freethought in Scotland was sent forth. A young Scotch deist of that school, William Dudgeon, published

---
[1] Work cited, p. 48.   [2] *Id.* p. 198.
[3] *Scotland and Scotsmen in the Eighteenth Century.* From the MSS. of John Ramsay, of Ochtertyre, 1888, i, 277. Ramsay describes Johnston as a "joyous, manly, honourable man," of whom Kames "was exceedingly fond" (p. 278).
[4] W. R. Scott, *Francis Hutcheson*, 1900, pp. 15, 20–21.
[5] *Id.* p. 52.

in 1732 a dialogue entitled *The State of the Moral World Considered*, wherein the optimistic position was taken up with uncommon explicitness; and in 1739 the same writer printed *A Catechism Founded upon Experience and Reason*, prefaced by an Introductory Letter on Natural Religion, which takes a distinctly anti-clerical attitude. The *Catechism* answers to its title, save in so far as it is a priori in its theism and optimistic in its ethic, as is another work of its author in the same year, *A View of the Necessarian or Best Scheme*, defending the Shaftesburyan doctrine against the criticism of Crousaz on Pope's *Essay*. Still more heterodox is his little volume of *Philosophical Letters Concerning the Being and Attributes of God* (1737), where the doctrine goes far towards pantheism. All this propaganda seems to have elicited only one printed reply—an attack on his first treatise in 1732. In the letter prefaced to his *Catechism*, however, he tells that "the bare suspicion of my not believing the opinions in fashion in our country hath already caused me sufficient trouble."[1] His case had in fact been raised in the church courts, the proceedings going through many stages in the years 1732-6; but in the end no decision was taken,[2] and the special stress of his rationalism in 1739 doubtless owes something alike to the prosecution and to its collapse. Despite such hostility, he must privately have had fair support.[3]

The prosecution of Hutcheson before the Glasgow Presbytery in 1738 reveals vividly the theological temper of the time. He was indicted for teaching to his students "the following two false and dangerous doctrines: first, that the standard of moral goodness was the promotion of the happiness of others; and,

[1] Cp. Alberti, *Briefe betreffend den Zustand der Religion in Gross-Brittannien*, 1752, pp. 430-1.
[2] See Dr. McCosh's *Scottish Philosophy*, 1875, pp. 111-113. Dr. McCosh notes that at some points Dudgeon anticipated Hume.
[3] Dr. McCosh, however, admits that the absence of the printer's name on the 1765 edition of Dudgeon's works shows that there was then no thorough freedom of thought in Scotland.

second, that we could have a knowledge of good and evil without and prior to a knowledge of God."[1] There has been a natural disposition on the orthodox side to suppress the fact that such teachings were ever ecclesiastically denounced as false, dangerous, and irreligious; and the prosecution seems to have had no effect beyond intensifying the devotion of Hutcheson's students, among whom was Adam Smith. Another prosecution soon afterwards showed that the new influences were vitally affecting thought within the church itself. Hutcheson's friend Leechman, whom he and his party contrived to elect as professor of theology in Glasgow University, was in turn prosecuted (1743-4) for a published sermon on Prayer, which Hutcheson and his sympathisers pronounced " noble,"[2] but which " resolved the efficacy of prayer into its reflex influence on the mind of the worshipper "[3]—a theorem which has chronically made its appearance in the Scottish church ever since, still ranking as a heresy, after having brought a clerical prosecution in the last generation on at least one divine, Professor William Knight, and rousing a scandal against another, the late Dr. Robert Wallace.[4]

Leechman in turn held his ground, and later became Principal of his University; but still the orthodox in Scotland fought bitterly against every semblance of rationalism. Even the anti-deistic essays of Lord-President Forbes of Culloden, head of the Court of Session, when collected and published after his death in 1747, were offensive to the church as laying undue stress on reason; as accepting the heterodox Biblical theories of Dr. John Hutchinson; and as making the awkward admission that " the freethinkers, with all their

---

[1] Rae, *Life of Adam Smith*, 1895, p. 13. Professor Fowler shows no knowledge of this prosecution in his monograph on Hutcheson (*Shaftesbury and Hutcheson*, 1882); and Mr. W. R. Scott, in his, seems to rely for the wording of the indictment solely on Mr. Rae, who gives no references.

[2] Scott, as cited, p. 87.

[3] Dr. James Orr, *David Hume and his Influence on Philosophy and Theology*, 1903, pp. 36-37.

[4] Also for a time a theological professor in Edinburgh University.

perversity, generally are sensible of the social duties, and act up to them better than others do who in other respects think more justly than they."[1] Such an utterance from such a dignitary told of a profound change; and, largely through the influence of Hutcheson and Leechman on a generation of students, the educated Scotland of the latter half of the eighteenth century was in large part either "Moderate" or deistic. After generations of barren controversy,[2] the very aridity of the Presbyterian life intensified the recoil among the educated classes to philosophical and historical interests, leading to the performances of Hume, Smith, Robertson, Millar, Ferguson, and yet others, all rationalists in method and sociologists in their interests.

Of these, Millar was known to be skeptical in a high degree;[3] while Smith and Ferguson were certainly deists, as was Henry Home (the judge, Lord Kames), who had the distinction of being attacked along with his friend Hume in the General Assembly of the Church of Scotland in 1755-56. Home wrote expressly to controvert Hume, alike as to utilitarianism and the idea of causation; but his book, *Essays on Morality and Natural Religion* (published anonymously, 1751), handled the thorny question of freewill in such fashion as to give no less offence than Hume had done; and the orthodox bracketed him with the subject of his criticism. His doctrine was indeed singular, its purport being that there can be no freewill, but that the deity has for wise purposes implanted in men the feeling that their wills are free. The fact of his having been made a judge of the Court of Session since writing his book had probably something to do with the rejection of the whole subject by the General Assembly,

---

[1] *Reflections on Incredulity*, in *Works*, 1747, ii, 141-2.
[2] As to which see *A Sober Enquiry into the Grounds of the Present Differences in the Church of Scotland*, 1723.
[3] See the *Autobiography of the Rev. Dr. A. Carlyle*, 1860, pp. 492-3. Millar's *Historical View of the English Government* (censured by Hallam) was once much esteemed; and his *Origin of Ranks* is still worth the attention of sociologists.

and afterwards by the Edinburgh Presbytery; but there had evidently arisen a certain diffidence in the church, which would be assiduously promoted by "moderates" such as Principal Robertson, the historian. It is noteworthy that while Home and Hume thus escaped, the other Home, John, who wrote the then admired tragedy of *Douglas*, was soon after forced to resign his position as a minister of the church for that authorship, deism having apparently more friends in the fold than drama.[1] While the theatre was thus being treated as a place of sin, many of the churches in Scotland were the scenes of repeated Sunday riots. A new manner of psalm-singing had been introduced, and it frequently happened that the congregations divided into two parties, each singing in its own way, till they came to blows. According to one of Hume's biographers, unbelievers were at this period wont to go to church to see the fun.[2] Naturally orthodoxy did not gain ground.

In Ireland, at least in Dublin, during the earlier part of the century, there occurred, on a smaller scale, a similar movement of rationalism, also largely associated with Shaftesbury. In Dublin towards the close of the seventeenth century we have seen Molyneux, the friend and correspondent of Locke, interested in "freethought," albeit much scared by the imprudence of Toland. In the next generation we find in the same city a coterie of Shaftesburyans, centring around Lord Molesworth, the friend of Hutcheson, a man of affairs devoted to intellectual interests. It was within a few years of his meeting Molesworth that Hutcheson produced his *Inquiry*, championing Shaftesbury's ideas;[3] and other literary men were similarly influenced. It is even suggested that Hutcheson's clerical friend Synge, whom we have seen[4] in 1713 attempting a ratiocinative answer

---

[1] Ritchie's *Account of the Life and Writings of David Hume*, 1807, pp. 52-81; Tytler's *Memoirs of the Life and Writings of Lord Kames*, 2nd ed. 1814, vol. i, ch. 5; Burton's *Life of David Hume*, 1846, i, 425-430.   [2] Ritchie, as cited, p. 57.
[3] W. R. Scott, *Francis Hutcheson*, p. 31.
[4] Above, p. 134, *note*.

to the unbelief he declared to be abundant around him, was not only influenced by Shaftesbury through Molesworth, but latterly "avoided publication lest his opinions should prejudice his career in the Church."[1] After the death of Molesworth, in 1725, the movement he set up seems to have languished ;[2] but, as we have seen, there were among the Irish bishops men given to philosophic controversy, and the influence of Berkeley cannot have been wholly obscurantist. When in 1756 we read of the Arian Bishop Clayton[3] proposing in the Irish House of Lords to drop the Nicene and Athanasian creeds, we realise that in Ireland thought was far from stagnant. The heretic bishop, however, died (February, 1758) just as he was about to be prosecuted for the heresies of his *Vindication of the Old and New Testaments* (2nd ed. 1757) ; and thenceforth Ireland plays no noticeable part in the development of rationalism, political interests soon taking the place of religious, with the result that orthodoxy recovered its ground.

§ 5.

In England, meanwhile, there was beginning a redistribution of energies which can be seen to have prepared for the intellectual and political reaction of the end of the century. There had been no such victory of

---

[1] Scott, pp. 28-29, 35-36. The suggestion is not quite convincing. Synge, after becoming Archbishop of Tuam, continued to publish his propagandist tracts, among them *An Essay towards Making the Knowledge of Religion Easy to the Meanest Capacity* (6th ed. 1734), which is quite orthodox, and which argues (p. 3) that the doctrine of the Trinity is to be believed and not pried into, "because it is above our understanding to comprehend." All the while there was being sold also his early treatise, "*A Gentleman's Religion : in Three Parts*......with an Appendix, wherein it is proved that nothing contrary to our Reason can possibly be the object of our belief, but that it is no just exception against some of the doctrines of Christianity that they are above our reason."

[2] Scott, p. 36.

[3] All that is told of this prelate by Mr. Lecky (*Hist. of Ireland in the 18th Cent.* 1892, i, 207) is that at Killala he patronised horse-races. He was industrious on more episcopal lines. He wrote an Introduction to the History of the Jews ; a Vindication of Biblical Chronology ; two treatises on prophecy ; an "Essay on Spirit" (1751), which aroused much controversy ; two volumes in answer to Bolingbroke (1752-54), which led to his being prosecuted ; and other works.

faith as is supposed to have been wrought by the forensic theorem of Butler. An orthodox German observer, making a close inquest about 1750, cites the *British Magazine* as stating in 1749 that half the educated people were then deists ; and he, after full inquiry, agrees.[1] In the same year, Richardson speaks tragically in the Postscriptum to *Clarissa Harlowe* of seeing "skepticism and infidelity openly avowed and *even* endeavoured to be propagated from the press ; the great doctrines of the gospel brought into question ;" and he describes himself as "seeking to steal in with a disguised plea for religion." Instead of being destroyed by the clerical defence, the deistic movement had really penetrated the church, which was become as rationalistic in its methods as its function would permit, and the educated classes, which had arrived at a state of compromise. The academic Conyers Middleton, whose *Letter from Rome* had told so heavily against Christianity in exposing the pagan derivations of much of Catholicism, had further damaged the doctrine of inspiration in his anonymous *Letter to Dr. Waterland* (1731), while professing to refute Tindal ; and in his famous *Free Inquiry* into the miracles of post-apostolic Christianity (1749), again professing to strike at Rome, he had laid the foundations of a new structure of comparative criticism, and had given fresh grounds for rejecting the miracles of the sacred books. In short, the deistic movement had done what it lay in it to do. The old evangelical or pietistic view of life was discredited among instructed people, and in this sense it was Christianity that had "decayed."

> Thus Skelton writes in 1751 that "our modern apologists for Christianity often defend it on deistical principles" (*Deism Revealed*, pref. p. xii). Cp. vol. ii, pp. 234, 237. Also Sir Leslie Stephen as cited above, p. 129, *note ;* and Gostwick, *German Culture and Christianity*, 1882, pp. 33-36. .
> An interesting instance of liberalising orthodoxy is furnished

[1] Dr. G. W. Alberti, *Briefe betreffende den Zustand der Religion in Gross-Brittannien*, Hannover, 1752, p. 440.

by the Rev. Arthur Ashley Sykes, who contributed many volumes to the general deistic discussion, some of them anonymously. In the preface to his *Essay on the Truth of the Christian Religion* (1732; 2nd ed. enlarged, 1755) Sykes remarks that "since...... systematical opinions have been received and embraced in such a manner that it has not been safe to contradict them, the burden of vindicating Christianity has been very much increased. Its friends have been much embarrassed through fear of speaking against *local truths;* and its adversaries have so successfully attacked those weaknesses that Christianity itself has been deemed indefensible, when in reality the follies of Christians alone have been so." Were Christians left to the simple doctrines of Christ and the Apostles, he contends, Infidelity could make no converts. And at the close of the book he writes: "Would to God that Christians would be content with the plainness and simplicity of the gospel.......That they would not vend under the name of evangelical truth the absurd and contradictory schemes of ignorant or wicked men! That they would part with that load of rubbish which makes thinking men almost sink under the weight, and gives too great a handle for Infidelity!" Such writing could not give satisfaction to the ecclesiastical authorities; and as little could Sykes's remarkable admission (*The Principles and Connection of Natural and Revealed Religion*, 1740, p. 242): "When the advantages of revelation are to be specified, I cannot conceive that it should be maintained as necessary to *fix a rule of morality.* For what one principle of morality is there which the heathen moralists had not asserted or maintained? Before ever any revelation is offered to mankind they are supposed to be so well acquainted with moral truths as from them to judge of the truth of the revelation itself." Again he writes: —

"Nor can revelation be necessary to *ascertain religion.* For religion consisting in nothing but doing our duties from a sense of the being of God, revelation is not necessary to this end, unless it be said that we cannot know that there is a God, and what our duties are, without it. *Reason* will teach us that there is a *God* that we are to be just and charitable to our neighbours; that we are to be temperate and sober in ourselves" (*Id.* p. 244).

This is simple Shaftesburyan deism, and all that the apologist goes on to contend for is that revelation "contains *motives* and *reasons* for the practice of what is right, more and different from what natural reason without this help can suggest." He seems, however, to have believed in miracles, though an anonymous *Essay on the Nature, Design, and Origin of Sacrifices* (1748), which is ascribed to him quietly undermines the whole evangelical doctrine. Throughout, he is remarkable for the amenity of his tone towards "infidels."

The next intellectual step in natural course would have been a revision of the deistic assumptions, in so far, that is, as certain positive assumptions were common to the deists. But, as we have seen, certain fresh issues were raised as among the deists themselves. In addition to those above noted, there was the profoundly important one as to ethics. Shaftesbury, who rejected the religious basis, held a creed of optimism ; and this optimism was assailed by Mandeville, who in consequence was opposed as warmly by the deist Hutcheson and others as by Law and Berkeley. To grapple with this problem, and with the underlying cosmic problem, there was needed at least as much general mental activity as went to the antecedent discussion ; and the main activity of the nation was now being otherwise directed. The negative process, the impeachment of Christian supernaturalism, had been accomplished so far as the current arguments went. Toland and Collins had fought the battle of free discussion, forcing ratiocination on the church ; Collins had shaken the creed of prophecy ; Shaftesbury had impugned the religious conception of morals ; and Mandeville had done so more profoundly, laying the foundations of scientific utilitarianism.[1] So effective had been the utilitarian propaganda in general that the orthodox Brown (author of the once famous *Estimate* of the life of his countrymen), in his criticism of Shaftesbury (1751), wrote as a pure utilitarian against an inconsistent one, and defended Christianity on strictly utilitarian lines. Woolston, following up Collins, had shaken the faith in New Testament miracles ; Middleton had done it afresh with all the decorum that Woolston lacked ; and Hume had laid down with masterly clearness the philosophic principle which rebuts all attempts to prove miracles as such.[2] Tindal had clinched the

[1] Cp. essay on *The Fable of the Bees* in the author's *Essays towards a Critical Method*, 1889.
[2] As against the objections of Mr. Lang, see the author's paper in *Studies in Religious Fallacy*.

case for "natural" theism as against revelationism; and the later deists, notably Morgan, had to some extent combined these results.[1] This literature was generally distributed; and so far the case had been thrashed out.

To carry intellectual progress much further there was needed a general movement of scientific study and a reform in education. The translation of La Mettrie's *Man a Machine* (1750) found a public no better prepared for the problems he raised than that addressed by Strutt eighteen years before; and his reply to himself, *Man More than a Machine*, of which the translator (1752) declared in his preface that "religion and infidelity overspread the land," probably satisfied what appetite there was for such a discussion. There had begun a change in the prevailing mental life, a diversion of interest from ideas as such to political and mercantile interests. The middle and latter part of the eighteenth century is the period of the rise of (1) the new machine industries, and (2) the new imperialistic policy of Chatham.[2] Both alike withdrew men from problems of mere belief, whether theological or scientific. That the reaction was not one of mere fatigue over deism we have already seen. It was a general diversion of energy, analogous to what had previously taken place in France in the reign of Louis XIV. As the poet Gray, himself orthodox, put the case in 1754, "the mode of freethinking has given place to the mode of not thinking at all."[3] In Hume's opinion the general pitch of national intelligence south of the Tweed was lowered.[4] This state of things of course was favourable to religious revival; but what took place was rather a new growth of emotional pietism in the new industrial masses (the population being now

---

[1] Cp. the summary of Farrar, *Critical History of Freethought*, 1862, pp. 177-8, which is founded on that of Pusey's early *Historical Enquiry concerning the causes of German Rationalism*, pp. 124-126.
[2] The point is further discussed in *Dynamics of Religion*, pp. 175-6.
[3] Letter xxxi, in Mason's *Memoir*.
[4] Letters to Smith, Elliot, and Gibbon. Hill Burton's *Life of Hume*, ii, 433, 434, 484-5, 487.

on a rapid increase), under the ministry of the Wesleys and Whitfield, and a further growth of similar religion in the new provincial middle-class that grew up on the industrial basis. The universities all the while were at the lowest ebb of culture, but officially rabid against philosophic freethinking.[1]

It would be a great mistake, however, to suppose that all this meant a dying out of deism among the educated classes. The statement of Goldsmith, about 1760, that deists in general "have been driven into a confession of the necessity of revelation, or an open avowal of atheism,"[2] is not to be taken seriously. Goldsmith, whose own orthodoxy is very doubtful, had a whimsical theory that skepticism, though it might not injure morals, has a "manifest tendency to subvert the literary merits" of any country;[3] and argued accordingly. Deism, remaining fashionable, did but fall partly into the background of living interests, the more concrete issues of politics and the new imaginative literature occupying the foreground. The literary status of deism after 1750 was really higher than ever. It was now represented by Hume; by ADAM SMITH (*Moral Sentiments*, 1759); by the scholarship of Conyers Middleton; and by the posthumous works (1754) of Lord BOLINGBROKE, who, albeit more of a debater than a thinker, debated with masterly power, in a style unmatched for harmony and energetic grace, which had already won him a great literary prestige, though the visible insincerity of his character always countervailed his charm. His influence, commonly belittled, was much greater than writers like Johnson would admit; and it

[1] Compare the verdicts of Gibbon in his *Autobiography*, and of Adam Smith, *Wealth of Nations*, B. v, ch. i, art. 2; and see the memoir of Smith in 1831 ed. and McCulloch's ed., and Rae's *Life of Adam Smith*, 1895, p. 24. It appears that about 1764 many English people sent their sons to Edinburgh University on account of the better education there. Letter of Blair, in Hill Burton's *Life of Hume*, ii, 229.
[2] *Essays*, iv, end.
[3] *Present State of Polite Learning*, 1765, ch. vi. His story of how the father of St. Foix cured the youth of the desire to rationalise his creed is not suggestive of conviction. The father pointed to a crucifix, saying, "Behold the fate of a reformer." The story has been often plagiarised since—*e.g.*, in Galt's *Annals of the Parish*.

went deep. Voltaire tells[1] that he had known some young pupils of Bolingbroke who altogether denied the historic actuality of the Gospel Jesus — a stretch of criticism beyond the assimilative power of that age.

In his lifetime, however, Bolingbroke had been extremely careful to avoid compromising himself. Mr. Arthur Hassall, in his generally excellent monograph on Bolingbroke (Statesmen Series: Allen & Co. 1889, p. 226), writes, in answer to the attack of Johnson, that "Bolingbroke, during his lifetime, had never scrupled to publish criticisms, remarkable for their freedom, on religious subjects." I cannot gather to what he refers; and Mr. Walter Sichel, in his copious biography (2 vols. 1901-2), indicates no such publications. In his letter to Swift of September 12th, 1724 (*Swift's Works*, Scott's ed. 1824, xvi. 448-9), Bolingbroke angrily repudiates the title of *esprit fort*, declaring, in the very temper in which pious posterity has aspersed himself, that "such are the pests of society, because they endeavour to loosen the bands of it........I therefore not only disown, but I detest, this character." In this letter he even affects to believe in "the truth of the divine revelation of Christianity." He began to write his essays, it is true, before his withdrawal to France in 1735, but with no intention of speedily publishing them. In his *Letter to Mr. Pope* (published with the *Letter to Wyndham*, 1753), p. 481, he writes: "I have been a martyr of faction in politics, and have no vocation to be so in philosophy." Cp. pp. 485-6. It is thus a complete blunder on the part of Bagehot to say (*Literary Studies*, Hutton's ed. iii, 137) that Butler's *Analogy*, published in 1736, was "designed as a confutation of Shaftesbury *and Bolingbroke*" It is even said (Warton, *Essay on Pope*, 4th ed. ii, 294-5) that Pope did not know Bolingbroke's real opinions; but Pope's untruthfulness was such as to discredit such a statement. Cp. Bolingbroke's *Letter* as cited, p. 521, and his *Philosophical Works*, 8vo-ed. 1754, ii, 405.

In seeking to estimate Bolingbroke's posthumous influence we have to remember that after the publication of his works the orthodox members of his own party, who otherwise would have forgiven him all his vices and insincerities, have held him up to hatred. Scott, for instance, founding on Bolingbroke's own dishonest denunciation of freethinkers as men seeking to loosen the bands of society, pronounced his arrangement for the posthumous issue of his works "an act of wickedness more purely diabolical than any hitherto upon record in the history of any age or nation" (Note to Bolingbroke's letter above cited in

---

[1] *Dieu et les Hommes*, ch. 39.

Swift's Works, xvi, 450). It would be an error, on the other hand, to class him among either the great sociologists or the great philosophers. Mr. Sichel undertakes to show (vol. ii, ch. x) that Bolingbroke had stimulated Gibbon to a considerable extent in his treatment of early Christianity. This is in itself quite probable, and some of the parallels cited are noteworthy; but Mr. Sichel, who always writes as a panegyrist, makes no attempt to trace the common French sources for both. He does show that Voltaire manipulated Bolingbroke's opinions in reproducing them. But he does not critically recognise the incoherence of Bolingbroke's eloquent treatises. Mr. Hassall's summary is nearer the truth; but that in turn does not note how well fitted was Bolingbroke's swift and graceful declamation to do its work with the general public, which (if it accepted him at all) would make small account of self-contradiction.

In view of such a reinforcement of its propaganda, deism could not be regarded as in the least degree written down. In 1765, accordingly, we find Diderot recounting, on the authority of d'Holbach, who had just returned from a visit to this country, that "the Christian religion is nearly extinct in England. The deists are innumerable; there are almost no atheists; those who are so, conceal it. An atheist and a scoundrel are almost synonymous terms for them."[1] Nor did the output of deistic literature end with the posthumous works of Bolingbroke. These were followed by translations of the new writings of VOLTAIRE,[2] who had assimilated the whole propaganda of English deism, and gave it out anew with a wit and brilliancy hitherto unknown in argumentative and critical literature. The freethinking of the third quarter of the century, though kept secondary to more pressing questions, was thus at least as deeply rooted and as convinced as that of the first quarter.

What was lacking to it, once more, was a social foundation on which it could not only endure but develop. In a nation of which the majority had no intellectual culture, such a foundation could not exist.

---

[1] *Mémoires de Diderot*, 1841, ii, 25.
[2] These had begun as early as 1753 (*Micromégas*).

Green exaggerates[1] when he writes that "schools there were none, save the grammar schools of Edward and Elizabeth ";[2] but by another account only twelve public schools were founded in the long reign of George III ;[3] and, as a result of the indifference of two generations, masses of the people "were ignorant and brutal to a degree which it is hard to conceive."[4] A great increase of population had followed on the growth of towns and the development of commerce and manufactures even between 1700 and 1760 ;[5] and thereafter the multiplication was still more rapid. There was thus a positive fall in the culture standards of the majority of the people. According to Massey, "hardly any tradesman in 1760 had more instruction than qualified him to add up a bill"; and "a labourer, mechanic, or domestic servant who could read or write possessed a rare accomplishment."[6] As for the Charity Schools established between 1700 and 1750, their express object was to rear humble tradesmen and domestics, not to educate in the proper sense of the term.

In the view of life which accepted this state of things the educated deists seem to have shared ; at least, there is no record of any agitation by them for betterment. The state of political thought was typified in the struggle over "Wilkes and Liberty," from which conservative temperaments like Hume's turned away in contempt ; and it is significant that poor men were persecuted for freethinking while the better-placed went

---

[1] I here extract a few sentences from my paper on *The Church and Education*, 1903.
[2] *Short History*, ed. 1881, p. 717. The *Concise Description of the Endowed Grammar Schools*, by Nicholas Carlisle, 1818, shows that schools were founded in all parts of the country by private bequest or public action in all periods since the seventeenth century.
[3] Collis, in *Transactions of the Social Science Association*, 1857, p. 126. According to Collis, 48 had been founded by James I, 28 under Charles I, 16 under the Commonwealth, 36 under Charles II, 4 under James II, 7 under William and Mary, 11 under Anne, 17 under George I, and 7 under George II. He does not indicate their size.
[4] Green, as last cited.
[5] Gibbins, *Industrial History of England*, 1894, p. 151.
[6] *Hist. of England under George III*, ed. 1865, ii, 83.

free. JACOB ILIVE, for denying in a pamphlet (1753) the truth of revelation, was pilloried thrice, and sent to hard labour for three years. In 1754 the Grand Jury of Middlesex "presented" the editor and publisher of Bolingbroke's posthumous works[1]—a distinction that in the previous generation had been bestowed on Mandeville's *Fable of the Bees;* and in 1761, as before noted, Peter Annet, aged seventy, was pilloried twice and sent to prison for discrediting the Pentateuch. The personal influence of George III, further, told everywhere against freethinking; and the revival of penalties would have checked publishing even if there had been no withdrawal of interest to politics.

> Yet freethinking treatises did appear at intervals in addition to the works of the better-known writers, such as Bolingbroke and Hume, after the period commonly marked as that of the "decline of deism." Like a number of the earlier works above mentioned, the following (save Evanson) are overlooked in Sir Leslie Stephen's survey:—
>
> 1746. *Essay on Natural Religion.* Attributed to Dryden.
> 1746. *Deism fairly stated and fully vindicated,* etc. Anon.
> 1749. Cooper, J. G. *Life of Socrates.*
> 1750. Dove, John. *A Creed founded on Truth and Common Sense.*
> ,,   *The British Oracle.* Two numbers only.
> 1752. *The Pillars of Priestcraft and Orthodoxy Shaken.* Four vols. of freethinking pamphlets, collected (and some written) by Thomas Gordon, formerly secretary to Trenchard. Edited by R. Barron. (Reprinted 1768.)
> 1765. Dudgeon, W. *Philosophical Works* (reprints of those of 1732,-4,-7,-9, above mentioned). Privately printed—at Glasgow?
> 1772. Evanson, E. *The Doctrines of a Trinity and the Incarnation.*
> 1777.   ,,   ,,   *Letter to Bishop Hurd.*
> 1781. Nicholson, W. *The Doubts of the Infidels.* Republished by Carlile.
> 1782. Turner, W. *Answer to Dr. Priestley's Letters to a Philosophical Unbeliever.*
> 1785. Toulmin, Dr. Joshua.[2] *The Antiquity and Duration of the World.*

---

[1] The document is given in Ritchie's *Life of Hume,* 1807, pp. 53-55.
[2] Toulmin was a Unitarian and a biographer of Socinus. He was much molested in 1791.

1789. Toulmin, Dr. Joshua. *The Eternity of the Universe.*
1789. Cooper, Dr. T. *Tracts, Ethical, Theological, and Political.*
1792. Evanson, E. *The Dissonance of the Four Evangelists.*
1795. O'Keefe, Dr. J. A. *On the Progress of the Human Understanding.*
1797. Davies, J. C. *The Scripturian's Creed.* Prosecuted and imprisoned.

On the other hand, apart from the revival of popular religion under Whitefield and Wesley, which won multitudes of the people whom no higher culture could reach, there was no recovery of educated belief upon intellectual lines; though there was a steady detachment of energy to the new activities of conquest and commerce which mark the second half of the eighteenth century in England. On this state of things supervened the massive performance of the greatest historical writer England had yet produced. GIBBON, educated not by Oxford but by the recent scholarly literature of France, had as a mere boy seen, on reading Bossuet, the theoretic weakness of Protestantism, and had straightway professed Romanism. Shaken as to that by a skilled Swiss Protestant, he speedily became a rationalist pure and simple, with as little of the dregs of deism in him as any writer of his age; and his great work begins, or rather signalises (since Hume and Robertson preceded him), a new era of historical writing, not merely by its sociological treatment of the rise of Christianity, but by its absolutely anti-theological handling of all things.

The importance of the new approach may be at once measured by the zeal of the opposition. In no case, perhaps, has the essentially passional character of religious resistance to new thought been more vividly shown than in that of the contemporary attacks upon Gibbon's *History*. By the admission of Macaulay, who thought Gibbon "most unfair" to religion, the whole troop of his assailants are now "utterly forgotten"; and those orthodox commentators who later sought to improve on their criticism have in turn, with a notable uniformity, been rebutted by their successors; till Gibbon's critical section ranks as the first systematically scientific handling of the problem of the rise of Christianity. He can be seen to have profited by all the relevant deistic work done before him, learning alike from Toland, from Middleton, and from Bolingbroke; though his acknowledgments are mostly paid to respectable Protestants and Catholics, as Basnage, Beausobre, Lardner, Mosheim, and Tillemont; and the sheer solidity of the work has sustained it against a hundred years of hostile comment. While Gibbon was thus earning for his country a new literary distinction, the orthodox interest was concerned above all things to convict him of ignorance, incompetence, and dishonesty; and Davis, the one of his assailants who most fully manifested all of these qualities, and who will long be remembered solely from Gibbon's deadly exposure, was rewarded with a royal pension. Another, Apthorp, received an archiepiscopal living; while Chelsum, the one who almost alone wrote against him like a gentleman, got nothing. But no cabal could avail to prevent the instant recognition, at home and abroad, of the advent of a new master in history; and in the worst times of reaction which followed, the *History of the Decline and Fall of the Roman Empire* impassively defied the claims of the ruling creed.

In a world which was eagerly reading Gibbon[1] and Voltaire,[2] there was a peculiar absurdity in Burke's famous question (1790) as to " Who now reads Bolingbroke " and the rest of the older deists.[3] The fashionable world was actually reading Bolingbroke even then;[4] and the work of the older deists was being done with

---

[1] Cp. Bishop Watson's *Apology for Christianity* (1776) as to the vogue of unbelief at that date. (*Two Apologies*, ed. 1806, p. 121. Cp. pp. 179, 399.)

[2] The panegyric on Voltaire delivered at his death by Frederick the Great (November 26th, 1778) was promptly translated into English (1779).

[3] *Reflections on the French Revolution*, 1790, p. 131.

[4] See Hannah More's letter of April, 1777, in her *Life*, abridged 16mo-ed. p. 36. An edition of Shaftesbury, apparently, appeared in 1773, and another in 1790.

new incisiveness and thoroughness by their successors.[1] Beside Burke in Parliament, all the while, was the Prime Minister, WILLIAM PITT the younger, an agnostic deist.

Whether or not the elder Pitt was a deist, the younger gave very plain signs of being at least no more. Mr. Gladstone (*Studies subsidiary to the Works of Bishop Butler*, ed. 1896, pp. 30-33) has sought to discredit the recorded testimony of Wilberforce (*Life of Wilberforce*, 1838, i, 98) that Pitt told him "Bishop Butler's work raised in his mind more doubts than it had answered." Mr. Gladstone points to another passage in Wilberforce's diary which states that Pitt "commended Butler's *Analogy*" (*Life*, i, 90). But the context shows that Pitt had commended the book for the express purpose of turning Wilberforce's mind from its evangelical bias. Wilberforce was never a deist, and the purpose accordingly could not have been to make him orthodox. The two testimonies are thus perfectly consistent; especially when we note the further statement credibly reported to have been made by Wilberforce (*Life*, i, 95), that Pitt later "*tried to reason me out of my convictions.*" We have yet further the emphatic declaration of Pitt's niece, Lady Hester Stanhope, that he "never went to church in his life......never even talked about religion" (*Memoirs of Lady Hester Stanhope*, 1845, iii, 166-7). This was said in emphatic denial of the genuineness of the unctuous death-bed speech put in Pitt's mouth by Gifford. Lady Hester's high veracity is accredited by her physician (*Travels of Lady Hester Stanhope*, 1846, i, pref. p. 11). No such character can be given to the conventional English biography of the period.

We have further to note the circumstantial account by Wilberforce in his letter to the Rev. S. Gisborne immediately after Pitt's death (*Correspondence*, 1840, ii, 69-70), giving the details he had had in confidence from the Bishop of Lincoln. They are to the effect that, after some demur on Pitt's part ("that he was not worthy to offer up any prayer, or was too weak"), the Bishop prayed with him once. Wilberforce adds his "fear" that "no further religious intercourse took place before or after, *and I own I thought what was inserted in the papers impossible to be true.*"

[1] The essays of Hume, including the *Dialogues concerning Natural Religion* (1779), were now circulated in repeated editions. Mr. Rae, in his valuable *Life of Adam Smith*, p. 311, cites a German observer, Wendeborn, as writing in 1785 that the *Dialogues*, though a good deal discussed in Germany, had made no sensation in England, and were at that date entirely forgotten. But a second edition had been called for in 1779, and they were added to a fresh edition of the essays in 1788. Any "forgetting" is to be set down to pre-occupation with other interests.

Among thinking men, too, the nascent science of geology was setting up a new criticism of " revelation "—this twenty years before the issue of the epoch-making works of Hutton.[1] The new phase of "infidelity" was of course furiously denounced, one of the most angry and most absurd of its opponents being the poet Cowper.[2] Still rationalism persisted. Paley, writing in 1786, protests that "Infidelity is now served up in every shape that is likely to allure, surprise, or beguile the imagination, in a fable, a tale, a novel, or a poem, in interspersed or broken hints, remote and oblique surmises, in books of travel, of philosophy, of natural history—in a word, in any form rather than that of a professed and regular disquisition."[3] The orthodox Dr. J. Ogilvie, in the introduction to his *Inquiry into the Causes of the Infidelity and Skepticism of the Times* (1783), begins : "That the opinions of the deists and skeptics have spread more universally during a part of the last century and in the present than at any former æra since the resurrection of letters, is a truth to which the friends and the enemies of religion will give their suffrage without hesitation." In short, until the general reversal of all progress which followed on the French Revolution, there had been no such change of opinion as Burke alleged. One of the most popular writers of the day was ERASMUS DARWIN, a deist, whose *Zoonomia* (1794) brought on him the charge of atheism. Even in rural Scotland, the vogue of the poetry of BURNS, who was substantially a deist, told of germinal doubt.

> With the infelicity in prediction which is so much commoner with him than the "prescience" for which he is praised, Burke announces that the whole deist school "repose in lasting oblivion." The proposition would be much more true of 999 out of every thousand writers on behalf of Christianity. It is characteristic of Burke, however, that he does

---

[1] See a letter in Bishop Watson's *Life*, i, 402 ; and cp. Buckle, ch. vii, *note*, 218.
[2] See his *Task*, B. iii, 150–190 (1783-4), for the prevailing religious tone.
[3] *Principles of Moral Philosophy*, B. v, ch. 9. The whole chapter tells of widespread freethinking.

not name Shaftesbury, a Whig peer of the sacred period. Mr. Lecky, writing in 1865, and advancing on Burke, has said of the whole school, including Shaftesbury, that "the shadow of the tomb rests on all: a deep, unbroken silence, the chill of death, surrounds them. They have long ceased to wake any interest" (*Rationalism in Europe*, i, 116). As a matter of fact, they had been discussed by Tayler in 1853; by Pattison in 1860; and by Farrar in 1862; and they have since been discussed at length by Dr. Hunt, by Cairns, by Lange, and by Sir Leslie Stephen.

A seeming justice was given to Burke's phrase by the undoubted reaction which took place immediately afterwards. In the vast panic which followed on the French Revolution, the multitude of mediocre minds in the middle and upper classes, formerly deistic or indifferent, took fright at unbelief as something now visibly connected with democracy and regicide; and orthodoxy became fashionable on political grounds just as skepticism had become fashionable at the Restoration. Class interest and political prejudice wrought much in both cases; only in opposite directions. Democracy was no longer Bibliolatrous, therefore aristocracy was fain to become so, or at least to grow respectful towards the Church as a means of social control. Gibbon, in his closing years, went with the stream. And as religious wars have always tended to discredit religion, so a war partly associated with the freethinking of the French revolutionists tended to discredit freethought. But even in the height of the revolutionary tumult, and while Burke was blustering about the disappearance of unbelief, THOMAS PAINE was laying deep and wide the English foundations of a new democratic freethought; and the upper-class reaction in the nature of the case was doomed to impermanency, though it was to arrest English intellectual progress for over a generation. The French Revolution had re-introduced freethought as a vital issue, even in causing it to be banned as a danger.

That freethought at the end of the century was rather driven inwards and downwards than expelled is made clear by the multitude of fresh treatises on Christian evidences.

Growing numerous after 1790, they positively swarm for a generation after Paley (1794). Cp. *Essays on the Evidence and Influence of Christianity*, Bath, 1790, pref. ; Andrew Fuller, *The Gospel its own Witness*, 1799, pref. and concluding address to deists ; Watson's sermon of 1795, in *Two Apologies*, ed. 1806, p. 399 ; Priestley's *Memoirs* (written in 1795), 1806, pp. 127-8 ; Wilberforce's *Practical View*, 1797, *passim* (*e.g.*, pp. 366-9, 8th ed. 1841) ; Rev. D. Simpson, *A Plea for Religion...... addressed to the Disciples of Thomas Paine*, 1797. The latter writer states (2nd ed. p. 126) that "infidelity is at this moment running like wildfire among the common people"; and Fuller (2nd ed. p. 128) speaks of the *Monthly Magazine* as "pretty evidently devoted to the cause of infidelity." A pamphlet on *The Rise and Dissolution of the Infidel Societies in this Metropolis* (London, 1800), by W. Hamilton Reid, describes the period as the first "in which the doctrines of infidelity have been extensively circulated among the lower orders"; and a *Summary of Christian Evidences*, by Bishop Porteous (1800 ; 16th ed. 1826), affirms, in agreement with the 1799 Report of the Lords' Committee on Treasonable Societies, that "new compendiums of infidelity, and new libels on Christianity, are dispersed continually, with indefatigable industry, through every part of the kingdom, and every class of the community." Freethought, in short, was becoming democratised.

Chapter XVI.

EUROPEAN FREETHOUGHT, FROM DESCARTES TO THE FRENCH REVOLUTION

§ 1. *France and Holland.*

1. WE have seen France, in the first quarter of the seventeenth century, pervaded in its upper classes by a freethought partly born of the knowledge that religion counted for little but harm in public affairs, partly the result of such argumentation as had been thrown out by Montaigne and codified by Charron. That it was not the freethinking of mere idle men of the world is clear when we note the names and writings of LA MOTHE LE VAYER, GUI PATIN, and GABRIEL NAUDÉ, all scholars, all heretics of the skeptical and rationalistic order. The first, one of the early members of the new Academy founded by Richelieu, is an interesting figure[1] in the history of culture, being a skeptic of the school of Sextus Empiricus, but practically a great friend of tolerance. Standing in favour with Richelieu, he wrote at that statesman's suggestion a treatise *On the Virtue of the Heathen*, justifying toleration by pagan example—a course which raises the question whether Richelieu himself was not strongly touched by the rationalism of his age. If it be true that the great Cardinal "believed as all the world did in his time,"[2] there is little more to be said, for unbelief, as we have seen, was already abundant, and even somewhat fashionable. Certainly no ecclesiastic in high power ever followed a less ecclesiastical policy;[3] and from the date of his appointment as Minister to Louis XIII (1624), for forty years, there

---

[1] See the notices of him in Owen's *Skeptics of the French Renaissance;* and in Sainte-Beuve, *Port Royal*, iii, 180, etc.
[2] Hanotaux, *Hist. du Cardinal de Richelieu*, 1893, i, pref. p. 7.
[3] Cp. Buckle, ch. viii, 1-vol. ed. pp. 305-10, 325-8.

was no burning of heretics or unbelievers in France. If he was orthodox, it was very passively.[1]

Le Vayer's *Dialogues of Orasius Tubero* (1633) is philosophically his most important work;[2] but its tranquil Pyrrhonism was not calculated to affect greatly the current thought of his day ; and he ranked rather as a man of all-round learning[3] than as a polemist, being reputed " a little contradictory, but in no way bigoted or obstinate, all opinions being to him nearly indifferent, excepting those of which faith does not permit us to doubt."[4] The last phrase tells of the fact that it affects to negate : Le Vayer's skepticism was well known. He was not indeed an original thinker, most of his ideas being echoes from the skeptics of antiquity ;[5] and it has been not unjustly said of him that he is rather of the sixteenth century than of the seventeenth or the eighteenth.[6]

2. Between this negative development of the doctrine of Montaigne and the vogue of upper-class deism, the philosophy of Descartes, with its careful profession of submission to the Church, had an easy reception ; and on the appearance of the *Discours de la Methode* (1637) it speedily affected the whole thought of France, the women of the leisured class, now much given to literature, being among its students.[7] From the first, the Jansenists, who were the most serious religious thinkers of the time, accepted the Cartesian system as in the main soundly Christian ; and its founder's authority has some such influence in keeping up the prestige of orthodoxy as had

---

[1] See the good criticism of M. Hanotaux in Perrens, *Les Libertins en France au xvii. siècle*, p. 95 sq.

[2] He wrote very many, the final collection filling three volumes folio, and fifteen in duodecimo.

[3] " On le régarde comme le Plutarque de notre siecle " (Perrault, *Les Hommes Illustres du XVIIe Siecle*, éd. 1701, ii, 131).

[4] Perrault, ii, 132.

[5] M. Perrens, who endorses this criticism, does not note that some passages he quotes from the *Dialogues*, as to atheism being less disturbing to States than superstition, are borrowed from Bacon's essay *Of Atheism*, of which Le Vayer would read the Latin version.

[6] Perrens, p. 132.

[7] Lanson, *Hist. de la litt. francaise*, 5e édit. p. 396 ; Brunetiere, *Études Critiques*, 3e série, p. 2 ; Buckle, 1-vol. ed. p. 338.

that of Locke later in England. Boileau is named among those whom he so influenced.[1] But a merely external influence of this kind could not counteract the whole social and intellectual tendency towards a secular view of life, a tendency revealed on the one hand by the series of treatises from eminent churchmen, defending the faith against unpublished attacks, and on the other hand by the prevailing tone in *belles lettres*. Malherbe, the literary dictator of the first quarter of the century, had died in 1628 with the character of a scoffer;[2] and the fashion now lasted till the latter half of the reign of Louis XIV. Two years after the burning of Vanini, a young man named Jean Fontanier had been burned alive on the Place de Greve at Paris, apparently for the doctrines laid down by him in a manuscript entitled *Le Tresor Inestimable*, written on deistic and anti-Catholic lines.[3] But the cases of the poet Theophile de Viau, who about 1623 suffered prosecution on a charge of impiety,[4] and of his companions Berthelot and Colletet—who like him were condemned but set free by royal favour—appear to be the only others of the kind for over a generation. Frivolity of tone sufficed to ward off legal pursuit. It was in 1665, some years after the death of Mazarin, who had maintained Richelieu's policy of tolerance, that Claude Petit was burnt at Paris for "impious pieces";[5] and even then there was no general reversion to orthodoxy, the upper-class tone remaining, as in the age of Richelieu and Mazarin, more or less unbelieving. When Corneille had introduced a touch of Christian zeal into his *Polyeucte* (1643) he had given general offence to the dilettants of both sexes.[6] Moliere, again, the disciple

---

[1] Lanson, p. 397.   [2] Perrens, pp. 81-85
[3] Cp. Perrens, pp. 68-69, and refs.
[4] See Duvernet, *Vie de Voltaire*, ch. i, and *note* 1; and Perrens, pp. 74-80.
[5] For all that is known of Petit see the Avertissement to Bibliophile Jacob's edition of *Paris ridicule et burlesque au 17ieme siecle*, and refs. in Perrens, p. 153. After Petit's death, his friend Du Pelletier defended him as being a deist; but he seems in his youthful writings to have blasphemed at large, and he had been guilty of assassinating a young monk. He was burned, however, for blaspheming the Virgin.
[6] Guizot, *Corneille et son temps*, ed. 1880, p. 200. The circle of the

of Gassendi[1] and "the very genius of reason,"[2] was unquestionably an unbeliever;[3] and only the personal protection of Louis XIV, which after all could not avail to support such a play as *Tartufe* against the fury of the bigots, enabled him to sustain himself at all against them. Equally freethinking was his brilliant predecessor and early comrade, CYRANO DE BERGERAC (1620–1655), who did not fear to indicate his frame of mind in one of his dramas. In *La Mort d'Agrippine* he puts in the mouth of Sejanus, as was said by a contemporary, "horrible things against the Gods," notably the phrase, "whom men made, and who did not make men,"[4] which, however, generally passed as an attack on polytheism; and though there was certainly no blasphemous intention in the phrase, *Frappons, voila l'hostie* [= *hostia*, victim], some pretended to regard it as an insult to the Catholic *host*.[5] At times Cyrano writes like a deist;[6] but in so many other passages does he hold the language of a convinced materialist, and of a scoffer at that,[7] that he can hardly be taken seriously on the former head.[8] In short, he was one of the first

Hotel Rambouillet were especially hostile. Cp. Pallisot's note to *Polyeucte*, end. On the other hand, Corneille found it prudent to cancel four skeptical lines which he had originally put in the mouth of the pagan Severus, the sage of the piece. Perrins, *Les Libertins*, p. 140.

[1] Under whom he studied in his youth with a number of other notably independent spirits, among them Cyrano de Bergerac. See Sainte-Beuve's essay on Moliere, prefixed to the Hachette edition.

[2] Constant Coquelin, art. "Don Juan" in the *International Review*, September, 1903, p. 61—an acute and scholarly study.

[3] "Moliere is a freethinker to the marrow of his bones" (Perrens, p. 280). Cp. Lanson, p. 520; Fournier, *Etudes sur Moliere*, 1885, pp. 122–3; Soury, *Brev. de l'hist. du matér.* p. 384. "Ginguene," writes Sainte-Beuve, "a publie une brochure pour montrer Rabelais précurseur de la révolution francaise; c'étoit inutile a prouver sur Moliere" (essay cited).

[4] Act II, sc. iv, in *Œuvres Comiques*, etc., ed. Jacob, rep. by Garnier, pp. 426–7.

[5] See Jacob's note *in loc.*, ed. cited, p. 455.

[6] *E.g.*, his *Lettre contre un Pédant* (No. 13 of the *Lettres Satiriques* in ed. cited, p. 181), which, however, appears to have been mutilated in some editions; as one of the deistic sentences cited by M. Perrens, p. 247, does not appear in the reprint of Bibliophile Jacob.

[7] *E.g.*, the *Histoire des Oiseaux* in the *Histoire comique des états et empires du Soleil*, ed. Jacob (Garnier), p. 278; and the *Fragment de Physique* (same vol.).

[8] See the careful criticism of Perrens, pp. 248–250.

of the hardy freethinkers who, under the tolerant rule of Richelieu and Mazarin, gave clear voice to the newer spirit. Under any other government, he would have been in danger of his life: as it was, he was menaced with prosecutions; his *Agrippine* was forbidden; the first edition of his *Pedant joue* was confiscated; during his last illness there was an attempt to seize his manuscripts; and down till the time of the Revolution the editions of his works were eagerly bought up and destroyed by zealots.[1] His recent literary rehabilitation thus hardly serves to realise his importance in the history of freethought. Between Cyrano and Molière it would appear that there was little less of rationalistic ferment in the France of their day than in England in the same period. Bossuet avows in a letter to Huet in 1678 that impiety and unbelief abound more than ever before.[2]

3. Even in the apologetic reasoning of the greatest French prose writer of that age, Pascal, we have the most pregnant testimony to the prevalence of unbelief; for not only were the fragments preserved as *Pensees* (1670) part of a planned defence of religion against contemporary rationalism,[3] but they themselves show their author profoundly unable to believe, save by a desperate abnegation of reason. The case of Pascal is that of Berkeley with a difference: the latter suffered from hypochondria, but reacted with nervous energy; Pascal, a physical degenerate, prematurely profound, was prematurely old; and his pietism in its final form is the expression of the physical collapse.[4]

---

[1] Bibliophile Jacob, pref. to ed. cited, pp. i-ii.
[2] Perrens, p. 302. Compare Bossuet's earlier sermon for the Second Sunday of Advent, 1665, cited by Perrens, pp. 253-4, where he speaks with something like fury of the free discussion around him.
[3] It is to be remembered that the work as published contained matter not Pascal's. Cp. Brunetiere, *Études*, iii, 46-47; and the editions of the *Pensées* by Faugere and Havet.
[4] This is disputed by M. Lanson, an always weighty authority. He writes (p. 464) that Pascal was "neither mad nor ill" when he gave himself up wholly to religion. But Pascal had *chronically* suffered from intense pains in the head from his eighteenth year; and M. Lanson admits (p. 451) that the *Pensées* were written in intervals of acute suffering. Cp. Pascal's *Priere pour demander a Dieu le bon usage des maladies;* and Owen, *French Skeptics*, pp. 746, 784.

Doubtless the levity and license of the *libertins* in high places[1] confirmed him in his revolt against unbelief; but his own credence was an act rather of despairing emotion than of rational conviction. The man who advised doubters to make a habit of causing masses to be said and following religious rites, on the score that *cela vous fera croire et vous abetira*—"that will make you believe and will stupefy you"[2]—was a pathological case; and though the whole Jansenist movement latterly stood for a reaction against freethinking, it can hardly be doubted that the *Pensees* generally acted as a solvent rather than as a sustainer of religious beliefs.[3] The same question arises concerning the famous *Lettres Provinciales* (1656), written by Pascal in defence of Arnauld against the persecution of the Jesuits, who carried on in Arnauld's case their campaign against Jansen, whom they charged with mis-stating the doctrine of Augustine in his great work expounding that Father. Once more the Catholic Church was swerving from its own established doctrine of predestination, the Spanish Jesuit Molina having set up a new movement in the Pelagian or Arminian direction. The cause of the Jansenists has been represented as that of freedom of thought and speech;[4] and this it relatively was insofar as Jansen and Arnauld sought for a hearing, while the Jesuit-ridden Sorbonne strove to silence and punish them. Pascal had to go from printer to printer as his Letters succeeded each other, the first three being successively prosecuted by the clerical authorities; and in their collected form they found publicity only by being printed at Rouen and published at Amsterdam,

---

[1] As to some of these see Perrens, pp. 158-169. They included the great Condé and some of the women in his circle; all of them unserious in their skepticism, and all "converted" when the physique gave the required cue.

[2] *Pensées*, ed. Faugere, ii, 168-9. The "abetira" comes from Montaigne.

[3] Thus Mr. Owen treats Pascal as a skeptic, which philosophically he was, insofar as he really philosophised and did not merely catch at pleas for his emotional beliefs.

[4] Vinet, *Etudes sur Blaise Pascal*, 3e édit. p. 267 sq.

with the rubric of Cologne. All the while Jansenism claimed to be strict orthodoxy ; and it was in virtue only of the irreducible element of rationalism in Pascal that the school of Port Royal made for freethought in any higher or more general sense. Indeed, between his own reputation for piety and that of the Jansenists for orthodoxy, the *Provincial Letters* have a conventional standing as orthodox compositions. It is strange, however, that those who charge upon the satire of the later philosophers the downfall of Catholicism in France should not realise the plain tendency of these brilliant satires to discredit the entire authority of the church, and, further, by their own dogmatic weaknesses, to put all dogma alike under suspicion.[1] Few men can read the *Provinciales* without being irresistibly impressed by the utter absurdity of the problem over which the entire religious intelligence of a great nation was engrossed. It was, in fact, the endless wrangles of the religious factions over unintelligible issues that more than any other single cause fostered unbelief ;[2] and Pascal's writings only deepened the trouble. Even Bossuet, in his *History of the Variations of the Protestant Churches*, did but throw a new light on the hollowness of the grounds of religion ; and for thoughtful readers gave a lead rather to atheism than to Catholicism. The converts it would make to the Catholic Church would be precisely those whose adherence was of least value, since they had not even the temperamental basis which, rather than argument, kept Bossuet a believer, and were Catholics only for lack of courage to put all religion aside.

[1] Cp. the *Éloge de Pascal* by Bordas Demoulin in Didot ed. of the *Lettres*, 1854, pp. xxii xxiii, and cit. from Sainte-Beuve. Mark Pattison, it seems, held that the Jesuits had the best of the argument. See the *Letters of Lord Acton to Mary Gladstone*, 1904, p. 207. As regards the effect of Jansenism on belief, we find De Tocqueville pronouncing that " Le Jansenisme ouvrit......la breche par laquelle la philosophie du 18e siecle devait faire irruption" (*Hist. philos. du regne de Louis XV*, 1849, i, 2).

[2] Cp. Voltaire's letter of 1768, cited by Mr. Morley, *Voltaire*, 4th ed. p. 159.

4. A similar fatality attended the labours of the learned Huet, bishop of Avranches, whose *Demonstratio Evangelica* (1679) is remarkable as anticipating Berkeley in the argument from the arbitrariness of mathematical assumptions. He, too, by that and by his later works, made for sheer philosophical skepticism,[1] always a dangerous basis for orthodoxy.[2] Such an evolution, on the part of a man of uncommon intellectual energy, challenges attention, the more so seeing that it typifies a good deal of thinking within the Catholic pale, on lines already noted as following on the debate with Protestantism. Honestly pious by bent of mind, but always occupied with processes of reasoning and research, Huet leant more and more, as he grew in years, to the skeptical defence against the pressures of Protestantism and rationalism, at once following and furthering the tendency of his age. A distinguished English critic, noting the general movement, pronounces that Huet took up philosophy "not as an end but as a means—not for its own sake but for the support of religion"; and that his attitude is thus quite different from Pascal's.[3] But the two cases are really on a level, Pascal too being driven to philosophy in reaction against incredulity; and though Pascal's work is of a more bitter and morbid intensity, Huet also had in him that psychic craving for a supernatural support which is the essence of latter-day religion. And if we credit this spirit to Pascal and to Huet, as we do to Newman, we must suppose that it partly touched the whole movement of pro-Catholic skepticism which has been above noted as following on the Reformation. It is ascribing to it as a whole too much of calculation and strategy to

---

[1] Cp. Owen, *French Skeptics*, pp. 762-3, 767.

[2] This was expressly urged against Huet by Arnauld. See the *Notice* in Jourdain's ed. of the *Logique de Port Royal*, 1854, p. xi; Perrens, *Les Libertins*, p. 301; and Bouillier, *Hist. de la philos. cartésienne*, 1854, i. 595-6, where are cited the letters of Arnauld (Nos. 830, 834, and 837 in *Œuvres Compl.* iii, 396, 404, 424) denouncing Huet's pyrrhonism as "impious" and perfectly adapted to the purposes of the freethinkers.

[3] Pattison, *Essays*, 1889, i, 303-4.

say of its combatants that "they conceived the desperate design of first ruining the territory they were prepared to evacuate; before philosophy was handed over to the philosophers the old Aristotelian citadel was to be blown into the air."[1] In reality they caught, as religious men will, with passion rather than with policy, at any plea that might seem fitted to beat down the presumption of "the wild, living intellect of man";[2] and their skepticism had a certain sincerity inasmuch as, trained to uncritical belief, they had never found for themselves the grounds of rational certitude.

Inasmuch, too, as Protestantism had no such ground, and rationalism was still far from having cleared its bases, Huet, as things went, was within his moral rights when he set forth his transcendentalist skepticism in his *Quæstiones Alnetanæ* in 1690. Though written in very limpid Latin,[3] that work attracted practically no attention; and though, having a repute for provincialism in his French style, Huet was loth to resort to the vernacular, he did devote his spare hours through a number of his latter years to preparing his *Traité Philosophique de la faiblesse de l'esprit humain*, which, dying in 1722, he left to be published posthumously (1723). The outcry against his criticism of Descartes and his *Demonstratio* had indisposed him for further personal strife; but he was determined to leave a completed message. Thus it came about that a sincere and devoted Catholic bishop "left, as his last legacy to his fellow-men, a work of the most outrageous skepticism."[4] It was immediately translated into English and German; and though it was probably found somewhat superfluous in deistic England, and supersubtle in Lutheran Germany, it went far to prepare the ground for the active unbelief

---

[1] Pattison, as cited.
[2] "After all, a book [the Bible] cannot make a stand against the wild, living intellect of man." Newman, *Apologia pro Vita Sua*, 1st ed. p. 382. The passage seems to disappear from later editions.
[3] Pattison disparages it as colourless, a fault he charges on Jesuit Latin in general. But by most moderns the Latin style of Huet will be found pure and pleasant.
[4] Pattison, *Essays*, i, 299. Cp. Bouillier, i, 595.

of the next generation in France. It is significant that whereas in the year of the issue of the *Demonstratio* the Duchesse d'Orleans could write that "every young man either is or affects to be an atheist," Le Vassor wrote in 1688: "People talk only of *reason*, of *good taste*, of *force of mind*, of the advantage of those who can raise themselves above the *prejudices* of education and of the society in which one is born. Pyrrhonism is the fashion in many things: men say that rectitude of mind consists in 'not believing lightly' and in being 'ready to doubt.'"[1]

On both lines, obviously, freethought was the gainer; and in a Jesuit treatise, *Le Monde Condamne par luy-mesme*, published in 1695, the *Préface contre l'incredulite des libertins* sets out with the avowal that "to draw the condemnation of the world out of its own mouth, it is necessary to attack first the incredulity of the unbelievers (*libertins*), who compose the main part of it, and who under some appearance of Christianity conceal a mind either Judaic [read *deistic*] or pagan." Such was France to a religious eye at the height of the Catholic triumph over Protestantism.

5. While the evolution had been to no small extent the outcome of defences of the faith, there had also been at work a directly rationalising influence in the teaching of Pierre Gassend or GASSENDI (1592–1655), who, living his life as a canon of the church, reverted in his doctrine to the philosophy of Epicurus, alike in physics and ethics. It seems clear that he never had any religious leanings, but simply entered the church on the advice of friends who pointed out to him how much better a provision it gave, in income and leisure, than the professorship he held in his youth at the university of Aix.[2] Professing like Descartes a strict submission to

---

[1] M. Le Vassor, *De la veritable religion*, 1688, pref. Le Vassor speaks in the same preface of "this multitude of *libertins* and of unbelievers which now terrifies us."

[2] Cp. Adam Smith, *Wealth of Nations*, B. v, ch. i (McCulloch's ed. 1839, pp. 364–5). It is told of him that when dying he said: "I know not who brought me into the world, neither do I know what was to do

the church, he yet set forth a theory of things which had in all ages been recognised as fundamentally irreconcilable with the Christian creed ; and his substantial exemption from penalties is one of the proofs of the permeation of the church at the time by the new spirit. The correspondent of Galileo and Kepler, he was the friend of La Mothe le Vayer and Naude ; and Gui Patin was his physician and intimate.[1] Strong as a physicist and astronomer where Descartes was weak, he divides with him the credit of practically renewing natural philosophy ; Newton following Gassendi rather than Descartes.[2] Indeed, Gassendi's youthful attack on the Aristotelian physics (1624) makes him the predecessor of Descartes ; and he expressly opposed his contemporary on points of physics and metaphysics on which he thought him chimerical, and so promoted unbelief where Descartes made for orthodoxy.[3] Of the criticisms on his *Meditations* to which Descartes published replies, those of Gassendi are distinctly the most searching and sustained. The later position of Hume, indeed, is explicitly taken up in the first objection of Craterus ;[4] but the persistent pressure of Gassendi on the theistic and spiritistic assumptions of Descartes reads like the reasoning of a modern atheist.[5] Yet the works of Descartes were placed on the *Index Librorum Prohibitorum*, and later even vetoed at Paris university,[6] and those of Gassendi were not, though his early work on Aristotelianism had to be stopped after the first volume

---

there, nor why I go out of it." *Reflections on the Death of Freethinkers*, by Deslandes (Eng. trans. of the *Réflexions sur les grands hommes qui sont morts en plaisantant*), 1713, p. 105.

[1] For a good account of Gassendi and his group (founded on Lange, § iii, ch. 1) see Soury, *Bréviaire de l'hist. du matérialisme*, Pt. iii, ch. 2.

[2] Voltaire, *Eléments de philos. de Newton*, ch. ii ; Lange, i, 232 (Eng. trans. i, 267) and *note*, and p. 269.

[3] Bayle, art. POMPONACE, Notes F and G. The complaint was made by Arnauld, who with the rest of the Jansenists was substantially a Cartesian.

[4] See it in Garnier's ed. of Descartes's *Œuvres Choisies*, p. 145.

[5] *Id.* pp. 158-164.

[6] Cartesian professors and cures were persecuted and exiled, or obliged to recant. Rambaud, *Hist. de la civilisation francaise*, 6e edit. ii, 336.

because of the anger it aroused.[1] Himself one of the most abstemious of men,[2] like his master Epicurus (of whom he wrote a Life, 1647), he attracted disciples of another temperamental cast as well as many of his own ; and as usual his system is associated with the former, who are duly vilified on the orthodox side, although certainly no worse than the average adherents of that.

Among his other practical services to rationalism was a curious experiment, made in a village of the Lower Alps, by way of investigating the doctrine of witchcraft. A drug prepared by one sorcerer was administered to others of the craft in presence of witnesses. It threw them into a deep sleep, on awakening from which they declared that they had been at a witches' Sabbath. As they had never left their beds, the experiment went far to discredit the superstition.[3] One significant result of the experiment was seen in the course taken by Colbert in overriding a decision of the Parlement of Rouen as to witchcraft (1670). That Parlement proposed to burn fourteen sorcerers. Colbert ordered that they should be dosed with hellebore—a medicine for brain disturbance.[4] In 1672, finally, the king issued a declaration forbidding the tribunals to admit charges of mere sorcery;[5] and any future condemnations were on the score of blasphemy and poisoning. Yet further, in the section of his posthumous *Syntagma Philosophicum* (1658) entitled *De Effectibus Siderum*,[6] Gassendi dealt the first great blow on the rationalist side to the venerable creed of astrology, assailed often, but to little purpose, from the side of faith ; bringing to his task, indeed, more asperity than he is commonly credited with, but also a stringent

---

[1] Apparently just because the Jansenists adopted Descartes and opposed Gassendi. But Gassendi is extremely guarded in all his statements, save, indeed, in his objections to the *Méditations* of Descartes.
[2] See Soury, pp. 397-8, as to a water-drinking "debauch" of Gassendi and his friends.
[3] Rambaud, as cited, p. 154.
[4] Rambaud, p. 155 ; Michelet, *La Sorcière*.
[5] Voltaire, *Siècle de Louis XIV*, ed. Didot, p. 366. "On ne l'eut pas osé sous Henri IV et sous Louis XIII," adds Voltaire.
[6] Translated into English in 1659, under the title "The Vanity of Judiciary Astrology."

scientific and logical method, lacking in the polemic of the churchmen, who had attacked astrology mainly because it ignored revelation. It is sobering to remember, however, that he was one of those who could not assimilate Harvey's discovery of the circulation of the blood.

6. Of the new Epicureans, the most famous in his day was SAINT-EVREMOND,[1] who, exiled from France for his politics, maintained both in London and in Paris, by his writings, a leadership in polite letters. In England he greatly influenced young men like Bolingbroke; and a translation (attributed to Dryden) of one of his writings seems to have given Bishop Butler the provocation to the first and weakest chapter of his *Analogy*[2] As to his skepticism there was no doubt in his own day; and his compliments to Christianity are much on a par with those paid later by the equally conforming and unbelieving Shaftesbury, whom he also anticipated in his persuasive advocacy of toleration.[3] REGNARD, the dramatist, had a similar private repute as an " Epicurean." And even among the nominally orthodox writers of the time in France a subtle skepticism touches nearly all opinion. La Bruyere is almost the only lay classic of the period who is pronouncedly religious; and his essay on the freethinkers,[4] against whom his reasoning is so forcibly feeble, testifies to their numbers. Even he, too, writes as a deist against atheists, hardly as a believing Christian.

> His posthumous *Dialogues sur le Quietisme*, of which he is credited with only the draft, seem to have been written to support his patron Bossuet in his dispute with Fenelon. They are so weak that some deny La Bruyere's authorship. His personal attitude, however, is indicated by his words: "If all religion is a respectful fear of God, what is to be thought of those who dare to wound him in his most living image, which is the sovereign?" (*Caracteres*, ed. Didot, 1865, p. 389).

---

[1] B. 1613; d. 1703. A man who lived to ninety can have been no great debauchee.
[2] Cp. *Dynamics of Religion*, p. 172.
[3] Cp. Gidel, *Etude* prefixed to *Œuvres Choisies de Saint-Evremond*, ed. Garnier, pp. 64-69.
[4] *Caracteres* (1687), ch. xvi: *Les Esprits Forts*.

FONTENELLE (1657-1757), whose *Conversations on the Plurality of Worlds* (1686) popularised for the elegant world the new cosmology, cannot but have undermined dogmatic faith in some directions ; above all by his graceful and skilful *Histoire des Oracles* (also 1686), where "the argumentation passes beyond the thesis advanced. All that he says of oracles could be said of miracles."[1] The Jesuits found the book essentially "impious"; and a French culture-historian sees in it "the first attack which directs the scientific spirit against the foundations of Christianity. All the purely philosophic arguments with which religion has been assailed are in principle in the work of Fontenelle."[2] Living to his hundredth year, he could join hands with the freethought of Gassendi and Voltaire, Descartes and Diderot.

7. Meanwhile the philosophy of Descartes, if less strictly propitious to science than that of Gassendi, was both directly and indirectly making for the activity of reason. In virtue of its formal "spiritualism," it found access where any clearly materialistic doctrine would have been tabooed ; so that we find the Cartesian ecclesiastic Regis not only eagerly listened to and acclaimed at Toulouse in 1665, but offered a civic pension by the magistrates[3]—this within two years of the placing of Descartes's works on the *Index*. After arousing a similar enthusiasm at Montpellier and at Paris, Regis was silenced by the Archbishop, whereupon he set himself to develop the Cartesian philosophy in his study. The result was that he ultimately went beyond his master, openly rejecting the idea of creation out of nothing,[4] and finally following Locke in rejecting the innate ideas which Descartes had affirmed.[5]

[1] Lanson, *Hist. de la litt. française*, p. 627.
[2] *Id. ib.* Cp. Demogeot, p. 468. Fontenelle was also credited with a heretical letter on the doctrine of Resurrection, an essay on the Infinite, and a *Traité sur la Liberté*, all pointing to unbelief. As the *Histoire des Oracles* was itself anonymous, the question remains open.
[3] Fontenelle, *Éloge sur Régis ;* Bouillier, *Philos. cartés.* i, 507.
[4] *Réponse* to Huet's *Censura philosophiæ cartes.* 1691 ; Bouillier, i, 515.
[5] *Usage de la raison et de la foi*, 1704, liv. i, ptie. i, ch. 7 ; Bouillier, p. 511.

Another young churchman, Desgabets, developing from Descartes and his pupil Malebranche, combined with their "spiritist" doctrine much of the virtual materialism of Gassendi, arriving at a kind of pantheism, and at a courageous pantheistic ethic, wherein God is recognised as the author alike of good and evil[1]—a doctrine which we find even getting a hearing in general society, and noticed in the correspondence of Madame de Sevigne in 1677.[2] And while an evolving Cartesianism was thus reacting on thought in all directions, the primary and proper impulse of Descartes was doing on the Continent what that of Bacon was doing in England—setting men on actual scientific observation and experiment, and turning them from traditionalism of every kind. Some of the school, as Malebranche, set their faces almost fanatically against erudition, thus making an enemy of the all-learned Huet,[3] but on the other hand preparing the way for the scientific age. For the rest we find the influence of Descartes at work in heresies at which he had not hinted. One of the first of the orthodox objections to his philosophy was that it was irreconcilable with the miracle of the eucharist ; and, as this was continually urged, Cartesianism tended at this point to be rationalistic even in spite of itself. Finally we shall see it in Holland, where it took deep root, furthering a rationalistic treatment of the Bible and of popular superstitions.

8. Yet another new departure was made in the France of Louis XIV by the scholarly performance of RICHARD SIMON (1638–1712), who was as regards the Scriptural texts what Spencer of Cambridge was as regards the culture-history of the Hebrews, one of the founders of modern methodical criticism. The congregation of the Oratory, where Simon laid the foundations of his learning, was so little inclined to his critical views that

[1] Bouillier, i, 521–5.
[2] Lettre de 10 aout, 1677, No. 591, éd. Nodier.
[3] Bouillier, i, 582, 588–90.

he decided to leave it, and though persuaded to stay, and to become for a time a professor of philosophy at Julli, he at length broke with the Order. Then, from his native town of Dieppe, came his strenuous series of critical works—*L'histoire critique du Vieux Testament* (1678), which among other things decisively impugned the Mosaic authorship of the Pentateuch; the *Histoire critique du texte du Nouveau Testament* (Rotterdam, 1689); numerous other volumes of critical studies on texts, versions, and commentators; and finally a French translation of the New Testament with notes. His *Bibliotheque Critique* (4 vols. under the name of Saint-Jarre) was suppressed by an order in council; the translation was condemned by Bossuet and the Archbishop of Paris; and the two first-named works were suppressed by the Parlement of Paris and attacked by a host of orthodox scholars; but they were translated promptly into Latin and English; and they gave a new breadth of footing to the deistic argument, though Simon always wrote as an avowed believer.

Before Simon, the Protestant Isaac la Peyrere, the friend of La Mothe le Vayer and Gassendi, and the librarian of Conde, had fired a somewhat startling shot at the Pentateuch in his *Præadamitæ*[1] and *Systema Theologica ex Præ-adamitarum Hypothesi* (both 1655: printed in Holland[2]), for which he was imprisoned at Brussels, with the result that he recanted and joined the Church of Rome, going to the Pope in person to receive absolution, and publishing an *Epistola ad Philotimum* (Frankfort, 1658), in which he professed to explain his reasons for abjuring at once his Calvinism and his treatise. It is clear that all this was done to save his skin, for there is explicit testimony that he held firmly

---

[1] *Præadamitæ, sive Exercitatio super versibus 12, 13, 14 cap. 5, Epist. D. Pauli ad Romanos, Quibus inducuntur Primi Homines ante Adamum conditi.* The notion of a pre-Adamite human race, as we saw, had been held by Bruno. (Above, p. 66.)

[2] My copies of the *Præadamitæ* and *Systema* bear no place-imprint, but simply "Anno Salutis MDCLV." They seem to have been at once reprinted in 12mo.

by his Preadamite doctrine to the end of his life, despite the seven or eight confutations of his work published in 1656.[1] Were it not for his constructive theses—especially his idea that Adam was a real person, but simply the father of the Hebrews and not of the human race—he would deserve to rank high among the scientific pioneers of modern rationalism, for his negative work is shrewd and sound. Like so many other early rationalists, collectively accused of "destroying without replacing," he erred precisely in his eagerness to build up, for his negations have all become accepted truths.[2] As it is, he may be ranked, after Toland, as a main founder of the older rationalism, developed chiefly in Germany, which sought to reduce as many miracles as possible to natural events misunderstood. But he was too far before his time to win a fair hearing. Where Simon laid a cautious scholarly foundation, Peyrere challenged immemorial beliefs, and failed accordingly.

9. Such an evolution could not occur in France without affecting the neighbouring civilisation of Holland. We have seen Dutch life at the beginning of the seventeenth century full of Protestant fanaticism and sectarian strife; and in the time of Descartes these elements, especially on the Calvinist side, were strong enough virtually to drive him out of Holland (1647) after nineteen years' residence.[3] He had, however, made disciples; and his doctrine bore fruit, finding doubtless some old soil ready. Thus in 1666 one of his disciples, the Amsterdam physician Louis Meyer, published a treatise entitled *Philosophia Sacrae Scripturae Interpres*,[4] in which, after

[1] Bayle, *Dictionnaire*, art. PEYRERE. A correspondent of Bayle's concludes his account of "le Preadamite" thus : "Le Pereire étoit le meilleur homme du monde, le plus doux, et qui tranquillement croyoit fort peu de chose."
[2] See the account of his book by Mr. Lecky, *Rationalism in Europe*, i, 295-7. Rejecting as he did the Mosaic authorship of the Pentateuch, he ranks with Hobbes and Spinoza among the pioneers of true criticism. Indeed, as his book seems to have been in MS. in 1645, he may precede Hobbes.
[3] Kuno Fischer, *Descartes and his School*, pp. 254-268.
[4] Colerus (*i.e.*, Kohler), *Vie de Spinoza*, in Gfrorer's ed. of the *Opera*, pp. xlv-xlvii.

formally affirming that the Scripture is the infallible Word of God, he proceeds to argue that the interpretation of the Word must be made by the human reason, and accordingly sets aside all meanings which are irreconcilable therewith, reducing them to allegories or tropes. As Meyer was one of the most intimate friends of Spinoza, being with him at death, and becoming the editor of his posthumous works, it can hardly be doubted that his treatise, which preceded Spinoza's *Tractatus* by four years, influenced the great Jew, who speedily eclipsed him.[1]

SPINOZA, however (1632-1677), was first led to rationalise by his Amsterdam friend and teacher, Van den Ende, a scientific materialist, hostile to all religion;[2] and it was while under his influence that he was excommunicated by his father's synagogue. From the first, apparently, Spinoza's thought was shaped partly by the medieval Hebrew philosophy[3] (which, as we have seen, combined Aristotelian and Saracen influences), partly by the teaching of Bruno, though he modified and corrected that at various points.[4] Later he was deeply influenced by Descartes, whom he specially expounded for a pupil in a tractate.[5] Here he endorses Descartes's doctrine of freewill, which he was later to repudiate and overthrow. But he drew from Descartes his retained principle that evil is not a real existence. In a much less degree he was influenced by Bacon, whose psychology he ultimately condemned; but from Hobbes he took not only his rationalistic attitude towards "revelation" but his doctrine of ecclesiastical subordination.[6]

---

[1] Cp. Bouillier, i, 293 4.
[2] Colerus, *Vie de Spinoza*, in Gfrorer's ed. of *Opera*, p. xxv; Martineau, *Study of Spinoza*, 1882, pp. 20-22; Willis, *Spinoza*, 1870, pp. 37, 79.
[3] As set forth by Joel, *Beiträge zur Gesch. der Philos.*, Breslau, 1876. See citations in Land's note to his lecture in *Spinoza: Four Essays*, 1882, pp. 51-53.
[4] Land, "In Memory of Spinoza," in *Spinoza: Four Essays*, pp. 57 58; Sigwart, as there cited; Willis, *Spinoza*, 1870, gen. introd. pp. x, xi. Cp. however, Martineau, *Study of Spinoza*, p. 101, *note*.
[5] *Renati Des Cartes Princip. Philos. more geometrico demonstratæ*, 1663.
[6] Cp. Martineau, pp. 46, 57.

Finally evolving his own conceptions, he produced a philosophic system which was destined to affect all European thought, remaining the while quietly occupied with the handicraft of lens-grinding by which he earned his livelihood. The Grand Pensionary of the Netherlands, John de Witt, seems to have been in full sympathy with the young heretic, on whom he conferred a small pension before he had published anything save his Cartesian *Principia* (1663).

The much more daring and powerful *Tractatus Theologico-Politicus* (1670[1]) was promptly condemned by a Dutch clerical synod, along with Hobbes's *Leviathan*, which it greatly surpassed in the matter of criticism of the scriptural text. It was the most stringent censure of supernaturalism that had thus far appeared in any modern language; and its preface is an even more mordant attack on popular religion and clericalism than the main body of the work. What seems to-day an odd compromise—the reservation of supra-rational authority for revelation, alongside of unqualified claims for the freedom of reason[2]—was but an adaptation of the old scholastic formula of "twofold truth," and was perhaps at the time the possible maximum of rationalism in regard to the current creed, since both Bacon and Locke, as we have seen, were fain to resort to it. As revealed in his letters, Spinoza in almost all things stood at the point of view of the cultivated rationalism of two centuries later. He believed in a historical Jesus, rejecting the Resurrection;[3] disbelieved in ghosts and spirits;[4] rejected miracles;[5] and refused to think of God as ever angry;[6] avowing that he could not understand the Scriptures, and had been able to learn nothing from them as to God's attributes.[7] The *Tractatus* could not go so far; but it went far enough to horrify many who counted themselves latitudinarian. It was only in

---

[1] Reprinted in 1674, without place-name, and with the imprint of an imaginary Hamburg publisher.
[2] *Tractatus*, c. 15.
[3] Ep. xxiv, to Oldenburg.
[4] Epp. lviii, lx, to Boxel.
[5] Ep. xxiii, to Oldenburg.
[6] Ep. xxiv.
[7] Ep. xxxiv, to W. van Bleyenberg.

Holland that so aggressive a criticism of Christian faith and practice could then appear; and even there neither publisher nor author dared avow himself. Spinoza even vetoed a translation into Dutch, foreseeing that such a book would be placed under an interdict.[1] It was as much an appeal for freedom of thought (*libertas philosophandi*) as a demonstration of rational truth; and Spinoza dexterously pointed (c. 20) to the social effects of the religious liberty already enjoyed in Amsterdam as a reason for carrying liberty further. There can be no question that it powerfully furthered alike the deistic and the Unitarian movements in England from the year of its appearance; and, though the States-General felt bound formally to prohibit it on the issue of the second edition in 1674, its effect in Holland was probably as great as elsewhere: at least there seems to have gone on there from this time a rapid modification of the old orthodoxy.

Still more profound, probably, was the effect of the posthumous *Ethica* (1677), which he had been prevented from publishing in his lifetime,[2] and which not only propounded in parts an absolute pantheism (= atheism[3]), but definitely grounded ethics in human nature. If more were needed to arouse theological rage, it was to be found in the repeated and insistent criticism of the moral and mental perversity of the defenders of the faith[4]—a position not indeed quite consistent with the primary teaching of the treatise on the subject of Will, of which it denies the entity in the ordinary sense. Spinoza was here reverting to the practical attitude of Bacon, which, under a partial misconception, he had repudiated; and he did not formally solve the contradiction. His purpose was to confute the ordinary orthodox dogma that unbelief is wilful sin; and to retort

---

[1] Ep. xlvii, to Jellis, Feb., 1671.
[2] Ep. xix, 1675, to Oldenburg.
[3] "Spinozism is atheistic, and has no valid ground for retaining the word 'God'" (Martineau, p. 349).
[4] *Ethica*, P. i, App.; P. ii, *end ;* P. v, prop. 41, schol. Cp. the Letters, *passim*.

the charge without reconciling it with the thesis was to impair the philosophic argument.[1] It was not on that score, however, that it was resented, but as an unpardonable attack on orthodoxy, not to be atoned for by any words about the spirit of Christ.[2] The discussion went deep and far. A reply to the *Tractatus* which appeared in 1674, by an Utrecht professor (then dead), is spoken of by Spinoza with contempt;[3] but abler discussion followed, though the assailants mostly fell foul of each other. Franz Cuper or Kuyper of Amsterdam, who in 1676 published an *Arcana Atheismi Revelata*, professedly refuting Spinoza's *Tractatus*, was charged with writing in bad faith and with being on Spinoza's side—an accusation which he promptly retorted on other critics, apparently with justice.[4]

10. The appearance in 1678 of a Dutch treatise "against all sorts of atheists,"[5] and in 1681, at Amsterdam, of an attack in French on Spinoza's Scriptural criticism,[6] points to a movement outside of the clerical and scholarly class. All along, indeed, the atmosphere of the Arminian or "Remonstrant" School in Holland must have been fairly liberal.[7] Already in 1685 Locke's friend Le Clerc had taken up the position of Hobbes and Spinoza and Simon on the Pentateuch in his *Sentimens de quelques*

---

[1] The solution is, of course, that the attitude of the will in the forming of opinion may or may not be passionally perverse, in the sense of being inconsistent. To show that it is inconsistent *may* be a means of enlightening it; and an aspersion to that effect *may* be medicinal. Spinoza might truly have said that passional perversity was at least as common on the orthodox side as on the other. In any case, he quashes his own criticism of Bacon.

[2] P. iv, prop. 68, schol.

[3] Ep. 1; 2 June, 1674.

[4] Colerus, as cited, p. liv. Cuper appears to have been genuinely anti-Spinozist, while his opponent, Breitburg, or Bredenburg, of Rotterdam, was a Spinozist. Both were members of the society of "Collegiants," a body of non-dogmatic Christians, which for a time was broken up through their dissensions. Mosheim, 17 Cent. sec. ii, Pt. ii, ch. vii, § 2, and *note*.

[5] *Theologisch, Philosophisch, en Historisch proces voor God, tegen allerley Atheisten*. By Francis Ridder, Rotterdam, 1678.

[6] *L'Impiété Convaincu*, "par Pierre Yvon," Amsterdam, 1681. Really by the Sieur Aubert de Verse.

[7] See Fox Bourne's *Life of Locke*, ii, 282-3, as to Locke's friendly relations with the Remonstrants in 1683-9.

theologiens de Hollande (translated into English and published in 1690 as "Five Letters Concerning the Inspiration of the Holy Scriptures"). And although Le Clerc always remained something of a Scripturalist, and refused to go the way of Spinoza, he had courage enough to revive an ancient heresy by urging, in his commentary on the fourth Gospel (1701), that "the Logos" should be rendered "Reason." A rationalising spirit now began to spread widely in Holland; and within twenty years of Spinoza's death there had arisen a Dutch sect, led by Pontiaan van Hattem, a pastor at Philipsland, which blended Spinozism with evangelicalism in such a way as to incur the anathema of the Church.[1] In the time of the English Civil War, the fear of the opponents of the new multitude of sects was that England should become "another Amsterdam."[2] This very multiplicity tended to promote doubt: and in 1713 we find Anthony Collins[3] pointing to Holland as a country where freedom to think has undermined superstition to a remarkable degree. During his stay, in the previous generation, Locke had found a measure of liberal theology, in harmony with his own; but in those days downright heresy was still dangerous. DEURHOFF (d. 1717), who translated Descartes and was accused of Spinozism, though he strongly attacked it,[4] had at one time to fly Holland, though by his writings he founded a pantheistic sect known as Deurhovians; and BALTHASAR BEKKER, a Cartesian, persecuted first for Socinianism, incurred so much odium by publishing in 1691 a treatise denying the reality of witchcraft that he had to give up his office as a preacher.

Cp. art. in *Biographie Universelle*, and Mosheim, 17 Cent. Pt. ii, ch. ii, § 35, and notes in Reid's ed. Bekker was not the

[1] Mosheim, Reid's ed. p. 836; Martineau, pp. 327-8. The first MS. of the treatise of Spinoza *De Deo et Homine*, found and published in the nineteenth century, bore a note which showed it to have been used by a sect of Christian Spinozists. See Janet's ed. 1878, p. 3. They altered the text, putting "faith" for "opinion." *Id.* p. 53, *notes*.
[2] Edwards, *Gangræna*, as before cited.
[3] *Discourse of Freethinking*, p. 28.
[4] Colerus, as cited, p. lviii.

first to combat demonology on scriptural grounds ; Arnold Geulincx, of Leyden, and the French Protestant refugee Daillon having less confidently put the view before him, the latter in his *Daimonologia*, 1687 (trans. in English, 1723), and the former in his system of ethics. Gassendi, as we saw, had notably discredited witchcraft a generation earlier; Reginald Scot had impugned its actuality in 1584 ; and Wier, still earlier, in 1583. And even before the Reformation the learned King Christian II. of Denmark (deposed 1523) had vetoed witch-burning in his dominions. (Allen, *Hist. de Danemark*, French trans. 1878, i, 281.) As Scot's *Discoverie* had been translated into Dutch in 1609, Bekker probably had a lead from him. Glanvil's *Blow at Modern Sadducism* (1688), reproduced in *Sadducismus Triumphatus*, undertakes to answer some objections of the kind later urged by Bekker; and the discussion was practically international. Bekker's treatise, entitled *De Betooverte Wereld*, was translated into English—first in 1695, from the French, under the title *The World Bewitched* (only 1 vol. published), and again in 1700 as *The World turned upside down*. In the French translation, *Le Monde Enchante* (4 tom. 1694), it had a great vogue. A refutation was published in English in *An historical treatise of spirits*, by J. Beaumont, in 1705. It is noteworthy that Bekker was included as one of "four modern sages (*vier neuer Welt-Weisen*)" with Descartes, Hobbes, and Spinoza, in a German folio tractate (hostile) of 1702.

In 1708 there was published at Amsterdam a more startling work, under the pseudonym of "Juan di Posos," wherein, by way of a relation of imaginary travels, something like atheism was said to be taught; but the pastor Leenhof had in 1703 been accused of atheism for his treatise, *Heaven on Earth*, which was at most Spinozistic.[1] Even as late as 1714 a Spinozist shoemaker, BOOMS, was banished for his writings ; but henceforth liberal influences, largely traceable to the works of Bayle, begin to predominate.

11. No greater service was rendered in that age to the spread of rational views than that embodied in the great *Dictionnaire* of PIERRE BAYLE (1647–1706), who, born in France, but driven out by the revocation of the Edict of Nantes, spent the best part of his life and did his main work at Rotterdam. Persecuted there to the

---

[1] Cp. Trinius, *Freydenker-Lexicon*, pp. 336–7; Colerus, as cited, p. lviii.

extent of having to give up his professorship, he yet produced a virtual encyclopedia for freethinkers in his incomparable Dictionary, baffling hostility by the Pyrrhonian impartiality with which he handled all religious questions. In his youth, when sent by his Protestant father to study at Toulouse, he had been temporarily converted, as was the young Gibbon later, to Catholicism;[1] and the retrospect of that experience seems in Bayle's case, as in Gibbon's, to have been a permanent motive to practical skepticism.[2] But, again, in the one case as in the other, skepticism was fortified by abundant knowledge. Bayle had read everything and mastered every controversy, and was thereby the better able to seem to have no convictions of his own. But even apart from the notable defences of the character of atheists dropped by him in the famous *Pensees diverses sur la Comete* (1682), and in the *Eclaircissements* in which he defended it, it is abundantly evident that he was an unbeliever. The only alternative view is that he was strictly or philosophically a skeptic, reaching no conclusions for himself; but this is excluded by the whole management of his expositions.[3] His ostensible Pyrrhonism was simply the tactic forced on him by his conditions; and it was the positive unbelievers who specially delighted in his volumes. He laid down no cosmic doctrines, but he illuminated all; and his air of repudiating such views as Spinoza's had the effect rather of forcing Spinozists to leave neutral ground than of rehabilitating orthodoxy.

On one theme he spoke without any semblance of

[1] Albert Cazes, *Pierre Bayle, sa vie, ses idées, son influence, son œuvre*, 1905, pp. 6, 7.

[2] A movement of skepticism had probably been first set up in the young Bayle by Montaigne, who was one of his favourite authors before his conversion (Cazes, p. 5). Montaigne, it will be remembered, had been a fanatic in his youth. Thus three typical skeptics of the sixteenth, seventeenth, and eighteenth centuries had known what it was to be Catholic believers.

[3] Cp. the essay on *The Skepticism of Bayle* in Sir J. F. Stephen's *Horæ Sabbaticæ*, vol. iii, and the remarks of Perrens, *Les Libertins*, pp. 331-7.

doubt. Above all men who had yet written he is the champion of toleration.[1] At a time when in England the school of Locke still held that atheism must not be tolerated, he would accept no such position, insisting that error as such is not culpable, and that, save in the case of a sect positively inciting to violence and disorder, all punishment of opinion is irrational and unjust.[2] On this theme, moved by the memory of his own life of exile and the atrocious persecution of the Protestants of France, he lost his normal imperturbability, as in his Letter to an Abbe, entitled *Ce que c'est que la France toute catholique sous le regne de Louis le Grand*, in which a controlled passion of accusation makes every sentence bite like an acid, leaving a mark that no dialectic can efface. But it was not only from Catholicism that he suffered, and not only to Catholics that his message was addressed. One of his most malignant enemies was the Protestant Jurieu, who it was that succeeded in having him deprived of his chair of philosophy and history at Rotterdam, on the score of the freethinking of his *Pensees sur la Comete*. But nothing could deprive him of his literary vogue, which was in the ratio of his unparalleled industry. As a mere writer he is admirable : save in point of sheer wit, of which, however, he has not a little, he is to this day as readable as Voltaire. By force of unfailing lucidity, wisdom, and knowledge, he made the conquest of literary Europe ; and fifty years after his death we find the Jesuit Delamare in his (anonymous) apologetic treatise, *La Foi justifiee de tout reproche de contradiction avec la raison* (1761), speaking of him to the deists as "their theologian, their doctor, their oracle."[3] He was indeed no less ; and his serene exposure of the historic failure of Christianity was all the more deadly as coming from a master of theological history.

[1] *Dictionnaire*, art. MAHOMET, § ix ; art. CONECTE ; art. SIMONIDE, notes H and G ; art. SPONDE, note C.
[2] *Commentaire philosophique sur la parabole : Contrains-les d'entrer*, 2e ptie, vi. Cp. the *Critique générale de l'histoire du Calvinisme du Pere Maimbourg*. [3] Ed. 1766, p. 7.

12. Welcomed by students everywhere, Bayle must have made powerfully for tolerance and rationalism in his adopted country, which after his time became a centre of culture for the States of northern Europe rather than a source of original works. Holland in the eighteenth century was receptive alike of French and English thought and literature, especially the former;[1] and, besides reprinting many of the French deists' works and translating some of the English, the Dutch cities harboured such heretics as the Italian Alberto Radicati, Count PASSERANO, who, dying at Rotterdam in 1736, left a collection of deistic treatises of a strongly freethinking cast to be posthumously published.

The German traveller Alberti,[2] citing the *London Magazine*, 1732, states that Passerano visited England and published works in English through a translator, Joseph Morgan, and that both were sentenced to imprisonment. This presumably refers to his anonymous *Philosophical Dissertation upon Death*, "by a friend to truth," published in English in 1732. It is a remarkable treatise, being a hardy justification of suicide, "composed for the consolation of the unhappy," from a practically atheistic standpoint. Two years earlier he had published in English, also anonymously, a tract entitled *Christianity set in a True Light, by a Pagan Philosopher newly converted;* and it may be that the startling nature of the second pamphlet elicited a prosecution which included both. The pamphlet of 1730, however, is a eulogy of the ethic of Jesus, who is deistically treated as a simple man, but with all the amenity which the deists usually brought to bear on that theme. His *Recueil des pieces curieuses sur les matieres les plus interessants*, published with his name at Rotterdam in 1736,[3] includes a translation of Swift's ironical *Project* concerning babies, and an *Histoire*

---

[1] See Texte, *Rousseau and the Cosmopolitan Spirit*, Eng. trans. p. 29.
[2] *Briefe*, 1752, p. 451.
[3] Reprinted, in French, at London in 1749, in a more complete and correct edition, published by J. Brindley.

abregee de la profession sacerdotale, which was published in a separate English translation.[1] Passerano is noticeable chiefly for the relative thoroughness of his rationalism. In the *Recueil* he speaks of deists and atheists as being the same, those called atheists having always admitted a first cause under the names God, Nature, Eternal Germs, movement, or universal soul.[2]

> In 1737 was published in French a small mystification consisting of a *Sermon preché dans la grande Assemblee des Quakers de Londres*, par la fameux Frere E. E., and another little tract, *La Religion Muhamedane comparee a la païenne de l'Indostan, par Ali-Ebn-Omar*. "E. E." stood for Edward Elwall, a well-known Unitarian of the time, who in 1742 published a treatise entitled *The Supernatural Incarnation of Jesus Christ proved to be false......and that our Lord Jesus Christ was the real son of Joseph and Mary*, and had been in 1726 tried at Stafford Assizes. The two tracts are both by Passerano, and are on deistic lines, the text of the *Sermon* being (in English) "The Religion of the Gospel is the true Original Religion of Reason and Nature." The proposition is of course purely ethical in its bearing.

The hospitality given in Holland to such literature tells of growing liberality of thought as well as of political freedom. But the conditions were not favourable to such general literary activity as prevailed in the larger States, though good work was done in medicine and the natural sciences. Not till the nineteenth century did Dutch scholars again give an original lead to Europe in religious thought.

13. Meantime, Spinoza had reinforced the critical movement in France,[3] where the later policy of Louis XIV sought as far as possible to extinguish freedom of thought. The crowning Catholic blunder and crime of

---

[1] The copy in the British Museum is dated 1737, and the title-page describes Passerano as "a Piemontæse exile *now in Holland*, a Christian Freethinker." It is presumably a re-issue.

[2] London ed. 1749, pp. 24-25.

[3] The *Tractatus Theologico-Politicus* had been translated into French in 1678 by Saint-Glain, a Protestant, who gave it no fewer than three other titles in succession to evade prosecution. (Note to Colerus in Gfrorer's ed. of Spinoza, p. xlix.) In addition to the work of Aubert de Verse, above mentioned, replies were published by Simon, De la Motte (minister of the Savoy Chapel, London), Lamy, a Benedictine, and others.

the revocation of the Edict of Nantes, forcing out of France some five hundred thousand industrious and educated inhabitants for the offence of Protestantism, wrought above all things for the ascendancy of rationalism. Abbadie, writing his *Traité de la Verité de la religion chretienne* at Berlin in 1684, speaks of an "infinity" of prejudiced deists as against the "infinity" of prejudiced believers,[1] and strives hard to refute both Hobbes and Spinoza on points of Biblical criticism. For a time, indeed, there was a falling away in French intellectual prestige,[2] the result, not of the mere "protective spirit" in literature, but of the immense diversion of national energy under Louis XIV to militarism;[3] and the freethinkers lost some of the confidence as well as some of the competence they had exhibited in the days of Moliere.[4] There had been too little solid thinking done to preclude a reaction when the king, led by Madame de Maintenon, went about to atone for his debaucheries by an old age of piety. But during the period of exhaustion and official orthodoxy there was no real building up of belief; and the forward movement at length recommenced. In 1700, at the height of the reign of the king's confessors, there appeared the *Lettre d'Hippocrate a Damagete*, described as "the first French work openly destructive of Christianity"; and it was ascribed to the Comte de Boulainvilliers, a pillar of the feudal system.[5] The king himself, so long morally discredited, could only discredit pietism by his adoption of it; the Jansenists and the Molinists fought incessantly; even on the side of authority there was dissension between Bossuet and Fenelon;[6] and the

---

[1] Tom. I, § ii, ch. ix (ed. 1864, i, 134, 177).
[2] Cp. Huet, *Huetiana*, § 1.
[3] The question is discussed in the author's *Buckle and his Critics*, pp. 324–342. Buckle's view, however, was held by Huet, *Huetiana*, § 73.
[4] Cp. Perrens, pp. 310–314.
[5] Lemontey, *Hist. de la régence et de la minorité de Louis XV*, 1835, ii, 358, *note*.
[6] For a brief view of the facts, usually misconceived, see Lanson, pp. 610–611. Fénelon seems to have been uncandid, while Bossuet, by common consent, was malevolent. There is probably truth, however,

movement of mysticism associated with the latter came to nothing, though he had the rare credit of converting, albeit to a doubtful orthodoxy, the emotional young Scotch deist, Chevalier Ramsay.[1] When the old king died (1715) even the fashion of conformity passed away;[2] and had not the exhausted and bankrupt country been kept for another half century on the rack of ruinous wars, alike under the regency of Orleans and the rule of Louis XV, the intellectual life might at once have gone fast and far. As it was, war after war absorbed its energy; and the debt of five milliards left by Louis XIV was never seriously lightened. Under such a system the last vestiges of constitutional government were swept away, and the autocracy kept the checks on printing insuperably strong, so that freethought could not attain to open speech. Any book with the least tendency to freethought had to seek printers in Holland. Huard, in publishing his anonymous translation of the *Hypotyposes* of Sextus Empiricus (1725), is careful to say in his preface that he "makes no application of the Pyrrhonian objections to any dogma that may be called theological"; but he goes on to add that the scandalous quarrels of Christian sects are well fitted to confirm Pyrrhonists in their doubts, the sects having no solid ground on which to condemn each other. As such an assertion was rank heresy, the translation had to be issued in Amsterdam, and even there without a publisher's name.[3] It was

---

in the view of Shaftesbury (*Characteristics*, ed. 1900, ii, 214), that the real grievance of Fénelon's ecclesiastical opponents was the tendency of his mysticism to withdraw devotees from ceremonial duties.

[1] Now remembered chiefly through the account of his intercourse with Fenelon (repr. in Didot ed. of Fénelon's misc. works), and Hume's long extract from his *Philosophical Principles of Natural and Revealed Religion* in the concluding note to the *Essays*. Cp. M. Matter, *Le Mysticisme en France au temps de Fénelon*, 1865, pp. 352-4.

[2] Cp. Duvernet, *Vie de Voltaire*, ch. i. Rivarol (*Lettres a Necker*, in *Œuvres*, ed. 1852, p. 138) wrote that under Louis XV there was a "general insurrection" of discussion, and that everybody then talked "only of religion and philosophy during half a century." But this exaggerates the beginnings, of which Rivarol could have no exact knowledge.

[3] A reprint in 1735 bears the imprint of London, with the note "Aux dépens de la Compagnie."

presumably in Holland that there were printed in 1738 the two volumes of *Lettres sur la religion essentielle a l'homme, distinguée de ce qui n'en est que l'accessoire*, by Marie Huber, a Genevese lady living in Lyons; also the two following parts (1739), replying to criticisms on the earlier. In its gentle way, the book stands very distinctly for the "natural" and ethical principle in religion, denying that the deity demands from men either service or worship, or that he can be wronged by their deeds, or that he can punish them eternally for their sins. This was one of the first French fruits, after Voltaire, of the English deistic influence;[1] and it is difficult to understand how the authoress escaped molestation.

> Some idea of the intensity of the tyranny over all literature in France under the Old Regime may be gathered from Buckle's compendious account of the books officially condemned, and of authors punished, during the two generations before the Revolution. Apart from the record of the treatment of Buffon, Marmontel, Morellet, Voltaire, and Diderot, it runs: "The......tendency was shown in matters so trifling that nothing but the gravity of their ultimate results prevents them from being ridiculous. In 1770, Imbert translated Clarke's *Letters on Spain*, one of the best works then existing on that country. This book, however, was suppressed as soon as it appeared; and the only reason assigned for such a stretch of power is that it contained some remarks respecting the passion of Charles III for hunting, which were considered disrespectful to the French crown, because Louis XV himself was a great hunter. Several years before this La Bletterie, who was favourably known in France by his works, was elected a member of the French Academy. But he, it seems, was a Jansenist, and had moreover ventured to assert that the Emperor Julian, notwithstanding his apostasy, was not entirely devoid of good qualities. Such offences could not be overlooked in so pure an age; and the king obliged the academy to exclude La Bletterie from their society. That the punishment extended no further was an instance of remarkable leniency; for Fréret, an eminent critic and scholar, was confined in the Bastille because he stated, in one of his memoirs, that the earliest Frankish chiefs had

---

[1] Cp. Staudlin, *Gesch. des Rationalismus und Supernaturalismus*, 1826, pp. 287–290; Hagenbach, *Kirchengeschichte des 18. und 19. Jahrhunderts*, 2te Aufl. 1848, i, 218–220.

received their titles from the Romans. The same penalty was inflicted four different times upon Lenglet du Fresnoy. In the case of this amiable and accomplished man, there seems to have been hardly the shadow of a pretext for the cruelty with which he was treated; though on one occasion the alleged offence was that he had published a supplement to the History of De Thou.

"Indeed, we have only to open the biographies and correspondence of that time to find instances crowding upon us from all quarters. Rousseau was threatened with imprisonment, was driven from France, and his works were publicly burned. The celebrated treatise of Helvétius on the Mind was suppressed by an order of the Royal Council; it was burned by the common hangman, and the author was compelled to write two letters retracting his opinions. Some of the geological views of Buffon having offended the clergy, that illustrious naturalist was obliged to publish a formal recantation of doctrines which are now known to be perfectly accurate. The learned *Observations on the History of France*, by Mably, were suppressed as soon as they appeared: for what reason it would be hard to say, since M. Guizot, certainly no friend either to anarchy or to irreligion, has thought it worth while to republish them, and thus stamp them with the authority of his own great name. *The History of the Indies*, by Raynal, was condemned to the flames, and the author ordered to be arrested. Lanjuinais, in his well-known work on Joseph II, advocated not only religious toleration, but even the abolition of slavery; his book, therefore, was declared to be 'seditious'; it was pronounced 'destructive of all subordination,' and was sentenced to be burned. The *Analysis of Bayle*, by Marsy, was suppressed, and the author was imprisoned. The *History of the Jesuits*, by Linguet, was delivered to the flames; eight years later his journal was suppressed; and, three years after that, as he still persisted in writing, his *Political Annals* were suppressed, and he himself was thrown into the Bastille. Delisle de Sales was sentenced to perpetual exile and confiscation of all his property on account of his work on the *Philosophy of Nature*. The treatise by Mey, on French Law, was suppressed; that by Boncerf, on Feudal Law, was burned. *The Memoirs of Beaumarchais* were likewise burned; the *Eloge on Fenelon*, by La Harpe, was merely suppressed. Duvernet, having written a *History of the Sorbonne*, which was still unpublished, was seized and thrown into the Bastille, while the manuscript was yet in his own possession. The celebrated work of De Lolme on the English constitution was suppressed by edict directly it appeared. The fate of being suppressed or prohibited also awaited the Letters of Gervaise in 1724; the Dissertations of Courayer in 1727; the Letters of Montgon in 1732; the *History of Tamerlane*, by Margat, also in 1732; the *Essay on Taste*, by Cartaud, in 1736; The *Life of Domat*, by Prévost de la Jannes, in 1742; the *History of Louis XI*, by Duclos, in 1745; the Letters of Bargeton in 1750; the *Memoirs on Troyes*, by Grosley, in the same year; the *History of Clement XI*, by Reboulet, in 1752; The *School of Man*, by Génard, also in 1752; the *Therapeutics* of Garlon in 1756; the celebrated thesis of Louis, on *Generation*, in 1754; the treatise on *Presidial Jurisdiction*, by Jousse, in 1755; the *Ericie* of Fontenelle in 1768; the *Thoughts of Jamin* in 1769; the *History of Siam*, by Turpin, and the *Eloge of Marcus Aurelius*, by Thomas, both in 1770; the works on Finance by Darigrand, in 1764, and by Le Trosne in 1779; the *Essay on Military Tactics*, by Guibert, in 1772; the Letters of Boucquet in the same year; and the *Memoirs of Terrai*, by Coquereau, in 1776. Such wanton destruction of property was, however, mercy itself compared to the treatment experienced by other literary men in France. Desforges, for example, having written against the arrest of the Pretender to the English throne, was, solely on that account, buried in a dungeon eight feet square and confined there for three years. This happened in 1749; and in 1770, Audra, professor at the College of Toulouse, and a man of some reputation, published the first volume of his *Abridgement of General History*. Beyond this the work never proceeded; it was at once condemned by the archbishop of the diocese, and the author was deprived of his office. Audra, held up to public opprobrium, the whole of his labours rendered useless, and the prospects of his life suddenly blighted, was unable to survive the shock. He was struck with apoplexy, and within twenty-four hours was lying a corpse in his own house."

14. One of the most comprehensive freethinking works of the century, the *Testament* of JEAN MESLIER, cure of Etrepigny, in Champagne (d. 1729 or 1733), though it inspired numbers of eighteenth-century freethinkers who read it in manuscript, was never printed till 1861–4. It deserves here some special notice. At his death, by common account, Meslier left two autograph copies of his book, after having deposited a third copy in the archives of the jurisdiction of Sainte-Menehould. By a strange chance one was permitted to circulate, and ultimately there were some hundred copies in Paris, selling at ten louis apiece. As he told on the wrapper

of the copy he left for his parishioners, he had not dared to speak out during his life ; but he had made full amends. He is recorded to have been an exceptionally charitable priest, devoted to his parishioners, whose interests he indignantly championed against a tyrannous lord of the manor ;[1] and his book reveals him as a man profoundly impressed at once by the sufferings of the people under heartless kings and nobles, and the immense imposture of religion which, in his eyes, maintained the whole evil system. Some men before him had impugned miracles, some the Gospels, some dogma, some the conception of deity, some the tyranny of kings. He impugns all.

He must have written during whole years, with a sombre, invincible patience, dumbly building up, in his lonely leisure, his unfaltering negation of all that the men around him held for sacred, and that he was sworn to preach—the whole to be his testament to his parishioners. In the slow, heavy style—the style of a cart horse, Voltaire called it—there is an indubitable sincerity, a smouldering passion, but no haste, no explosion. The long-drawn, formless, prolix sentences say everything that can be said on their theme ; and when the long book was done it was slowly copied, and yet again copied, by the same heavy, unwearying hand. He had read few books, it seems—only the Bible, some of the Fathers, Montaigne, the "Turkish Spy," Naude, Charron, Pliny, and Fenelon on the existence of God, with some history, and Moreri's Dictionary ; but he had re-read them often. He does not cite Bayle ; and Montaigne is evidently his chief master. But on his modest reading he had reached as absolute a conviction of the untruth of the entire Judæo-Christian religion as any freethinker ever had. Moved above all by his sense of the corruption and misgovernment around him, he sets out with a twofold indictment against religion

---

[1] The details are dubious. See the memoir compiled by "Rudolf Charles" (R. C. D'Ablaing van Giessenburg), the editor of the *Testament*, Amsterdam, 3 tom, 1861-4.

and government, of which each sustains the other, and he tells his parishioners how he had been "hundreds of times"[1] on the point of bursting out with an indignant avowal of his contempt for the rites he was compelled to administer, and the superstitions he had to inculcate. Then, in a grimly-planned order, he proceeds to demolish, section by section, the whole structure.

Religions in general he exhibits as tissues of error, illusion, and imposture, the endless sources of troubles and strifes for men. Their historical proofs and documentary bases are then assailed, and the Gospels in particular are ground between the slow millstones of his dialectic; miracles, promises, and prophecies being handled in turn. The ethic and the doctrine are next assailed all along the line, from their theoretic bases to their political results; and the kings of France fare no better than their creed. As against the theistic argument of Fenelon, the entire theistic system is then oppugned, sometimes with precarious erudition, generally with cumbrous but solid reasoning; and the eternity of matter is affirmed with more than Averroïstic conviction, the Cartesians coming in for a long series of heavy blows. Immortality is further denied, as miracles had been; and the treatise ends with a stern affirmation of its author's rectitude, and, as it were, a massive gesture of contempt for all that will be said against him when he has passed into the nothingness which he is nearing. "I have never committed any crime," he writes,[2] "nor any bad or malicious action: I defy any man to make me on this head, with justice, any serious reproach"; but he quotes from the Psalms, with grim zest, phrases of hate towards workers of iniquity. There is not even the hint of a smile at the astonishing bequest he was laying up for his parishioners and his country. He was sure he would be read, and he was right.

To the general public, however, he was never known

---

[1] *Testament*, as cited, i, 25. [2] iii, 396.

save by the "Extract"—really a deistic adaptation—made by Voltaire,[1] and the re-written summary by d'Holbach and Diderot entitled *Le Bon Sens du Curé Meslier* (1772). Even this publicity was delayed for a generation, as Voltaire, who heard of the Testament as early as 1735, seems to have made no use of it till 1762. But the entire group of fighting freethinkers of the age was in some sense inspired by the old priest's legacy.

15. With the ground prepared as we have seen, freethought was bound to progress in France in the age of Louis XV; but it chanced that the lead fell into the hands of the most brilliant and fecund of all the writers of the century. VOLTAIRE[2] (1694–1778) was already something of a freethinker when a mere child. So common was deism already become in France at the end of the seventeenth century that his godfather, an abbe, is said to have taught him, at the age of three, a poem by J. B. ROUSSEAU,[3] then privately circulated, in which Moses in particular and religious revelations in general are derided as fraudulent.[4] Knowing this poem by heart in his childhood, the boy was well on the way to his life's work. It is on record that many of his school-fellows were, like himself, already deists, though his brother, a juvenile Jansenist, made vows to propitiate the deity on the small unbeliever's behalf.[5] It may have

[1] First published in 1762, with the date 1742; and reprinted in the *Evangile de la Raison*, 1766. This was condemned to be burned by the Parlement of Paris in 1775, and no fewer than four times ordered to be destroyed in the Restoration period.

[2] Name assumed for literary purposes, and probably composed by anagram from the real name AROUET, with "le jeune" (junior) added, thus: A. R. O. V. E. T. L(e). I(eune).

[3] Not to be confounded with the greater and later Jean Jacques Rousseau.

[4] See the poem in note 4 to ch. ii of Duvernet's *Vie de Voltaire*. Duvernet calls it "one of the first attacks on which philosophy in France had ventured against superstition" (*Vie de Voltaire*, ed. 1797, p. 19).

[5] Duvernet, ch. ii. The free-hearted NINON DE L'ENCLOS, brightest of old ladies, is to be numbered among the pre-Voltairean freethinkers, and to be remembered as leaving young Voltaire a legacy to buy books. She refused to "sell her soul" by turning devote on the invitation of her old friend Madame de Maintenon. Madame du Deffand and Madame Geoffrin were among the later freethinking *grandes dames* of the Voltairean period; and so, presumably, was the Madame de Créqui, quoted by Rivarol, who remarked that "Providence" is "the baptismal name of Chance."

been a general reputation for audacious thinking that led to his being charged with the authorship of a stinging philippic published in 1715, after the death of Louis XIV. The unknown author, a young man, enumerated the manifold abuses and iniquities of the reign, concluding : " I have seen all these, and I am not twenty years old." Voltaire was then twenty-two ; but D'Argenson, who in the poem had been called "the enemy of the human race," finding no likelier author for the verses, put him under surveillance and exiled him from Paris; and on his imprudent return imprisoned him for nearly a year in the Bastille (1716), releasing him only when the real author of the verses avowed himself. Unconquerable then as always, Voltaire devoted himself in prison to his literary ambitions, planning his *Henriade* and completing his *Œdipe*, which was produced in 1718 with signal success.

Voltaire was thus already a distinguished young poet and dramatist when, in 1726, after enduring the affronts of an assault by a nobleman's lacqueys, and of imprisonment in the Bastille for seeking amends by duel, he came to England. Four years previously, in the powerful poem, *For and Against* [1] he had put his early deistic conviction in a vehement impeachment of the immoral creed of salvation and damnation, making the declaration, "I am not a Christian." Thus what he had to learn in England was not deism, but the details of the deist campaign against revelationism ; and these he mastered.[2] Not only was he directly and powerfully influenced by Bolingbroke, who became his intimate friend, but he read widely in the philosophic, scientific, and deistic English literature of the day, and went back to France, after three years' stay, not only equipped for his ultimate battle with tyrannous religion, but deeply

---

[1] *Pour et Contre, ou Epître a Uranie.* It was of course not printed till long afterwards.

[2] He has been alternately represented as owing everything and owing very little to England. Cp. Texte, *Rousseau and the Cosmopolitan Spirit*, Eng. trans. p. 58. Neither view is just.

impressed by the moral wholesomeness of free discussion.[1] Not all at once, indeed, did he become the mouthpiece of critical reason for his age: his literary ambitions were primarily on the lines of *belles lettres*, and secondarily on those of historical writing. After his *Pour et Contre*, his first freethinking production was the *Lettres Philosophiques* or *Lettres Anglaises*, published in English in 1728, and in French in 1733; and the official burning of the book by the common hangman was a sufficient check on such activity for the time. Save for the jests about Adam and Eve in the *Mondaine* (1736), a slight satire for which he had to fly from Paris, and the indirect though effective thrusts at bigotry in the tragedy of *Mahomet* (written in 1739; printed in 1742), in the tales of *Memnon* and *Zadig* (1747-8) and in the *Idees de La Mothe le Vayer* (1751), he produced nothing markedly deistic till 1755, when he published the "Poem to the King of Prussia," otherwise named *Sur la loi naturelle* (which appears to have been written in 1751, while he was on a visit to the Margravine of Bayreuth), and that on the Earthquake of Lisbon. So definitely did the former poem base all morality on natural principles that it was ordered to be burned by the Parlement of Paris, then equally alarmed at freethinking and at Molinism.[2] And so impossible was it still in France to print any specific criticism of Christianity, that when in 1759 he issued his verse translations of the Song of Solomon and Ecclesiastes they also were publicly burned, though he had actually softened instead of heightening the eroticism of the first and the "materialism" of the second.[3]

It is thus a complete mistake on the part of Buckle to affirm that the activity of the French reformers up to 1750 was directed against religion, and that it was thereafter turned against the State. He has probably mistaken

---

[1] Mr Morley (*Voltaire*, 4th ed. p. 40) speaks of the English people as having then won "a full liberty of thought and speech and person." This, as we have seen, somewhat overstates the case. But discussion was much more nearly free than in France.
[2] Condorcet, *Vie de Voltaire*, ed. 1792, p. 92.
[3] *Id.* p. 99.

the meaning of the summing up of some previous writer to the effect that up to 1750 the political opposition to the Court was religious, in the sense of ecclesiastical or sectarian, and that it afterwards turned to matters of public administration.[1] It would be truer to say that the early *Lettres Anglaises*, the reading of which later made the boy Lafayette a republican at nine, were a polemic for political and social freedom, and as such a more direct criticism of the French administrative system than Voltaire ever penned afterwards, save in the *Voix du Sage et du Peuple* (1750). In point of fact, as will be shown below, only a few scattered freethinking works had appeared in French up to 1750, almost none of them directly attacking Christian beliefs; and, despite the above-noted sallies of Voltaire, Condorcet comes to the general conclusion that it was the hardihood of Rousseau's deism in the "Confession of a Savoyard Vicar" in his *Emile* (1762) that spurred Voltaire to new activity.[2] This is perhaps not quite certain: there is some reason to believe that his "Sermon of the Fifty," his "first frontal attack on Christianity,"[3] was written a year before; but in any case that and other productions of his at once left Rousseau far in the rear. Even now he had perhaps no fixed purpose of continuous warfare against so powerful and cruel an enemy as the church, which in 1757 had actually procured an edict pronouncing the death penalty against all writers of works attacking religion; though the fall of the Jesuits in 1764 raised new hopes of freedom. But when, after that hopeful episode, there began a new movement of Jansenist fanaticism, and when, after the age of religious savagery had seemed to be over, there began a new series of religious atrocities in France itself (1762-66), he girded on a sword that was not to be laid down till his death.

The misconception of Buckle, above discussed, has been

[1] The case has been thus correctly put by M. Rocquain.
[2] "Cette hardiesse étonna Voltaire, et excita son emulation" (ed. cited, p. 118).
[3] *Avertissement des éditeurs* in Basle ed. of 1792, vol. xlv, p. 92.

widely shared even among students. Thus Mr. Morley, discussing the "Creed of the Savoyard Vicar" in Rousseau's *Emile* (1762), writes that "Souls weary of the fierce mockeries that had so long been flying like fiery shafts against the far Jehovah of the Hebrews, and the silent Christ of the later doctors and dignitaries," may well have turned to it with ardour (*Rousseau*, ed. 1886, ii, 266). He further speaks of the "superiority of the skeptical parts of the Savoyard Vicar's profession......over the biting mockeries which Voltaire had made the fashionable method of assault" (p. 294). No specifications are offered, and the chronology is seen to be astray. The only mockeries which Voltaire could be said to have made fashionable before 1760 were those of his *Lettres Anglaises*, his *Mondaine*, and his philosophically humorous tales, as *Candide*, *Zadig*, *Micromegas*, etc.; and all his distinctive attacks on Judaism and Christianity were yet to come. Mr. Morley, as it happens, does not make this chronological mistake in his earlier work on Voltaire, where he rightly represents him as beginning his attack on "the Infamous" after he had settled at Ferney (1758). His "fierce mockeries" begin at the earliest in 1761. The mistake may have arisen through taking as true the fictitious date of 1736 for the writing of the *Examen Important de Milord Bolingbroke*. It belongs to 1767. Buckle's mistake, it may be noted, is repeated by so careful a student as Dr. Redlich, *Local Government in England*, Eng. trans. 1903, i, 64.

The rest of his long life was a sleepless and dexterous warfare, by all manner of literary stratagem,[1] facilitated by vast literary fame and ample acquired wealth, against what he called "the Infamous"—the church and the creed which he found still swift to slay for mere variation of belief, and slow to let any good thing be wrought for the bettering of men's lives. Of his prodigious literary performance it is probably within the truth to say that in respect of swift influence on the general intelligence of the world it has never been equalled by any one man's writing; and that, whatever its measure of error and of personal misdirection, its broader influence was invariably for peace on earth, for tolerance among men, and for reason in all things. His faults were many, and some were serious; but to no other man of his age, save

[1] It has been counted that he used no fewer than a hundred and thirty different pseudonyms.

possibly Beccaria, can be attributed so much beneficent accomplishment. If in a literary way he hated his personal foes, much more did he hate cruelty and bigotry ; and it was his work more than any that made impossible a repetition in Europe of such clerical crimes as the hanging of the Protestant pastor, La Rochette ; the execution of the Protestant, Calas, on an unproved and absurdly false charge ; the torture of his widow and children ; the beheading of the lad La Barre for ill-proved blasphemy.[1] As against his many humanities, there is not to be charged on him one act of public malevolence. In his relations with his fickle admirer, FREDERICK THE GREAT, and with others of his fellow-thinkers, he and they painfully brought home to free-thinkers the lesson that for them as for all men there is a personal art of life that has to be learned, over and above the rectification of opinion. But he and they wrought much towards that liberation alike from unreason and from bondage which must precede any great improvement of human things.

Voltaire's constant burden was that religion was not only untrue but pernicious, and when he was not dramatically showing this of Christianity, as in his poem *La Ligue* (1723), he was saying it by implication in such plays as *Zaïre* (1732) and *Mahomet* (1742), dealing with the fanaticism of Islam ; while in the *Essai sur les mœurs* (1756), really a broad survey of general history, and in the *Siecle de Louis XIV*, he applied the method of Montesquieu, with pungent criticism thrown in. Later, he added to his output direct criticisms of the Christian books, as in the *Examen important de Milord*

[1] See details in Mr. Morley's *Voltaire*, 4th ed. pp. 165-170, 257-8. The erection by the French freethinkers of a monument to La Barre in 1905, opposite the Cathedral of the Sacred Heart, Montmartre, Paris, is an expression at once of the old feud with the church and the French appreciation of high personal courage. La Barre was in truth something of a scapegrace, but his execution was an infamy, and he went to his death as to a bridal. The erection of the monument has been the occasion of a futile pretence on the clerical side that for La Barre's death the church had no responsibility, the movers in the case being laymen. Nothing, apparently, can teach Catholic churchmen that the church's past sins ought to be confessed like those of individuals.

Bolingbroke (1767), and the *Recherches historiques sur le Christianisme* (? 1769), continuing all his former lines of activity. Meanwhile, with the aid of his companion the MARCHIONESS DU CHATELET, an accomplished mathematician, he had done much to popularise the physics of Newton and discredit the fallacies of the system of Descartes; all the while preaching a Newtonian but rather agnostic deism. This is the purport of his *Philosophe Ignorant*, his longest philosophical essay.[1] The destruction of Lisbon by the earthquake of 1755 seems to have shaken him in his deistic faith, since the upshot of his poem on that subject is to leave the moral government of the universe an absolute enigma; and in the later *Candide* (1759) he attacks theistic optimism with his matchless ridicule. Indeed, as early as 1749, in his *Traité de la Métaphysique*, written for the Marquise du Chatelet, he reaches virtually pantheistic positions in defence of the God-idea, declaring with Spinoza that deity can be neither good nor bad. But, like so many professed pantheists, he relapsed, and he never accepted the atheistic view; on the contrary, we find him arguing absurdly enough, in his *Homily on Atheism* (1765), that atheism had been the destruction of morality in Rome;[2] and his tale of *Jenni, or, the Sage and the Atheist* (1775), is a polemic against the atheism of d'Holbach. By this time the inconsistent deism of his youth had itself been discredited among the more thoroughgoing freethinkers; and for years it had been said in one section of literary society that Voltaire after all "is a bigot: he is a deist!"[3]

But for freethinkers of all schools the supreme service of Voltaire lay in his twofold triumph over the spirit of religious persecution. He had contrived at once to

---

[1] M. Lanson seems to overlook it when he writes (p. 747) that "the affirmation of God, the denial of Providence and miracles, is the whole metaphysic of Voltaire."

[2] Mr. Morley writes (p. 209): "We do not know how far he ever seriously approached the question......whether a society can exist without a religion." This overlooks the *Homélie sur l'Athéisme*, where it is discussed seriously and explicitly.

[3] Horace Walpole, Letter to Gray, Nov. 19th, 1765.

make it hateful and to make it ridiculous; and it is a great theistic poet of our own day that has pronounced his blade the

"sharpest, shrewdest steel that ever stabbed
To death Imposture through the armour joints."[1]

To be perfect, the tribute should have noted that he hated cruelty much more than imposture; and such is the note of the whole movement of which his name was the oriflamme. It is notable that most of the humanitarian ideas of the latter half of the century—the demand for the reform of criminal treatment, the denunciation of war and slavery, the insistence on good government, and toleration of all creeds—are more definitely associated with the freethinking than with any religious party, excepting perhaps the laudable but uninfluential sect of Quakers.

16. From Voltaire onwards the rationalistic movement in eighteenth-century France so rapidly widens and deepens that it is impossible in the present survey to do more than note its main features. The number of rationalistic writers, despite the press laws which in that age inflicted the indignity of imprisonment on half the men of letters, increased from decade to decade, especially after 1765; the audacious example of Voltaire, and the rising prestige of the *philosophes* in connection with the *Encyclopedie* (1751-72), giving new courage to writers and printers. At once the ecclesiastical powers saw in the *Encyclopedie* a dangerous enemy; and in 1752 the Sorbonne condemned a thesis by the Abbe de Prades, which had at first been received with applause, but which was found on study to breathe the spirit of the new work, whose editor, Diderot, was the Abbe's friend. Soon after came the formal condemnation of the first two volumes of the *Encyclopedie*, of which the second had just appeared.[2]

A new era of propaganda and struggle had visibly

[1] Browning, *The Two Poets of Croisic*, st. cvii.
[2] Rocquain, *L'Esprit Révolutionnaire avant la Révolution*, 1878, pp. 149-151; Morley, *Diderot*, ch. v.

begun. In the earlier part of the century freethought had been disseminated largely by way of manuscripts[1] and reprints of foreign books in translation ; but from the middle onwards, despite denunciations and prohibitions, new books multiply. Voltaire single-handed produced a library ; and d'Holbach is credited with at least a dozen freethinking treatises, every one noticeable in its day. But there were many more combatants. The reputation of Voltaire has overshadowed even that of his leading contemporaries, and theirs and his have further obscured that of the lesser men ; but a partial list of miscellaneous freethinking works by minor French writers during the century, up to the Revolution, will serve to show how general was the activity after 1750. It will be seen that very little was published in France in the period in which English deism was most fecund. It was when the long period of chronic warfare ended for France with the peace of Paris (1763) ; when she had lost India and North America ; when she had expelled the Jesuits (1764) ; and when England had in the main turned from intellectual interests to the pursuit of empire and the development of manufacturing industry, that the released French intelligence turned with irresistible energy to the rational criticism of established opinions. The following table is thus symbolic of the whole century's development :—

1700. *Lettre d'Hippocrate a Damagete*, attributed to the Comte de Boulainvilliers.

,, Gilbert (Claude). *Histoire de Calejava, ou de l'isle des hommes raisonnables, avec le parallele de leur Morale et du Christianisme.* (Dijon.) Suppressed : only one copy known to have escaped.

1704. *Dialogues de M. le Baron de la Houtan et d'un sauvage dans l'Amerique.* By Gueudeville, Amsterdam.

1710. Tissot de Patot. *Voyages et Avantures de Jaques Masse.* (Bourdeaux.)

1712. Deslandes. A. F. B. *Reflexions sur les grands hommes qui sont morts en plaisantant.*[2]

[1] Cp. pref. (*La Vie de Salvian*) to French trans. of Salvian, 1734, p. lxix.
[2] Given by Brunet, who is followed by Wheeler, as appearing in 1732,

1714. *Discours sur la liberté de penser* [French trans. of Collins's *Discourse of Freethinking*], traduit de l'anglois et augmenté d'une Lettre d'un Médecin Arabe.
1725. Huard's trans. of the *Hypotyposes* of Sextus Empiricus.
1732. Re-issue of Deslandes's *Réflexions*.
1737. D'Argens, Marquis. *La philosophie du Bon Sens.* (Berlin.)
1738. ———, *Lettres Juives.* 6 tom. (Berlin.)
,, Marie Huber. *Lettres sur la religion essentielle a l'homme, distingue de ce qui n'en est que l'accessoire.* 2 tom. (Nominally London). Rep. 1739.
1739. ———, *Suite* to the foregoing, "servant de reponse aux objections," etc. Also *Suite de la troisieme partie.*
1741. Deslandes, A. F. B. *Pygmalion, ou la Statue animée.* Condemned to be burnt by Parlement of Dijon, 1742.
1743. *Nouvelles libertés de penser* (Amsterdam).
1745. De la Serre (Lieut.). *Examen de la Religion.* Appeared under other titles. Condemned to be burnt by Parlement of Paris.
,, La Mettrie, *Histoire naturelle de l'âme.*
1747. Deslandes, A. F. B. *De la Certitude des connaissances humaines.*
1748. Esteve, P. *L'Origine de l'Univers expliquée par un principe de matière.*
,, La Mettrie. *L'Homme Machine.*
1750. *Nouvelles libertés de penser.* Rep. (?) Containing Dumarsais's *Dissertation du Philosophe* (the *Essai sur les préjujes*).
1751. Mirabaud, J. B. de. *Le Monde, son origine et son antiquite.*
,, De Prades. *Sorbonne Thesis.*
1752. Maubert de Gouvest. *Lettres Iroquoises.*
,, Génard, F. *L'Ecole de l'homme, ou Parallele des Portraits du siecle et des tableaux de l'écriture sainte.* Author imprisoned.
1753. Baume-Desdossat, Canon of Avignon. *La Christiade.* Book suppressed. Author fined.
1754. Premontval, A. l. le Guay de. *Le Diogene de d'Alembert, ou Pensées libres sur l'homme.* (Berlin : 2nd ed. enlarged, 1755.)
,, Burigny, J. L. *Théologie payenne.*

and as translated into English, under the title *Dying Merrily*, in 1745. But I possess an English translation of *1713* (pref. dated March 25), entitled *A Philological Essay : or, Reflections on the Death of Freethinkers By Monsieur D——, of the Royal Academy of Sciences in France, and author of the Poetae Rusticantis Literatum Otium.* Translated from the French by Mr. B——, with additions by the author, now in London, and the translator. [A note in a contemporary hand makes "B" Boyer.]

1754.	Beausobre, L. de (the Younger). *Pyrrhonisme du Sage.* (Berlin.) Burnt by Paris Parlement.
1755.	*Les Trois Imposteurs.* Attributed to Boulainvilliers.
,,	*Analyse de Bayle.* Begun by Marsy, continued by Robinet.
1756.	*Le Christianisme devoile.* Attributed to Boulanger, Damilaville, and d'Holbach. 3 tom. Rep. 1766 and 1777.
1757.	Premontval. *Vues Philosophiques.* (Amsterdam.) [In this year was pronounced the death penalty against all writers attacking religion. Hence a suspension of publication. In 1764 the Jesuits were expelled, and the policy of suppression was soon paralysed.]
1760.	Dumarsais (d. 1756). *Essai sur les préjugés* (the *Dissertation du Philosophe*, with additions).
1762.	Meister, J. H. *De l'origine des principes religieux.*
1764.	*Discours sur la liberte de penser.* (Rep. of trans. of Collins.)
,,	*Recherches sur l'origine du despotisme oriental, et des superstitions.* Ouvrage posthume de Mr. D. J. D. P. E. C.
,,	*L'Evangile de la Raison*, par M——y, M.D. [ed. by Abbe Dulaurens; containing the *Testament de Jean Meslier* (greatly abridged and adapted by Voltaire)]; Voltaire's *Catechisme de l'honnete homme*, *Sermon des cinquante*, *Examen de la religion*, etc. [Rep. 1766.]
1765.	Castillon, J. L. *Essai de philosophie morale.*
1766.	Boulanger, N. A. *L'Antiquite devoilee.* Recast by d'Holbach.
,,	De Prades. **Abrégé de l'histoire ecclésiastique de Fleury.** (Berlin.) Pref. by Frederick the Great.
,,	Burigny, J. L. *Examen critique des Apologistes de la religion chretienne.* Published by Naigeon under the name of Freret. [Twice rep. in 1767.]
1767.	Castillon, J. L. *Almanach Philosophique.*
,,	*Doutes sur la religion.* Attributed to Boulainvilliers and others.
,,	Dulaurens, Abbé H. J. **L'Antipapisme revélé.**
,,	Freret, N. *Lettre de Thrasybule a Leucippe.* [Written long before.]
,,	Damilaville. · **L'Honnêteté Théologique.**
,,	Reprint of *Le Christianisme devoile.* [Condemned to be burnt, 1770.]
,,	*Questions sur les Miracles.* Par un Proposant.
,,	*Seconde partie* of the *Recherches sur l'origine du despotisme.*
1768.	*Catalogue raisonné des esprits forts, depuis le cure Rabelais jusqu'au curé Meslier.*
,,	D'Holbach. *La Contagion Sacree.*
,,	*Theologie Portative.* "Par l'abbe Bernier." [By d'Holbach.]
,,	D'Argens. *Œuvres completes.* 24 tom. (Berlin.)

1768. Naigeon, J. A. *Le militaire philosophe.*
,, Robinet, J. B. *Considerations Philosophiques.*
1769–1780. *L'Evangile du jour.* 18 tom. Scores of pieces, chiefly by Voltaire, but with some by others.
1769. Castillon, J. L. *Histoire generale des dogmes et opinions philosophiques.*
,, Isoard-Delisle (otherwise Delisle de Sales). *La Philosophie de la Nature.* Author imprisoned.
,, *L'Enfer Detruit,* traduit de l'Anglois [by d'Holbach].
1770. *Histoire critique de Jesus Christ.* [By d'Holbach.]
,, Dumarsais. *Essai sur les préjugés.* Rep.
,, *Recueil Philosophique.* Edited by Naigeon.
[In this year appeared the *Systeme de la Nature* of d'Holbach, which checked deism and turned discussion on atheism. In 1776 appeared Condorcet's *Lettres d'un Theologue,* also atheistic.]
1772. *Le Bon Sens.* [Adaptation from Meslier by Diderot and d'Holbach.]
1773. Carra, J. L. *Systeme de la Raison, ou le prophete philosophe.*
,, Burigny (?). *Recherches sur les miracles.*
1774. D'Holbach. *La politique naturelle.*
,, ———. *Systeme Sociale.*
,, Abauzit, F. *Réflexions impartiales sur les Évangiles,* suivies d'une essai sur l'Apocalypse. (Abauzit died 1767).
1776. D'Holbach. *La morale universelle.*
,, ———. *Ethocratie.*
1777. Carra, J. L. *Esprit de la morale et de la philosophie.*
,, *Examen critique du nouveau Testament.*
Attrib. to J. B. de Mirabaud. Appd. in 1769 as *Réflexions impartiales sur l'evangile.*
1778. Barthez, P. J. *Nouveaux Élements de la Science de l'Homme.*
1780. Duvernet, Abbé Th. J. *L'Intolerance religieuse.*
,, Clootz, Anacharsis. *La Certitude des preuves du Mahometisme.* [Reply by way of parody to Bergier's work, noted on p. 229.]
1781. Marechal, Sylvain. *Le nouveau Lucrece.*
1783. Brissot de Warville. *Lettres philosophiques sur S. Paul.*
1784. Doray de Longrais. *Faustin, ou le siecle philosophique.*
,, Pougens, M. C. J. de. *Recreations de philosophie et de morale.*
1787. Pastoret, Marquis. *Zoroastre, Confucius, et Mahomet.*
1788. Meister, J. H. *De la Morale Naturelle.*
,, Pastoret, Marquis. *Moïse consideré comme legislateur et comme moraliste.*
,, Marechal. *Almanach des honnetes gens.*

1789. Duvernet, Abbe. *Les Dévotions de Madame de Betzamooth.*
  ,,   Cerutti (Jesuit Father). *Breviaire Philosophique, ou Histoire du Judaisme, du Christianisme, et du Déisme.*
1791-93. Naigeon. *Dictionnaire de la philosophie ancienne et moderne.*

Of these works the merit is of course very various; but the total effect of the propaganda was formidable, and some of the treatises are extremely effective. The *Examen critique* of Burigny, for instance, which quickly won a wide circulation, is one of the most telling attacks thus far made on the Christian system, raising as it does most of the issues fought over by recent criticism. It tells indeed of a whole generation of private investigation and debate. The *Lettre de Thrasybule a Leucippe*, said to have been written by Freret (d. 1749) as early as 1722, but never printed in his lifetime, is a no less mordant attack on theism; and the powerful *Essai sur les Préjuges* of DUMARSAIS (1676-1756), first published in 1750,[1] sets forth such a stern indictment alike of religions and governments that few copies of the book were allowed to survive.[2] In him we have already the note of the Revolution. Making no such conciliatory concessions to religion in the abstract as were offered by other deists, he thunders on the text that "Under unjust Gods proclaimed by lying priests, under licentious and cruel chiefs, subjects will never be either virtuous or happy. Morality is forced to break for ever with religion and policy."[3]

Of both Freret and Dumarsais the arguments are to be found reproduced in d'Holbach's *Systeme de la Nature* as well as in the anonymous *Bon Sens* given forth (1772), presumptively by Diderot and d'Holbach, as the work of Jean Meslier, but really an independent

---

[1] In that issue, under the title *Dissertation du Philosophe*, it was prefaced by a letter to La Harpe, then a freethinker, in entire sympathy with the work.

[2] Mirabeau spoke of the *Essai* as "le livre le moins connu, et celui qui merite le plus l'etre." Even the reprint of 1793 had become "extremely rare" in 1822. The book seems to have been specially disquieting to orthodoxy, and was hunted down accordingly.

[3] Ch. xiii. Rep. of 1822, p. 338.

compilation, embodying other arguments with his, and putting the whole with a concision and brilliancy to which he could make no approach. Premontval, a bad writer,[1] contrives to say many pungent things of a deistic order in his *Diogene de d'Alembert*, and, following Marie Huber, puts forward the formula of religion *versus* theology, which has done so much duty in the nineteenth century. Of the whole literature it is not too much to say that it covered cogently most of the important grounds of latter-day debate, from the doctrine of torments to the bases of ethics and the problem of deity; and it would be hard to show that the nineteenth century has handled the main issues with more sincerity, lucidity, or logic than were attained by Frenchmen in the eighteenth. It is only in the analysis of the historical problem by the newer tests of anthropology and hierology, and in the light of latterly discovered documents, that our generation has made much advance on the strenuous pioneers of the age of Voltaire.

17. Though the bibliographers claim to have traced the authorship in most cases, such works were in the first instance nearly always published anonymously,[2] as were those of Voltaire, d'Holbach, and the leading freethinkers; and the clerical policy of suppression had the result of leaving them generally unanswered, save in anonymous writings, when they nevertheless got into private circulation. It was impolitic that an official answer should appear to a book which was officially held not to exist; so that the orthodox defence was mainly confined to the classic performances of Pascal, Bossuet, Huet, Fenelon, and some outsiders such as the Protestant Abbadie, who settled first in Berlin and later in London. The polemic of every one of the writers named is a work of great ability; even that of Abbadie (*Traite de la Verite de la religion chretienne*, 1684), though

---

[1] Like Huard, however, he strives for a reform in spelling, dropping many doubled letters, and writing *home, bone, acuse, fole, apelle, honete, afreux*, etc.

[2] The exceptions were books published outside of France.

now little known, being in its day much esteemed.[1] In the age of Louis XIV those classic answers to unbelief were by believers held to be conclusive; and thus far the French defence was certainly more thorough and philosophical than the English. But French freethought, which in Herbert's day had given the lead to English, now drew new energy from the English growth; and the general arguments of the old apologists did not explicitly meet the new attack. Their books having been written to meet the mostly unpublished objections of previous generations, the church through its chosen policy had the air of utter inability to confute the newer propaganda, though some apologetic treatises of fair power did appear, in particular those of the Abbé Bergier.[2] By the avowal of a Christian historian, "So low had the talents of the once illustrious Church of France fallen, that in the latter part of the eighteenth century, when Christianity itself was assailed, not one champion of note appeared in its ranks; and when the convocation of the clergy, in 1770, published their famous anathema against the dangers of unbelief, and offered rewards for the best essays in defence of the Christian faith, the productions called forth were so despicable that they sensibly injured the cause of religion."[3]

Merit apart, the defence was belated. After the expulsion of the Jesuits (1762)[4] the press grew practically

---

[1] Madame de Sévigné, for instance, declared that she would not let pass a year of her life without re-reading the second volume of Abbadie.
[2] *Le Déisme réfuté par lui-même* (largely a reply to Rousseau), 1765; 1770, *Apologie de la religion chrétienne;* 1773, *La certitude des preuves du christianisme*. Previously had appeared the *Lettres sur le Déisme* of the younger Salchi, professor at Lausanne. It deals chiefly with the English deists, and with D'Argens. There were also two journals, Jesuit and Jansenist, which fought the *philosophes* (Lanson, p. 721); and sometimes even a manuscript was answered—*e.g.*, the *Réfutation du Celse moderne* of the Abbé Gautier (1752), a reply to Mirabaud's unpublished *Examen critique*.
[3] Alison, *History of Europe*, ed. 1849, i, 180–1.
[4] The Jesuits were expelled from Portugal in 1759; from Bohemia and Denmark in 1766; from Spain, Genoa, and Venice in 1767; and from Naples, Malta, and Parma in 1768. At first the Pope, Clement VIII, strove to defend them, but in 1773 the Society was suppressed by papal bull.

more and more free; and when, after the accession of Pope Clement XIV (1769), the freethinking books circulated with less and less restraint, Bergier opened fire on deism, and deists and clerics joined in answering the atheistic *Systeme de la Nature* of d'Holbach. But by this time the deistic books were legion, and the political battle over the taxation of church property had become the more pressing problem, especially seeing that the mass of the people remained conforming.

The English view that French orthodoxy made a "bad" defence to the freethinking attack as compared with what was done in England (Sir J. F. Stephen, *Horæ Sabbaticæ*, 2nd ser. p. 281; Alison, as cited above) proceeds on some misconception of the circumstances, which, as has been shown, were substantially different in the two countries. Could the English clergy have resorted to official suppression of deistic literature, they too would doubtless have done so. Swift and Berkeley bitterly desired to. But the view that the English defence was relatively "good," and that Butler's in particular was decisive, is also, as we have seen, fallacious. In Sir Leslie Stephen's analysis, as apart from his preamble, the orthodox defence is exhibited as generally weak, and often absurd. In France, the defence began sooner, and was more profound and even more methodical. Pascal at least went deeper, and Bossuet (in his *Discours sur l'Histoire Universelle*) more widely, into certain inward and outward problems of the controversy than did any of the English apologists; Huet produced, in his *Demonstratio Evangelica*, one of the most methodical of all the defensive treatises of the time; Abbadie, as before noted, gave great satisfaction, and certainly grappled zealously with Hobbes and Spinoza; Allix, though no great dialectician, gave a lead to English apologetics against the deists (above, p. 107), and was even adapted by Paley; and Fenelon, though his *Traite de l'Existence et des Attributs de Dieu* (1712) and *Lettres sur la Religion* (1716) are not very powerful processes of reasoning, contributed through his reproduced conversations (1710) with Ramsay a set of arguments at least as plausible as anything on the English side, and, what is more notable, marked by an amenity which almost no English apologist attained.

The ground had been thus very fully covered by the defence in France before the main battle in England began; and, when a new French campaign commenced with Voltaire, the defence against that incomparable attack, so far as the system allowed of any, was probably as good as it could have been made in

England. As we have seen, the very principle of suppression disallowed notice of books secretly printed, and therefore officially non-existent. But, as Paley admitted with reference to Gibbon ("Who can refute a sneer?"), the new attack was very hard to meet. A sneer is not hard to refute when it is unfounded, inasmuch as it implies a proposition, which can be rebutted or turned by another sneer. The Anglican church had been well enough pleased by the polemic sneers of Swift and Berkeley; but the other side had the heavier guns, and of the mass of defences produced in England nothing remains save in the neat compilation of Paley. Alison's whole avowal might equally well apply to anything produced in England as against Voltaire. The skeptical line of argument for faith had been already employed by Huet and Pascal and Fenelon, with visibly small success; Berkeley had achieved nothing with it as against English deism; and Butler had no such effect in his day in England as to induce French Catholics to use him. (He does not appear to have been translated into French till 1821.) On the other hand, Voltaire circulated widely in England, and was no better answered there than in France. His attack was, in truth, at many points peculiarly baffling, were it only by its inimitable wit. The English replies to Spinoza, again, were as entirely inefficient or deficient as the French; the only intelligent English answers to Hume on Miracles (the replies on other issues were of no account) made use of the French investigations of the Jansenist miracles; and the replies to Gibbon were in general ignominious failures.

Finally, though the deeper reasonings of Diderot were over the heads alike of the French and the English clergy, the *Systeme de la Nature* of d'Holbach was met skilfully enough at many points by G. J. Holland (1772), who, though not a Frenchman, wrote excellent French, and supplied for French readers a very respectable rejoinder; whereas in England there was practically none. In this case, of course, the defence was deistic; as was that of Voltaire, who criticised d'Holbach as Bolingbroke attacked Spinoza and Hobbes. But the *Examen du Materialisme* of the Abbe Bergier (1771), who was a member of the Academy of Sciences, was at least as good as anything that could then have been done in the Church of England. Broadly speaking, as we have said, much more of French than of English intelligence had been turned to the dispute in the third quarter of the century. In England, political and industrial discussion relieved the pressure on creed; in France, before the Revolution, the whole habit of absolutism tended to restrict discussion to questions of creed; and the attack would in any case have had the best of it, because it embodied all the critical forces hitherto available. The controversy thus went much further than the pre-Humian issues raised in England; and the English orthodoxy of the end of the century was, in comparison, intellectually as weak as politically and socially it was strong.

18. Above the scattered band of minor combatants rises a group of writers of special power, several of whom, without equalling Voltaire in ubiquity of influence, rivalled him in intellectual energy and industry. The names of DIDEROT, D'HOLBACH, D'ALEMBERT, HELVETIUS, and CONDORCET are among the first in literary France of the generation before the Revolution; after them come VOLNEY and DUPUIS; and in touch with the whole series stands the line of great mathematicians and physicists (to which also belongs D'Alembert), LAPLACE, LAGRANGE, LALANDE, DELAMBRE. When to these we add the names of MONTESQUIEU, BUFFON, CHAMFORT, RIVAROL, VAUVENARGUES; of the materialists LA METTRIE and CABANIS; of the philosophers CONDILLAC and DESTUTT DE TRACY; of the historian RAYNAL; of the poet ANDRE CHENIER; of the politicians TURGOT, MIRABEAU, DANTON, DESMOULINS, ROBESPIERRE—all (save perhaps Raynal) deists or else pantheists or atheists—it becomes clear that the intelligence of France was predominantly rationalistic before the Revolution, though the mass of the nation certainly was not.

> It is necessary to deprecate Mr. Lecky's statement (*Rationalism in Europe*, i, 176) that "Raynal has taken, with Diderot, a place in French literature which is probably permanent"—an estimate as far astray as the declaration on the same page that the English deists are buried in "unbroken silence." Raynal's vogue in his day was indeed immense (cp. Morley, *Diderot*, ch. xv); and Edmond Scherer (*Etudes sur la litt. du 18e Siecle*, 1891, pp. 277-8) held that Raynal's *Histoire philosophique des deux Indes* had had more influence on the French Revolution than even Rousseau's *Contrat Social*. But the book has long been discredited (cp. Scherer, pp. 275-6). Although the first edition (1770) passed the censure only by means of bribery, and the second was publicly burned, and its author forced to leave France, he was said to reject, in religion, "only the pope, hell,

and monks" (*Id.* p. 286); and most of the anti-religious declamation in the *Histoire* is said to be from the pen of Diderot, who wrote it very much at random, at Raynal's request.

No list of orthodox names remotely comparable with these can be drawn from the literature of France, or indeed of any other country of that time. JEAN JACQUES ROUSSEAU (1712-1778), the one other pre-eminent figure, though not an anti-Christian propagandist, is distinctly on the side of deism. In the *Contrat Social*[1] writing with express approbation of Hobbes, he declares that "the Christian law is at bottom more injurious than useful to the sound constitution of the State"; and even the famous *Confession of Faith of a Savoyard Vicar* in the *Emile* is anti-revelationist, and practically anti-clerical. He was accordingly anathematised; and, although his temperamental way of regarding things has a clear affinity with some later religious philosophy of a more systematic sort, he undoubtedly made for freethought as well as for the revolutionary spirit in general. Thus the cause of Christianity stood almost denuded of intellectually eminent adherents in the France of 1789; for even among the writers who had dealt with public questions without discussing religion, or who had criticised Rousseau and the *philosophes*—as the Abbes Mably, Morellet, Millot — the tone was essentially rationalistic.

> It has been justly enough argued, concerning Rousseau (see below, p. 253), that the generation of the Revolution made him its prophet in his own despite, and that had he lived twenty years longer he would have been its vehement adversary. But this does not alter the facts as to his influence. A great writer of emotional genius, like Rousseau, inevitably impels men beyond the range of his own ideals, as in recent times Ruskin and Tolstoy, both anti-Socialists, have led thousands towards Socialism. In his own generation and the next, Rousseau counted essentially for criticism of the existing order; and it was the revolutionaries, never the conservatives, who acclaimed him. De Tocqueville (*Hist. philos. du regne de Louis XV*, 1849, i, 33) speaks of his "impiete dogmatique."

[1] Liv. i, ch. 8.

Martin du Theil, in his *J. J. Rousseau apologiste de la religion chretienne* (2e edit. 1840), makes out his case by identifying emotional deism with Christianity, as did Rousseau himself when he insisted that "the true Christianity is only natural religion well explained." Rousseau's praise of the gospel and of the character of Jesus was such as many deists acquiesced in. Similar language, in the mouth of Matthew Arnold, gave rather more offence to Gladstone, as a believing Christian, than did the language of simple unbelief; and a recent Christian polemist, at the close of a copious monograph, has repudiated the association of Rousseau with the faith (see J. F. Nourrisson, *J. J. Rousseau et le Rousseauisme*, 1903, p. 497 sq.). What is true of him is that he was more religiously a theist than Voltaire, whose impeachment of Providence in the poem on the Earthquake of Lisbon he sought strenuously though not very persuasively to refute in a letter to the author. But, with all his manifold inconsistencies, which may be worked down to the neurosis so painfully manifest in his life and in his relations to his contemporaries, he never writes as a believer in the dogmas of Christianity or in the principle of revelation; and it was as a deist that he was recognised by his Christian contemporaries. The work of the Abbe Bergier, *Le Deisme refute par lui-meme* (1765, and later), takes the form of letters addressed to Rousseau, and is throughout an attack on his works, especially the *Emile*. When, therefore, Buckle (1-vol. ed. p. 475) speaks of him as not having attacked Christianity, and Mr. Morley (*Rousseau*, ch. xiv) treats him as creating a religious reaction against the deists, they do not fully represent his influence on his time. As we have seen, he stimulated Voltaire to new audacities by his example.

19. A certain broad development may be traced throughout the century. MONTESQUIEU, who in his early *Persian Letters* (1721) had revealed himself as "fundamentally irreligious,"[1] proceeded in his masterly little book on the *Greatness and Decadence of the Romans* (1734) and his famous *Spirit of Laws* (1748) to treat the problems of human history in an absolutely secular and scientific spirit, making only a few such polite allusions to religion[2] as were advisable in an age when all heretical works were suppressible. In his posthumous *Pensees*

---

[1] Lanson, p. 702. The *Persian Letters*, like the *Provincial Letters* of Pascal, had to be printed at Rouen and published at Amsterdam.

[2] "Au point de vue religieux, Montesquieu tirait poliment son coup de chapeau au christianisme." Lanson, p. 714.

his anti-clericalism is sufficiently emphatic. "Churchmen," he writes, "are interested in keeping the people ignorant." He expresses himself as a convinced deist, and, with no great air of conviction, as a believer in immortality. But there his faith ends. "I call piety," he says, "a malady of the heart, which plants in the soul a malady of the most ineradicable kind." "The false notion of miracles comes of our vanity, which makes us believe we are important enough for the Supreme Being to upset Nature on our behalf." "Three incredibilities among incredibilities: the pure mechanism of animals [the doctrine of Descartes]; passive obedience; and the infallibility of the Pope."[1] Even in his lifetime, Jesuits and Jansenists combined to attack the *Spirit of Laws*, which was denounced at an assembly of the clergy, put on the Roman Index, and prohibited by the censure until Malesherbes came into office in 1750.[2] By this time the repute of Voltaire and others had made the idea of unbelief privately familiar, and thereafter the movement rapidly deepens, the authorities zealously advertising the arch-critic by causing many of his freethinking books to be publicly burnt by the hangman, and putting others under the censure.[3] With a friend like Malesherbes at headquarters, official condemnation of a book tended more than ever to promote its sale. It is told of him that he once warned Diderot that there would be an official raid next day on his editorial premises in connection with the *Encyclopedie;* and when Diderot protested that he could not within the time get all his papers removed and put in safety, Malesherbes replied: "Send them to my office: they will be safe there";

---

[1] *Pensees Diverses: De la religion.* Lanson, p. 714, *note.*
[2] The *Lettres philosophiques* (otherwise the *Lettres anglaises*) were so treated on their appearance in 1734, and the bookseller put in the Bastille; the *Voix du Sage et du Peuple* was officially and clerically condemned in 1751; the poem on *Natural Religion* (otherwise *Natural Law*) was burned at Paris in 1758; *Candide* at Geneva in 1759; and the *Dictionnaire philosophique* at Geneva in 1764; and many of his minor pseudonymous performances had the same advertisement. But even the *Henriade*, the *Charles XII*, and the first chapters of the *Siecle de Louis XIV* were prohibited.

which was accordingly done, with the promised impunity.[1]

20. Alongside of the more strictly literary or humanist movement, there went on one of a scientific kind, which divided into two lines, a speculative and a practical. On the former the philosopher LA METTRIE gave a powerful initial push by his materialistic theses; and others after him continued the impulse. La Mettrie produced his *Natural History of the Mind* in 1745;[2] and in 1746 appeared the *Essay on the Origin of Human Knowledge* of the Abbe CONDILLAC, both essentially rationalistic and anti-theological works, though differing in their psychological positions, Condillac being a non-materialist, though a strong upholder of "sensism." The impulse towards physical science was further reinforced by BUFFON, who like the others was a freethinker, though like them he avoided religious issues. La Mettrie followed up his system with the works *L'Homme Plante* and *L'Homme Machine* (1748), the second of which, published at Leyden[3] and wickedly dedicated to the pious Baron von Haller, was burned by order of the magistrates, its author being at the same time expelled from Holland. Though he professed to think the "balance of probability" was in favour of the existence of a personal God,[4] his other writings gave small support to the hypothesis. It is notable that he, the typical materialist of his age, seems to have been one of its kindliest men, by the consent of all who knew him.[5]

[1] *Mémoires, etc., de Diderot*, ed. 1841, ii, 352. (*Mémoires par sa fille*.)
[2] Published anonymously as a translation from the English : *Histoire naturelle de l'ame*, traduite de l'Anglais de M. Charp, par feu M. H   , de l'Academie des Sciences. À La Haye, 1745.
[3] By Elie Luzac, to whom is ascribed the reply entitled *L'Homme plus que Machine* (1748 also).
[4] Soury, *Bréviaire de l'hist. du matérialisme,* p. 689.
[5] Lange, *Gesch. des Materialismus*, i, 326 sq. (Eng. trans. ii, 78 80); Soury, pp. 663, 666-668 ; Voltaire, *Homélie sur l'athéisme,* end. The conventional denunciation of La Mettrie (endorsed by Mr. Morley, *Voltaire*, p. 122) proceeds upon those of his writings in which he discussed sexual questions with absolute scientific freedom. He, however, insisted that his theoretic discussion had nothing whatever to do with his practice ; and there is no evidence that he lived otherwise than as most men did in his age and ours. Still, the severe censure passed on him by the kindly Diderot seems to convict him of, at least, great levity of character.

A more general influence, naturally, attached to the simple concrete handling of scientific problems. The interest in such questions, noticeable in England at the Restoration and radiating thence, is seen widely diffused in France after the publication of Fontenelle's *Entretiens*, and thenceforward it rapidly strengthens. Barren theological disputations set men not merely against theology but upon the study of Nature, where real knowledge was visibly possible. Even in hidebound Protestant Switzerland, the sheer ennui of Puritanism is seen driving the descendants of the Huguenot refugees to the physical sciences for an interest and an occupation, before any free-thinking can safely be avowed; and in France, as Buckle has shown in abundant detail, the study of the physical sciences became for many years before the Revolution almost a fashionable mania. And at the start the church had contrived that such study should rank as unbelief, and so make unbelievers. When Buffon in 1749 published his *Histoire Naturelle*, the delight which its finished style gave to most readers was paralleled by the wrath which its *Theorie de la Terre* aroused among the clergy. After much discussion, Buffon received early in 1751 from the Sorbonne an official letter specifying as reprehensible in his book fourteen propositions which he was invited to retract. He stoically obeyed in a declaration to the effect that he had "no intention to contradict the text of Scripture," and that he believed "most firmly all there related about the creation," adding "I abandon everything in my book respecting the formation of the earth."[1] During the rest of his life he outwardly conformed to religious usage, but all men knew that in his heart he believed what he had written; and the memory of the affront that the church had thus put upon so honoured a student helped to identify her cause no less with ignorance than with insolence and oppression. For all such insults,

---

[1] Lyell, *Principles of Geology*, 12th ed. 1875, i, 57-58.

and for the long roll of her cruelties, the church was soon to pay a tremendous penalty.

But science, like theology, had its schisms, and the rationalising camp had its own strifes. MAUPERTUIS, for instance, is remembered mainly as one of the victims of the mockery of Voltaire; yet he was really an energetic man of science, and had preceded Voltaire in setting up in France the Newtonian against the Cartesian physics. In his *System of Nature* (not to be confused with the later work of d'Holbach under the same title) he in 1751 propounded a new version of the hylozoisms of ancient Greece, and at the same time anticipated some of the special philosophic positions of Kant.[1] Next in the materialistic series came J. B. ROBINET, whose *Nature* (1761) is a remarkable attempt to reach a strictly naturalistic conception of things.[2] He founds at once on Descartes and Leibnitz, but in his *Philosophical Considerations on the natural gradation of living forms* (1768) he definitely sets aside theism as illusory, and puts ethics on a strictly scientific and human footing,[3] extending the arguments of Hume and Hutcheson somewhat on the lines of Mandeville. On another line of reasoning a similar application of Mandeville's thesis had already been made by HELVETIUS in his *Traité de l'Esprit*[4] (1758), a work which excited a hostility now difficult to understand, but still reflected in censures no less surprising.[5] Its faults are lack of system, undue straining after popularity, some hasty generalisation,

---

[1] Soury, p. 579. The later speculations of Maupertuis by their extravagance discredited the earlier.
[2] Lange, ii, 27, 29; Soury, pp. 603-644.
[3] Soury, pp. 596-600; Lange, ii, 27.
[4] This may best be translated *Treatise on the Mind*.
[5] One of the worst misrepresentations in theological literature is the account of Helvetius by the late Principal Cairns (*Unbelief in the Eighteenth Century*, 1881, p. 158) as appealing to government "to promote luxury, and, through luxury, public good, by abolishing all those laws that cherish a false modesty and restrain libertinage." Helvetius simply pressed the consequences of the existing theory of luxury, which for his own part he disclaimed. *De l'Esprit*, Disc. ii, ch. 15. Dr. Pünjer (i, 462) falls so far below his usual standard as to speak of Helvetius in a similar fashion. As against such detraction it is fitting to note that Helvetius, like La Mettrie, was one of the most lovable and most beloved men of his time.

and a greater concern for paradox than for persuasion; but it abounds in acuteness and critical wisdom, and it definitely and seriously founds public ethics on utility.[1] Its most serious error, the assumption that all men are born with equal faculties, and that education is the sole differentiating force, was repeated in our own age by John Stuart Mill; but in Helvetius the error is balanced by the thoroughly sound and profoundly important thesis that the general superiorities of *nations* are the result of their culture-conditions and politics.[2] The overbalance of his stress on self-interest[3] is an error easily soluble. On the other hand, we have the memorable testimony of BECCARIA that it was the work of Helvetius that inspired him to his great effort for the humanising of penal laws and policy.[4] It may be doubted whether any such fruits can be claimed for the teachings of the whole of the orthodox moralists of the age. For the rest, Helvetius is not to be ranked among the great abstract thinkers; but it is noteworthy that his thinking went on advancing to the end. Always greatly influenced by Voltaire, he did not philosophically harden as did his master; and though in his posthumous work, *Les Progres de la Raison dans la recherche du Vrai* (published in 1775), he stands for deism against atheism, the argument ends in the pantheism to which Voltaire had once attained, but did not adhere.

21. Over all of these men, and even in some measure over Voltaire, DIDEROT (1713–1784) stands pre-eminent, on retrospect, for variety of power and depth and subtlety of thought; though for these very reasons, as well as because some of his most masterly works were never printed in his lifetime, he was less of a recognised popular force than many of his friends. In his own

---

[1] As Mr. Morley notes, Bentham acknowledged Helvetius as his teacher and inspirer. *Diderot*, ed. 1884, p. 329.
[2] *De l'Esprit*, Disc. iii, ch. 30.
[3] Cp. Mr. Morley's criticism, *Diderot*, pp. 331-2.
[4] Beccaria's Letter to Morellet, cited in ch. i of Mr. J. A. Farrer's ed. of the *Crimes and Punishments*, p. 6. It is noteworthy that the partial reform effected earlier in England by Oglethorpe, on behalf of imprisoned debtors (1730-2), belongs to the time of propagandist deism there.

mental history he reproduces the course of the French thought of his time. Beginning as a deist, he assailed the contemporary materialists ; in the end, with whatever of inconsistency, he was substantially an atheist and a materialist.[1] It is recorded that his last words in serious conversation were : "The beginning of philosophy is incredulity"; and it may be inferred from his writings that his first impulses to searching thought came from his study of Montaigne, who must always have been for him one of the most congenial of spirits.[2] At an early stage of his independent mental life we find him turning to the literature which in that age yielded to such a mind as his the largest measure both of nutriment and stimulus—the English. In 1745 he translated Shaftesbury's *Inquiry concerning Virtue and Merit;* and he must have read with prompt appreciation the other English freethinkers then famous. Ere long, however, he had risen above the deistical plane of thought, and grappled with the fundamental issues which the deists took for granted, partly because of an innate bent to psychological analysis, partly because he was more interested in scientific problems than in scholarly research. The *Pensées Philosophiques*, published in 1746, really deserve their name ; and though they exhibit him as still a satisfied deist, and an opponent of the constructive atheism then beginning to suggest itself, they contain abstract reasonings sufficiently disturbing to the deistic position.[3] The *Promenade du Sceptique* (written about 1747, published posthumously) goes further, and presents explicitly the reply to the design argument which was adopted by Hume. Then comes

---

[1] Cp. Soury's contention (p. 577) that we shall never make an atheist and a materialist out of "this enthusiastic artist, this poet-pantheist" (citing Rosenkranz in support), with his own admissions, pp. 589-590, and with Mr. Morley's remarks, pp. 33, 401, 418. See also Lange, i, 310 sq. ; ii, 63 (Eng. trans. ii, 32, 256). Lange points out in this connection (i, 310) that the Hegelian schema of philosophic evolution, "with its sovereign contempt for chronology," has wrought much confusion as to the real developments of the seventeenth and eighteenth centuries.

[2] Cp. Morley, *Diderot*, ed. 1884, p. 32.

[3] *E.g.* § 21.

the *Letter on the Blind, for the use of those who see* (1749), in which a logical rebuttal alike of the ethical and the cosmological assumptions of theism, developed from hints in the *Pensees*, is put in the mouth of the blind English mathematician, Professor Sanderson. It is not surprising that whereas the *Pensees* had been, with some other books, ordered by the Paris Parlement to be burnt by the common hangman, the *Lettre sur les Aveugles* led to his arrest and imprisonment. Both had of course been published without license ;[1] but the second book was more than a defiance of the censorship : it was a challenge alike to the philosophy and the faith of Christendom ; and as such could not have missed denunciation.[2]

But Diderot was not the kind of man to be silenced by menaces. In the famous Sorbonne thesis of the Abbe de Prades (1751), calling in question the positions of theism, he was believed to have a considerable share ; and when De Prades was condemned and deprived of his license (1752), Diderot wrote in whole or in part the *Apology* which defended his positions and arraigned the Jansenists ; imputing to their fanaticism and superstition, their wrangles and their sectarian bitterness, the discredit which among thinking men had latterly fallen upon church and creed alike.[3] Thenceforward he never faltered on his path. It is his peculiar excellence to be an original and innovating thinker not only in philosophy but in psychology, in æsthetics, in ethics, in dramatic art ; and his endless and miscellaneous labours in the *Encyclopedie*, of which he was the most loyal and devoted producer, represent an extraordinary range of

[1] The *Lettre* purports, like so many other books of that and the next generation, to be published "À Londres."

[2] Diderot's daughter in her memoir of him speaks of his imprisonment in the Bastille as brought about through the resentment of a lady of whom he had spoken slightingly ; but the narrative is untrustworthy. The prosecution was quite in the spirit of the period, and the earlier *Pensées* were made part of the case against him. Delort, *Hist. de la détention des philosophes*, 1829, ii, 208-216. Buckle (1-vol. ed. p. 425) does not seem to have fully read the *Lettre*, which he describes as merely discussing the differentiation of thought and sensation among the blind.

[3] Cp. Morley, *Diderot*, pp. 98-99.

interests. He suffered from his position as a hack writer and as a forced dissembler in his articles on religious matters; and there is probably a very real connection between his compulsory insincerities in the *Encyclopedie* —to say nothing of the official prosecution of that and of others of his works—and his misdeeds in the way of indecent fiction. When organised society is made to figure as the heartless enemy of thinking men, it is no great wonder if they are careless at times about the effect of their writings on society. But it stands to his lasting honour that his sufferings at the hands of priests, printers, and *parlements* never soured his natural goodness of heart.[1] Having in his youth known a day's unrelieved hunger, he made a vow that he would never refuse help to any human being; and, says his daughter, no vow was ever more faithfully kept. No one in trouble was ever turned away from his door; and even his enemies were helped when they were base enough to beg of him. It seems no exaggeration to say that the bulk of his life was given to helping other people, physically and mentally; and the indirect effect of his work, which is rather intellectually disinterested than didactic, is no less liberative and humanitarian. "To do good, and to find truth," were his mottoes for life. He was, in his way, as beneficent as Voltaire, without Voltaire's faults of private malice; and his life's work was a great ministry of light. It was Goethe who said of him in the next generation that "whoever holds him or his doings cheaply is a Philistine." His large humanity reaches from the planes of expert thought to that of popular feeling; and while by his *Letter on the Blind* he could advance speculative psychology and pure philosophy, he could by his tale *The Nun* (*La Religeuse*, written about 1760, published 1796) enlist the sympathies of the people against the rule of the church.

[1] Buckle's account of him (1-vol. ed. p. 426) as "burning with hatred against his persecutors" after his imprisonment seems overdrawn. He was a poor hater.

22. With Diderot were specially associated, in different ways, D'ALEMBERT, the mathematician, for some years his special colleague on the *Encyclopedie*, and Baron D'HOLBACH. The former, one of the staunchest friends of Voltaire, though a less invincible fighter than Diderot, counted for practical freethought by his miscellaneous articles, his little book on the Jesuits (1765), his *Pensees Philosophiques*, his physics, and the general rationalism of his Preliminary Discourse to the *Encyclopedie*. D'HOLBACH, a naturalised German of large fortune, was on the other hand one of the most strenuous propagandists of freethought in his age. Imitating the tactic of Voltaire, he produced, with some assistance from Diderot, NAIGEON, and others, a whole series of anti-Christian treatises under a variety of pseudonyms;[1] and his principal work, the famous *System of Nature* (1770), was put out under the name of Mirabaud, an actual person, then dead. Summing up as it does with stringent force the whole anti-theological propaganda of the age, it has been described as a "thundering engine of revolt and destruction."[2] It was the first published atheistic[3] treatise of a systematic kind, if we except that of Robinet, issued two years before; and it significantly marks the era of modern freethought by its stern impeachment of the sins of monarchy—here carrying on the note struck by Jean Meslier in his manuscript of half-a-century earlier. Rather a practical argument than a dispassionate philosophic research, its polemic against human folly laid it open to the regulation retort

[1] See a full list of his works, compiled by JULIAN HIBBERT, prefixed to Watson's ed. (1834 and later) of the English translation of the *System of Nature*. The principal freethinking books apart from that work, ascribed in whole or in part to d'Holbach, are:—*Le Christianisme Dévoilé*, 1756, and later; *La Contagion Sacrée*, 1768, and later; *Théologie Portative*, 1768, and later; *Histoire critique de Jésus Christ*, about 1770; *Le Bon Sens*, 1772, and later; *La politique naturelle*, 1774; *Systeme social*, 1774; *La morale universelle*, 1776; *Ethocratie*, 1776.

[2] Morley, *Diderot*, p. 341. The chapter gives a good account of the book. Cp. Lange, i, 364 sq. (Eng. trans. ii, 26 sq.) as to its materialism.

[3] It is to be noted that the English translation (3 vols. 3rd ed. 1817; 4th ed. 1820) deliberately tampers with the language of the original to the extent of making it deistic. This perversion has been by oversight preserved in all the reprints.

that on its own necessarian principles no such polemic was admissible. That retort is, of course, ultimately invalid when the denunciation is resolved into demonstration. If, however, it be termed "shallow" on the score of its censorious treatment of the past,[1] the term will have to be applied to the Hebrew books, to the Gospel Jesus, to Pascal, Milton, Carlyle, Ruskin, and a good many other prophets, ancient and modern. The synthesis of the book is really emotional rather than philosophic, and hortatory rather than scientific.

23. The death of d'Holbach (1789) brings us to the French Revolution. By that time all the great freethinking propagandists and non-combatant deists of the Voltairean group were gone, save CONDORCET. Voltaire and Rousseau had died in 1778, Helvetius in 1771, Turgot in 1781, D'Alembert in 1783, Diderot in 1784. After all their labours, only the educated minority, broadly speaking, had been made freethinkers; and of these, despite the vogue of the *System of Nature*, only a minority were atheists. Deism prevailed, as we have seen, among the foremost revolutionists; but atheism was relatively rare, though Voltaire, impressed by the number of cultured men of his acquaintance who avowed it, latterly speaks[2] of them as very numerous; and after 1789 the new freethinking works run to critical and ethical attack on the Christian system rather than on theism. VOLNEY combined both lines of attack in his famous *Ruins of Empires* (1791); and the learned DUPUIS, in his voluminous *Origin of all Cults* (1795), took an important step, not yet fully reckoned with by later mythologists, towards the mythological analysis of the Gospel narrative. After these vigorous performances, the popular progress of French freethought

---

[1] So Mr. Morley, p. 347. It does not occur to Mr. Morley, and to the Comtists who take a similar tone, that in thus disparaging past thinkers they are doing exactly the thing they blame.
[2] *Lettres de Memmius a Cicéron* (1771); *Histoire de Jenni* (1775). In the earlier article, ATHÉE, in the *Dictionnaire Philosophique*, he speaks of having met in France very good physicists who were atheists.

was for long practically suspended[1] by the tumult of the Revolution and the reaction which followed it, though LAPLACE went on his way with his epoch-making theory of the origin of the solar system, for which, as he told Napoleon, he had " no need of the hypothesis " of a God. The admirable CONDORCET had died, perhaps by his own hand, in 1794, when in hiding from the Terrorists, leaving behind him his *Esquisse d'un tableau historique des progres de l'esprit humain*, in which the most sanguine convictions of the rationalistic school are reformulated without a trace of bitterness or of despair.

24. No part of the history of freethought has been more distorted than that at which it is embroiled in the French Revolution. The conventional view in England still is that the Revolution was the work of deists and atheists, but chiefly of the latter; that they suppressed Christianity and set up a worship of a Goddess of Reason, represented by a woman of the town; and that the bloodshed of the Terror represented the application of their principles to government, or at least the political result of the withdrawal of religious checks.[2] Those who remember in the briefest summary the records of massacre connected with the affirmation of religious beliefs—the furious strifes of Christian sects under the Roman Empire; the massacres of the period of propagation in Northern Europe, from Charlemagne onwards; the story of the Crusades, in which nine millions of human beings are estimated to have been destroyed; the generation of wholesale murder of the heretics of Languedoc by the Papacy; the protracted savageries of the Hussite War; the early slaughter of Protestant heretics in France; the massacres of German peasants and Anabaptists; the reciprocal persecutions in England; the civil strifes of sectaries in Switzerland; the ferocious wars of the French Huguenots and the League; the

---

[1] Though in 1797 we have Maréchal's *Code d'une Société d'hommes sans Dieu*, and in 1798 his *Pensées libres sur les prêtres*.

[2] Thus Dr. Cairns (*Unbelief in the Eighteenth Century*, p. 165) gravely argues that the French Revolution proves the inefficacy of theism without a Trinity to control conduct.

long-drawn agony of the war of thirty years in Germany; the annihilation of myriads of Mexicans and Peruvians by the conquering Spaniards in the name of the Cross— those who recall these things need spend no time over the proposition that rationalism stands for a removal of restraints on bloodshed. But it is necessary to put concisely the facts as against the legend in the case of the French Revolution.

(*a*) That many of the leading men among the revolutionists were deists is true; and the fact goes to prove that it was chiefly the men of ability in France who rejected Christianity. Of a number of these the normal attitude was represented in the work of Necker, *Sur l'importance des idees religieuses* (1787), which repudiated the destructive attitude of the few, and may be described as an utterance of pious theism or Unitarianism.[1] But the majority of the Constituent Assembly was never even deistic; it professed itself cordially Catholic;[2] and the atheists there might be counted on the fingers of one hand.

> The Abbe Bergier, in answering d'Holbach (*Examen du Materialisme*, ii, ch. i, § 1), denies that there has been any wide spread of atheistic opinion. This is much more probable than the statement of the Archbishop of Toulouse, on a deputation to the king in 1775, that "le monstrueux athéisme est devenu l'opinion dominante" (Soulavie, *Regne de Louis XVI*, iii, 16; cited by Buckle, 1-vol. ed. p. 488, *note*). Joseph Droz, a monarchist and a Christian, writing under Louis Philippe, sums up that "the atheists formed only a small number of adepts" (*Hist. de la Regne de Louis XVI*, ed. 1839, p. 42). And Rivarol, who at the time of writing his *Lettres a M. Necker* was substantially an atheist, says in so many words that, while Rousseau's "Confession of a Savoyard Vicar" was naturally very attractive to many, such a book as the *Systeme*

---

[1] In translation (1788) it found a welcome in England among churchmen by reason of its pro-Christian tone and its general vindication of religious institutions.

[2] Cp. Aulard, *Le Culte de la Raison et le Culte de l'Être Suprême*, 1892, pp. 17-19. M. Gazier (*Etudes sur l'histoire religieuse de la révolution française*, 1877, pp. 48, 173, 189 sq.) speaks somewhat loosely of a prevailing anti-Christian feeling when actually citing only isolated instances, and giving proofs of a general orthodoxy. He points out the complete misconception of Thiers on the subject (p. 202).

de la Nature, " were it as attractive as it is tedious, would win nobody" (*Œuvres*, éd. 1852, p. 134).

Nor were there lacking vigorous representatives of orthodoxy : the powerful Abbe Gregoire, in particular, was a convinced Jansenist Christian, and at the same time an ardent democrat and anti-royalist.[1] He saw the immense importance to the church of a good understanding with the Revolution, and he accepted the constitution of 1790. With him went a very large number of priests. M. Leonce de Lavergne, who was pious enough to write that "the philosophy of the eighteenth century had had the audacity to lay hands on God ; and this impious attempt has had for punishment the revolutionary expiation," also admits that "of the clergy, it was not the minority but the majority which went along with the Tiers Etat."[2] Many of the clergy, however, being refractory, the Assembly pressed its point, and the breach widened. It was solely through this *political* hostility on the part of the church to the new constitution that any civic interference with public worship ever took place. Gregoire was extremely popular with the advanced types,[3] though his piety was conspicuous ;[4] and there were not a few priests of his way of thinking,[5] among them being some of the ablest bishops.[6] On the flight of the king, he and they went with the democracy ; and it was the obstinate refusal of the others to accept the constitution that provoked the new Legislative Assembly to coerce them. Though the new body was more anti clerical than the old, however, it was simply doing what successive Protestant monarchs had done in England and Ireland ; and probably no Government in the world would then have acted otherwise in a similar case.[7] Patience might perhaps have

---

[1] Gazier, *Études sur l'hist. relig. de la révol.* pp. 2, 4, 12, 19-21, 71, etc.
[2] *Les Assemblées Provinciales sous Louis XVI*, 1864, pref. pp. viii-ix.
[3] Gazier, L. ii, ch. 1.   [4] *Id.* p. 67.
[5] *Id.* p. 69.   [6] Léonce de Lavergne, as cited.
[7] The authority of Turgot himself could be cited for the demand that the State clergy should accept the constitution of the State. Cp. Aulard, *Le Culte de la Raison et le Culte de l'Être Suprême*, p. 12 ; Tissot, *Étude sur Turgot*, 1878, p. 160.

won the day; but the Revolution was fighting for its life, and the conservative church, as all men knew, was eager to strangle it. Had the clergy left politics alone, or simply accepted the constitutional action of the State, there would have been no religious question. To speak of such a body of priests, who had at all times been eager to put men to death for heresy, as vindicating "liberty of conscience" when they refused fealty to the constitution,[1] is somewhat to strain the terms. The expulsion of the Jesuits under the Old Regime had been a more coercive measure than the demand of the Assembly on the allegiance of the State clergy. And all the while the reactionary section of the priesthood was known to be in active conspiracy with the royalists abroad. It was only when, in 1793, the conservative clergy were seen to be the great obstacle to the levy of an army of defence, that the more radical spirits began to think of interfering with their functions.[2]

(b) For the rest, the legend falsifies what took place. The facts are now established by exact documentary research.[3] The Government never substituted any species of religion for the Catholic.[4] The Festival of Reason at Notre Dame was an act not of the Convention but of the Commune of Paris and the Department; the Convention had no part in promoting it; half the members stayed away when invited to attend; and there was no Goddess of Reason in the ceremony, but only a Goddess of Liberty, represented by an actress who cannot even be identified.[5] Throughout, the devoutly theistic Rousseau was the chief literary hero of the movement. The two executive Committees in no way countenanced the dechristianisation of the churches, but on the contrary imprisoned persons who removed church properties; and these in turn protested that they

[1] Gazier, p. 113.   [2] Aulard, pp. 19-20.
[3] See the whole details in the definitive work of M. Aulard.
[4] The grave misstatement of Michelet on this head is exposed by M. Aulard, p. 60.
[5] Yet it is customary among Christians to speak of this lady in the most opprobrious terms.

had no thought of abolishing religion. The acts of irresponsible violence did not amount to a hundredth part of the "sacrilege" wrought in Protestant countries at the Reformation, and do not compare with the acts charged on Cromwell's troopers. The policy of inviting priests and bishops to abdicate their functions was strictly political; and the Archbishop Gobel did *not* abjure Catholicism, but only surrendered his office. That a number of priests did gratuitously abjure their religion is only a proof of what was well known—that a good many priests were simple deists. Diderot in a letter of 1769 tells of a day which he and a friend had passed with two monks who were atheists. "One of them read the first draft of a very fresh and very vigorous treatise on atheism, full of new and bold ideas: I learned with edification that this doctrine was the current doctrine of their cloisters. For the rest, these two monks were the 'big bonnets' of their monastery: they had intellect, gaiety, good feeling, knowledge."[1] And a priest of the cathedral of Auxerre, whose recollections went back to the revolutionary period, has confessed that at that time "philosophic" opinions prevailed in most of the monasteries. His words even imply that the unbelieving monks were the majority.[2]

In the provinces, where the movement went on with various degrees of activity, it had the same general character. "Reason" itself was often identified with deity, or declared to be an emanation thereof. Hebert, commonly described as an atheist for his share in the movement, expressly denied the charge, and claimed to have exhorted the people to read the Gospels and obey Christ.[3] Even Chaumette was not an atheist;[4] and the Prussian Clootz, who probably was, had certainly no doctrinary influence; while the two or three other

---

[1] *Mémoires*, ed. 1841, ii, 166.
[2] Pere F.-J.-F. Fortin, *Souvenirs*, Auxerre, 1867, ii, 41.
[3] See the speech in Aulard, p. 240; and cp. pp. 79-85.
[4] *Id.* pp. 81-82.

professed atheists of the Assembly had no part in the public action.

(c) Finally, Robespierre was all along thoroughly hostile to the movement: in his character of Rousseauist and deist he argued that atheism was "aristocratic"; he put to death the leaders of the Cult of Reason; and he set up the Worship of the Supreme Being as a counter-move. Broadly speaking, he affiliated to Necker, and stood very much at the standpoint of the English Unitarianism of the present day. Thus the bloodshed of the Reign of Terror, if it is to be charged on any species of philosophic doctrine rather than on the unscrupulous policy of the enemies of the Revolution in and out of France, stands to the credit of the belief in a God, the creed of Frederick, Turgot, Necker, Franklin, Pitt, and Washington. The one convinced and reasoning atheist among the publicists of the time, the journalist SALAVILLE,[1] opposed the Cult of Reason with sound and serious and persuasive argument, and strongly blamed all forcible interference with worship, while at the same time calmly maintaining atheism as against theism. The age of atheism had not come, any more than the triumph of Reason.

25. The anti-atheistic and anti-philosophic legend was born of the exasperation and bad faith of the dethroned aristocracy, themselves often unbelievers in the day of their ascendency, and, whether unbelievers or not, responsible with the church and the court for that long insensate resistance to reform which made the revolution inevitable. In the life of the brilliant Rivarol, who associated with the noblesse while disdained by many of them because of his obscure birth, we may read the intellectual history of the case. Brilliant without patience, keen without scientific coherence,[2] Rivarol in 1787 met the pious deism of Necker with a dialectic in

[1] Concerning whom see Aulard, pp. 86-96.
[2] Cp. the admissions of Curnier (*Rivarol, sa vie et ses œuvres*, 1858, p. 149) in deprecation of Burke's wild likening of Rivarol's journalism to the Annals of Tacitus.

which cynicism as often disorders as illuminates the argument. With prompt veracity he first rejects the ideal of a beneficent reign of delusion, and insists that religion is seen in all history powerless alike to overrule men's passions and prejudices, and to console the oppressed by its promise of a reversal of earthly conditions in another world. But in the same breath, by way of proving that the atheist is less disturbing to convention than the deist, he insists that the unbeliever soon learns to see that "irreverences are crimes against society"; and then, in order to justify such conformity, asserts what he had before denied. And the self-contradiction recurs.[1] The underlying motive of the whole polemic is simply the grudge of the upper class diner-out against the serious and conscientious *bourgeois* who strives to reform the existing system. Conscious of being more enlightened, the wit is eager at once to disparage Necker for his religiosity and to discredit him politically as the enemy of the socially useful ecclesiastical order. The due sequence is that when the Revolution breaks out Rivarol sides with the court and the noblesse, while perfectly aware of the ineptitude and malfeasance of both ;[2] and, living in exile, proceeds to denounce the philosophers as having caused the overturn by their universal criticism. In 1787 he had declared that he would not even have written his Letters to Necker if he were not certain that "the people does not read." Then the people had not read the philosophers any more than it did him. But in exile he must needs frame for the *emigres* a formula, true or false. It is the falsity of men divided against themselves, who pay themselves with recriminations rather than realise their own deserts.[3] And in the end Rivarol is but a deist.

[1] *Œuvres*, ed. cited, pp. 136–140, 147–155.
[2] Cp. the critique of Sainte-Beuve, prefixed to ed. cited, pp. 14–17, and that of Arsene Houssaye, *id.* pp. 31–33.
[3] Charles Comte is thus partly inaccurate in saying (*Traité de Législation,* 1835, i, 72) that the charge against the philosophers began "on the day on which there was set up a government in France that sought

If the slightest attempt be made to analyse the situation, the thesis as to the activity of the *philosophes* must at once be restricted to the cases of Rousseau, Raynal, and d'Holbach. Voltaire was in things political a conservative, save in so far as he fought for toleration and for the most necessary reforms. Only by heedless misreading or malice can support be given to the pretence that Diderot wrought for the violent overthrow of the existing political system. A phrase about strangling kings in the bowels of priests is expressly put by him in the mouth of an *Éleuthéromane* or Liberty-maniac ;[1] which shows that the type had arisen in his lifetime in opposition to his own bias. The tyranny of the French Government he did indeed detest, as he had cause to do, and as every man of good feeling did with him; but no writing of his wrought measurably for its overthrow.[2] Some of the philosophers, it is true, themselves gave colour to the view that they were the makers of the Revolution, as when D'Alembert said to Romilly that "philosophy" had produced in his time that change in the popular mind which exhibited itself in the indifference with which they received the news of the birth of the dauphin.[3] The error is none the less plain. It was the whole political and social evolution of two generations that had wrought the change; and the people were still for the most part believing Catholics. Frederick the Great was probably right when he reminded the more optimistic philosophers that their entire public did not number above 200,000 people.

And this is the answer to any pretence that the Revolution was the work of the school of d'Holbach. Bergier the priest, and Rivarol the conservative

to re-establish the abuses of which they had sought the destruction." What is true is that the charge, framed at once by the backers of the Old Regime, has always since done duty for reaction.

[1] Cp. Morley, *Diderot*, p. 407. Mr. Morley points to the phrase in another form in a letter of Voltaire's in 1761. It really derives from Jean Meslier, who quotes it from an unlettered man (*Testament*, i, 19).

[2] As Mr. Morley points out, Henri Martin absolutely reverses the purport of a passage in order to convict Diderot of justifying regicide.

[3] *Memoirs of Sir Samuel Romilly*, 3rd ed. 1841, i, 46.

unbeliever, alike denied that d'Holbach's systematic writings had any wide public. Doubtless the same men were ready to eat their words for the satisfaction of vilifying an opponent. It has always been the way of orthodoxy to tell atheists alternately that they are an impotent handful, and that they are the ruin of society. But by this time it ought to be a matter of elementary knowledge that a great political revolution can be wrought only by far-reaching political forces, whether or not these may concur with a propaganda of rationalism in religion.[1] If any "philosopher" so-called is to be credited with specially promoting the Revolution, it is either Rousseau, who is so often hailed as the engineer of a religious reaction, and whose works, as has been repeatedly remarked, "contain much that is utterly and irreconcilably opposed" to the Revolution,[2] or Raynal, who was only anti-clerical, not anti-Christian, and who actually censured the revolutionary procedure. They were the two most popular writers of their day who dealt with social as apart from religious or philosophical issues, and to both is imputed a general subversiveness. But here, too, the charge rests upon a sociological fallacy. Rousseau was influential towards change because change was essential, not because he was restless. He was influential because he set forth what so many felt. In brief, the evils of the Revolution lie at the door not of the reformers, but of the men, the classes, and the institutions which first provoked and then resisted it.[3]

---

[1] This is the sufficient comment on a perplexing page of Mr. Morley's second monograph on Burke (pp. 110–111), which I have never been able to reconcile with the rest of his writing.
[2] Lecky, *Hist. of England in the Eighteenth Century,* small ed. vi, 263.
[3] On this complicated issue, which cannot be here handled at any further length, see Professor P. A. Wadia's essay *The Philosophers and the French Revolution* (Social Science Series, 1904), which, however, needs revision; and compare the argument of Nourrisson, *J.-J. Rousseau et le Rousseauisme,* 1903, ch. xx.

§ II. *Germany.*

1. When two generations of Protestant strife had turned to naught the intellectual promise of the Reformation, and much of the ground first won by it had lapsed to Catholicism, the general forward movement of European thought availed to set up in Germany as elsewhere a measure of critical unbelief. There is abundant evidence that the Lutheran clergy not only failed to hold the intelligence of the country with them, but in large part fell into personal disrepute.[1] "The scenes of clerical immorality," says an eminently orthodox historian, "are enough to chill one's blood even at the distance of two centuries."[2] A Church Ordinance of 1600 acknowledges information to the effect that a number of clergymen and schoolmasters are guilty of "whoredom and fornication," and commands that "if they are *notoriously* guilty they shall be suspended." Details are preserved of cases of clerical drunkenness and ruffianism; and the women of the priests' families do not escape the pillory.[3] It is noted that "the great moral decline of the clergy was confined chiefly to the Lutheran Church. The Reformed [Calvinistic] was earnest, pious, and aggressive"[4]—the usual result of official hostility.

In such circumstances, the active freethought existing in France at the beginning of the seventeenth century could not fail to affect Germany; and even before the date of the polemic of Garasse and Mersenne there appeared (1615) a counterblast to the new thought in the *Theologia Naturalis* of J. H. Alsted, of Frankfort, directed *adversus atheos, Epicureos, et sophistas hujus temporis.* The preface to this solid quarto (a remarkable

---

[1] Cp. Pusey, *Histor. Enquiry into the Probable Causes of the Rationalist Character......of the Theology of Germany,* 1828, p. 79.
[2] Bishop Hurst, *History of Rationalism,* ed. 1867, p. 56.
[3] *Id.* pp. 57-58 (last ed. pp. 74-76), citing Tholuck, *Deutsche Universitäten,* i, 145-148, and Dowding, *Life and Correspondence of Calixtus,* pp. 132-3.
[4] Hurst, p. 59.

sample of good printing for the period) declares that
"there are men in this diseased *(exulcerato)* age who
dare to oppose science to revelation, reason to faith,
nature to grace, the creator to the redeemer, and truth
to truth"; and the writer undertakes to rise argumentatively from nature to the Christian God, without,
however, transcending the logical plane of De Mornay.
The trouble of the time, unhappily, was not rationalism,
but the inextinguishable hatreds of Protestant and
Catholic, and the strife of economic interests dating
from the appropriations of the first reformers. At
length, after a generation of gloomy suspense, came
the explosion of the hostile ecclesiastical interests, and
the long-drawn horror of the Thirty Years' War, which
left Germany mangled, devastated, drained of blood and
treasure, decivilised, and well-nigh destitute of the
machinery of culture. No such printing as that of
Alsted's book was to be done in the German world for
many generations. But as in France, so in Germany,
the exhausting experience of the moral and physical
evil of religious war wrought something of an antidote,
in the shape of a new spirit of rationalism.

Not only was the Peace of Westphalia an essentially
secular arrangement, subordinating all religious claims
to a political settlement,[1] but the drift of opinion was
markedly freethinking. Already in 1630 one writer
describes "three classes of skeptics among the nobility
of Hamburg: first, those who believe that religion is
nothing but a mere fiction, invented to keep the masses
in restraint; second, those who give preference to no
faith, but think that all religions have a germ of truth;
and third, those who, confessing that there must be one
true religion, are unable to decide whether it is papal,
Calvinist, or Lutheran, and consequently believe nothing
at all."[2] No less explicit is the written testimony of
Walther, the court chaplain of Ulrich II of East

---

[1] Cp. Buckle, 1-vol. ed. pp. 308-9.
[2] Quoted by Bishop Hurst, ed. cited, p. 60.

Friesland, 1637:—" These infernal courtiers, among whom I am compelled to live against my will, doubt those truths which even the heathen have learned to believe."[1] In Germany as in France the freethinking which thus grew up during the religious war expanded after the peace. As usual, this is to be gathered from the orthodox propaganda against it, setting out in 1662 with a *Preservative against the Pest of Present-day Atheists* [2] by one Theophilus Gegenbauer. So far was this from attaining its end that there ensued ere long a more positive and aggressive development of freethinking than any other country had yet seen. A wandering scholar, MATTHIAS KNUTZEN (b. 1645), who had studied philosophy at Konigsberg, went about teaching a hardy Religion of Humanity, rejecting alike immortality, God and Devil, churches and priests, and insisting that conscience could perfectly well take the place of the Bible as a guide to conduct. His doctrines are to be gathered chiefly from a curious Latin letter, written by him for circulation, entitled *Amicus Amicis Amica;* and in this the profession of atheism is explicit: "*Insuper Deum negamus.*" His followers, as holding by conscience, were called *Gewissener;* and he is reported to have said that at Jena alone, about 1674, there were seven hundred of them. Yet he and the whole movement passed rapidly out of sight—hardly by reason of the orthodox refutations, however. Germany was in no state to sustain such a party; and what happened was a necessarily slow gestation of the seed of new thought thus cast abroad.

> Knutzen's letter is given in full by a Welsh scholar settled in Germany, Jenkinus Thomasius (Jenkin Thomas), in his *Historia Atheismi*, 1709, pp. 97-101. Thomasius thus codifies its doctrine:—" 1. There is neither God nor Devil. 2. The magistrate is nothing to be esteemed; temples are to be condemned, priests to be rejected. 3. In place of the magistrate and the priest are to be put knowledge and reason, joined with

---

[1] Quoted by Bishop Hurst, ed. cited, p. 60 (78).
[2] *Preservatio wider die Pest der heutigen Atheisten.*

conscience, which teaches to live honestly, to injure none, and to give each his own. 4. Marriage and free union do not differ. 5. This is the only life : after it, there is neither reward nor punishment. 6. The Scripture contradicts itself." Knutzen admittedly wrote like a scholar (Thomasius, p. 97). As to the numbers of the movement see Trinius, *Freydenker Lexicon*, 1759, s.v. KNUTZEN. Kurtz (*Hist. of the Christian Church*, Eng. trans. 1864, i, 213) states that a careful academic investigation proved the claim to a membership of 700 to be an empty boast (citing H. Rossel, *Studien und Kritiken*, 1844, iv). It is difficult to attach any weight to an academic pronouncement on the subject, at a time when avowal of membership in an atheistic movement meant the peril of grave penalties, if not of death. "Examples of total unbelief come only singly to knowledge," says Tholuck ; "but total unbelief had still to the end of the century to bear penal treatment." He gives the instances (1) of the Swedish Baron Skytte, reported in 1669 by Spener to the Frankfort authorities for having said at table, before the court preacher, that the Scriptures were not holy, and not from God but from men ; and (2) "a certain minister" who at the end of the century was prosecuted for blasphemy. (*Das kirchliche Leben des 17ten Jahrhunderts*, 2 Abth. pp. 56-57.) Even anabaptists were still liable to banishment in the middle of the century. *Id.*, 1 Abth. 1861, p. 36. As to clerical intolerance see pp. 40-44. On the merits of the Knutzen movement cp. Pünjer, *Hist. of the Christian Philos. of Religion*, Eng. trans. i, 437-8.

2. While, however, clerical action could drive such a movement under the surface, it could not prevent the spread of rationalism in all directions ; and there was now germinating a philosophic unbelief[1] under the influence of Spinoza. Nowhere were there more prompt and numerous answers to Spinoza than in Germany,[2] whence it may be inferred that within the educated class he soon had a good many adherents. In point of fact the Elector Palatine offered him a professorship of philosophy at Heidelberg in 1673, promising him "the most ample freedom in philosophical teaching," and

---

[1] Even Knutzen seems to have been influenced by Spinoza. Pünjer, *Hist. of the Christ. Philos. of Religion*, Eng. trans. i, 437. Dr. Pünjer, however, seems to have exaggerated the connection.

[2] Cp. Lange, *Gesch. des Materialismus*, 3te Aufl. i, 318 (Eng. trans. ii, 35).

merely stipulating that he should not use it "to disturb the religion publicly established."[1] On the other hand, Professor Rappolt, of Leipzig, attacked him as an atheist, in an *Oratio contra naturalistas* in 1670; Professor Musæus, of Jena, assailed him in 1674;[2] and the Chancellor Kortholt, of Kiel, grouped him, Herbert, and Hobbes as *The Three Great Impostors* in 1680.[3] After the appearance of the *Ethica* the replies multiplied. On the other hand, Cuffelaer vindicated Spinoza in 1684; and in 1691 F. W. STOSCH, a court official, and son of the court preacher, published a stringent attack on revelationism, entitled *Concordia rationis et fidei*, partly on Spinozistic lines, which created much commotion, and was forcibly suppressed and condemned to be burnt by the hangman at Berlin,[4] as it denied not only the immateriality but the immortality of the soul and the historical truth of the Scriptural narratives. This seems to have been the first work of modern freethought published by a German,[5] apart from Knutzen's letter; but a partial list of the apologetic works of the period, from Gegenbauer onwards, may suffice to suggest the real vogue of heterodox opinions:—

1662. Th. Gegenbauer. *Preservatio wider die Pest des heutigen Atheisten.* Erfurt.
1668. J. Musæus. *Examen Cherburianismi. Contra E. Herbertum de Cherbury.*
1670. Rappolt. *Oratio contra Naturalistas.* Leipzig.
1672. J. Müller. *Atheismus devictus* (in German). Hamburg.
,, J. Lassen. *Arcana-Politica-Atheistica* (in German).
1673. ——— *Besiegte Atheisterey.*
,, Chr. Pfaff. *Disputatio contra Atheistas.*
1674. J. Musæus. *Spinozismus.* Jena.

[1] *Epistolæ ad Spinozam et Responsiones*, liii.
[2] Colerus, *Vie de Spinoza*, in Gfrorer's ed. of the *Opera*, 1830, pp. lv, lvi.
[3] Pünjer, as cited, i, 434-6; Lange, last cit. Lange notes that Genthe's *Compendium de impostura religionum*, which has been erroneously assigned to the 16th century, must belong to the period of Kortholt's work.
[4] Pünjer, p. 439; Lange, last cit.; Tholuck, *Das Kirchliche Leben*, 2 Abth. pp. 57-58.
[5] It was nominally issued at Amsterdam, really at Berlin.

1677.	Val. Greissing. *Corona Transylvani: Exerc. 2, de Atheismo, contra Cartesium et Math. Knutzen.* Wittemberg.	
,,	Tobias Wagner. *Examen......atheismi speculativi.* Tübingen.	
,,	Rudrauf, Theol. Giessenis, **Dissertatio de Atheismo.**	
1680.	Chr. Kortholt. *De tribus impostoribus magnis liber.* Kiloni.	
1689.	Th. Undereyck. *Der Närrische Atheist in seiner Thorheit ueberzeugt.* Bremen.	
1696.	J. Lassen. *Arcana-Politica-Atheistica.* Reprint.	
1697.	Grapius. *An Atheismus necessario ducat ad corruptionem morum.* Rostock.	
,,	Em. Weber. *Beurtheilung der Atheisterei.*	
1700.	Tribbechov. *Historia Naturalismi.* Jena.	
1708.	Loescher. *Prænotiones Theologicæ contra Naturalistarum et Fanaticorum omne genus, Atheos, Deistas, Indifferentistas,* etc. Wittemberg.	
,,	Schwartz. *Demonstrationes Dei.* Leipzig.	
,,	Rechenberg. **Fundamenta veræ religionis Prudentum,** *adversus Atheos,* etc.	
1709.	Jenkinus Thomasius. *Historia Atheismi.* Basel.	
1710.	J. C. Wolfius. *Dissertatio de Atheismi falso suspectis.* Wittemberg.	
1713.	J. N. Fromman. *Atheus Stultus.* Tubingen.	
,,	Anon. *Widerlegung der Atheisten, Deisten, und neuen Zweifeler.* Frankfort.	

[Later came the works of Buddeus (1716) and Reimmann and Fabricius, noted above, vol. i, ch. i, § 2.]

3. For a community in which the reading class was mainly clerical and scholastic, the seeds of rationalism were thus in part sown in the seventeenth century; but the ground was not yet propitious. Leibnitz (1646–1716), the chief thinker produced by Germany before Kant, lived in a state of singular intellectual isolation;[1] and showed his sense of it by writing his philosophic treatises chiefly in French. One of the most widely learned men of his age, he was wont from his boyhood to grapple critically with every system of thought that came in his way; and, while claiming to be always eager to learn,[2] he was as a rule strongly concerned to affirm his own powerful bias. Early in life he writes that it horrifies him to think how many men he has met who

---

[1] Cp. *Buckle and his Critics,* pp. 171–2; Punjer, i, 515.
[2] Letter cited by Dr. Latta, *Leibniz,* 1898, p. 2, *note.*

were at once intelligent and atheistic;[1] and his propaganda is always dominated by the desire rather to confute unbelief than to find out the truth. As early as 1668 (aet. 22) he wrote an essay to that end, which was published as a *Confessio naturæ contra Atheistas*. Against Spinoza he reacted instantly and violently, pronouncing the *Tractatus* on its first (anonymous) appearance an "unbearably bold (*licentiosum*) book," and resenting the Hobbesian criticism which it "dared to apply to sacred Scripture."[2] Yet in the next year we find him writing to Arnauld in earnest protest against the hidebound orthodoxy of the Church. "A philosophic age," he declares, "is about to begin, in which the concern for truth, flourishing outside the schools, will spread even among politicians. Nothing is more likely to strengthen atheism and to upset faith, already so shaken by the attacks of great but bad men [a pleasing allusion to Spinoza], than to see on the one side the mysteries of the faith preached upon as the creed of all, and on the other hand become matter of derision to all, convicted of absurdity by the most certain rules of common reason. The worst enemies of the church are in the church. Let us take care lest the latest heresy —I will not say atheism, but—naturalism, be publicly professed."[3] For a time he seemed thus disposed to liberalise. He wrote to Spinoza on points of optics before he discovered the authorship; and he is represented later as speaking of the *Tractatus* with respect. He even called on Spinoza in 1676, and obtained a perusal of the manuscript of the *Ethica;* but he remained hostile to him in theology and philosophy. To the last he called Spinoza a mere developer of Descartes,[4] whom he also resisted. This was not hopeful; and Leibnitz,

[1] *Philosophische Schriften*, ed. Gerhardt, i, 26; trans. in Martineau's *Study of Spinoza*, p. 77.
[2] Letter to Thomas, December 23rd, 1670.
[3] Quoted by Tholuck, as last cited, p. 61. Spener took the same tone.
[4] Latta, p. 24; Martineau, *Study of Spinoza*, p. 75; *Philos. Schriften von Leibniz*, ed. Gerhardt, i, 34; ii, 563. Cp. *Refutation of Spinoza by Leibnitz*, ed. by Foucher de Careil, Eng. trans. 1855.

with all his power and originality, really wrought little for the direct rationalisation of religious thought.[1] His philosophy, with all its ingenuity, has the common stamp of the determination of the theist to find reasons for the God in whom he believed beforehand; and his principle that all is for the best is the fatal rounding of his argumentative circle. Nominally he adhered to the entire Christian system, though he declared that his belief in dogma rested on the agreement of reason with faith, and claimed to keep his thought free on unassailed truths;[2] and he always discussed the Bible as a believer; yet he rarely went to church;[3] and the Low German nickname *Lovenix* (= *Glaubet nichts*, "believes nothing") expressed his local reputation. No clergyman attended his funeral; but indeed no one else went, save his secretary.[4]

4. It is on the whole difficult to doubt that his indirect influence not only in Germany but elsewhere had been for deism and atheism.[5] He and Newton were the most distinguished mathematicians and theists of the age; and Leibnitz, as we saw, busied himself to show that the philosophy of Newton[6] tended to atheism, and that that of their theistic predecessor Descartes would not stand criticism.[7] Spinoza being, according to him, in still worse case, and Locke hardly any sounder,[8] there remains for theists only his cosmology of monads and his ethic of optimism—all for the best in the best of all possible worlds—which seems at least as well fitted as

---

[1] His notable surmise as to gradation of species (see Latta, pp. 38–39) was taken up among the French materialists, but did not then modify current science.

[2] Cp. Tholuck, *Das kirchliche Leben*, as cited, 2 Abth. 1862, pp. 52-55.

[3] Cp. Pünjer, i, 509, as to his attitude on ritual.

[4] Latta, as cited, p. 16; *Vie de Leibnitz*, par De Jaucourt, in ed. 1747 of the *Essais de Théodicée*, i, 235-9.

[5] As to his virtual deism, see Pünjer, i, 513-5. But he proposed to send Christian missionaries to the heathen. Tholuck, p. 55.

[6] *Lettres entre Leibnitz et Clarke.*

[7] *Discours de la conformité de la foi avec la raison*, §§ 68-70; *Essais sur la bonté de Dieu*, etc., §§ 50, 61, 164, 180, 292-3.

[8] The *Nouveaux Essais sur l'Entendement humain*, refuting Locke, appeared posthumously in 1765. Locke in his turn had treated his theistic critic with contempt. (Latta, p. 13.)

any other theism to make thoughtful men give up the principle. Other culture-conditions concurred to set up a spirit of rationalism in Germany. After the Thirty Years' War there arose a religious movement, called *Pietism* by its theological opponents, which aimed at an emotional inwardness of religious life as against what its adherents held to be an irreligious orthodoxy around them.[1] Though its first leaders grew embittered with their unsuccess and the attacks of their religious enemies,[2] their impulse went far, and greatly influenced the clergy through the university of Halle, which turned out 6,000 clergymen in one generation.[3] Against the Pietists were furiously arrayed the Lutherans of the old order, who even contrived in many places to suppress their schools.[4] Religion was thus represented by a species of extremely unattractive and frequently absurd formalists on the one hand, and on the other by a school tending alternately to fanaticism and cant.[5] Thus "the rationalist tendencies of the age were promoted by this treble exhibition of the aberrations of belief."[6] "How sorely," says Tholuck, "the hold not only of ecclesiastical but of Biblical belief on men of all grades had been shaken at the beginning of the eighteenth century is seen in many instances."[7] Orthodoxy selects that of a Holstein student who hanged himself at Wittemberg in 1688, leaving written in his New Testament, in Latin, the declaration that "Our soul is mortal; religion is a popular delusion, invented to gull the ignorant and so govern the world the better."[8] But again there is the testimony of the mint-master at Hanover that at court

---

[1] Amand Saintes, *Hist. crit. du Rationalisme en Allemagne*, 1841, ch. vi.
[2] Hagenbach, *German Rationalism*, Eng. trans. 1865, p. 9.
[3] *Id.* p. 39; Pusey, *Historical Enquiry into the Causes of German Rationalism*, 1828, pp. 88, 97.
[4] Pusey, pp. 86, 87, 98.
[5] Cp. Pusey, pp. 37-38, 45, 48, 49, 53-4, 79, 101-9; Saintes, pp. 28, 79-80; Hagenbach, pp. 41, 72, 105.
[6] Pusey, p. 110. Cp. Saintes, ch. vi.
[7] *Das kirchliche Leben*, as cited, 2 Abth. p. 58.
[8] *Id.* pp. 56-57.

there all lived as "free atheists." And though the name "freethinker" was not yet much used in discussion, it had become current in the form of *Freigeist*[1]—the German equivalent still used. This was probably a survival from the name of the old sect of the "Free Spirit," rather than an adaptation from the French *esprit fort* or the English "freethinker."

5. After the collapse of the popular movement of Matthias Knutzen, the thin end of the new wedge may be seen in the manifold work of CHRISTIAN THOMASIUS (1655-1728), who at the age of twenty-two published a treatise on "Divine Jurisprudence," in which the principles of Puffendorf on natural law were carried so far as to give much offence. Innovating in all things, he began, while still a *Privatdocent* at Leipzig University, a campaign on behalf of the German language; and, not content with arousing much pedantic enmity by delivering lectures for the first time in his mother tongue, and deriding at the same time the bad scholastic Latin of his compatriots, he set on foot the first German periodical,[2] which ran for two years (1688-90), and caused so much anger that he was twice prosecuted before the ecclesiastical court of Dresden, the second time on a charge of contempt of religion. Other satirical writings, and a defence of intermarriage between Calvinists and Lutherans,[3] at length put him in such danger that, to escape imprisonment, he sought the protection of the Elector of Brandenburg at Halle, where he ultimately became professor of jurisprudence in the new university, founded by his advice. In philosophy an unsystematic pantheist, he taught, after Plutarch, Bayle, and Bacon, that "superstition is worse than atheism"; but his great practical service to German civilisation, over and above

---

[1] *E.g.*, the reference to "Alten Quacker und neuen Frey-Geister" in the title-page of the folio *Anabaptisticum et Enthusiasticum Pantheon*, 1702.

[2] *Freimüthige, lustige und ernsthafte, jedoch vernunft- und gesetzmässige Gedanken, oder Monatgespräche über allerhand, vornehmlich über neue Bücher.*

[3] Pusey, p. 86, *note*.

his furthering of the native speech, was his vigorous polemic against prosecutions for heresy, trials for witchcraft, and the use of torture, all of which he did more than any other German to discredit, though judicial torture subsisted for another half-century.[1] In such a battle he of course had the clergy against him all along the line ; and it is as an anti-clerical that he figures in clerical history. The perturbed Mosheim pronounces that the "famous jurists" who were led by Thomasius "set up a new fundamental principle of church polity—namely, the supreme authority and power of the civil magistrate," so tending to create the opinion "that the ministers of religion are not to be accounted ambassadors of God, but vicegerents of the chief magistrates. They also weakened not a little the few remaining prerogatives and advantages which were left of the vast number formerly possessed by the clergy ; and maintained that many of the maxims and regulations of our churches which had come down from our fathers were relics of popish superstition. This afforded matter for long and pernicious feuds and contests between our theologians and our jurists.......It will be sufficient for us to observe, what is abundantly attested, that they diminished much in various places the respect for the clergy, the reverence for religion, and the security and prosperity of the Lutheran Church."[2]

6. A personality of a very different kind emerges in the same period in Johann Conrad Dippel (1673-1734), who developed a system of rationalistic mysticism, and as to whom, says an orthodox historian, "one is doubtful whether to place him in the class of pietists or of rationalists, of enthusiasts or of scoffers, of mystics or of

---

[1] Compare Weber, *Geschichte der deutschen Literatur*, § 81 (ed. 1880, pp. 90-91) ; Enfield's *History of Philosophy* (an abstract of Brucker's *Historia critica philosophiæ*), 1840, pp. 610-612 ; Ueberweg, ii, 115 ; and Schlegel's note in Reid's Mosheim, p. 790, with Karl Hillebrand, *Six Lectures on the History of German Thought*, 1880, pp. 64-65. There is a modern monograph by A. Nicoladoni, *Christian Thomasius ; ein Beitrag zur Geschichte der Aufklärung*, 1888.
[2] *Ec. Hist.* 17 Cent. Sect. ii, Pt. ii, ch. i, § 14.

freethinkers."[1] The son of a preacher, he yet "exhibited in his ninth year strong doubts as to the catechism." After a tolerably free life as a student he turned Pietist at Strasburg, lectured on astrology and palmistry, preached, and got into trouble with the police. In 1698 he published under the pen-name of "Christianus Democritus" his book, *Gestäuptes Papstthum der Protestirenden* ("The Popery of the Protestantisers Whipped"), in which he so attacked the current Christian ethic of salvation as to exasperate both churches.[2] The stress of his criticism fell firstly on the unthinking Scripturalism of the average Protestant, who, he said, while reproaching the Catholic with setting up in the crucifix a God of wood, was apt to make for himself a God of paper.[3] In his repudiation of the "bargain" or "redemption" doctrine of the historic church he took up positions which were one day to become respectable; but in his own life he was much of an Ishmaelite, with wild notions of alchemy and gold-making; and after predicting that he should live till 1808, he died suddenly in 1734, leaving a doctrine which appealed only to those constitutionally inclined, on the lines of the earlier English Quakers, to set the inner light above Scripture.[4]

7. Among the pupils of Thomasius at Halle was Theodore Louis Lau, who, born of an aristocratic family, became Minister of Finances to the Duke of Courland, and after leaving that post held a high place in the service of the Elector Palatine. While holding that office Lau published a small Latin volume of *pensees* entitled *Meditationes Theologicæ-Physicæ*, notably deistic in tone. This gave rise to such an outcry among the clergy that he had to leave Frankfort, only, however, to be summoned before the consistory of Konigsberg,

---

[1] Hagenbach, *Kirchengeschichte des 18. und 19. Jahrh.* 2te Aufl. i, 164. (This matter is not in the abridged translation.)
[2] See the furious account of him by Mosheim, 17 Cent. sec. ii, Pt. ii, ch. i, § 33.
[3] *Id.* p. 169.
[4] Noack, *Die Freidenker in der Religion*, Th. iii, Kap. 1; Bruno Bauer, *Einfluss des englischen Quäkerthums auf die deutsche Cultur und auf das englisch-russische Projekt einer Weltkirche*, 1878, pp. 41-44.

his native town, and charged with atheism (1719). He thereupon retired to Altona, where he had freedom enough to publish a reply to his clerical persecutors.[1]

8. While Thomasius was still at work, a new force arose of a more distinctly academic cast. This was the adaptation of the Leibnitzian system made by Wolff, who first came into prominence by a rectorial address at Halle (1722) in which he warmly praised the ethics of Confucius. Such praise was naturally held to imply disparagement of Christianity; and as a result of the pietist outcry Wolff was condemned by the king to exile from Prussia, under penalty of death,[2] all "atheistical" writings being at the same time forbidden. Wolff's system, however, prevailed, though he refused to return on any invitation till the accession (1740) of Frederick the Great; and his teaching, which for the first time popularised philosophy in the German language, in turn helped to promote the rationalistic temper,[3] though orthodox enough from the modern point of view. Under the new reign, however, pietism and Wolffism alike lost prestige,[4] and the age of anti-Christian and Christian rationalism began.

9. Even before the generation of active pressure from English and French deism there were clear signs that rationalism had taken root in German life. In the so-called *Wertheim Bible* (1735) Johann Lorenz Schmidt, in the spirit of the Leibnitz-Wolffian theology, "undertook to translate the Bible, and to explain it according to the principle that in revelation only that can be accepted as true which does not contradict the reason."[5] To the same period belong the first activities of JOHANN CHRISTIAN EDELMANN (1698-1767), one of the most energetic freethinkers of his age. Trained philosophically at Jena under the theologian Budde, a

---

[1] Pref. to French trans. of the *Meditationes*, 1770, pp. xii-xvii. Lau died in 1740.
[2] Hagenbach, trans. pp. 35-36; Saintes, p. 61.
[3] Cairns, *Unbelief in the Eighteenth Century*, 1881, p. 173; Pusey pp. 115-119; Pünjer, p. 529; Lechler, pp. 448-9.
[4] Hagenbach, pp. 37-39. [5] Punjer, i, 544.

bitter opponent of Wolff, and theologically in the school of the Pietists, he was strongly influenced against official orthodoxy through reading the "Impartial History of the Church and of Heretics," by Godfrey Arnold, an eminently anti-clerical work, which nearly always takes the side of the heretics.[1] In the same heterodox direction he was swayed by the works of Dippel. At this stage Edelmann produced his *Unschuldige Wahrheiten* ("Innocent Truths"), in which he takes up a pronouncedly rationalist and latitudinarian position, but without rejecting "revelation"; and in 1736 he went to Berleburg, where he worked on the Berleburg translation of the Bible, a Pietist undertaking, somewhat on the lines of Dippel's mystical doctrine, in which a variety of incredible Scriptural narratives, from the six days' creation onwards, are turned to mystical purpose.[2] In this occupation Edelmann seems to have passed some years. Gradually, however, he came more and more under the influence of the English deists; and he at length withdrew from the Pietist camp, attacking his former associates for the fanaticism into which their thought was degenerating. It was under the influence of Spinoza, however, that he took his most important steps. A few months after meeting with the *Tractatus* he began (1740) the first part of his treatise *Moses mit aufgedecktem Angesichte* ("Moses with unveiled face"), an attack at once on the doctrine of inspiration and on that of the Mosaic authorship of the Pentateuch. The book was intended to consist of twelve parts; but after the appearance of three it was prohibited by the imperial fisc, and the published parts burned by the hangman at

---

[1] *Unpartheyische Kirchen- und Ketzerhistorie*, 1699-1700, 2 tom. fol.— fuller ed. 3 tom. fol. 1740. Compare Mosheim's angry account of it with Murdock's note in defence: Reid's ed. p. 804. Bruno Bauer describes it as epoch-making (*Einfluss des englischen Quäkerthums*, p. 42). This history had a great influence on Goethe in his teens, leading him, he says, to the conviction that he like so many other men should have a religion of his own, which he goes on to describe. It was a re-hash of Gnosticism. (*Wahrheit und Dichtung*, B. viii: *Werke*, ed. 1866, xi, 344 sq.)

[2] Cp. Hagenbach, *Kirchengeschichte*, i, 171; Pünjer, i, 279.

Hamburg and elsewhere. Nonetheless, Edelmann continued his propaganda, publishing in 1741 or 1742 *Die Göttlichkeit der Vernunft* (" The Divinity of Reason "), and in 1741 *Christ and Belial*. In 1749 or 1750 his works were again publicly burned at Frankfurt by order of the imperial authorities ; and he had much ado to find anywhere in Germany safe harbourage, till he found protection under Frederick at Berlin, where he died in 1767.

Edelmann's teaching was essentially Spinozist and pantheistic,[1] with a leaning to the doctrine of metempsychosis. As a pantheist he of course entirely rejected the divinity of Jesus, pronouncing inspiration the appanage of all ; and the Gospels were by him dismissed as late fabrications, from which the true teachings of the founder could not be learned ; though, like all the freethinkers of that age, he estimated Jesus highly. A German theologian complains, nevertheless, that he was "more just toward heathenism than toward Judaism ; and more just toward Judaism than toward Christianity"; adding : "What he taught had been thoroughly and ingeniously said in France and England ; but from a German theologian, and that with such eloquent coarseness, such mastery in expatiating in blasphemy, such things were unheard of."[2]

Even from decorous and official exponents of religion, however, there came "naturalistic" and semi-rationalistic teaching, as in the *Reflections on the most important truths of religion*[3] (1744) of J. F. W. Jerusalem, Abbot of Marienthal in Brunswick, and later of Riddagshausen (1709-1789). Though really written

---

[1] Noack, Th. iii, Kap. 2 ; Saintes, pp. 85 86 ; Pünjer, p. 442.
[2] Kahnis, cited by Bishop Hurst, *Hist. of Rationalism*, ed. 1867, p. 118; ed. 1901, pp. 138-9. A collection of extracts from Edelmann's works, entitled *Der neu eröffnete Edelmann*, was published at Bern in 1847 ; and the *Unschuldige Wahrheiten* was reprinted in 1846. His Autobiography, written in 1752, was published in 1849.
[3] *Betrachtungen über die vornehmsten Wahrheiten der Religion*. Another apologetic work of the period marked by rational moderation and tolerance was the *Vertheidigten Glauben der Christen* of A. W. F. Sack (1754).

by way of defending Christianity against the freethinkers, in particular against Bolingbroke and Voltaire,[1] the very title of the book is suggestive of a process of disintegration ; and in it certain unedifying Scriptural miracles are actually rejected.[2] It was probably this measure of adaptation to new needs that gave it its great popularity in Germany, and secured its translation into several other languages. Jerusalem was, however, at most a semi-rationalist, taking a view of the fundamental Christian dogmas which approached closely to that of Locke.[3] It was, as Goethe said later, the epoch of common sense ; and the very theologians tended to a " religion of nature."[4]

10. Alongside of home-made heresy there had come into play a new initiative force in the literature of English deism, which began to be translated after 1740,[5] and was widely circulated till, in the last third of the century, it was superseded by the French. The English answers to the deists were frequently translated likewise, and notoriously helped to promote deism[6]—another proof that it was not their influence that had changed the balance of activity in England. Under a freethinking king, even clergymen began guardedly to accept the deistic methods ; and the optimism of Shaftesbury began to overlay the optimism of Leibnitz ;[7] while a French scientific influence began with La Mettrie,[8] Maupertuis, and Robinet. Even the Leibnitzian school, proceeding on the principle of immortal monads,

---

[1] Hagenbach, *Kirchengeschichte*, i, 355.
[2] Pünjer, i, 542.
[3] Cp. Hagenbach, i, 353 ; trans. p. 120. Jerusalem was the father of the youth whose fate moved Goethe to write *The Sorrows of Werther*. He had considerable influence in purifying German style. Cp. Goethe, *Wahrheit und Dichtung*, Th. II, B. vii ; *Werke*, ed. 1866, xi, 272.
[4] *Id.* pp. 268-9.
[5] Lechler, *Gesch. des englischen Deismus*, pp. 447-452. The translations began with that of Tindal (1741), which made a great sensation.
[6] Puscy, pp. 125, 127, citing Twesten ; Gostwick, *German Culture and Christianity*, p. 36, citing Ernesti. Thorschmid's *Freidenker Bibliothek*, issued in 1765-67, collected both translations and refutations. Lechler, p. 451.
[7] Lange, *Gesch. des Materialismus*, i, 405 (Eng. trans. ii, 146-7).
[8] Lange, i, 347, 399 (Eng. trans. ii, 76, 137).

developed a doctrine of the immortality of the souls of animals[1]—a position not helpful to orthodoxy. There was thus a general stirring of doubt among educated people,[2] and we find mention in Goethe's Autobiography of an old gentleman of Frankfort who avowed, as against the optimists, "Even in God I find defects (*Fehler*)."[3]

On the other hand, there were instances in Germany of the phenomenon, already seen in England in Newton and Boyle, of men of science devoting themselves to the defence of the faith. The most notable cases were those of the mathematician Euler and the biologist von Haller. The latter wrote Letters (to his Daughter) *On the Truth of the Christian Religion* (1772)[4] and other apologetic works. Euler in 1747 published at Berlin, where he was professor, his *Defence of Revelation against the Reproaches of Freethinkers;*[5] and in 1769 his *Letters to a German Princess,* of which the argument notably coincides with part of that of Berkeley against the freethinking mathematicians. Haller's position comes to the same thing. All three men, in fact, grasped at the argument of despair—the inadequacy of the human faculties to sound the mystery of things; and all alike were entirely unable to see that it logically cancelled their own judgments. Even a theologian, contemplating Haller's theorem of an incomprehensible omnipotence countered in its merciful plan of salvation by the set of worms it sought to save, comments on the childishness of the philosophy which confidently described the plans of deity in terms of what it declared to be the blank ignorance of the worms in question.[6] Euler and von Haller, like some later men of

---

[1] Lange, i, 396-7 (ii, 134-5).
[2] Goethe tells of having seen in his boyhood, at Frankfurt, an irreligious French romance publicly burned, and of having his interest in the book thereby awakened. But this seems to have been during the French occupation. (*Wahrheit und Dichtung*, B. iv; *Werke*, xi, 146.)
[3] *Id.* B. iv, *end.*
[4] Translated into English as *Letters against the Freethinkers.*
[5] *Rettung der Offenbarung gegen die Einwürfe der Freigeister.*
[6] Baur, *Gesch. der christl. Kirche,* iv, 599.

science, kept their scientific method for the mechanical or physical problems of their scientific work, and brought to the deepest problems of all the self-will, the emotionalism, and the irresponsibility of the ignorant average man. Each did but express in his own way the resentment of the undisciplined mind at attacks upon its prejudices; and Haller's resort to poetry as a vehicle for his religion gives the measure of his powers on that side. Thus in Germany as in England the "answer" to the freethinkers was a failure. Men of science playing at theology and theologians playing at science alike failed to turn the tide of opinion, now socially favoured by the known deism of the king. German orthodoxy, says a recent Christian apologist, fell "with a rapidity reminding one of the capture of Jericho."[1] Goethe, writing of the general attitude to Christianity about 1768, sums up that "the Christian religion wavered between its own historic-positive base and a pure deism, which, grounded on morality, was in turn to re-establish ethics."[2]

> Frederick's attitude, said an early Kantian, had had "an almost magical influence" on popular opinion (Willich, *Elements of the Critical Philosophy*, 1798, p. 2). With this his French teachers must have had much to do. Mr. Morley pronounces (*Voltaire*, 4th ed. p. 123) that French deism "never made any impression on Germany," and that "the teaching of Leibnitz and Wolff stood like a fortified wall against the French invasion." This is contradicted by much German testimony; in particular by Lange's (*Gesch. des Mater.* i, 318), though he notes that French materialism could not get the upper hand. Baur, even in speaking disparagingly of the French as compared with the English influence, admits (*Lehrbuch der Dogmengeschichte*, 2te Aufl. p. 347) that the former told upon Germany. Cp. Tennemann, Bohn. trans. pp. 385, 388. Hagenbach shows great ignorance of English deism, but he must have known something of German; and he writes (trans. p. 57) that "the imported deism soon swept through the rifts of the church and gained supreme control of literature." Cp. pp. 67-8. And see Professor Croom Robertson's *Hobbes*, pp. 225-6, as to the persistence of a succession of Hobbes and

---
[1] Gostwick, p. 15.
[2] *Wahrheit und Dichtung*, B. viii: *Werke*, xi, 329

Locke in Germany in the teeth of the Wolffian school. It is further noteworthy that Brucker's copious *Historia Critica Philosophiæ* (1742-44), which as a mere learned record has great merit, and was long the standard authority in Germany, gives great praise to Locke and little space to Wolff. (See Enfield's abstract, pp. 614, 619 sq.) The Wolffian philosophy, too, had been rejected and disparaged by both Herder and Kant—who were alike deeply influenced by Rousseau—in the third quarter of the century; and was generally discredited, save in the schools, when Kant produced the *Critique of Pure Reason.* See below, pp. 293, 302.

11. Frederick, though a Voltairean freethinker from his youth, showed himself at first disposed to act on the old maxim that freethought is bad for the common people. In 1743-4 he caused to be suppressed two German treatises by one Gebhardt, attacking the Biblical miracles; and in 1748 he sent a young man named Rüdiger to Spandau for six months' confinement for printing an anti-Christian work by one Dr. Pott.[1] But as he grew more confident in his own methods he extended to men of his own way of thinking the toleration he allowed to all religionists, save insofar as he vetoed the mutual vituperation of the sects, and such proselytising as tended to create strife. With an even hand he protected Catholics, Greek Christians, and Unitarians, letting them have churches where they would;[2] and when, after the battle of Striegau, a body of Protestant peasantry asked his permission to slay all the Catholics they could find, he answered with the Gospel precept, "Love your enemies."[3] Beyond the toleration of all forms of religion, however, he never went; and he himself, chiefly by way of French verses, added to the literature of deism. Bayle was his favourite study; and as the then crude German literature had no attraction for him, he drew to his court many distinguished Frenchmen, including La Mettrie, Maupertuis, D'Alembert, D'Argens, and above all Voltaire, between

---

[1] Schlosser, *Hist. of the Eighteenth Century*, Eng. trans. 1843, i, 150; Hagenbach, trans. p. 66.
[2] Hagenbach, trans. p. 63.   [3] *Id.*, *Kirchengeschichte*, i, 232.

whom and him there was an incurable incompatibility of temper and character, which left them admiring without respecting each other, and unable to abstain from mutual vituperation. Under Frederick's vigorous rule all speech was free save such as he considered personally offensive, as Voltaire's attack on Maupertuis; and after a stormy reign he could say, when asked by Prince William of Brunswick whether he did not think religion one of the best supports of a king's authority, " I find order and the laws sufficient.......Depend upon it, countries have been admirably governed when your religion had no existence."[1]

> As the first modern freethinking king, Frederick is something of a test case. Son of a man of narrow mind and odious character, he was himself no admirable type, being neither benevolent nor considerate, neither truthful nor generous; and in international politics he played the old game of unscrupulous aggression. Yet he was not only the most competent, but, as regards home administration, the most conscientious king of his time. To find a rival we must go back to the pagan Antonines and Julian, or at least to St. Louis of France, who, however, was rather worsened than bettered by his creed (cp. the argument of Faure, *Hist. de Saint Louis*, 1866, i, 242-3; ii, 597).
>
> The effect of Frederick's training is seen in his final attitude to the advanced criticism of the school of d'Holbach, which assailed governments and creeds with the same unsparing severity of logic and moral reprobation. Stung by the uncompromising attack, Frederick retorts by attacking the rashness which would plunge nations into civil strife because kings miscarry where no human wisdom could avoid miscarriage. He who had wantonly plunged all Germany into a hell of war for his sole ambition, bringing myriads to misery, thousands to violent death, and hundreds of his own soldiers to suicide, could be virtuously indignant at the irresponsible audacity of writers who indicted the whole existing system for its imbecility and injustice. But he did reason on the criticism; he did ponder it; he did feel bound to meet argument with argument; and he gave his arguments to the world. The advance on previous regal practice is enormous: the whole problem of

---

[1] Thiébault, *Mes Souvenirs de Vingt Ans de Sejour a Berlin*, 1804, i, 77-79. See ii, 78-80, as to the baselessness of the stories (*e.g.*, Pusey, *Histor. Inquiry into German Rationalism*, p. 123) that Frederick changed his views in old age.

politics is at once brought to the test of judgment and persuasion. Beside the Christian Georges and the Louis's of his century, and beside his Christian father, his superiority in judgment and even in character is signal. Such was the great deist king of the deist age ; a deist of the least religious temper and of no very fine moral material to begin with.

The one contemporary monarch who in any way compares with him in enlightenment, Joseph II of Austria, belonged to the same school. The main charge against Frederick as a ruler is that he did not act up to the ideals of the school of Voltaire. In reply to the demand of the French deists for an abolition of all superstitious teaching, he observed that among the 16,000,000 inhabitants of France at most 200,000 were capable of philosophic views, and that the remaining 15,800,000 were held to their opinions by "insurmountable obstacles." Such an answer meant that he had no idea of so spreading instruction that all men should have a chance of reaching rational beliefs. (*Examen de l'Essai sur les préjuges*, 1769. See the passage in Lévy-Bruhl, *L'Allemagne depuis Leibniz*, p. 89.) This attitude was his inheritance from the past. Yet it was under him that Germany began to figure as a first-rate culture force in Europe.

12. The most systematic propaganda of the new ideas was that carried on in the periodical published by F. NICOLAI under the title of *The General German Library* (founded 1765), which began with fifty contributors, and at the height of its power had a hundred and thirty, among them being Lessing, Eberhard, and Moses Mendelssohn. To Nicolai is fully due the genial tribute paid to him by Heine,[1] were it only for the national service of his "Library." Its many translations from the English and French freethinkers, older and newer, concurred with native work to spread a deistic rationalism, now known as *Aufklarung*, or enlightenment, through the whole middle class of Germany.[2] Native writers in independent works added to the propaganda. ANDREAS RIEM (1749-1807), a Berlin preacher, appointed by Frederick a hospital

---

[1] *Zur Gesch. der Relig. und Philos. in Deutschland—Werke*, ed. 1876, iii, 63-64. Goethe's blame (*W. und D.*, B. vii) is passed on purely literary grounds.

[2] Hagenbach, trans. pp. 103-4 ; Cairns, p. 177.

chaplain,[1] wrote anonymously against priestcraft as no other priest had yet done. "No class of men," he declared, "has ever been so pernicious to the world as the priesthood. There were laws at all times against murderers and bandits, but not against the assassin in the priestly garb. War was repelled by war, and it came to an end. The war of the priesthood against reason has lasted for thousands of years, and it still goes on without ceasing."[2] GEORG SCHADE (1712-1795), who appears to have been one of the believers in the immortality of animals, and who in 1770 was imprisoned for his opinions in the island of Christiansœ, was no less emphatic, declaring, in a work on Natural Religion on the lines of Tindal (1760), that "all who assert a supernatural religion are godless impostors."[3] Constructive work of great importance, again, was done by J. B. BASEDOW (1723-1790), who early became an active deist, but distinguished himself chiefly as an educational reformer, on the inspiration of Rousseau's *Emile*,[4] setting up a system which "tore education away from the Christian basis,"[5] and becoming in virtue of that one of the most popular writers of his day. It is latterly admitted even by orthodoxy that school education in Germany had in the seventeenth century become a matter of learning by rote, and that such reforms as had been set up in some of the schools of the Pietists had in Basedow's day come to nothing.[6] As Basedow was the first to set up vigorous reforms, it is not too much to call him an instaurator of rational education, whose chief fault was to be too far ahead of his age. This, rather than any personal defect, was the cause of the failure of his "Philanthropic Institute," established in 1771, on the invitation of the Prince of Dessau, to

---

[1] This post he left to become secretary of the Academy of Painting.
[2] Cited by Pünjer, i, 545-6.
[3] *Id.* p. 546.
[4] Hagenbach, trans. pp. 100-3; Saintes, pp. 91-92; Pünjer, p. 536; Noack, Th. iii, Kap. 7.
[5] Hagenbach, *Kirchengeschichte*, i, 298, 351.
[6] *Id.* i, 294 sq.

carry out his educational ideals. Quite a number of other institutions, similarly planned, after his lead, by men of the same way of thinking, as Canope and Salzmann, in the same period, had no better success.

> Goethe, who was clearly much impressed by Basedow, and travelled with him, draws a somewhat antagonistic picture of him on retrospect (*Wahrheit und Dichtung*, B. xiv). He accuses him in particular of always obtruding his anti-orthodox opinions; not choosing to admit that religious opinions were being constantly obtruded on Basedow. Praising Lavater for his more amiable nature, Goethe reveals that Lavater was constantly obtruding *his* orthodoxy. Goethe, in fine, was always lenient to pietism, in which he had been brought up, and to which he was wont to make sentimental concessions. Hagenbach notes (i, 298, *note*), without any deprecation, that after Basedow had published in 1763-4 his *Philalethie*, a perfectly serious treatise on natural as against revealed religion, one of the many orthodox answers, that by Pastor Goeze, so inflamed against him the people of his native town of Hamburg that he could not show himself there without danger. And this is the man accused of "obtruding his views." Baur is driven, by way of disparagement of Basedow and his school, to censure their self-confidence—precisely the quality which, in religious teachers with whom he agreed, he as a theologian would treat as a mark of superiority. Baur's attack on the moral utilitarianism of the school is still less worthy of him. (*Gesch. der christlichen Kirche*, iv, 595-6.)

Yet another influential deist was JOHANN AUGUST EBERHARD (1739-1809), for a time a preacher at Charlottenburg, but driven out of the church for the heresy of his *New Apology of Sokrates; or the Final Salvation of the Heathen* (1772). The work in effect placed Sokrates on a level with Jesus,[1] which was blasphemy.[2] But the outcry attracted the attention of Frederick, who made Eberhard a Professor of Philosophy at Halle, where, later, he opposed the idealism of both Kant and Fichte. Substantially of the same school was the less pronouncedly deistic cleric STEINBART,[3] author of a utilitarian *System of Pure Philosophy*,

---

[1] Hagenbach, trans. p. 109.
[2] Eberhard, however, is respectfully treated by Lessing in his discussion on Leibnitz's view as to eternal punishment.
[3] Noack, Th. iii, Kap. 8.

or Christian doctrine of Happiness, now forgotten, who had been variously influenced by Locke and Voltaire.[1] Among the less heterodox but still rationalising clergy of the period were J. J. Spalding, author of a work on *The Utility of the Preacher's Office*, a man of the type labelled "Moderate" in the Scotland of the same period, and as such antipathetic to emotional pietists;[2] and Zollikofer, of the same school—both inferribly influenced by the deism of their day. Considerably more of a rationalist than these was the clergyman W. A. Teller (1734-1804), author of a New Testament Lexicon, who reached a position virtually deistic, and intimated to the Jews of Berlin that he would receive them into his church on their making a deistic profession of faith.[3]

13. If it be true that even the rationalising defenders of Christianity led men on the whole towards deism,[4] much more must this hold true of the new school who applied rationalistic methods to religious questions in their capacity as theologians. Of this school the founder was JOHANN SALOMO SEMLER (1725-1791), who, trained as a Pietist at Halle, early thought himself into a more critical attitude,[5] albeit remaining a theological teacher. As early as 1750, in a *Treatise on the Canon of Scripture*, he set forth the view, developed a century later by Baur, that the early Christian Church contained a Pauline and a Petrine party, mutually hostile. The merit of his research won him a professorship at Halle; and this position he held till his death, despite such heresy as his rejection from the canon of the books of Ruth, Esther, Ezra, Nehemiah, the Song

---

[1] Saintes, pp. 92-3.

[2] Cp. Hagenbach, *Kirchengeschichte*, i, 318, 363.

[3] *Id.* i, 367; trans. pp. 124-5; Saintes, p. 94. Pusey (150-1, *note*) speaks of Teller and Spalding as belonging, with Nicolai, Mendelssohn, and others, to a "secret institute, whose object was to remodel religion and alter the form of government." This seems to be a fantasy.

[4] So Steffens, cited by Hagenbach, trans. p. 124.

[5] See Pusey, 140-1, *note*, for Semler's account of the rigid and unreasoning orthodoxy against which he reacted. (Citing Semler's Autobiography, Th. ii, pp. 171-161.)

of Solomon, the two books of Chronicles, and the Apocalypse, in his *Freie Untersuchung des Canons* (1771) —a work apparently inspired by the earlier performance of Richard Simon.[1] His intellectual life was a long advance, always in the direction of a more rationalistic comprehension of religious history ; and he reached, for his day, a remarkably critical view of the mythical element in the Old Testament.[2] Thus he recognised the mythical character of the story of Samson, and was at least on the way towards a scientific handling of the New Testament.[3] But in his period and environment a systematic rationalism was impossible; and his powers were expended in an immense number of works,[4] which failed to yield any orderly system, while setting up a great general stimulus. In his latter days he strongly opposed and condemned the more radical rationalism of his pupil Bahrdt, and of the posthumous work of Reimarus ; but his own influence in promoting rationalism is obvious and unquestioned,[5] and he is rightly to be reckoned the main founder of "German rationalism"—that is, academic rationalism on theological lines.

14. Much more notorious than any other German deist of his time was CARL FRIEDRICH BAHRDT (1741–1792), a kind of Teutonic Voltaire, and the most popularly influential German freethinker of his age. In all he is said to have published a hundred and twenty-six books and tracts,[6] thus approximating to Voltaire in quantity if not in quality. Theological hatred has so pursued him that it is hard to form a fair opinion as to his character ; but the record runs that he led a somewhat Bohemian and disorderly life, though a very industrious one. While a preacher in Leipzig in 1768 he first got into trouble—"persecution," by his own

---

[1] Cp. Saintes, pp. 129-131.
[2] Cp. Gostwick, p. 51 ; Pünjer, i, 561.
[3] Cp. Saintes, p. 132 sq.
[4] A hundred and seventy-four in all. Pünjer, i, 560.
[5] Pusey, p. 142 ; A. S. Farrar, *Crit. Hist. of Freethought*, p. 313.
[6] Gostwick, p. 53 ; Pünjer, i, 546, *note*.

account; "disgrace for licentious conduct," by that of his enemies. That there was no serious disgrace is suggested by the fact that he was appointed Professor of Biblical Antiquities at Erfurt; and soon afterwards, on the recommendation of Semler and Ernesti, at Giessen (1771). While holding that post he published his translation of the New Testament, done from the point of view of belief in revelation, following it up by his *New Revelations of God in Letters and Tales* (1773), which aroused Protestant hostility. After teaching for a time in a new Swiss "Philanthropin"—an educational institution on Basedow's lines—he obtained a post as a district ecclesiastical superintendent in Turkheim; whereafter he was enabled to set up a "Philanthropin" of his own in the castle of Heidenheim, near Worms. The second edition of his translation of the New Testament, however, aroused Catholic hostility in the district; the edition was confiscated, and he found it prudent to make a tour in Holland and England, only to receive, on his return, a missive from the imperial consistory declaring him disabled for any spiritual office in the Holy German Empire. Seeking refuge in Halle, he found Semler grown hostile; but made the acquaintance of Eberhard, with the result of abandoning the remains of his orthodox faith. Henceforth he regarded Jesus, albeit with admiration, as simply a great teacher, like Moses, Confucius, Sokrates, Semler, Luther; and to this view he gave effect in the third edition of his New Testament translation, which was followed in 1782 by his *Letters on the Bible in Popular Style* (*Volkston*). More and more fiercely antagonised, he duly retaliated on the clergy in his *Church and Heretic Almanack* (1781); and after for a time keeping a tavern, ended not very happily his troublous life in Halle in 1792.

The weakest part of Bahrdt's performance is now seen to be his application of the empirical method of the early rationalists, who were wont to take every Biblical prodigy as a merely perverted account of an incident which certainly happened. That method—which is not yet discarded by rationalising theologians—is reduced to open absurdity in his hands, as when he makes Moses employ fireworks on Mount Sinai, and Jesus feed the five thousand by stratagem, without miracle. But it was not by such extravagances that he won and kept a hearing throughout his life. It is easy to see on retrospect that the source of his influence lay above all things in his healthy ethic, his own mode of progression being by way of simple common sense and natural feeling, not of critical research. His first step in rationalism was to ask himself "how Three Persons could be One God"—this while believing devoutly in revelation, miracles, the divinity of Jesus, and the Atonement. Under the influence of a naturalist travelling in his district, he gave up the orthodox doctrine of the Atonement, feeling himself "as if new-born" in being freed of what he had learned to see as a "pernicious and damnable error."[1] It was for such writing that he was hated and persecuted, despite his habitual eulogy of Christ as "the greatest and most venerable of mortals." His offence was not against morals, but against theology.

> Bahrdt's real power may be inferred from the fury of some of his opponents. "The wretched Bahrdt" is Dr. Pusey's Christian account of him. The American translators of Hagenbach, Messrs. Gage and Stuckenberg, have thought fit to insert in their chapter-heading the phrase "Bahrdt, the Theodore Parker of Germany." As Hagenbach has spoken of Bahrdt with special contempt, the intention can be appreciated; but the intended insult may now serve as a certificate of merit to Bahrdt. Bishop Hurst solemnly affirms that "What Jeffreys is to the judicial history of England, Bahrdt is to the religious history of German Protestantism. Whatever he touched was disgraced by the vileness of his heart and the Satanic daring of his mind" (*History of Rationalism*, ed. 1867, p. 119; ed. 1901, p. 139). This concerning doctrines of an invariable moral soundness, which to-day would be almost universally received with approbation. Pünjer, who cannot at any point indict the doctrines, falls back on the professional

---

[1] *Geschichte seines Lebens.*

device of classing them with the "platitudes" of the *Aufklärung;* and, finding this insufficient to convey a disparaging impression to the general reader, intimates that Bahrdt, connecting ethic with rational sanitation, "does not shrink from the coarseness of laying down" a rule for bodily health, which Pünjer does not shrink from quoting (pp. 549-50). Finally Bahrdt is dismissed as "the theological public-house-keeper of Halle." So hard is it for men clerically trained to attain to a manly rectitude in their criticism of anti-clericals. Bahrdt was a great admirer of the Gospel Jesus ; so Cairns (p. 178) takes a lenient view of his life. On that and his doctrine cp. Hagenbach, pp. 107-110; Pünjer, i, 546-550; Noack, Th. iii, Kap. 5. Goethe satirised him in a youthful *Prolog*, but speaks of him not unkindly in the *Wahrheit und Dichtung*.

15. Alongside of these propagators of popular rationalism stood a group of companion deists usually considered together — LESSING, HERMANN SAMUEL REIMARUS, and MOSES MENDELSSOHN. The last-named, a Jew, "lived entirely in the sphere of deism and of natural religion,"[1] and sought, like the deists in general, to give religion an ethical structure ; but he was popular chiefly as a constructive theist and a defender of the doctrine of immortality on non-Christian lines. His *Phædon* (1767), setting forth that view, had a great vogue.[2] One of his more notable teachings was an earnest declaration against any connection between Church and State ; but like Locke and Rousseau he so far sank below his own ideals as to agree in arguing for a State enforcement of a profession of belief in a God[3]— a negation of his own plea. With much contemporary popularity, he had no permanent influence ; and he seems to have been finally broken-hearted by Jacobi's disclosure of the pantheism of Lessing.

See the monograph of Rabbi Schreiber, of Bonn, *Moses Mendelssohn's Verdienste um die deutsche Nation* (Zurich, 1880), pp. 41-42. The strongest claim made for Mendelssohn by

---

[1] Baur, *Gesch. der chr. Kirche*, iv, 597.
[2] Translated into English in 1789.
[3] Mendelssohn, *Jerusalem*, Abschn. I— *Werke*, 1838, p. 239 (Eng. trans. 1838, pp. 50-51); Rousseau, *Contrat Social*, liv. iv, ch. viii, near end; Locke, as cited above, p. 117. Cp. Bartholmess, *Hist. crit. des doctr. relig. de la philos. moderne*, 1855, i, 145; Baur, as last cited.

Rabbi Schreiber is that he, a Jew, was much more of a German patriot than Goethe, Schiller, or Lessing. Heine, however, pronounces that "As Luther against the Papacy, so Mendelssohn rebelled against the Talmud" (*Zur Gesch. der Relig. und Philos. in Deutschland: Werke*, ed. 1876. iii, 65).

LESSING, on the other hand, is one of the outstanding figures in the history of Biblical criticism, as well as of German literature in general. The son of a Lutheran pastor, Lessing became in a considerable measure a rationalist, while constantly resenting, as did Goethe, the treatment of religion in the fashion in which he himself treated non-religious opinions with which he did not agree.[1] It is clear that already in his student days he had become an unbeliever, and that it was on this as well as other grounds that he refused to become a clergyman.[2] Nor was he unready to jeer at the bigots when they chanced to hate where he was sympathetic.[3] But when the rationalism of the day seriously or otherwise assailed the creed of his parents, whom he loved and honoured, sympathy in his case as in Goethe's always predetermined his attitude; and it is not untruly said of him that he "did prefer the orthodox to the heterodox party, like Gibbon,"[4] inasmuch as "the balance of learning which attracted his esteem was [then] on that side." We thus find him rather nervously rejecting alike the popular freethought,[5] represented by

---

[1] See his *Werke*, ed. 1866, v, 317—*Aus dem Briefe, die neueste Literatur betreffend*, 49ter Brief.

[2] If Lessing's life were sketched in the spirit in which orthodoxy has handled that of Bahrdt, it could be made unedifying enough. Even Goethe remarks that Lessing "enjoyed himself in a disorderly tavern life" (*Wahrheit und Dichtung*, B. vii); and all that Hagenbach maliciously charges against Basedow in the way of irregularity of study is true of him. On that and other points, usually glosed over, see the sketch in Taylor's *Historic Survey of German Poetry*, 1830, i, 332–7. All the while, Lessing is an essentially sound-hearted and estimable personality; and he would probably have been the last man to echo the tone of the orthodox towards the personal life of the freethinkers who went further than he.

[3] *E.g.* his fable *The Bull and the Calf* (*Fabeln*, ii, 5), apropos of the clergy and Bayle.

[4] Taylor, as cited, p. 361.

[5] See his rather crude comedy, *Der Freigeist*, and Sime's *Life of Lessing*, i, 41–2.

his friend Mylius,[1] and the attempts of the rationalising clergy to put religion on a common-sense basis. For himself, he framed (or perhaps adopted)[2] a theory of the *Education of the Human Race* (1780), which has served the semi-rationalistic clergy of our own day in good stead ; and adapted Rousseau's catching doctrine that the true test of religion lies in feeling and not in argument.[3] Neither doctrine has a whit more philosophical value than the other " popular philosophy " of the time, and neither was fitted to have much immediate influence; but both pointed a way to the more philosophic apologists of religion, while baulking the orthodox.[4] " Christianity " he made out to be a " universal principle," independent of its pseudo-historical setting ; thus giving to the totality of the admittedly false tradition the credit of an ethic which in the terms of the case is simply human, and in all essentials demonstrably pre-Christian. Lessing, in short, bore himself from first to last as the son of a pastor, always finding for the errors of his own people defences of a kind which he would never have tolerated in a discussion on any other issue. Nonetheless, he must be credited with some measure of science, and a large measure of courage, for going so far as he did. As the orthodox historian of rationalism has it, " Though he did not array himself as a champion of rationalism, he proved himself one of the strongest promoters of its reign."[5]

It was by him that there were published the " Anonymous Fragments" known as the " Wolfenbüttel Fragments " (1774-1778), wherein the methods of the English and French deists are applied with a new severity to

---

[1] Mylius for a short time ran in Leipzig a journal called the *Freethinker*.
[2] As to the authorship, see Saintes, pp. 101-2 ; and Sime's *Life of Lessing*, i, 261-2, where the counter-claim is rejected.
[3] *Zur Geschichte und Literatur*, aus dem 4ten Beitr.—*Werke*, vi, 142 sq. See also in his *Theologische Streitschriften* the *Axiomata* written against Pastor Goeze. Cp. Schwarz, *Lessing als Theologe*, pp. 146, 151 ; and Pusey, as cited, p. 51, *note*.
[4] Compare the regrets of Pusey (pp. 51, 155), Cairns (p. 195), Hagenbach (pp. 89-97), and Saintes (p. 100).
[5] Hurst, *History of Rationalism*, 3rd ed. p. 130.

both the Old and the New Testament narratives. It is now put beyond doubt that they were the work of Reimarus,[1] who had in 1755 published a defence of "Natural Religion"—that is, of the theory of a Providence—against La Mettrie, Maupertuis, and older materialists, which had a great success in its day.[2] At his death, accordingly, Reimarus ranked as an admired defender of theism and of the belief in immortality.[3] He was the son-in-law of the famous scholar Fabricius, and was for many years Professor of Oriental Languages in the Hamburg Academy. The famous research which preserves his memory was begun by him at the age of fifty, for his own satisfaction, and was elaborated by him during twenty years, while he silently endured the regimen of the intolerant Lutheranism of his day.[4] As he left the book, it was a complete treatise, entitled *An Apology for the Rational Worshipper of God;* but the friends to whom he left the MS., of whom Lessing was the accepted representative, ventured only to publish certain "Fragments"[5] dealing with the problems of the gospel history and of revelation in general. These, however, constituted the most serious attack yet made in Germany on the current creed, though its theory of the true manner of the gospel history of course smacks of the pre-scientific period. A generation later, however, they were still "the radical book of the anti-supernaturalists" in Germany.[6]

The method is, to accept as real occurrences all the non-

---

[1] Stahr, *Lessing, sein Leben und seine Werke*, 7te Aufl. ii, 243. Lessing said the report to this effect was a lie; but this and other mystifications appear to have been by way of fulfilling his promise of secresy to the Reimarus family. Cairns, pp. 203, 209. Cp. Farrar, *Crit. Hist. of Freethought*, note 29.
[2] See it analysed by Bartholmess, *Hist. crit. des doctr. relig. de la philos. moderne*, i, 147-167.
[3] Gostwick, p. 47; Bartholmess, i, 166. His book was translated into English (*The Principal Truths of Natural Religion Defended and Illustrated*) in 1766; into Dutch in 1758; in part into French in 1768; and seven editions of the original had appeared by 1798.
[4] Stahr, ii, 241-4.
[5] These were republished separately with the title *Von dem Zwecke Jesus und seiner Junger*, Braunschweig, 1778.
[6] W. Taylor, *Historic Survey of German Poetry*, 1830, i, 365.

miraculous episodes, and to explain them by a general theory. Thus the appointment of the seventy apostles—a palpable myth—is taken as a fact, and explained as part of a scheme by Jesus to obtain temporal power; and the scourging of the money-changers from the Temple, improbable enough as it stands, is made still more so by supposing it to be part of a scheme of insurrection. See the sketch in Cairns, p. 197 sq., which indicates the portions of the treatise produced later by Strauss. Cp. Pünjer, i, 550-7; Noack, Th. iii, Kap. 4. It is but fair to say that Reimarus' fallacy of method has not yet disappeared from criticism.

Though Lessing professed to combat the positions of the *Fragments*, he was led into a fiery controversy over them, and the series was finally stopped by authority. There can now be no doubt that Lessing at heart agreed with Reimarus on most points of negative criticism,[1] while reaching a different emotional estimate and attitude. Thereafter, as a final check to his opponents, he produced his famous drama *Nathan the Wise*, which embodies Boccaccio's story of *The Three Rings*, and has ever since served as a popular lesson of tolerance in Germany.[2] In the end, he seems to have become to some extent a pantheist;[3] but he never expounded any coherent and comprehensive set of opinions, preferring, as he put it in an oft-quoted sentence, the state of search for truth to any consciousness of possessing it.

16. Deism was now as prevalent in educated Germany as in France or England; and, according to a contemporary preacher, "Berliner" was about 1777 a synonym for "rationalist."[4] Wieland, one of the foremost

---

[1] Stahr, ii, 254.

[2] Cp. Introd. to Willis's trans. of *Nathan*.

[3] See Cairns, *Appendix*, Note I, and Willis, *Spinoza*, pp. 149-162, giving the testimony of Jacobi. Cp. Pünjer, i, 564-585. But Heine laughingly adjures Moses Mendelssohn, who grieved so intensely over Lessing's Spinozism, to rest quiet in his grave: "Thy Lessing was indeed on the way to that terrible error......but the Highest, the Father in Heaven, saved him in time by death. He died a good deist, like thee and Nicolai and Teller and the Universal German Library" (*Zur Gesch. der Rel. und Philos. in Deutschland*, B. ii, near end.—*Werke*, ed. 1876, iii, 69).

[4] Cited by Hurst, *Hist. of Rationalism*, 3rd ed. p. 125. Outside Berlin, however, matters went otherwise till late in the century. Kurz tells (*Gesch. der deutschen Literatur*, ii, 461 b) that "the indifference of the

German men of letters of his time, is known to have been a deist of the school of Shaftesbury;[1] and in the leading journal of the day he wrote on the free use of reason in matters of faith.[2] Some acts of persecution by the church show how far the movement had gone. In 1774 we find a Catholic professor at Mayence, Lorenzo Isenbiehl, deposed and sent back to the seminary for two years on the score of "deficient theological knowledge," because he argued that the text Isaiah vii, 14 applied not to the mother of Jesus but to a contemporary of the prophet; and when, four years later, he published a book on the same thesis, in Latin, he was imprisoned. Three years later still, a young Jesuit of Salzburg, named Steinbuhler, was actually condemned to death for writing some satires on Roman Catholic ceremonies, and, though afterwards pardoned, died of the ill-usage he had undergone in prison.[3]

The spirit of rationalism, however, was now so prevalent that it began to dominate the work of the more intelligent theologians, to whose consequent attempts to strain out by the most dubious means the supernatural elements from the Bible narratives[4] the name of "rationalism" came to be specially applied, that being the kind of criticism naturally most discussed among the clergy. Taking rise broadly in the work of Semler, reinforced by that of the English and French deists and that of Reimarus, the method led stage by stage to the scientific performance of Strauss and Baur, and the recent "higher criticism" of the Old and New Testaments. Noteworthy at its outset as exhibiting the

learned towards native literature was so great that even in the year 1761 Abbt could write that in Rinteln there was nobody who knew the names of Moses Mendelssohn and Lessing."

[1] Karl Hillebrand, *Six Lectures on the History of German Thought*, 1880, p. 109.
[2] *Deutsche Merkur*, January and March, 1788 (*Werke*, ed. 1797, vol. xxix, pp. 1-144: cited by Staudlin, *Gesch. der Rationalismus und Supernaturalismus*, 1826, p. 233).
[3] Kurtz, *Hist. of the Chr. Church*. Eng. trans. 1864, ii, 224.
[4] The method had been broached in the modern period in the *Evangelium medici* of Connor. See above, p. 124. But see also vol. i, p. 368, as to its earlier employment by Pomponazzi.

tendency of official believers to make men, in the words of Lessing, irrational philosophers by way of making them rational Christians,[1] this order of "rationalism" in its intermediate stages belongs rather to the history of Biblical scholarship than to that of freethought, since more radical work was being done by unprofessional writers outside, and deeper problems were raised by the new systems of philosophy. Within the Lutheran pale, however, there were some hardy thinkers. A striking figure of the time, in respect of his courage and thoroughness, is the Lutheran pastor SCHULZ,[2] who so strongly combated the compromises of the Semler school in regard to the Pentateuch, and argued so plainly for a severance of morals from religion, as to bring about his own dismissal (1792).[3]

This appears to have been the only juridical result of the orthodox edict (1788) of the new king, Frederick William, the brother of Frederick, who succeeded in 1786. It announced him as the champion of religion and the enemy of freethinking; forbade all proselytising, and menaced with penalties all forms of heresy,[4] while professing to maintain freedom of conscience. The edict seems to have been specially provoked by fresh literature of a pronouncedly freethinking stamp. In 1785 appeared the anonymous *Moroccan Letters*,[5] wherein, after the model of the *Persian Letters* and others, the life and creeds of Germany are handled in a quite Voltairean fashion. The writer is evidently familiar with French and English deistic literature, and draws freely on both, making no pretence of systematic treatment. Such writing, quietly turning a disenchanting light of common sense on Scriptural incredibilities

---

[1] Letter to his brother, February 2nd, 1774.
[2] Known as Zopf-Schulz from his wearing a pigtail in the fashion then common among the laity.
[3] Hagenbach, *Kirchengeschichte*, i, 372; Gostwick, pp. 52, 54.
[4] See the details in Hagenbach, *Kirchengeschichte*, i, 368-372.
[5] *Marokkanische Briefe. Aus dem Arabischen*. Frankfurt and Leipzig, 1785. The Letters purport to have been written by one of the Moroccan embassy at Vienna in 1783.

and Christian historical scandals, without a trace of polemical zeal, illustrated at once the futility of Kant's claim, in the second edition of his *Critique of Pure Reason*, to counteract "freethinking unbelief" by transcendental philosophy. And though the writer is careful to point to the frequent association of Christian fanaticism with regicide, his very explicit appeal for a unification of Germany,[1] his account of the German Protestant peasant and labourer as the most dismal figure in Germany, Holland, and Switzerland,[2] and his charge against Germans of degrading their women,[3] would not enlist the favour of the authorities for his work. Within two years (1787) appeared an even more strongly anti-Christian and anti-clerical work, *The Only True System of the Christian Religion*,[4] ascribed to Jakob von Mauvillon[5] (1743-1794), a historian and economist, and also an officer in the service of the Duke of Brunswick, who nevertheless became a great admirer of the French Revolution. To such propaganda the edict of repression was the official answer. It naturally roused a strong opposition;[6] but though it ultimately failed, through the general breakdown of European despotisms, it was not without injurious effect. The first edict was followed in a few months by one which placed the press and all literature, native and foreign, under censorship. This policy, which was chiefly inspired by the new king's Minister of Religion, Woellner, was followed up in 1791 by the appointment of a committee of three reactionaries—Hermes, Hilmer, and Woltersdorf—who not only saw to the execution of the edicts, but supervised the schools and churches. Such a regimen, aided by the reaction against the Revolution, for a time prevented any open propaganda

---

[1] *Briefe*, xxi.   [2] P. 49.   [3] P. 232.
[4] *Das einzig wahre System der christlichen Religion.* It was at first composed under the title *False Reasonings of the Christian Religion.*
[5] Noack, Th. III, Kap. 9, p. 194.
[6] It was a test of the depth of the freethinking spirit in the men of the day. Semler justified the edict; Bahrdt vehemently denounced it. Hagenbach, i, 372.

on the part of men officially placed ; and we shall see it hampering and humiliating Kant ; but it left the leaven of anti-supernaturalism to work all the more effectively among the increasing crowd of university students.

Many minds of the period, doubtless, are typified by Herder, who, though a practising clergyman, was clearly a Spinozistic theist, accommodating himself to popular Christianity in a genially latitudinarian spirit.[1] When in his youth he published an essay discussing Genesis as a piece of oriental poetry, not to be treated as science or theology, he evoked an amount of hostility which startled him.[2] Learning his lesson, he was for the future guarded enough to escape persecution. He was led by his own temperamental bias, however, to a transcendental position in philosophy. Originally in agreement with Kant,[3] as against the current metaphysic, in the period before the issue of the latter's *Critique of Pure Reason*, he nourished his religious instincts by a discursive reading of history, which he handled in a comparatively scientific yet above all poetic or theosophic spirit, while Kant, who had little or no interest in history, developed his thought on the side of physical science.[4] The philosophic methods of the two men thus became opposed ; and when Herder found Kant's philosophy producing a strongly rationalistic cast of thought among the divinity students who came before him for examination, he directly and sharply antagonised it[5] in a theistic sense. Yet his own influence on his age was on the whole latitudinarian and anti-theological.

[1] Cp. Crabb Robinson's *Diary*, iii, 48 ; Martineau, *Study of Spinoza*, p. 328 ; Willis, *Spinoza*, pp. 162-8. Bishop Hurst laments (*Hist. of Rationalism*, 3rd ed. p. 145) that Herder's early views as to the mission of Christ "were, in common with many other evangelical views, doomed to an unhappy obscuration upon the advance of his later years by frequent intercourse with more skeptical minds."
[2] On the clerical opposition to him at Weimar on this score see Düntzer, *Life of Goethe*, Eng. trans. 1883, i, 317.
[3] Cp. Dr. Moritz Kronenberg, *Herder's Philosophie nach ihrem Entwickelungsgang*, 1889.
[4] Kronenberg, p. 90.
[5] Stuckenberg, *Life of Immanuel Kant*, 1882, pp. 381-7 ; Kronenberg, *Herder's Philosophie*, pp. 91, 103.

17. Meanwhile, the drift of the age of *Aufklärung* was apparent in the practically freethinking attitude of the two foremost men of letters in the new Germany— GOETHE and SCHILLER. Of the former, despite the bluster of Carlyle, and despite the æsthetic favour shown to Christianity in *Wilhelm Meister*, no religious ingenuity can make more than a pantheist,[1] who, in so far as he touched on Biblical questions, copied the half-grown rationalism of the school of Semler.[2] "The great Pagan" was his common label among his orthodox or conformist contemporaries.[3] He has told how, when Lavater insisted that he must choose between orthodox Christianity and atheism, he answered that, if he were not free to be a Christian in his own way (*wie ich es bisher gehegt hatte*), he would as soon turn atheist as Christian, the more so as he saw that nobody knew very well what either signified.[4] Nor did he ever yield to the Christian creed more than a Platonic amity ; so that much of the peculiar hostility that was long felt for his poetry and was long shown to his memory in Germany is to be explained as an expression of the normal malice of pietism against unbelievers.[5] To-day belief is glad to claim Goethe as a friend in respect of his many concessions to it, as well as of his occasional flings at more consistent freethinkers. But a "great

---

[1] The chief sample passages in his works are the poem *Das Göttliche* and the speech of Faust in reply to Gretchen in the garden scene It was the surmised pantheism of Goethe's poem *Prometheus* that, according to Jacobi, drew from Lessing *his* avowal of a pantheistic leaning. The poem has even an atheistic ring ; but we have Goethe's own account of the influence of Spinoza on him from his youth onwards (*Wahrheit und Dichtung*, Th. III, B. xiv ; Th. IV, B. xvi). See also his remarks on the "natural" religion of "conviction" or rational inference, and that of "faith" (*Glaube*) or revelationism, in B. iv (*Werke*, ed. 1866, xi, 134) ; also Kestner's account of his opinions at twenty-three, in Düntzer's *Life*, Eng. trans. i, 185 ; and again his letter to Jacobi, January 6th, 1813, quoted by Düntzer, ii, 290.
[2] See the *Alt-Testamentliches* Appendix to the *West-Oestlicher Divan*.
[3] Heine, *Zur Gesch. der Rel. u. Phil. in Deutschland* (*Werke*, ed. 1876, iii, 92).
[4] *Wahrheit und Dichtung*, Th. III, B. xiv, par. 20 (*Werke*, ed. 1886, xii, 159).
[5] Compare, as to the kinds of hostility he aroused, Düntzer's *Life*, i, 152, 317, 329 30, 451 , ii, 291 *note*, 455, 461 ; and Heine, last cit. p. 93.

pagan" he remains for the student. In the opinion of later orthodoxy his "influence on religion was very pernicious."[1] He indeed showed small concern for religious susceptibilities when he humorously wrote that from his youth up he believed himself to stand so well with his God as to fancy that he might even "have something to forgive Him."[2]

One passage in Goethe's essay on the Pentateuch, appended to the *West-Oestlicher Divan*, is worth noting here as illustrating the ability of genius to cherish and propagate historical fallacies. It runs: "The peculiar, unique, and deepest theme of the history of the world and man, to which all others are subordinate, is always the conflict of belief and unbelief. All epochs in which belief rules, under whatever form, are illustrious, inspiriting, and fruitful for that time and the future. All epochs, on the other hand, in which unbelief, in whatever form, secures a miserable victory, even though for a moment they may flaunt it proudly, disappear for posterity, because no man willingly troubles himself with knowledge of the unfruitful" (First ed. pp. 424-5). Goethe goes on to speak of the four latter books of Moses as occupied with the theme of unbelief, and of the first as occupied with belief. Thus his formula was based, to begin with, on purely fabulous history, into the nature of which his poetic faculty gave him no true insight. (See his idyllic recast of the patriarchal history in B. iv of the *Wahrheit und Dichtung*.) Applied to real history, his formula has no validity save on a definition which implies either an equivoque or an argument in a circle. If it refer, in the natural sense, to epochs in which any given religion is widely rejected and assailed, it is palpably false. The Renaissance and Goethe's own century were ages of such unbelief; and they remain much more deeply interesting than the Ages of Faith. St. Peter's at Rome is the work of a reputedly unbelieving Pope. If on the other hand his formula be meant to apply to belief in the sense of energy and enthusiasm, it is still fallacious. The crusades were manifestations of energy and enthusiasm; but they were profoundly "unfruitful," and they are not deeply interesting. The only sense in which Goethe's formula could stand would be one in which it is recognised that all vigorous intellectual life stands for "belief"—that is to say, that Lucretius and Voltaire, Paine and d'Holbach, stand for "belief" when confidently attacking beliefs. The formula is

---

[1] Hurst, *Hist. of Rationalism*, 3rd ed. p. 150.
[2] *Wahrheit und Dichtung*, B. viii; *Werke*, xi, 331.

thus true only in a strained and non-natural sense ; whereas it is sure to be read and to be believed, by thoughtless admirers, in its natural and false sense, though the whole history of Byzantium and modern Islam is a history of stagnant and unfruitful belief, and that of modern Europe a history of fruitful doubt, disbelief, and denial, involving new affirmations. Goethe's own mind on the subject was in a state of verbalising confusion, the result or expression of his temperamental aversion to clear analytical thought ("Above all," he boasts, "I never thought about thinking") and his habit of poetic allegory and apriorism. Where he himself doubted and denied current creeds, as in his work in natural science, he was most fruitful (though he was not always right—*e.g.*, his polemic against Newton's theory of colour) ; and the permanently interesting teaching of his *Faust* is precisely that which artistically utters the doubt through which he passed to a pantheistic Naturalism.

18. No less certain is the unbelief of Schiller (1759–1805), whom Hagenbach even takes as "the representative of the rationalism of his age." In his juvenile *Robbers*, indeed, he makes his worst villains freethinkers ; and in the preface he stoutly champions religion against all assailants; but hardly ever after that piece does he give a favourable portrait of a priest.[1] He himself soon joined the *Aufklärung;* and all his æsthetic appreciation of Christianity never carried him beyond the position that it virtually had the tendency (*Anlage*) to the highest and noblest, though that was in general tastelessly and repulsively represented by Christians. He added that in a certain sense it is the only æsthetic religion, whence it is that it gives such pleasure to the feminine nature, and that only among women is it to be met with in a tolerable form.[2] Like Goethe, he sought to reduce the Biblical supernatural to the plane of possibility,[3] in the manner of the liberal theologians of the period ; and like him he often writes as a deist,[4] though professedly for a time a Kantist. On the other hand, he does not hesitate to say that a healthy nature (which Goethe had said needed no

---

[1] Remarked by Hagenbach, trans. p. 238.
[2] Letter to Goethe, August 17th, 1795 (*Briefwechsel*, No. 87). The passage is given in Carlyle's essay on Schiller.
[3] In *Die Sendung Moses*.   [4] See the *Philosophische Briefe*.

Morality, no *Natur-recht*,[1] and no political metaphysic) required neither Deity nor Immortality to sustain it.[2]

19. The critical philosophy of Kant may be said to represent most comprehensively the outcome in German intelligence of the higher freethought of the age, in so far as its results could be at all widely assimilated. In its most truly critical part, the analytic treatment of previous theistic systems in the *Critique of Pure Reason* (1781), he is fundamentally anti-theological; the effect of the argument being to negate all previously current proofs of the existence and cognisableness of a "supreme power" or deity. Already the metaphysics of the Leibnitz-Wolff school were discredited;[3] and so far Kant could count on a fair hearing for a system which rejected that of the schools. Certainly he meant his book to be an antidote to the prevailing religious credulity. "Henceforth there were to be no more dreams of ghost-seers, metaphysicians, and enthusiasts."[4] On his own part, however, no doubt in sympathy with the attitude of many of his readers, there followed a species of intuitional reaction; and in the *Critique of Practical Reason* (1788) he makes an almost avowedly unscientific attempt to restore the reign of theism on a basis of a mere emotional and ethical necessity assumed to exist in human nature—a necessity which he never even attempts to demonstrate. With the magic wand of the Practical Reason, as Heine has it, be reanimated the corpse of theism, which the Theoretic Reason had slain.[5] In

---

[1] Carlyle translates, "No Rights of Man," which was probably the implication.

[2] Letter to Goethe, July 9th, 1796 (*Briefwechsel*, No. 188). "It is evident that he was estranged not only from the church but from the fundamental truths of Christianity" (Rev. W. Baur, *Religious Life of Germany*, Eng. trans. 1872, p. 22).

[3] Cp. Liettrunk, as cited by Stuckenberg, *Life of Immanuel Kant*, 1882, p. 225.

[4] *Id.* p. 376.

[5] For an able argument vindicating the unity of Kant's system, however, see Professor Adamson, *The Philosophy of Kant*, 1879, p. 21 sq. as against Lange. With the verdict in the text compare that of Heine, *Zur Gesch. der Relig. u. Philos. in Deutschland*, B. iii (*Werke*, as cited, iii, 81-82), and that of Professor G. Santayana, *The Life of Reason*, vol. i, 1905, p. 91 sq.

this adjustment he was perhaps consciously copying Rousseau, who had greatly influenced him,[1] and whose theism is an avowedly subjectivist predication. But the same attitude to the problem had been substantially adopted by Lessing;[2] and indeed the process is at bottom identical with that of the quasi-skeptics, Pascal, Huet, Berkeley, and the rest, who at once impugn and employ the rational process, reasoning that reason is not reasonable. Kant did but set up the "practical" against the "pure" reason, as other theists before him had set up faith against science, or the "heart" against the "head," and as theists to-day exalt the "will" against "knowledge," the emotional nature against the logical. It is tolerably clear that Kant's motive at this stage was an unphilosophic fear that Naturalism would work moral harm[3]—a fear shared by him with the mass of the average minds of his age.

> The process of Kant's adjustment of his philosophy to social needs as he regarded them is to be understood by following the chronology and the vogue of his writings. The first edition of the *Critique of Pure Reason* "excited little attention" (Stuckenberg, *The Life of Immanuel Kant*, 1882, p. 368); but in 1787 appeared the second and modified edition, with a new preface, clearly written with a propitiatory eye to the orthodox reaction. "All at once the work now became popular, and the praise was as loud and as fulsome as at first the silence had been profound. The literature of the day began to teem with Kantian ideas, with discussions of the new philosophy, and with the praises of its author.......High officials in Berlin would lay aside the weighty affairs of State to consider the *Kritik*, and among them were found warm admirers of the work and its author." *Id.* p. 369. Cp. Heine, *Rel. und Phil. in Deutschland*, B. iii—*Werke*, iii, 75, 82.
>
> This popularity becomes intelligible in the light of the new edition and its preface. To say nothing of the alterations in the text, pronounced by Schopenhauer to be cowardly accommodations (as to which question see Adamson, as cited, and Stuckenberg, p. 461, *note* 94), Kant writes in the preface that

---

[1] Stuckenberg, pp. 225, 332.
[2] Cp. Haym's *Herder nach seinem Leben......dargestellt*, 1877, i, 33, 48; Kronenberg, *Herder's Philosophie*, 1889, p. 10.
[3] Cp. Hagenbach, Eng. trans. p. 223.

he had been "obliged to destroy knowledge in order to make room for faith"; and, again, that "only through criticism can the roots be cut of materialism, fatalism, atheism, freethinking unbelief (*freigeisterischen Unglauben*), fanaticism and superstition, which may become universally injurious; also of idealism and scepticism, which are dangerous rather to the Schools, and can hardly reach the general public." (Meiklejohn mistranslates: "which *are* universally injurious" Bohn ed. p. xxxvii.) This passage virtually puts the popular religion and all philosophies save Kant's own on one level of moral dubiety. It is, however, distinctly uncandid as regards the "freethinking unbelief," for Kant himself was certainly an unbeliever in Christian miracles and dogmas. His want of philosophic candour, or at least his readiness to make an appeal to prejudice, again appears in the second *Critique* when he asks: "Whence does the freethinker derive his knowledge that there is, for instance, no Supreme Being?" (*Kritik der reinen Vernunft, Transc. Methodenlehre*, 1 H. 2 Absch., ed. Kirchmann, 1879, p. 587; Bohn trans. p. 458.) He had just before professed to be dealing with denial of the "existence of God" a proposition of no significance whatever unless "God" be defined. He now without warning substitutes the undefined expression "Supreme Being" for "God," thus imputing a proposition probably never sustained with clear verbal purpose by any human being. Either, then, Kant's own proposition was the entirely vacuous one that nobody can demonstrate the impossibility of an alleged *undefined* existence, or he was virtually asserting that no one can disprove *any* alleged supernatural existence—witch, demon, Moloch, Krishna, Bel, Siva, Aphrodite, or Isis and Osiris. In the latter case he would be absolutely stultifying his own claim to cut the roots of "superstition" and "fanaticism" as well as of freethinking and materialism; for, if the freethinker cannot disprove Jehovah, neither can the Kantist disprove Allah and Satan; and Kant had no basis for denying, as he did with Spinoza, the existence of ghosts or spirits. From this dilemma Kant's argument cannot be delivered. And as he finally introduces Deity as a psychologically and morally necessary regulative idea, howbeit indemonstrable, he leaves every species of superstition exactly where it stood before—every superstition being practically held, as against "freethinking unbelief," on just such a tenure.

Concerning the age-long opposition between rationalism (*Verstandesaufklärung*) and intuitionism or emotionalism (*Gefuhlsphilosophie*), it is claimed by modern transcendentalists that Kant, or Herder, or another, has effected a solution on a plane higher than either. (*E.g.*, Kronenberg, *Herder's Philosophie nach ihrem Entwickelungsgang und ihrer historischen*

Stellung, 1889, p. 6.) The true solution certainly must account for both points of view; but no solution is really attained by either of these writers. Kant alternately stood at the two positions; and his unhistorical mind did not seek to unify them in a study of human evolution. Herder, recognisant of evolution, would not follow out any rational analysis.

All the while, however, Kant's theism was radically irreconcilable with the prevailing religion. As appears from his cordial hostility to the belief in ghosts, he really lacked the religious temperament. " He himself," says a recent biographer, "was too suspicious of the emotions to desire to inspire any enthusiasm with reference to his own heart."[1] This misstates the fact that his "Practical Reason" was but an abstraction of his own emotional predilection; but it remains true that that predilection was nearly free from the commoner forms of pious psychosis; and typical Christians have never found him satisfactory. " From my heart," writes one of his first biographers, " I wish that Kant had not regarded the Christian religion merely as a necessity for the State, or as an institution to be tolerated for the sake of the weak (which now so many, following his example, do even in the pulpit), but had known that which is positive, improving, and blessed in Christianity."[2] He had in fact never kept up any theological study;[3] and his plan of compromise had thus, like those of Spencer and Mill in a later day, a fatal unreality for all men who have discarded theology with a full knowledge of its structure, though it appeals very conveniently to those disposed to retain it as a means of popular influence. All his adaptations, therefore, failed to conciliate the mass of the orthodox; and even after the issue of the second *Critique* he had been the subject of discussion among the reactionists.[4] But that *Critique*, and the preface to the second edition of the first, were at bottom only pleas for a revised ethic,

---

[1] Stuckenberg, *Life of Immanuel Kant*, p. 329.
[2] Borowski, *Darstellung des Lebens und Charakters Immanuel Kant's*, 1804, cited by Stuckenberg, p. 357.
[3] Stuckenberg, pp. 359-60. [4] *Id*, p. 361.

Kant's concern with current religion being solely ethical; and the force of that concern led him at length, in what was schemed as a series of magazine articles,[1] to expound his notion of religion in relation to morals. When he did so he aroused a resentment much more energetic than that felt by the older academics against his philosophy. The title of his treatise on *Religion within the Boundaries of Mere Reason*[2] (1792-94) is obviously framed to parry criticism; yet so drastic is its treatment of its problems that the College of Censors at Berlin under the new theological regime vetoed the second part. By the terms of the law as to the censorship, the publisher was entitled to know the reason for the decision; but on his asking for it he was informed that "another instruction was on hand, which the censor followed as his law, but whose contents he refused to make known."[3] Greatly incensed, Kant submitted the rejected article with the rest of his book to the theological faculty of his own university of Konigsberg, asking them to decide in which faculty the censorship was properly vested. They referred the decision to the philosophical faculty, which duly proceeded to license the book (1793). As completed, it contained an article markedly hostile to the church. His opponents in turn were now so enraged that they procured a royal cabinet order (October, 1794) charging him with "distorting and degrading many of the chief and fundamental doctrines of the Holy Scriptures and of Christianity," and ordering all the instructors at the university not to lecture on the book.[4] Such was the reward for a capitulation of philosophy to the philosophic ideals of the police.

Kant, called upon to render an account of his conduct to the Government, formally defended it, but in conclusion decorously said: "I think it safest, in order to obviate the least suspicion in this respect, as your

---

[1] The first, on "Radical Evils," appeared in a Berlin monthly in April, 1792, and was then reprinted separately.
[2] *Religion innerhalb der Grenzen der blossen Vernunft.*
[3] Stuckenberg, p. 361.
[4] Ueberweg, ii, 141; Stuckenberg, p. 363.

Royal Majesty's most faithful subject, to declare solemnly that henceforth I will refrain altogether from all public discussion of religion, whether natural or revealed, both in lectures and in writings." After the death of Frederick William, Kant held himself free to speak out again, and published (1798) an essay on "The Strife of the [University] Faculties," wherein he argued that philosophers should be free to discuss all questions of religion so long as they did not handle Biblical theology as such. The belated protest, however, led to nothing. By this time the philosopher was incapable of further efficient work; and when he died in 1804 the chief manuscript he left, planned as a synthesis of his philosophic teaching, was found to be hopelessly confused.[1]

The attitude in which Kant stood to the reigning religion in his latter years was thus substantially hostile. Religion was for him essentially ethic; and there is no reconciling the process of propitiation of deity, in the Christian or any other cult, with his express declaration that all attempts to win God's favour save by simple right-living are sheer fetishism.[2] He thus ends practically at the point of view of the deists, whose influence on him in early life is seen in his work on cosmogony.[3] He had, moreover, long ceased to go to church or follow any religious usage, even refusing to attend the services on the installation of a new university rector, save when he himself held the office. "He did not like the singing in the churches, and pronounced it mere bawling. In prayer, whether public or private, he had not the least faith; and in his conversation as well as his writings he treated it as a superstition, holding that to address anything unseen would open the way for fanaticism. Not only did he argue against prayer: he also ridiculed it, and declared that a man would be ashamed to be caught by another in the attitude of

---

[1] Stuckenberg, pp. 304-9.
[2] *Religion innerhalb der Grenzen der blossen Vernunft*, B. iv, c. 2.
[3] Cp. Stuckenberg, p. 332.

prayer." One of his maxims was that "To kneel or prostrate himself on the earth, even for the purpose of symbolising to himself reverence for a heavenly object, is unworthy of man."[1] So too he held that the doctrine of the Trinity had no practical value, and had a "low opinion" of the Old Testament.

Yet his effort at compromise had carried him to positions which are the negation of some of his own most emphatic ethical teachings. While he carries his "categorical imperative," or a priori conception of duty, so extravagantly far as to argue that it is wrong even to tell a falsehood to a would-be murderer in order to mislead him, he approves of the systematic employment of the pulpit function by men who do not believe in the creed they there expound. The priest, with Kant's encouragement, is to "draw all the practical lessons for his congregation from dogmas which he himself cannot subscribe with a full conviction of their truth, but which he can teach, since it is not altogether impossible that truth may be concealed therein," while he remains free as a scholar to write in a contrary sense in his own name. And this doctrine, set forth in the censured work of 1793, is repeated in the moralist's last treatise (1798), wherein he explains that the preacher, when speaking doctrinally, "can put into the passage under consideration his own rational views, whether found there or not." Kant thus ended by reviving for the convenience of churchmen the medieval principle of a "twofold truth." So little efficacy is there in a transcendental ethic for any of the actual emergencies of life.

> On this question compare Kant's *Religion innerhalb der Grenzen der blossen Vernunft*, B. iii, Apotome i, Sect. 6; B. iv, Apot. ii, preamble and Sect. i, 3 and 4; with the essay in reply to Constant in App. to Rosenkranz's ed. of *Werke*, vii, 295— given by T. K. Abbott in his trans. of the *Critique of Judgment*. See also Stuckenberg, pp. 341-5, and the general comment of Baur, *Kirchengeschichte des 19ten Jahrhunderts*, 1862, p. 65. "Kant's recognition of Scripture is purely a matter of

[1] Stuckenberg, pp. 340, 346, 354, 468.

expedience. The State needs the Bible to control the people ; the masses need it in order that they, having weak consciences, may recognise their duty ; and the philosopher finds it a convenient vehicle for conveying to the people the faith of reason. Were it rejected it might be difficult, if not impossible, to put in its place another book which would inspire as much confidence." All the while " Kant's principles of course led him to deny that the Bible is authoritative in matters of religion, or that it is of itself a safe guide in morals.......Its value consists in the fact that, owing to the confidence of the people in it, reason can use it to interpret into Scripture its own doctrines, and can thus make it the means of popularising rational faith. If anyone imagines that the aim of the interpretation is to obtain the real meaning of Scripture, he is no Kantian on this point " (Stuckenberg, p. 341).

20. The total performance of Kant thus left Germany with a powerful lead on the one hand towards that unbelief in religion which in the last reign had been fashionable, and on the other hand a series of prescriptions for compromise ; the monarchy all the while throwing its weight against all innovation in doctrine and practice. In 1799 Fichte is found expressing the utmost alarm at the combination of the European despotisms to " root out freethought " ;[1] and so strong did the official reaction become that in the opinion of Heine all the German philosophers and their ideas would have been suppressed by wheel and gallows but for Napoleon,[2] who intervened in the year 1805. The Prussian despotism being thus weakened, what actually happened was an adaptation of Kant's teaching to the needs alike of religion and of rationalism. The religious world was assured by it that, though all previous arguments for theism were philosophically worthless, theism was now safe on the fluid basis of feeling. On the other hand, rationalism alike in ethics and in historical criticism was visibly reinforced on all sides. Herder, as before noted, found divinity students grounding their unbelief on Kant's teaching. Staüdlin begins the

[1] Letter of May 22nd, 1799, reproduced by Heine.
[2] *Zur Gesch. der Rel. u. Philos. in Deutschland.* *Werke*, as cited, iii, 96, 98.

preface to his *History and Spirit of Skepticism* (1794) with the remark that "Skepticism begins to be a disease of the age"; and Kant is the last in his list of skeptics. At the close of the century "the number of Kantian theologians was legion," and it was through the Kantian influence that "the various anti-orthodox tendencies which flourished during the period of Illumination were concentrated in Rationalism"[1]—in the tendency, that is, to bring rational criticism to bear alike on history, dogma, and philosophy. Borowski in 1804 complains that "beardless youths and idle babblers" devoid of knowledge "appeal to Kant's views respecting Christianity."[2] These views were partly accommodating, partly subversive in the extreme. Kant regards Jesus as an edifying ideal of perfect manhood, "belief" in whom as such makes a man acceptable to God, because of following a good model. "While he thus treats the historical account of Jesus as of no significance, except as a shell into which the practical reason puts the kernel, his whole argument tends to destroy faith in the historic person of Jesus as given in the Gospel, treating the account itself as something whose truthfulness it is not worth while to investigate."[3] In point of fact we find his devoted disciple Erhard declaring: "I regard Christian morality as something which has been falsely imputed to Christianity; and the existence of Christ does not at all seem to me to be a probable historical fact"—this while declaring that Kant had given him "the indescribable comfort of being able to call himself openly, and with a good conscience, a Christian."[4]

While therefore a multitude of preachers availed themselves of Kant's philosophic license to rationalise in the pulpit and out of it as occasion offered, and yet

---

[1] Stuckenberg, p. 311.

[2] *Id.* p. 357.

[3] Stuckenberg, p. 351. "It is only necessary," adds Dr. Stuckenberg (p. 468, *note* 142), "to develop Kant's hints in order to get the views of Strauss in his *Leben Jesu.*"

[4] *Id.* p. 375. Erhard also stated that Pestalozzi shared his views on the ethics of Christianity.

others opposed them only on the score that all divergence from orthodoxy should be avowed, the dissolution of orthodoxy in Germany was rapid and general; and the anti-supernaturalist handling of Scripture, prepared for as we have seen, went on continuously. Even the positive disparagement of Christianity was carried on by Kantian students; and Hamann, dubbed "the Magician of the North" for his alluring exposition of emotional theism, caused one of them, a tutor, to be brought before a clerical consistory for having taught his pupil to throw all specifically Christian doctrines aside. The tutor admitted the charge, and with four others signed a declaration "that neither morality nor sound reason nor public welfare could exist in connection with Christianity."[1]

21. Against the intellectual influence thus set up there was none in contemporary Germany capable of resistance. Philosophy for the most part went in Kant's direction, having indeed been so tending before his day. Rationalism of a kind had already had a representative in Crusius (1712–1775), who in treatises on logic and metaphysics opposed alike Leibnitz and Wolff, and taught for his own part a kind of Epicureanism, nominally Christianised. To his school belonged Platner (much admired by Jean Paul Richter, his pupil) and Tetens, "the German Locke," who attempted a common-sense answer to Hume. His ideal was a philosophy "at once intelligible and religious, agreeable to God and accessible to the people."[2] Platner on the other hand, leaning strongly towards a psychological and anthropological view of human problems,[3] opposed alike to atheism[4] and to Kantian theism[5] a moderate

[1] Stuckenberg, p. 358.
[2] Bartholmess, *Hist. crit. des doctr. relig. de la philos. moderne*, 1855, i, 136–140.
[3] In demanding a "history of the human conscience" (*Neue Anthropologie*, 1790) Platner seems to have anticipated the modern scientific approach to religion.
[4] *Gespräche uber den Atheismus*, 1781.
[5] *Lehrbuch der Logik und Metaphysik*, 1795.

Pyrrhonic skepticism; here following a remarkable lead from the younger Beausobre, who in 1755 had published in French, at Berlin, a treatise entitled *Le Pyrrhonisme Raisonnable*, taking up the position, among others, that while it is hard to prove the existence of God by reason it is impossible to disprove it. This was virtually the position of Kant a generation later; and it is clear that thus early the dogmatic position was discredited.

Some philosophic opposition there was to Kant, alike on intuitionist grounds, as in the cases of Hamann and Herder, and on grounds of academic prejudice, as in the case of Kraus; but the more important thinkers who followed him were all as heterodox as he. In particular, Fichte, who began by being a Kantian zealot, gave even greater scandal than the Master had done. Passing rapidly, under Spinoza's influence, to pantheism, he rejected Kant's anti-rational ground for affirming a God not immanent in things, and claimed, as did his contemporaries Schelling and Hegel, to establish theism on rational grounds. Rejecting Kant's reiterated doctrine that religion is ethic, Fichte ultimately insisted that, on the contrary, religion is knowledge, and that "it is only a corrupt society that has to use religion as an impulse to moral action." But alike in his Kantian youth and later, he was definitely anti-revelationist. In his *Essay towards a Critique of all Revelation*, published with some difficulty, Kant helping (1792), he in effect negates the orthodox assumption, and, in the spirit of Kant and Lessing, but with more directness than they had shown, concludes that belief in revelation "is an element, and an important element, in the moral education of humanity, but it is not a final stage for human thought."[1] In Kant's fashion, he had professed[2] to "silence the opponents of positive religion not less than its dogmatical defenders"; but that result did not

---

[1] Professor Adamson, *Fichte*, 1881, p. 32; W. Smith, *Memoir of Fichte*, 2nd ed. pp. 64-65.
[2] Letter to Kant, cited by Smith, p. 63.

follow on either side; and ere long he was figuring as one of the most aggressive of the opponents.

It does not appear to be true that he ever told his students at Jena: "In five years there will be no more Christian religion: reason is our religion";[1] and the charges alike of subverting Christianity and of teaching atheism, brought against him soon after his appointment to the Jena chair, seem to have been unjustified at that time.[2] On the provocation given, however, by his lecturing on Sunday to his students, those charges were furiously pressed against him; opinion running so high that he was personally maltreated, and his wife insulted in the streets. Leaving Jena, despite an official vindication, he found harbourage at Berlin, Erlangen, and Konigsberg; but his philosophy was in no way modified, becoming more definitely pantheistic and non-Christian as it developed.[3] Thus Fichte's final pantheism is even more fundamentally atheistic than that of Spinoza. In one of his minor essays[4] he says in so many words that "the living and active moral order is itself God: we need no other God, and can make no other." And that he was conscious of a vital sunderance between his thought and that of the past is made clear by his answer, in 1805, to the complaint that the people had lost their "religious feeling" (*Religiosität*). His retort is that a new religious feeling has taken the place of the old;[5] and that was the position taken up by the generation which swore by him, in the German manner, as the last had sworn by Kant.

But the successive philosophies of Kant, Fichte, Schelling, and Hegel, all rising out of the "Illumination" of the eighteenth century, have been alike

---

[1] Asserted by Stuckenberg, *Life of Kant*, p. 386.
[2] Cp. Robins, *A Defence of the Faith*, 1862, Pt. i, pp. 132-3; Professor Adamson, *Fichte*, pp. 50-67; W. Smith, *Memoir of Fichte*, pp. 106-7.
[3] Compare the complaints of Hurst, *Hist. of Rationalism*, 3rd ed. pp. 136-7.
[4] Summarised by Baur, *Kirchengeschichte des 19ten Jahrh.* pp. 66-67. Heine insists that Fichte's Idealism is "more Godless than the crassest Materialism" (as last cited, p. 75).
[5] *Grundzüge des gegenwärtigen Zeitalters*, 1805-6, 16te Vorlesung.

impermanent. Nothing is more remarkable in the history of thought than the internecine strife of the systems which insisted on "putting something in the place" of the untenable systems of the past. They have been but so many "toppling spires of cloud." Fichte, like Herder, broke away from the doctrine of Kant; and later became bitterly opposed to that of his former friend Schelling, as did Hegel in his turn. Schleiermacher, hostile to Kant, was still more hostile to Fichte; and Hegel, developing Fichte, gave rise to schools arrayed against each other. All that is permanent in the product of the age of German Rationalism is the fundamental principle upon which it proceeded, the confutation of the dogmas and legends of the past, and the concrete results of the historical, critical, and physical research to which the principle and the confutation led.

The emancipation, too, was but partial in the German-speaking world. In Austria, despite a certain amount of French culture, the rule of the Jesuits in the eighteenth century was too effective to permit of any intellectual developments. Maria Theresa, who knew too well that the boundless sexual licence against which she fought had nothing to do with innovating ideas, had to issue a special order to permit the importation of Montesquieu's *Esprit des Lois;* and works of more subversive doctrine could not openly pass the frontiers at all. An attempt to bring Lessing to Vienna in 1774, with a view to founding a new literary Academy, collapsed before the opposition; and when Professor Jahn, of the Vienna University—described as "free-thinking, latitudinarian, supernaturalistic"—developed somewhat anti-clerical tendencies in his teaching and writing, he was forced to resign, and died a simple Canon.[1] "Austria, in a time of universal effervescence, produced only musicians, and showed zest only for pleasure."[2] Yet among the music-makers was the

---

[1] Kurtz, *Hist. of the Chr. Church,* Eng. trans. 1864, ii, 225.
[2] A. Sorel, *L'Europe et la révolution francaise,* i (1885), p. 458.

German-born BEETHOVEN, the greatest master of his age. Kindred in spirit to Goethe, and much more of a revolutionist than he in all things, Beethoven spent the creative part of his life at Vienna without ceasing to be a freethinker.[1]

§ III. *The remaining European States.*

1. Traces of new rationalistic life are to be seen in the Scandinavian countries at least as early as the time of Descartes. There, as elsewhere, the Reformation had been substantially a fiscal or economic revolution, proceeding on various lines. In Denmark the movement, favoured by the king, began among the people; the nobility rapidly following, to their own great profit; and finally Christian III, who ruled both Denmark and Norway, acting with the nobles, suppressed Catholic worship, and confiscated to the crown the "castles, fortresses, and vast domains of the prelates."[2] In Sweden the king, Gustavus Vasa, took the initiative, moved by sore need of funds, and a thoroughly anti-ecclesiastical temper,[3] the clergy having supported the Danish rule which he threw off. The burghers and peasants promptly joined him against the clergy and nobles, enabling him to confiscate the bishops' castles and estates, as was done in Denmark; and he finally secured himself with the nobles by letting them reclaim lands granted by their ancestors to monasteries.[4] His anti-feudal reforms having stimulated new life in many ways, further evolution followed.

Towards the middle of the seventeenth century there are increasing traces of rationalism at the court of the

---

[1] See articles on Beethoven by Macfarren in *Dict. of Univ. Biog.*, and by Grove in the *Dict. of Music and Musicians.*
[2] Koch, *Histor. View of the European Nations*, Eng. trans. 3rd ed. p. 103. Cp. Crichton and Wheaton, *Scandinavia*, 1837, i, 383-396; Otte, *Scandinavian History*, 1874, pp. 222-4; Villiers, *Essay on the Reformation*, Eng. trans. 1836, p. 105. But cp. Allen, *Histoire de Danemark*, Fr. trans. i, 298-300.
[3] Otte, pp. 232-6; Crichton and Wheaton, i, 398-400; Geijer, *History of the Swedes*, Eng. trans. i, 125.
[4] Koch, p. 104; Geijer, i, 129.

famous Christina, who already in her youth is found much interested in the objections of "Jews, heathens, and philosophers against Christian doctrine ";[1] and her invitation of Descartes to her court (1649) suggests that Sweden had been not a little affected by the revulsion of popular thought which followed on the Thirty Years' War in Germany. In the course of a few years, the new spirit had gone so far as to make church-going matter for open scoffing at the Swedish court;[2] and the Queen's adoption of Romanism soon after her abdication appears to have been by way of revulsion from a state of mind approaching atheism, to which she had been led by her freethinking French physician, Bourdelot, after Descartes's death.[3] It is confidently asserted, however, that she really cared for neither creed, and embraced Catholicism only by way of conformity for social purposes, retaining her freethinking views.[4] No important literary results, however, could follow in the then state of Swedish culture, when the studies at even the new colleges were mainly confined to Latin and theology.[5] Puffendorf, indeed, by his great treatise *On the Law of Nature and Nations* (published at Lund, 1672), did much to establish the utilitarian and naturalistic tendency in ethics which was promoted at the same time by Bishop Cumberland in England ;[6] but his latent deism had no great direct influence, his Scripture-citing orthodoxy countervailing it, although he argued strongly for a separation of Church and State.[7] Such being the culture conditions, the Scandinavian countries all round, though strongly affected like the Russian aristocracy by the French freethinking influence in the eighteenth century,[8] have only in our own age begun to contribute weightily to the serious thought of Europe.

[1] Geijer, i, 324. [2] *Id.* p. 343; Otte, p. 292. [3] Geijer, i, 342.
[4] Crichton and Wheaton, ii, 88–9, and refs. [5] Geijer, i, 342.
[6] Cp. Hallam, *Lit. of Europe*, iv, 171 8.
[7] See his treatise, *Of the Nature and Qualification of Religion in Reference to Civil Society*, Eng. trans. by Crull, 1698.
[8] Schweitzer, *Geschichte der skandinavischen Literatur*, ii, 175, 225; C. F. Allen, *Histoire de Danemark*, Fr. trans. ii, 190–1.

The most celebrated northern unbeliever of the French period was Count Struensee, who for some years (1770-2) virtually ruled Denmark as the favourite of the queen, the king being half-witted. Struensee was an energetic and capable reformer: he abolished torture; emancipated the enslaved peasantry; secured toleration for all sects; encouraged the arts and industry; established freedom of the press; and reformed the finances, the police, the law courts, and sanitation.[1] His very reforms made his position untenable, and his enemies soon effected his downfall and death. There is an elaborate account of his conversion to Christianity in prison by the German Dr. Munter,[2] which makes him out by his own confession an excessive voluptuary. It is an extremely suspicious document, exhibiting strong political bias, and giving Struensee no credit for reforms; the apparent assumption being that the conversion of a reprobate was of more evidential value than that of a reputable and reflective type.

2. In Poland, where, as we saw, Unitarian heresy had spread considerably in the sixteenth century, positive atheism is heard of in 1688-9, when Count LISZINSKI (or Lyszczynski), among whose papers, it was said, had been found the written statement that there is no God, or that man had made God out of nothing, was denounced by the bishops of Posen and Kioff, tried, beheaded (his tongue being first torn out), and then burned, his ashes being scattered from a cannon.[3] But even had a less murderous treatment been meted out to such heresy, anarchic Poland, ridden by Jesuits, was in no state to

---

[1] Crichton and Wheaton, ii, 190; Otté, p. 322; C.-F. Allen, as cited, ii, 194-201.
[2] Trans. from the German, 1774; 2nd ed. 1825. See it also in the work, *Converts from Infidelity*, by Andrew Crichton; vols. vi and vii of Constable's Miscellany, 1827. This singular compilation includes lives of Boyle, Bunyan, Haller, and others, who were never "infidels."
[3] He claimed that certain remarks penned by him in an anti-atheistic work, challenging its argument, represented not unbelief but the demand for a better proof, which he undertook to produce. See Krasinski, *Sketch of the Religious History of the Slavonic Nations*, 1851, pp. 224-5. It is remarkable that the Pope, Innocent XI, bitterly censured the execution.

develop a rationalistic literature. In Russia, again, though in the fourteenth century the Strigolniks, who abounded at Novgorod, had held strongly by anti-ecclesiastical doctrines of the Paulician and Lollard type,[1] literature and culture, as distinguished from folk-lore and monastic writing, begin only in the sixteenth century. At this stage we find the usual symptom of criticism of the lives of the monks.[2] But the culture was almost wholly ecclesiastical, and in the seventeenth century the effort of the Patriarch Nicon to correct the sacred texts was furiously resisted.[3] Gradually there arose a new secular fiction, under western influence; and Peter the Great, who promoted printing and literature as he did every other new activity, took the singular step of actually withdrawing writing materials from the monks, whose influence he held to be wholly reactionary. Now began the era of translations from the French; and in the day of the great Catherine the ideas of the *philosophes* were the ruling ones at her court,[4] till the outbreak of the Revolution put the whole school in disgrace with her. This did not alter the tone of thought of the educated classes; but in Russia as in the Scandinavian States it was not till the nineteenth century that original serious literature began.

3. Returning to Italy, no longer the leader of European thought, but still full of veiled freethinking, we find in the seventeenth century the proof that no amount of such predisposition can countervail thoroughly bad political conditions. Ground down by the matchless misrule of Spain, from which the conspiracy of the monk Campanella vainly sought to free her, and by the kindred tyranny of the Papacy, Italy could produce in its educated class, save for the students of economics,

---

[1] Hardwick, *Church History: Middle Age*, 1853, pp. 386-7.
[2] L. Sichler, *Hist. de la litt. Russe*, 1887, pp. 88-9, 139. Cp. Rambaud, *History of Russia*, Eng. trans. 1879, i, 309, 321, 328.
[3] Rambaud, i, 414-417. The struggle (1654) elicited old forms of heresy, going back to Manicheism and Gnosticism.
[4] She bought the library of Diderot when he was in need, constituted him its salaried keeper, and actually had him for a time at her court.

only triflers, whose unbelief was of a piece with their cynicism. While Naples and the south decayed, mental energy had for a time flourished in Tuscany, where, under the grand dukes from Ferdinando I onwards, industry and commerce had revived; and even after a time of retrogression Ferdinando II encouraged science, now made newly glorious by the names of Galileo and Torricelli. But again there was a relapse; and at the end of the century, under a bigoted duke, Florence was priest-ridden and, at least in outward seeming, gloomily superstitious; while, save for the better conditions secured at Naples under the viceroyalty of the Marquis of Carpi,[1] the rest of Italy was cynically corrupt and intellectually superficial.[2] Yet it only needed the breathing time and the improved conditions under the Bourbon rule in the eighteenth century to set up a wonderful intellectual revival. First came the great work of VICO, the *Principles of a New Science* (1725), whereof the originality and the depth—qualities in which, despite its incoherences, it on the whole excels Montesquieu's *Spirit of Laws*—place him among the great freethinkers in philosophy. It was significant of much that Vico's book, while constantly using the vocabulary of faith, grappled with the science of human development in an essentially secular and scientific spirit. This is the note of the whole eighteenth century in Italy.[3] Vico posits Deity and Providence, but proceeds nevertheless to study the laws of civilisation inductively from its phenomena. He permanently obscured his case, indeed, by insisting on putting it theologically, and

[1] See Bishop Burnet's *Letters*, iv, ed. Rotterdam, 1686, pp. 187-191. Burnet observes that "there are societies of men at Naples of freer thoughts than can be found in any other place of Italy"; and he admits a general tendency of intelligent Italians to recoil from Christianity by reason of Catholic corruption. But at the same time he insists that, though the laity speak with scorn of the clergy, "yet they are masters of the spirits of the people" (*Id.* pp. 195-7).
[2] Zeller, *Histoire d'Italie*, pp. 426-432, 450; Procter, *History of Italy*, 2nd ed. pp. 240, 268.
[3] Professor Flint, who insists on the deep piety of Vico, notes that he "appears to have had strangely little interest in Christian systematic theology" (*Vico*, 1884, p. 70).

condemning Grotius and others for separating the idea of law from that of religion. Only in a pantheistic sense has Vico's formula any validity; and he never avows a pantheistic view, refusing even to go with Grotius in allowing that Hebrew law was akin to that of other nations. But a rationalistic view, had he held it, would have been barred. The wonder is, in the circumstances, not that he makes so much parade of religion, but that he could venture to undermine so vitally its pretensions, especially after he had found it prudent to renounce the project of annotating the great work of Grotius, *De Jure Belli ac Pacis*, on the score that (as he puts it in his Autobiography) a good Catholic must not endorse a heretic. It is noteworthy, indeed, that the "New Science," as Vico boasted, arose in the Catholic and not in the Protestant world. The reason probably was that the energy which elsewhere ran to criticism of religion as such had in Catholic Italy to take other channels. As it was, Vico's sociology aroused on the one hand new rationalistic speculation as to the origin of civilisation, and on the other orthodox protest on the score of its fundamentally anti-Biblical character. It was thus attacked in 1749 by Damiano Romano, and later by Finetti, a professor at Padua, apropos of the propaganda raised by Vico's followers as to the animal origin of the human race. This began with Vico's disciple, Emmanuele Duni, a professor at Rome, who published a series of sociological essays in 1763. Thenceforth for many years there raged, "under the eyes of Pope and cardinals," an Italian debate between the *Ferini* and *Antiferini*, the affirmers and deniers of the animal origin of man, the latter of course taking up their ground on the Bible, from which Finetti drew twenty-three objections to Vico.[1] Duni found it prudent to declare that he had "no intention of discussing the origin of the world, still less that of the Hebrew nation, but solely that of the Gentile nations"; but even when

[1] Professor Siciliani, *Sul Rinnovamento della filosofia positiva in Italia*, 1871, pp. 37-41.

thus limited the debate set up far-reaching disturbance. At this stage Italian sociology doubtless owed something to Montesquieu and Rousseau; but the fact remains that the *Scienza Nuova* was a book "truly Italian; Italian *par excellence*."[1] It was Vico, too, who led the way in the critical handling of early Roman history, taken up later by Beaufort, and still later by Niebuhr; and it was he who began the scientific analysis of Homer, followed up later by Wolf.[2] In the same age Muratori and Giannone amassed their unequalled historical learning; and a whole series of Italian writers broke new ground on the field of social science, Italy having led the way in this as formerly in philosophy and physics.[3] The Hanoverian Dr. G. W. Alberti, of Italian descent, writes in 1752 that "Italy is full of atheists."[4]

4. Between 1737 and 1798 may be counted twenty-eight Italian writers on political economy; and among them was one, CESARE BECCARIA, who on another theme produced perhaps the most practically influential single book of the eighteenth century,[5] the treatise on *Crimes and Punishments* (1764), which affected penal methods for the better throughout the whole of Europe. Even were he not known to be a deist, his strictly secular and rationalist method would have brought upon him priestly suspicion; and he had in fact to defend himself against pertinacious and unscrupulous attacks,[6] though he had

---

[1] Siciliani, p. 36.
[2] Introduction (by Mignet?) to the Princess Belgiojoso's trans. *La Science Nouvelle*, 1844, p. cxiii. Cp. Flint, *Vico*, p. 231.
[3] See the *Storia della economia pubblica in Italia* of G. Pecchio, 1829, p. 61 sq., as to the claim of Antonio Serra (*Breve trattato*, etc., 1613) to be the pioneer of modern political economy. Cp. Hallam, *Lit. of Europe*, iii, 164-6. Buckle (1-vol. ed. p. 122, *note*) has perhaps with more justice claimed the title for William Stafford, whose *Compendious or briefe Examination of certain ordinary Complaints* (otherwise called *A Briefe Conceipt of English Policy*) appeared in 1581. But cp. Ingram (*Hist. of Pol. Econ.* 1888, pp. 43-45) as to the prior claims of Bodin.
[4] *Briefe*, as before cited, p. 408.
[5] The *Dei delitti e delle pene* was translated into twenty-two languages. Pecchio, p. 144.
[6] See in the 6th ed. of the *Dei delitti* (Harlem, 1766) the appended *Risposta ad uno scritto*, etc., *Parte prima, Accuse d'empietà*.

sought in his book to guard himself by occasionally "veiling the truth in clouds."[1] As we have seen, Beccaria owed his intellectual awakening first to Montesquieu and above all to Helvetius—another testimony to the reformative virtue of all freethought.

5. Of the aforesaid eight-and-twenty writers on economics, probably the majority were freethinkers. Among them, at all events, were ALGAROTTI, the distinguished æsthetician, one of the group round Frederick at Berlin; FILANGIERI, whose work on legislation (put on the *Index* by the Papacy) won the high praise of Franklin; GALIANI, one of the brightest and soundest wits in the circle of the French *philosophes;* GENOVESI, the "redeemer of the Italian mind,"[2] and the chief establisher of economic science for modern Italy. To these names may be added those of ALFIERI, one of the strongest anti-clericalists of his age; BETTINELLI, the correspondent of Voltaire and author of *The Resurrection of Italy* (1775); Count DANDOLO, author of a French work on *The New Men* (1799); and the learned GIANNONE, author of the great anti-papal *History of the Kingdom of Naples* (1723), who, after more than one narrow escape, was thrown in prison by the King of Sardinia, and died there (1748) after twelve years' confinement. Italy had done her full share, considering her heritage of burdens and hindrances, in the intellectual work of the century; and in the names of Galvani and Volta stands the record of one more of her great contributions to human enlightenment. Under Duke Leopold of Tuscany, the Papacy was so far defied that books put on the *Index* were produced for him under the imprint of London;[3] and the papacy itself at length gave way to the spirit of reform, Clement XIV consenting among other things to abolish the Order of Jesuits (1773), after his predecessor had died of grief

---

[1] See his letter to the Abbe Morellet, cited by Mr. Farrer in ch. i of his ed. of *Crimes and Punishments*, 1880, p. 5. It describes the Milanese as deeply sunk in prejudices.

[2] Pecchio, p. 123.   [3] Zeller, p. 473.

over his proved impotence to resist the secular policy of the States around him.[1] Such was the dawn of the new Italian day that has since slowly but steadily broadened, albeit under many a cloud.

6. For the rest of Europe during the eighteenth century, we have to note only traces of receptive thought. Spain under Bourbon rule, as already noted, experienced an administrative renascence. Such men as Count ARANDA (1718–99) and Aszo y del Rio (1742–1814) wrought to cut the claws of the Inquisition and to put down the Jesuits; but not yet, after the long work of destruction accomplished by the church in the past, could Spain produce a fresh literature of any far-reaching power. When Aranda was about to be appointed in 1766, his friends the French *Encyclopédistes* prematurely proclaimed their exultation in the reforms he was to accomplish; and he sadly protested that they had thereby limited his possibilities.[2] None the less he wrought much, the power of the Inquisition being already on the wane. Between 1746 and 1759 it had burned only ten persons; from 1759 until 1781 it burned only four; thereafter none,[3] the last case having provoked an amount of comment which testified to the moral change wrought in Europe by a generation of freethought. The trouble was that the enlightened administration of Charles III in Spain did not build up a valid popular education, the sole security for durable rationalism. Its school policy, though not without zeal, was undemocratic, and so left the priests in control of the mind of the multitude; and throughout the reign the ecclesiastical revenues had been allowed to increase greatly from private sources.[4] When, accordingly, the weak and pious Charles IV succeeded in 1788, three of

---

[1] Zeller, pp. 478–9.
[2] Coxe, *Memoirs of the Bourbon Kings of Spain*, ed. 1815, iv, 408.
[3] Buckle, iii, 547–8 (1-vol. ed. 599–600). The last victim seems to have been a woman accused of witchcraft. Her nose was cut off before her execution. See the *Marokkanische Briefe*, 1785, p. 36; and Buckle's *note* 272.
[4] Buckle, p. 618.

the anti-clerical Ministers of his predecessor, including Aranda, were put under arrest,[1] and clericalism resumed full sway, to the extent even of vetoing the study of moral philosophy in the universities.[2] Mentally and materially alike, Spain relapsed to her former state of indigence; and the struggle for national existence against Napoleon evoked rather traditionalist sentiment than the spirit of innovation.

7. Portugal in the same period, despite the anti-clerical policy of the famous Marquis of Pombal, made no noticeable intellectual progress. Though that powerful statesman in 1761 abolished slavery in the kingdom,[3] he too failed to see the need for popular education, while promoting that of the upper classes.[4] His expulsion of the Jesuits, accordingly, did but raise up against him a new set of enemies in the shape of the *Jacobeos*, "the Blessed," a species of Catholic Puritan, who accused him of impiety. His somewhat forensic defence[5] leaves the impression that he was in reality a deist; but though he fought the fanatics by imprisoning the Bishop of Coimbra, their leader, and by causing Moliere's *Tartufe* to be translated and performed, he does not seem to have shown any favour to the deistical literature of which the Bishop had composed a local *Index Expurgatorius*.[6] In Portugal, as later in Spain, accordingly, a complete reaction set in with the death of the enlightened king. Dom Joseph died in 1777, and Pombal was at once disgraced and his enemies released, the pious Queen Maria and her Ministers subjecting him to persecution for some years. In 1783, the Queen, who became a religious maniac, and died insane,[7] is found establishing new nunneries, and so adding to one of the main factors in the impoverishment, moral and financial, of Portugal.

8. During the period we have been surveying, up to the French Revolution, Switzerland, which owed much

---

[1] Buckle, p. 612. [2] *Id.* p. 613.
[3] Carnota, *The Marquis of Pombal*, 2nd ed. 1871, p. 242.
[4] *Id.* p. 240. [5] *Id.* pp. 261-2. [6] *Id.* p. 262. [7] *Id.* p. 375.

of new intellectual life to the influx of French Protestants at the revocation of the Edict of Nantes,[1] contributed to the European movement some names, of which by far the most famous is Rousseau ; and the potent presence of Voltaire cannot have failed to affect Swiss culture. The chief native service to intellectual progress thus far, however, was rendered in the field of the natural sciences, Swiss religious opinion being only passively liberalised, mainly in a Unitarian direction.

[1] P. Godet, *Hist. litt. de la Suisse française*, 1900.

Chapter XVII.

EARLY FREETHOUGHT IN THE UNITED STATES

1. PERHAPS the most signal of all the proofs of the change wrought in the opinion of the civilised world in the eighteenth century is the fact that at the time of the War of Independence the leading statesmen of the American colonies were deists. Such were BENJAMIN FRANKLIN, the diplomatist of the Revolution; THOMAS PAINE, its prophet and inspirer; WASHINGTON, its commander; and JEFFERSON, its typical legislator. But for these four men the American Revolution probably could not have been accomplished in that age; and they thus represent in a peculiar degree the power of new ideas, in fit conditions, to transform societies, at least politically. On the other hand, the fashion in which their relation to the creeds of their time has been garbled, alike in American and English histories, proves how completely they were in advance of the average thought of their day: and also how effectively the mere institutional influence of creeds can arrest a nation's mental development. It is still one of the stock doctrines of religious sociology in England and America that deism, miscalled atheism, wrought the Reign of Terror in the French Revolution; when as a matter of fact the same deism was at the head of affairs in the American.

2. The rise of rationalism in the colonies must be traced in the main to the imported English literature of the eighteenth century; for the first Puritan settlements had contained at most only a fraction of freethought; and the conditions, so deadly for all manner even of

devout heresy, made avowed unbelief impossible. The superstitions and cruelties of the Puritan clergy, however, must have bred a silent reaction, which prepared a soil for the deism of the next age.[1] "The perusal of Shaftesbury and Collins," writes Franklin with reference to his early youth, "had made me a sceptic," after being "previously so as to many doctrines of Christianity."[2] This was in his seventeenth or eighteenth year, about 1720, so that the importation of deism had been prompt.[3] Throughout life he held to the same opinion, conforming sufficiently to keep on fair terms with his neighbours,[4] and avoiding anything like critical propaganda; though on challenge, in the last year of his life, he avowed his negatively deistic position.[5]

3. Similarly prudent was JEFFERSON, who, like Franklin and Paine, extolled the Gospel Jesus and his teachings, but rejected the notion of supernatural revelation.[6] In a letter written so late as 1822 to a Unitarian correspondent, while refusing to publish another of similar tone, on the score that he was too old for strife, he declared that he "should as soon undertake to bring the crazy skulls of Bedlam to sound understanding as to inculcate reason into that of an Athanasian."[7] His experience of the New England clergy is expressed in allusions to Connecticut as having been "the last retreat of monkish darkness, bigotry, and abhorrence of those advances of the mind which had

---

[1] John Wesley in his Journal, dating May, 1737, speaks of having everywhere met many more "converts to infidelity" than "converts to Popery," with apparent reference to Carolina.

[2] Such is the wording of the passage in the *Autobiography* in the Edinburgh edition of 1803, p. 25, which follows the French translation of the original MS. In the edition of the *Autobiography and Letters* in the Minerva Library, edited by Mr. Bettany (1891, p. 11), which follows Mr. Bigelow's edition of 1879, it runs: "Being then, from reading Shaftesbury and Collins, become a real doubter in many points of our religious doctrine........"

[3] Only in 1784, however, appeared the first anti-Christian work published in America, Ethan Allen's *Reason the only Oracle of Man*. As to its positions, see Conway, *Life of Paine*, ii, 192-3.

[4] *Autobiography*, Bettany's ed. pp. 56, 65, 74, 77, etc.

[5] Letter of March 9th, 1790. *Id.* p. 636.

[6] Cp. J. T. Morse's *Thomas Jefferson*, pp. 339-340.

[7] MS. cited by Dr. Conway, *Life of Paine*, ii, 310-311.

carried the other States a century ahead of them "; and in congratulations with John Adams (who had written that "this would be the best of all possible worlds if there were no religion in it"), when "this den of the priesthood is at last broken up."[1] John Adams, whose letters with their "crowd of scepticisms" kept even Jefferson from sleep,[2] seems to have figured as a member of a Congregationalist church, while in reality a Unitarian.[3] Still more prudent was Washington, who seems to have ranked habitually as a member of the episcopal church; but concerning whom Jefferson relates that, when the clergy, having noted his constant abstention from any public mention of the Christian religion, so penned an address to him on his withdrawal from the Presidency as almost to force him to some declaration, he answered every part of the address but that, which he entirely ignored. It is further noted that only in his valedictory letter to the governors of the States, on resigning his commission, did he speak of the "benign influence of the Christian religion"[4]—the common tone of the American deists of that day. It is further established that Washington avoided the Communion in church.[5] For the rest, the broad fact that all mention of deity was excluded from the Constitution of the United States must be historically taken to signify a profound change in the convictions of the leading minds among the people as compared with the beliefs of their ancestors. At the same time, the fact

[1] *Memoirs of Jefferson*, 1829, iv, 300-1. The date is 1817. These and other passages exhibiting Jefferson's deism are cited in Rayner's *Sketches of the Life*, etc., *of Jefferson*, 1832, pp. 513-517.
[2] *Memoirs of Jefferson*, iv, 331.
[3] Dr. Conway, *Life of Paine*, ii, 310.
[4] Extract from Jefferson's Journal under date February 1st, 1800, in the *Memoirs*, iv, 512. Gouverneur Morris, whom Jefferson further cites as to Washington's unbelief, is not a very good witness; but the main fact cited is significant.
[5] Compare the testimony given by the Rev. Dr. Wilson, of Albany, in 1831, as cited by R. D. Owen in his *Discussion on the Authenticity of the Bible* with O. Bacheler (London, ed. 1840, p. 231), with the replies on the other side (pp. 233-4). Washington's death-bed attitude was that of a deist. See all the available data for his supposed orthodoxy in Sparks' *Life of Washington*, 1857, app. iv.

that they as a rule dissembled their unbelief is a proof that, even where legal penalties do not attach to an avowal of serious heresy, there inheres in the menace of mere social ostracism a power sufficient to coerce the outward life of public and professional men of all grades, in a democratic community where faith maintains and is maintained by a competitive multitude of priests. With this force the freethought of our own age has to reckon, after Inquisitions and blasphemy laws have become obsolete.

4. Nothing in American culture-history more clearly proves the last proposition than the case of THOMAS PAINE, the virtual founder of modern democratic freethought in Great Britain and the States.[1] It does not appear that Paine openly professed any heresy while he lived in England, or in America before the French Revolution. Yet the first sentence of his *Age of Reason*, of which the first part was written shortly before his imprisonment, under sentence of death from the Robespierre Government, in Paris (1793), shows that he had long held pronounced deistic opinions.[2] They were probably matured in the States, where, as we have seen, such views were often privately held, though there, as Franklin is said to have jesuitically declared in his old age, by way of encouraging immigration: " Atheism is unknown; infidelity rare and secret, so that persons may live to a great age in this country without having their piety shocked by meeting with either an atheist or an infidel." Paine did an unequalled service to the American Revolution by his *Common Sense* and his series of pamphlets headed *The Crisis:* there is, in fact, little question that but for the intense stimulus thus given by him at critical moments the movement might have collapsed at an early stage. Yet he seems to have had no thought there and then of avowing his deism.

[1] So far as is known, Paine was the first writer to use the expression, "the religion of Humanity." See Conway's *Life of Paine*, 1892, ii, 206. To Paine's influence, too, appears to be due the founding of the first American Anti-Slavery Society. *Id.* i, 51-2, 60, 80, etc.
[2] Cp. Dr. Conway's *Life of Paine*, ii, 205-7.

It was in part for the express purpose of resisting the ever-strengthening attack of atheism in France on deism itself that he undertook to save it by repudiating the Judæo-Christian revelation ; and it is not even certain that he would have issued the *Age of Reason* when it did appear, had he not supposed he was going to his death when put under arrest, on which score he left the manuscript for publication.[1]

5. Its immediate effect was much greater in Britain, where his *Rights of Man* had already won him a vast popularity in the teeth of the most furious reaction, than in America. There, to his profound chagrin, he found that his honest utterance of his heresy brought on him hatred, calumny, ostracism, and even personal and political molestation. In 1797 he had founded in Paris the little " Church of Theo-philanthropy," beginning his inaugural discourse with the words : " Religion has two principal enemies, Fanaticism and Infidelity, or that which is called atheism. The first requires to be combated by reason and morality ; the other by natural philosophy."[2] These were his settled convictions ; and he lived to find himself shunned and vilified, in the name of religion, in the country whose freedom he had so puissantly wrought to win.[3] The Quakers, his father's

---

[1] A letter of Franklin to someone who had shown him a freethinking manuscript, advising against its publication (Bettany's ed. p. 620), has been conjecturally connected with Paine, but was clearly not addressed to him. Franklin died in 1790, and Paine was out of America from 1787 onwards. But the letter is in every way inapplicable to the *Age of Reason*. The remark : " If men are so wicked *with* religion, what would they be *without* it ?" could not be made to a devout deist like Paine.

[2] Conway, *Life of Paine*, 1892, ii, 254-5.

[3] See Dr. Conway's chapter, " The American Inquisition," vol. ii, ch. 16 ; also pp. 361-2, 374, 379. The falsity of the ordinary charges against Paine's character is finally made clear by Dr. Conway, ch. xix, and pp. 371, 383, 419, 423. Cp. the author's pamphlet, *Thomas Paine : An Investigation* (Bonner). The chronically revived story of his deathbed remorse for his writings—long ago exposed (Conway, ii, 420)—is definitively discredited in the latest reiteration. That occurs in the *Life and Letters of Dr. R. H. Thomas* (1905), the mother of whose stepmother was the Mrs. Mary Hinsdale, neé Roscoe, on whose testimony the legend rests. Dr. Thomas, a Quaker of the highest character, accepted the story without question, but incidentally tells of the old lady (p. 13) that "*her wandering fancies* had all the charm of a present fairy-tale to us." No further proof is needed, after the previous exposure, of the worthlessness of the testimony in question.

sect, refused him a burial-place. He has had sympathy and fair play, as a rule, only from the atheists whom he distrusted and opposed, or from thinkers who no longer hold by deism. There is reason to think that in his last years the deistic optimism which survived the deep disappointments of the French Revolution began to give way before deeper reflection on the cosmic problem,[1] if not before the treatment he had undergone at the hands of Unitarians and Trinitarians alike. The Butlerian argument, that Nature is as unsatisfactory as revelation, had been pressed upon him by Bishop Watson in a reply to the *Age of Reason;* and though, like most deists of his age, he regarded it as a vain defence of orthodoxy, he was not the man to remain long blind to its force against deistic assumptions. Like Franklin, he had energetically absorbed and given out the new ideals of physical science ; his originality in the invention of a tubular iron bridge, and in the application of steam to navigation,[2] being nearly as notable as that of Franklin's great discovery concerning electricity. Had the two men drawn their philosophy from the France of the latter part of the century instead of the England of the first, they had doubtless gone deeper. As it was, temperamental optimism had kept both satisfied with the transitional formula ; and in the France of before and after the Revolution they lived pre-occupied with politics.

6. The habit of reticence or dissimulation among American public men was only too surely confirmed by the treatment meted out to Paine. Few stood by him ; and the vigorous deistic movement set up in his latter years by Elihu Palmer soon succumbed to the conditions,[3] though Palmer's book, *The Principles of Nature* (1802, rep. by Richard Carlile, 1819), is a powerful attack on the Judaic and Christian systems all along the

---

[1] Conway, ii, 371.
[2] See the details in Conway's *Life*, ii, 280-1, and *note.* He had also a scheme for a gunpowder motor (*Id.* and i, 240), and various other remarkable plans.
[3] Conway, ii, 362-371.

line. George Houston, leaving England after two years' imprisonment for his translation of d'Holbach's *Ecce Homo*, went to New York, where he edited the *Minerva* (1822), reprinted his book, and started a freethought journal, *The Correspondence*. That, however, lasted only eighteen months. All the while, such statesmen as Madison and Monroe, the latter Paine's personal friend, seem to have been of his way of thinking,[1] though the evidence is scanty. The essential evil is that the baseness of partisan politics is at all times ready to turn a man's heresy to his political ruin; such being in part the explanation of the gross ingratitude shown to Paine. Thus it came about that, save for the liberal movement of the Hicksite Quakers,[2] the secret American deism of Paine's day was decorously transformed into the later Unitarianism, the extremely rapid advance of which in the next generation is the best proof of the commonness of private unbelief. The influence of Priestley, who, persecuted at home, went to end his days in the States, had doubtless much to do with the Unitarian development there, as in England; but it seems certain that the whole deistic movement, including the work of Paine and Palmer, had tended to move out of orthodoxy many of those who now, recoiling from the fierce hostility directed against the outspoken freethinkers, sought a more rational form of creed than that of the orthodox churches. The deistic tradition in a manner centred in the name of Jefferson, and the known deism of so popular a leader would do much to make fashionable a heresy which combined his philosophy with a decorous attitude to the Sacred Books.

---

[1] Testimonies quoted by R. D. Owen, as cited, pp. 231-2.
[2] Conway, ii, 422.

Chapter XVIII.

FREETHOUGHT IN THE NINETEENTH CENTURY

As with the cause of democracy, so with the cause of rationalism, the forward movement which was checked for a generation by the reaction against the French Revolution grew only the deeper and more powerful through the check; and the nineteenth century closed on a record of freethinking progress which may be said to outbulk that of all the previous centuries of the modern era together. So great has been the activity of the century in point of mere quantity that it is impossible, within the scheme of a " Short History," to treat it on even such a reduced scale of narrative as has been applied to the past. A detailed history from the French Revolution onwards probably requires a separate book as large as the present. It must here suffice, therefore, to take a series of broad and general views of the century's work, leaving adequate critical and narrative treatment for a separate undertaking. The most helpful method seems to be that of a conspectus (1) of the main movements and forces that have affected in varying degrees the thought of the civilised world, and (2) of the advance made and the point reached in the culture of the nations, separately considered. At the same time, the forces of rationalism may be discriminated into Particular and General. We may then roughly represent the lines of movement, in non-chronological order, as follows :—

>I.—*Forces of criticism and corrective thought bearing expressly on religious beliefs.*

> 1. In Great Britain and America, the new movements of popular freethought deriving immediately from Paine, and lasting continuously to the present day.

2. In France and elsewhere, the reverberation of the attack of Voltaire, d'Holbach, Dupuis, and Volney, carried on most persistently in Catholic countries by the Freemasons, as against official orthodoxy after 1815.

3. German "rationalism," proceeding from English deism, moving towards naturalist as against supernaturalist conceptions, dissolving the notion of the miraculous in both Old and New Testament history, and all along affecting studious thought in other countries.

4. The compromise of Lessing, claiming for all religions a place in a scheme of "divine education."

5. In England, the neo-Christianity of the school of Coleridge, a disintegrating force, promoting the "Broad Church" tendency, which in Dean Milman is so pronounced as to bring on him charges of rationalism.

6. The utilitarianism of the school of Bentham, carried into moral and social science.

7. Comtism, making little direct impression on the "constructive" lines laid by the founder, but affecting critical thought in all directions.

8. German philosophy, Kantian and post-Kantian, in particular the Hegelian, turned to anti-Christian and anti-supernaturalist account by Strauss, Vatke, Bruno Bauer, Feuerbach, and Marx.

9. German atheism and scientific "materialism"—represented by Feuerbach and Büchner (who, however, rejected the term "materialism" as inappropriate).

10. Revived English deism, involving destructive criticism of Christianity, as in Hennell, F. W. Newman, R. W. Mackay, W. R. Greg, Theodore Parker, and Thomas Scott, partly in co-operation with Unitarianism.

11. American transcendentalism or pantheism—the school of Emerson.

12. Colenso's preliminary attack on the Pentateuch, a systematised return to Voltairean common-sense, rectifying the unscientific course of the "higher criticism" on the historical issue.

13. The later or scientific "higher criticism" of the Old Testament—represented by Kuenen, Wellhausen, and their successors.

14. New historical criticism of Christian origins, in particular the work of Strauss and Baur in Germany, Renan and Havet in France, and their successors.

15. Exhibition of rationalism within the churches, as in Germany, Holland, and Switzerland generally; in England in the *Essays and Reviews;* later in multitudes of essays and

books, and in the documentary criticism of the Old Testament; in America in popular theology.

16. Association of rationalistic doctrine with the Socialist movements, new and old, from Owen to Marx.

17. Communication of doubt and questioning through poetry and *belles-lettres* as in Shelley, Byron, Coleridge, Clough, Tennyson, Carlyle, Arnold, Browning, Swinburne, Heine, Victor Hugo, Leconte de Lisle, Leopardi, and some recent French and English novelists.

II.—*Modern Science, physical, mental, and moral, sapping the bases of all supernaturalist systems.*

1. Astronomy, newly directed by Laplace.

2. Geology, gradually connected (as in Britain by Chambers) with

3. Biology, made definitely non-deistic by Darwin.

4. The comprehension of all science in the Evolution Theory, as by Spencer, advancing on Comte.

5. Psychology, as regards localisation of brain functions.

6. Comparative mythology, as yet imperfectly applied to **Christism**.

7. Sociology, as outlined by Comte, Buckle, Spencer, Winwood Reade, Lester Ward, Giddings, Tarde, Durkheim, and others, on strictly naturalistic lines.

8. Comparative Hierology; the methodical application of principles insisted on by all the deists, and formulated in the interests of deism by Lessing, but latterly freed of his implications.

On the other hand, we may group somewhat as follows the general forces of retardation of freethought operating throughout the century :—

1. Penal laws, still operative in Germany against popular freethought propaganda, and till recently in Britain against any endowment of freethought.

2. Class interests, involving in the first half of the century a social conspiracy against rationalism in England.

3. Commercial pressure thus set up, and always involved in the influence of churches.

4. In England, identification of orthodox Dissent with political Liberalism a sedative.

5. Concessions by the clergy, especially in England and the United States—to many, another sedative.

6. Above all, the production of new masses of popular ignorance in the industrial nations, and continued lack of education in the others.

7. On this basis, business-like and in large part secular-minded organisation of the endowed churches, as against a freethought propaganda hampered by the previously named causes, and in England by laws which veto all direct endowment of anti-Christian heresy.

It remains to make, with forced brevity, the surveys thus outlined.

§ 1. *Popular Propaganda.*

1. If any one circumstance more than another differentiates the life of to-day from that of older civilisations, or from that of previous centuries of the modern era, it is the diffusion of rationalistic views among the "common people." In no other age is to be found the phenomenon of widespread critical skepticism among the labouring masses; in all previous ages, though chronic complaint is made of *some* unbelief among the uneducated, the constant and abject ignorance of the mass of the people has been the sure foothold of superstitious systems. And this vital change in the distribution of knowledge is largely to be attributed to the written and spoken teaching of a line of men who made popular enlightenment their great aim. Their leading type among the English-speaking races is THOMAS PAINE, whom we have seen combining a gospel of democracy with a gospel of critical reason in the midst of the French Revolution. Never before had rationalism been made popular. The English and French deists had written for the middle and upper classes. Peter Annet was practically the first who sought to reach the multitude; and his punishment expressed the special resentment aroused in the governing classes by such a policy. Of all the English freethinkers of the earlier deistical period he alone was selected for reprinting by the propagandists of the Paine period. Paine was to Annet, however, as a cannon to a musket, and through the democratic ferment of his day he won an audience a hundredfold wider than Annet could dream of reaching. The anger of the governing classes,

in a time of anti-democratic panic, was proportional. Paine would have been at least imprisoned for his *Rights of Man* had he not fled from England in time ; and the sale of all his books was furiously prohibited and ferociously punished. Yet they circulated everywhere, even in Protestant Ireland,[1] hitherto affected only under the surface of upper-class life by deism. The circulation of Bishop Watson's *Apology* in reply only served to spread the contagion, as it brought the issues before multitudes who would not otherwise have heard of them.[2] All the while, direct propaganda was carried on by translations and reprints as well as by fresh English tractates. Diderot's *Thoughts on Religion*, and Freret's *Letter from Thrasybulus to Leucippus*, seem to have been great favourites among the Painites, as was Elihu Palmer's *Principles of Nature ;* and Volney's *Ruins of Empires* had a large vogue. Condorcet's *Esquisse* had been promptly translated in 1795 ; the translation of d'Holbach's *System of Nature* reached a third edition in 1817 ;[3] that of Raynal's History had been reprinted in 1804 ; and that of Helvetius *On the Mind* in 1810 ; while an English abridgment of Bayle in four volumes, on freethinking lines, appeared in 1826.

Meantime, new writers arose to carry into fuller detail the attacks of Paine, sharpening their weapons on those of the more scholarly French deists. A *Life of Jesus Christ, including his Apocryphal History*,[4] was published in 1818, with such astute avoidance of all comment that it escaped prosecution. Others, taking a more daring course, fared accordingly. George Houston translated the *Ecce Homo* of d'Holbach, first

---

[1] Lecky, *Hist. of Ireland in the Eighteenth Century*, ed. 1892, iii, 382.
[2] Cp. Conway's *Life of Paine*, ii, 252-3.
[3] This translation, issued by "Sherwood, Neely, and Jones, Paternoster Row, and all booksellers," purports to be "with additions." The translation, however, has altered d'Holbach's atheism to deism.
[4] By W. Huttman. The book is "embellished with a head of Jesus" —a conventional religious picture. Huttman's opinions may be divined from the last sentence of his preface, alluding to "the high pretentions and inflated stile of the lives of Christ which issue periodically from the English press."

publishing it at Edinburgh in 1799, and reprinting it in London in 1813. For the second issue he was prosecuted, fined £200, and imprisoned for two years in Newgate. Robert Wedderburn, a mulatto calling himself "the Rev.," in reality a superannuated journeyman tailor who officiated in Hopkins Street Unitarian Chapel, London, was in 1820 sentenced to two years' imprisonment in Dorchester Jail for a "blasphemous libel" contained in one of his pulpit discourses. His Letters to the Rev. Solomon Herschell (the Jewish Chief Rabbi) and to the Archbishop of Canterbury show a happy vein of orderly irony and not a little learning, despite his profession of apostolic ignorance; and at the trial the judge admitted his defence to be "exceedingly well drawn up." His publications naturally received a new impetus, and passed to a more drastic order of mockery.

As the years went on, the persecution in England grew still fiercer; but it was met with a stubborn hardihood which wore out even the malice of piety. One of the worst features of the religious crusade was that it affected to attack not unbelief but "vice," such being the plea on which Wilberforce and others prosecuted, during a period of more than twenty years, the publishers and booksellers who issued the works of Paine.[1] But even that dissembling device did not ultimately avail. A name not to be forgotten by those who value obscure service to human freedom is that of RICHARD CARLILE, who between 1819 and 1835 underwent nine years' imprisonment in his unyielding struggle for the freedom of the Press, of thought, and of speech.[2] John Clarke, an ex-Methodist, became one of Carlile's shopmen, was tried in 1824 for selling one of his publications, and "after a spirited

---

[1] Cp. *Dynamics of Religion*, pp. 208-9.
[2] See Harriet Martineau's *History of the Peace*, ed. 1877, ii, 87, and Mrs. Carlile Campbell's *The Battle of the Press* (Bonner, 1899) passim, as to the treatment of those who acted as Carlile's shopmen. Women were imprisoned as well as men—*e.g.*, SUSANNA WRIGHT, as to whom see Wheeler's *Dictionary*, and last ref. Carlile's wife and sister were likewise imprisoned with him; and over twenty volunteer shopmen in all went to jail.

defence, in which he read many of the worst passages of the Bible," was sentenced to three years' imprisonment, and to find securities for good behaviour during life. The latter disability he effectively anticipated by writing, while in prison, *A Critical Review of the Life, Character, and Miracles of Jesus*, wherein Christian feelings were treated as Christians had treated the feelings of freethinkers, with a much more destructive result. Published first, strangely enough, in the *Newgate Magazine*, it was republished in 1825 and 1839, with impunity. Thus did a brutal bigotry bring upon itself ever a deadlier retaliation, till it sickened of the contest. Those who threw up the struggle on the orthodox side declaimed as before about the tone of the unbeliever's attack, failing to read the plain lesson that, while noisy bigotry deterred from utterance all the gentler and more sympathetic spirits on the side of reason, the work of reason could be done only by the harder natures, which gave back blow for blow and insult for insult, rejoicing in the encounter. Thus championed, freethought could not be crushed. The propagandist and publishing work done by Carlile was carried on diversely by such free lances as ROBERT TAYLOR (ex-clergyman, author of the *Diegesis*, 1829, and *The Devil's Pulpit*, 1830), CHARLES SOUTHWELL (1814-1860), and William Hone,[1] who ultimately became an independent preacher. Southwell, a disciple of Robert Owen, who edited *The Oracle of Reason*, was imprisoned for a year in 1840 for publishing in that journal an article entitled "The Jew Book"; and was succeeded in the editorship by GEORGE JACOB HOLYOAKE (1817-1906), another Owenite missionary, who met a similar sentence; whereafter George Adams and his wife, who continued to publish the journal, were

[1] Hone's most important service to popular culture was his issue of the *Apocryphal New Testament*, which, by coordinating work of the same kind, gave a fresh scientific basis to the popular criticism of the Gospel history. As to his famous trial for blasphemy on the score of his having published certain parodies, political in intention, see B. I, ch. x (by Knight) of Harriet Martineau's *History of the Peace*.

imprisoned in turn. Matilda Roalfe and Mrs. Emma Martin about the same period underwent imprisonment for like causes.[1] In this fashion, by the steady courage of a much-enduring band of men and women, was set on foot a systematic Secularist propaganda—the name having relation to the term "Secularism," coined by Mr. Holyoake.

In this evolution political activities played an important part. Henry Hetherington (1792–1849), the strenuous democrat who in 1830 began the trade union movement, and so became the founder of Chartism, fought for the right of publication in matters of freethought as in politics. After undergoing two imprisonments of six months each (1832), and carrying on for three and a half years the struggle for an untaxed press, which ended in his victory (1834), he was in 1840 indicted for publishing *Haslam's Letters to the Clergy of all Denominations*, a freethinking criticism of Old Testament morality. He defended himself so ably that Lord Denman, the judge, confessed to have "listened with feelings of great interest and sentiments of respect too," and Justice Talfourd later spoke of it as marked by "great propriety and talent." Nevertheless, he was punished by four months' imprisonment.[2] In the following year, on the advice of Francis Place, he brought a test prosecution for blasphemy against Moxon, the poet-publisher, for issuing Shelley's complete works, including *Queen Mab*. Talfourd, then Serjeant, defended Moxon, and pleaded that there "must be some alteration of the law, or some restriction of the right to put it in action"; but the jury were impartial enough to find the publisher guilty, though he received no punishment.[3] Among other works published by Hetherington was one entitled *A Hunt after*

---

[1] Holyoake, *Sixty Years of an Agitator's Life*, i, 109–110. See p. 111 as to other cases.
[2] Art. by G. J. Holyoake in *Dict. of Nat. Biog.* Cp. Holyoake's *Sixty Years of an Agitator's Life*, per index.
[3] Articles in *Dict. of Nat. Biog.*

the *Devil*, "by Dr. P. Y." (really by Lieutenant Lecount), in which the story of Noah's ark was subjected to a destructive criticism.[1]

2. Mr. Holyoake had been a missionary and martyr in the movement of Socialism set up by ROBERT OWEN, whose teaching, essentially scientific on its psychological or philosophical side, was the first effort to give systematic effect to democratic ideals by organising industry. It was in the discussions of the "Association of all Classes of all Nations," formed by Owen in 1835, that the word "Socialism" first became current.[2] Owen was a freethinker in all things;[3] and his whole movement was so penetrated by an anti-theological spirit that the clergy as a rule became its bitter enemies, though such publicists as Macaulay and John Mill also combined with them in scouting it on political and economic grounds. None the less, "his secularistic teaching gained such influence among the working classes as to give occasion for the statement in the *Westminster Review* (1839) that his principles were the actual creed of a great portion of them."[4] To a considerable extent it was furthered by the popular deistic philosophy of GEORGE and ANDREW COMBE, which then had a great vogue;[5] and by the implications of phrenology, then also in its most scientific and progressive stage. When, for various reasons, Owen's movement dissolved, the freethinking element seems to have been absorbed in the secular party, while the others appear to have gone in part to build up the movement of Co-operation. The imprisonment of Mr. Holyoake (1842) for six months, on a trifling charge of blasphemy, is an illustration of the brutal spirit of

[1] Holyoake, *Sixty Years*, i, 47.
[2] Kirkup, *History of Socialism*, 1892, p. 64.
[3] "From an early age he had lost all belief in the prevailing forms of religion" (Kirkup, p. 59).
[4] Kirkup, as cited, p. 64.
[5] Of George Combe's *Constitution of Man*, a deistic work, over 50,000 copies were sold in Britain within twelve years, and 10,000 in America. Advt. to 4th ed. 1839.

public orthodoxy at the time.¹ Where bigotry could thus only injure and oppress without suppressing heresy, it stimulated resistance ; and the result of the stimulus was the founding of a Secular Society in 1852. Six years later there was elected to the presidency of the London Society of that name the young CHARLES BRADLAUGH, one of the greatest orators of his age, and one of the most powerful personalities ever associated with a progressive movement. A personal admirer of Owen, he never accepted his social polity, but was at all times the most zealous of democratic reformers. Thenceforward the working masses in England were in large part kept in touch with a freethought which drew on the results of the scientific and scholarly research of the time, and wielded a dialectic of which trained opponents confessed the power.²

The inspiration and the instruction of the popular movement thus maintained were at once literary, scientific, ethical, historical, scholarly, and philosophic. Shelley was its poet ; Voltaire its story-teller ; and Gibbon its favourite historian. In philosophy, Bradlaugh learned less from Hume than from Spinoza ; in Biblical criticism—himself possessing a working knowledge of Hebrew—he collated all the work of English and French specialists, down to and including Colenso, applying all the while to the consecrated record the merciless tests of a consistent ethic. At the same time, the whole battery of argument from the natural sciences was turned against traditionalism and supernaturalism, alike in the lectures of Bradlaugh and the other speakers of his party, and in the pages of his journal, *The National Reformer*. The general outcome was an unprecedented diffusion of critical thought among the English masses, and a proportionate antagonism to those who had wrought such a result. When, therefore, Bradlaugh, as deeply concerned for political as for intellectual

---

[1] See the details in his *Last Trial by Jury for Atheism in England*.
[2] See Professor Flint's tribute to the reasoning power of Bradlaugh and Holyoake in his *Anti-Theistic Theories*, 4th ed. pp. 518 519.

righteousness, set himself to the task of entering Parliament, he commenced a struggle which shortened his life, though it promoted his main objects. Not till after a series of electoral contests extending over twelve years was he elected for Northampton in 1880; and the House of Commons in a manner enacted afresh the long resistance made to him in that city. When, however, on his election in 1880, the Conservative Opposition began the historic proceedings over the Oath question, they probably did even more to deepen and diffuse the popular freethought movement than Bradlaugh himself had done in the whole of his previous career. The process was furthered by the policy of prosecuting and imprisoning Mr. G. W. Foote, editor of the *Freethinker*, under the Blasphemy Laws—a course not directly ventured on as against Bradlaugh, though it was sought to connect him with the publication of Mr. Foote's journal.

To this day, it is common to give a false account of the origin of the episode, representing Bradlaugh as having "forced" his opinions on the attention of the House. Rather he strove unduly to avoid wounding religious feeling. Wont to make affirmation by law in the courts of justice, he felt that it would be unseemly on his part to take the oath of allegiance if he could legally affirm. On this point he expressly consulted the law officers of the Crown, and they gave the opinion that he had the legal right, which was his own belief. The faction called the "fourth party," however, saw an opportunity to embarrass the Gladstone Government by challenging the act, and thus arose the protracted struggle. Only when a committee of the House decided that he could not affirm did Bradlaugh propose to take the oath, in order to take his seat.

The pretence of zeal for religion, made by the politicians who had raised the issue, was known by all men to be the merest hypocrisy. Lord Randolph Churchill, who distinguished himself by insisting on the moral necessity for a belief in "some divinity or other," is recorded to have professed a special esteem for Mr. John Morley, a Positivist.[1] The whole procedure, in Parliament and out, was so visibly that of the lowest political malice, exploiting the crudest religious intolerance, that it turned into active freethinkers many who had before been only passive doubters, and raised the secularist party to an intensity of zeal never before seen. At no period in modern British history had there been so constant and so keen a platform propaganda of unbelief; so unsparing an indictment of Christian doctrine, history, and practice; such contemptuous rebuttal of every Christian pretension; such asperity of spirit against the creed which was once more being championed by chicanery, calumny, and injustice. In those five years of indignant warfare were sown the seeds of a more abundant growth of rationalism than had ever before been known in the British Islands. When Bradlaugh at length took the oath and his seat in 1886, under a ruling of the Speaker which stultified the whole action of the Speaker and majorities of the previous Parliament, and no less that of the Law Courts, straightforward freethought stood three-fold stronger in England than in any previous generation. Apart from their educative work, the struggles and sufferings of the secularist leaders had now secured for Great Britain the abolition within one generation of the old burden of suretyship on newspapers, and of the disabilities of non-theistic witnesses;[2] the freedom of public meeting in the London parks; the right of avowed atheists to sit in Parliament (Bradlaugh having secured in 1888 their title to make affirmation instead of oath); and the virtual discredit of the Blasphemy Laws as such. It is probable also that the treatment meted out to Mrs. BESANT marked the end of another form of tyrannous outrage, already made historic in the case of Shelley. Secured the custody of her children under a marital deed of separation,

---

[1] After Bradlaugh had secured his seat, the noble lord, when leader of the House, even sought his society.
[2] See Mrs. Bradlaugh Bonner's *Charles Bradlaugh*, i, 149, 288-9.

she was deprived of it at law (1879) on her avowal of atheistic opinions, with the result that her influence as a propagandist was immensely increased.

3. Only in the United States has the public lecture platform been made a means of propaganda to anything like the extent seen in Britain ; and the greatest part of the work in the States has thus far been done by the late Colonel INGERSOLL, the leading American orator of the last generation, and the most widely influential platform propagandist of the last century. No other single freethinker, it is believed, has reached such an audience by public speech. In other countries, popular freethought has been spread, as apart from books, mainly by pamphlets and journalism, and, in the Latin countries, by the organisation of freemasonry, which is there normally anti-clerical. In France, the movement of FOURIER (1772-1837) may have counted for something as organising the secular spirit among the workers in the period of the monarchic and Catholic reaction ; but at no time was the proletariat of Paris otherwise than largely Voltairean after the Revolution, of which one of the great services (carried on by Napoleon) was an improvement in popular education. The new non-Christian systems of SAINT-SIMON[1] (1760-1823) and AUGUSTE COMTE (1798-1857) never took any practical hold among them ; but throughout the century they have been fully the most freethinking working-class population in the world. During the period of reaction after the restoration, numerous editions of Volney's *Ruines* and of the *Abrege*[2] of Dupuis's *Origine de tous les Cultes* served to maintain among the more intelligent an almost scientific rationalism, which can hardly be said to be improved on by such historiography as that of Renan's *Vie de Jesus*.

[1] Saint-Simon, who proposed a "new Christianity," expressly guarded against direct appeals to the people. See Weil, *Saint-Simon et son Œuvre*, 1894, p. 193. As to the Saint-Simonian sect, see an interesting testimony by Renan, *Les Apôtres*, p. 148.

[2] Louis Philippe sought to suppress this book, of which many editions had appeared before 1830. See Blanco White's *Life*, 1845, ii, 168.

In other Catholic countries the course of popular culture in the first half of the century was not greatly dissimilar to that seen in France, though less rapid and expansive. Thus we find the Spanish Inquisitor-General in 1815 declaring that "all the world sees with horror the rapid progress of unbelief," and denouncing "the errors and the new and dangerous doctrines" which have passed from other countries to Spain.[1] This evolution was to some extent checked; but in the latter half of the century, especially in the last twenty years, freethinking journalism has counted for much in the most Catholic parts of Southern Europe. The influence of such journals is to be measured not by their circulation, which is never great, but by their keeping up a habit of more or less instructed freethinking among readers, to many of whom the instruction is not otherwise easily accessible. Probably the least ambitious of them is an intellectual force of a higher order than the highest grade of popular religious journalism; while some of the stronger, as *De Dageraad* of Amsterdam, have ranked as high-class serious reviews. In the more free and progressive countries, however, freethought affects all periodical literature; and in France it partly permeates the ordinary newspapers. In England, where a series of monthly or weekly publications of an emphatically freethinking sort has been nearly continuous from about 1840,[2] new ones rising in place of those which succumbed to the commercial difficulties, such periodicals suffer an economic pinch in that they cannot hope for much income from advertisements, which are the chief sustenance of popular journals and magazines. The same law holds elsewhere; but in England and America the high-priced reviews have been gradually opened to rationalistic articles, the way being led by the

---

[1] Llorente, *Hist. crit. de l'Inquisition de l'Espagne*, 2e édit. iv, 153.

[2] Before 1840 the popular freethought propaganda had been partly carried on under cover of Radicalism, as in Carlile's *Republican*, and *Lion*, and in publications of William Hone. Cp. H. B. Wilson's article "The National Church," in *Essays and Reviews*, 9th ed. p. 152.

English *Westminster Review*[1] and *Fortnightly Review*, both founded with an eye to freer discussion.

Among the earlier freethinking periodicals may be noted *The Republican*, 1819-26 (edited by Carlile) ; *The Deist's Magazine*, 1820 ; *The Lion*, 1828 (Carlile) ; *The Prompter*, 1830 (Carlile) ; *The Gauntlet*, 1833 (Carlile) ; *The Atheist and Republican*, 1841 2 ; *The Blasphemer*, 1842 ; *The Oracle of Reason* (founded by Southwell), 1842, etc. ; *The Reasoner* and *Herald of Progress* (largely conducted by Mr. Holyoake), 1846-1861 ; *Cooper's Journal; or, unfettered Thinker*, etc., 1850, etc.; *The Movement*, 1843 ; *The Freethinker's Information for the People* (undated : after 1840) ; *Freethinker's Magazine*, 1850, etc. ; *London Investigator*, 1854, etc. Mr. Bradlaugh's *National Reformer*, begun in 1860, lasted till 1893. Mr. Foote's *Freethinker*, begun in 1881, still subsists. Various freethinking monthlies have risen and fallen since 1880— *e.g.*, *Our Corner*, edited by Mrs. Besant, 1883-88 ; *The Liberal* and *Progress*, edited by Mr. Foote, 1879-87 ; the *Free Review*, transformed into the *University Magazine*, 1893-1898. The *Reformer*, a monthly, edited by Mrs. Bradlaugh Bonner, subsisted from 1897 to 1904. *The Literary Guide*, which began as a small sheet in 1885, flourishes. Recently, a popular Socialist journal, *The Clarion*, has declared for rationalism through the pen of its editor, Mr. R. Blatchford ("Nunquam"), whose polemic has caused much controversy. For a generation back, further, rationalistic essays have appeared from time to time not only in the *Fortnightly Review* (founded by G. H. Lewes, and long edited by Mr. John Morley, much of whose writing on the French *philosophes* appeared in its pages), but in the *Nineteenth Century*, wherein was carried on, for instance, the famous controversy between Mr. Gladstone and Professor Huxley. Latterly, the *Independent Review* has given space to a number of outspoken criticisms of current religion ; and in the *Hibbert Journal* some opening is given to advanced views.

4. In Germany the relative selectness of culture, the comparative aloofness of the "enlightened" from the mass of the people, made possible after the War of Independence a certain pietistic reaction, in the absence of any popular propagandist machinery or purpose on the side of the rationalists. In the opinion of an evangelical authority, at the beginning of the nineteenth

---

[1] Described as "our chief atheistic organ" by the late Professor F. W. Newman "because Dr. James Martineau declined to continue writing for it, *because* it interpolated atheistical articles between his theistic articles" (*Contributions......to the early history of the late Cardinal Newman*, 1891, p. 103). The review was for a time edited by J. S. Mill.

century, "through modern enlightenment (*Aufklärung*) the people had become indifferent to the church; the Bible was regarded as a merely human book, the Saviour merely as a person who had lived and taught long ago, not as one whose almighty presence is with his people still."[1] According to the same authority, "before the war, the indifference to the word of God which prevailed among the upper classes had penetrated to the lower; but after it, a desire for the Scriptures was everywhere felt."[2] A pietistic movement had, however, begun during the period of the French ascendancy;[3] and inasmuch as the freethinking of the previous generation had been in large part associated with French opinion, it was natural that on this side anti-French feeling should promote a reversion to older and more "national" forms of feeling. Thus after the fall of Napoleon the tone of the students who had fought in the war seems to have been more religious than that of previous years.[4] Inasmuch, however, as the "enlightenment" of the scholarly class was maintained, and applied anew to critical problems, the religious revival did not turn back the course of progress.[5] Alongside of the pietistic reaction of the Liberation period there went on an open ecclesiastical strife, dating from an anti-rationalist declaration by the Court preacher Reinhard at Dresden in 1811,[6] between the rationalists or "Friends of Light" and the Scripturalists of the old school; and the effect was a general disintegration of orthodoxy, despite, or it may be largely in virtue of, the governmental policy of rewarding the Pietists and discouraging their opponents in the way of official

[1] Pastor W. Baur, Hamburg, *Religious Life in Germany during the Wars of Independence*, Eng. trans. 1872, p. 41.
[2] *Id*. p. 481.   [3] See the same volume, *passim*.
[4] Karl von Raumer, *Contrib. to the Hist. of the German Universities*, Eng. trans. 1859, p. 79. The intellectual tone of W. Baur and K. von Raumer certainly protects them from any charge of "enlightenment."
[5] "When the third centenary commemoration, in 1817, of the Reformation approached, the Prussian people were in a state of stolid indifference, apparently, on religious matters" (Laing, *Notes of a Traveller*, 1842, p. 181).
[6] C. H. Cotterill, *Relig. Movements of Germany in the Nineteenth Century*, 1849, pp. 39-40.

appointments.[1] The Prussian measure (1817) of forcibly uniting the Lutheran and Calvinistic churches, with a neutral sacramental ritual in which the eucharist was treated as a historical commemoration, tended to the same consequences, though it also revived old Lutheran zeal;[2] and when the new revolutionary movement broke out in 1848, popular feeling was substantially non-religious. "In the South of Germany especially, the conflict of political opinions and revolutionary tendencies produced, in the first instance, an entire prostration of religious sentiment." The bulk of society showed entire indifference to worship, the churches being everywhere deserted; and "atheism was openly avowed, and Christianity ridiculed as the invention of priestcraft."[3] One result was a desperate effort of the clergy to "effect a union among all who retained any measure of Christian belief, in order to raise up their national religion and faith from the lowest state into which it has ever fallen since the French Revolution."

But the clerical effort evoked a counter effort. Already, in 1846, official interference with freedom of utterance led to the formation of a "free religious" society by Dr. Rupp, of Konigsberg, one of the "Friends of Light" in the State church; and he was followed by Wislicenus, of Halle, a Hegelian, and by Uhlich, of Magdeburg.[4] As a result of the determined pressure, social and official, which ensued on the collapse of the revolution of 1848, these societies failed to develop on the scale of their beginnings; and that of Magdeburg, which at the outset had 7,000 members, has now only 500; though that of Berlin has nearly 4,000.[5] There is further a *Freidenker Bund*, with branches in many towns; and the two organisations, with their total membership of some fifty thousand, may be held to represent the militant side of popular freethought in Germany. This, however, constitutes only a fraction of the total amount

[1] *Id.* pp. 27–28, 41–42.   [2] Cp. Laing, as cited, pp. 206-7, 211.
[3] Cotterill, as cited.   [4] Cotterill, as cited, pp. 43-47.
[5] Rapport de Ida Altmann, in *Almanach de Libre Pensée*, 1906, p. 20.

of passive rationalism. In no country, perhaps, is there a larger measure of enlightenment in the working class ; and the ostensible force of orthodoxy among the official and conformist middle class is illusory in the extreme. The German police laws put a rigid check on all manner of platform and press propaganda which could be indicted as hurting the feelings of religious people ; so that a jest at the Holy Coat of Treves can send a journalist to jail, and the platform work of the militant societies is closely trammelled. Yet there are over a dozen journals which so far as may be take the freethought side ;[1] and the whole stress of Bismarckian reaction and of official orthodoxy under the present Kaiser has never availed to make the tone of popular thought pietistic. KARL MARX, the prophet of the German Socialist movement (1818-1883), laid it down as part of its mission " to free consciousness from the religious spectre ;" and his two most influential followers in Germany, BEBEL and LIEBKNECHT, have been avowed atheists, the former even going so far as to avow officially in the Reichstag that " the aim of our party is on the political plane the republican form of State ; on the economic, Socialism ; and on the plane which we term the religious, atheism ;"[2] though the party attempts no propaganda of the latter order. " Christianity and Social-Democracy," says Bebel again, " are opposed as fire and water."[3]

Some index to the amount of popular freethought that normally exists under the surface in Germany is furnished, further, by the strength of the German freethought movement in the United States, where, despite

[1] The principal are : *Das freie Wort* and *Frankfurter Zeitung*, Frankfort-on-Main ; *Der Freidenker*, Friedrichshagen, near Berlin ; *Der freireligioses Sonntagsblatt*, Breslau ; *Die freie Gemeinde*, Magdeburg ; *Der Atheist*, Nuremberg ; *Menschentum*, Gotha ; *Vossische Zeitung*, Berlin ; *Berliner Volkszeitung*, Berlin ; *Vorwarts* (Socialist), Berlin ; *Weser Zeitung*, Bremen ; *Hartungsche Zeitung*, Konigsberg ; *Kölnische Zeitung*, Cologne.

[2] Studemund, *Der moderne Unglaube in den unteren Ständen*, 1901, p. 14.

[3] *Id.* p. 22.

the tendency to the adoption of the common speech, there grew up in the last quarter of the nineteenth century many German freethinking societies, a German federation of atheists, and a vigorous popular organ, *Der Freidenker*.

5. "Free-religious" societies, such as have been noted in Germany, may be rated as forms of moderate freethought propaganda, and are to be found in all Protestant countries, with all shades of development. A movement of the kind has existed for a number of years back in America, in the New England States and elsewhere, and may be held to represent a theistic or agnostic thought too advanced to adhere even to the Unitarianism which during the two middle quarters of the century was perhaps the predominant creed in New England. One of the best types of such a gradual and peaceful evolution is the South Place Institute (formerly "Chapel") of London, where, under the famous orator W. J. Fox, nominally a Unitarian, there was preached between 1824 and 1852 a theism tending to pantheism, perhaps traceable to elements in the doctrine of Priestley, and passed on by Mr. Fox to Robert Browning.[1] In 1864 the charge passed to MONCURE D. CONWAY, under whom the congregation quietly advanced during twenty years from Unitarianism to a non-scriptural rationalism, embracing the shades of philosophic theism, agnosticism, and anti-theism. The Institute then became an open platform for rationalist and non-theological ethics, and social and historical teaching, and it now stands as an "Ethical Society" in touch with the numerous groups so named which have come into existence in England in the last dozen years, on lines originally laid down by Dr. Felix Adler in New York. At the time of the present writing the English societies of this kind number between twenty and thirty, the majority being in London and its environs. Their open adherents, who are some thousands

---

[1] Cp. Priestley, *Essay on the First Principles of Government*, 2nd ed. 1771, pp. 257-261, and Conway's *Centenary History of South Place*, pp. 63, 77, 80.

strong, are in most cases non-theistic rationalists, and include many former members of the Secularist movement, of which the organisation has somewhat dwindled. On partly similar lines have been developed in provincial towns a small number of "Labour Churches," in which the tendency is to substitute a rationalist humanitarian ethic for supernaturalism; and the same lecturers frequently speak from their platforms and from those of Ethical and Secularist societies.

6. Alongside of the lines of movement before sketched, there has subsisted in England during the greater part of the nineteenth century a considerable organisation of Unitarianism. The precise evolution of this body in its incipient stages is not easily to be traced. In England during the eighteenth century specific Anti-trinitarianism was not much in evidence. The most distinguished names associated with the position were those of Lardner and Priestley, of whom the former, trained as a simple "dissenter," avowedly reached his conclusions without much reference to Socinian literature;[1] and the second, who was similarly educated, no less independently gave up the doctrines of the Atonement and the Trinity, passing later from the Arian to the Socinian position after reading Lardner's *Letter on the Logos*.[2] As Priestley derived his determinism from Collins,[3] it would appear that the deistical movement had set up a general habit of reasoning which thus wrought even on Christians who, like Lardner and Priestley, undertook to rebut the objections of unbelievers to their faith. It thus becomes intelligible how, after a period in which Dissent, contemned by the State church, learned to criticise that church's creed, there emerged in England early in the nineteenth century a movement of specific Unitarianism, manifested mainly among the remaining churches of the English Presbyterian body. Such a development is to be explained by the relative freedom

---

[1] *Life of Lardner*, by Dr. Kippis, prefixed to *Works*, ed. 1835, i, p. xxxii.
[2] *Memoirs of Priestley*, 1806, pp. 30-32, 35, 57.
[3] *Id.* p. 19.

from authority enjoyed by dissenting sects, in compensation for their social disabilities. In the State church, as we saw, there had been many traces of deism among the clergy in the deistic age. In the freer self-governing churches, especially those which had a tradition of learning and clerical culture, the same tendencies could emerge as Unitarianism.[1] But inasmuch as the Presbyterian churches alone had non-dogmatic trust deeds, they alone made the transition in large numbers—a fact which tells the whole story of institutional causation.

When the heretical preachers of the Presbyterian sect began openly to declare themselves as Unitarians, there naturally arose a protest from the orthodox, and an attempt was made to save from its new destination the property owned by the heretical congregations. This was frustrated by the Dissenters' Chapels Act of 1844, which gave to each group singly the power to interpret its trust in its own fashion. Thenceforward the sect, formally founded in 1825, prospered considerably, albeit not so greatly as in the United States. During the century, English Unitarianism has been associated with scholarship through such names as Samuel Sharpe, the historian of Egypt, and J. J. Tayler; and, less directly, with philosophy in the person of Dr. James Martineau, who, however, was rather a coadjutor than a champion of the sect. In the United States the movement, greatly aided to popularity by the eloquent humanism of Channing, lost the prestige of the name of Emerson, who had been one of its ministers, by the inability of his congregation to go the whole way with him in his opinions. Latterly, Unitarians have been entitled to say that the Trinitarian churches are approximating to their position. Such an approach, however, involves rather a weakening than a strengthening of the smaller body; though a number of its teachers are to the full as bigoted and embittered in their propaganda as the bulk of the traditionally orthodox. Others adhere to their ritual practices in the

[1] The penal laws against anti-trinitarianism were repealed in 1813.

spirit of use and wont, as Emerson found when he sought to rationalise in his own church the usage of the eucharist.[1] On the other hand, numbers have passed from Unitarianism to thoroughgoing rationalism; and some whole congregations, following more or less the example of that of South Place Chapel, have latterly reached a position scarcely distinguishable from that of the Ethical Societies.

7. A partly similar evolution has taken place among the Protestant churches of France, Switzerland, Hungary, and Holland. French Protestantism could not but be intellectually moved by the intense ferment of the Revolution; and, when finally secured against active oppression from the Catholic side, could not but develop an intellectual opposition to the Catholic Reaction after 1815. As early as 1828 we find the Protestant Coquerel avowing that in his day the Bourbonism of the Catholic clergy had revived the old anti-clericalism, and that it was common to find the most high-minded patriots unbelievers and materialists.[2] But still more remarkable was the persistence in the Catholic church itself of deep freethinking currents. About 1830 freethinking had become normal among the younger students at Paris;[3] and the revolution of that year elicited a charter putting all religions on an equality.[4] Soon the throne and the chambers were on a footing of practical hostility to the church.[5] Under Louis Philippe men dared to teach in the College de France that "the Christian dispensation is but *one* link in the chain of divine revelations to man."[6] Such

[1] Conway, *Emerson at Home and Abroad*, 1883, ch. vii.
[2] Coquerel, *Essai sur l'histoire générale du christianisme*, 1828, pref.
[3] Dr. Christopher Wordsworth, *Diary in France*, 1845, pp. 75-77.
[4] "The miserable and deistical principle of the *equality* of *all* religions" (*Id.* p. 188). Cp. pp. 151, 153.
[5] *Id.* pp. 15, 37, 45, 181, 185, 190.
[6] *Id.* pp. 157-161. Some such position was reached by Lamennais. *Id.* p. 196. As to the general vogue of rationalism in France at that period, see pp. 35, 204; and compare Saisset, *Essais sur la philosophie et la religion*, 1845; *The Progress of Religious Thought as illustrated in the Protestant Church of France*, by Dr. J. R. Beard, 1861; and Wilson's article in *Essays and Reviews*. As to the other countries named, see Pearson, *Infidelity, its Aspects*, etc., 1853, pp. 560 4, 575-84.

speculation could not go on in the Catholic pale without contagion to the Protestant; and in Switzerland, always in intellectual touch with France and Germany, the tendencies which had been stamped as Socinian in the days of Voltaire reasserted themselves so strongly as to provoke fanatical reaction.[1] The nomination of Strauss to a chair of theology at Zurich by a Radical Government in 1839 actually gave rise to a violent revolt, inflamed and led by Protestant clergymen. The Executive Council were expelled, and a number of persons killed in the strife.[2] In the canton of Aargau in 1841, again, the cry of "religion in danger" sufficed to bring about a Catholic insurrection against a Liberal Council; and yet again in 1844 it led, among the Catholics of the Valais canton, to the bloodiest insurrection of all. Since these disgraceful outbreaks the progress of Rationalism in Switzerland has been steady. In 1847 a chair was given at Berne to the rationalistic scholar Zeller, without any such resistance as was made to Strauss at Zurich. In 1892, out of a total number of 3,151 students in the five universities of Switzerland and in the academies of Fribourg and Neuchatel, the number of theological students was only 374, positively less than that of the teaching staff, which was 431. Leaving out the academies named, which had no medical faculty, the number of theological students stood at 275 out of 2,917.

The church in Switzerland has thus undergone the relative restriction in power and prestige seen in the other European countries of long-established culture. The evolution, however, remains negative rather than positive. Though a number of pastors latterly call themselves *libres penseurs* or *penseurs libres*, and a

---

[1] Hagenbach, *Kirchengeschichte des 18. und 19. Jahrhunderts*, 1848, ii, 422. Rationalism seems to have spread soonest in the canton of Zurich. *Id.* ii, 427.
[2] See Grote's *Seven Letters concerning the Politics of Switzerland*, ed. 1876, pp. 34-35. Hagenbach (*Kirchengeschichte*, ii, 427-8) shows no shame over the insurrection at Zurich. But cp. Beard, in the compilation *Voices of the Church in Reply to Dr. Strauss*, 1845, pp. 17-18.

movement of ethical culture (*morale sociale*) is making progress, the forces of positive freethought are not numerically strong. An economic basis still supports the churches, and the lack of it leaves rationalism non-aggressive.[1]

A somewhat similar state of things exists in Holland, where the "higher criticism" of both the Old and New Testaments made notable progress in the middle decades of the century. There then resulted not only an extensive decay of orthodoxy within the Protestant Church, but a movement of aggressive popular freethought, which was for a number of years well represented in journalism. To-day, orthodoxy and freethought are alike less demonstrative; the broad explanation being that the Dutch people in the mass has ceased to be pietistic, and has secularised its life. Even in the Bible-loving Boer Republic of South Africa (Transvaal), one of the most orthodox of the civilised communities of the world, there was seen a generation ago the phenomenon of an agnostic ex-clergyman's election to the post of president, in the person of T. F. Burgers, who succeeded Pretorius in 1871. His election was of course on political and not on religious grounds; and panic fear on the score of his heresy, besides driving some fanatics to emigrate, is said to have disorganised a Boer expedition under his command;[2] but his views were known when he was elected. In the past few years the terrible experience of the last Boer War, in South Africa as in Britain, has perhaps done more to turn critical minds against supernaturalism than has been accomplished by almost any other agency in the same period. In Britain the overturn was by way of the revolt of many ethically-minded Christians against the attitude of the orthodox churches, which were so generally and so unscrupulously

---

[1] Cp. the *rapport* of Ch. Fulpius in the *Almanach de Libre Pensée*, 1906.
[2] G. M. Theal, *South Africa* ("Story of the Nations" series), pp. 340, 345. Mr. Theal's view of the mental processes of the Boers is somewhat *a priori*, and his explanation seems in part inconsistent with his own narrative.

belligerent as to astonish many even of their enemies.[1] As regards the Boers and the Cape Dutch the resultant unbelief was among the younger men, who harassed their elders with challenges as to the justice or the activity of a God who permitted the liberties of his most devoted worshippers to be wantonly destroyed. Among the more educated burghers in the Orange Free State commandos unbelief asserted itself with increasing force and frequency.[2] An ethical rationalism thus motived is not likely to be displaced save by a successful movement, religiously inspired, for the recovery of the lost liberties; and the Christian churches of Britain have thus the sobering knowledge that the war which they so vociferously glorified[3] has wrought to the discredit of their creed alike in their own country and among the vanquished.

8. It is a significant fact that freethought propaganda is often most active in countries where the Catholic Church is most powerful. Thus in Belgium there are at least three separate federations, standing for hundreds of freethinking "groups"; in Spain, a few years ago, there were freethought societies in all the large towns, and at least half-a-dozen freethought journals; in Portugal there have been a number of societies, a weekly journal, *O Seculo*, of Lisbon; and a monthly review, *O Livre Exame*. In France and Italy, where educated society is in large measure rationalistic, the Masonic lodges do most of the personal and social propaganda; but there are federations of freethought societies in both countries. In Switzerland freethought is more aggressive in the Catholic than in the Protestant

---

[1] An English acquaintance of my own at Cape Town, who before the war not only was an orthodox believer, but found his chief weekly pleasure in attending church, was so astounded by the general attitude of the clergy on the war that he severed his connection, once for all. Thousands did the same in England.

[2] I write on the strength of personal testimonies spontaneously given to me in South Africa, some of them by clergymen of the Dutch Reformed Church.

[3] See the evidence collected in the pamphlet *The Churches and the War*, by Alfred Marks. *New Age* Office, 1905.

cantons.[1] In the South American republics again, as in Italy and France, the Masonic Lodges are predominantly freethinking ; and in Peru there was, a few years ago, a Freethought League, with a weekly organ. That the movement is also active in the other republics of the Continent may be inferred from the facts that a Positivist organisation has long subsisted in Brazil ; that its members were active in the peaceful revolution which there substituted a republic for a monarchy ; and that at the Freethought Congresses of Rome and Paris in 1904 and 1905 there was an energetic demand for a Congress at Buenos Ayres, which was finally agreed to for 1906.

9. The history of popular freethought in Sweden yields a good illustration, in a compact form,[2] of the normal play of forces and counter-forces. Since the day of Christina, as we saw, rationalism has been little known in her kingdom down till modern times. Bishop Jesper Svedberg (d. 1735) is notable as being anti-trinitarian, and an opponent of the Lutheran doctrine of salvation ; and his son followed in his footsteps ; but Sweden as a whole was little touched by the great ferment of the eighteenth century. Only in the poets J. H. Kjellgren and J. M. Bellman (both d. 1795) is there seen the influence of the German *Aufklärung* and the spirit of Voltaire. The prose-writer Tomas Torild (d. 1812), who wrote among other things a pamphlet on *The Freedom of the General Intelligence*, shows more markedly the revolutionary temper. Tegner, the poet-bishop, author of the once-famous *Frithiof's Saga*, was further notable in his day for a determined rejection of the evangelical doctrine of salvation ; and his letters contain much criticism of the ruling system. But the first recognisable champion of freethought in Sweden is the thinker and historian E. G. Geijer (d. 1847), whose history of his native land is one of the best European performances of his

[1] *Rapport* of Ch. Fulpius, before cited.
[2] For the survey here reduced to outline I am indebted to two Swedish friends.

generation. In 1820 he was prosecuted for his attack upon the dogmas of the Trinity and redemption—long the special themes of discussion in Sweden—in his book *Thorild;* but was acquitted by the jury.

Thenceforth Sweden follows the general development of Europe. In 1841 Strauss's *Leben Jesu* was translated in Swedish, and wrought its usual effect. On the popular side the poet Wilhelm von Braun carried on an anti-Biblical warfare ; and a blacksmith in a provincial town contrived to print in 1850 a translation of Paine's *Age of Reason.* Once more the spirit of persecution blazed forth, and he was prosecuted and imprisoned. H. B. Palmaer (d. 1854) was likewise prosecuted for his satire, *The Last Judgment in Cocaigne* (Krakwinkel), with the result that his defence extended his influence. In the same period the Stockholm curate Nils Ignell (d. 1864) produced a whole series of critical pamphlets and a naturalistic *History of the Development of Man*, besides supplying a preface to the Swedish translation of Renan's *Vie de Jesus.* Meantime translations of the works of Thomas Parker, by V. Pfeiff and A. F. Akerberg, had a large circulation and a wide influence ; and the stringent rationalism of the gymnasium rector N. J. Cramer (d. 1893), author of *The Farewell to the Church*, gave an edge to the new movement. The partly rationalistic doctrine of Victor Rydberg (d. 1895) was in comparison uncritical, and was proportionally popular.

On another line the books of Dr. Nils Lilja (d. 1870), written for working people, created a current of rationalism among the masses ; and in the next generation G. J. Leufstedt maintained it by popular lectures and by the issue of translations of Colenso, Ingersoll, Büchner, and Renan. Hjalmar Stromer (d. 1886) did similar platform work. Meantime the followers of Parker and Rydberg founded in 1877 a monthly review, *The Truthseeker*, which lasted till 1894, and an association of " Believers in Reason," closely resembling the British Ethical Societies of our own day. Among its leading adherents has been K. P. Arnoldson, the well-known peace advocate. Liberal clerics were now fairly numerous; Positivism, represented by Dr. Anton Nystrom's *General History of Civilisation*, played its part; and the more radical freethinking movement, nourished by new translations, became specially active, with the usual effect on orthodox feeling. August Strindberg, author and lecturer, was prosecuted in 1884 on a charge of ridiculing the eucharist, but was declared not guilty. The strenuous Victor Lennstrand, lecturer and journalist, prosecuted in 1888 and later for his anti-Christian propaganda, was twice fined and imprisoned, with the inevitable result of extending his influence and discrediting his opponents. "Utilitarian Associations," created by his activity, were set up in many parts of the country; and his movement survives his death.

§ II. *Scholarly and Other Biblical Criticism.*

1. While in France, under the restored monarchy, rationalistic activity was mainly headed into historical, philosophical, and sociological study, and in England orthodoxy predominated in theological discussion, the German rationalistic movement went on among the specialists, despite the liberal religious reaction of Schleiermacher,[1] who himself gave forth such an uncertain sound. His case and that of his father, an army chaplain, tell signally of the power of the mere clerical occupation to develop a species of emotional belief in one who has even attained rationalism. When the son, trained for the church, avowed to his father (1787) that he had lost faith in the supernatural Jesus, the father professed to mourn bitterly, but three years

---

[1] As to the absolute predominance of rationalistic unbelief in educated Germany in the first third of the century, see the *Memoirs of F. Perthes*, Eng. trans. 2nd ed. ii, 240-5, 255, 266-275. Despite the various reactions asserted by Perthes and others, it is clear that the tables have not since been turned. Cp. Pearson, *Infidelity*, pp. 554-9, 569-574. Schleiermacher is charged on his own side with making fatal concessions. Robins, *A Defence of the Faith*, 1862, i, 181; and Quinet as there cited.

later avowed that he in his own youth had preached Christianity for twelve years while similarly disbelieving its fundamental tenet.[1] He professionally counselled compromise, which the son duly practised, with such success that, whereas he originally addressed his *Discourses on Religion* (1799) to "its despisers among the educated," he was able to say in the preface to the third edition, twenty years later (1821), that the need now was to reason with the pietists and literalists, the ignorant and bigoted, the credulous and superstitious.[2] He had himself promoted such irrationalism by his resistance to the critical spirit. When, however, soon after his funeral, in which his coffin was borne and followed by troops of students, his church was closed to the friends who wished there to commemorate him, it was fairly clear that his own popularity lay mainly with the progressive spirits, and not among the orthodox; and in the end his influence tended to merge in that of the critical movement.[3]

That went forward with a new precision of method. Beginning with the Old Testament, criticism gradually saw more and more of mere myth where of old men had seen miracle, and where the first rationalists saw natural events misconceived. In time the process reached the New Testament, every successive step being resisted in the old fashion; and after much laborious work, now mostly forgotten, by a whole company of scholars, among whom Paulus, Eichhorn, De Wette, G. L. Bauer, Wegscheider, Bretschneider, and Gabler were prominent,[4] the train as it were exploded on the world in the great *Life of Jesus* by STRAUSS (1835).

[1] *Aus Schleiermachers Leben: In Briefen*, 1860, i, 42, 84. The father's letters, with their unctuous rhetoric, are a revelation of the power of declamatory habit to eliminate sincere thought.
[2] *Werke*, 1843, i, 140.
[3] For an estimate of his work cp. Baur, *Kirchengeschichte des 19ten Jahrh.* p. 45, and art. by Rev. F. J. Smith in *Theological Review*, July, 1869.
[4] See a good account of the development in Strauss's Introduction. He notes (§ 11, *end*) that the most extended application of the mythical principle to the Gospels before his time was in an anonymous work on *Religion and Mythology* published in 1799.

Before this time, "German Rationalism" had become the terror of the English orthodox; and henceforth a scholarly "infidelity" had to be faced throughout the educated world.

Orthodoxy was at first fain to resort, even in "intellectually free" Germany, to its old methods of repression. The authorities of Berlin discussed with Neander the propriety of suppressing Strauss's *Leben Jesu*;[1] and after a time those who shared his views were excluded even from philosophical chairs.[2] Later, the *brochure* in which Edgar Bauer defended his brother Bruno against his opponents (1842) was seized by the police; and in the following year, for publishing *The Strife of Criticism with Church and State*, the same writer was sentenced to four years' imprisonment. In private life, persecution was carried on in the usual ways. Still, the research and the discussion were irrepressible.

Naturally the most advanced and uncompromisingly scientific positions were least discussed, the stress of dispute going on around the criticism which modified without annihilating the main elements in the current creed, or that which did the work of annihilation on a popular level of thought. Only to-day is German "expert" criticism beginning openly to reckon with propositions fairly and fully made out by German writers of three or more generations back. Thus in 1781 Corodi in his *Geschichte des Chiliasmus* dwelt on the pre-Hebraic origins of the belief in angels, in immortality, and heaven and hell, and on the Persian derivation of the Jewish seven archangels; Wegscheider in 1819 in his *Institutes of Theology* indicated further connections of the same order, and cited pagan parallels to the virgin-birth; J. A. L. Richter in the same year pointed to Indian and Persian precedents for the Logos

---

[1] Dr. J. R. Beard, in *Voices of the Church in Reply to Strauss*, 1845, pp. 16-17.

[2] Zeller, D. F. Strauss, Eng. trans. 1879, p. 56.

and many other Christian doctrines ; and several other writers, Strauss included, pointed to both Persian and Babylonian influences on Jewish theology and myth.[1] When even these theses were in the main ignored, more mordant doctrine was necessarily burked. Such subversive criticism of religious history as Ghillany's *Die Menschenopfer der alten Hebräer* (1842), insisting that human sacrifice had been habitual in early Jewry, and that ritual cannibalism underlay the paschal eucharist, found even fewer students prepared to appreciate it than did the searching ethico-philosophical criticism passed on the Christian creed by Feuerbach. Daumer, who in 1842 published a treatise on the same lines as Ghillany's (*Der Feuer und Molochdienst*), and followed it up in 1847 with another on the Christian mysteries, nearly as drastic, wavered later in his rationalism and avowed his conversion to a species of faith. Hence a certain setback for his school. In France, the genial German revolutionist and exile Ewerbeck published, under the titles of *Qu' est ce que la Religion?* and *Qu' est ce que la Bible?* (1850), two volumes of very freely edited translations from Feuerbach, Daumer, Ghillany, Lützelberger (on the simple humanity of Jesus), and Bruno Bauer, avowing that after vainly seeking a publisher for years he had produced the books at his own expense. He had, however, so mutilated the originals as to make the work ineffectual for scholars, without making it attractive to the general public ; and there is nothing to show that his formidable-looking arsenal of explosives had much effect on contemporary French thought, which developed on other lines.

2. On other lines as well as Strauss's, however—notably on those of the famous Tubingen school, led by F. C. Baur, perhaps the ablest Christian scholar of his day, and certainly the most intellectual of Christian historians—German critical research proceeded continuously, with a notable effect on the supply of students

---

[1] See Gunkel, *Zum religionsgeschichtlichen Verständnis des Neuen Testaments*, 1903, pp. 1–2, *note*.

for the theological profession. The numbers of Protestant and Catholic theological students in all Germany have varied as follows :—*Protestant:* 1831, 4,147 ; 1851, 1,631 ; 1860, 2,520 ; 1876, 1,539 ; 1882-3, 3,168. *Catholic:* 1831, 1,801 ; 1840, 866 ; 1850, 1,393 ; 1860, 1,209, 1880, 619.[1] Thus, under the reign of Bismarckian reaction which set in after 1848 there was a prolonged recovery; and again since 1876 the figures rise for Protestantism through financial stimulus. When, however, we take population into account, the main movement is clear. In an increasing proportion, the theological students come from the rural districts (69.4 in 1861-70), the towns furnishing ever fewer;[2] so that the conservative measures do but outwardly and formally affect the course of thought; the clergy themselves showing less and less inclination to make clergymen of their sons.[3] Even among the Catholic population, though that has increased from ten millions in 1830 to sixteen millions in 1880, the number of theological students has fallen from eleven to four per 100,000 inhabitants.[4] Thus, after many "reactions" and much Bismarckism, the *Zeit-Geist* in Germany was still pronouncedly skeptical in all classes in 1881,[5] when the church accommodation in Berlin provided only two per cent. of the population, and even that provision outwent the demand.[6] And though there have been yet other alleged reactions since, and the imperial influence is zealously used for orthodoxy, the mass of the intelligent workers remain socialistic and freethinking; and the mass of the educated classes remain unorthodox in the teeth of the socialist menace. Reactionary professors can at most make an academic fashion : the great body of instructed men remains tacitly naturalistic.[7]

---

[1] Conrad, *The German Universities for the last Fifty Years*, Eng. trans. 1885, p. 74. See p. 100 as to the financial measures taken; and p. 105 as to the essentially financial nature of the "reaction."
[2] *Id.* p. 103.   [3] *Id.* p. 104.
[4] *Id.* p. 112. See pp. 118-119 as to Austria   [5] *Id.* pp. 97-98.
[6] Professor A. D. White, *Warfare*, i, 239.
[7] As against reactionary views of Christian origins, the German laity

3. On a less extensive scale than in Germany, critical study of the sacred books made some progress in England, France, and America in the first half of the century. The Unitarian C. C. HENNELL produced an *Inquiry Concerning the Origin of Christianity* (1838), so important for its time as to be thought worth translating into German by Strauss; and this found a considerable response from the educated English public of its day. In the preface to his second edition (1841) Hennell spoke very plainly of "the large and probably increasing amount of unbelief in all classes around us"; and made the then remarkably courageous declarations that in his experience " neither deism, pantheism, nor even atheism indicate modes of thought incompatible with uprightness and benevolence"; and that "the real or affected horror which it is still a prevailing custom to exhibit towards their names would be better reserved for those of the selfish, the cruel, the bigot, and other tormentors of mankind." In the next generation, THEODORE PARKER in the United States, developing his critical faculty chiefly by study of the Germans, at the cost of much obloquy, forced some knowledge of critical results and a measure of theistic or pantheistic rationalism on the attention of the orthodox world; promoting at the same time a semi-philosophic, semi-ethical reaction against the Calvinistic theology of Jonathan Edwards, theretofore prevalent among the orthodox of New England. In the old country a number of writers developed new movements of criticism from theistic points of view. F. W. NEWMAN, the scholarly brother of John Henry,[1] produced a book entitled *The Soul* (1849), and another, *Phases of Faith* (1853), which had much influence in

has recently been supplied with an excellent conspectus of the Gospel problem in the *Vergleichende Uebersicht der vier Evangelien*, by S. G. Verus (Leipzig: Van Dyk, 1897), a work of the most laborious kind, issued at a low price.

[1] A third brother, Charles Robert, became an atheist. This, as well as his psychic infirmity, insures him sufficiently severe treatment at the hands of his theistic brother in the introduction to the latter's *Contributions Chiefly to the Early History of the late Cardinal Newman*, 1891.

promoting rationalism of a rather rigidly theistic cast. R. W. MACKAY in the same period published two learned treatises, *A Sketch of the Rise and Progress of Christianity* (1854), notably scientific in method for its time ; and *The Progress of the Intellect as Exemplified in the Religious Development of the Greeks and Hebrews* (1850), which won the admiration of Buckle ; "George Eliot" translated Feuerbach's *Essence of Christianity* (1854) under her own name, Marian Evans ; and W. R. GREG, one of the leading publicists of his day, put forth a rationalistic study of *The Creed of Christendom: Its Foundations Contrasted with its Superstructure* (1850), which has gone through many editions and is still reprinted. Another zealous theist, THOMAS SCOTT, whose pamphlet-propaganda on deistic lines had so wide an influence during many years, produced an *English Life of Jesus* (1871), which, though less important than the works of Strauss and less popular than those of Renan, played a considerable part in the disintegration of the traditional faith among Engish churchmen. Still the primacy in critical research on scholarly lines lay with the Germans, till the results of their work were co-ordinated, from a theistic standpoint,[1] in the anonymous work, *Supernatural Religion* (1874-77), a massive and decisive performance, too powerful to be disposed of by the episcopal and other attacks made upon it.[2] Since its assimilation the orthodox or inspirationist view of the Gospels has lost credit among competent scholars even within the churches. The battleground is now removed to the problem of the historicity of the ostensible human origins of the cult ; and scholarly orthodoxy takes for granted many of the positions which fifty years ago were typical of "German rationalism."

---

[1] Now abandoned by the learned author, who has latterly disclosed his name—W. R. Cassels.
[2] See the testimonies of Pfleiderer, *The Development of Theology since Kant*, Eng. trans. 1890, p. 397, and Dr. Samuel Davidson, *Introd. to the Study of the New Testament*, pref. to 2nd ed.

4. In France systematic criticism of the sacred books recommenced in the second half of the century with such writings as those of P. LARROQUE (*Examen Critique des doctrines de la religion chretienne*, 1860); GUSTAVE D'EICHTHAL (*Les Evangiles*, Ptie. I, 1863); and ALPHONSE PEYRAT (*Histoire elementaire et critique de Jesus*, 1864); whereafter the rationalistic view was applied with singular literary charm, if with imperfect consistency, by RENAN in his series of seven volumes on the origins of Christianity, and with more scientific breadth of view by ERNEST HAVET in his *Christianisme et ses Origines* (1872, etc.). Renan's *Vie de Jesus* especially has been read throughout the civilised world.

5. Old Testament criticism, methodically begun by scholars before that of the New Testament, has in the last generation been carried to new lengths, after having long missed some of the first lines of advance. Starting from the clues given by Hobbes, Spinoza, and Simon, and above all on the suggestion of Astruc (whose work on the subject had appeared in 1753) as to the twofold element implied in the God-names Jehovah and Elohim, it had proceeded, for sheer lack of radical skepticism, on the assumption that the Pentateuchal history was true. On this basis, modern Old Testament criticism of a professional kind may be said to have been founded by Eichhorn, who hoped by a quasi-rationalistic method to bring back unbelievers to belief.[1] Of his successors, some, like Ilgen, were ahead of their time; some, like De Wette, failed to make progress in their criticism; some, like Ewald, remained always arbitrary; and some of the ablest and most original, as Vatke, failed to coordinate fully their critical methods and results.[2] Thus little sure progress had been made, apart from discrimination of sources, between the issue

---

[1] Cheyne, *Founders of Old Testament Criticism*, 1893, p. 16. Eichhorn seems to have known Astruc's work only at second-hand, yet, without him, it might be contended, Astruc's work would have been completely lost to science. (*Id.* p. 23.)

[2] See Dr. Cheyne's surveys, which are those of a liberal ecclesiastic— a point of view on which he has since notably advanced.

of the *Critical Remarks on the Hebrew Scriptures* of the Scotch Catholic priest, Dr. GEDDES, in 1800, and the publication of the first part of the work of Bishop COLENSO on *The Pentateuch* (1862). This, by the admission of KUENEN, who had begun as a rather narrow believer,[1] corrected the initial error of the specialists by applying to the narrative the common-sense tests suggested long before by Voltaire.[2] Thenceforward the "higher criticism" proceeded with such substantial certainty on the scientific lines of KUENEN and WELLHAUSEN that, whereas Professor Robertson Smith thirty years ago had to leave the Free Church of Scotland for propagating Kuenen's views, Canons of the English Church are now doing the work with the acquiescence of perhaps nine clergymen out of ten; and American preachers are found promoting an edition of the Bible which exhibits the critical results to the general reader. Heresy on this score is "become merchandise." Nevertheless, the professional tendency to compromise (a result of economic and other pressures) keeps most of the ecclesiastical critics far short of the outspoken utterances of KALISCH, who in his *Commentary on Leviticus* (1867-72) repudiates every vestige of the doctrine of inspiration.[3] Later clerical critics, notably Canon Driver, use language on that subject which cannot be read with critical respect.[4]

The analytical treatment of the New Testament on the same principles naturally lagged somewhat; but at the beginning of the twentieth century we find the long series of textual studies by German and other specialists culminating in such a survey as that of the Swiss

[1] Cheyne, pp. 187-8.
[2] Kuenen, *The Hexateuch*, Eng. trans., introd. pp. xiv-xvii.
[3] These utterances were noted for their "vigour and independence" by Kuenen, and also by Dr. Cheyne, who remarks that the earlier work of Kalisch on *Exodus* (1855) was somewhat behind the critical standpoint of contemporary investigators on the Continent. (*Founders of Old Testament Criticism*, p. 207.)
[4] See his *Introduction to the Study of the Old Testament*, pref. "It is the spirit of compromise that I chiefly dread for our younger students," wrote Dr. Cheyne in 1893 (*Founders*, p. 247). His courteous criticism of Dr. Driver does not fail to point the moral in that writer's direction.

theologian Dr. SCHMIEDEL, which may be said to come within sight of a surrender of the historicity of the Gospel Jesus. His searching analysis has found a place in the *Encyclopædia Biblica*, edited by Dr. Cheyne and Mr. A. Sutherland Black, which presents many other results of advanced research by professional theologians. Less radical but still disintegrating views of the Gospel texts had been already to some extent popularised for general readers in England by such works as that of Mr. J. E. Carpenter on *The First Three Gospels*—a Unitarian publication—and *The Synoptic Problem*, by Mr. Jolley.

6. The outcome of Old Testament criticism is worth noting in connection with the results of Assyrian research. Whereas the defenders of the faith even a generation ago habitually stood to the "argument from prophecy," the conception of prophecy as prediction has now become meaningless as regards the so-called Mosaic books; and the constant disclosure of interpolations and adaptations in the others has discredited it as regards the "prophets" themselves. At the same time, a comparison of Biblical with Assyrian and Babylonian texts reduces the cosmology and anthropology of Genesis once for all to the level of normal mythology. The old argument for the compatibility of the Genesaic creation story with geology is thus welcome now only to those who are ignorant of the results of Assyriology. That the clerical exponents of the higher criticism should in the face of their own results continue to speak of the "inspiration" of their texts will not surprise the reader who has noted the analogous phenomena in the history of the religious systems of antiquity.

§ III. *The Natural Sciences.*

1. The power of intellectual habit and tradition had preserved among the majority of educated men, to the end of the eighteenth century, a notion of deity either slightly removed from that of the ancient Hebrews or

ethically modified without being philosophically transformed, though the astronomy of Copernicus, Galileo, and Newton had immensely modified the Hebraic conception of the physical universe. We have seen that Newton did not really hold by the Christian scheme—he wrote, at times, in fact, as a pantheist—but some later astronomers seem to have done so. When, however, the great LAPLACE developed the nebular hypothesis, previously guessed at by Bruno and outlined by Kant, orthodox psychological habit was rudely shaken as regards the Biblical account of creation; and like every other previous advance in physical science this was denounced as atheistic[1]—which, as we know, it was, Laplace having declared in reply to Napoleon that he had no need of the God hypothesis. Confirmed by all subsequent science, Laplace's system negates once for all the historic theism of the Christian era; and the subsequent concrete developments of astronomy, giving as they do such an insistent and overwhelming impression of physical infinity, have made the "Christian hypothesis"[2] fantastic save for minds capable of enduring any strain on the sense of consistency. Paine had brought the difficulty vividly home to the common intelligence; and though the history of orthodoxy is a history of the success of institutions and majorities in imposing incongruous conformities, the perception of the incongruity on this side must have been a force of disintegration. The freethinking of the French astronomers of the Revolution period marks a decisive change; and as early as 1826 we find in a work on Jewish antiquities by a Scotch clergyman a very plain indication[3] of disbelief in the Hebrew story of the stopping of the sun and moon, or (alternatively) of the

[1] See Professor A. D. White's *History of the Warfare of Science with Theology*, 1896, i, 17, 22.
[2] The phrase is used by a French Protestant pastor. *La vérité chrétienne et la doute moderne* (Conférences), 1879, pp. 24-25.
[3] *Antiquities of the Jews*, by William Brown, D.D., Edinburgh, 1826, i, 121-2. Brown quotes "from a friend" a demonstration of the monstrous consequences of a stoppage of the earth's rotation.

rotation of the earth. It is typical of the tenacity of religious delusion that a quarter of a century later this among other irrational credences was contended for the Swiss theologian Gaussen,[1] and by the orthodox majority elsewhere, when for all scientifically trained men they had become untenable. And that the general growth of scientific thought was disintegrating among scientific men the old belief in miracles, may be gathered from an article, remarkable in its day, which appeared in the *Edinburgh Review* of January, 1814 (No. 46), and was "universally attributed to Professor Leslie,"[2] the distinguished physicist. Reviewing the argument of Laplace's essay, *Sur les probabilites*, it substantially endorsed the thesis of Hume, that miracles cannot be proved by any testimony.

2. In the same period of reaction, some cultivators of the other sciences applied their results to the discredit of faith. Professor William Lawrence (1783-1867), the physiologist, published in 1816 an *Introduction to Comparative Anatomy and Physiology*, containing some remarks on the nature of life, which elicited from the then famous Dr. Abernethy a violent attack in his *Physiological Lectures* delivered before the College of Surgeons. Lawrence was charged with belonging to the party of French physiological skeptics, whose aim was to "loosen those restraints on which the welfare of mankind depends."[3] In the introductory lecture of his course of 1817 before the College of Physicians, Lawrence severely retaliated, repudiating the general charge, but reasserting that the dependence of life on organisation is as clear as the derivation of daylight from

---

[1] *Theopneustia: The Plenary Inspiration of the Holy Scriptures*, Eng. trans. Edinburgh, 1850, pp. 246-9. Gaussen elaborately argues that if eighteen minutes were allowed for the stoppage of the earth's rotation, no shock would occur. Finally, however, he argues that there may have been a mere refraction of the sun's rays—an old theory, already set forth by Brown.

[2] Dr. C. R. Edmonds, Introd. to rep. of Leland's *View of the Deistical Writers*, Tegg's ed. 1837, p. xxiii.

[3] Lawrence's *Lectures on Physiology, Zoology, and the Natural History of Man*, 8th ed. 1840, pp. 1-3.

the sun. The war was adroitly carried at once into the enemy's territory in the declaration that "The profound, the virtuous, and fervently pious Pascal acknowledged, what all sound theologians maintain, that the immortality of the soul, the great truths of religion, and the fundamental principles of morals, cannot be demonstrably proved by mere reason; and that revelation alone is capable of dissipating the uncertainties which perplex those who inquire too curiously into the sources of these important principles. All will acknowledge that, as no other remedy can be so perfect and satisfactory as this, no other can be necessary, if we resort to this with firm faith."[1] The value of this pronouncement is indicated later in the same volume by subacid allusions to "those who regard the Hebrew Scriptures as writings composed with the assistance of divine inspiration," and who receive Genesis "as a narrative of actual events." Indicating various "grounds of doubt respecting inspiration," the lecturer adds that the stories of the naming of the animals and their collection in the ark, "if we are to understand them as applied to the living inhabitants of the whole world, are zoologically impossible."[2] On the principle then governing such matters, Lawrence was in 1822, on the score of his heresies, refused copyright in his lectures, which were accordingly reprinted many times in a cheap stereotyped edition, and thus widely diffused.[3]

3. A more direct effect, however, was probably wrought by the science of geology, which in a stable and tested form belongs to the nineteenth century. Of its theoretic founders in the eighteenth century, Werner and Dr. JAMES HUTTON (1726-1797), the latter and more important[4] is known from his *Investigation of the Principles of Knowledge* (1794) to have been consciously a freethinker on more grounds than that of his naturalistic science; and his *Theory of the World* (1795) was duly denounced

---

[1] Lawrence's *Lectures*, p. 9, note.   [2] *Id.* pp. 168-9.
[3] Yet Lawrence was created a baronet two months before his death.
[4] Cp. Whewell, *Hist. of the Inductive Sciences*, 3rd ed. iii, 505.

as atheistic.[1] Whereas the physical infinity of the universe almost forced the orthodox to concede a vast cosmic process of some kind as preceding the shaping of the earth and solar system, the formation of these within six days was one of the plainest assertions in the sacred books ; and every system of geology excluded such a conception. As the evidence accumulated, in the hands of men mostly content to deprecate religious opposition,[2] there was duly evolved the quaint compromise of the doctrine that the Biblical six "days" meant six ages—a fantasy still cherished in the pulpit. Even this thesis, and others of the same order, drew upon their supporters angry charges of "infidelity." Hugh Miller, whose natural gifts for geological research were chronically turned to confusion by his orthodox bias, was repeatedly so assailed, when in point of fact he was perpetually tampering with the facts to salve the Scriptures.[3] Of all the inductive sciences, geology had been most retarded by the Christian canonisation of error.[4] Even the plain fact that what is dry land had once been sea was obstinately distorted through centuries, though Ovid[5] had put the observations of Pythagoras in the way of all scholars ; and though Leonardo da Vinci had insisted on the visible evidence ; nay, deistic habit could keep even Voltaire preposterously incredulous on the subject.[6] When the scientific truth began to force its way in the

---

[1] White, as cited i, 222-3, gives a selection of the language in general use among theologians on the subject.

[2] The early policy of the Geological Society of London (1807), which professed to seek for facts and to disclaim theories as premature (cp. Whewell, iii, 428 ; Buckle, iii, 392), was at least as much socially as scientifically prudential.

[3] See the excellent monograph of W. M. Mackenzie, *Hugh Miller : A Critical Study*, 1905, ch. vi ; and cp. Spencer's essay on *Illogical Geology - Essays*, vol. i. Miller's friend Dick, the Thurso naturalist, being a freethinker, escaped such error. (Mackenzie, pp. 161-4.)

[4] Cp. the details given by Whewell, iii, 406-8, 411 13, 506-7, as to early theories of a sound order, all of which came to nothing. Steno, a Dane resident in Italy in the seventeenth century, had reached non-Scriptural and just views on several points. Cp. White, *Hist. of the Warfare of Science with Theology*, i, 215.

[5] *Metamorphoses*, lib. xv.

[6] See his essay, *Des Singularités de la Nature*, ch. xii ; and his *Dissertation sur les changements arrivés dans notre globe*.

teeth of such authorities as Cuvier, who stood for the
"Mosaic"doctrine, the effect was proportionately marked;
and whether or not the suicide of Miller (1856) was in
any way due to despair on perception of the collapse
of his reconciliation of geology with Genesis,[1] the
scientific demonstration made an end of revelationism
for many.

4. Still more rousing, finally, was the effect of the
science of zoology, as placed upon a broad scientific
foundation by CHARLES DARWIN. Here again steps had
been taken in previous generations on the right path,
without any general movement on the part of scientific
and educated men. Darwin's own grandfather, ERASMUS
DARWIN, had in his *Zoonomia* (1794) anticipated many
of the positions of the French LAMARCK, who in 1801
began developing the views he fully elaborated in 1815,
as to the descendance of all existing species from earlier
forms.[2] As early as 1795 GEOFFROY SAINT-HILAIRE
had begun to suspect that all species are variants on a
primordial form of life ; and at the same time (1794-5)
GOETHE in Germany had reached similar convictions.[3]
That views thus reached almost simultaneously in
Germany, England, and France, at the time of the
French Revolution, should have to wait for two generations before even meeting the full stress of battle, must
be put down as one of the results of the general reaction.
Saint-Hilaire, publishing his views in 1828, was officially
overborne by the Cuvier school in France. In England,
indeed, so late as 1855, we find Sir David Brewster
denouncing the Nebular Hypothesis : "that dull and
dangerous heresy of the age.......An omnipotent arm
was required to give the planets their position and
motion in space, and a presiding intelligence to assign

---

[1] He had just completed a work on the subject at his death. Cp.
Mackenzie, *Hugh Miller*, as cited, pp. 134-5, 146-7.
[2] See Charles Darwin's *Historical Sketch* prefixed to the *Origin of Species*.
[3] Meding, as cited by Darwin, 6th ed. i, p. xv. Goethe seems to
have had his general impulse from Kielmeyer, who also taught Cuvier.
Virchow, *Gothe als Naturforscher*, 1861, Beilage x.

to them the different functions they had to perform."[1]
And Murchison the geologist was no less emphatic
against Darwinism, which he rejected till his dying day
(1871).

5. Other anticipations of Darwin's doctrine in England
and elsewhere came practically to nothing,[2] as regarded
the general opinion, until ROBERT CHAMBERS in 1844
published anonymously his *Vestiges of the Natural
History of Creation*, a work which found a wide
audience, incurring bitter hostility not only from the
clergy but from some specialists who, like Huxley, were
later to take the evolutionist view on Darwin's persuasion. Chambers it was that brought the issue within
general knowledge; and he improved his position in
successive editions. A hostile clerical reader, Whewell,
admitted of him, in a letter to a less hostile member
of his profession, that, "as to the degree of resemblance
between the author and the French physiological
atheists, he uses reverent phrases: theirs would not
be tolerated in England"; adding: "You would be
surprised to hear the contempt and abhorrence with
which Owen and Sedgwick speak of the *Vestiges* "[3]
Hugh Miller, himself accused of "infidelity" for his
measure of inductive candour, held a similar tone
towards men of greater intellectual rectitude, calling
the liberalising religionists of his day "vermin" and
"reptiles,"[4] and classifying as "degraded and lost"[5]
all who should accept the new doctrine of evolution,
which, as put by Chambers, was then coming forward
to evict his own delusions from the field of science.

6. "Contempt and abhorrence" had in fact at all
times constituted the common Christian temper towards
every form of critical dissent from the body of received
opinion; and only since the contempt and abhorrence

---
[1] *Memoirs of Newton*, i, 131. [2] See Darwin's *Sketch*, as cited.
[3] Letter of March 16th, 1845, in *Life of Whewell*, by Mrs. Stair Douglas,
2nd ed. 1882, pp. 318 319.
[4] Mackenzie, *Hugh Miller*, p. 185.
[5] *Foot-Prints of the Creator*, end.

have been in a large degree retorted on the bigots by instructed men has a better spirit prevailed. Such a reaction was greatly promoted by the establishment of the Darwinian theory. It was after the above-noted preparation, popular and academic, and after the theory of transmutation of species had been definitely pronounced erroneous by the omniscient Whewell,[1] that Darwin produced (1859) his irresistible arsenal of arguments and facts, the *Origin of Species*, expounding systematically the principle of Natural Selection, suggested to him by the economic philosophy of Malthus, and independently and contemporaneously arrived at by Dr. Alfred Russel Wallace. The outcry was enormous; and the church, as always, arrayed itself violently against the new truth. Bishop Wilberforce affirmed in the *Quarterly Review* that "the principle of natural selection is absolutely incompatible with the word of God,"[2] which was perfectly true; and at a famous meeting of the British Association in 1860 he so travestied the doctrine as to goad Huxley into a fierce declaration that he would rather be a descendant of an ape than of a man who (like the Bishop) plunged into questions with which he had no real acquaintance, only to obscure them and distract his hearers by appeals to religious prejudice.[3] The mass of the clergy kept up the warfare of ignorance; but the battle was practically won within twenty years. In France, Germany, and the United States leading theologians had made the same suicidal declarations, entitling all men to say that, if evolution proved to be true, Christianity was false. Professor Luthardt, of Leipzig, took up the same position as Bishop Wilberforce, declaring that "the whole superstructure of personal religion is built upon the doctrine of creation";[4] leading American

[1] *Hist. of the Inductive Sciences*, 3rd. ed. iii, 479-483; *Life*, as above cited. Whewell is said to have refused to allow a copy of the *Origin of Species* to be placed in the Trinity College Library. White, i, 84.
[2] White, i, 70 sq.
[3] Clodd's *Thomas Henry Huxley*, 1902, pp. 19-20.
[4] Luthardt, *Fundamental Truths of Christianity*, Eng. trans. 1865, p. 74.

theologians pronounced the new doctrine atheistic; and everywhere gross vituperation eked out the theological argument.

> See the many examples cited by White. As late as 1885 the Scottish clergyman Dr. Lee is quoted as calling the Darwinians "gospellers of the gutter," and charging on their doctrine "utter blasphemy against the divine and human character of our incarnate Lord" (White, i, 83). Carlyle is quoted as calling Darwin "an apostle of dirt-worship." His admirers appear to regard him as having made amends by admitting that Darwin was personally charming.

7. Thus the idea of a specific creation of all forms of life by an originating Deity—the conception which virtually united the deists and Christians of the eighteenth century against the atheists—was at length scientifically exploded. The principle of personal divine rule or providential intervention had now been philosophically excluded successively (1) from astronomy by the system of Newton; (2) from the science of earth-formation by the system of Laplace and the new geology; (3) from the science of living organisms by the new zoology. It only needed that the deistic conception should be further excluded from the human sciences—from anthropology, from the philosophy of history, and from ethics—to complete, at least in outline, the rationalisation of modern thought. Not that the process was complete in detail even as regarded zoology. Despite the plain implications of the *Origin of Species,* the doctrine of the *Descent of Man* (1871) came on many as a shocking surprise, and evoked a new fury of protest. The lacunæ in Darwin, further, had to be supplemented; and much speculative power has been spent on the task by HAECKEL, without thus far establishing complete agreement. But the desperate stand so long made on the score of the "missing link" was finally discredited in 1894; and the Judæo-Christian doctrine of special creation and providential design appears, even in the imperfectly educated and largely ill-placed society of our day, to be already a lost cause.

§ IV. *Abstract Philosophy and Ethics.*

1. The philosophy of Kant, while giving the theological class a new apparatus of defence as against common-sense freethinking, forced none the less on theistic philosophy a great advance from the orthodox positions. Thus his immediate successors, Fichte and Schelling, produced systems of which one was loudly denounced as atheistic, and the other as pantheistic,[1] despite its dualism. Neither seems to have had much influence on concrete religious opinion outside the universities;[2] and when Schelling in old age turned Catholic obscurantist, the gain to clericalism was not great. Hegel in turn loosely wrought out a system of which the great merit is to substitute the conception of existence as relation for the nihilistic idealism of Fichte and the unsolved dualism of Schelling. This system he latterly adapted to practical exigencies[3] by formulating a philosophic Trinity and hardily defining Christianity as "Absolute Religion" in comparison with the various forms of "Natural Religion." Nevertheless, he counted in a great degree as a disintegrating influence, and was in a very practical way anti-Christian.

> Compare Hagenbach, *German Rationalism* (Eng. trans. of *Kirchengeschichte*), pp. 364-9; Renan, *Etudes d'histoire religieuse*, 5e édit. p. 406; J. D. Morell, *Histor. and Crit. View of the Spec. Philos. of Europe in the Nineteenth Century*, 2nd ed. 1847, ii, 189 191; Robins, *A Defence of the Faith*, 1862, Pt. i, pp. 135-141, 176; Eschenmenger, *Die Hegel'sche Religionsphilosophie*, 1834, quoted in Beard's *Voices of the Church*, p. 8; Leo, *Die Hegelingen*, 1838; and Reinhard, *Lehrbuch der Geschichte der Philosophie*, 2nd ed. 1839, pp. 753-4—also cited by Beard, pp. 9-12.

Not only does his conception of the Absolute make deity simply the eternal process of the universe, and the

---

[1] Such is Saintes's view of Schelling. *Hist. crit. du rationalisme en Allemagne*, p. 323.
[2] *Id.* pp. 372-4.
[3] As to Hegel's mental development, cp. J. R. Beard, D.D., on "Strauss, Hegel, and their Opinions," in *Voices of the Church in Reply to Strauss*, 1845, pp. 3-4.

divine consciousness indistinguishable from the total consciousness of mankind,[1] but his abstractions lend themselves equally to all creeds ;[2] and some of the most revolutionary of the succeeding movements of German thought—as those of Strauss,[3] Feuerbach, and Marx— professedly founded on him. In 1854, Heine told his French readers that there were in Germany " fanatical monks of atheism " who would willingly burn Voltaire as a besotted deist ;[4] and Heine himself, in his last years of suffering and of revived religiosity, could see in Hegel's system only atheism. BRUNO BAUER at first opposed Strauss, and afterwards went even further than he, professing Hegelianism all the while.[5] SCHOPEN- HAUER and HARTMANN in turn being even less sustain- ing to orthodoxy, and later orthodox systems failing to impress, there came in due course the cry of " Back to Kant," where at least orthodoxy had some formal semblance of sanction. Hegel himself was indeed, in his last days, avowedly bent on championing the Christian creed at all its main points ; but here his method, arbitrary even for him, appealed neither to the orthodox nor, with a few exceptions,[6] to his own disciples, some of whom, as Ruge, at length definitely renounced Christianity.[7] Hartmann's work on *The Self- Reparation of Christianity*[8] is a stringent exposure of the unreality of what passed for " liberal Christianity " in Germany a generation ago, and an appeal for a " new concrete religion " of monism or pantheism as a bulwark against Ultramontanism. On this monism, however,

---

[1] Cp. Morell, as cited, and pp. 195-6 ; and Feuerbach, as summarised by Baur, *Kirchenges. des 19ten Jahrh.*, p. 390.
[2] Cp. Michelet as cited by Morell, ii, 192-3.
[3] As to Strauss, cp. Beard, as above cited, pp. 21-2, 30 ; and Zeller, *David Friedrich Strauss*, Eng. trans. 1899, pp. 35, 47-8, 71-2, etc.
[4] *Geständnisse*. Werke, iv, 33. Cp. iii, 110.
[5] Cp. Hagenbach, pp. 369-372 ; Farrar, *Crit. Hist. of Freethought*, pp. 387-8. On Bauer's critical development and academic career see Baur, *Kirchengesch. des 19ten Jahrh.*, pp. 386-9.
[6] *E.g.*, Dr. Hutchison Stirling. See his trans. of Schwegler's *Hand- book of the History of Philosophy*, 6th ed. p. 438 sq.
[7] Baur, last cit. p. 389.
[8] *Das Selbstersetzung des Christenthums*, 2te Aufl. 1874.

Hartmann insists on grounding his pessimism. On the whole, the effect of all German philosophy has probably been to make for the general discredit of theistic philosophy, the surviving forms of Hegelianism being little propitious to current religion. And though Schopenhauer and NIETZSCHE can hardly be said to carry on the task of philosophy either in spirit or in effect, yet the rapid intensification of hostility to current religion which their writings in particular manifest[1] must be admitted to stand for a deep revolt against the Kantian compromise.

2. From the collisions of philosophic systems in Germany there emerged two great practical freethinking forces, the teachings of LUDWIG FEUERBACH (1804–76), who was deprived of his chair at Erlangen in 1830 for his *Thoughts upon Death and Immortality*, and LUDWIG BUCHNER, who was deprived of his chair of clinic at Tubingen in 1855 for his *Force and Matter*. The former, originally a Hegelian, expressly broke away from his master, declaring that whereas Hegel belonged to the "Old Testament" of modern philosophy, he himself would set forth the New, wherein Hegel's fundamentally incoherent treatment of deity (as the total process of things on the one hand, and an objective personality on the other) should be cured.[2] Feuerbach accordingly, in his *Essence of Christianity* (1841) and *Essence of Religion* (1851), supplied one of the first adequate modern statements of the positively rationalistic position as against Christianity and theism, in terms of philosophic as well as historical insight, a statement to which there is no characteristically modern answer save in terms of the refined sentimentalism of Renan,[3]

---

[1] See Schopenhauer's dialogues on *Religion* and *Immortality*, and his essay on *The Christian System* (Eng. trans. in Schopenhauer Series by T. B. Saunders), and Nietzsche's *Antichrist*. The latter work is discussed by the writer in *Essays in Sociology*, vol. ii.

[2] Baur gives a good summary, *Kirchengeschichte*, pp. 390–4. Vatke similarly grew out of his original Hegelianism. Cheyne, *Founders*, pp. 135–140.

[3] See his paper, *M. Feuerbach et la nouvelle école hégélienne*, in *Études d'histoire religieuse*. Baur, who pronounced Feuerbach a nobler and

fundamentally averse alike to scientific precision and intellectual consistency.

On Feuerbach's *Essence of Religion* followed the resounding explosion of Büchner's *Force and Matter* (1855), which in large measure, but with much greater mastery of scientific detail, does for the plain man of his century what d'Holbach in his chief work sought to do for his day. Constantly vilified, even in the name of philosophy, in the exact tone and spirit of animal irritation which marks the religious vituperation of all forms of rationalism in previous ages; and constantly misrepresented as professing to explain an infinite universe when it does but show the hollowness of all supernaturalist explanations,[1] the book steadily holds its ground as a manual of anti-mysticism.[2] Between them, Feuerbach and Büchner may be said to have framed for their age an atheistic "System of Nature," concrete and abstract, without falling into the old error of substituting one apriorism for another.

3. In France, the course of thought had been hardly less revolutionary. Philosophy, like everything else, had been affected by the legitimist restoration; and between Victor Cousin and the other "classic philosophers" of the first third of the century, orthodoxy was nominally reinstated. Yet even among these there was no firm coherence. Maine de Biran, one of the shrinking spirits who passed gradually into an intolerant authoritarianism from fear of the perpetual pressures of reason, latterly declared (1821) that a philosophy which ascribed to deity only infinite thought or supreme intelligence,

---

more important personality than Bruno Bauer, makes an oddly weak answer to his philosophy (fairly stated by Baur), saying merely that it is extremely one-sided, that it favours the communistic and other extreme tendencies of the time, and that it brings everything "under the rude rule of egoism" (*Kirchengeschichte*, p. 396).

[1] Büchner expressly rejected the term "materialism" because of its misleading implications or connotations. Cp., in Mrs. Bradlaugh Bonner's *Charles Bradlaugh*, the discussion in Part II, ch. i, § 3 (by J. M. R.).

[2] While the similar works of CARL VOGT and MOLESCHOTT have gone out of print, Büchner's, recast again and again, continues to be republished.

eliminating volition and love, was pure atheism ; and this pronouncement struck at the philosophy of Cousin. Nor was this species of orthodoxy any more successful than the furious irrationalism of Joseph De Maistre in setting up a philosophic form of faith, as distinct from the cult of rhetoric and sentiment founded by Chateaubriand. Cousin was deeply distrusted by those who knew him, and at the height of his popularity he was contemned by the more competent minds around him, such as Sainte-Beuve and Edgar Quinet.[1] The latter thinker himself counted for a measure of rationalism, though he argued for theism, and undertook to make good the historicity of Jesus against those who challenged it. For the rest, even among the ostensibly conservative and official philosophers, Theodore Jouffroy, an eclectic, who held the chair of moral philosophy in the Faculte des Lettres at Paris, was at heart an unbeliever from his youth up,[2] and even in his guarded writings was far from satisfying the orthodox. "God," he wrote,[3] "interposes as little in the regular development of humanity as in the course of the solar system." He added a fatalistic theorem of divine predetermination, which he verbally salved in the usual way by saying that predetermination presupposed individual liberty. Eclecticism thus fell, as usual, between two stools ; but it was not orthodoxy that would gain. On another line Jouffroy openly bantered the authoritarians on their appeal to a popular judgment which they declared to be incapable of pronouncing on religious questions.[4]

On retrospect, the whole official French philosophy of the period, however conservative in profession, is found

[1] Cp. Paul Deschanel, *Figures Littéraires*, 1889, pp. 130-2, 171-3, and Ch. Adam, *La Philosophie en France*, 1894, p. 228.

[2] Adam, as cited, pp. 227-230.

[3] In his *Mélanges Philosophiques* (1833), Eng. trans. (incomplete) by George Ripley, *Philos. Essays of Th. Jouffroy*, Edinburgh, 1839, ii, 32. Ripley, who was one of the American transcendentalist group, and a member of the Brook Farm Colony, indicates his own semi-rationalism in his Introductory Note, p. xxv.

[4] *Mélanges philosophiques*, trans. as cited, ii, 95.

to have been at bottom rationalistic, and only superficially friendly to faith. Lamennais declaimed warmly against *l'Indifférence en matière de religion* (1818-24), and Damiron, writing his *Essai sur l'histoire de la philosophie en France au XIXe Siecle* in 1834, replies in a fashion more amiable than reassuring, commenting on the "strange skepticism" of Lamennais as to the human reason.[1] For himself, he takes up the parable of Lessing, and declares that where Lessing spoke doubtfully, men had now reached conviction. It was no longer a question of whether, but of when, religion was to be recast in terms of fuller intelligence. "In this religious regeneration we shall be to the Christians what the Christians were to the Jews, and the Jews to the patriarchs: we shall be Christians and something more." The theologian of the future will be half-physicist, half-philosopher. "We shall study God through nature and through men; and a new Messiah will not be necessary to teach us miraculously what we can learn of ourselves and by our natural lights." Christianity has been a useful discipline; but "our education is so advanced that henceforth we can be our own teachers; and, having no need of an extraneous inspiration, we draw faith from science."[2] "Prayer is good, doubtless," but it "has only a mysterious, uncertain, remote action on our environment."[3] All this under Louis Philippe, from a professor at the Ecole Normale. Not to this day has official academic philosophy in Britain ventured to go so far. In France the brains were never out, even under the Restoration.

4. But the one really energetic and characteristic philosophy produced in the new France was that of AUGUSTE COMTE, which as set forth in the *Cours de Philosophie Positive* (1830-42) practically reaffirmed while it recast and supplemented the essentials of the anti-theological rationalism of the previous age, and in that sense rebuilt French positivism, giving that new

[1] *Essai*, cited, i, 232, 237.   [2] *Id.* pp. 241-243.   [3] *Id.* p. 221.

name to the naturalistic principle. Though Comte's direct following was never large, it is significant that soon after the completion of his *Cours* we find Saisset lamenting that the war between the clergy and the philosophers, " suspended by the great political commotion of 1830," had been "revived with a new energy."[1] The later effort of Comte to frame a politico-ecclesiastical system never succeeded beyond the formation of a politically powerless sect ; but both in France and England his philosophy tinged all the new thought of his time, his leading English adherents in particular being among the most esteemed publicists of the day. In France, the general effect of the rationalistic movement had been such that when TAINE, under the Third Empire, assailed the whole "classic" school in his *Philosophes Classiques* (1857), his success was at once generally recognised, and a non-Comtist positivism was thenceforth the ruling philosophy. The same thing has happened in Italy, where quite a number of university professors are explicitly positivist in their philosophic teaching.[2]

5. In Britain, where abstract philosophy after Berkeley had been left to Hume and the Scotch thinkers who opposed him, metaphysics was for a generation practically overridden by the moral and social sciences ; Hartley's Christian Materialism making small headway as formulated by him. The proof of the change wrought in the direction of native thought is seen in the personalities of the men who, in the teeth of the reaction, applied rationalistic method to ethics and psychology. BENTHAM and JAMES MILL were in their kindred fields among the most convinced and active freethinkers of their day, the former attacking both clericalism and orthodoxy :[3] while the latter, no less

---

[1] Article in 1844, rep. in *Essais de la philosophie et religion*, 1845, p. 1.
[2] Cp. Professor Botta's chapter in Ueberweg's *Hist. of Philos.* ii, 513 516.
[3] In his *Church of Englandism and its Catechism Examined* (1818) and *Not Paul but Jesus* (1823), " by Gamaliel Smith."

pronounced in his private opinions, more cautiously built up a rigorously naturalistic psychology in his *Analysis of the Human Mind* (1829). Bentham's utilitarianism was so essentially anti-Christian that he could hardly have been more disliked by discerning theists if he had avowed his share in the authorship of the atheistic *Analysis of the Influence of Natural Religion*, which, elaborated from his manuscript by no less a thinker than GEORGE GROTE, was published in 1822;[1] but his ostensible restriction of his logic to practical problems of law and morals secured him a wider influence than was wielded by any of the higher publicists of his day. The whole tendency of his school was intensely rationalistic; and it indirectly affected all thought by its treatment of economics, which from Hume and Smith onwards had been practically divorced from theology. Even clerical economists, such as Malthus and Chalmers, alike orthodox in religion, furthered naturalism in philosophy in spite of themselves. A not unnatural result was a religious fear of all reasoning whatever, and a disparagement of the very faculty of reason. This, however, was sharply resisted by the more cultured champions of orthodoxy,[2] to the great advantage of critical discussion.

6. When English metaphysical philosophy revived with Sir William Hamilton and Dean Mansel, they gave the decisive proof that the orthodox cause had been philosophically lost while being socially won, since their theism emphasised in the strongest way the negative criticism of Kant, leaving Deity void of all cognisable qualities. Their metaphysic thus served as an open and avowed basis for the naturalistic *First Principles* (1860-62)

---

[1] Under the pseudonym of Philip Beauchamp. See *The Minor Works of George Grote*, edited by Professor Bain, 1873, p. 18; *Athenæum*, May 31, 1873; J. S. Mill's *Autobiography*, p. 69; and *Three Essays on Religion*, p. 76. This remarkable treatise, which greatly influenced Mill, is the most stringent attack made on theism between d'Holbach and Feuerbach.

[2] Cp. Morell, *Spec. Philos. of Europe in the Nineteenth Century*, ii, 620; and *Life and Corr. of Whately*, by E. Jane Whately, abridged ed. p. 159.

of HERBERT SPENCER, wherein, with an unfortunate laxity of metaphysic on the author's own part, and a no less unfortunate lack of consistency as regards the criticism of religious and anti-religious positions,[1] the new cosmic conceptions are unified in a masterly conception of evolution as a universal law. Strictly, the book is a " System of Nature " rather than a philosophy in the sense of a study of the grounds and limitations of knowledge : that is to say, it is on the former ground alone that it is coherent and original. But its very imperfections on the other side have probably promoted its reception among minds already shaken in theology by the progress of concrete science ; while at the same time such imperfections give a hostile foothold to the revived forms of theism. Even these, however, in particular the neo-Hegelian system associated with the name of the late Professor T. H. Green, fail to give any shelter to Christian orthodoxy. In England, as on the Continent, the bulk of philosophical activity is now dissociated from the Christian creed.[2]

7. The effect of the ethical pressure of the deistic attack on the intelligence of educated Christians was fully seen even within the Anglican Church before the middle of the century. The unstable Coleridge, who had gone round the whole compass of opinion[3] when he began to wield an influence over the more sensitive of the younger churchmen, was strenuous in a formal affirmation of the doctrine of the Trinity, but no less anxious to modify the doctrine of Atonement on which the conception of the Trinity was historically founded. In the

---

[1] Mr. Spencer has avowed in his *Autobiography* (ii, 75) what might be surmised by critical readers, that he wrote the First Part of *First Principles* in order to guard against the charge of "materialism." This motive led him to misrepresent "atheism," and there was a touch of retribution in the general disregard of his disavowal of materialism, at which he expresses surprise. The broad fact remains that for prudential reasons he set forth at the very outset of his system a set of conclusions which could properly be reached only at the end, if at all.

[2] For instance, the *Appearance and Reality* of Mr. F. Bradley. See pp. 448, 500, 509, 558, 3rd ed.

[3] As to his fluctuations, which lasted till his death, cp. the author's *New Essays towards a Critical Method*, 1897, pp. 144-7, 149-154, 168-9.

hands of Maurice, the doctrine of sacrifice became one of example to the end of subjective regeneration of the sinner. This view, which was developed by John the Scot—perhaps from hints in Origen[1]—and again by Bernardino Ochino,[2] is specially associated with the teaching of Coleridge ; but it was quite independently held in England before him by the Anglican Dr. Parr (1747–1825), who appears to have been heterodox upon most points in the orthodox creed,[3] and who, like Servetus and Coleridge and Hegel, held by a modal as against a "personal" Trinity. Such Unitarian accommodations presumably reconciled to Christianity and the Church many who would otherwise have abandoned them ; and the only orthodox rebuttal seems to have been the old and dangerous resort to the Butlerian argument, to the effect that the God of Nature shows no such benign fatherliness as the anti-sacrificial school ascribe to him.[4]

8. The same pressure of moral argument was doubtless potent in the development of "Socinian" or other rationalistic views in the Protestant churches of Germany, Holland, Hungary, Switzerland, and France in the first half of the century. Such development had gone so far that by the middle of the century the churches in question were, to the eye of an English evangelical champion, predominantly rationalistic, and in that sense "infidel."[5] Reactions have been claimed before and since ; but in our own age there is little to show for them. In the United States, again, the ethical element probably predominated in the recoil of EMERSON from Christian orthodoxy even of the Unitarian stamp, as well as in the heresy of THEODORE PARKER, whose aversion to the

---

[1] Baur, *Die christliche Lehre der Versöhnung*, 1838, pp. 54-63, 124-131.
[2] Benrath, *Bernardino Ochino*, Eng. trans. pp. 284-7.
[3] Field's *Memoirs of Parr*, 1828, ii, 363, 374-9.
[4] See Pearson's *Infidelity, its Aspects, Causes, and Agencies*, 1853, p. 215 sq. The position of Maurice and Parr (associated with other and later names) is there treated as one of the prevailing forms of "infidelity," and called spiritualism. In Germany, the orthodox made the same dangerous answer to the theistic criticism. See the *Memoirs of F. Perthes*, Eng. trans. 2nd ed. ii, 242-3.
[5] Pearson, as cited, pp. 560-2, 568-579, 583-4.

theistic ethic of Jonathan Edwards was so strong as to make him blind to the reasoning power of that stringent Calvinist. At the same time, all such moral accommodations in Protestant churches, while indirectly countenancing freethought, have served to maintain Christian organisations, with their too common accompaniments of social intolerance, as against more open freethinking ; and in themselves they represent a partial perversion of the ethics of the intellectual life.

§ V. *The Sociological Sciences.*

1. A rationalistic treatment of human history had been explicit or implicit in the whole literature of Deism ; and had been attempted with various degrees of success by Bodin, Vico, Montesquieu, Mandeville, Hume, Smith, Voltaire, and Condorcet, as well as by lesser men. So clear had been the lead to naturalistic views of social growth in the *Politics* of Aristotle, and so strong the influence of the new naturalistic spirit, that it is seen even in the work of Goguet (1769), who sets out as biblically as Bossuet ; while in Germany Herder and Kant framed really luminous generalisations ; and a whole group of sociological writers rose up in the Scotland of the middle and latter parts of the century. Here again there was reaction ; but in France the orthodox Guizot did much to promote broader views than his own ; EUSEBE SALVERTE in his essay *De la Civilisation* (1813) made a highly intelligent effort towards a general view ; and CHARLES COMTE in his *Traité de Législation* (1826) made a marked scientific advance on the suggestive work of Herder. As we have seen, the eclectic Jouffroy put human affairs in the sphere of natural law equally with cosmic phenomena. At length, in the great work of AUGUSTE COMTE, scientific method was applied so effectively and concretely to the general problem that, despite his serious fallacies, social science again took rank as a solid study. In England and America, by the works of DRAPER and BUCKLE, in the sixth and later decades of the century, the conception of law in human

history was at length widely popularised, to the due indignation of the supernaturalists, who saw the last great field of natural phenomena passing like others into the realm of science. Draper's avowed theism partly protected him from attack ; but Buckle's straightforward attacks on creeds and on churches brought upon him a peculiarly fierce hostility, which was unmollified by his incidental avowal of belief in a future life. For long this hostility told against his sociological teaching. Mr. Spencer's *Principles of Sociology* nevertheless clinched the scientific claim by taking sociological law for granted ; and the new science has continually progressed in acceptance. In the hands of all its leading exponents in all countries—Lester Ward, Giddings, Guyau, Letourneau, Tarde, Ferri, Durkheim, De Greef, Gumplowicz, Lilienfeld, Schaffle—it is entirely naturalistic, though some Catholic professors continue to inject into it theological assumptions. It cannot be said, however, that a general doctrine of social evolution is even yet fully established. The problem is complicated by the profoundly contentious issues of practical politics ; and in the resulting diffidence of official teachers there arises a notable opening for obscurantism, which has been duly forthcoming. In the first half of the century, such an eminent churchman as Dean Milman incurred at the hands of J. H. Newman and others the charge of writing the history of the Jews and of early Christianity in a rationalistic spirit, presenting religion as a "human" phenomenon.[1] Later churchmen, with all their preparation, have rarely gone further.

2. Two lines of scientific study, it would appear, must be thoroughly followed up before the ground can be pronounced clear for authoritative conclusions—those of anthropological archæology (including comparative mythology and comparative hierology) and economic analysis. On both lines great progress has been made ; but on both occurs a resistance of vested interests. Such

[1] See *The Dynamics of Religion*, pp. 227-233.

students as TYLOR, WAITZ, and SPENCER have sifted and classified our knowledge as to primitive social life; and a whole line of comparative mythologists, from Dupuis and Volney to Mannhardt and Frazer, have enlarged and classified our knowledge of primitive religious norms and tendencies. As regards economics, less work has been done. Buckle applied the economic principle with force and accuracy to the case of the great primary civilisations, but only in a partial and biassed way to modern history; and the school of Marx incurs reaction by applying it somewhat fanatically. Thus economic interests and clericalism join hands to repel an economic theory of history; and clericalism itself represents a vast economic interest when it wards off the full application of the principle of comparative mythology to Christian lore. The really great performance of Dupuis was not scientifically improved upon, Strauss failing to profit by it. In Strauss's hands the influence of Pagan myth counts almost for nothing; and Renan practically waived the whole principle. The searching anthropology of Ghillany, again, as we have seen, made no general impression on the theological world, which had not in his day begun to realise that there is an anthropology. Thus the "higher criticism" of both the Old and New Testaments remains radically imperfect; and specialists in mythology are found either working all round Gospel myth without once touching it, or unscientifically claiming to put it, as "religion," on a plane above science. All scientific thought, however, turns in the direction of a complete law of historical evolution; and such a law must necessarily make an end of the supernaturalist conception as regards every aspect of human life, ethical, social, religious, and political. The struggle lies finally between the scientific or veridical instinct and the sinister interests founded on economic endowments, and buttressed by use and wont.

3. Psychology, considered as a department of anthropology, may perhaps as fitly be classed among the sociological sciences as under philosophy; though it

strictly overlaps on that as well as on biology. However defined, it has counted for much in the dissolution of supernaturalist beliefs, from the tentatives of Diderot to the latest refinements of physiological experiment. It was the perception of this tendency that, two generations ago, secured the abandonment of phrenology to the disastrous devotion of amateurs, after men like GEORGE and ANDREW COMBE, sincere theists, as were GALL and SPURZHEIM before them, had made it a basis of a great propaganda of social and educational reform. The development of the principle of brain localisation, however, is only a question of time, there being between the procedure of the early scientific phrenologists and those of the later anatomists only a difference of method. All the ethical implications of phrenology belong to the science of brain in any of its developments, being indeed implicit in the most general principles of biological science ; and the abstention of later specialists from all direct application of their knowledge to religious and ethical issues is simply the condition of their economic existence as members of university staffs. But the old principle, *ubi tres medici, duo athei,* is more nearly true to-day than ever, being countervailed only by the fact signified just as truly in the other saw, *ubi panis, ibi Deus.* While the priest's bread depends on his creed, the physician's must be similarly implicated.

§ VI. *Poetry and Fine Letters.*

1. The whole imaginative literature of Europe, in the generation after the French Revolution, reveals directly or indirectly the transmutation that the eighteenth century had worked in religious thought. In France, the literary reaction is one of the first factors in the orthodox revival. Its leader and type was Chateaubriand, in whose typical work, the *Genie du Christianisme* (1802), lies the proof that, whatever might be the "shallowness" of Voltairism, it was profundity beside the philosophy of the majority who repelled it. On one who now reads it with the slightest scientific

preparation the book makes an impression in parts of something like imbecility. The handling of the scientific question at the threshold of the inquiry is that of a man incapable of a scientific idea. All the accumulating evidence of geology and palæontology is disposed of by the grotesque theorem that God made the world out of nothing with all the marks of antiquity upon it—the oaks at the start bearing "last year's nests"—on the ground that, " if the world were not at once young and old, the great, the serious, the moral would disappear from nature, for these sentiments by their essence attach to antique things."[1] In the same fashion the fable of the serpent is with perfect gravity homologated as a literal truth, on the strength of an anecdote about the charming of a rattlesnake with music.[2] It is humiliating, but instructive, to realise that only a century ago a " Christian reaction," in a civilised country, was inspired by such an order of ideas ; and that in the nation of Laplace, with his theory in view, it was the fashion thus to prattle in the taste of the Dark Ages.[3] The book is merely the eloquent expression of a nervous recoil from everything savouring of cool reason and clear thought, a recoil partly initiated by the sheer stress of excitement of the near past ; partly fostered by the vague belief that freethinking in religion had caused the Revolution ; partly enhanced by the tendency of every warlike period to develop emotional rather than reflective life. What was really masterly in Chateaubriand was the style ; and sentimental pietism had now the prestige of fine writing, so long the specialty of the other side. Yet a generation of monarchism served to wear out the ill-based credit of the literary reaction ; and *belles lettres* began to be rationalistic as soon as politics began again to be radical.

Thus the prestige of the neo-Christian school was

[1] Ptie. i, liv. i, ch. 5. [2] *Id.* i, liv. iii, ch. 2.
[3] It is further to be remembered, however, that Mr. Matthew Arnold saw fit to defend Chateaubriand, calling him "great," when his fame was being undone by common-sense.

already spent before the revolution of 1848;[1] and the inordinate vanity of Chateaubriand, who died in that year, had undone his special influence still earlier. For the rest, the belief that he had brought back Christianity to a France denuded of worship by atheists is part of the mythology of the Revolution. Already in February, 1795, on the principle of a separation between church and State, public worship had been put on a perfectly free footing; and in 1796 the 36,000 parishes were served by 25,000 cures.[2] Napoleon's arrangement with the Papacy had restored the old political connections; and Chateaubriand had created merely a literary mode and sentiment.

2. The literary history of France since his death decides the question, so far as it can be thus decided. From 1848 till our own day it has been predominantly naturalistic and non-religious. After Guizot and the Thierrys, the nearest approach to Christianity in a French historian is perhaps in the case of Edgar Quinet. MICHELET was a mere heretic in the eyes of the faithful, Saisset describing his book *Du Pretre, de la Femme, et de la Famille* (1845), as a "renaissance of Voltaireanism."[3] His whole brilliant History, indeed, is from beginning to end rationalistic, challenging as it does all the decorous traditions, exposing the failure of the faith to civilise, pronouncing that "the monastic Middle Age is an age of idiots" and the scholastic world which followed it an age of artificially formed fools,[4] flouting dogma and discrediting creed over each of their miscarriages. And he was popular not only because of his vividness and unfailing freshness, but

---

[1] C. Wordsworth, *Diary in France*, 1845, pp. 55–6, 124, 204.

[2] See the details in the *Appendice* to the *Etudes* of M. Gazier, before cited. That writer's account is the more decisive seeing that his bias is clerical, and that, writing before M. Aulard, he had to a considerable extent retained the old illusion as to the "decreeing of atheism" by the Convention (p. 313). See pp. 230–260 as to the readjustment effected by Gregoire, while the conservative clergy were still striving to undo the Revolution.

[3] *Essais sur la philosophie et la religion*, 1845, p. 193.

[4] *Histoire*, tom. vii, *Renaissance*, introd. § 6.

because his convictions were those of the best intelligence around him. In poetry and fiction the predominance of one or other shade of freethinking is signal. Balzac, who grew up in the age of reaction, makes essentially for rationalism by his intense analysis; and after him the difficulty is to find a great French novelist who is not frankly rationalistic. George Sand will probably not be claimed by orthodoxy; and BEYLE, CONSTANT, FLAUBERT, MERIMEE, ZOLA, DAUDET, MAUPASSANT, and the DE GONCOURTS make a list against which can be set only the names of the distinguished *decadent* Huysmans, who has become a Trappist after a life marked by a philosophy of an extremely different complexion, and of M. Bourget, an artist of the second order.

3. In French poetry the case is hardly otherwise. BERANGER, who passed for a Voltairean, did indeed claim to have "saved from the wreck an indestructible belief";[1] and Lamartine goes to the side of Christianity; but De Musset, the most inspired of *decadents*, was no more Christian than Heine, save for what a critic has called "la banale religiosite de *l'Espoir en Dieu*";[2] and the pessimist Baudelaire had not even that to show. De Musset's absurd attack on Voltaire in his Byronic poem, *Rolla*, well deserves the same epithets. It is a mere product of hysteria, representing neither knowledge nor reflection. The grandiose theism of VICTOR HUGO, again, is stamped only with his own image and superscription; and in his great contemporary LECONTE DE LISLE we have one of the most convinced and aggressive freethinkers of the century, a fine scholar and a self-controlled pessimist, who felt it well worth his while to write a little *Popular History of Christianity* (1871) which would have delighted d'Holbach. It is significant, on the other hand, that the exquisite religious verse of Verlaine was the product of an incurable neuropath, like the later work of Huysmans, and stands

---

[1] Letter to Sainte-Beuve, cited by Levallois, *Sainte-Beuve*, 1872, p. 14.
[2] Lanson, *Hist. de la litt. française*, p. 951.

for decadence pure and simple. While French *belles lettres* thus in general made for rationalism, criticism was naturally not behindhand. Sainte-Beuve, the most widely appreciative though not the most scientific or just of critics, had only a literary sympathy with the religious types over whom he spent so much effusive research;[1] EDMOND SCHERER was an unbeliever almost against his will; TAINE, though reactionary on political grounds in his latter years, was the typical French rationalist of his time; and though M. Brunetiere, whose preferences are all for Bossuet, makes "the bankruptcy of science" the text of his somewhat facile philosophy, the most scientific and philosophic head in the whole line of French critics, the late EMILE HENNEQUIN, was wholly a rationalist; and even the rather reactionary Jules Lemaître has not maintained his early attitude of austerity towards Renan.

4. In England it was due above all to Shelley that the very age of reaction was confronted with unbelief in lyric form. His immature *Queen Mab* was vital enough with conviction to serve as an inspiration to a whole host of unlettered freethinkers not only in its own generation but in the next. Its notes preserved, and greatly expanded, the tract entitled *The Necessity of Atheism*, for which he was expelled from Oxford; and against his will it became a people's book, the law refusing him copyright in his own work, on the memorable principle that there could be no "protection" for a book setting forth pernicious opinions. Whether he would not in later life, had he survived, have passed to a species of mystic Christianity, reacting like Coleridge, but with a necessary difference, is a question raised by parts of the *Hellas*. But Shelley's work, as

---

[1] "L'incredulité de Sainte-Beuve était sincere, radicale, et absolue. Elle a été invariable et invincible pendant trente ans. Voila la verite" (Jules Levallois, *Saint-Beuve*, 1872, pref. p. xxxiii). M. Levallois, who writes as a Christian, was one of Sainte-Beuve's secretaries. M. Zola, who spoke of the famous critic's rationalism as "une negation n'osant conclure," admitted later that it was hardly possible for him to speak more boldly than he did (*Documents Littéraires*, 1881, pp. 314, 325-8).

done, sufficed to keep for radicalism and rationalism the crown of song as against the Tory orthodoxy of the elderly Wordsworth and of Southey ; and Coleridge's zeal for (amended) dogma came upon him after his hour of poetic transfiguration was past.

 And even Coleridge, who held the heresies of a modal Trinity and the non-expiatory character of the death of Christ, was widely distrusted by the pious, and expressed himself privately in terms which would have outraged them. Miracles, he declared, "are supererogatory. The law of God and the great principles of the Christian religion would have been the same had Christ never assumed humanity. It is for these things, and for such as these, for telling unwelcome truths, that I have been termed an atheist. It is for these opinions that William Smith assured the Archbishop of Canterbury that I was (what half the clergy are in *their lives*) an atheist. Little do these men know what atheism is. Not one man in a thousand has either strength of mind or goodness of heart to be an atheist. I repeat it. Not one man in ten thousand has goodness of heart or strength of mind to be an atheist." Allsopp's *Letters, Conversations, and Recollections of S. T. Coleridge*, 3rd ed. 1864, p. 47.

On the other side, Scott's honest but unintellectual romanticism, as we know from Newman, certainly favoured the Tractarian reaction, to which it was æsthetically though hardly emotionally akin ; but the far more potent influence of BYRON, too wayward to hold a firm philosophy, but too intensely alive to realities to be capable of Scott's feudal orthodoxy, must have counted for heresy even in England, and was one of the literary forces of revolutionary revival for the whole of Europe. Though he never came to a clear atheistical decision as did Shelley,[1] and often in private gave himself out for a Calvinist, he so handled theological problems in his *Cain* that he, like Shelley, was refused copyright in his work ;[2] and it was widely appropriated for freethinkers'

[1] At the age of twenty-five we find him writing to Gifford : " I am no bigot to infidelity, and did not expect that because I doubted the immortality of man I should be charged with denying the existence of God " (letter of June 18th, 1813).
[2] By the Court of Chancery, in 1822, the year in which copyright was refused to the *Lectures* of Dr. Lawrence. Harriet Martineau, *History of the Peace*, ii, 87.

purposes. The orthodox Southey was on the same grounds denied the right to suppress his early revolutionary drama, *Wat Tyler*, which accordingly was made to do duty in Radical propaganda by freethinking publishers. Keats, again, though he melodiously declaimed, in a boyish mood, against the scientific analysis of the rainbow, and though he never assented to Shelley's impeachments of Christianity, was in no active sense a believer in it, and after his long sickness met death gladly without the "consolations" ascribed to creed.[1]

5. Nor has the balance of English poetry ever reverted to the side of faith. Even Tennyson, who more than once struck at rationalism below the belt, is in his own despite the poet of doubt as much as of credence, however he might wilfully attune himself to the key of faith; and the unparalleled optimism of Browning evolved a form of Christianity sufficiently alien to the historic creed.[2] In CLOUGH and MATTHEW ARNOLD, again, we have the positive record of surrendered faith. Alongside of Arnold, Mr. SWINBURNE put into his verse the freethinking temper that Leconte de Lisle reserved for prose; and the ill-starred but finely gifted JAMES THOMSON (" B.V.") was no less definitely though despairingly an unbeliever. Among our younger poets, finally, the balance is pretty much the same; Mr. Watson declaring in worthily noble diction for a high agnosticism, and Mr. Davidson defying orthodox ethics in the name of his very antinomian theology;[3] while on the side of the regulation religion—since Mr. Yeats is but a stray Druid—can be cited at best the regimental psalmody of Mr. Kipling, lyrist of trumpet and drum;

[1] W. Sharp, *Life of Severn*, 1892, pp. 86-7, 90, 117-118.
[2] Cp. Mrs. Sutherland Orr's article on *The Religious Opinions of Robert Browning* in the *Contemporary Review*, December, 1891, p. 878; and the present writer's *Tennyson and Browning as Teachers*, 1903.
[3] Recently, apropos of his *Theatrocrat*, which he pronounces "the most profound and original of English books," Mr. Davidson has in a newspaper article proclaimed himself on socio-political grounds an anti-Christian. "I take the first resolute step out of Christendom," is his claim (*Daily Chronicle*, December 20th, 1905).

the stained-glass Mariolatries of Mr. Francis Thompson; and the Godism of Mr. Henley, whereat the prosaic godly look askance.

6. One of the best-beloved names in English literature, Charles Lamb, is on several counts to be numbered with those of the freethinkers of his day—who included Godwin and Hazlitt—though he had no part in any direct propaganda. Himself at most a Unitarian, but not at all given to argument on points of faith, he did his work for reason partly by way of the subtle and winning humanism of such an essay as *New Year's Eve*, which seems to have been what brought upon him the pedantically pious censure of Southey, apparently for its lack of allusion to a future state; partly by his delicately-entitled letter, *The Tombs in the Abbey*, in which he replied to Southey's stricture. "A book which wants only a sounder religious feeling to be as delightful as it is original" had been Southey's pompous criticism, in a paper on *Infidelity*. In his reply, Lamb commented on Southey's life-long habit of scoffing at the Church of Rome, and gravely repudiated the test of orthodoxy for human character.

> Lamb's words are not generally known, and are worth remembering. "I own," he wrote, "I never could think so considerably of myself as to decline the society of an agreeable or worthy man upon difference of opinion only. The impediments and the facilitations to a sound belief are various and inscrutable as the heart of man. Some believe upon weak principles; others cannot feel the efficacy of the strongest. One of the most candid, most upright, and single-meaning men I ever knew was the late Thomas Holcroft. I believe he never said one thing and meant another in his life; and, as near as I can guess, he never acted otherwise than with the most scrupulous attention to conscience. Ought we to wish the character false for the sake of a hollow compliment to Christianity?" Of the freethinking and unpopular Hazlitt, who had soured towards Lamb in his perverse way, the essayist spoke still more generously. Of Leigh Hunt he speaks more critically, but with the same resolution to stand by a man known as a heretic. But the severest flout to Southey and his church is in the next paragraph, where, after the avowal that "the last sect with which you can remember me to have made common

profession were the Unitarians," he tells how, on the previous Easter Sunday, he had attended the service in Westminster Abbey, and, when he would have lingered afterwards among the tombs to meditate, was "turned, like a dog or some profane person, out into the common street, with feelings which I could not help, but not very congenial to the day or the discourse. I do not know," he adds, "that I shall ever venture myself again into one of your churches."

These words were published in the *London Magazine* in 1825; but in the posthumous collected edition of the *Essays of Elia* all the portions above cited were dropped, and the paragraph last quoted from was modified, leaving out the last words. The essay does not seem to have been reprinted in full till it appeared in R. H. Shepherd's edition of 1878. But the original issue in the *London Magazine* created a tradition among the lovers of Lamb, and his name has always been associated with some repute for freethinking. There is further very important testimony as to Lamb's opinions in one of Allsopp's records of his conversations with Coleridge :—

"No, no; Lamb's skepticism has not come lightly, nor is he a skeptic [*sic;* Query, *scoffer?*]. The harsh reproof to Godwin for his contemptuous allusion to Christ before a well-trained child proves that he is not a skeptic [? scoffer]. His mind, never prone to analysis, seems to have been disgusted with the hollow pretences, the false reasonings and absurdities of the rogues and fools with whom all establishments, and all creeds seeking to become established, abound. I look upon Lamb as one hovering between earth and heaven ; neither hoping much nor fearing anything. It is curious that he should retain many usages which he learnt or adopted in the fervour of his early religious feelings, now that his faith is in a state of suspended animation. Believe me, who know him well, that Lamb, say what he will, has more of the *essentials* of Christianity than ninety-nine out of a hundred professing Christians. He has all that would still have been Christian had Christ never lived or been made manifest upon earth." (Allsopp's *Letters, Conversations, and Recollections of S. T. Coleridge*, 3rd ed. 1864, p. 46.). In connection with the frequently cited but doubtful anecdote as to Lamb's religious feeling given in Leigh Hunt's *Autobiography* (rep. p. 253), may be noted the following, given by Allsopp : "After a visit to Coleridge, during which the conversation had taken a religious turn, Leigh Hunt......expressed his surprise that such a man as Coleridge should, when speaking of Christ, always call him Our Saviour. Lamb, who had been exhilarated by one glass of that gooseberry or raisin cordial which he has so often anathematised, stammered out, 'Ne-ne-never mind what Coleridge says ; he is full of fun.'"

7. To *belles lettres* belongs, broadly speaking, that part of the work of Carlyle which, despite his anxious caution, conveyed to susceptible readers a non-Christian view of things. We know from a posthumous writing of Mr. Froude's that, when that writer had gone through the university and taken holy orders without ever having had a single doubt as to his creed, Carlyle's books "taught him that the religion in which he had been reared was but one of many dresses in which spiritual truth had arrayed itself, and that the creed was not literally true so far as it was a narrative of facts."[1] It was presumably from the *Sartor Resartus* and some of the Essays, such as that on Voltaire—perhaps, also, negatively from the general absence of Christian sentiment in Carlyle's works—that such lessons were learned; and though it is certain that many non-zealous Christians saw no harm in Carlyle, there is reason to believe that for multitudes of readers he had the same awakening virtue. It need hardly be said that his friend Emerson exercised it in no less degree. Of Ruskin, again, the same may be asserted in respect of his many searching thrusts at clerical and lay practice, his defence of Colenso, and the obvious disappearance from his later books of the evangelical orthodoxy of the earlier.[2] Thus the three most celebrated writers of English prose in the latter half of the century were in a measure associated with the spirit of critical thought on matters religious. In a much stronger degree, the same thing may be predicated finally of the writer who in the field of English *belles lettres*, apart from fiction, came nearest them in fame and influence. Matthew Arnold, passing insensibly from the English attitude of academic orthodoxy to that of the humanist for whom Christ is but an admirable teacher and God a "Something not ourselves which makes for righteousness," became for the England of his later years the favourite pilot across the bar between supernaturalism and naturalism. Only in England,

---

[1] *My Relations with Carlyle*, 1903, p. 2.
[2] Cp. the author's *Modern Humanists*, pp. 189-194.

perhaps, could his curious gospel of church-going and Bible-reading atheism have prospered, but there it prospered exceedingly. Alike as poet and as essayist, even when essaying to disparage Colenso or to confute the Germans where they jostled his predilection for the Fourth Gospel, he was a disintegrator of tradition, and, in his dogmatic way, a dissolver of dogmatism. When, therefore, beside the four names just mentioned the British public placed those of the philosophers Spencer, Lewes, and Mill, and the scientists Darwin, Huxley, Clifford, and Tyndall, they could not but recognise that the mind of the age was divorced from the nominal faith of the church.

8. In English fiction, the beginning of the end of genuine faith was apparent to the prophetic eyes of Wilberforce and Robert Hall, of whom the former lamented the total absence of Christian sentiment from nearly all the successful fiction even of his day;[1] and the latter avowed the pain with which he noted that Miss Edgeworth, whom he admired for her style and art, put absolutely no religion in her books,[2] while Hannah More, whose principles were so excellent, had such a vicious style. With Thackeray and Dickens, indeed, serious fiction might seem to be on the side of faith, both being liberally orthodox, though neither ventured on religious romance; but with GEORGE ELIOT the balance began to lean the other way, her sympathetic treatment of religious types counting for little as against her known rationalism. At the end of the century, almost all of the leading writers of the higher fiction were known to be either rationalists or simple theists; and against the heavy metal of Mr. Meredith, Mr. Conrad, Mr. Hardy,

---

[1] *Practical View of the Prevailing Religious System* (1797), 8th ed. p. 368. Wilberforce points with chagrin to the superiority of Mohammedan writers in these matters.

[2] "In point of tendency I should class her books among the most irreligious I ever read," delineating good characters in every aspect, "and all this without the remotest allusion to Christianity, the only true religion." Cited in O. Gregory's *Brief Memoir of Robert Hall*, 1833, p. 242. The context tells how Miss Edgeworth avowed that she had not thought religion necessary in books meant for the upper classes.

Mr. Moore (whose sympathetic handling of religious motives suggests the influence of Huysmans), and the didactic-deistic Mrs. Humphry-Ward, orthodoxy can but claim artists of the third or lower grades. The championship of some of the latter may be regarded as the last humiliation of faith.

> In 1905 there was current a vulgar novel entitled *When it was Dark*, wherein was said to be drawn a blood-curdling picture of what would happen in the event of a general surrender of Christian faith. Despite some episcopal approbation, the book excited much disgust among the more enlightened clergy. The preface to Miss Marie Corelli's *Mighty Atom* may serve to convey to the many readers who cannot peruse the works of that lady an idea of the temper in which she vindicates her faith. Another popular novelist of a low artistic grade, the late Mr. Seton-Merriman, has avowed his religious soundness in a romance with a Russian plot, entitled *The Sowers*. Referring to the impressions produced by great scenes of Nature, he writes: "'These places and these times are good for convalescent atheists and such as pose as unbelievers—the cheapest form of notoriety'" (p. 168). The novelist's own Christian ethic is thus indicated: "He had Jewish blood in his veins, which carried with it the usual tendency to cringe. It is in the blood; it is part of that which the people who stood without Pilate's palace took upon themselves and their children" (p. 59). But the enormous mass of modern novels includes some tolerable pleas for faith, as well as many manifestoes of agnosticism, One of the works of the late "Edna Lyall," *We Two*, was notable as the expression of the sympathy of a devout, generous, and amiable Christian lady with the personality and career of Mr. Bradlaugh.

9. Among the most artistically gifted of the English story-writers and essayists of the last generation of the century was RICHARD JEFFERIES (d. 1887), who in *The Story of My Heart* (1883) has told how "the last traces and relics of superstitions acquired compulsorily in childhood" finally passed away from his mind, leaving him a Naturalist in every sense of the word. In the *Eulogy of Richard Jefferies* published by Sir Walter Besant in 1888 it is asserted that on his deathbed Jefferies returned to his faith, and "died listening with faith and love to the words contained in the Old Book."

A popular account of this "conversion" accordingly became current, and was employed to the usual purpose. As has been shown by a careful student, and as was admitted on inquiry by Sir Walter Besant, there had been no conversion whatever, Jefferies having simply listened to his wife's reading without hinting at any change in his convictions.[1] Despite his biographer's express admission of his error, Christian journals, such as the *Spectator*, have burked the facts; one, the *Christian*, has piously charged dishonesty on the writer who brought them to light; and a third, the Salvationist *War Cry*, has pronounced his action " the basest form of chicanery and falsehood."[2] The episode is worth noting as indicating the qualities which still attach to orthodox propaganda.

10. Of the imaginative literature of the United States, as of that of England, the same generalisation broadly holds good. The incomparable Hawthorne, whatever his psychological sympathy with the Puritan past, wrought inevitably by his art for the loosening of its intellectual hold; POE, though he did not venture till his days of downfall to write his *Eureka*, thereby proves himself an entirely non-Christian theist; and EMERSON'S poetry, no less than his prose, constantly expresses his pantheism; while his gifted disciple THOREAU, in some ways a more stringent thinker than his master, was either a pantheist or a Lucretian theist, standing aloof from all churches.[3] The economic conditions of American life have till recently been unfavourable to the higher literature, as apart from fiction; but the unique figure of WALT WHITMAN stands for a thoroughly naturalistic view of life;[4] Mr. HOWELLS appears to be at most a

---

[1] Art. "The Faith of Richard Jefferies," by H. S. Salt, in *Westminster Review*, August, 1905, rep. as pamphlet by the R. P. A., 1906.
[2] The writer of these scurrilities is Mr. Bramwell Booth, *War Cry*, May 27th, 1905.
[3] See *Talks with Emerson*, by C. J. Woodbury, 1890, pp. 93 94.
[4] It was in his old age that Whitman tended most to "theise" Nature. In conversation with Dr. Moncure Conway, he once used the expression that "the spectacle of a mouse is enough to stagger a sextillion of

theist; Mr. HENRY JAMES has not even exhibited the bias of his gifted brother to the theism of their no less gifted father; and some of the most esteemed men of letters since the Civil War, as Dr. WENDELL HOLMES and Colonel WENTWORTH HIGGINSON, have been avowedly on the side of rationalism, or, as the term goes in the States, "liberalism." Though the tone of ordinary conversation is more often reminiscent of religion in the United States than in England, the novel and the newspaper have been perhaps more thoroughly secularised there than here; and in the public honour lately done to so thorough a rationalist as Dr. Moncure Conway at the hands of his *alma mater*, the Dickinson College, West Virginia, may be seen the proof that the official orthodoxy of his youth has disappeared from the region of his birth.

11. Of the vast modern output of *belles lettres* in continental Europe, finally, a similar account is to be given. The supreme poet of modern Italy, LEOPARDI, is one of the most definitely rationalistic as well as one of the greatest philosophic poets in literature; and despite all the claims of the Catholic socialists, there is no modern Catholic literature in Italy of any European value. In Germany we have seen Goethe and Schiller distinctly counting for naturalism; and the line is found to be continued in HEINRICH VON KLEIST, the unhappy but masterly dramatist of *Der Zerbrochene Krug*, one of the truest geniuses of his time; and above all in HEINE, whose characteristic profession of reconciling himself on his deathbed with the deity he imaged as "the Aristophanes of heaven"[1] serves so scantily to console the orthodox lovers of his matchless song. His criticism of Kant and Fichte is a sufficient clue to his serious convictions; and that "God is all that there is"[2] is the

---

infidels." Dr. Conway replied: "And the sight of the cat playing with the mouse is enough to set them on their feet again"; whereat Whitman tolerantly smiled.

[1] *Gestandnisse*, end (*Werke*, ed. 1876, iv, 59).

[2] *Zur Gesch. der Relig. und Philos.*, in *Werke*, ed. cited, iii, 80.

sufficient expression of his pantheism. The whole purport of his brilliant sketch of the *History of Religion and Philosophy in Germany* (1834; 2nd ed. 1852) is a propaganda of the very spirit of freethinking, which now constitutes for Germany at once a literary classic and a manifesto of rationalism—certainly not to be taken as scientific history, but often, for the later period, perfectly just. As he himself said of the return of the aged Schelling to Catholicism, we may say of Heine that a deathbed reversion to early beliefs is a pathological phenomenon, and the reverse of a good argument for the belief so recovered.

> The use latterly made of Heine's deathbed re-conversion by orthodoxy in England is characteristic. The late letters and conversations in which he said edifying things of God and the Bible are cited for readers who know nothing of the context, and almost as little of the speaker. He had similarly praised the Bible in 1830 (Letter of July, in B. iii of his volume on Borne—*Werke*, vii, 160). To the reader of the whole it is clear that, while Heine's verbal renunciation of his former pantheism, and his characterisation of the pantheistic position as a "timid atheism," might have been made independently of his physical prostration, his profession of the theism at which he had formerly scoffed is only momentarily serious, even at a time when such a reversion would have been in no way surprising. His return to and praise of the Bible, the book of his childhood, during years of extreme suffering and utter helplessness, was in the ordinary way of physiological reaction. But inasmuch as his thinking faculty was never extinguished by his tortures, he chronically indicated that his religious talk was a half-conscious indulgence of the overstrained emotional nature, and substantially an exercise of his poetic feeling—always as large a part of his psychosis as his reasoning faculty. Even in deathbed profession he was neither a Jew nor a Christian, his language being that of a deism "scarcely distinguishable in any essential element from that of Voltaire or Diderot" (Strodtmann, *Heine's Leben und Werke*, 2te Aufl. ii, 386). "My religious convictions and views," he writes in the preface to the late *Romancero*, "remain free of all churchism.......I have abjured nothing, not even my old heathen Gods, from whom I have parted in love and friendship." In his will he peremptorily forbade any clerical procedure at his funeral; and his feeling on that side is revealed in his sad jests to his friend Meissner in 1850. "If I could only go out on crutches!" he exclaimed;

adding: "Do you know where I should go? Straight to church." On his friends expressing disbelief, he went on: "Certainly, to church! Where should a man go on crutches? Naturally, if I could walk without crutches, I should go to the laughing boulevards or the Jardin Mabille." The story is told in England *without* the conclusion, as a piece of "Christian Evidence."

But even as to his theism Heine was never more than wilfully and poetically a believer. In 1849 we find him jesting about "God" and "the Gods," declaring he will not offend the *lieber Gott*, whose vultures he knows and respects. "Opium is also a religion," he writes in 1850. "Christianity is useless for the healthy for the sick it is a very good religion." "If the German people in their need accept the King of Prussia, why should not I accept the personal God?" And in speaking of the postscript to the *Romancero* he writes in 1851: "Alas, I had neither time nor mood to say there what I wanted—namely, that I die as a Poet, who needs neither religion nor philosophy, and has nothing to do with either. The Poet understands very well the symbolic idiom of Religion, and the abstract jargon of Philosophy, but neither the religious gentry nor those of philosophy will ever understand the Poet." A few weeks before his death he signs a New Year letter, "Nebuchadnezzar II, formerly Prussian Atheist, now Lotosflower-adorer." At this time he was taking immense doses of morphia to make his tortures bearable. A few hours before his death a querying pietist got from him the answer: "God will pardon me; it is his business." The *Geständnisse*, written in 1854, ends in absolute irony; and his alleged grounds for giving up atheism, sometimes quoted seriously, are purely humorous (*Werke*, iv, 33). If it be in any sense true, as he tells in the preface to the *Romancero*, that "the high clerisy of atheism pronounced its anathema" over him—that is to say, that former friends denounced him as a weak turncoat—it needed only the publication of his Life and Letters to enable freethinkers to take an entirely sympathetic view of his case, which may serve as a supreme example of "the martyrdom of man." On the whole question see Strodtmann, as cited, ii, 372 sq., and the *Geständnisse*, which should be compared with the earlier written fragments of *Briefe über Deutschland* (*Werke*, iii, 119), where there are some significant variations in statements of fact.

Since Heine, German *belles lettres* has hardly been a first-rate influence in Europe; but some of the leading novelists, as AUERBACH and HEYSE, are well known to have shared in the rational philosophy of their age; and the Christianity of Wagner, whose precarious support to the cause of faith has been welcomed chiefly by its heteroclite adherents, counts for nothing in the critical scale.[1]

12. But perhaps the most considerable evidence, in *belles lettres*, of the predominance of rationalism in modern Europe is to be found in the literary history of the Scandinavian States and Russia. The Russian development indeed had gone far ere the modern Scandinavian literatures had well begun. Already in the first quarter of the century the poet Poushkine was an avowed heretic ; and Gogol even let his art suffer from his preoccupations with the new humanitarian ideas ; while the critic BIELINSKY, classed by Tourguenief as the Lessing of Russia,[2] was pronouncedly rationalistic,[3] as was his contemporary the critic GRANOVSKY,[4] reputed the finest Russian stylist of his day. At this period *belles lettres* stood for every form of intellectual influence in Russia,[5] and all educated thought was moulded by it. The most perfect artistic result is the fiction of the freethinker TOURGUENIEF,[6] the Sophocles of the modern novel. His two great contemporaries, Dostoyevsky and Tolstoy, count indeed for supernaturalism ; but the truly wonderful genius of the former is something apart from his philosophy, which is merely childlike ; and the latter, the least masterly if the most strenuous artist of the three, makes his religious converts in Russia chiefly among the uneducated, and is in any case sharply antagonistic to orthodox Christianity. It does not appear that the younger writer, Potapenko, a fine artist, is orthodox, despite his extremely sympathetic

---

[1] See Ernest Newman's *Study of Wagner*, 1899, p. 390, *note*, as to the vagueness of Wagnerians on the subject.
[2] Tikhomirov, *La Russie*, 2e édit. p. 343.
[3] See Comte de Vogüé's *Le roman russe*, p. 218, as to his propaganda of atheism.
[4] Arnaudo, *Le Nihilisme et les Nihilistes*, French trans. p. 50.
[5] Tikhomirov, p. 344.
[6] " Il [Tourguénief] etait libre-penseur, et détestat l'apparat religieux d'une maniere toute particuliere." I. Pavlovsky, *Souvenirs sur Tourguénief*, 1887, p. 242.

presentment of a superior priest; and the still younger Gorky is an absolute Naturalist.

In the Scandinavian States, again, there are hardly any exceptions to the freethinking tendency among the leading living men of letters. In the person of the abnormal religionist Soren Kierkegaard (1813-1855) a new force of criticism began to stir in Denmark. Setting out as a theologian, Kierkegaard gradually developed, always on quasi-religious lines, into a vehement assailant of conventional Christianity, somewhat in the spirit of Pascal, somewhat in that of Feuerbach, again in that of Ruskin; and in a temper recalling now a Berserker and now a Hebrew prophet. The general effect of his teaching may be gathered from the mass of the work of HENRIK IBSEN, who was his disciple, and in particular from Ibsen's *Brand*, of which the hero is partly modelled on Kierkegaard.[1] Ibsen, though his *Brand* was counted to him for righteousness by the churches, has shown himself a profound naturalist in all his later work; BJORNSON is an active freethinker; the eminent Danish critic, GEORG BRANDES, early avowed himself to the same effect; and his brother, the dramatist, EDWARD BRANDES, was elected to the Danish Parliament in 1881 despite his declaration that he believed in neither the Christian nor the Jewish God. Most of the younger *litterateurs* of Norway and Sweden seem to be of the same cast of thought.

---

[1] See the article "Un Précurseur d'Henrik Ibsen, Soeren Kierkegaard," in the *Revue de Paris*, July 1st, 1901.

Chapter XIX.

THE STATE OF THOUGHT IN THE NATIONS

If it be a sound general principle that freethought is a natural variation which prospers according to the environment, it will follow that where, culture-opportunities being roughly equal, there are differences in the amount of ostensible freethinking, the explanation lies in some of the social conditions. We have seen rationalism, in the sense of a free play of critical reason on traditional creeds, flourish variously in various ages and civilisations according to its opportunities; till in our own day, with a maximum of political freedom, a minimum of priestly power, a maximum of popular culture, and a maximum development of science and special research, there has occurred by far the greatest diffusion and the most thorough cultivation of antisupernaturalist ideas. Yet in some of the most civilised countries countenance is given by the greater part of the newspaper press, and by the machinery of government in general, to the assumption that the doctrine of the Christian churches is still in full possession of the educated intelligence, and that "unbelief" is a noxious weed. This phenomenon is to be explained like any other, after a comparison of the conditions.

§ 1. *Britain and the United States.*

In this country we have noted the natural collusion of the clerical and propertied classes to put down freethought, as a dangerously democratic force, after the French Revolution. Between the positive persecution of the popular forms and the social ostracism of the others, it had come about that up to the middle of the century few writers ventured to avow even a guarded hostility to the current creed.[1] Such proceedings as the persecution of the writers and publishers of heterodox books, and the refusal of copyright to their authors, had a very practical influence. Only after the death of Romilly was it tacitly avowed, by the publication of a deistic prayer found among his papers, that he had had no belief in revelation.[2] Eminent authors who are known to have rejected the Christian creed, as Carlyle and John Mill, avoided any open breach, and received much orthodox approbation. Privately they would speak of the need for speaking out, without speaking out;[3] and Carlyle was so far false to his own doctrine of veracity as even to disparage all who did.[4] Mill, it is true, spoke out to some extent in his latter years, as in his address to the St. Andrews students (1867), when, "in the reception given to the Address, he was most struck by the vociferous applause of the divinity students at the freethought passage. He was privately thanked by others among the hearers for this part."[5] But as the pressure of freethought is always increasing, the total timidity seems to remain much the same, the latest heresy being shunned in its day as was the earlier, which now ranks as orthodoxy. And in the first half of the century displays of courage were rare indeed. Mr. Froude was remarkable for his surrender of the clerical profession after taking orders, in the teeth of a bitter opposition from his family, and further for his publication of a freethinking romance, *The Nemesis of Faith* (1849); but he did not continue an "aggressive" course, and went far to conciliate Anglican orthodoxy by his *History*. Thus the air of fixity was in large part maintained by the

---

[1] See *The Dynamics of Religion*, pp. 191-233, as to the prevailing tone among publicists.
[2] See Brougham's letters in the *Correspondence of Macvey Napier*, 1879, pp. 333-7. Brougham is deeply indignant, not at the fact, but at the indiscreet revelation of it—as also at the similar revelation concerning Pitt (p. 334).
[3] See Professor Bain's *J. S. Mill*, pp. 157, 191.
[4] Cp. Froude's *London Life of Carlyle*, i, 458.
[5] Bain, *J. S. Mill*, p. 128.

educated class, while it was well known privately that educated doubters abounded. On the one hand the bigots held the language of fanaticism, and on the other hand the less bigoted blustered against the braver gainsayers. A professed man of science could write in 1838 that "the new mode of interpreting the Scriptures which has sprung up in Germany is the darkest cloud which lowers upon the horizon of that country.......The Germans have been conducted by some of their teachers to the borders of a precipice, one leap from which will plunge them into deism." He added that in various parts of Europe "the heaviest calamity impending over the whole fabric of society in our time is the lengthening stride of bold skepticism in some parts, and the more stealthy onwards-creeping step of critical cavil in others."[1] Such declamation could terrorise the timid and constrain the prudent in such a society as that of early Victorian England. The prevailing note is struck in Macaulay's description of Charles Blount as "an infidel, and the head of a small school of infidels who were troubled with a morbid desire to make converts."[2] All the while, Macaulay was himself privately "infidel";[3] but he cleared his conscience by thus denouncing those who had the courage of their opinions. In this simple fashion some of the sanest writers in history were complacently put below the level of the commonplace dissemblers who aspersed them ; and the average educated man saw no baseness in the procedure. It was assumed that a sanhedrim of shufflers could make courage ridiculous by calling themselves "the wise"; and it

---

[1] *Germany*, by Bisset Hawkins, M.D., F.R.S., F.R.C.P., Inspector of Prisons, late Professor at King's College, etc., 1838, p 171.

[2] *History*, ch. xix. Student's ed. ii, 411.

[3] Sometimes he gives a clue ; and we find Brougham privately denouncing him for his remark (Essay on *Ranke's History of the Popes*, 6th par.) that to try "without the help of revelation to prove the immortality of man," is vain. "It is next thing to preaching atheism," shouts Brougham (Letter of October 20th, 1840, in *Correspondence of Macvey Napier*, p. 333), who at the same time hotly insisted that Cuvier had made an advance in Natural Theology by proving that there must have been *one* divine interposition after the creation of the world—to create species. (*Id.* p. 337.)

became current doctrine that "the wise man" conceals his opinions when they are unpopular.

> The opinion deliberately expressed in this connection by the late Professor Bain is worth noting :—
>
> "It can at least be clearly seen what was the motive of Carlyle's perplexing style of composition. We now know what his opinions were when he began to write, and that to express them would have been fatal to his success; yet he was not a man to indulge in rank hypocrisy. He accordingly adopted a studied and ambiguous phraseology, which for long imposed upon the religious public, who put their own interpretation upon his mystical utterances, and gave him the benefit of any doubt. In the *Life of Sterling* he threw off the mask, but still was not taken at his word. Had there been a perfect tolerance of all opinions, he would have begun as he ended; and his strain of composition, while still mystical and high-flown, would never have been identified with our national orthodoxy.
>
> "I have grave doubts as to whether we possess Macaulay's real opinions on religion. His way of dealing with the subject is so like the hedging of an unbeliever that, without some good assurance to the contrary, I must include him also among the imitators of Aristotle's 'caution.' Some future critic will devote himself, like Professor Mohl, to expounding his ambiguous utterances.
>
> "When Sir Charles Lyell brought out his *Antiquity of Man*, he too was cautious. Knowing the dangers of his footing, he abstained from giving an estimate of the extension of time required by the evidences of human remains. Society in London, however, would not put up with this reticence, and he had to disclose at dinner parties what he had withheld from the public - namely, that in his opinion the duration of man could not be less than fifty thousand years" (*Practical Essays*, 1884, pp. 274-5).

In this way honest and narrow-minded believers were trained to suppose that their views were triumphant over all attacks,[1] and to see in "infidelity" a disease of an ill-informed past; and as the church had really gained in conventional culture as well as in wealth and prestige in the period of reaction, the power of mere convention to override ideas was still enormous. Above all, social

---

[1] In 1830, for instance, we find a Scottish episcopal D.D. writing that "Infidelity has had its day; it, depend upon it, will never be revived— NO MAN OF GENIUS WILL EVER WRITE ANOTHER WORD IN ITS SUPPORT." Morehead, *Dialogues on Natural and Revealed Religion*, p. 266.

and religious prejudices were aided by the vast leverage of economic interest throughout a thoroughly commercialised community. This holds good alongside of a clear balance of literary power on the side of unbelief. The commercial history of England and America throughout the century has been broadly one of ever-increasing competition in all classes; and to avow an "unpopular" view is in general to stand at a serious disadvantage in business and professional life. Even of the known rationalists among the serious writers of the latter half of the century, many have perforce confined themselves to pure science or scholarly research; and others have either held safe official posts or enjoyed private means.

In one or other of these classes stand such names as those of GROTE, the two MILLS, Professors BAIN, HUXLEY, TYNDALL, and CLIFFORD, DARWIN, ARNOLD, F. W. NEWMAN, LEWES, and in a measure SPENCER, who, however, long felt the pinch of unpopularity severely enough. Detached men of letters like Mr. Morley and Sir Leslie Stephen, while taking up freethinking positions, have perhaps not been uninfluenced by the hostile environment. In any case it is perfectly well known to all freethinkers that there are many of their way of thinking on all hands who dare not publicly declare themselves. And whereas religious sects, if at all numerous, can in large measure indemnify themselves against others by holding together, rationalists are under the difficulty that their special opinions do not call for institution-making save of the most disinterested kind. Every religionist is under some religious compulsion from his own creed to worship; and every priest preaches for the institutions by which he lives. We have seen how impossible it is to set up freethinking *institutions* in a primitive society. The difficulty is still great, though different, in a commercial community, where even among freethinkers the disinterested concern for the diffusion of truth is constantly dulled by the social struggle for existence; while, moreover, the instructed man's dislike of sectarianism is a further dissuasive from action that he thinks might tend to further it. And as regards the main source of most religious endowments, bequest by will, freethought is in this country absolutely interdicted from any save circuitous provision. Not till the present President of the National Secular Society discovered that bequests to a registered company escape the old law could any such provision be made.[1] Various bequests for specifically freethinking purposes have been quashed under the Blasphemy Laws; and all the while ingenuous Christians have taunted freethinkers with their lack of sectarian institutions.

Thus, educated reason standing aloof or inhibited, while educated self-interest conspires with ignorance, an enormous revenue is annually devoted to the maintenance of beliefs not held by multitudes of the clergy themselves; and the propaganda of freethought, down till the other day, has rested with the "quixotic" few. Nearly every freethinking writer is still advised by prudent friends to give up such unprofitable work; and the very desire to wield an influence for good, as in politics, makes many rationalists conceal the opinions which they know would restrict their audience. Only great orators, as Bradlaugh and Ingersoll, can make a good income by platform propaganda; and Bradlaugh was prematurely worn out by the atrocious burdens laid upon him in his Parliamentary struggle, with the active connivance of many Conservative partisans who believed no more than he.

It would thus appear that until the "social problem" is solved in some fashion which shall make intellectual honesty a much safer thing than at present, the profession of supernaturalism and the vogue of real superstition among the mass of the less intelligent of all classes are likely to continue in many communities alongside of

[1] The amount of propaganda that has been achieved by the Rationalist Press Association in the few years of its existence is a proof of the importance of the economic basis.

the fullest scientific disproof of the beliefs in question. Any creed whatever can subsist under the modern system of endowments. Had a church of Isis and Osiris by any chance survived with good endowments through the ages of Christian destruction and confiscation of other systems, it could to-day find educated priests and adherents in such a society as ours. The general faculty for consistent thought is at best not great. Scientific rationalists, finding excuses for their official conformities to the current creeds, argue privately that all that is needed is non-contentiously to put true doctrines in circulation —that without argument they must needs expel the false. All modern culture-history proves this to be a fallacy. Even gifted brains can harbour childish errors on the side on which they are undeveloped. We need not go back to Faraday to find scientific men clinging to the religion of their nurseries. An eminent mathematician, entirely unqualified in moral fields, pays tribute to Paley; and the average churchgoer straightway claims that "science" is with him. To say nothing of the habitual employment of the Bible in the churches, the vogue of such a book as the late Mr. Henry Drummond's *Natural Law in the Spiritual World* is a sufficient proof of the general capacity for digesting the grossest inconsistencies in science. It was possible for multitudes of people to suppose that Darwin, buried as he was in Westminster Abbey, had died a Christian, until it was shown by his letters that he had definitely abandoned theism. On the other hand, it takes a rare combination of intellectual power, moral courage, and official freedom to permit of such a directly rationalistic propaganda as was carried on by the late Professor CLIFFORD, or even such as has been accomplished by President ANDREW WHITE in America under the comparatively popular profession of deism. It was only in his leisured latter years that Professor HUXLEY carried on a general conflict with orthodoxy. In middle age he frequently covered himself by attacks on professed freethinkers; and he did more than any other man of his time to conserve the Bible as a school manual by his politic panegyric of it in that aspect at a time when bolder rationalists were striving to get it excluded from the State schools.[1]

The survival of theism itself, as well as the common preference in England of such a term as "agnosticism" to either "naturalism" or "atheism," is in part a psychological result of social pressure. Mr. Spencer in his earlier works used the language of deism,[2] at a time when Comte had discarded it; and he and many other rationalists have later made a serious stand for their property in the word "religion," though the reasons urged are as applicable to the word "God," and even in part to "Christ." Draper and White in the United States, again, and Buckle and others in England, have shown how some elements of essentially emotional and traditionary supernaturalism, in the shape of theism, can be long clung to by able men engaged in rationalistic and even in anti-theological argument. The opposition still made by some English Comtists to straightforward freethinking propaganda illustrates the same normal tendency. In the English-speaking countries the coinage of the term "agnostic," though objected to by some Comtists, is largely on all fours with their own practice. In France and Italy, freethinkers do not find it necessary to refine on the term "atheist" and draw paralogistic distinctions; the necessity, when felt, is the psychological product of special social conditions.

In the United States, with all the relative freedom of social and political life, the pressure against open freethought, before noted as subsisting in the early part of the nineteenth century, is perhaps still as great as in Britain. In the middle decades of the century the conditions had been so little changed that after the death of

[1] I am informed on good authority that in later life Huxley changed his views on the subject. He had abundant cause. As early as 1879 he is found complaining (pref. to Eng. trans. of Haeckel's *Freedom in Science and Teaching*, p. xvii) of the mass of "falsities at present foisted upon the young in the name of the church."

[2] E.g., the *Education*, small ed. pp. 41, 155.

President LINCOLN, who was certainly a non-Christian deist, and an agnostic deist at that,[1] it was sought to be established that he was latterly orthodox. In his presidential campaign of 1860 he escaped attack on his opinions simply because his opponent, Stephen A. Douglas, was likewise an unbeliever.[2] The great negro orator, FREDERICK DOUGLAS, was as heterodox as Lincoln.[3] It is even alleged that President Grant[4] was of the same cast of opinion. Such is the general drift of intelligent thought in the United States, from Washington onwards; and still the social conditions impose on public men the burden of concealment, while popular history is garbled for the same reasons. Despite the great propagandist power of the late Colonel Ingersoll, therefore, American freethought remains dependent largely on struggling organisations and journals,[5] and its special literature is rather of the popularising than of the scholarly order. Nowhere else has every new advance of rationalistic science been more angrily opposed by the priesthood; because nowhere is the ordinary prejudice of the priest more voluble or better-bottomed in self-complacency. As late as 1891 the Methodist Bishop Keener delivered a ridiculous attack on the evolution theory before the Œcumenical Council of Methodism at Washington, declaring that it had been utterly refuted by a certain "wonderful deposit of the Ashley beds."[6] Various professors in ecclesiastical colleges have been driven from their posts for accepting in turn the discoveries of geology, biology, and the "higher criticism" — for instance, Woodrow of Columbia, South Carolina; Toy of Louisville; Winchell of Vanderbilt University; and more than one professor in the American college at Beyrout.[7] In

[1] Cp. Lamon's *Life of Lincoln*, and J. B. Remsburg's *Abraham Lincoln: Was He a Christian?* (New York, 1893.)
[2] Remsburg, pp. 318-19.   [3] Personal information.
[4] Remsburg, p. 324.
[5] Of these the New York *Truthseeker* has been the most energetic and successful.
[6] White, *Warfare*, i, 81.   [7] *Id.* i, 84, 86, 314, 317, 318.

every one of the three former cases, it is true, the denounced professor has been called to a better chair; and, as before mentioned, latterly some of the more liberal clergy have even commercially exploited the higher criticism by producing the " Rainbow Bible." In England, still more recently, the demand raised by some zealots for the dismissal of so distinguished a scholar as Professor Cheyne from his chair, on the score of his heresy, has come to nothing. But the demand has collapsed rather because of the impossibility of drawing a line which shall not exclude many more teachers of less advanced views, and impeach many of the clergy of all grades, than because of any learning of the lesson of tolerance by men who themselves to-day hold opinions that were viewed with horror a generation ago.

From these surveys there emerges the general result that in the British Islands and the United States the avowal of unbelief and the disinterested effort to enlighten others are relatively more common among the hand-workers, whose incomes are not as a rule affected thereby, than among the middle classes, where the economic motive is strong, and the upper, where the social motive specially operates. Wealthy Conservatives never publicly avow unbelief; yet it is well known that many disbelieve. In the House of Commons and the American Congress there are probably scores of such on both sides. It is easy to blame them; as it is easy to blame the many clergymen who hold office without conviction. But such insincerities, in which laymen so abundantly share, are at worst on the same ethical footing as the endless immoralities of ordinary commerce; the clergy being under economic pressure like other men. They have further the justification that in most cases they have in youth been led or pushed into the clerical career by elders who did nothing to enlighten them on the difficulties they were bound to meet with in later life. Nor is it finally desirable, from any point of view, that all the more reasonable minds should be eliminated from the churches, leaving only the most ignorant, the most unteachable, and the most intolerant to misguide the more ignorant laity. In any case, the church bids fair to subsist by the adherence of large numbers of men who do not hold its creed. Of recent years some of the Ethical Societies have sought to carry on a non-theological teaching that guards against being anti-theological. Such a policy escapes a number of the ordinary social and economic obstacles, while incurring the special difficulties involved in the application of ethics to the social problem. It does not operate, however, as a dissolvent of theology save in so far as theology is incidentally criticised; at least, the fact that the same view of ethics was proclaimed nearly three hundred years ago by Charron, and nearly two hundred years ago in some of the British churches, makes it seem unlikely that its simple affirmation can undermine the economic bases of supernaturalism.

In sum, other things being equal, open freethought is least common where commercialism is most stringent, and in communities where social pressure is most easily felt. In Scotland, where the culture-movement of the eighteenth century was succeeded in the nineteenth by a pietistic reaction and a new ecclesiastical ferment and schism, the intellectual life is less free than in England. It was so when the clergy proposed to sit in judgment on Hume in 1756; it was emphatically so when Buckle summed up Scotch life forty years ago; it is so to-day, when the economic conditions send to England and the colonies most of the innovating elements, leaving the rival churches in undisturbed possession, with their numerous rationalistic clergy afraid to declare themselves against the conservative mass. An important advance, indeed, has lately been forced upon the Scottish churches by the unexpected sequel of the amalgamation of the Free and United Presbyterian churches. This was resented by a small section of the former, partly on the ground that they adhered to the original polity of the Free Church, which the majority had abandoned; partly in resentment of the proclivities of a number of the innovating clergy to the higher criticism. When the Free Church was established in 1843, by secession from the State Church, it still affirmed the duty of the State to maintain *a* church, though refusing to accept certain of the conditions then enforced. Latterly the great majority of its members have accepted the voluntary basis and declared for disestablishment; whence the amalgamation with the voluntary church formerly named the United Presbyterian. It is probable that the ecclesiastico-political objection to this course weighed much less with the recalcitrant minority than did their objection to the new theology they saw gaining ground among the modernisers. Bringing an action at law against the majority, they won it on appeal to the House of Lords, and were accordingly given possession of the whole former property of the Free Church. The decision being an outrage on the national sense of justice, there became necessary a legislative Act of relief (1905), which, in restoring the bulk of the property to the majority, provided that their organisation should be collectively free to modify its principles and formulas at will. On the introduction of this measure the leading clergy of the Establishment claimed a similar power for their church, which a Conservative Parliament gave, foreseeing that a church which could not modify its creed would be intellectually discredited in comparison with one which could. The creeds of the Scottish churches are thus at present in the melting-pot. It is avowed that almost no minister now accepts the Westminster Confession of Faith; and there is an edifying uncertainty as to what is really believed all round. Under such circumstances, though the later developments of rationalism are still scouted by those who accept the earlier, orthodoxy is unquestionably weakened; and it is confessed that the strife between the " Free " sections, accompanied as it finally was by some unseemly disturbances, has been " injurious to religion."

In the United States, sheer preoccupation with business, and lack of leisure, counteract in a measure the relative advantage of social freedom ; and while culture is much more widely diffused than in England, it remains on the whole less radical in the "educated" classes so-called. So far as it is possible to make a quantitative estimate, it may be said that in the more densely populated parts of the States there is less of studious freethinking because there is less leisure than in England ; but that in the Western States there is a relative superiority, class for class, because of the special freedom of the conditions and the independent character of many of the immigrants who constitute the new populations.[1]

In the Australasian colonies, again, there is some such relative superiority in freedom as is seen in the American West, and for similar reasons. In New Zealand, prominent statesmen, as Sir ROBERT BALLANCE and Mr. JOHN STOUT, have held office despite their avowed freethinking ; and in Australia a popular freethought journal has subsisted for over twenty years. But there too the commercial environment and the ecclesiastical basis of endowment tell adversely.

From the fact that in New England the supremacy appears to be passing from Unitarianism to Episcopalianism, it may be inferred that the more religiously biassed types in the former sect tend to gravitate to the more emotional worship, and the more rationalistic to withdraw; though the economic interest of the Unitarian clergy conserves their institutions. In England is seen the analogous phenomenon of the advance of Romanist ritualism in the Church of England. While the more emotional and unintellectual believers thus zealously promote what may be termed the most religious form of religion, there is a prospect that the many semi-rational conformists will be in part driven to a more rationalist

---

[1] This view is not inconsistent with the fact that popular forms of credulity are also found specially flourishing in the West. Cp. Bryce, *The American Commonwealth*, 3rd ed. ii, 832–3.

attitude; since, save for the certainly great power of the purse—seen in the outward collapse of the Tractarian movement on Newman's conversion—Anglican moderation is as powerless against ritualism as is modern Protestantism against Catholicism in general. For the rest, all the forces of religious conservatism in commercial communities are backed by the economic interest of the general newspaper press, wherein multitudes of unbelieving journalists perforce treat orthodoxy as being what it claims to be, and at best describe their own opinions as " peculiar " when openly avowed by public men. The determining force is revenue, which depends on advertisements, which depend on circulation. For lack of these bases freethinking journals, even when aiming at comparative popularity, must be relatively expensive. In the United States the habitual freedom of the newspapers allows of more fairplay to avowed freethought; but the main economic forces are similar. Thus on every ground the organised forms of freethought are restricted and apparently uninfluential in comparison with the known amount of rationalism, which nevertheless quietly increases from decade to decade; so that within a generation the intellectual balance has shifted, till the "sensations" of serious literature are no longer produced by attacks on the popular creed, but by the few noteworthy attempts to justify it.

This last phenomenon seems decisively significant as to the real state of opinion among educated people, under all the conformities of the commercial system. The popular works of Mr. Drummond, Mr. Benjamin Kidd, and Mr. A. J. Balfour are the most prominent pleas for Christianity put forth in England in the past twenty years. The first was recognised even by many theologians as a tissue of fallacy; the second (*Social Evolution*) is a suicidal formula of professed irrationalism; and the third (*The Foundations of Belief*) is a more skilful revival of the old resort to skepticism, so often and so vainly employed by apologists in the past.

Meanwhile the few remaining churchmen of high literary standing, as the late Bishop Stubbs and the late Bishop Creighton, rank as simple historians, not as thinkers ; and the apologetic labours of the churches in general range between respectable reiterations of Paley and a popular traffic in " Christian Evidences " that is beneath criticism.

Meanwhile, new forces of advance assert themselves. Under all the social stress set up by orthodoxy, women are found in ever-increasing numbers giving up the faith, and even doing effective rationalist propaganda. Thus HARRIET MARTINEAU and GEORGE ELIOT (Marian Evans) are specially significant names in the history of modern English freethought. The popularisation of the Positive Philosophy by the former, and the translations of Strauss and Feuerbach by the latter, were services as workmanlike as any done by their male contemporaries ; and though the reversion of Mrs. BESANT to mysticism in the form of Theosophy was a chagrin to many, it could not undo the work she had done as a rationalist teacher.[1] Even in the time of persecution, in the first half of the century, women did unflinching service to the ostracised cause. The second wife of Richard Carlile was his worthy helpmate ; and FRANCES WRIGHT (Madame D'Arusmont) was in the front of all the rational and ethical[2] propaganda of her time (1795-1852).

§ 2. *The Catholic Countries.*

As already noted, there prevails in the Catholic countries a more general and a more direct division between faith and rationalism than usually exists under Protestantism, where the possibilities of gradation and

[1] The argument, sometimes heard, that such a reversion, and such recurrences of religious emotion as may be noted in the latter years of George Eliot, point to a special and permanent unfitness for the rationalist life among women, is worth notice only for the sake of pointing to the quite contrary conclusion deducible from the case of Miss Martineau.
[2] " She bought 2,000 acres in Tennessee, and peopled them with slave families she purchased and redeemed " (Wheeler, *Biog. Dict.*).

adjustment, as well as the admission of the laity to a share in church administration, moderate matters. The very stress of papalism, accordingly, generates an opposing energy. In Italy, as elsewhere, the reaction after the French Revolution, especially after 1815, was very powerful, and clericalism flourished to a disastrous degree. All criticism of Catholicism was a penal offence ; and in the kingdom of Naples alone, in 1825, there were 27,612 priests, 8,455 monks, 8,185 nuns, 20 archbishops, and 73 bishops, though in 1807 the French influence had caused the dissolution of some 250 convents.[1] If, accordingly, the mind of Italy was to survive, it must be by the assimilation of the culture of freer States ; and this culture, reinforced by the writings of Leopardi, generated a new intellectual life, which was a main factor in the achievement of Italian liberation from Austrian rule. This association of political liberalism with heresy seems to be natural alike in Catholic countries and in Russia, where the Church-and-State principle works with only a difference in the positions of the partners. Thus Mazzini was a simple theist ; Garibaldi held with Renan ;[2] and Gambetta was a Voltairean. In the Catholic countries, too, commercialism has come later on the scene, and is much less developed than in England and America ; so that social pressure tells only partially on the side of the church. The result is that as a rule in France and Italy, and to a large extent also in Spain, educated men are unbelievers, and atheism is no bar to political influence. One of the most distinguished of Italian scholars, Professor A. DE GUBERNATIS, has in his *Letture sopra la mitologia vedica* (1874) explicitly treated the Christian legend as a myth like another ; and in France to-day prominent scholars, politicians, and thinkers freely proclaim their adherence to the movement of freethought. Not only has the legislature in the past year made an end of the old

[1] Dr. Ramage, *Nooks and Bye-Ways of Italy*, 1868, pp. 76, 105-113. Ramage describes the helplessness of the better minds before 1830.
[2] See Mr. Morley's *Life of Gladstone*, 1903, ii, 110-111.

connection between Church and State, but for many years the Paris Municipal Council has been a predominantly freethinking body. After a period in which such teachers as Michelet and Renan could suffer suspension, university teaching in all three countries is substantially open, and professors can freely indicate their opinions.

On the other hand, the higher life of all Catholic countries suffers from the common assumption that a religion of prayer and penance is a necessity for women. Women there are accordingly found as a rule on the side of faith and churchgoing : and it results that in all social and domestic matters in which they are intimately concerned the church has still a strong footing. Baptisms, marriages, and funerals are in the great majority of cases religious functions, the men shrugging their shoulders and making no general effort to enlighten their wives and daughters.[1] In this state of things there is as constant an element of loss to progress as takes place in our own society through the organised activity of the churches ; a continual reproduction of artificial ignorance, so to speak, going on in both cases. A reform in the education and status of women is therefore as peculiarly necessary to the advance of freethought in the Catholic countries as is a correction of commercialist conditions in ours. English and American experience goes to show that women under fair conditions can live the rationalist life as well as men, their relapses to mysticism being no more frequent than those of men, and much less frequent than their abandonment of supernaturalist beliefs. Indeed, there have been cases enough of freethinking educated women in France and Italy to show the error of the conventional assumption among the other sex. It is so far satisfactory that the Socialist movement, which gains ground among all the "Latin" peoples, makes substantially for the more

[1] The case of M. Littré, whose family pressed him to recant on his deathbed and destroyed his papers after his death, is a painful illustration of the frequent outcome of such a policy.

equal culture of the sexes, as against the contrary policy of the church.

§ 3. *Germany.*

Alongside of the inveterate rationalism of modern Germany, a no less inveterate bureaucratism preserves a certain official conformity to religion. University freedom does not extend to open and direct criticism of the orthodox creed.[1] On the other hand, the applause won by Virchow in 1877 on his declaration against the doctrine of evolution, and the tactic resorted to by him in putting upon that doctrine the responsibility of Socialist violence, are instances of the normal operation of the lower motives against freedom in scientific teaching.[2] The pressure operates in other spheres in Germany, especially under such a regimen as the present. Men who never go to church save on official occasions, and who have absolutely no belief in the church's doctrine, nevertheless remain nominally its adherents;[3] and the Press laws make it peculiarly difficult to reach the common people with freethinking literature, save through Socialist channels. Thus the Catholic Church is perhaps nowhere—save in Ireland and the United States—more practically influential than in nominally "Protestant" Germany, where it wields a compact vote of a hundred or more in the Reichstag, and can generally count on well-filled churches as beside the half-empty temples of Protestantism.

Another circumstance partly favourable to reaction is the simple maintenance of all the old theological chairs in the universities. As the field of scientific work widens, and increasing commerce raises the social standard of comfort, men of original intellectual power

---

[1] It is recorded by the friends of UEBERWEG, author of the fairest of modern histories of philosophy, that he was an atheist and materialist. But this could only here and there be divined from his writing.

[2] See Haeckel's *Freedom in Science and Teaching*, Eng. trans. with pref. by Huxley, 1879, pp. xix, xxv, xxvii, 89-90; and Clifford.

[3] Büchner, for straightforwardly renouncing his connection with the State Church, was blamed by many who held his philosophic opinions.

grow less apt to devote themselves to theological pursuits even under the comparatively free conditions which so long kept German Biblical scholarship far above that of other countries. It can hardly be said that men of the mental calibre of Strauss, Baur, Volkmar, and Wellhausen continue to arise among the specialists in their studies. Harnack, the most prominent German Biblical scholar of our day, despite his great learning, creates no such impression of originality and insight, and, though latterly forced forward by more independent minds, exhibits often a very uncritical orthodoxy. Thus it is *a priori* possible enough that the orthodox reactions so often claimed have actually occurred, in the sense that the experts have reverted to a prior type. A scientifically-minded "theologian" in Germany has now little official scope for his faculty save in the analysis of the Hebrew Sacred Books and the New Testament documents as such ; and this has there been on the whole very well done ; but there is a limit to the attraction of such studies for minds of a modern cast. Thus there is always a chance that chairs will be filled by men of another type.[1]

Meanwhile, under the sounder moral and economic conditions of the life of the proletariate, straightforward rationalism, as apart from propaganda, is becoming more and more the rule. A Protestant pastor some years ago made an investigation into the state of religious opinion among the working Socialists of some provincial towns and rural districts, and found everywhere a determined attitude of rationalism. The formula of the Social Democrats, " Religion is a private matter," he bitterly perceives to carry the implication " a private matter for the fools"; and while he holds that the belief in a speedy collapse of the Christian religion is latterly less common than formerly among the upper and middle classes, he complains that the Socialists are

[1] Cp. Zeller's pref. to his work on *The Acts of the Apostles*, Eng. trans. 1875, i, 89, as to the tendency of German Protestantism to stagnate in " Byzantine conditions."

not similarly enlightened.[1] Bebel's drastic teaching as to the economic and social conditions of the rise of Christianity,[2] and the materialistic theory of history set forth by Marx and Engels, he finds generally accepted. Not only do most of the party leaders declare themselves to be without religion, but those who do not so declare themselves are so no less.[3] Nor is the unbelief a mere sequel to the Socialism : often the development is the other way.[4] The opinion is almost universal, further, that the clergy in general do not believe what they teach.[5] Atheists are numerous among the peasantry ; more numerous among the workers in the provincial towns ; and still more numerous in the large towns ;[6] and while many take a sympathetic view of Jesus as a man and teacher, not a few deny his historic existence[7] —a view set forth in non-Socialist circles also.[8]

§ 4. *Russia and the Scandinavian States.*

Under the widely-different political conditions in Russia and the Scandinavian States, it is the more significant that in all alike rationalism is in the ascendant among the educated classes. In Norway the latter, perhaps, include a larger proportion of working people than can be so classed even in Germany ; and rationalism is relatively hopeful, though social freedom is still far from perfect. It is the old story of toleration for a dangerously well-placed freethought, and intolerance for that which reaches the common people. The Scandinavian churches, however, though backward and bigoted, have no such relative wealth and power as the English, or even the American ; and the intellectual balance, as already noted, is distinctly on the freethought side, though in Sweden, of late years, there is

[1] Pastor W. Studemund, *Der moderne Unglaube in den unteren Ständen*, 1901, pp. 17, 21.
[2] *Glossen zu Yves Guyot's und Sigismund Lacroix's "Die wahre Gestalt des Christentums."*
[3] Studemund, p. 22.   [4] *Id.* p. 23.   [5] *Id.* p. 27.   [6] *Id.* pp. 37-38.
[7] *Id.* pp. 40-42. Cp. p. 43. Pastor Studemund cites other inquirers, notably Rade, Gebhardt, Lorenz, and Dietzgen, all to the same effect.
[8] *E.g.*, Pastor A. Kalthoff's *Was wissen wir von Jesus?* 1904.

seen the common tendency to a slackening in the freethought attack now that the old orthodoxy is undermined and shaken. There, as elsewhere, the stress of intellectual strife runs for the time rather to social than to religious problems ; and commercialism dulls the edge of educative zeal. But the transition from faith to reason cannot be undone. It would be well if the rationalist temper could so far assert itself as to check the unhappy racial jealousies of the three Scandinavian peoples, and discredit their irrationalist belief in fundamental differences of " national character " among them. But that problem, like those of industry and social structure, is still to solve, for them as for other races.

In Russia, rationalism has before it the still harder task of transmuting a system of tyranny into one of self-government. In no European country, perhaps, is rationalism more general among the educated classes ; and in none is there a greater mass of popular ignorance.[1] The popular icon-worship in Moscow can hardly be paralleled outside of Asia. On the other hand, the aristocracy became Voltairean in the eighteenth century, and has remained more or less incredulous since, though it now joins hands with the church ; while the democratic movement, in its various phases of socialism, constitutionalism, and Nihilism, has been markedly antireligious since the second quarter of the century.[2] Subsidiary revivals of mysticism, such as are chronicled in other countries, are of course to be seen in Russia ; but the instructed class, the *intelliguentia*, is essentially naturalistic in its cast of thought. This state of things subsists despite the readiness of the government to suppress the slightest sign of official heterodoxy in the universities.[3] The struggle is thus substantially between

---

[1] "The people in the country do not read ; in the towns they read little. The journals are little circulated. In Russia one never sees a cabman, an artisan, a labourer reading a newspaper" (Ivan Strannik, *La pensée russe contemporaine*, 1903, p. 5).

[2] Cp. E. Lavigne, *Introduction a l'histoire du nihilisme russe*, 1880, pp. 149, 161, 224 ; Arnaudo, *Le Nihilisme*, French trans. pp. 37, 58, 61, 63, 77, 86, etc. ; Tikhomirov, *La Russie*, p. 290.

[3] Tikhomirov, *La Russie*, pp. 325-6, 338-9.

the spirit of freedom and that of despotism; and the fortunes of freethought will go with the former. Were Russia an isolated community, both alike might be strangled by the superior brute force of the autocracy, resting on the loyalty of the ignorant mass; but the unavoidable contact of surrounding civilisations seems to make such suppression impossible. Such was the critical forecast in the closing years of the nineteenth century. In 1906 the prediction can be made with a new confidence.

§ 5. *Modern Jewry.*

In the culture-life of the dispersed Jews, in the modern period, there is probably as much variety of credence in regard to religion as occurs in the life of Christendom so called. Such names as those of Spinoza, Jacobi, Moses Mendelssohn, Heine, and Karl Marx tell sufficiently of Jewish service to freethought; and each one of these must have had many disciples of his own race. Deism among the educated Jews of Germany in the eighteenth century was probably common.[1] The famous Rabbi Elijah of Wilna (d. 1797), entitled the Gaon, "the great one," set up a movement of relatively rationalistic pietism which led to the establishment in 1803 of a Rabbinical college at Walosin, which has flourished ever since, and had in 1888 no fewer than 400 students, among whom goes on a certain amount of independent study.[2] In the freer world outside, critical thought has asserted itself within the pale of orthodox Judaism; witness such a writer as Nachman Krochmal (1785–1840), whose posthumous *Guide to the Perplexed of the Time* (1851), though not a scientific work, is ethically and philosophically in advance of the orthodox Judaism of its age. Of Krochmal it has been said that he "was inspired in his work by the study of Hegel, just as Maimonides

---

[1] Cp. Schechter, *Studies in Judaism*, 1896, pp. 59, 71. Schechter writes with a marked Judaic prejudice.
[2] *Id.* pp. 117–118.

had been by the study of Aristotle."[1] The result is only a liberalising of Jewish orthodoxy in the light of historic study,[2] such as went on among Christians in the same period; but it is thus a stepping-stone to further science.

To-day, educated Jewry is divided in somewhat the same proportions as Christendom into absolute rationalists and liberal and fanatical believers; and representatives of all three types, of different social grades, may be found among the Zionists, whose movement for the acquisition of a new racial home has attracted so much attention and sympathy in recent years. Whether or not that movement attains to any decisive political success, Judaism clearly cannot escape the solvent influences which affect all European opinion. As in the case of the Christian church, the synagogue in the centres of culture keeps the formal adherence of some who no longer think on its plane; but while attempts are made from time to time to set up more rationalistic institutions for Jews with the modern bias, the general tendency is to a division between devotees of the old forms and those who have decided to live by reason.

§ 6. *The Oriental Civilisations.*

We have already seen, in discussing the culture histories of India, China, and Moslem Persia, how ancient elements of rationalism continue to germinate more or less obscurely in the unpropitious soils of Asiatic life. Ignorance is in most oriental countries too immensely preponderant to permit of any other species of survival. But sociology, while recognising the vast obstacles to the higher life presented by conditions which with a fatal facility multiply the lower, can set no limit to the possibilities of upward evolution. The case of Japan is a sufficient rebuke to the thoughtless iterators of the formula of the "unprogressiveness

---

[1] Zunz, cited by Schechter, p. 79.
[2] Whence Krochmal is termed the Father of Jewish Science. *Id.* p. 81.

of the East." While a cheerfully superstitious religion is there still normal among the mass, the transformation of the political ideals and practice of the nation under the influence of European example is so great as to be unparalleled in human history; and it has inevitably involved the substitution of rationalism for supernaturalism among the great majority of the educated younger generation. The late Yukichi Fukuzawa, who did more than any other man to prepare the Japanese mind for the great transformation effected in his time, was spontaneously a freethinker from his childhood;[1] and through a long life of devoted teaching he trained thousands to a naturalist way of thought. That they should revert to Christian or native orthodoxy seems as impossible as such an evolution is seen to be in educated Hindostan, where the higher orders of intelligence are probably not relatively more common than among the Japanese. The final question, there as everywhere, is one of social reconstruction and organisation; and in the enormous population of China the problem, though very different in degree of imminence, is the same in kind. Perhaps the most hopeful consideration of all is that of the ever-increasing inter-communication which makes European and American progress tend in every succeeding generation to tell more and more on Asiatic life.

As to Japan, Professor B. H. Chamberlain, a writer with irrationalist leanings, pronounces that the Japanese "now bow down before the shrine of Herbert Spencer" (*Things Japanese*, 3rd ed. 1898, p. 321. Cp. *Religious Systems of the World*, 3rd ed. p. 103), proceeding in another connection (p. 352) to describe them as *essentially* an undevotional people. Such a judgment somewhat shakes trust. The Japanese people in the past have exhibited the amount of superstition normal in their culture stage (cp. the *Voyages de C. P. Thunberg au Japon*, French trans. 1796, iii, 206); and in our own day they differ from Western peoples on this side merely in respect of their greater general serenity of temperament. There were in Japan in 1894 no fewer than 71,831 Buddhist

[1] *A Life of Mr. Yukichi Fukuzawa*, by Asataro Miyamori, revised by Professor E. H. Vickers, Tokyo, 1902, pp. 9-10.

temples, and 190,803 Shinto temples and shrines; and the largest temple of all, costing "several million dollars," was built in the last dozen years of the nineteenth century. To the larger shrines there are habitual pilgrimages, the numbers annually visiting one leading Buddhist shrine reaching from 200,000 to 250,000, while at the Shinto shrine of Kompira the pilgrims are said to number about 900,000 each year. (See *The Evolution of the Japanese*, 1903, by L. Gulick, an American missionary organiser.)

Professor Chamberlain appears to construe "devotional" in the light of his personal conception of true devotion. Yet a Christian observer testifies, of the revivalist sect of Nichirenites, "the Ranters of Buddhism," that "the wildest excesses that seek the mantle of religion in other lands are by them equalled if not excelled" (Griffis, *The Mikado's Empire*, 1876, p. 163); and Professor Chamberlain admits that "the religion of the family binds them [the Japanese in general, including the 'most materialistic'] down in truly sacred bonds"; while another writer, who thinks Christianity desirable for Japan, though he apparently ranks Japanese morals above Christian, declares that in his travels he was much reassured by the superstition of the innkeepers, feeling thankful that his hosts were "not Agnostics or Secularists," but devout believers in future punishments (Tracy, *Rambles through Japan without a Guide*, 1892, pp. 131, 276, etc.).

A third authority with Japanese experience, Professor W. G. Dixon, while noting that "among certain classes in Japan not only religious earnestness but fanaticism and superstition still prevail," decides that "at the same time it remains true that the Japanese are not in the main a very religious people, and that at the present day religion is in lower repute than probably it has ever been in the country's history. Religious indifference is one of the prominent features of new Japan" (*The Land of the Morning*, 1882, p. 517). The reconciliation of these estimates lies in the recognition of the fact that the Japanese populace is religious in very much the same way as those of Italy and England, while the more educated classes are rationalistic, not because of any "essential" incapacity for "devotion," but because of enlightenment, and lack of countervailing social pressure. To the eye of the devotional Protestant, the Catholics of Italy, with their regard to externals, seem "essentially" irreligious; and *vice versa*. Buddhism triumphed over Shintoism in Japan both in ancient and modern times precisely because its lore and ritual make so much more appeal to the devotional sense. (Cp. Chamberlain, pp. 358-362; Dixon, ch. x; *Religious Systems of the World*, pp. 103, 111;

Griffis, p. 166.) But the æsthetically charming cult of the family, with its poetic recognition of ancestral spirits (as to which see Lafcadio Hearn, *Japan : An Attempt at Interpretation*, 1904), seems to hold its ground as well as any.

So universal is sociological like other law, that we find in Japan, among some freethinkers, the same disposition as among some in Europe to decide that religion is necessary for the people. Professor Chamberlain (p. 352) cites Mr. Fukuzawa, "Japan's most representative thinker and educationist," as openly declaring that " It goes without saying that the maintenance of peace and security in society requires a religion. For this purpose any religion will do. I lack a religious nature, and have never believed in any religion. I am thus open to the charge that I am advising others to be religious while I am not so. Yet my conscience does not permit me to clothe myself with religion when I have it not at heart.......Of religions there are several kinds Buddhism, Christianity, and what not. From my standpoint there is no more difference between those than between green tea and black.......See that the stock is well selected and the prices cheap " (*Japan Herald*, September 9th, 1897). Further reflection, marked by equal candour, may lead the pupils of Mr. Fukuzawa to see that nations cannot be led to adore any form of " tea " by the mere assurance of its indispensableness from leaders who confess they never take any. His view is doubtless shared by those priests concerning whom "it may be questioned whether in their fundamental beliefs the more scholarly of the Shinshiu priests differ very widely from the materialistic agnostics of Europe " (Dixon, p. 516). In this state of things the Christian thinks he sees his special opportunity. Professor Dixon writes (p. 518), in the manner of the missionary, that "decaying shrines and broken gods are to be seen everywhere. Not only is there indifference, but there is a rapidly-growing skepticism. ......The masses too are becoming affected by it.......Shintoism and Buddhism are doomed. What is to take their place ?

It must be either Christianity or Atheism. We have the brightest hopes that the former will triumph in the near future......."

The American missionary before cited, Mr Gulick, argues alternately that the educated Japanese are religious and that they are not, meaning that they have "religious instincts," while rejecting current creeds. The so-called religious instinct is in fact simply the spirit of moral and intellectual seriousness. Mr. Gulick's summing-up, as distinct from his theory and forecast, is as follows : " For about three hundred years the intelligence of the nation has been dominated by Confucian thought, which rejects active belief in supra-human beings. The tendency of all persons trained in Confucian classics was towards thoroughgoing skepticism as to divine beings and their relation to this world. For this reason, beyond doubt, has Western agnosticism found so easy an entrance into Japan. *Complete indifference to religion is characteristic of the educated classes of to-day*. Japanese and foreigners, Christians and non-Christians alike, unite in this opinion. The impression usually conveyed by this statement, however, is that agnosticism is a new thing in Japan. In point of fact, the old agnosticism is merely reinforced by the agnosticism of the West" (*The Evolution of the Japanese*, pp. 286–7). This may be taken as broadly accurate. Cp. the author's paper on "Freethought in Japan" in the *Agnostic Annual* for 1906. Professor E. H. Parker notes (*China and Religion*, 1905, p. 263) that "the Japanese in translating Western books are beginning, to the dismay of our missionaries, to leave out all the Christianity that is in them."

The intellectual evolution, however, must depend on the economic and social. Rationalism on any large scale is always a product of culture ; and culture for the mass of the people of Japan has only recently begun. Down till the middle of the nineteenth century nothing more than sporadic freethought existed. Some famous captains were irreverent as to omens,[1] and the great founder of modern feudalism, Iyeyasu, in the seventeenth century, denounced the sacrifices of vassals at graves, and even cited Confucius as ridiculing the burial of effigies in substitution.[2] But, as elsewhere under similar conditions, such displays of originality were confined to the ruling caste.[3] I have seen, indeed, a delightful popular satire, apparently a product of mother-wit, on the methods of popular Buddhist shrine-making; but, supposing it to be genuine and vernacular, it can stand only for that measure of freethought which is never absent from any society not pithed by a long

---

[1] Lafcadio Hearn, *Japan : An Attempt at Interpretation*, 1904, p. 168.
[2] *Id.* p. 313 ; cp. p. 46.
[3] Thus the third emperor of the Ming dynasty in China (1425–1435), referring to the belief in a future life, makes the avowal : " I am fain to sigh with despair when I see that in our own day men are just as superstitious as ever " (Professor E. H. Parker, *China and Religion*, 1905, p. 99).

process of religious tyranny. Old Japan, with its intense feudal discipline and its indurated etiquette, exhibited the social order, the grace, the moral charm, and the intellectual vacuity of a hive of bees. The higher mental life was hardly in evidence ; and the ethical literature of native inspiration is of no importance.[1] To this day the educated Chinese, though lacking in Japanese "efficiency" and devotion to drill of all kinds, are the more freely intellectual in their habits of mind. The Japanese feudal system, indeed, was so immitigably ironbound, so incomparably destructive of individuality in word, thought, and deed, that only in the uncodified life of art and handicraft was any free play of faculty possible. What has happened of late is the rapid and docile assimilation of western science. Another and a necessarily longer step is the independent development of the speculative and critical intelligence ; and in the East, as in the West, this is subject to economic conditions.

A similar generalisation holds good as to the other Oriental civilisations. Analogous developments to those seen in the latter-day Mohammedan world, and equally marked by fluctuation, have been noted in the mental life alike of the non-Mohammedan and the Mohammedan peoples of India ; and at the present day the thought of the relatively small educated class is undoubtedly much affected by the changes going on in that of Europe, and especially of England. The vast Indian masses, however, are far from anything in the nature of critical culture ; and though some system of education for them is probably on the way to establishment,[2] their life must long remain quasi-primitive, mentally as well as physically. Buddhism is theoretically more capable of adaptation to a rationalist view of life than is Christianity ; but its intellectual activities at present seem to tend more towards an "esoteric"

[1] See Hearn, as cited, *passim*.
[2] Cp. Sir F. S. P. Lely, *Suggestions for the Better Governing of India*, 1906, p. 59.

credulity than towards a rational or scientific adjustment to life.

Of the nature of the influence of Buddhism in Burmah, where it has prospered, a vivid and thoughtful account is given in the recent work of H. Fielding, *The Soul of a People*, 1898. At its best, the cult there deifies the Buddha; elsewhere, it is interwoven with aboriginal polytheism and superstition (Davids, *Buddhism*, pp. 207-211 ; Max Müller, *Anthropological Religion*, p. 132).

Within Brahmanism, again, there have been at different times attempts to set up partly naturalistic reforms in religious thought—*e.g.*, that of Chaitanya in the sixteenth century; but these have never been pronouncedly freethinking, and Chaitanya preached a "surrender of all to Krishna," very much in the manner of evangelical Christianity. Finally he has been deified by his followers. (Müller, *Nat. Rel.* p. 100 ; *Phys. Rel.* p. 356.)

More definitely freethinking was the monotheistic cult set up among the Sikhs in the fifteenth century, as the history runs, by Nanak, who had been influenced both by Parsees and by Mohammedans, and whose ethical system repudiated caste. But though Nanak objected to any adoration of himself, he and all his descendants have been virtually deified by his devotees, despite their profession of a theoretically pantheistic creed. (Cp. De la Saussaye, *Manual of the Science of Religion*, Eng. trans. pp. 659-662 ; Müller, *Phys. Rel.* p. 355.) Trumpp (*Die Religion der Sikhs*, 1881, p. 123) tells of other Sikh sects, including one of a markedly atheistic character belonging to the nineteenth century; but all alike seem to sink towards Hinduism.

Similarly among the Jainas, who compare with the Buddhists in their nominal atheism as in their tenderness to animals and in some other respects, there has been decline and compromise ; and their numbers appear steadily to dwindle, though in India they survived while Buddhism disappeared. Cp. De la Saussaye, *Manual,* pp. 557-563; Rev. J. Robson, *Hinduism*, 1874, pp. 80-86 ; Tiele, *Outlines*, p. 141. Finally, the Brahmo-Somaj movement of the present century appears to have come to little in the way of rationalism (Mitchell, *Hinduism*, pp. 224-246 ; De la Saussaye, pp. 669-671 ; Tiele, p. 160).

The principle of the interdependence of the external and the internal life, finally, applies even in the case of Turkey. The notion that Turkish civilisation in Europe is unimprovable, though partly countenanced by despondent thinkers even among the enlightened Turks,[1] has no justification in social science; and though Turkish freethinking has not in general passed the theistic stage,[2] and its spread is grievously hindered by the national religiosity,[3] which the age-long hostility of the Christian States so much tends to intensify, a gradual improvement in the educational and political conditions would suffice to evolve it, according to the observed laws of all civilisation. It may be that a result of the rationalistic evolution in the other European States will be to make them intelligently friendly to such a process, where at present they are either piously malevolent towards the rival creed or merely self-seeking as against each other's influence on Turkish destinies. In any case, it cannot seriously be pretended that the mental life of Christian Greece in modern times has yielded, apart from services to simple scholarship, any better result to the world at large than has that of Turkey. Despite the political freedom of the Christian State, there has thus far occurred there no such general fertilisation by the culture of the rest of Europe as is needed to produce a new intellectual evolution of any importance. The mere geographical isolation of modern Greece from the main currents of European thought and commerce is probably the most retardative of her conditions; and it is hard to see how it can be countervailed. Italy, in comparison, is pulsating with original life, industrial and intellectual. But, given a renascence of Mohammedan civilisation, the whole life of the nearer East may take a new departure; and in such an evolution Greece would be likely to share.

[1] See article on "The Future of Turkey" in the *Contemporary Review*, April, 1899, by "A Turkish Official."
[2] Yet, as early as the date of the Crimean War, it was noted by an observer that "young Turkey makes profession of atheism." Ubicini, *La Turquie actuelle*, 1855, p. 361. Cp. Sir G. Campbell, *A Very Recent View of Turkey*, 2nd ed. 1878, p. 65. Vambéry makes somewhat light of such tendencies (*Der Islam im 19ten Jahrhundert*, 1875, pp. 185, 187); but admits cases of atheism even among mollahs, as a result of European culture (p. 101).
[3] Ubicini (p. 344), with Vambéry and most other observers, pronounces the Turks the most religious people in Europe.

The general conclusion, then, is that the spirit of freethought, which has survived and modified the long malaria of primeval superstition, the systematically destructive aggression of the medieval Christian church, and even the forces of decivilisation in most of the more backward communities, will be able to survive the economic pressure which in some of the leading States is now its most formidable obstacle. Unquestionably tolerance is being rapidly extended; and the deadly stress of religious conviction which has wrought such incalculable harm in political, social, and mental life is year by year being lightened. Perhaps a new danger lies now in the tendency of many who recognise the economic side of the case to concentrate their whole effort on the problem of social justice, and leave the cause of disinterested truth to the future : which is as if, in indignation at the ill-distribution of the heritage of art among the multitude, one should propose to suspend all artistry till a new society be established. But it seems incredible that those who are concerned to solve the greatest of all human problems should ever be led in the mass to suppose that the solution can be hastened by dropping from their hands one of the main instruments of intellectual discipline and moral enlightenment.

INDEX

Abailard, i, 302, 313, 328 sq., 341
Abauzit, ii, 226
Abbadie, ii, 208, 228
Abbas Effendi, i, 282
Abbot, Archbishop, ii, 39
Abdera, i, 157
Aben-Ezra, i, 335
Abernethy, ii, 362
Aboul-ala el Marri, i, 269
Abraham and Isaac, i, 101
Abraxas, i, 230
Abubacer, i, 277
Academy, the New, i, 183
Aconzio, ii, 4, 14
Adamites, the, i, 431
Adams, John, ii, 319
— George, ii, 330
Adamson, Professor, cited, ii, 83 n., 115
Addison, ii, 331
Adler, Felix, ii, 342
Adonai, i, 104
Adonis, i, 101
Æneas Sylvius, i, 356, 427, 431 n.
Ænesidemus, i, 177 n., 186
Aerius, i, 244
Æschylus, i, 131-5, 145 n.
African tribes, religion of, i, 24 sq., 29
—— unbelief in, i, 32, 34, 35
Agathon, i, 163 n.
Agni, cult of, i, 46
"Agnostic," use of word, ii, 407
Agnosticism, Chinese, i, 82, 83
— Greek, i, 145, 146, 161, 162
Agobard, i, 292 3
Agur, i, 117
Ahriman (Angra Mainyu), i, 67, 69, 112
Ahura Mazda, i, 65 sq.
Aikenhead, ii, 158
Akbar, i, 283
Akerberg, ii, 350
Altaladian religion, i, 60 sq.
Alberti, cited, ii, 136 n., 166, 206, 312
Albertus Magnus, i, 339, 349 n., 368 n., 406
—— of Saxony, i, 404

Albigenses, i, 317 sq.
Alciati, i, 469
Alexander VI, i, 362
—— of Aphrodisias, i, 367
Alexandria, religion at, i, 185
—— culture at, i, 184
Alfarabi, i, 274
Alfieri, ii, 313
Algazel, i, 267, 272, 273, 274
Algarotti, ii, 313
Algeria, freethought in, i, 284
Ali Syed, i, 280 n.
Alison, cited, ii, 229
Alkaios, i, 197
Alkibiades, i, 159
Al Kindi, i, 274
Al Kindy, i, 266
Allbutt, Professor T. C., cited, i, 38, 411 n.; ii, 113 n.
Allegory, freethinking, i, 143
Allen, Ethan, ii, 318 n.
Allix, ii, 107, 230
Allsopp, cited, ii, 390
Almoravides and Almohades, i, 276
Alphabetic writing, age of, i, 192
Alphonso X (the Wise), i, 341, 346-7, 382
—— II, i, 381
—— of Naples, i, 356
Alsted, ii, 254 sq.
Amadeo de' Landi, i, 359
Amalrich (Amaury) of Bena, i, 336, 374
Ambrose, i, 236
Ames, ii, 90
Ammianus Marcellinus, i, 237-8
Ammonios Saccas, i, 227
Amos, i, 104 sq.
Amsterdam i, 4 n.; ii, 197-8
Amun, i, 70
Anabaptists, the, i, 431, 453, 470
Anaita, i, 68
Anatomy, ii, 7
Anav, i, 126
Anaxagoras, i, 139, 152 sq., 157, 161, 168
Anaximandros, i, 139, 141
Anaximenes, i, 139, 141-2, 152

Ancestor-worship, i, 82
Andamanese, religion and ethics of, i, 94
Angels, belief in, i, 112; ii, 353
Anglo-Saxons, i, 115
Annet, ii, 146-7, 174, 327
Anomeans, the, i, 247
Anselm, St., i, 302, 326 sq.
   of Laon, i, 333 *n*.
Anstruther, ii, 115, 125
Anthropomorphism, i, 178
Anti-clericalism, i, 53, 289, 309, 312, 350, 357, 358-9, 371 sq.
Antisthenes, i, 179
Antonines, the, i, 208, 216
Aphrodite, i, 126
Apthorp, ii, 176
Apistos, early use of word, i, 1, 129 *n*.
Apocalypse, i, 225 *n*.
Apollo, i, 126, 129
Apologetics, Christian, i, 240, 360 sq., 392, 417; ii, 95 7, 100, 102 sq., 140, 179, 180, 230 sq., 414
Apostolici, i, 379-80
Apotheosis, imperial, i, 181-2
Apuleius, i, 210; cited, i, 75
Aquinas, Thomas, i, 337 sq., 339, 366, 378, 403
Arabs, influence of, on Europe, i, 275, 293, 319 sq., 334, 336, 345
—— —— on negro life, i, 284
—— civilisation of, i, 255, 257, 259, 274 sq.
—— science of, i, 265, 267, 275, 319 sq.
—— decadence of, i, 267 sq., 269 sq., 275 sq.
—— persecution of, ii, 56
—— Himyarite, i, 113, 117
Aranda, Count, ii, 314
Arcadia, religion in, i, 43
Archelaos, i, 139, 161
Archilochos, i, 125 *n*., 143
Aristarchos, i, 184
Aristippos, i, 179
Aristo, i, 181
Aristophanes, i, 152, 167
Aristotle, i, 165, 169 *n*., 172 sq.; ii, 81-2, 379
Aristotelianism, i, 333, 334, 336, 338 sq., 344, 11, 81
Arius and Arianism, i, 74, 231 sq., 235
Ark, the Hebrew, i, 100
Arkesilaos, i, 183
Arminianism, i, 477; ii, 201
Arnauld, ii, 186
Arnold of Brescia, i, 313, 329 *n*.
—— the legate, i, 322

Arnold, Godfrey, ii, 267
—— Matthew, ii, 326, 388, 391, 404
Arnoldo of Villanueva, i, 383
Arnoldson, K. P., ii, 351
Artemis, i, 125
Arts, effect of, on religion, i, 95
   affected by religion, i, 343
Aryabhata, i, 55
Aryans, i, 46 sq.
Asceticism, i, 248-251, 308
Ascham, ii, 3, 24
Asgill, ii, 133
Ashari, Al, i, 267
Ashtoreths, i, 80
Asmodeus, i, 112
Asoka, i, 58
Aspasia, i, 155-6
Assassins, the, i, 272
Assyria, religion of, i, 60 sq., 127
Assyriology, ii, 360
Astrology, i, 410
—— assailed by Gassendi, ii, 192
Astronomy, Arab, i, 270, 275
—— Hindu, i, 55
—— Greek, i, 140, 148 sq., 184
—— Babylonian, i, 61, 62, 95, 140, 175
—— Modern, ii, 326
Astruc, ii, 358
Asvamedha, rite of, i, 51, 94
Aszo y del Rio, ii, 314
Athanasius, i, 74
Athanasianism, i, 235
Atheism, and atheist, use of words, i, 1, 4, 225
—— Arab, i, 255, 258, 263, 264 *n*., 279
—— Brahmanic, i, 49 sq.
—— Buddhistic, i, 55, 57
—— —— among Sikhs, ii, 428
—— —— in Phœnicia, i, 78, 79
—— —— in Greece, i, 18, 141, 146, 159, 161, 179, 180, 188
—— at Rome, i, 209
—— —— under Islam, i, 259 sq., 269; ii, 429 *n*.
—— in modern Germany, i, 455
—— in Poland, ii, 308
—— —— in England, ii, 24, 25, 88, 130, 142, 157
—— in Scotland, ii, 159
—— —— in the French Revolution, ii, 244 sq.
—— rise of modern, ii, 1
—— in Turkey, ii, 429 *n*.
—— —— in Japan, ii, 426
Athenagoras, i, 225, 232
Athene, i, 126

INDEX

Athens, culture of, i, 135-6, 154-7, 164-5, 166, 245
Atheos, early use of word, i, 129
Atomic theory, i, 157
Audra, ii, 212
Auerbach, ii, 397
Aufklarung, ii. 274, 290, 292
Augsburg, Peace of, ii, 49
Augustine, St., i, 214, 233 sq., 239
Augustus, i, 204 sq., 210
Aulus Gellius, cited, i, 197 n.
Auspices, Roman, i, 195
Austore d'Orlac, i, 344 n.
Australian aborigines, ethics and religion of, i, 94, 98
—— freethought, ii, 412
Austria, freethought in, ii, 305 sq.
Avempace, i, 277, 335
Avenar, ii, 27
Averroes and Averroism, i, 277 sq., 320, 334, 336 sq., 338 sq., 348, 352, 353-4, 359, 367, 370, 381 sq., 383 sq., 388-9, 409, 414
Avicebron, i, 335
Avicenna, i, 274
Avignon, the papacy at, i, 351 sq., 398, 443
Aztec religion, i, 87 sq.

BAALS, i, 76-77
Bab sect, i, 281 sq.
Babylon, religion of, i, 44, 66 sq., 110-112
—— freethought in, i, 61-4
—— science in, i, 62-3, 95, 138, 140, 148, 157
Bacchic mysteries, i, 196, 208
Bacon, Francis, i, 5, 6, 158, 172 n., 369; ii, 40, 41 sq., 60
—— Roger, i, 338, 387 sq.
Baden Powell, Rev., cited, ii, 33
Bagehot, W., criticised, ii, 171
Bahrdt, ii, 278 sq.
Bain, Professor, ii, 404; quoted, i, 169 n., 173; ii, 118, 403
Bainham, i, 473
Baker, Sir S., i, 35
Balfour, A. J., ii, 413
Balguy, ii, 150
Ball, John, i, 392
Ballance, ii, 417
Balzac, ii, 385
Bantu, the, i, 24
Banvan, i, 445
Baptism, i, 289
Barmekides, the, i, 265
Barrington, ii, 149
Barthez, ii, 226
Barthogge, ii, 103

Bartoli, cited, i, 372
Basedow, ii, 275 sq.
Basileus, i, 126
Basilides, i, 230
Bathenians, the, i, 264
Baudelaire, ii, 385
Bauer, A., quoted, i, 156 n.
—— Bruno, ii, 325, 354, 370
—— Edgar, ii, 353
—— G. L., ii, 352
Baume-Desdossat, ii, 224
Baur, F. C., ii, 325, 354; cited, i, 454
—— Rev. W., cited, ii, 293 n., 339
Baxter, ii, 98-9, 103
Bayle, ii, 129, 203 sq., 328; cited, ii, 19
Beard, C., cited, i, 478
Beausobre, ii, 225, 303
Bebel, August, ii, 341, 419
—— Heinrich, i, 452
Beccaria, ii, 220, 239, 312
Beethoven, ii, 306
Beghards and Beguins, i, 375, 377, 390, 398
Beha, i, 282
Bekkar, ii, 202
Belgium, freethought in, ii, 348
"Believers in Reason," ii, 350
Bellay, Jean du, ii, 8
—— Joachim du, ii, 12
Bellman, ii, 349
Bel Merodach, i, 45, 62, 64
Benn, A., cited, i, 140 n., 141 n., 173, 174-5, 183 n.
Bentham, ii, 325, 375
Bentley, ii, 108, 135, 149, 150
—— cited, i, 7 n.
Beranger, ii, 385
Berault, ii, 108
Berengar, i, 300 sq., 459
Bergier, ii, 230, 231, 233
Berkeley, i, 7 n.; ii, 129, 132, 138 sq., 145, 168, 231
Bernard, St., i, 312, 329, 331, 378
Berquin, i, 445-6
Berthelot, ii, 183
Berti, quoted, ii, 77, 80
Besant, Mrs., ii, 335-6, 338, 414
Bettinelli, ii, 313
Bevan, E. R., cited, i, 182 n.
Beverland, ii, 54
Beyle, ii, 385
Beza, i, 463; ii, 82
Bezold, ii, 414, 452, 460
Biandrata, i, 135, 441, 469; ii, 4
Bibliolatry, i, 457, 469
Bickell, i, 113
Biddle, ii, 94, 116

VOL. II 2F

Biélinsky, ii, 389
Biology, ii, 326, 365 sq.
Bion, i, 180
Biran, ii, 372
Bjornson, ii, 399
Black, A. S., ii, 360
Black Death, i, 32, 351
Blackmore, ii, 149
Blasphemy, i, 164, 166, 195 ; ii, 92, 109, 126
Blatchford, ii, 338
Bleckly, H., i, 167 *n.*
Bletterie, ii, 210
Blind, ideas of the, i, 39
Blount, ii, 106-7, 109, 129, 150
Boas, Professor, cited, ii, 32
Boccaccio, i, 349 sq.
Bodin, i, 1 ; ii, 12, 379
Boeheim, i, 416 *n.*
Boethius, i, 252-3
Bogomilians, the, i, 291
Bohemia, Reformation in, i, 427 sq.
Boileau, ii, 183
Boissier, cited, i, 193
Boleslav, i, 437
Bolingbroke, ii, 141, 155, 170 sq., 231
Bolsec, i, 461, 467
Bonaventure Desperiers, ii, 5 sq.
Boncerf, ii, 211
Boniface, St. i, 291-2
Bonner, Mrs., ii, 338
Booms, ii, 203
Borowski, cited, ii, 296, 301
Bossuet, ii, 187, 196
—— cited, ii, 185
Bouchier, Jean, i, 474
Bougre, origin of word, i, 291
Bouillier, cited, i, 368 *n.*
Boulainvilliers, ii, 208, 223, 225
Boulanger, ii, 225
Bourdelot, ii, 307
Bourget, ii, 385
Bourgeville, ii, 15
Bourne, cited, ii, 118 *n.*
Bouterwek, cited, ii, 59
Boyle, i, 4 ; ii, 103, 143
Boyle lectures, ii, 107
Bradke, Von, cited, i, 48
Bradford, Bishop, ii, 108
Bradlaugh, ii, 333 sq., 405
Bradley, J., ii, 108
Brahmanism, i, 48 sq.
—— Dravidian influence on, i, 54 *n.*
Brahmo-Somaj movement, ii, 428
Brandes, G., ii, 399
—— E., ii, 399
Braun, ii, 350
Breitburg, ii, 201 *n.*

Brethren of the Free Spirit, i, 2, 374, 377, 380, 406, 466
—— Sincere (of Purity), i, 263
—— Bohemian, i, 430
—— of the Common Lot, i, 456
Bretschneider, ii, 352
Brewster, cited, ii, 123, 154, 365
Briconnet, i, 444
Brihaspati, i, 52
"Broad Church," ii, 375
Brougham, ii, 401 *n.*, 402 *n.*
Brown, ii, 168
—— W., ii, 361
Browne, Sir T., i, 11 ; ii, 111
—— Bishop, ii, 129
Browning, ii, 326, 388
—— quoted, ii, 222
Brunetière, ii, 386
Brunetto Latini, i, 348, 398 *n.*
Bruno, Giordano, i, 22, 422 *n.*, 471 ; ii, 5, 60, 62 sq., 361
Bruyere, ii, 193
Bryce, cited, i, 18-19, 311
Bucer, i, 468
Buchner, ii, 325, 350, 371, 372, 417 *n.*
Buckingham, ii, 107
Buckle, i, 14 ; ii, 19 ; cited, i, 325 ; ii, 115, 149, 210-2, 217, 234, 241, 242, 326, 379, 381, 407
Buddeus, i, 11
Buddha, traditions of, i, 54 sq., 57
Buddhism, i, 54 sq., 148
Budny, ii, 55
Buffon, ii, 211, 232, 236 sq.
Bulgarians, i, 290
Bullen, cited, ii, 111 *n.*
Burckhardt, cited, i, 133, 351 *n.*, 357 *n.*, 420
Burgers, ii, 347
Burghley, cited, ii, 3
Buridan, i, 404
Burigny, ii, 224, 227
Burke, ii, 176
Burnet, Bishop, cited, i, 6, 475 ; ii, 94, 310
—— Dr. J., cited, i, 150, 156 *n.*, 189-190
—— Dr. T., ii, 119, 124, 153, 158
Burns, ii, 178
Bury, A., ii, 120
Busone da Gubbio, i, 350 *n.*
Butler, ii, 145, 155, sq., 231
Byron, ii, 326, 387
Byzantium, civilisation of, i, 250 sq.
—— freethought in, i, 287 sq.

CABANIS, ii, 232
Cælestius, i, 232
Cæsar, i, 202 sq., 210

Caird, E., i, 460
Cairns, ii, 238, 245 n.
Calas, ii, 220
Calderon, ii, 58
Calendar, reform of, i, 472-3
Callidius, ii, 51
Callimachus, i, 137 n.
Calovius, i, 472
Calvin, i, 2, 448, 457 sq., 461; ii, 8, 11
Calvinism, i, 461 sq., 477
Cambyses, i, 74
Campanella, ii, 309
Campanus, i, 453
Cannibalism, i, 41
Cantu, i, 13; cited, 349
Cardan, i, xv, 349 n.
Carlile, ii, 329, 338
Carlyle, ii, 326, 368, 391, 401
Carneades, i, 183, 187 n.
Carnesecchi, i, 423
Carpenter, J. E., ii, 360
Carranza, ii, 63
Carra, ii, 226
Carrol, ii, 119
Cartaud, ii, 212
Cartesianism, ii, 113 sq., 182, 194
Casaubon, Isaac, i, 477
—— Meric, ii, 102
Casimir the Great, i, 438
Cassels, W. R., ii, 357
Castalio, i, 461, 467; ii, 14, 15
Castelnau, ii, 64
Castillon, ii, 225, 226
Casuistry, ii, 90
Cathari, i, 308 sq., 314
Catherine the Great, ii, 309
Cavalcanti, the two, i, 347
Cecco d'Ascoli, i, 349
Celsus, i, 240 sq.
Celso, ii, 15
Censorship, Roman, i, 210
Cerinthus, i, 226 n.
Cerutti, ii, 226
Cervantes, ii, 58
Cesalpini, ii, 81 n.
Chaeremon, i, 208
Chaitanya, ii, 428
Chalmers, ii, 376; cited, i, 84
Chaloner, ii, 94
Chamberlain, B. H., cited, ii, 423-4
Chambers, R., ii, 326, 366
Chamfort, ii, 232
Chandragupta, i, 58
Channing, ii, 344
Charlemagne, i, 309
Charles II, ii, 89, 99 n.
    III of Spain, ii, 314
  – IV of Spain, ii, 314
  —— V, i, 410, ii, 49

Charleton, W., ii, 97
Charron, ii, 19 sq.
Chastellain, i, 445
Chateaubriand, ii, 373, 382 sq.
Chatelet, Marquise du, ii, 221
Chatham. (See Pitt.)
Chaucer, i, 389
Chaumette, ii, 249
Chazars, the, i, 308 n.
Cheffontaines, ii, 16
Chelsum, ii, 176
Chenier, A., ii, 232
Cheyne, Dr., ii, 358 n., 360, 409
—— cited, i, 105 n., 107, 113, 117;
  ii, 144 n., 151, 359 n.
Chillingworth, ii, 115-6
China, thought in, i, 80 sq.
—— evolution of, i, 136
Chivalry and religion, i, 399 sq.
Cholmeley, ii, 32
Christian II of Denmark, ii, 203,
  306
Christianity, theory of, i, 19 sq.
—— rise of, i, 215, 217 sq.
—— hostility of to freethought, i,
  224
—— strifes of, i, 214
—— and conduct, i, 19, 20
Christina, Queen, ii, 307
Chrysostom, i, 246-7, 250
Chubb, ii, 146, 150
Chuen-Aten, i, 72 sq.
Church, popular hostility to, ii, 91
Church, Dean, cited, ii, 18 n., 45 n.
Churchill, Lord Randolph, ii, 334-5
Cicero, i, 199 sq.
Clarke, ii, 109, 143, 150
  John, ii, 329
Clarkson, ii, 93
Claudius of Turin, i, 292-3, 316 n.
  of Savoy, ii, 3
Clayton, Bishop, ii, 165
Cleanthes, i, 181
Clemens Alexandrinus, i, 226, 228
—— Romanus, i, 228
Clement IV, i, 387
—— VII, i, 418; ii, 8
—— XIV, ii, 313
Clergy, extortion by, i, 309, 328
 – vice among, i, 309, 350, 355
——— hostility to, i, 289, 309, 312,
  350, 357-9, 371 sq.
Clifford, M., ii, 105
—— Professor, i, 448 n.; ii, 404, 406
Clitomachos, i, 183
Clootz, ii, 226, 249
Clough, ii, 326, 388
Coifi, i, 36
Coimbra, Bishop of, ii, 315

Colbert, ii, 192
Cole, P., ii, 26
Colenso, i, 35; ii, 325, 350, 359
Coleridge, ii, 31, 325-6, 377-8, 387
Colet, i, 413 n.
Colletet, ii, 183
Collins, Anthony, i, 7, 22; ii, 121, 123, 134 sq., 142, 150-1, 168, 202, 224
Collis, cited, ii, 173 n.
Columbus, i, 388
Combe, G. and A., ii, 332, 382
Comenius, i, 5
Comines, i, 399
Comparison of creeds, effect of, i, 42, 194
Comte, Auguste, ii, 326, 336, 374, 379, 407
—— Charles, ii, 379; cited, ii, 251 n.
Comtism, ii, 325, 407
Conches. (See William.)
Condillac, ii, 232, 236
Condorcet, ii, 218, 232, 244 sq., 328, 379
Confucius, i, 80 sq.
Connor, ii, 124
Conrad, Joseph, ii, 392
Conrad the Inquisitor, i, 324 n.
—— of Waldhausen, i, 428
Constance, Council of, i, 355, 429
Constans, i, 245 n
Constant, i, 31; ii, 385
Constantine, i, 236
Constantine Copronymus, i, 290
Constantius, i, 237, 245 n.
Conway, M. D., ii, 342, 394 n., 395
—— cited, i, 220 n.
Conybeare, ii, 149, 150
—— F. C., quoted, i, 289
Cooper, J. G., ii, 174
Coornhert, ii, 51 sq.
Copernicus, i, 460; ii, 13, 17 n., 49, 60 sq.
Coquereau, ii, 212
Coquerel, ii, 345
Corelli, Miss, ii, 393
Corneille, ii, 183
Cornutus, i, 188
Corodi, ii, 353
Cosimo dei Medici, i, 361
Cosmas Indicopleustes, i, 246
Cosmology, ancient, i, 61, 77-9, 139 sq.
Cotta, i, 190 sq.
Cousin, ii, 372
Coward, ii, 133, 143
Cowell, Professor, cited, i, 270
Cowper, ii, 178
Craig, ii, 124

Craik, cited, ii, 128 n.
Cramer, ii, 350
Cranmer, i, 474
Creation, doctrine of, i, 121, 178; ii, 363, 368
Creator-Gods, i, 61, 89, 178
Credulity, evolution of, i, 90
Creighton, Bishop, ii, 414
Cremonini, ii, 75
Crequi, Madame de, ii, 215 n.
Cromwell, i, 203 n.; ii, 89, 94
Crotus, i, 452
Cruelty, Christian and pagan, i, 251, 315
—— Moslem, i, 264
Crusades, effects of, i, 45 n., 319
Crusius, ii, 302
Cudworth, 4; ii, 104, 129
Cuffelaer, ii, 258
Culverwel, ii, 96-7
Cumberland, i, 30; ii, 114, 307
Cuper, Franz, ii, 201
Curtius, E., cited, i, 125 n., 126 n., 129
Cuvier, ii, 365
Cybele, cult of, i, 63
Cynics, the, i, 179
Cyrano de Bergerac, ii, 184, 185
Cyrenaics, the, i, 179
Cyril, i, 238, 243
Cyrus, i, 64, 66
Czechowicz, ii, 55

DAILLÉ, i, 479
Daillon, ii, 203
D'Alembert, ii, 232, 243, 244, 272
Damilaville, ii, 225
Damiron, ii, 374
Damon, i, 154
Dandolo, ii, 313
Dante, i, 347, 348 sq., 353 n.
Danton, ii, 232
Daoud, i, 101
D'Argens, ii, 224, 225, 272
D'Argenson, ii, 216
Darigrand, ii, 212
Darius, i, 65, 66
Darmesteter, cited, i, 68
Darwin, C., ii, 326, 365 sq., 404, 406
—— E., ii, 178, 365
Darwinism, early, ii, 365, 366
Daudet, ii, 385
Daumer, ii, 354
David, King, i, 101
David of Dinant, i, 336, 374
Davides, i, 435; ii, 55
Davids, Rhys, cited, i, 53 n., 57
Davidson, J., ii, 388
Davies, J. C., ii, 175

Davies, Archbishop, ii, 108
—— Sir John, ii, 38
Davis, ii, 176
Deaf-mutes, beliefs of, i, 39
Decameron, The, i, 350 sq.
Decharme, i, 13
Deffand, Madame du, ii, 215 n.
Degeneration in religion, i, 91 sq.
Deification, i, 205, 207
"Deism" and "deist," use of words, i, 4; ii, 1, 105
—— early Italian and French, i, 350
—— English, ii, 41, 85 sq., 325, 356 sq.
—— French, ii, 215 sq.
—— German, ii, 281 sq.
—— American, ii, 317 sq.
"*Déiste*," introduction of word, i, 1
Delamare, cited, ii, 205
Delambre, ii, 232
Delmedigo, E. and J. S., i, 371
De Lolme, ii, 211
Delphi, oracle of, i, 128, 137, 183
Demetrius Phalereus, i, 179
—— Poliorketes, i, 182
Democracy and freethought, i, 155, 160, 175, 191; ii, 327 sq.
Demokritos, i, 139, 157 sq., 169
Demonax, i, 187
Denk, i, 453
Denman, Lord, ii, 331
Dersdon, ii, 104
Descartes, i, 337 n.; ii, 54, 60, 83 sq., 88, 129, 182, 197, 198
Desdouits, Professor, ii, 69 sq
Desforges, ii, 212
Desgabets, ii, 195
Deslandes, i, 7; ii, 223, 224; cited, ii, 190 n.
Desmoulins, ii, 232
Destutt de Tracy, ii, 232
Deurhoff, ii, 202
Diagoras, i, 159 160
Dick, ii, 364 n.
Dickens, ii, 392
Dickinson, T. L., cited, i, 99
Diderot, ii, 232, 235, 239 sq., 249, 328; cited, ii, 172
Dikaiarchos, i, 181
Dillon, Dr., cited, i, 113, 117
Diodoros, cited, i, 71
Diogenes of Apollonia, i, 141 n., 154
—— Laertius, i, 142
—— the Babylonian, i, 181 n.
Dionysios, the younger, i, 170 n.
—— the Areopagite, i, 231 n.
Dionysos, i, 126, 128, 136, 143
Diopeithes, i, 154
Dippel, J. Conrad, ii, 265 sq.

Dissent, English, and Liberalism, ii, 326
Dissenters' Chapels Act, ii, 334
Divination, i, 247
Dixon, Professor, cited, ii, 424-5
Doddridge, ii, 149
Dodwell, senr., ii, 133, 143
—— junr., ii, 147
Dolcino, i, 379
Dolet, i, 22; ii, 5, 8, 9
Dominic, St., i, 375, 383
Dominicans, i, 375-6, 384, 385; ii, 62
Domitian, i, 211
Domitius, i, 202 n.
Dostoyevsky, ii, 398
Douglas, S. A., ii, 408
Douglass, Frederick, ii, 408
Dove, Dr. John, ii, 39
—— J., ii, 174
Drama, freethought in, i, 135
Draper, i, 13; ii, 379, 407
Driver, Canon, ii, 359; cited, i, 106, 113
Droz, ii, 246
Drummond, H., ii, 406, 413
Dryden, ii, 174
Dualism, i, 67, 114, 149, 169, 289
Ducket, ii, 144
Duclos, ii, 212
Dudgeon, ii, 160 sq., 174
Duels, veto on, i, 293 n.
Dulaurens, ii, 225
Dumarsais, ii, 225, 227
Dunbar, W., quoted, ii, 159, 160
Duni, ii, 311
Duns Scotus, i, 337-8, 378, 402, 403
Dupuis, ii, 232, 244, 336, 381
Durand, i, 403
Durkheim, ii, 326, 380
Duvernet, ii, 211, 226

EARTHQUAKES, i, 288
Eberhard, ii, 274, 276
Ebionites, i, 226
Ecclesiastes, i, 112 sq., 116-7
Eckhart, i, 406
Economic causation, i, 33, 37, 38, 59, 72, 85, 205, 236 sq., 297 sq., 308 sq., 354, 356, 369, 372, 375 sq., 382 sq., 384, 413 sq., 430 sq., 431; ii, 34, 50, 131, 209, 306, 327, 347, 406, 409 sq.
Ecphantos, i, 149
Edelmann, ii, 266 sq.
Edersheim, cited, i, 121
Edgeworth, Miss, ii, 392
Education and Protestantism, i, 456
—— in England in eighteenth century, ii, 173

Edwards, T., cited, ii, 94
—— Jonathan, ii, 356, 379
—— John, ii, 108, 119
Egypt, ancient, religion of, i, 69 sq.
—— freethought in, i, 110
—— influence of on Greece, i, 123, 131-2
—— modern, i, 25, 282-3
Eichhorn, ii, 352, 358
d'Eichthal, ii, 358
Eleatic School, i, 139, 144-6
Eleusinian mysteries, i, 179 n.
Elias, i, 376
Eliezer, Rabbi, i, 334
Elijah and Elisha, i, 101
—— Rabbi, ii, 421
Eliot, George, ii, 357, 392, 414
Elizabeth, Queen, ii, 25
—— St., i, 324 n.
Elohim, i, 97, 104
Ellis, C., ii, 108
Elwall, ii, 138, 207
Emerson, ii, 325, 344, 378, 391, 394
Emes, ii, 108
Emin, Khalif, i, 265
Empedokles, i, 158-9
Encyclopédie, ii, 220, 241
England, medieval, freethought in, i, 297, 315-316, 387 sq.
—— Tudor, freethought in, i, 473 sq.
—— Reformation in, i, 449, 473 sq.; ii, 23 sq.
—— seventeenth century, freethought in, ii, 85 sq.
—— eighteenth century, freethought in, ii, 126 sq.
—— nineteenth century, freethought in, 327 sq., 342, 356 sq., 375 sq., 386 sq., 400 sq.
—— arrest of culture in, ii, 173, 179
—— social conditions in, ii, 169, 173, 400 sq.
English influence on France, ii, 210, 216
—— —— Germany, ii, 269
Ennius, i, 193, 194 sq.
Enrique IV, i, 384
Ephesos, i, 125
Ephoros, i, 176
Epic, rise of, i, 128
Epicharmos, i, 152, 196
Epictetus, i, 185-6, 209-210, 214
Epicurus, i, 176 sq., 179, 182
Epicureanism, i, 118, 176 sq., 179 n., 182, 185, 199 sq., 306, 346, 347, 356
Erasmus, i, 413, 425, 446, 459, 463
Erastianism, ii, 87 n.
Eratosthenes, i, 184

Erdmann, cited, i, 332, 387-8
Erhard, ii, 301
Erigena. (See John Scotus.)
Esoteric religion, i, 71
Esprit fort, use of term, ii, 171
Essays and Reviews, ii, 325
Essenes, i, 148
Essex, Earl of, ii, 23
Esteve, P., ii, 224
Estienne, ii, 14
"Ethical Culture" movement, ii, 347
Ethical Societies, ii, 342, 410
Ethics, progress in, i, 135, 180
—— of Chinese, i, 82 sq.
—— of Greeks, i, 129, 135
—— of Hebrews, i, 97 sq., 110 sq., 121, 122
—— of primitive peoples, i, 28, 87, 92-3
Etruscan religion, i, 195-6
Eucharist, doctrine of the, i, 296, 300 sq., 312, 419, 435
Euchite heresy, i, 289 n., 310
Euclides, i, 180, 294
Eudemus, i, 141
Eudo, i, 313
Eugenius IV, i, 357
Euler, ii, 270
Eunomians, i, 247
Euripides, i, 159, 161-4, 196
Evanson, ii, 174
Evelyn, cited, ii, 146
Evemeros, i, 78, 181, 195-6
Evemerism among Semites, i, 78
—— —— Christians, i, 225 sq.
—— —— Romans, i, 195-6
Everlasting Gospel, the, i, 377 sq., 398, 420
Evolution theory, ii, 326, 365, 377
Ewald, ii, 358
Ewerbeck, ii, 354
Exeter, ii, 3
Eye, S., ii, 108

FABRICIUS, i, 11
Fairbanks, i, 139 n.
Falkland, ii, 115
"Family of Love," ii, 25
Faraday, ii, 406
Farel, i, 444
Farinata degli Uberti, i, 347
Farrar, A. S., i, 14-15; cited, i, 341 n.; ii, 151
Fathers, the Christian, i, 226
Faye, La, ii, 64
Fear in religion, i, 207-8, 351
Feargal, i, 291, 358
Federation, i, 140

Fenelon, i, 497; ii, 208
Ferdinand, King, i, 384
Ferguson, ii, 163
Ferini and *Antiferini*, ii, 311
Ferri, ii, 380
Fetishism, i, 34
Feuerbach, ii, 325, 354, 370, 371
Fichte, ii, 300, 303 sq., 369
Fiji, unbelief in, i, 33 *n.*, 41
— religion in, i, 34-35, 41
Filangieri, ii, 313
Finetti, ii, 311
Finlay, quoted, i, 288 *n.*
Finow, i, 36
Firdausi, i, 270
Firmin, ii, 123
Fisher, Dr. L., quoted, i, 47
—— Kuno, quoted, ii, 84
Fitzgerald, i, 270-1
Flade, ii, 51
Flagellants, i, 378
Flanders, civilisation of, i, 312-3
Flaubert, ii, 385
Fletcher, ii, 37
Flint, Professor, cited, ii, 53, 310
Florence, culture of, i, 306, 361 sq.
Fogg's Weekly Journal, quoted, ii, 136
Fontane, cited, i, 48
Fontanier, ii, 183
Fontenelle, ii, 194, 212
Foote, G. W., ii, 334, 338, 405
Forbes, Lord President, ii, 114, 162
Forchhammer, i, 167 *n.*
Foster, ii, 149
Fotherby, Bishop, ii, 40-1
Founders, religious, i, 68
Fourier, ii. 336
Fowler, Dr., cited, ii, 115, 121 *n.*
Fox, W. J., ii, 342
France, early freethought in, i, 306 sq., 315, 326 sq., 396 sq.
—— Reformation in, i, 442 sq.
—— influence of, on Germany, ii, 269
—— influence of, on Italy, i, 396-7 *n.*; ii, 312
—— freethought in, ii, 529, 181 sq., 336, 372 sq., 384 sq.
—— culture-history of, i, 326 sq., 396 sq., 443 sq.; ii, 5 sq., 210 sq., 237 sq.
Francis, King, i, 443, 447
Francis of Assisi, i, 375
Franciscans, i, 375 sq., 398
Franck, Sebastian, i, 461
Francois de Rues, i, 373
Francklin, T., ii, 156

Franklin, B., ii, 317 sq.
Fraticelli, the, i, 336, 376-80
Fraud in religion, i, 27 sq., 109, 248
Frazer, J. G., ii, 381
Frederick II, Emperor, i, 336, 344 *n.*, 384
—— —— of Aragon, i, 383
—— the Great, ii, 220, 252, 271 sq., 286, 325
—— William, ii, 287
Free Church of Scotland, ii, 410 sq.
Freeke, ii, 123 *n.*
Freeman, cited, i, 269
Freemasonry, i, 401-2; ii, 336
" Free religious " societies, ii, 340, 342-3
Freeseekers, sect of, 6
Free Spirit. (See Brethren.)
" Freethinker," origin of word, i, 1, 4, 6 sq.
—— meaning of word, i, 4 sq., 8 sq.
Freethinker, early journal, i, 7
Freethought, meaning of, i, 1 sq.
—— and conduct, i, 21
—— continuity of, i, 35 sq., 45 sq., 48 sq., 410 sq.
—— histories of, i, 10 sq.
—— psychology of, i, 8 sq., 16 sq.
—— resistance to, i, 24 sq.
—— in religion, i, 33 *n.*
—— primitive, i, 33, 115
—— early Arab, i, 113, 117
—— Babylonian, i, 61-64
—— Chinese, i, 80 sq.
—— Christian, i, 217 sq.
—— Egyptian, i, 70 sq.
—— Greek, i, 129 sq., 138 sq.
—— Hebrew, i, 96, 115, 114-120
—— Hindu, i, 47 sq.
—— in medieval schools, i, 293 sq.
—— in the Renaissance, i, 343 sq.
—— in Tudor England, i, 473 sq.; ii, 23 sq.
—— in Austria. ii, 305
—— in France in the 16th and 17th centuries ii, 5 sq., 181 sq.
—— in France in the 18th century, ii, 207 sq.
—— in France in the 19th century, ii, 336, 372 sq., 384 sq.
—— in England in the 17th century, ii, 85 sq.
—— in England in the 18th century, ii, 126 sq.
—— in England in the 19th century, ii, 327 sq., 356 sq., 375 sq., 386 sq., 400 sq.
—— in Germany, ii, 51, 254 sq., 338 sq., 352 sq., 395 sq., 417 sq.

Freethought in Holland, i, 407 sq.;
ii, 51 sq., 197 sq., 347
—— in Italy, ii, 309 sq., 395
—— in Spain, i, 381 sq. : ii, 337, 348
—— in Switzerland, ii, 315, 346, 348
—— in Russia and Scandinavia, ii, 306, 349, 398, 419 sq.
—— in South Africa, ii, 347
—— in the United States, ii, 317 sq., 336, 407
—— in Catholic countries to-day, ii, 337, 345, 348 9, 414 sq.
—— in the Catholic Church, ii, 345
—— in Oriental countries to-day, ii, 422 sq.
—— Phœnician, i, 73 sq.
—— psychology of, i, 8 sq., 16 sq.
—— Roman, i, 192 sq., 207
—— under Islam, i, 254 sq., 350
Free-will, doctrine of, i, 8
Frei-geist, use of word, ii, 263
Freret, ii, 210, 225, 227
Fresnoy, L. du, ii, 211
"Friends of Light," ii, 339
Froissart, i, 399
Fromman, ii, 259
Fronto, i, 239
Froude, 1, 3 *n*.; ii, 401
Fry, ii, 119
Fuegians, i, 94
Fukuzawa, ii, 423, 425
Fuller, cited, ii, 180
Furnival, F. J., cited, ii, 36

GABLER, ii, 352
Gabriele de Salo, i, 359
Gaetano of Siena, i, 359
Galen, ii, 7
Galeotto Marcio, i, 359
Galiani, ii, 313
Galileo, i, 369, 411, 471; ii, 60, 74 sq., 310
Gall and Spurzheim, ii, 382
Galvani, ii, 313
Garasse, ii, 19 *n*., 21 sq.
Garcilasso, cited, i, 89
Gardiner, cited, i, 415; ii, 39, 40
Garibaldi, ii, 415
Garlon, ii, 212
Gassendi, ii, 60, 83, 114, 130, 190 sq.
Gastrell, ii, 108
Gaul, Christian, freethought in, ii, 239
—— —— vice in, i, 250
Gaunilo, i, 327
Gaussen, ii, 362
Gautama. (See Buddha.)
Gazier, ii, 384 *n*.
Gazzali, i, 267, 272, 273, 274

Gebhardt, ii, 272
Gebhart, discussed, i, 420
Gebler, criticised, ii, 76-7
Geddes, Dr., ii, 359
Gegenbauer, Theophilus, ii, 256
Geijer, ii, 349; cited, ii, 307
Gemistos Plethon, i, 361
Genard, ii, 212, 224
Genesis, criticism of, i, 463
Geneva, thought in, i, 468
Gennadios, i, 361
Genovesi, ii, 313
Gentilis, Valentinus, i, 469
Geoffrand, Madame, ii, 215 *n*.
Geology, ii, 326, 363 sq.
Georgios Trapezuntios, i, 361
Gerbert, i, 319 *n*.
Gerhard, Bishop, i, 307
Germany, religion in, ii, 355
—— Reformation in, i, 413 sq., 452 sq.
—— freethought in, i, 405; ii, 254 sq., 338 sq., 352 sq., 395 sq., 417 sq.
Gerson, i, 407,
Geulincx, ii, 203
Gewissener, ii, 256
Ghailan of Damascus, i, 260
Ghibellines, i, 347
Ghillany, ii, 353, 381
Giannone, ii, 312, 313
Gibbon, i, 176 *n*.; ii, 150, 175 sq.
Gibson, Bishop, ii, 137, 149, 150
Giddings, ii, 326, 380
Gilbert, i, 471
    Claude, ii, 223
Gildon, ii, 109, 145-6
Giorgio di Novara, i, 359
Girard, i, 133, 164
Gladiatorial games, i, 251
Gladstone, i, 199 *n*.; ii, 338
Glanvill, ii, 113, 203
Glisson, ii, 113
Gnosticism, i, 227 sq.
Go, the chief, i, 36
Gobel, ii, 249
God-idea, evolution of, i, 194, 326
Godwin, ii, 389
Goethe, ii, 290 sq., 365
—— cited, ii, 269, 270, 271, 282
Gogol, ii, 398
Goguet, ii, 379
Golden Rule, i, 83-4
Goldsmith, ii, 170
Goliards, i, 318, 348, 373
Gomates, i, 67
Goncourt, de, ii, 385
Goniondzki, i, 440-1
Good, Dr. T., ii, 103
Goodman, ii, 108

Gordon, T., ii, 174
Gorgias, i, 165
Gorky, ii, 399
Gorlæus, ii, 53
Gospels, freethought in, i, 217 sq.
Gostwick, cited, ii, 271
Gottschalk, i, 294 sq.
Gouvest, ii, 224
Granovsky, ii, 398
Grant, Sir A., i, 173 *n.*
—— General, ii, 408
Grapius, ii, 259
Grassi, ii, 77
Gray, cited, ii, 169
Greef, de, ii, 380
Greek civilisation, i, 122 sq., 136 sq.
—— religion, i, 99, 124 sq., 137 sq., 155, 178, 185, 193
—— influence in India, i, 55
—— influence on Jews, i, 118
—— Rome, i, 192, 194 sq.
—— Saracens, i, 262, 264
Green, J. R., cited, i, 413 *n.*, 476; ii, 25 *n.*, 35
—— criticised, ii, 61-2
—— T. H., ii, 377
Greene, ii, 28
Greg, W. R., ii, 325, 357
Grégoire, ii, 247
Gregorovius, cited, i, 364 *n.*
Gregory VII, i, 311
—— IX, i, 324, 344 sq., 354, 366
—— XIII, i, 472
Greissing, ii, 259
Greville, ii, 38
Gribaldo, i, 469
Griffis, cited, ii, 424
Grimm, cited, i, 37
Gringoire, i, 443; ii, 6
Grosley, ii, 212
Grosstete, Robert, i, 340, 387, 391
Grote, ii, 376; quoted, i, 135, 143, 167 *n.*
Grotius, i, 477; ii, 53, 311
Gruet, Jacques, i, 461, 465 sq.
Gruppe, i, 39
Guardati, i, 357
Gubernatis, ii, 415
Gueudeville, ii, 223
Guibert, ii, 212
—— de Nogent, i, 306
Guicciardini, i, 366
Guirlando, ii, 4
Guizot, ii, 379, 384; cited, i, 448
Gulick, cited, ii, 425-6
Gumplowicz, ii, 380
Gustavus Vasa, ii, 306
Gutschmid, cited, i, 69
Guyau, ii, 380

HADI, Khalif, i, 264
Haeckel, ii, 368
Hafiz, i, 272
Hagenbach, i, 13; ii, 271 *n.*, 292
Hahn, i, 13
Haigh, cited, i, 133, 162 *n.*, 164
Hale, ii, 153
Hall, Robert, ii, 392
Hallam, cited, i, 356 *n.*, 360; ii, 96
Halle, university of, ii, 262
Haller, Von, ii, 270 sq.
Halley, ii, 130, 150
Halyburton, ii, 159; cited, ii, 142 *n.*
Hamann, ii, 302
Hamilton, ii, 376
Hammurabi, i, 60
Hamond, ii, 26
Hampden, Dr., quoted, i, 230 *n.*, 303, 329 *n.*
Hancock, ii, 109
Hanyfism, i, 255 sq.
Hanyfites, the, i, 255 *n.*
Hardy, ii, 392
Harnack, cited, i, 233 *n.*
Haroun Alraschid, i, 264
Harrington, ii, 93
Harriott, i, 471; ii, 31-2
Harris, ii, 108
Harrison, F., i, 331 *n.*
Hartley, ii, 375
Hartmann, ii, 370
Harvey, ii, 47
—— Gabriel, ii, 28
Haslam, ii, 331
Hassall, cited, ii, 171
Hassan, i, 272
Hatch, quoted, i, 169 *n.*, 228 *n.*
Hattem, P. van, ii, 202
Havet, i, 108-9; ii, 325, 358
Hawaii, freethought in, i, 35
Hawkins, B., quoted, ii, 402
Hawthorne, ii, 394
Haynes, E. S. P., i, 14, 299
Hazlitt, ii, 389
Hebert, ii, 249
Hebrews, religion and ethics of, i, 96 sq.
—— mythology of, i, 101 sq.
—— freethought among, i, 112 sq.
Hegel, i, 12; ii, 303, 305, 325, 369, 370, 378
Heine, ii, 326, 370, 395 sq.; quoted, ii, 285
Heiric, i, 337 *n.*
Hekataios, i, 142, 146-7
Helchitsky, i, 432
Helena, i, 130
Helvetius, ii, 232, 238 sq., 244, 328
Hemming, ii, 27

Henley, ii, 389
Hennell, C. C., ii, 325, 356
Hennequin, ii, 386
Henotheism, i, 48
Henry, the monk, i, 312
   of Clairvaux, i, 313
   IV, of France, ii, 20
—— VIII, of England, i, 449, 473
—— P. E., cited, i, 462 n., 466 n., 467
Hensel, i, 472
Herakleides, i, 143, 188
Herakleitos, i, 139, 142-4
Herbert of Cherbury, Lord, ii, 41, 85 sq., 109, 150
Herder, ii, 289, 379
Here, i, 126
Hermippos, i, 155
—— i, 154 n.
Hermits, Hindu, i, 52
Hermogenes, i, 211
Hermotimos, i, 139
Herodotos, i, 123, 127 n., 132, 147, 156
Hesiod, i, 126-8, 130, 137, 144, 151
Hetherington, ii, 331
Hetzer, i, 453
Heyse, ii, 397
Hibbert, Julian. ii, 243 n.
Hicksites, the, ii, 323
Hiero, i, 152
Hierocles, i, 240
Hierology, ii, 87, 112-3, 157, 326, 380
Hieronymos, i, 154 n.
Higginson, Colonel T. W., ii, 395
High Priests, i, 112
Hiketas. (See Iketas.)
Hildebrand, i, 311
Hillel, i, 120, 217
Hilton, ii, 27
Hincmar, i, 294, 297
Hinduism, i, 64 sq.
Hipparchia, i, 180 n.
Hipparchos, i, 184, 208
Hippias, i, 165
Hippo, i, 141
Hippokrates, i, 166, 175 ; ii, 7
Hittites, i, 138
Hobbes, ii, 87 sq., 150
Hoffding, Professor, criticised, ii, 151
d'Holbach, ii, 223, 225, 266, 231, 232, 243 sq., 328
Holcroft, ii, 389
Holland. (See Netherlands.)
—— G. J., ii, 231
Holm, cited, i, 156 n.
Holmes, O. W., ii, 395

"Holy," early meaning of, i, 103
Holyoake, G. J., ii, 330, 332, 338
Home, H. (See Kames.)
—— John, ii, 164
Homer, i, 124-5, 128 sq., 137, 143, 151, 193
Homeric poems, i, 128 sq., 144
Hone, ii, 330
Honorius of Autun, i, 330
Hooker, i, 394 ; ii, 33-4
   cited, i, 3
Hooper, i, 474
Horace, i, 206, 213
Hosea, i, 104 sq.
Hosius, i, 442
Houston, ii, 323, 328-9
Howe, ii, 98, 105
Howells, ii, 394
Huard, ii, 209, 224
Huber, Marie, ii, 210
Huet, ii, 188 sq.
Hugo, Victor, ii, 326, 385
Hull, John, ii, 38
Humanists, Italian, i, 355 sq., 369 sq.
Hume, i, 201 ; ii, 150, 155, 156 sq., 168, 170 ; cited, ii, 169, 376, 379
Humiliati, i, 376
Hungary, thought in, i, 435
—— Reformation in, i, 433 sq.
Hunt, Leigh, ii, 389, 390
Hurst, Bishop, i, 5, 14
—— cited, ii, 254, 280, 283, 289 n.
Huss, i, 304, 355, 427 sq.
Hutcheson, F., ii, 160 sq., 168
Hutchinson, Mrs., cited, ii, 92
—— J., ii, 130, 162
—— Roger, i, 473-4
Huttman, ii, 328
Hutton, ii, 178, 363
Huxley, ii, 338, 367, 404, 406
Huysmans, ii, 385
Hygiainon, i, 163 n.
Hyksos, the, i, 73

IBN EZRA, i, 335
Ibn Gebriol, i, 335
Ibn Khaldun, i, 279
Ibsen, ii, 399
Iconoclasm, i, 287 sq.
Idolatry, i, 62
—— early opposition to, i, 62-3
—— Christian, i, 287 sq., 290 n.
Ignell, ii, 350
Iketas, i, 149
Ilgen, ii, 358
Ilive, J., ii, 174
Imitatio Christi, i, 407
Immortality, belief in, i, 98-9, 114, 119

INDEX

Immortality, denial of, i, 53, 117-8, 338-9, 347, 367, 404, 440; ii, 93, 214
—— of animals, ii, 270, 275
Impostors, the Three, i, 26, 344 sq.
Incas, rationalistic, i, 90
Index Expurgatorius, i, 424; ii, 18, 76, 191, 234, 313, 80
India, freethought in, ii, 427 sq.
—— magic in, i, 43
—— religious evolution in, i, 46 sq.; ii, 427 sq.
Indra, cult of, i, 47
Indulgences, i, 321, 355
Industrialism, ii, 169
Infanticide, Arab, i, 260
"Infidel," use of word, i, 3, 8, 259
"Infidelity," use of word, i, 3, 4, 8; ii, 126
Ingelo, ii, 102-3
Ingersoll, ii, 336, 350, 405
Innocent III, i, 317-323
—— IV, i, 342
—— VIII, i, 362
Inquisition, the, i, 317, 321, 325, 340, 348, 356, 358 sq., 366, 381, 382 sq., 384, 398, 419, 438; ii, 4, 57, 59, 66, 68, 74, 314
Institutions, power of, in religion, i, 33, 38
—— lack of rationalist, i, 33, 38
Intolerance, Greek, i, 154, 156 sq., 171, 179, 182, 189-190
—— Christian, i, 226, 235, 237. (See Persecution.)
Ionia, culture of, i, 122 sq., 136 sq., 175
Ireland, ancient, culture in, i, 293-4
—— Protestantism in, i, 450
—— freethought in, ii, 164
Irenæus, i, 235
Isabella, i, 384
Isaiah, i, 105, 106, 108
Isenbiehl, ii, 286
Isis, cult of, i, 75
Islam, i, 254 sq., 350
Ismailites, the, i, 264, 272
Israel, relative freethought in, i, 96 sq.
Italy, freethought in, i, 343 sq., 419 n.; ii, 309 sq., 395
—— influence of, on Europe, ii, 1 sq.
—— Reformation in, i, 417 sq.
Iyeyasu, ii, 426

Jaafer, i, 265
Jabarites, the, i, 261
Jacob, i, 101
Jacobeos, the, ii, 315
Jahedians, the, i, 273 n.
Jahn, ii, 305
Jainism, i, 56; ii, 428
Jamblichos, i, 239
James, Professor W., 17 n.
—— Henry, ii, 395
Jami, i, 272
Jannes, P. de la, ii, 212
Jansenists, ii, 182, 186, 187, 208, 235
Japan, freethought in, ii, 422 sq.
—— reform in, i, 25
Jeanne d'Arc, i, 394
Jeannin, ii, 20
Jefferies, R., ii, 393
Jefferson, ii, 317 sq., 323
Jehovah. (See Yahweh.)
Jenghiz Khan, i, 268
Jerome, St., i, 244
Jerome of Prague, i, 428, 430
Jerusalem, J. F. W., ii, 268
Jesuits, i, 436, 442; ii, 4, 50, 81, 186, 229 n., 235, 313
Jesus, i, 22
—— horoscope of, i, 349 n.
Jevons, F. B., criticised, i, 43
Jews in Middle Ages, i, 320, 333, 370-1
—— persecutions of, i, 381, 386; ii, 57
—— modern, ii, 421-2
Joachim, Abbot, i, 377
Job, i, 112 sq., 116
Joel, i, 106
John the Scot, i, 293 sq., 304-5, 331, 336; ii, 378
—— of Gaunt, i, 391
—— of Jandun, i, 402
—— of Parma, i, 378
—— of Salisbury, i, 327, 332, 366
—— Pannonicus, i, 433
—— Pirnensis, i, 438
—— Zapoyla, i, 434
—— Zimisces, Emperor, i, 290
—— Pope, XXI, i, 339 n.
—— Pope, XXIII, i, 429
Johnston, H. H., cited, i, 284-5
Johnstone, John, ii, 160
Joinville, i, 335, 399
Jolley, ii, 360
Jonas al Aswari, i, 260
Joseph, myth of, i, 101
Joseph II, ii, 274
Joshua, i, 101
Jouffroy, ii, 373
Journalism, freethinking, ii, 337 sq., 341, 348, 413
Jousse, ii, 212
Jovinian, i, 244
Juan de Peratallada, i, 383
"Juan di Posos," ii, 293

INDEX

Julian, i, 185, 242-3
Jurieu, ii, 205
Justin Martyr, i, 239 sq., 249
Juvenal, i, 120, 209, 223

KADARITES, i, 261
Kalam, the, i, 269
Kalisch, ii, 359
Kames, Lord, ii, 163
Kant, ii, 289, 293 sq., 361, 369, 379
Kantsa, i, 50
Kapila, i, 50
Karaites, i, 333, 334 *n*.
Karians, i, 122 sq.
Karma, doctrine of, i, 56
Karmathians, the, i, 268
Karneades, i, 183, 187 *n*.
Keats, ii, 388
Keener, Bishop, ii, 408
Kepler, i, 471 ; ii, 83
Kett, ii, 26, 31, 32
Ketzer, origin of word, i, 308
Kharejites, the, i, 261
Kharvakas, the, i, 51
Kidd, B., ii, 413
Kidder, ii, 108
Kiellgren, ii, 349
Kierkegaard, ii, 399
Kindi, Al, i, 274
Kindy, Al, i, 266
King, Archbishop, ii, 129, 134
Kings, deification of, i, 181-2
Kipling, ii, 388
Kirkup, cited, ii, 332 *n*.
Kleist, ii, 395
Klitomachos, i, 183
Knaggs, ii, 108
Knight, ii, 162
Knutzen, ii, 256 sq.
Koerbagh, ii, 54
Koheleth, i, 109, 116-7
Koran, the, i, 256 sq., 264, 266
Kortholt, ii, 258
Krake, Rolf, i, 37
Krishna myth, i, 55
Kritias, i, 160
Krochmal, ii, 421
Kronos, i, 126
Kropf, cited, i, 36 *n*.
Ktesilochos, i, 164 *n*.
Kuenen, ii, 325, 359
Kumarila, i, 51
Kuyper, ii, 201
Kyd, ii, 32

LA BARRE, ii, 220
Labitte, cited, ii, 22
Labour churches, ii, 343
La Bruyere, ii, 193; cited, i, 45 *n*.

Lachares, i, 183
Lactantius, i, 213 *n*., 246
Lagrange, ii, 232
La Harpe, ii, 211, 227
Laing, cited, ii, 339 *n*.
Lalande, i, 11 ; ii, 232
Lamarck, ii, 365
Lamartine, ii, 385
Lamb, C., ii, 389
Lambert, François, i, 455
Lamennais, ii, 374
La Mettrie, ii, 169, 224, 232, 236, 272
La Mothe le Vayer, ii, 22, 181, 182
Lanjuinais, ii, 211
La Peyrere, ii, 196 sq.
La Placette, i, 479
Landau, cited, i, 350 *n*.
Lane, cited, i, 25, 283
Lang, A., criticised, i, 42, 89, 93, 98-9; cited, i, 35
Lange, cited, i, 10, 137, 173, 175; ii, 240
Langland, i, 389
Languedoc, civilisation in, i, 317 sq.
Lanson, cited, ii, 185, 194, 221, 234
Lao-Tsze, i, 80, 82 sq.
Laplace, ii, 232, 326, 361
La Primaudaye, ii, 27
Lardner, ii, 149, 343
La Rochette, ii, 220
Larroque, ii, 358
Lassen, ii, 258
Lasson, Dr., cited, i, 407
Latini, Brunetto, i, 348, 398 *n*.
Latitudinarians, ii, 124
Lau, ii, 265 sq.
Lavater, ii, 276
Lavergne, cited, ii, 247
Law, William, ii, 119, 149, 168
Lawrence, Dr., ii, 362 sq.
Lea, H. C., cited, i, 325
Lechler, cited, i, 13
Lecky, i, 14 ; quoted, i, 337 *n*.
—— cited, ii, 36, 165 *n*., 179, 232
Le Clerc, i, 478 ; ii, 91, 107, 129, 201
Leconte de Lisle, ii, 326, 385
Lecount, ii, 332
Lee, Dr., ii, 368
Leechman, ii, 162
Leenhof, ii, 203
Lefevre, i, 444, 446
Legate, ii, 39, 40
Legge, Dr., cited, i, 81
Leibnitz, ii, 13 *n*., 46, 130, 259 sq.
Leicester, Lollardry in, i, 390
Leland, ii, 146, 149
Lemaître, ii, 386
Lennstrand, ii, 351
Lenormant, cited, i, 69 *n*.

Leo the Isaurian, i, 286-7
— X, Pope, i, 368
Leopardi, ii, 326, 395
Leopold of Tuscany, ii, 313
Leslie, C., ii, 107, 134 *n*., 149
—— Professor, ii, 362
Lessing, i, 350; ii, 274, 282 sq., 325-6
Letourneau, ii, 380
Le Trosne, ii, 212
Leufstedt, ii, 350
Leukippos, i, 139, 157
Leukothea, i, 145
Levallois, cited, ii, 386 *n*.
Levellers, the, ii, 93
Levi ben Gershom, i, 334
Levites, origin of, i, 44, 112
Lewes, G. H , ii, 338, 404
Lewis, ii, 26
L'Hopital, ii, 13
Libanius, quoted, i, 237
Libertin, use of word, i, 2
Libertini, or "libertines," use of word, i, 2, 379-80, 466, 473-4; ii, 11
—— tenets of, i, 466 sq.
Libraries, public, i, 205 *n*.
Lidgould, ii, 108
Liebknecht, ii, 341
Lightfoot, Bishop, cited, i, 148
Lilienfeld, ii, 380
Lilja, ii, 350
Lillie, cited, i, 53 *n*.
Lincoln, President, ii, 408
Linguet, ii, 211
Liszinski, ii, 308
Littré, cited, i, 398
—— death of, ii, 416 *n*.
Livy, i, 206
Llorente, i, 386 *n*.
Localisation of Gods, i, 43 sq.
Locke, ii, 108, 116 sq., 126, 150
Loescher, ii, 259
Logos, the, i, 83, 169
Lokayata, i, 51, 52
Lollards, i, 390, 449
Long, G., cited, i, 202 *n*., 203 *n*.
Longrais, ii, 226
Lope de Vega, ii, 58
Lord's Prayer, the, i, 212 sq.
Lorenzo dei Medici, i, 362
Louis, Saint, i, 335
—— Philippe, ii, 336 *n*.
Lowndes, Miss, cited ii, 16
Lubbock, cited, i, 30
Lucian, i, 179, 115-6, 208, 242
Lucilius, i, 199 *n*.
Lucretius, i, 178, 198 sq.
— influence of, i, 306
Ludovicus Vives, ii, 82

Luthardt, Professor, ii, 367
Luther, i, 190, 415-417, 454, 457 sq., 460 sq., 463, 470; ii, 82
Lützelberger, ii, 354
Lyall, Edna, ii, 393
Lydia, civilisation in, i, 138
Lyell, ii, 403
Lyly, cited, ii, 24, 31 *n*.
Lyons, ii, 135 *n*.
Lysimachos, i, 179 *n*.
Lyttleton, ii, 149

MABAD AL JHONI, i, 260
Mably, ii, 211, 233
Macaulay, ii, 332, 402; cited, i, 45 *n*.; ii, 175; criticised, ii, 106 *n*.
McCosh, cited, ii, 161
McCrie, i, 418 *n*., 419 *n*., 425 *n*.
Machiavelli, i, 363 sq., 373-4; ii, 28
Mackay, R. W., i, 12; ii, 325, 357
—— quoted, i, 146 *n*., 228 *n*.
Mackenzie, George, ii, 101, 158
Macrobius, i, 244
Madison, ii, 323
Magi, i, 66, 67
Magian religion, i, 66 sq.
Magic and religion, i, 43, 410 sq.
—— in Middle Ages, i, 369
Magna Graecia, culture of, i, 144, 150-1
Mahabharata, the, i, 58
Mahaffy, quoted, i, 127-8, 131, 134, 185 *n*.
Mahdi, Khalif, i, 264
Mahmoud, Sultan, i, 269, 270
Maimonides, i, 320, 334
Maistre, J. de, ii, 373
Malebranche, ii, 195
Malesherbes, ii, 235
Malherbe, ii, 183
Malik, i, 270
Malthus, i, 174; ii, 367, 376
Mamoun, i, 265, 268
Mandard, ii, 7
Mandeville, ii, 136, 150, 168, 174, 379
Manfred, i, 346
Manichæism, i, 229, 231, 307, 310
Mannhardt, ii, 381
Mansel, ii, 376
Mansour, Khalif, i, 263
Marcion and Marcionites, i, 229
Marcus Aurelius, i, 214, 216
Mardouk-nadinakhe, i, 45
Maréchal, Sylvain, i, 11; ii, 226, 245 *n*.
Margat, ii, 212
Marguerite of Navarre, i, 2; ii, 5, 11 sq., 446

Maria Theresa, ii, 305
Mariner, cited, i, 36
Mariolatry, i, 378
Marius, i, 203
Marlowe, ii, 28 sq.
Marot, ii, 5, 6
Marri, El, i, 269
Marriage, ancient, i, 249
Marsiglio of Padua, i, 402
Marsilio Ficino, i, 304, 361, 363
Marsy, ii, 211
Marten, ii, 94
Martin Marprelate, ii, 28
Martin, Mrs. Emma, ii, 331
Martineau, J., ii, 338 *n.*, 344
—— cited, ii, 200 *n.*
—— Harriet, ii, 414
Martyrs, i, 249 *n.*
Mary of Hungary, i, 433
Marx, ii, 325, 341, 370, 381
Massey, cited, ii, 173
Mass, the, i, 298
Masuccio, i, 298 *n.*,'357
Materialism, i, 70, 127, 146-9, 152-3, 156, 161, 334, 338; ii, 88, 127, 130, 143, 236, 240, 325, 372
Mathematics, rise of, i, 148
—— English in 18th century, ii, 154
Matter, doctrines concerning, i, 146 *n.*, 149, 169, 334
Matthias of Janow, i, 428
— Corvinus, i, 433
Maupassant, ii, 385
Maupertuis, ii, 238, 272
Maurice, ii, 378; cited, i, 253 *n.*, 331
Mauvillon, ii, 288
Maximillian II, ii, 49
Maximus Tyrius, i, 214
Mazarin, ii, 183, 185
Mazdeism, i, 65 sq.
Mazzini, ii, 415
Medicine, Renaissance, i, 369
Meister, ii, 225, 226
Melanchthon, i, 410, 454, 459, 460, 463, 468, 470, 471; ii, 3
Melissos, i, 145
Menander, i, 183
Mencius, i, 85
Mendelssohn, Moses, ii, 274, 281
Mendicant Friars, i, 375, 377
Menippus, i, 185
Menzel, cited, i, 471
Menzies, Dr., cited, i, 68, 81, 82, 97
Meredith, ii, 392
Merivale, criticised, i, 203-4
Merodach, i, 45, 62, 64
Mersenne, i, 4; ii, 22-3, 89 *n.*
Meslier, ii, 212 sq.

Mesopotamia, cults of, i, 44
—— religious evolution in, i, 60 sq.
Metempsychosis, ii, 66, 268
Metrodoros, i, 161
  (the second), i, 177
Meung, Jean de, i, 373
Mexico, religions of, i, 87 sq.
Mey, ii, 211
Meyer, E., quoted, i, 68, 77, 80, 126 *n.*, 128, 130, 155 *n.*
—— Louis, ii, 197 sq.
Mezentius, i, 37
Mezieres, i, 353
Mezzanotte, i, 360 *n.*
Michael, Emperor, i, 288
—— Scotus, i, 345-6
Michelet, ii, 384; cited, i, 380, 414, 463 *n.*, 464 sq.
Middleton, i, 299; ii, 136, 150, 166, 170
Miletos, i, 125, 139, 146
Militarism, ii, 208, 347-8
Militz, i, 427
Mill, James, ii, 375, 404
—— J. S., ii, 239, 332, 338 *n.*, 401, 404
Millar, J., ii, 163
Miller, Hugh, ii, 364, 366
Millot, ii, 233
Milman, ii, 325, 380; cited, i, 318 *n.*
Milner, Rev. J., ii, 119
Milton, ii, 47 *n.*, 116
Minnesingers, i, 405
Mirabaud, ii, 224
Mirabeau, ii, 232
Miracles, i, 246 *n.*
Miriam, i, 101
Mirza Ali, i, 281
Mithra, i, 67
Mithraism, i, 67, 69, 230, 231, 245
Mitra, cult of, i, 47
Moabite Stone, i, 105 *n.*
Mocenigo, ii, 65
Moffat, cited, i, 27 *n.*, 32
Mohammed, i, 27, 254 sq.
Mohl, ii, 403
Moktader, i, 268, 272
Molech, i, 102
Moleschott, ii, 372 *n.*
Molesworth, ii, 164
Moliere, ii, 184
Molinists, ii, 208
Mollio, i, 422
Molyneux, i, 6; ii, 164
Mommsen, i, 192 *n.*, 193, 195
Monarchism and religion, i, 45
Monk, ii, 144
Monolatry, i, 56, 81, 97
Monotheism, i, 60 sq., 67, 77, 81, 97, 100, 121, 173

INDEX

Monroe, ii, 323
Montagu, Lady Mary Wortley, ii, 141
Montaigne, i, 479; ii, 16 sq., 181, 204 n., 240; cited, i, 2
Montalembert, cited, i, 322 n., 324 n.
Montesquieu, ii, 232, 234 sq., 379
Moore, G., ii, 393
Moors. (See Arabs.)
More, Sir T., i, 172, 475 sq.; ii, 1
—— Henry, ii, 97-8, 114
—— Hannah, ii, 392
Morehead, ii, 403 n.
Morellet, ii, 233
Morgan, Professor de, cited, ii, 32
Morgan, T., ii, 146, 150, 168
Morison, J. Cotter, i, 331 n.
Morley, J., i, 464; ii, 338, 404
—— cited, ii, 219, 221, 234, 243, 271
Mornay, de, ii, 15, 36
Moroccan Letters, ii, 287
Morris, Rev. J., ii, 119
Morton, Bishop, ii, 27
Moschus, i, 79
Moses, i, 101
Mosheim, cited, i, 209, 231, 464; ii, 90, 264
Motadhed, i, 267
Motamid, i, 267
Motasim, i, 266, 268
Motawakkel, i, 266, 268
Motazilites, the, i, 260 sq., 280, 350 n.
Motecallemin, the, i, 274, 278, 350 n.
Moxon, ii, 331
Mozdar, i, 264
Muller, J., ii, 258
—— K. O., 124, 133, 163 n.; cited, i
—— Max, cited, i, 57; criticised, i, 46 n., 94 n.
Munter, ii, 308
Muratori, ii, 312
Murchison, ii, 366
Murray, Professor G., cited, i, 137 n., 167 n.
Musaeus, ii, 258
Musset, ii, 385
Mutianus, i, 452
Mylius, ii, 283
Mysteries, Eleusinian, i, 179 n.
—— Pythagorean, i, 131
—— Bacchic, i, 208
Mystery-plays, Christian, i, 320
Mysticism, i, 230 n.
—— Arab, i, 266, 271 sq.
Mythology, ii, 326, 380 sq.

Nabonidos, i, 44, 64

Naigeon, ii, 226, 243
Nanak, ii, 428
Nantes, revocation of Edict of, ii, 208
Napier, ii, 158
Naples, freethought in, i, 356-7, 419, 426
Napoleon, i, 203; ii, 384
Nash, ii, 28, 37
Natura naturans, i, 337
"Naturalist," use of word, i, 2
Naudé, Gabriel, ii, 13 n., 181
Neander, cited, i, 467-8
Nebo, i, 45
Necker, ii, 246
"Negative criticism," i, 17; ii, 197
Neo-Platonism, i, 75, 185
Nero, i, 211
Nestorians, the, i, 246, 262
Netherlands, i, 407 sq., 414, 426, 476 sq.; ii, 51 sq., 197 sq., 347
Netzahuatlcoyotl, i, 39, 88 n.
Nevill, ii, 95
Newman, J. H., ii, 189 n., 356, 380
—— F. W., ii, 325, 338 n., 356, 404
—— C. R., ii, 356 n.
New Testament, criticism of, ii, 124, 146, 214, 220, 285, 325, 352 sq.
Newton, ii, 81, 116, 120 sq., 150, 361
New Zealand, freethought in, ii, 412
—— superstition in, i, 44 n.
Nichirenites, ii, 424
Nicholas, the painter, i, 315 n.
—— of Amiens, i, 328
Nichols, ii, 108
Nicholson, ii, 174
Nicolai, ii, 274
Nicolaus of Autricuria, i, 358, 405
—— of Cusa, i, 356, 358, 407; ii, 61
Nicholas III, Pope, i, 387
—— V, Pope, i, 357
Nicoletto, Vernias, i, 359
Nicon, ii, 309
Nietzsche, ii, 371
Nifo, i, 359-360
Niketas. (See Iketas.)
Ninon de l'Enclos, ii, 215
Niphus. (See Nifo.)
Nirvana, doctrine of, i, 55
Nodier, cited, ii, 11 n.
Nominalism, i, 293, 302 sq., 329, 341, 402, 430
Nous, doctrine of, i, 153
Numa, i, 364
Numbers, doctrine of, i, 148-9
Nystrom, ii, 351

Occam. (See William.)

Ochino, i, 419, 468; ii, 2, 378
Ogilvie, cited, ii, 178
Oglethorpe, ii, 239 n.
Okeanos, i, 127
O'Keefe, ii, 175
Oldcastle, i, 390
Oldfield, ii, 109
Old Testament, criticism of, ii, 105, 107, 124, 144, 153, 196, 199, 277 sq., 325, 331-2, 352 sq.
Omar, the Khalif, i, 257, 259 n.
Omar Khayyam, i, 269 sq.
Omens, belief in, i, 195
Origen, i, 228, 240 sq.; ii, 378
Orléans, Duchesse d', cited, ii, 190
Ormazd. (See Ahura Mazda.)
Orpheus, i, 127 n.
Orphicism, i, 147 n., 148
Ortlieb, i, 374
Orzechowski, i, 440
Osborn, Major, cited, i, 262 n.
—— Francis, cited, ii, 31 n.
Ostrorog, i, 438
Overton, ii, 95
Ovid, i, 206, 213; ii, 364
Owen, Rev. John, i, 11; cited, i, 318 n., 319 n., 364 n., 368 n.; ii, 18, 19, 22
—— Robert, ii, 326, 332
—— Robert Dale, ii, 319 n.
Oxford in 16th century, ii, 24, 64
—— in 18th century, ii, 136
Ozanam, cited, i, 232 n.

PACHACAMAC, i, 89
Padua, school of, i, 354, 370, 438
Paganism, suppression of, i, 237
Pagitt, ii, 96
Paine, ii, 179, 317, 320 sq., 324, 327, 350, 361
Paleario, i, 423
Palestrina, ii, 4
Paley, ii, 231; cited, ii, 178
Palmaer, ii, 350
Palmer, Professor, i, 255 n., 256 n.
—— Elihu, ii, 322, 328
Pannonicus, i, 433
Pantheism, i, 2, 48, 74, 83, 132, 280, 361, 363, 374, 466; ii, 69, 195, 200, 221, 325
Paolo Giovio, i, 364 n.
Papacy, growth of, i, 310 sq., 354 sq.
—— power of, i, 317 sq., 355
—— hostility to, i, 311, 357, 366, 371, 391, 442 sq.
Paris, university of, i, 336, 338-9, 352, 397, 398, 404-5
Parker, Archdeacon, ii, 106

Parker, Theodore, ii, 325, 356
—— Thomas, ii, 350
Parkes, Professor, cited, ii, 426
Parmenides, i, 139, 145
Parr, ii, 378
Parsees, the, i, 112, 280
Parsons, ii, 30
Parvish, ii, 144
Pascal, ii, 185, 186, 188
Paschasius Radbert, i, 296
Passerano, ii, 206
Pastoret, ii, 226
Pastoris, i, 439
Paterini, i, 313, 315, 398
Patin, Gui, ii, 181
—— Professor, i, 133
Patot, Tissot de, ii, 223
Pattison, Mark, i, 461, 464-5; ii, 156, 189
Paul, i, 224, 249
—— of Samosata, i, 233
—— II, Pope, i, 360
—— III, Pope, i, 421
—— IV, Pope, i, 423
Paul, Herbert, ii, 143 n.
Pauli, Gregorius, i, 441
Paulicians, the, i, 288 sq., 304 sq., 306 sq.
Paulus, ii, 352
Pavlovsky, cited, ii, 398 n.
Pazmany, i, 436
Pearson, Bishop, ii, 31
Peasant wars, i, 430, 433, 454
Pecock, i, 393 sq.; ii, 34
Pedro II, i, 381
Pedro de Osma, i, 384
Peele, ii, 37
Pelagianism, i, 233 sq., 286
Pelagius, i, 232
Pelham, Professor, i, 197 n.
Pellicier, ii, 11
Pelling, E., ii, 108
Penn, ii, 123
Pentateuch, criticism of, i, 463; ii, 124, 144, 146, 195 sq., 267
Pericles, i, 153-6
Perrault, cited, ii, 182
Perrens, cited, i, 2 n., 13, 358
Persecution, primitive, i, 33 n.
—— Christian, i, 226, 235, 237, 299, 317 sq., 325, 445 sq.; ii, 4, 5, 26, 39, 40, 54, 73, 123, 127, 147, 158, 161 sq., 183, 210 sq., 257, 328 sq., 350-1, 353. (See Inquisition.)
—— Greek, i, 154, 156 sq., 171, 179, 182, 189-190
—— Roman, i, 196-7, 214
Persia, religions of, i, 64 sq.
—— freethought in, i, 64, 271

Persia, culture-history of, i, 148, 271, 280 sq.
Peru, ancient freethought in, i, 38, 89-90
—— religion of, i, 88
—— modern freethought in, ii, 349
Perugino, i, 360
Pessimism, i, 132
Pestalozzi, ii, 301 n.
Peter the Hermit, i, 312
    the Great, ii, 309
    of Alliaco, i, 388
    de Brueys, i, 312
—— Martyr, i, 419
—— of St. Cloud, i, 372
— of Vaux, i, 316
Petit, Claude, ii, 183
Petrarch, i, 351 n., 352 sq., 368
Petrie, W. M. F., cited, i, 73 notes
Petrobrussians, the, i, 312
Petronius, i, 208
Peucer, i, 472
Peyrat, ii, 358
Peyrere, ii, 196 sq.
Pfaff, ii, 258
Pfeiff, ii, 350
Pfeiffer, i, 472
Pheidias, i, 156
Pherekydes, i, 147
Philanthropic Institute, ii, 275
Philips, A., i, 7
Philiskos, i, 197
Phillips, Stephen, quoted, ii, 74
Philo, i, 119, 333; cited, i, 180 n.
Philolaos, i, 149
Phœnicia, religious evolution in, i, 75 sq., 99
—— freethought in, i, 78-9
Photinus, i, 247
Photius, i, 288
Phrenology, ii, 332, 382
Pico della Mirandola, i, 361, 362 sq.
Pierre Aureol, i, 402
Pierre d'Ailly, i, 349 n., 404
Piers Ploughman, vision of, i, 389
Pietism, ii, 262
Pietro of Abano, i, 348, 366
Pilkington, Bishop, cited, ii, 33
Pindar, i, 130-1
Pinkerton, cited, i, 294
Pionensis, i, 148
Pitt, the elder, ii, 146, 169
    the younger, ii, 177
Pius II, i, 356
 — IV, i, 423
—— V, i, 423; ii, 4
Platner, ii, 302
Plato, i, 146, 165, 166, 168 sq.
Platonism, i, 227 sq., 361

layfair, ii, 154
Pliny, i, 184, 207-8, 209
lotinus, i, 74
Plutarch, i, 140, 153, 155 n., 156, 180 n., 188-9
Poe, ii, 394
Poetry, Greek, i, 128
Poland, culture-history of, i, 437; ii, 55, 308
Pole, Cardinal, i, 364 n.
Polybius, i, 187, 365 n
Polytheism, i, 42 sq., 59, 71, 226
Pomare, i, 35
Pombal, ii, 315
Pompeius, i, 203 n.
Pomponazzi, i, 367 sq., 369
Pomponius Lætus, i, 370
Poole, R. L., cited, i, 304
Pope, ii, 141-2, 150
Porphyry, i, 242-3
Porteous, Bishop, cited, ii, 180
Portugal, inquisition in, i, 316
—— freethought in, ii, 315
Posidonius, i, 245
Postell, ii, 11
Potapenko, ii, 398
Pougens, ii, 226
Poushkine, ii, 398
Prades, Abbé de, ii, 222, 224, 225, 241
Praxeas, i, 233
Prayer, popular view of, i, 33
Preaching, early, i, 215 n.
Premontval, ii, 224, 225, 227
Press Licensing Act, ii, 99, 109, 110
Prideaux, ii, 108
Priestcraft, i, 26, 33 n.
Priesthoods, evolution of, i, 59, 61, 69, 91, 136-7
Priestley, ii, 156, 343
Printing, rise of, i, 456, 457 n.
Proclus, i, 246
Prodikos, i, 165
Progress, i, 143
Prophecy, i, 107, 108, 110
Prophets, Hebrew, i, 104 sq., 110 sq.
Protagoras, i, 139, 157
Protestantism in Italy, i, 417 sq.
    fortunes of, i, 425, 436, 455, 459, 469, 471. (See Reformation.)
Provence, civilisation of, i, 315, 317 sq.
Providence, popular view of, i, 33
Psammetichus, i, 132
Psychology, ii, 326, 381 sq.
Ptolemy, i, 184 n., 225 n.
Puffendorf, ii, 307
Pulci, i, 358
Punjaub, ancient, freethought in, i, 53, 56

VOL. II   2G

Pünjer, cited, ii, 280, 281
Puritanism, ii, 89, 99, 317-8
Pusey, cited, ii, 262, 280
Pyrrho, i, 176-7, 187
Pyrrhonism, i, 186-7
Pythagoras, i, 139, 147 sq.; ii, 364
Pythagoreanism, i, 148 sq.

QUAKERS, ii, 222, 321
Quetzalcoatl, i, 88
Quinet, ii, 373, 384.

RABANUS, i, 293, 298-9
Rabelais, i, 471; ii, 6 sq.
Rabia, i, 271
Race-character, theories of, i, 64, 101-2, 123 sq., 174-5, 193, 417 sq., 448, 449
Raleigh, ii, 28 sq.
Ramsay, Chevalier de, ii, 209
—— W. M., cited, i, 126 n.
Ramus, ii, 60, 82-3
Ranke, cited, i, 415, 457 n.
Raoul de Houdan, i, 319
Rappolt, ii, 258
Rashdall, Dr., cited, i, 331, 370
Rastus, i, 25 n.
Rationalism and Rationalist, use of terms, i, 5, 8; ii, 95, 125, 285, 286
Rationalist Press Association, ii, 405 n.
Ratramnus, i, 296-7
Rawley, ii, 32
Rawlinson, Canon, cited, i, 69
Ray, John, ii, 108
Raymond Berenger, i, 319 sq.
  of Sebonde, i, 408; ii, 16
—— Archbishop, of Toledo, i, 381
Raynal, ii, 211, 232, 253, 328
Reade, Winwood, ii, 326
Realism, philosophic, i, 146, 302 sq., 402, 430
Reason, deification of, i, 213; ii, 248 sq.
—— religious defence of, i, 293
Reboult, ii, 212
Recared, i, 381
Rechenberg, ii, 259
Reformation, the, politically considered, i, 413 sq.
—— in Britain, i, 449 sq., 473 sq.
—— in France, i, 443 sq.
—— in Germany, i, 413 sq.
—— in Hungary, i, 433 sq.
—— in Italy, i, 417 sq.
—— in the Netherlands, i, 476 sq.
—— in Poland, i, 439 sq.
—— in Spain, i, 425
Reformers, anti-pagan, i, 237

Regis, ii, 194
Regnard, ii, 193
Reimarus, ii, 278, 284
Reimmann, i, 11
Reinach, i, 122 n.
Reinhard, ii, 339
Reinhold, i, 472
Religion and conquest, i, 43-5, 47
—— psychology of, i, 26
—— of lower races, influence of, i, 43
Remigius, i, 297
Renaissance in Italy, freethought in, i, 343 sq.
—— in France, i, 371, 396
—— in England, i, 371, 387 sq.
Renan, ii, 325, 350, 358, 381
—— cited, i, 101, 102, 209, 274 n., 279 n., 335, 348, 353, 378
Renee, Princess, i, 421
Reuchlin, i, 413
Reuter, H., cited, i, 13, 293 n.
Réville, Dr. A., i, 88 n., 97
Revolution, French, ii, 179, 245 sq.
  American, ii, 317
Rewandites, the, i, 264
Reynard the Fox, i, 372-3, 405
Rheticus, i, 472
Richardson, cited, ii, 166
Richelieu, ii, 181
Richter, ii, 353
Riddle, i, 14, 15
Riem, ii, 274
Rihoriho, i, 35
Rings, the Three, i, 350
Ripley, G., ii, 373 n.
Ritchie, cited, ii, 164
Ritual and ritualism, i, 29
Rivarol, ii, 232, 250 sq.; cited, ii, 209 n.
Roalfe, Matilda, ii, 331
Robertson, W., ii, 164
—— Professor Croom, cited, ii, 83 n.
Robespierre, ii, 232, 250
Robinet, ii, 226, 238
Rolf Krake, i, 37
Roman religion, i, 193, 204 sq., 209, 212
—— law, i, 214
Romano, ii, 311,
Rome, papal, i, 311, 354
Romilly, ii, 401
Ronsard, ii, 12
Roos, ii, 3
Roscelin, i, 302 sq., 328
Rose, roman de la, i, 373
Rossi, M. A. de, i, 370
Rousseau, J. B., ii, 215
—— J. J., ii, 211 sq., 218, 233, 244, 253

Royal Society, ii, 95
Rüdiger, ii, 272
Rudrauf, ii, 259
Ruge, ii, 370
Rum Bahadur, i, 25 *n.*
Rupp, ii, 340
Ruskin, ii, 391
Russia, ii, 306, 398, 419 sq.
Rust, ii, 107
Rutebœuf, i, 319
Rutherford, ii, 158
Rydberg, ii, 350
Ryswyck, i, 408

SABBATH, origin of, i, 111
Sabellius, i, 233
Sack, ii, 268 *n.*
Sacraments, Mexican, i, 87, 89
Sacred Books, i, 40-41, 137, 191, 215
Sacrifices, causation of, i, 49, 93 sq.
—— early disbelief in, i, 41, 49, 62, 85, 89, 213
—— human, i, 63, 85, 87, 89
Sadducees, i, 120
Sadi, i, 272
Saga, ii, 4
Sahagun, i, 90
Sainte-Beuve, ii, 373, 386
—— cited, ii, 184 *n.*
St. Bartholomew, massacre of, ii, 13
St. Evremond, ii, 193
St. Glain, ii, 207 *n.*
St. Hilaire, B., cited, i, 57
—— Geoffroy, ii, 365
St. Simon, ii, 336
Saintsbury, cited, i, 373
Saisset, cited, ii, 375
Saladin, i, 350
Salaville, ii, 250
Sales, Deslisle de, ii, 211, 226
Salverte, ii, 379
Salvian, i, 239, 250
Samaritans, i, 111 *n.*
Samoans, religion of, i, 34-35
Samson, ii, 278
Sanchez, ii, 60, 74
Sanchoniathon, i, 77
Sand, George, ii, 385
Sankara, i, 51
Saracen culture, i, 119, 274 sq., 319, 350. (See Arabs.)
Satan, i, 112, 114
Saturninus, i, 229
Satyre Menippée, ii, 20
Saul, i, 101
Saunderson, ii, 131
Savages, freethought among, i, 32, 33 sq., 38 sq., 42
—— religion of, i, 25, 30 sq.

Savages, ethics of, i, 28
—— mental life of, i, 24 sq.
Savile, ii, 121
Saviour-Gods, i, 87
Savonarola, i, 351, 360, 363, 417 sq.
Sayce, cited, i, 62
Sayous, i, 13
Sbinko, i, 429
Scævola, i, 200 *n.*
Scaliger, cited, ii, 5
Scandinavia, freethought in ancient, i, 37
—— in modern, ii, 399
Scaurus, i, 202
Sceptic. (See Skeptic.)
Schade, ii, 275
Schaffie, ii, 380
Schelling, ii, 303, 305, 369
Scherer, E., ii, 232, 386
Schiller, ii, 292
Schism, the Great Papal, i, 354 sq.
Schlegel, A., quoted, i, 163
Schleiermacher, ii, 305, 351
Schmidt, W. A., cited, i, 12, 189, 204 *n.*, 210 *n.*
Schmidt, J. L., ii, 266
Schmiedel, ii, 360
Scholastics, the, i, 302 sq., 333 sq.
Schoner, ii, 56
Schopenhauer, ii, 370
Schopp, ii, 70-1
Schrader, i, 126
Schulz, ii, 287
Schurer, i, 148
Schwartz, ii, 259
Schwegler, i, 192 *n.*
Schweizer, cited, i, 37 *n.*
Science, ancient, i, 61-3, 95, 138, 140, 141, 149, 152, 157, 166, 175, 184
Scot, Reginald, i, 3 ; ii, 25, 203
—— W., ii, 108
Scotland, Reformation in, i, 415, 450
—— freethought in, ii, 101, 158 sq., 410 sq.
Scott, Thomas, ii, 325, 357
—— Walter, ii, 387
Secularism, ii, 331
Sedillot, cited, i, 257 *n.*
Segarelli, i, 378 sq.
Selden, ii, 91
Sembat, i, 289 *n.*
Semele, i, 126
Semites, religions of, i, 44, 97 sq., 123 sq., 139
—— theories concerning, i, 64, 80, 101-2
Semitic influence on Greeks, i, 122 sq., 138

Semler, ii, 277 sq.
Seneca, i, 207, 214
Serre, De la, ii, 224
Serra, ii, 312 *n.*
Servetus, i, 461 sq. ; ii, 3, 378
Seton-Merriman, ii, 393
Sevigné, Madame de, i, 2 *n.*; ii, 195
Sextus Empiricus, i, 186-7 ; ii, 14, 17, 30, 224
Shaftesbury, i, 6 ; ii, 109, 120, 132, 143, 149, 150, 168, 240
—— cited, i, 7 *n.*
Shakespeare, ii, 34 sq.
Sharpe, i, 113 ; ii, 344
Shelley, ii, 326, 386
Sherlock, W., i, 4 ; ii, 123, 149, 150
Shîites, the, i, 261 sq., 281 *n.*
Sibylline books, i, 202 *n.*
Sichel, W., criticised, ii, 171, 172
Sicily, culture of, i, 319, 337, 344
Sidgwick, H., cited, ii, 91 *n.*
Sidney, A., ii, 95
Sidney, Sir P., i, ii, 64-5
Sifatites, the, i, 261
Sikhs, ii, 428
Silvanus, i, 289
Simeon Duran, Rabbi, i, 350
Simon de Montfort, i, 321, 323, 324
Simon of Tournay, i, 326-7, 333
Simon, Richard, ii, 195 sq.
Simonides, i, 152
Simpson, cited, ii, 180
Simson, ii, 131
Sismondi, quoted, i, 329 *n.*; ii, 58 *n.*
Sixtus IV, i, 359, 367
Skelton, cited, ii, 166
Skeptic, meaning of word, i, 12
Skepticism, academic, i, 183 sq.
—— Pyrrhonic, i, 12, 176-7
—— dialectic, among Christians, i, 479 ; ii, 139, 140, 188
—— popular, among Christians, i, 33, 479
Skytte, ii, 257
Slavery, Christianity and, i, 225
—— Paine and, ii, 320 *n.*
Smalbroke, ii, 149
Smith, Adam, ii, 162, 170, 376, 379
—— John, ii, 97
—— W. Robertson, i, 49, 359
—— S., i, 6
Smyrna, ancient, i, 124-5
Social causation, ii, 148, 153, 172, 173, 179, 253, 320, 326-7, 340-1, 450-1
Socialism, ii, 326, 341, 418 sq.
Socinianism, ii, 2, 54, 56, 115 sq., 131, 378

Sociology, i, 365 sq., 410; ii, 326, 379 sq.
Sokrates, i, 160, 165 sq., 172, 173
Solomon, i, 101
—— ben Gebirol, i, 335
Sorbonne, the, i, 447 ; ii, 8
Sorcery, belief in, 24
Sorel, cited, ii, 305
Soury, cited, ii, 240
South, Dean, ii, 124
Southey, ii, 387-8, 389
South Place Institute, ii, 342
Southwell, ii, 330
Sozzini, the, i, 435, 441 ; ii, 2, 15, 55 sq.
Spain, culture history of, i, 380 sq.; ii, 57, 314
—— freethought in, i, 381 sq.; ii, 337
—— Reformation in, i, 425
Spalding, ii, 277
Spencer, J., ii, 112
—— H., ii, 326, 377, 380-1, 404, 407 ; cited, i, 34
Speusippos, i, 180
Spiegel, cited, i, 69 *n.*
Spina, Alfonso, i, 366
Spinoza, i, 4, 17, 335, 340, 478 ; ii, 46, 107, 145, 193 sq., 257 sq., 260
Spinozism, ii, 204, 268
Spirituales, the sect, i, 2
Sprat, i, 3
Sprenger, cited, i, 255 *n.*, 256 *n.*
Stafford, Sir W., ii, 312 *n.*
Stancari, i, 440
Stanhope, ii, 108
Stationers' Company, ii, 110
Statius, i, 208
Staudlin, i, 12 ; ii, 300
Stebbing, ii, 149
Steele, ii, 132
Steinbart, ii, 276
Steinbuhler, ii, 286
Steno, ii, 364 *n.*
Stephen, Sir J., cited, i, 399 *n.*
—— Sir Leslie, i, 13 ; ii, 404 ; cited, ii, 114, 129 *n.*, 130 *n.*; criticised, ii, 130 *n.*, 149 sq.
Stesichoros, i, 130
Stewart, H. F., cited, i, 252-3
Stillingfleet, i, 4 ; ii, 98-9, 104, 105, 119
Stilpo, i, 180
Stoicism, i, 176, 199, 207
Stosch, ii, 258
Stout, Sir R., ii, 412
Strabo, i, 168 *n.*, 187-8
Strannik, cited, ii, 420 *n.*
Strasburg Cathedral, i, 405 *n.*

Strato, i, 180
Strauss, ii, 325, 346, 350, 352 sq., 370, 381
Strigolniks, the, ii, 309
Strindberg, ii, 351
Stromer, ii, 350
Struensee, ii, 308
Strutt, ii, 143, 169
Stuart, Dean, ii, 97
Stubbs, Bishop, ii, 414
Stuckenberg, cited, ii, 296, 298, 301
Studemund, cited, i, 418
Suarez, i, 407
Suetonius, i, 209
Sufiism, i, 271, 280
Sulla, i, 203
Sully, Professor, cited, i, 39
Sun-Gods, worship of, i, 70, 76, 87, 88, 101, 125
Sunnites, the, i, 261
Svedberg, ii, 349
Swift, ii, 132-3, 149, 150; cited, i, 6
Swinburne, ii, 326, 388
Switzerland, reformation in, i, 414, 421, 456, 459 sq.
—— freethought in, ii, 315, 346
Sykes, A. A., ii, 149; quoted, ii, 167
Sylvester II, i, 319 n.
— Bernard, i, 329
Symonds, J. A., cited, i, 343 n., 421
Synge, ii, 134 n., 164

TABARI, cited, i, 264 n.
Taborites, the, i, 431
Tacitus, i, 209
Taillandier, cited, i, 294
Taine, ii, 375, 386
Talfourd, ii, 331
Talmud, thought in, i, 120-1
Tamerlane, i, 268
Tammuz, i, 101
Tanquelin, i, 313
Tarde, ii, 326, 380
Taouism, i, 82 sq.
Tasmanians, religion of, i, 99
Tau, i, 83
Tauler, i, 406
Tayler, ii, 344
Taylor, Jeremy, ii, 112
—— Robert, ii, 330
Tegnér, ii, 349
Telesio, ii, 82
Teller, ii, 277
Templars, the Knights, i, 383, 400-2
Temple, Sir W., ii, 103
Ten, theories of, i, 150
Tenison, ii, 107
Tenneman, cited, ii, 117
Tennyson, ii, 326

Teodori, i, 422
Tertullian, i, 235, 239, 249; ii, 111
Tetens, ii, 302
Tetzel, i, 416
Teuffel, i, 193-4
Texte, cited, ii, 141-2
Thackeray, ii, 392
Thales, i, 138 sq.
Thallos, i, 78
Thamamians, the, i, 273 n.
Theagenes, i, 151, 153
Theodora, i, 250
Theodore of Mopsuestia, i, 247
Theodoric, i, 252
Theodoros, i, 179-180
Theodosius II, i, 245 n.
Theodotos, i, 232
Theophilanthropy, ii, 321
Theophrastos, i, 182
Thierrys, the two, ii, 384
Thirlwall, i, 124 n.
Thirty-nine Articles, the, i, 475
Thirty Years' War, ii, 255
Tholuck, i, 12-13; cited, ii, 257, 262
Thomas Aquinas, i, 337, 339, 340, 366, 378, 403
Thomas a Kempis, i, 407
Thomas, Dr. R. H., ii, 321 n.
Thomasius, Jenkin, i, 11; ii, 259; cited, ii, 256
—— Christian, ii, 263
Thompson, F., ii, 389
Thomson, J., ii, 388
Thonrakians, i, 289 n.
Thoreau, ii, 394
Thrakians, the, i, 124 n.
Thukydides, i, 156 n., 168
Thunder-Gods, i, 97
Tiberius, i, 210-212
Ticknor, cited, i, 385
Tiele, cited, i, 68; criticised, i, 44
Tillotson, ii, 104, 123
Tindal, ii, 133, 137, 145, 149, 168
Tocco, i, 13
Tocqueville, cited, ii, 233
Toland, i, 6; ii, 109, 126 sq., 149, 150-1, 168, 197
Tolstoy, ii, 398
Toltecs, the, i, 88
Tonga Islands, freethought in, i, 36
Torild, ii, 349
Torquemada, i, 386
Torricelli, ii, 310
Torture, ecclesiastical, i, 342
Toulmin, ii, 174, 175
Tourguenief, ii, 398
Tourneur, ii, 37-8
Towers, ii, 98
Toy, ii, 408

Tractarianism, ii, 387
Transubstantiation, i, 296 sq.
Transvaal, freethought in, ii, 347
Trebonian, i, 250
Trenchard, ii, 132
Triads, i, 70
Tribbechov, i, 11 ; ii, 259
Trinity, dogma of, i, 74, 227, 232-3, 247, 296, 304, 328, 329, 333, 339, 404, 419, 440, 461. (See Unitarianism.)
Trinius, i, 11
Trouveres and Troubadours, i, 318 sq., 373
Turgot, ii, 232, 244
Turkey, civilisation of, ii, 428-9
—— freethought in, ii, 429 n.
Turlupins, i, 375
Turner, ii, 174
Turpin, ii, 212
Turretin, i, 473
Twelve, sacred number, i, 96, 126
Twofold truth, doctrine of, i, 339, 368, 388, 404 ; ii, 117, 199, 299
Tylor, Dr., ii, 381 ; cited, i, 24, 31
Tyndall, ii, 404
Tyrannos, i, 126

UBALDINI, i, 347 n.
Ueberweg, quoted, i, 171-2, 294, 305
—— opinions of, ii, 417 n.
Uhlich, ii, 340
Uladislaus II, i, 433
Ulrich von Hutten, i, 413, 426
Undereyck, ii, 259
Unitarianism, early, i, 255, 335, 351, 414, 453, 474
—— in England, ii, 32, 39, 94, 122-3, 133, 139, 200, 343 sq.
—— in Hungary, i, 435
—— in Poland, i, 439 sq.; ii, 55 sq.
—— in Italy, ii, 3
—— in Holland, ii, 54
—— in America, ii, 323, 412
United States, freethought in, ii, 317 sq., 394 sq., 407 sq.
—— German freethinkers in, 341-2
Universalism, i, 63
Universities, low ebb of culture in, ii, 170
—— German, i, 413, 470; ii, 355, 417 sq.
—— Swiss, ii, 346
Upanishads, philosophy of, i, 49 sq.
Urban VIII, ii, 77
Urstitius, ii, 60
Utilitarianism, i, 213; ii, 168
"Utilitarian Associations," ii, 351

VALENTINUS, i, 230
Gentilis, i, 469
Valla, Lorenzo, i, 355-6, 368
Vallée, ii, 14
Vambery, cited, i, 281
Van der Ende, ii, 198
Vanini, i, 22 ; ii, 60, 71 sq.
Van Mildert, i, 14, 15
Varro, i, 200 n.
Varuna, i, 47 sq.
Vasari, cited, i, 360 n.
Vassor, ii, 190
Vatke, ii, 325, 358
Vaudois, the, i, 316 sq.
Vaughan, cited, ii, 95
Vauvenargues, ii, 232
Vedanta, i, 49 n., 53
Vedas, i, 30, 46
—— translations of, i, 30 n.
—— skepticism in, i, 30, 47-8
—— attacks on, i, 50-1
Vejento, i, 211
Velasquez, ii, 59
Verlaine, ii, 385
Verrall, i, 163-4
Verus, S. G., ii, 356 n.
Viau, ii, 183
Vico, i, 26 n. ; ii, 310, 379
Vigilantius, i, 244, 316 n.
Villani, G., i, 305
Villari, cited, i, 361, 362 n.
Vinci, Leonardo da, ii, 364
Virchow, ii, 417
Viret, ii, 1
Virgil, i, 206
Virgilius, St., i, 291, 358
Virgin-Mother-Goddess, i, 87
Voelkel, ii, 54
Vogt, ii, 372 n.
Volney, ii, 232, 244, 328, 336, 381
Volta, ii, 313
Voltaire, i, 22, 135, 352 ; ii, 172, 215 sq., 231, 239, 244, 272, 359, 364, 379
—— cited, i, 2 n., 286 ; ii, 136 n., 138, 171
Vorstius, ii, 39

WAGNER, RICHARD, ii, 398
Tobias, ii, 259
Wahabi sect, i, 284
Waitz, ii, 381
Waldenses, i, 2, 316 sq., 422, 427, 448
Waldus, i, 316
Walid, i, 263
Wallace, A. R., ii, 367
Dr. Robert, ii, 162
—— Professor W., cited, i, 177 n.

INDEX

Walter Von der Vogelweide, i, 405
Walther, cited, ii, 255-6
Walwyn, ii, 95
War in South Africa, effect of, ii, 347-8
Warburton, ii, 136, 149, 150
Ward, Mrs. Humphry, ii, 393
—— Lester, ii, 326, 380
Warton, cited, ii, 142
Warville, ii, 226
Washington, ii, 317, 319 sq.
Wasil Ibn Atta, i, 260
Waterland, ii, 149, 150
Wathek, Khalif, i, 267
Watson, Bishop, ii, 176 n., 322, 328
— W., ii, 388
Watts, C., i, 11,
—— H. E., cited, ii, 59 n
Wazon, Bishop, i, 310
Weber, A., cited, i, 43, 49 n., 54
—— Em., ii, 259
Wedderburn, ii, 329
Wegscheider, ii, 352, 353
Wellhausen, ii, 325, 359
— quoted, i, 103, 139
Wen, Emperor, i, 85
Werner, ii, 363
Wesley, cited, ii, 318 n.
Wesleyanism, ii, 170, 175
Westphalia, Peace of, ii, 255
Wette, de, ii, 144, 352, 358
Wheeler, J. M., i, 11
Whewell, ii, 366, 367
— cited, ii, 90, 115
Whiston, ii, 131, 153
White, A. D., i, 14, 40; ii, 406, 407
Whitfield, ii, 170
Whitman, ii, 394
Wiclif, i, 376, 390, 391 sq., 428
Wieland, ii, 285-6
Wier, ii, 51, 203
Wightman, ii, 39, 40
Wilamowitz, i, 126 n.
Wilberforce, ii, 329, 367, 392
—— cited, ii, 177
Wildman, ii, 95
Wilkes, ii, 173
Wilkins, Bishop, ii, 104
"Will to believe," i, 17
William of Auvergne, i, 338 n.
—— of Conches, i, 330
—— of Occam, i, 397, 402 sq.
—— of St. Amour, i, 376
Williams, Speaker, cited, ii, 2
Willich, cited, ii, 271

Winchell, ii, 408
Wireker, i, 405 n.
Wisdom of Solomon, i, 118, 119
Wise, ii, 109, 142 n.
Wislicenus, ii, 340
Witchcraft, belief in, i, 24, 366, 411; ii, 13, 50, 112
—— assailed, ii, 25, 51, 192, 203, 264
Witt, John de, ii, 199
Wolff and Wolffianism, ii, 266
Wolfius, ii, 259
Wolseley, Sir C., ii, 108
Women, freethought among, i, 364 n.; ii, 186 n., 414 n., 416
—— orthodoxy among, ii, 148, 416
— position of early Christian, i, 250
Wood, Anthony a, cited, ii, 33
Woodrow, ii, 408
Woodward, ii, 153
Woolston, ii, 136, 137-8, 149, 150, 168
Wordsworth, ii, 387
— Bishop, cited, ii, 345
Wright, Susanna, ii, 329 n.
—— Frances, ii, 414
Writing, antiquity of, i, 105 n., 192 n.

XENOPHANES, i, 142, 144-5
Xenophon, i, 195

YAHWEH, i, 97, 100, 102, 104
Yaska, i, 50
Yeats, ii, 388
Young, ii, 149

ZAID, i, 254-5
Zapoyla, i, 434
Zarathustra, i, 68
Zebrzydowski, i, 440
Zeller, ii, 346
—— cited, i, 148, 167 n.; ii, 418 n.
Zendavesta,
Zendekism (Arab atheism), i, 255 sq., 258, 263, 264 n., 279
Zeno (the elder), i, 139, 145
— (the Stoic), i, 176 sq., 183, 213 n.
Zeus, i, 126, 132 sq.
Ziska, i, 430 sq.
Zola, ii, 385
Zollikofer, ii, 277
Zoroastrianism, i, 69
Zulus, freethought among, i, 35
Zwingli, i, 458 sq.

CORRIGENDA

Vol. I.

P. 14, line 11. *For* "Baynes" *read* "Haynes."
P. 35. *After* line 13 *insert* "§ 2."
P. 37, line 15. *For* "is declared that" *read* "is told that one chief declared."
P. 154, note 2. For "*de*" read "*des*."
P. 189, line 16. *For* "than" *read* "that."
P. 272, line 4. *For* "Moktadir" *read* "Moktader."
P. 304, note 1. *After* "scolastique" *insert* "î."
P. 357, line 8 from bottom of text. *For* "Masaccio" *read* "Masuccio."
P. 368, line 6. *For* "Lozenzo" *read* "Lorenzo."
P. 449, line 10. *For* "revelation" *read* "revolution."

Vol. II.

P. 191, note. *For* "sout" *read* "sont."
P. 198. *For* "Van den Ende" *read* "Van der Ende."
P. 355, line 24. *After* "provided" *read* "for."
P. 362, line 3. *After* "for" *read* "by."
P. 364, line 10. *After* "that" *read* "the."

K
2750

UNIVERSITY OF CALIFORNIA
Santa Barbara College Library
Santa Barbara, California

Return to desk from which borrowed.
This book is DUE on the last date stamped below.

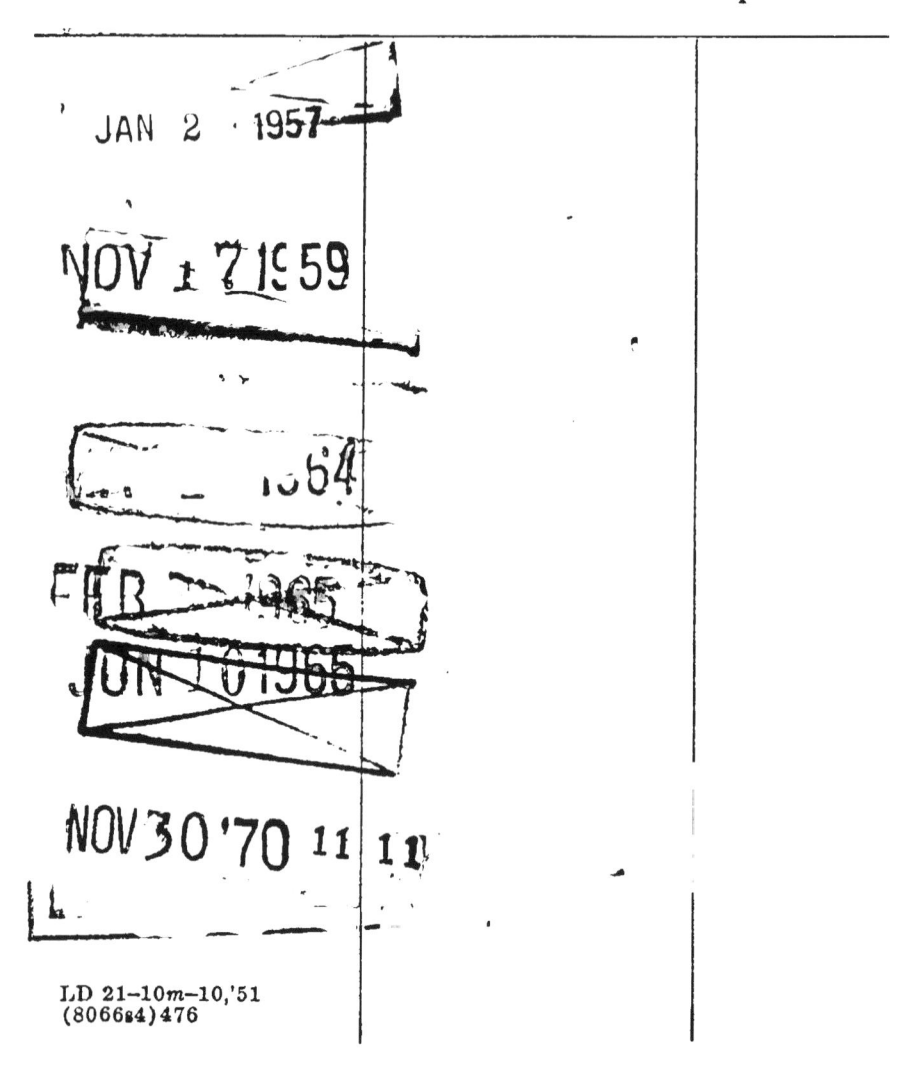

JAN 2 1957

NOV 17 1959

NOV 30 '70 11 11

LD 21-10m-10,'51
(8066s4)476

Printed in Great Britain
by Amazon